About the Authors

John P. McKay Born in St. Louis, Missouri, John P. McKay received his B.A. from Wesleyan University (1961), his M.A. from the Fletcher School of Law and Diplomacy (1962), and his Ph.D. from the University of California, Berkeley (1968). He began teaching history at the University of Illinois in 1966 and became a professor there in 1976. John won the Herbert Baxter Adams Prize for his book *Pioneers for Profit: Foreign Entrepreneurship and Russian Industrialization, 1885–1913* (1970). He has also written *Tramways and Trolleys: The Rise of Urban Mass Transport in Europe* (1976) and has translated Jules Michelet's *The People* (1973). His research has been supported by fellowships from the Ford Foundation, the Guggenheim Foundation, the National Endowment for the Humanities, and IREX. He has written well over a hundred articles, book chapters, and reviews, which have appeared in numerous publications, including *The American Historical Review, Business History Review, The Journal of Economic History,* and *Slavic Review.* He contributed extensively to C. Stewart and P. Fritzsche, eds., *Imagining the Twentieth Century* (1997).

Bennett D. Hill A native of Philadelphia, Bennett D. Hill earned an A.B. from Princeton (1956) and advanced degrees from Harvard (A.M., 1958) and Princeton (Ph.D., 1963). He taught history at the University of Illinois at Urbana, where he was department chairman from 1978 to 1981. He has published *English Cistercian Monasteries and Their Patrons in the Twelfth Century* (1968), *Church and State in the Middle Ages* (1970), and articles in *Analecta Cisterciensia, The New Catholic Encyclopaedia, The American Benedictine Review,* and *The Dictionary of the Middle Ages.* His reviews have appeared in *The American Historical Review, Speculum, The Historian,* the *Journal of World History,* and *Library Journal.* He is one of the contributing editors to *The Encyclopedia of World History* (2001). He has been a Fellow of the American Council of Learned Societies and served on the editorial board of *The American Benedictine Review,* on committees of the National Endowment for the Humanities, and as Vice President of the American Catholic Historical Association (1995–1996). A Benedictine monk of St. Anselm's Abbey in Washington, D.C., he is also a Visiting Professor at Georgetown University.

John Buckler Born in Louisville, Kentucky, John Buckler received his B.A. (summa cum laude) from the University of Louisville in 1967. Harvard University awarded him the Ph.D. in 1973. From 1984 to 1986 he was an Alexander von Humboldt Fellow at the Institut für Alte Geschichte, University of Munich. He has lectured at the Fondation Hardt at the University of Geneva and at the University of Freiburg. He has also participated in numerous international conferences. He is currently a professor of Greek history at the University of Illinois. In 1980 Harvard University Press published his *Theban Hegemony, 371–362* B.C. He has also published *Philip II and the Sacred War* (Leiden 1989) and co-edited *BOIOTIKA: Vorträge vom 5. Internationalen Böotien-Kolloquium* (Munich 1989). He has contributed articles to *The American Historical Association's Guide to Historical Literature* (Oxford 1995), *The Oxford Classical Dictionary* (Oxford 1996), and *Encyclopedia of Greece and the Hellenic Tradition* (London 1999). His other articles have appeared in journals both in the United States and abroad, including the *American Journal of Ancient History, Classical Philology, Rheinisches Museum für Philologie, Klio, Classical Quarterly, Wiener Studien,* and many others.

A History of Western Society

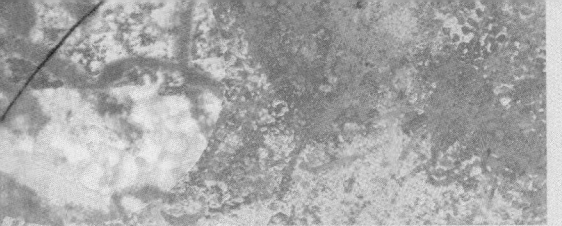

A History of Western Society

Volume C
From the Revolutionary Era to the Present

Seventh Edition

John P. McKay

University of Illinois at Urbana-Champaign

Bennett D. Hill

Georgetown University

John Buckler

University of Illinois at Urbana-Champaign

HOUGHTON MIFFLIN COMPANY
Boston   New York

Editor-in-Chief: Jean L. Woy
Senior Sponsoring Editor: Nancy Blaine
Development Editor: Julie Dunn
Senior Project Editor: Christina M. Horn
Editorial Assistant: Talia M. Kingsbury
Manufacturing Manager: Florence Cadran
Senior Marketing Manager: Sandra McGuire

Text credits:
Page 877: Parody by Henry Labouchère, quoted in *The Social History of the Machine Gun,* by John Ellis. Reprinted by permission of Pantheon Books, a division of Random House, Inc.

Volume C cover image: *Lynford* (1969), by Karen Armitage. Private Collection/Bridgeman Art Library.

Printed in the U.S.A.

Library of Congress Control Number: 2001133313

ISBN: 0-618-17053-7

3 4 5 6 7 8 9 DOW 08 07 06 05 04

Brief Contents

Chapter 21   The Revolution in Politics, 1775–1815   691

Chapter 22   The Revolution in Energy and Industry   725

Chapter 23   Ideologies and Upheavals, 1815–1850   755

Chapter 24   Life in the Emerging Urban Society   787

Chapter 25   The Age of Nationalism, 1850–1914   823

Chapter 26   The West and the World   855

Chapter 27   The Great Break: War and Revolution   887

Chapter 28   The Age of Anxiety   921

Chapter 29   Dictatorships and the Second World War   953

Chapter 30   Cold War Conflicts and Social Transformations, 1945–1985   989

Chapter 31   Revolution, Rebuilding, and New Challenges:
              1985 to the Present   1027

Contents

Preface   xvii

Acknowledgments   xxiii

Chapter 21

The Revolution in Politics, 1775–1815   691

Liberty and Equality   691

The American Revolutionary Era, 1775–1789   693

The Origins of the Revolution 694
Independence 695
Framing the Constitution 696
The Revolution's Impact on Europe 697

The French Revolution, 1789–1791   697

The Breakdown of the Old Order 697
Legal Orders and Social Realities 698
The Formation of the National Assembly 699
The Revolt of the Poor and the Oppressed 700
A Limited Monarchy 703

World War and Republican France, 1791–1799   704

Foreign Reactions and the Beginning of War 704
The Second Revolution 706
Total War and the Terror 708
The Thermidorian Reaction and the Directory, 1794–1799 711

The Napoleonic Era, 1799–1815   712

Napoleon's Rule of France 712
Napoleon's Wars and Foreign Policy 714

• **Individuals in Society:** *Jakob Walter, German Draftee with Napoleon* 719

Summary 718 • *Key Terms* 720

Notes 720 • *Suggested Reading* 720

LISTENING TO THE PAST: *Revolution and Women's Rights*   722

Chapter 22

The Revolution in Energy and Industry   725

The Industrial Revolution in Britain   726

Eighteenth-Century Origins 726
The First Factories 727
The Problem of Energy 729
The Steam Engine Breakthrough 730
The Coming of the Railroads 732
Industry and Population 733

Industrialization in Continental Europe   734

National Variations 735
The Challenge of Industrialization 736
Agents of Industrialization 738

Capital and Labor   740

The New Class of Factory Owners 741
The New Factory Workers 742
Conditions of Work 744
The Sexual Division of Labor 746
The Early Labor Movement in Britain 748

• **Individuals in Society:** *The Strutt Family* 743

Summary 750 • *Key Terms* 750

Notes 750 • *Suggested Reading* 750

LISTENING TO THE PAST: *The Testimony of Young Mine Workers*   752

Chapter 23

Ideologies and Upheavals, 1815–1850   755

The Peace Settlement   757

The European Balance of Power 757
Intervention and Repression 759
Metternich and Conservatism 759

Radical Ideas and Early Socialism   **761**

Liberalism 762
Nationalism 762
French Utopian Socialism 764
The Birth of Marxian Socialism 765

The Romantic Movement   **766**

Romanticism's Tenets 766
Literature 768
Art and Music 770

• **Individuals in Society:** *Germaine de Staël 769*

Reforms and Revolutions   **770**

National Liberation in Greece 771
Liberal Reform in Great Britain 773
Ireland and the Great Famine 776
The Revolution of 1830 in France 777

The Revolutions of 1848   **778**

A Democratic Republic in France 778
The Austrian Empire in 1848 780
Prussia and the Frankfurt Assembly 781

Summary 782 • *Key Terms* 782
Notes 782 • *Suggested Reading* 783

LISTENING TO THE PAST: *Faith in
Democratic Nationalism*   **784**

Chapter 24

Life in the Emerging Urban Society   **787**

Taming the City   **787**

Industry and the Growth of Cities 788
Public Health and the Bacterial Revolution 791
Urban Planning and Public Transportation 792

Rich and Poor and Those in Between   **796**

Social Structure 796
The Middle Classes 797
Middle-Class Culture 798
The Working Classes 799
Working-Class Leisure and Religion 804

The Changing Family   **805**

Premarital Sex and Marriage 805
Prostitution 806
Kinship Ties 807
Gender Roles and Family Life 807
Child Rearing 810

• **Individuals in Society:** *Franziska Tiburtius 809*

Science and Thought   **812**

The Triumph of Science 812
Social Science and Evolution 813
Realism in Literature 815

Summary 817 • *Key Terms* 817
Notes 817 • *Suggested Reading* 818

LISTENING TO THE PAST: *Middle-Class
Youth and Sexuality*   **820**

Images in Society: Class and Gender Boundaries in
Women's Fashion, 1850–1914 800

Chapter 25

The Age of Nationalism, 1850–1914   **823**

Napoleon III in France   **823**

The Second Republic and Louis Napoleon 824
Napoleon III's Second Empire 824

Nation Building in Italy and Germany   **826**

Italy to 1850 826
Cavour and Garibaldi in Italy 828
Germany Before Bismarck 829
Bismarck and the Austro-Prussian War, 1866 830
The Taming of the Parliament 831
The Franco-Prussian War, 1870–1871 832

Nation Building in the United States   **833**

The Modernization of Russia   **835**

The "Great Reforms" 835
The Industrialization of Russia 835
The Revolution of 1905 837

The Responsive National State, 1871–1914   **838**

The German Empire 839
Republican France 841
Great Britain and Ireland 843
The Austro-Hungarian Empire 844
Jewish Emancipation and Modern Anti-
Semitism 845

Marxism and the Socialist Movement   **846**

The Socialist International 846
Unions and Revisionism 848

• Individuals in Society: *Theodor Herzl 847*

Summary 850 • Key Terms 850

Notes 850 • Suggested Reading 850

LISTENING TO THE PAST: *The Making of a Socialist*   852

Chapter 26

The West and the World   855

Industrialization and the World Economy   855

The Rise of Global Inequality 856
The World Market 857
The Opening of China and Japan 860
Western Penetration of Egypt 862

The Great Migration   863

The Pressure of Population 863
European Migrants 865
Asian Migrants 867

Western Imperialism   868

The Scramble for Africa 869
Imperialism in Asia 872
Causes of the New Imperialism 872
Critics of Imperialism 876

• Individuals in Society: *Cecil Rhodes 873*

Responses to Western Imperialism   877

Empire in India 878
The Example of Japan 879
Toward Revolution in China 881

Summary 882 • Key Terms 882

Notes 882 • Suggested Reading 883

LISTENING TO THE PAST: *A French Leader Defends Imperialism*   884

Chapter 27

The Great Break: War and Revolution   887

The First World War   887

The Bismarckian System of Alliances 888
The Rival Blocs 890

The Outbreak of War 891
Reflections on the Origins of the War 894
The First Battle of the Marne 895
Stalemate and Slaughter 895
The Widening War 897

The Home Front   900

Mobilizing for Total War 900
The Social Impact 902
Growing Political Tensions 902

The Russian Revolution   904

The Fall of Imperial Russia 904
The Provisional Government 905
Lenin and the Bolshevik Revolution 906
Trotsky and the Seizure of Power 908
Dictatorship and Civil War 909

The Peace Settlement   911

The End of the War 911
Revolution in Germany 911
The Treaty of Versailles 912
American Rejection of the Versailles Treaty 914

• Individuals in Society: *Rosa Luxemburg 913*

Summary 916 • Key Terms 916

Notes 916 • Suggested Reading 917

LISTENING TO THE PAST: *The Experience of War*   918

Chapter 28

The Age of Anxiety   921

Uncertainty in Modern Thought   921

Modern Philosophy 924
The Revival of Christianity 925
The New Physics 926
Freudian Psychology 928
Twentieth-Century Literature 929

Modern Art and Music   930

Architecture and Design 930
Modern Painting 932
Modern Music 933

Images in Society: Pablo Picasso and Modern Art 934

Movies and Radio   936

The Search for Peace and Political Stability   937

Germany and the Western Powers 937
Hope in Foreign Affairs, 1924–1929 939
Hope in Democratic Government 940

• **Individuals in Society:** *Gustav Stresemann 941*

The Great Depression, 1929–1939   942

The Economic Crisis 942
Mass Unemployment 944
The New Deal in the United States 945
The Scandinavian Response to the
Depression 946
Recovery and Reform in Britain and
France 947

Summary 948 • Key Terms 948

Notes 948 • Suggested Reading 949

LISTENING TO THE PAST: *Life on the
Dole in Great Britain*   950

Chapter 29

**Dictatorships and the Second
World War**   953

Authoritarian States   954

Conservative Authoritarianism 954
Radical Totalitarian Dictatorships 954

Stalin's Soviet Union   957

From Lenin to Stalin 957
The Five-Year Plans 959
Life and Culture in Soviet Society 961
Stalinist Terror and the Great Purges 963

Mussolini and Fascism in Italy   964

The Seizure of Power 964
The Regime in Action 965

Hitler and Nazism in Germany   966

The Roots of Nazism 967
Hitler's Road to Power 967
The Nazi State and Society 969
Hitler's Popularity 970

Nazi Expansion and the Second World War   971

Aggression and Appeasement, 1933–1939 971
Hitler's Empire, 1939–1942 975
The Grand Alliance 979
The Tide of Battle 980

• **Individuals in Society:** *Le Chambon, a Refuge
for the Persecuted 981*

Summary 984 • Key Terms 984

Notes 984 • Suggested Reading 984

LISTENING TO THE PAST: *Witness to the
Holocaust*   986

Chapter 30

**Cold War Conflicts and Social
Transformations, 1945–1985**   989

The Division of Europe   990

The Origins of the Cold War 990
West Versus East 992

The Western Renaissance, 1945–1968   993

The Postwar Challenge 995
Toward European Unity 997
Decolonization 999
America's Civil Rights Revolution 1000

Soviet Eastern Europe, 1945–1968   1001

Stalin's Last Years, 1945–1953 1001
Reform and De-Stalinization, 1953–1964 1002
The End of Reform 1004

• **Individuals in Society:** *Tito and the Rise of
Independent Communism 1003*

Postwar Social Transformations, 1945–1968   1006

Science and Technology 1006
The Changing Class Structure 1007
New Roles for Women 1009
Youth and the Counterculture 1011

**Conflict and Challenge in the Late Cold
War, 1968–1985**   1013

The United States and Vietnam 1013
Détente or Cold War? 1015
The Women's Movement 1017
The Troubled Economy 1018
Society in a Time of Economic Uncertainty 1020

Summary 1021 • Key Terms 1021

Notes 1021 • Suggested Reading 1022

LISTENING TO THE PAST: *A Feminist
Critique of Marriage*   1024

Chapter 31

Revolution, Rebuilding, and New Challenges: 1985 to the Present   1027

The Decline of Communism in Eastern Europe   1028

The Soviet Union to 1985 1028
Solidarity in Poland 1030
Gorbachev's Reforms in the Soviet
    Union 1032

The Revolutions of 1989   1034

The Collapse of Communism in Eastern
    Europe 1035
The Disintegration of the Soviet Union 1038
German Unification and the End of the
    Cold War 1040

• **Individuals in Society:** *Václav Havel 1037*

Building a New Europe in the 1990s   1041

Common Patterns and Problems 1042
Recasting Russia 1044
Progress and Tragedy in Eastern Europe 1046
Unity and Identity in Western Europe 1050

New Challenges in the Twenty-first Century   1052

The Prospect of Population Decline 1052
The Growth of Immigration 1054
Europe's Role in the Global Era 1055

The Future in Perspective   1058

Key Terms 1060 • *Notes* 1060
Suggested Reading 1060

LISTENING TO THE PAST: *A Solidarity
    Leader Speaks from Prison*   1062

Index   I-1

Maps

21.1	Napoleonic Europe in 1810	716
22.1	Cottage Industry and Transportation in Eighteenth-Century England	726
22.2	The Industrial Revolution in England, ca 1850	734
22.3	Continental Industrialization, ca 1850	737
23.1	Europe in 1815	756
23.2	Peoples of the Habsburg Monarchy, 1815	760
24.1	European Cities of 100,000 or More, 1800 and 1900	788
24.2	The Modernization of Paris, ca 1850–1870	794
25.1	The Unification of Italy, 1859–1870	827
25.2	The Unification of Germany, 1866–1871	832
25.3	Slavery in the United States, 1860	834
26.1	European Investment to 1914	859
26.2	The Partition of Africa	870
26.3	Asia in 1914	874
27.1	The Balkans After the Congress of Berlin, 1878	892
27.2	The Balkans in 1914	892
27.3	The First World War in Europe	898
27.4	Shattered Empires and Territorial Changes After World War I	915
28.1	The Great Depression in the United States, Britain, and Europe	943
29.1	The Growth of Nazi Germany, 1933–1939	972
29.2	World War II in Europe	976
29.3	World War II in the Pacific	982
30.1	The Results of World War II in Europe	994
30.2	European Alliance Systems, 1949–1989	996
30.3	The New States in Africa and Asia	998
31.1	Democratic Movements in Eastern Europe, 1989	1034
31.2	Russia and the Successor States	1039
31.3	Contemporary Europe	1048
31.4	The Ethnic Composition of Yugoslavia, 1991	1049

Listening to the Past

Chapter 21   Revolution and Women's Rights   722

Chapter 22   The Testimony of Young Mine Workers   752

Chapter 23   Faith in Democratic Nationalism   784

Chapter 24   Middle-Class Youth and Sexuality   820

Chapter 25   The Making of a Socialist   852

Chapter 26   A French Leader Defends Imperialism   884

Chapter 27   The Experience of War   918

Chapter 28   Life on the Dole in Great Britain   950

Chapter 29   Witness to the Holocaust   986

Chapter 30   A Feminist Critique of Marriage   1024

Chapter 31   A Solidarity Leader Speaks from Prison   1062

Preface

A History of Western Society grew out of the authors' desire to infuse new life into the study of Western civilization. We knew that historians were using imaginative questions and innovative research to open up vast new areas of historical interest and knowledge. We also recognized that these advances had dramatically affected the subject of European economic, intellectual, and, especially, social history, while new research and fresh interpretations were also revitalizing the study of the traditional mainstream of political, diplomatic, and religious development. Despite history's vitality as a discipline, however, it seemed to us that both the broad public and the intelligentsia were generally losing interest in the past.

It was our conviction, based on considerable experience introducing large numbers of students to the broad sweep of Western civilization, that a book reflecting current trends could excite readers and inspire a renewed interest in history and our Western heritage. Our strategy was twofold. First, we made social history a core element of our work. We not only incorporated recent research by social historians but also sought to recreate the life of ordinary people in appealing human terms. At the same time we were determined to give great economic, political, cultural, and intellectual developments the attention they unquestionably deserve. We wanted to give individual readers and instructors a balanced, integrated perspective so that they could pursue—on their own or in the classroom—those themes and questions that they found particularly exciting and significant. In an effort to realize fully the potential of our fresh yet balanced approach, we made many changes, large and small, in the editions that followed.

Changes in the Seventh Edition

In preparing the Seventh Edition we have worked hard to keep our book up-to-date and to strengthen our distinctive yet balanced approach. Six main lines of revision guided our many changes.

New "Images in Society" Feature

A photo essay, "Images in Society," represents a new and distinctive feature of this Seventh Edition. The complete text contains four essays, each consisting of a short narrative with questions, accompanied by several images. The goal of the feature is to encourage students to think critically: to view and compare visual images and draw conclusions about the societies and cultures that produced those images. Thus, "The Roman Villa at Chedworth" in Britain mirrors Roman provincial cuture (Chapter 6). The essay "From Romanesque to Gothic" treats the architectural shift in medieval church building and aims to show how the Gothic cathedral reflected the ideals and values of medieval society (Chapter 11). Moving to modern times, the essay "Class and Gender Boundaries in Women's Fashion, 1850–1914" studies women's clothing in relationship to women's evolving position in society and gender relations (Chapter 24), while "Pablo Picasso and Modern Art" looks at Picasso's greatest paintings to gain insight into his principles and practices and the modernist revolution in art (Chapter 28).

"Individuals in Society" Feature

In the Sixth Edition of the text, we introduced the feature "Individuals in Society," including in each chapter a brief study of a woman, man, or group that informed us about the societies in which they lived; each study or biographical sketch was carefully integrated into the body of the text. Readers' positive response to this feature encouraged us to continue it in the Seventh Edition. The "Individuals in Society" feature grew out of our longstanding focus on people's lives and the varieties of historical experience, and we believe that readers will empathize with these human beings as they themselves seek to define their own identities. The spotlighting of individuals, both famous and obscure, perpetuates the greater attention to cultural and intellectual developments that we used to invigorate our social history in earlier editions, and it reflects changing interests within the historical profession as well as the development of "micro history."

The range of men and women we consider is broad. For this edition, and sometimes at readers' suggestion, we have dropped eight individuals and replaced them with others who we believe will prove more exciting or significant. Several are famous historical actors, such as Queen Nefertiti, the fourteenth-century B.C. queen of Egypt (Chapter 1); the mystical Saint Teresa of Ávila (Chapter 14); the charismatic Russian rebel Stenka Razin (Chapter 17); the ruthless British imperialist Cecil Rhodes (Chapter 26); the great Renaissance artist and polymath Leonardo da Vinci (Chapter 13); and the creator of communist Yugoslavia, Marshal Tito (Chapter 30). Other individuals illuminate aspects of their times but are not well known: a Roman soldier stationed in the provinces (Chapter 6); a serf who gained freedom and success in thirteenth-century France (Chapter 10); a Jewish businesswoman and mother of thirteen in seventeenth-century Germany (Chapter 16); Madame du Coudray, who traveled through eighteenth-century France instructing, in the king's name, midwives on the safest delivery practices (Chapter 20); and the Zionist leader Theodor Herzl, who made the creation of a Jewish state in Palestine his life's work (Chapter 25). Creative artists and intellectuals include the Muslim-Spanish mulatto artist Juan de Pareja (Chapter 15) and the controversial German statesman Gustav Stresemann (Chapter 28).

Expanded Ethnic and Geographic Scope

In this edition we have added significantly more discussion of groups and regions that are frequently short-changed in the general histories of Europe and Western civilization. This expanded scope is, we feel, an important improvement. It reflects the renewed awareness within the profession of Europe's enormous historical diversity, as well as the efforts of contemporary Europeans to understand the ambivalent and contested meanings of their national, regional, ethnic, and pan-European identities. Examples of this enlarged scope include early Greek influence in the western Mediterranean (Chapter 3) and subsequent developments there (Chapter 4); greatly expanded treatment of Europe's borderlands—Iberia, Ireland, Scotland, eastern Europe, and the Baltic area—in the Middle Ages and coverage of racism in these regions (Chapters 9, 11, 12); developments in absolutist Sweden and southern Russia (Chapter 17); Spanish urban life (Chapter 24); and completely new and detailed discussion of twentieth-century eastern Europe (Chapters 27, 30, and 31). A broader treatment of Jewish his-

tory has been integrated into the text throughout this edition, just as the history of women and gender was integrated in the Fifth Edition. Examples include anti-Semitism and Europeans' hostility toward Muslims (Chapter 9); anti-Semitism in the period of the Black Death (Chapter 12), in the Spanish inquisition (Chapter 13), and in tsarist Russia (Chapter 27); Jewish Enlightenment thought in Germany (Chapter 18); a new section on Jewish emancipation in nineteenth-century Europe, which is tied to the "Individuals in Society" feature on Theodor Herzl (Chapter 25); and the unfolding of the Holocaust before and during the Second World War (Chapter 29).

Organizational Changes

Our expanded ethnic and geographic scope is one of several organizational improvements. Chapter 23 has undergone extensive revision, including a reconceptualized section on nationalism and an entirely new section on Ireland and the Great Famine. In Chapter 28, material on the United States has been tightened. Perhaps most important, the book's final chapter dealing with the period from 1985 to the present has been greatly reorganized. Material on the cold war has been reduced, there are new sections on the 1990s, and Western relations with the Islamic world are treated, leading up to the fall of the Taliban. The book concludes with a discussion of European population decline, the surge of immigration, and the European Union's search for identity in the global age.

Incorporation of Recent Scholarship

As in all previous revisions we have made a conscientious effort to keep our book up-to-date with new and significant scholarship. Because the authors are committed to a balanced approach that reflects the true value of history, we have continued to incorporate important new findings on political, economic, cultural, and intellectual developments in this edition. Revisions of this nature include extensive work on early Judaism based on archaeological evidence, and on the Phoenicians (Chapter 2); on the origins and development of the polis, revised in cooperation with the Copenhagen Polis Center (Chapter 3); on the catacombs as pilgrimage sites (Chapter 6); on Muslim-Christian relations (Chapters 7 and 9); on the work of ordinary and elite women in the Renaissance (Chapter 13); on recent interpretations of the sixteenth-century Reformations (Chapter 14); on the Atlantic economy, including a new subsection on the slave trade (Chapter 19); on nationalism in the French Revolution (Chapter 21); and on women and the women's movement in the post–World War II era (Chapter 30). In short, recent research keeps the broad sweep of our history fresh.

Revised Full-Color Art and Map Programs

Finally, the illustrative component of our work has been carefully revised. We have added many new illustrations to our extensive art program, which includes nearly two hundred color reproductions, letting great art and important events come alive. As in earlier editions, all illustrations have been carefully selected to complement the text, and all carry informative captions, based on thorough research, that enhance their value. Artwork remains an integral part of our book; the past can speak in pictures as well as in words. The use of full color serves to clarify the maps and graphs and to enrich the textual material. The maps and map captions have been updated to correlate directly to the text, and new maps have been added in Chapters 7, 14, and 15.

*D*istinctive Features

In addition to the new "Images in Society" studies and the revised "Individuals in Society" essays, distinctive features from earlier editions guide the reader in the process of historical understanding. Many of these features also show how historians sift through and evaluate evidence. Our goal is to suggest how historians actually work and think. We want the reader to think critically and to realize that history is neither a list of cut-and-dried facts nor a senseless jumble of conflicting opinions. To help students and instructors realize this goal, we have significantly expanded the discussion of "what is history" in Chapter 1 of this edition.

Revised Primary-Source Feature

In the Fifth Edition we added a two-page excerpt from a primary source at the end of each chapter. This important feature, entitled "Listening to the Past," extends and illuminates a major historical issue considered in the chapter, and it has been well received by instructors and students. In the new edition we have reviewed our selections and made judicious substitutions. For example, in Chapter 4 Antiochus III meets the Jews, and in Chapter

5, students may explore Titus Flamininus on the liberty of the Greeks. In Chapter 13 Desiderius Erasmus explains why his era was an "Age of Gold," while in Chapter 14 students may reflect on Martin Luther's concept of liberty. Chapter 20 provides a new selection from Rousseau's influential treatise *Emile,* which deals with the gendered needs of education for girls; in Chapter 26 the French political leader Jules Ferry gives a spirited defense of French imperialism before the French Assembly, and in Chapter 28 the novelist and critic George Orwell analyzes the multiple consequences of prolonged unemployment in Britain during the Great Depression.

Each primary source opens with a problem-setting introduction and closes with "Questions for Analysis" that invite students to evaluate the evidence as historians would. Drawn from a range of writings addressing a variety of social, cultural, political, and intellectual issues, these sources promote active involvement and critical interpretation. Selected for their interest and importance and carefully fitted into their historical context, these sources do indeed allow the student to "listen to the past" and to observe how history has been shaped by individual men and women, some of them great aristocrats, others ordinary folk.

Problems of Historical Interpretation

The addition of more problems of historical interpretation in the Fifth Edition was well received, and so we have increased their number again in this edition. We believe that the problematic element helps our readers develop the critical-thinking skills that are among the most precious benefits of studying history. New examples of this more open-ended, interpretive approach include the debate over the transition from Antiquity to the early Middle Ages (Chapter 6), the question of European racism in the Middle Ages (Chapter 12), the issue of gender in the Italian cities of the Renaissance (Chapter 13), the renewed debate on personal and collective responsibilities for the Holocaust (Chapter 29), the dynamics of the great purges in the Soviet Union (Chapter 29), the process of reconstruction in eastern Europe, and the debate over globalization (Chapter 31).

Improved Chapter Features

Other distinctive features from earlier editions have been reviewed and improved in this Seventh Edition. To help guide the reader toward historical understanding, we pose specific historical questions at the beginning of each chapter. These questions are then answered in the course of each chapter, and each chapter concludes with a concise summary of its findings. All of the questions and summaries have been re-examined and frequently revised in order to maximize the usefulness of this popular feature.

A list of Key Terms concludes each chapter, another new feature of this edition. These terms are highlighted in boldface in the text. The student may use these terms to test his or her understanding of the chapter's material.

In addition to posing chapter-opening questions and presenting more problems in historical interpretation, we have quoted extensively from a wide variety of primary sources in the narrative, demonstrating in our use of these quotations how historians evaluate evidence. Thus primary sources are examined as an integral part of the narrative as well as presented in extended form in the "Listening to the Past" chapter feature. We believe that such an extensive program of both integrated and separate primary source excerpts will help readers learn to interpret and think critically.

Each chapter concludes with carefully selected suggestions for further reading. These suggestions are briefly described to help readers know where to turn to continue thinking and learning about the Western world. Also, chapter bibliographies have been thoroughly revised and updated to keep them current with the vast amount of new work being done in many fields.

Revised Timelines

New comparative timelines now begin each chapter. These timelines organize historical events into three categories: political/military, social/economic, and intellectual/religious. In addition, the topic-specific timelines appearing in earlier editions have been revised for this edition. Once again we provide a unified timeline in an appendix at the end of the book. Comprehensive and easy to locate, this useful timeline allows students to compare simultaneous political, economic, social, cultural, intellectual, and scientific developments over the centuries.

Flexible Format

Western civilization courses differ widely in chronological structure from one campus to another. To accommodate the various divisions of historical time into intervals that fit a two-quarter, three-quarter, or two-semester period, *A History of Western Society* is being published in four versions, three of which embrace the complete work:

- One-volume hardcover edition: A HISTORY OF WESTERN SOCIETY
- Two-volume paperback: A HISTORY OF WESTERN SOCIETY, *Volume I: From Antiquity to the Enlightenment* (Chapters 1–17); *Volume II: From Absolutism to the Present* (Chapters 16–31)
- Three-volume paperback: A HISTORY OF WESTERN SOCIETY, *Volume A: From Antiquity to 1500* (Chapters 1–13); *Volume B: From the Renaissance to 1815* (Chapters 12–21); *Volume C: From the Revolutionary Era to the Present* (Chapters 21–31)
- A HISTORY OF WESTERN SOCIETY, *Since 1300* (Chapters 12–31), for courses on Europe since the Renaissance

Note that overlapping chapters in both the two- and the three-volume sets permit still wider flexibility in matching the appropriate volume with the opening and closing dates of a course term.

Ancillaries

Learning and teaching ancillaries, listed below, also contribute to the usefulness of the text.

- *Study Guide*
- *Online Study Guide*
- *Instructor's Resource Manual*
- *Test Items*
- *Computerized Test Items*
- *ClassPrep: an instructor's resource CD-ROM*
- *Web site for instructors and students*
- *Blackboard™ and WebCT™ course cartridges*
- *Mosaic: Perspectives on Western Civilization web site*
- *GeoQuest™: an interactive map CD-ROM*
- *Bibliobase™: custom coursepacks in Western civilization*
- *Map Transparencies*

The excellent *Study Guide* has been thoroughly revised by Professor James Schmiechen of Central Michigan University. Professor Schmiechen has been a tower of strength ever since he critiqued our initial prospectus, and he has continued to give us many valuable suggestions as well as his warmly appreciated support. His *Study Guide* contains learning objectives, chapter summaries, chapter outlines, review questions, extensive multiple-choice exercises, self-check lists of important concepts and events, and a variety of study aids and suggestions. The Seventh Edition also retains the study-review exercises on the interpretation of visual sources and major political ideas, as well as suggested issues for discussion and essay, chronology reviews, and sections on studying effectively. These sections take the student through reading and studying activities such as underlining, summarizing, identifying main points, classifying information according to sequence, and making historical comparisons. For the Seventh Edition, new essay activities have been added for each of the four "Images in Society" features. The multiple-choice questions now offer five potential responses to coincide more directly with the Advanced Placement examination.

To enable both students and instructors to use the *Study Guide* with the greatest possible flexibility, the guide is available in two volumes, with considerable overlapping of chapters. Instructors and students who use only Volumes A and B of the text have all the pertinent study materials in a single volume, *Study Guide, Volume I* (Chapters 1–21); likewise, those who use only Volumes B and C of the text also have all the necessary materials in one volume, *Study Guide, Volume II* (Chapters 12–31). An *Online Study Guide* is also available for students. Accessible through Houghton Mifflin's @history web site (college.hmco.com), it functions as a tutorial, providing rejoinders to all multiple-choice questions that explain why the student's response is or is not correct.

The *Instructor's Resource Manual* and *Test Items* have been thoroughly revised for this edition by Professor Matthew Lenoe of Assumption College. The *Instructor's Resource Manual* contains instructional objectives, annotated chapter outlines, suggestions for lectures and discussion, term paper and class activity topics, primary-source exercises, map activities, and lists of audiovisual resources. For the Seventh Edition, a new section has been added on the "Images in Society" photo essays. The accompanying *Test Items* offer identification, multiple-choice, map, and essay questions for a total of approximately two thousand test items. In order to make the multiple-choice questions more useful to the Advanced Placement market, a fifth answer option has been added. These test items are available to adopters in a Windows™ version that includes editing capability.

New to this edition is the *ClassPrep CD-ROM* for instructors. This resource includes an electronic version of the *Instructor's Manual* and *Test Items,* PowerPoint™ maps from the text, a testbank of questions from Geo-Quest™, a transition guide, and other teaching aids.

The text-specific web site has been thoroughly revised and expanded for this edition. It now includes a glossary of Key Terms, a searchable bibliography, web activities, links to web resources, interactive exercises on the "Individuals in Society" and "Images in Society" features, chronological ordering activities, and the ACE self-testing quiz program. Visitors to the site can also access some of the older "Individuals in Society" features that did not make it into the Seventh Edition.

For institutions using either the Blackboard™ or WebCT™ platforms, we have designed a premium version of the course cartridge. Students can access a wealth of information, including learning objectives, chapter summaries, study outlines, review questions and self-quizzes, web research projects, and geography activities.

Houghton Mifflin is pleased to announce *Mosaic: Perspectives on Western Civilization.* This web site is a comprehensive, interactive resource that includes primary and secondary documents, interactive maps, fine art, and audio files, providing students with a direct connection to the raw material of Western civilization. Please contact your Houghton Mifflin Company representative for more information about this innovative multimedia program.

An exciting addition to our map program is a CD-ROM of thirty interactive maps—GeoQuest™, available for both instructors and students.

We are also proud to call attention to our on-line primary-source collection, Bibliobase™. This resource allows instructors to select from over six hundred documents to create their own customized readers for courses in Western civilization. Visit our web site at **www.bibliobase.com** for more information.

Finally, a set of full-color Map Transparencies of all the maps in the text is available on adoption.

Acknowledgments

It is a pleasure to thank the many instructors who read and critiqued the manuscript through its development:

Mary Elizabeth Ailes
University of Nebraska at Kearney

Ann Taylor Allen
University of Louisville

Robert J. Antony
Western Kentucky University

James Rushton Bishop
Holmes Community College

Gary B. Blumenshine
Indiana University, Fort Wayne

Donna L. Boutelle
California State University, Long Beach

Denvy A. Bowman
Coastal Carolina University

Jerry H. Brookshire
Middle Tennessee State University

James Burns
Clemson University

David Cherry
Montana State University, Bozeman

Stephanie Christelow
Idaho State University

Marc Cooper
Southwest Missouri State University

Jeffrey Cox
University of Iowa

Robert L. Dise, Jr.
University of Northern Iowa

Peter Dykema
University of Arizona

Carla C. Falkner
Northeast Mississippi Community College

James Felak
University of Washington

Malia B. Formes
Western Kentucky University

J. Drew Harrington
Troy State University, Montgomery

Jeffrey Hyson
Saint Joseph's University

Allen E. Jones
Troy State University

Sarah A. Kent
University of Wisconsin, Stevens Point

Danton Kostandarithes
Bolles School

Lisa M. Lane
MiraCosta College

Oliver L. Larkin
Hawkeye Community College

Michael V. Leggiere
Louisiana State University, Shreveport

Paul Douglas Lockhart
Wright State University

Martin C. J. Miller
Metropolitan State College of Denver

Michael Mini
Montgomery County Community College

R. Scott Moore
University of Dayton

Kathleen Paul
University of South Florida

Penne L. Prigge
Rockingham Community College

John B. Reid
Truckee Meadows Community College

Thomas S. Reid
Valencia Community College

Anna Marie Roos
University of Minnesota, Duluth

Thomas Schaeper
St. Bonaventure University

Richard Schellhammer
University of West Alabama

Linda Bregstein Scherr
Mercer County Community College

Jeffrey Smith
Northwestern State University

Philip M. Soergel
Arizona State University

Janet Thompson
Tallahassee Community College

Victoria E. Thompson
Arizona State University

Rosemary Fox Thurston
New Jersey City University

Laura Trauth
*The Community College of Baltimore County,
    Essex Campus*

George S. Vascik
Miami University

Sydney E. Watts
University of Richmond

Henry Weisser
Colorado State University

Terri York
Kilgore College

Mary E. Zamon
Marymount University

It is also a pleasure to thank our many editors at Houghton Mifflin for their efforts over many years. To Christina Horn, who guided production in the ever-more intensive email age, and to Julie Dunn, our development editor, we express our special appreciation. And we thank Carole Frohlich for her contributions in photo research and selection.

Many of our colleagues at the University of Illinois and at Georgetown University continued to provide information and stimulation, often without even knowing it. We thank them for it. Bennett Hill wishes to express his appreciation to Donald Franklin for his support and encouragement in the preparation of this Seventh Edition. John Buckler thanks Professor Jack Cargill for his advice on topics in Chapter 2. And he wishes to thank Professor Nicholas Yalouris, former General Inspector of Antiquities, for his kind permission to publish the newly discovered mosaic from Elis, Greece, in Chapter 3. He also wishes to thank Dr. Amy C. Smith, Curator of the Ure Museum of Archaeology of the University of Reading for her kind permission to publish the vase on page 61. John McKay happily acknowledges the excellent research assistance provided by Bryan Ganaway and Irina Gigova and he thanks them for it. He also expresses his deep appreciation to Jo Ann McKay for her sharp-eyed editorial support and unfailing encouragement.

Each of us has benefited from the criticism of his co-authors, although each of us assumes responsibility for what he has written. John Buckler has written the first six chapters; Bennett Hill has continued the narrative through Chapter 16; and John McKay has written Chapters 17 through 31. Finally, we continue to welcome the many comments and suggestions that have come from our readers, for they have helped us greatly in this ongoing endeavor.

J. P. M.   B. D. H.   J. B.

Dans l'enthousiasme de cette Li...
s'être donné, on imagina de pl...
en perpetuer la mémoire, ce q...
section avec grand appareil. Le...
accompagnoient le Maire, et u...
rendoit cette fete interessante...

The Planting of a Liberty Tree, by Pierre Antoine Leseur.
(Giraudon/Art Resource, NY)

21 The Revolution in Politics, 1775–1815

chapter outline

- Liberty and Equality

- The American Revolutionary Era, 1775–1789

- The French Revolution, 1789–1791

- World War and Republican France, 1791–1799

- The Napoleonic Era, 1799–1815

*T*he last years of the eighteenth century were a time of great upheaval. A series of revolutions and revolutionary wars challenged the old order of monarchs and aristocrats. The ideas of freedom and equality, ideas that have not stopped shaping the world since that era, flourished and spread. The revolutionary era began in North America in 1775. Then in 1789 France, the most influential country in Europe, became the leading revolutionary nation. It established first a constitutional monarchy, then a radical republic, and finally a new empire under Napoleon. The armies of France also joined forces with patriots and radicals abroad in an effort to establish new governments based on new principles throughout much of Europe. The world of modern domestic and international politics was born.

- What caused this era of revolution?
- What were the ideas and objectives of the men and women who rose up violently to undo the established system?
- What were the gains and losses for privileged groups and for ordinary people in a generation of war and upheaval?

These are the questions underlying this chapter's examination of the revolutionary era.

Liberty and Equality

Two ideas fueled the revolutionary period in both America and Europe: **liberty and equality.** What did eighteenth-century politicians and other people mean by liberty and equality, and why were those ideas so radical and revolutionary in their day?

The call for liberty was first of all a call for individual human rights. Even the most enlightened monarchs customarily claimed that it was their duty to regulate what people wrote and believed. Liberals of the revolutionary era protested such controls from on high. They demanded freedom to worship according to the dictates of their consciences, an end to censorship, and freedom from arbitrary laws and from judges who simply obeyed orders from the government. The Declaration of the Rights of Man, issued at the beginning of the French Revolution, proclaimed, "Liberty consists in being able to do anything that does not harm another person." In the context of the monarchical and absolutist forms of government then dominating Europe, this was a truly radical idea.

The call for liberty was also a call for a new kind of government. Revolutionary liberals believed that the people had **sovereignty**—that is, that the people alone had the authority to make laws limiting an individual's freedom of action. In practice, this system of government meant choosing legislators who represented the people and were accountable to them.

Equality was a more ambiguous idea. Eighteenth-century liberals argued that, in theory, all citizens should have identical rights and civil liberties and that the nobility had no right to special privileges based on the accident of birth. However, liberals accepted some well-established distinctions.

First, most eighteenth-century liberals were *men* of their times, and they generally shared with other men the belief that equality between men and women was neither practical nor desirable. Women played an important political role in the French Revolution at several points, but the men of the French Revolution limited formal political rights—the right to vote, to run for office, to participate in government—to men.

Second, liberals never believed that everyone should be equal economically. Quite the contrary. As Thomas Jefferson wrote in an early draft of the American Declaration of Independence (before he changed "property" to the more noble-sounding "happiness"), everyone was equal in "the pursuit of property." Jefferson and other liberals certainly did not expect equal success in that pursuit. Great differences in wealth and income between rich and poor were perfectly acceptable to liberals. The essential point was that everyone should legally have an equal chance.

In eighteenth-century Europe, however, such equality of opportunity was a truly revolutionary idea. Society was still legally divided into groups with special privileges, such as the nobility and the clergy, and groups with special burdens, such as the peasantry. And in most countries, various middle-class groups—professionals, business people, townspeople, and craftsmen—enjoyed privileges that allowed them to monopolize all sorts of economic activity. Liberals criticized not economic inequality itself but this kind of economic inequality based on legal distinctions for different social groups.

Although the ideas of liberty and equality—the central ideas of classical liberalism—had deep roots in Western history dating back to ancient Greece and the Judeo-

Christian tradition, classical liberalism first crystallized at the end of the seventeenth century and during the Enlightenment of the eighteenth century. Liberal ideas reflected the Enlightenment's stress on human dignity, personal liberty, and human happiness on earth and its faith in science, rationality, and progress.

Certain English and French thinkers were mainly responsible for joining the Enlightenment's concern for personal freedom and legal equality to a theoretical justification of liberal self-government. The two most important were John Locke and the baron de Montesquieu. Locke maintained that England's long political tradition rested on "the rights of Englishmen" and on representative government through Parliament. He argued that if a government oversteps its proper function of protecting the natural rights of life, liberty, and private property, it becomes a tyranny. Montesquieu was also inspired by English constitutional history. He, too, believed that powerful "intermediary groups"—such as the judicial nobility of which he was a proud member—offered the best defense of liberty against despotism.

The belief that representative institutions could defend their liberty and interests appealed powerfully to well-educated, prosperous, middle-class groups, which historians have traditionally labeled as the **bourgeoisie.** Yet liberal ideas about individual rights and political freedom also appealed to much of the hereditary nobility, at least in western Europe and as formulated by Montesquieu. **Representative government** did not mean democracy, which liberal thinkers tended to equate with mob rule. Rather, they envisioned voting for representatives as being restricted to those who owned property—those with "a stake in society." England had shown the way. After 1688 it had combined a parliamentary system and considerable individual liberty with a restricted franchise and unquestionable aristocratic pre-eminence. In the course of the eighteenth century, many leading French nobles, led by high-ranking noble judges, who were inspired by the doctrines of Montesquieu, were increasingly eager to follow the English example. Thus eighteenth-century liberalism in western Europe found broad support among the prosperous, well-educated elites in both the nobility and the bourgeoisie.

What liberalism lacked from the beginning was strong popular support, for at least two reasons. First, for common people, the great questions were not theoretical and political but immediate and economic; getting enough to eat was a crucial challenge. Second, some of the traditional practices and institutions that liberals wanted to abolish were dear to peasants and urban workers. Comfortable elites had already come into conflict with the

1770	1780	1790	1800	1810	1820

Political/Military

- 1773 Boston Tea Party
- 1775–1783 American Revolution
- 1789 Ratification of U.S. Constitution
- 1789 Storming of the Bastille
- 1789–1799 French Revolution
- 1793–1794 Robespierre's Reign of Terror
- 1793 Execution of Louis XVI
- 1794 Robespierre deposed and executed
- 1794–1799 Thermidorian reaction
- 1799–1815 Napoleonic era
- 1812 Napoleon invades Russia
- 1814–1815 Napoleon defeated and exiled

Social/Economic

- 1786–1789 Financial crisis in France
- 1789 Feudalism abolished in France
- 1793–1794 Economic controls to help poor in France

Intellectual/Religious

- 1775 Paine, *Common Sense*
- 1790 Burke, *Reflections on the Revolution in France*
- 1792 Wollstonecraft, *A Vindication of the Rights of Woman*

people in the eighteenth century over the enclosure of common lands and the regulation of food prices. This conflict would sharpen in the revolutionary era as differences in outlook and well-being led to many misunderstandings and disappointments for both groups.

The American Revolutionary Era, 1775–1789

The era of liberal political revolution began in the New World. The thirteen mainland colonies of British North America revolted against their home country and then succeeded in establishing a new, unified government.

Americans have long debated the meaning of their revolution. Some have even questioned whether it was a real revolution, as opposed to a war for independence. According to some scholars, the Revolution was conservative and defensive in that its demands were for the traditional liberties of English citizens; Americans were united against the British, but otherwise they were a satisfied people, not torn by internal conflict. Other scholars have argued that, on the contrary, the American Revolution was quite radical. It split families between patriots and Loyalists and divided the country. It achieved goals that were as fully advanced as those obtained by the French in their great Revolution a few years later.

How does one reconcile these positions? Both contain large elements of truth. The American revolutionaries did believe that they were demanding only the traditional rights of English men and women. But those traditional rights were liberal rights, and in the American context they had very strong democratic and popular overtones. Thus the American Revolution was fought in the name of established ideals that were still quite radical in the context of the times. And in founding a government firmly based on liberal principles, the Americans set an example that had a forceful impact on Europe and sped up political development there.

The Origins of the Revolution

The American Revolution had its immediate origins in a squabble over increased taxes. The British government had fought and decisively won the Seven Years' War (see pages 647–648) on the strength of its professional army and navy. The American colonists had furnished little real aid. The high cost of the war to the British, however, had led to a doubling of the British national debt. Anticipating further expense defending its recently conquered

Toward Revolution in Boston   The Boston Tea Party was only one of many angry confrontations between British officials and Boston patriots. On January 27, 1774, an angry crowd seized a British customs collector and then tarred and feathered him. This French engraving of 1784 commemorates the defiant and provocative action. *(The Granger Collection, New York)*

western lands from native American uprisings, the British government in London set about reorganizing the empire with a series of bold, largely unprecedented measures. Breaking with tradition, the British decided to maintain a large army in North America after peace was restored in 1763 and to tax the colonies directly. In 1765 the government pushed through Parliament the Stamp Act, which levied taxes on a long list of commercial and legal documents, diplomas, pamphlets, newspapers, almanacs, dice, and playing cards. A stamp glued to each article indicated the tax had been paid.

This effort to increase taxes as part of a tightening up of the empire seemed perfectly reasonable to the British. Heavier stamp taxes had been collected in Great Britain for two generations, and Americans were being asked only to pay a share of their own defense costs. Moreover, Americans had been paying only very low local taxes. The Stamp Act would have doubled taxes to about 2 shillings per person per year, whereas the British paid the highest taxes in the Western world—26 shillings per person. The colonists protested the Stamp Act vigorously and violently, however, and after their rioting and boycotts against British goods, Parliament reluctantly repealed the new tax.

As the fury over the Stamp Act revealed, much more was involved than taxes. The key questions were political. To what extent could the home government refashion the empire and reassert its power while limiting the authority of colonial legislatures and their elected representatives? Accordingly, who should represent the colonies, and who had the right to make laws for Americans? The British government replied that Americans were represented in Parliament, albeit indirectly (like most British people themselves), and that the absolute supremacy of Parliament throughout the empire could not be questioned. Many Americans felt otherwise. As John Adams put it, "A Parliament of Great Britain can have no more rights to tax the colonies than a Parliament of Paris." Thus imperial reorganization and parliamentary supremacy came to appear as grave threats to Americans' existing liberties and time-honored institutions.

Americans had long exercised a great deal of independence. In British North America, unlike England and Europe, no powerful established church existed, and personal freedom in questions of religion was taken for granted. The colonial assemblies made the important laws, which were seldom overturned by the home government. The right to vote was much more widespread than in England. In many parts of colonial Massachusetts, for example, as many as 95 percent of the adult males could vote.

Moreover, greater political equality was matched by greater social and economic equality. Neither a hereditary nobility nor a hereditary serf population existed, although the slavery of the Americas consigned blacks to a legally oppressed caste. Independent farmers were the largest group in the country and set much of its tone. In short, the colonial experience had slowly formed a people who felt themselves separate and distinct from the home country, and the controversies over taxation intensified those feelings.

In 1773 the dispute over taxes and representation flared up again. The British government had permitted the financially hard-pressed East India Company to ship its tea from China directly to its agents in the colonies rather than through London middlemen who sold to independent merchants in the colonies. Thus the company secured a vital monopoly on the tea trade, and colonial merchants were suddenly excluded from a lucrative business. The colonists were quick to protest.

In Boston men disguised as Indians had a rowdy "tea party" and threw the company's tea into the harbor. This led to extreme measures. The so-called Coercive Acts closed the port of Boston, curtailed local elections and town meetings, and greatly expanded the royal governor's power. County conventions in Massachusetts protested vehemently and urged that the acts be "rejected as the attempts of a wicked administration to enslave America." Other colonial assemblies joined in the denunciations. In September 1774, the First Continental Congress met in Philadelphia, where the more radical members argued successfully against concessions to the Crown. Compromise was also rejected by the British Parliament, and in April 1775 fighting began at Lexington and Concord.

Independence

The fighting spread, and the colonists moved slowly but inevitably toward open rebellion and a declaration of independence. The uncompromising attitude of the British government and its use of German mercenaries went a long way toward dissolving long-standing loyalties to the home country and rivalries among the separate colonies. *Common Sense* (1775), a brilliant attack by the recently arrived English radical Thomas Paine (1737–1809), also mobilized public opinion in favor of independence. A runaway bestseller with sales of 120,000 copies in a few months, Paine's tract ridiculed the idea of a small island ruling a great continent. In his call for freedom and republican government, Paine expressed Americans' growing sense of separateness and moral superiority.

On July 4, 1776, the Second Continental Congress adopted the Declaration of Independence. Written by Thomas Jefferson, the Declaration of Independence boldly listed the tyrannical acts committed by George III (r. 1760–1820) and confidently proclaimed the natural rights of mankind and the sovereignty of the American states. Sometimes called the world's greatest political editorial, the Declaration of Independence in effect universalized the traditional rights of English people and made them the rights of all mankind. It stated that "all men are created equal. . . . They are endowed by their Creator with certain unalienable rights. . . . Among these are life, liberty, and the pursuit of happiness." No other American political document has ever caused such excitement, either at home or abroad.

Many American families remained loyal to Britain; many others divided bitterly. After the Declaration of Independence, the conflict often took the form of a civil war pitting patriot against Loyalist. The Loyalists tended to be wealthy and politically moderate. Many patriots, too, were wealthy—individuals such as John Hancock and George Washington—but willingly allied themselves with farmers and artisans in a broad coalition. This coalition harassed the Loyalists and confiscated their property to help pay for the American war effort. The broad social base of the revolutionaries tended to make the liberal revolution democratic. State governments extended the right to vote to many more men (but not to any women) in the course of the war and re-established themselves as republics.

On the international scene, the French sympathized with the rebels and supplied guns and gunpowder from the beginning. The French wanted revenge for the humiliating defeats of the Seven Years' War. By 1777 French volunteers were arriving in Virginia, and a dashing young nobleman, the marquis de Lafayette (1757–1834), quickly became one of Washington's most trusted generals. In 1778 the French government offered a formal alliance to the American ambassador in Paris, Benjamin Franklin, and in 1779 and 1780 the Spanish and Dutch declared war on Britain. Catherine the Great of Russia helped organize the League of Armed Neutrality in order to protect neutral shipping rights, which Britain refused to recognize.

Thus by 1780 Great Britain was engaged in an imperial war against most of Europe as well as the thirteen colonies. In these circumstances, and in the face of severe reverses in India, in the West Indies, and at Yorktown in Virginia, a new British government decided to cut its losses. American negotiators in Paris were receptive. They feared that France wanted a treaty that would bottle up the new United States east of the Allegheny Mountains and give British holdings west of the Alleghenies to

The Signing of the Declaration of Independence, July 4, 1776   John Trumbull's famous painting shows the dignity and determination of America's revolutionary leaders. An extraordinarily talented group, they succeeded in rallying popular support without losing power to more radical forces in the process. *(The Granger Collection, New York)*

France's ally, Spain. Thus the American negotiators deserted their French allies and accepted the extraordinarily favorable terms Britain offered.

By the Treaty of Paris of 1783, Britain recognized the independence of the thirteen colonies and ceded all its territory between the Allegheny Mountains and the Mississippi River to the Americans. Out of the bitter rivalries of the Old World, the Americans snatched dominion over a vast territory.

Framing the Constitution

The liberal program of the American Revolution was consolidated by the federal Constitution, the Bill of Rights, and the creation of a national republic. Assembling in Philadelphia in the summer of 1787, the dele-gates to the Constitutional Convention were determined to end the period of economic depression, social uncertainty, and very weak central government that had followed independence. The delegates thus decided to grant the federal, or central, government important powers: regulation of domestic and foreign trade, the right to tax, and the means to enforce its laws.

Strong rule would be placed squarely in the context of representative self-government. Senators and congressmen would be the lawmaking delegates of the voters, and the president of the republic would be an elected official. The central government would operate in Montesquieu's framework of **checks and balances.** The executive, legislative, and judicial branches would systematically balance one another. The power of the federal government would in turn be checked by the powers of the individual states.

When the results of the secret deliberations of the Constitutional Convention were presented to the states for ratification, a great public debate began. The opponents of the proposed constitution—the Antifederalists—charged that the framers of the new document had taken too much power from the individual states and made the federal government too strong. Moreover, many Antifederalists feared for the personal liberties and individual freedoms for which they had just fought. In order to overcome these objections, the Federalists solemnly promised to spell out these basic freedoms as soon as the new Constitution was adopted. The result was the first ten amendments to the Constitution, which the first Congress passed shortly after it met in New York in March 1789. These amendments formed an effective bill of rights to safeguard the individual. Most of them—trial by jury, due process of law, right to assemble, freedom from unreasonable search—had their origins in English law and the English Bill of Rights of 1689. Other rights—the freedoms of speech, the press, and religion—reflected natural-law theory and the American experience.

The American Constitution and the Bill of Rights exemplified the great strengths and the limits of what came to be called **classical liberalism.** Liberty meant individual freedoms and political safeguards. Liberty also meant representative government but did not necessarily mean democracy, with its principle of one person, one vote. Equality—slaves excepted—meant equality before the law, not equality of political participation or wealth. The radicalism of liberal revolution in America was primarily legal and political, *not* economic or social.

The Revolution's Impact on Europe

Hundreds of books, pamphlets, and articles analyzed and romanticized the American upheaval. Thoughtful Europeans noted, first of all, its enormous long-term implications for international politics. A secret report by the Venetian ambassador to Paris in 1783 stated what many felt: "If only the union of the Provinces is preserved, it is reasonable to expect that, with the favorable effects of time, and of European arts and sciences, it will become the most formidable power in the world."[1] More generally, American independence fired the imaginations of those aristocrats who were uneasy with their hereditary privileges and those commoners who yearned for legal equality. Many Europeans believed that the world was advancing and that America was leading the way.

Europeans who dreamed of a new era were fascinated by the political lessons of the American Revolution. The

Americans had begun with a revolutionary defense against tyrannical oppression, and they had been victorious. They had then shown how rational beings could assemble together to exercise sovereignty and write a permanent constitution—a new social contract. All this gave greater reality to the concepts of individual liberty and representative government and reinforced one of the primary ideas of the Enlightenment: that a better world was possible.

The French Revolution, 1789–1791

No country felt the consequences of the American Revolution more directly than France. Hundreds of French officers served in America and were inspired by the experience. The most famous of these, the young and impressionable marquis de Lafayette, left home as a great aristocrat determined only to fight France's traditional foe, England. He returned with a love of liberty and firm republican convictions. French intellectuals and publicists engaged in passionate analysis of the federal Constitution as well as the constitutions of the various states of the new United States. The American Revolution undeniably hastened upheaval in France.

Yet the French Revolution did not mirror the American example. It was more radical and more complex, more influential and more controversial, more loved and more hated. For Europeans and most of the rest of the world, it was the great revolution of the eighteenth century, *the* revolution that opened the modern era in politics.

The Breakdown of the Old Order

Like the American Revolution, the French Revolution had its immediate origins in the financial difficulties of the government. The efforts of Louis XV's ministers to raise taxes had been thwarted by the high courts, led by the Parlement of Paris, which was strengthened in its opposition by widespread popular support (see page 622). When renewed efforts to reform the tax system met a similar fate in 1776, the government was forced to finance all of its enormous expenditures during the American war with borrowed money. As a result, the national debt and the annual budget deficit soared. By the 1780s, fully 50 percent of France's annual budget went for ever-increasing interest payments on the ever-increasing debt. Another 25 percent went to maintain the military, while 6 percent was absorbed by the costly and extravagant king and his court at Versailles. Less than 20 percent of

The Three Estates In this political cartoon from 1789 a woman of the third estate struggles under the burden of a nun and an aristocrat. The third estate is being represented in a new way as the true nation, oppressed by the parasitic clergy and nobility. *(Musée Carnavalet/Photo Bulloz)*

the entire national budget was available for the productive functions of the state, such as transportation and general administration. This was an impossible financial situation.

One way out would have been for the government to declare partial bankruptcy, forcing its creditors to accept greatly reduced payments on the debt. The powerful Spanish monarchy had regularly repudiated large portions of its debt in earlier times, and France had done likewise after an attempt to establish a French national bank had ended in financial disaster in 1720. Yet by the 1780s, the French debt was being held by an army of aristocratic and bourgeois creditors, and the French monarchy, though absolute in theory, had become too weak for such a drastic and unpopular action.

Nor could the king and his ministers, unlike modern governments, print money and create inflation to cover their deficits. Unlike England and Holland, which had far larger national debts relative to their populations, France had no central bank, no paper currency, and no means of creating credit. French money was good gold coin. Therefore, when a depressed economy and a lack of public confidence made it increasingly difficult for the government to obtain new gold loans in 1786, it had no alternative but to try increasing taxes. And since France's tax system was unfair and out-of-date, increased revenues were possible only through fundamental reforms. Such reforms, which would affect all groups in France's complex and fragmented society, opened a Pandora's box of social and political demands. Thus historians have usually looked to social forces and social relationships in their efforts to understand the Revolution, as we shall now see.

Legal Orders and Social Realities

As in the Middle Ages, France's 25 million inhabitants were still legally divided into three orders, or **estates**— the clergy, the nobility, and everyone else. As the nation's first estate, the clergy numbered about 100,000 and had important privileges. It owned about 10 percent of the land and paid only a "voluntary gift," rather than regular taxes, to the government every five years. Moreover, the church levied a tax (the tithe) on landowners, which averaged somewhat less than 10 percent. Much of the church's income was actually drained away from local parishes by political appointees and worldly aristocrats at the top of the church hierarchy—to the intense dissatisfaction of the poor parish priests.

The second legally defined estate consisted of some 400,000 noblemen and noblewomen—the descendants of "those who fought" in the Middle Ages. The nobles owned outright about 25 percent of the land in France, and they, too, were taxed very lightly. Moreover, nobles continued to enjoy certain **manorial rights,** or privileges of lordship, that dated back to medieval times and allowed them to tax the peasantry for their own profit. This was done by means of exclusive rights to hunt and fish, village monopolies on baking bread and pressing grapes for wine, fees for justice, and a host of other "useful privileges." In addition, nobles had "honorific privileges," such as the right to precedence on public occasions and the right to wear a sword. These rights conspicuously proclaimed the nobility's legal superiority and exalted social position.

Everyone else was a commoner, legally a member of the third estate. A few commoners—prosperous merchants or lawyers and officials—were well educated and rich, and might even buy up manorial rights as profitable investments. Many more commoners were urban artisans and unskilled day laborers. The vast majority of the third estate consisted of the peasants and agricultural workers in the countryside. Thus the third estate was a conglomeration of vastly different social groups united only by their shared legal status as distinct from the nobility and clergy.

In discussing the long-term origins of the French Revolution, historians have long focused on growing tensions between the nobility and the comfortable members of the third estate, usually known as the *bourgeoisie,* or middle class. A dominant historical interpretation, which held sway for at least two generations, maintained that the bourgeoisie was basically united by economic position and class interest. Aided by the general economic expansion discussed in Chapter 19, the middle class grew rapidly in the eighteenth century, tripling to about 2.3 million persons, or about 8 percent of France's population. Increasing in size, wealth, culture, and self-confidence, this rising bourgeoisie became progressively exasperated by archaic "feudal" laws restraining the economy and by the pretensions of a reactionary nobility, which was closing ranks against middle-class needs and aspirations. As a result, the French bourgeoisie eventually rose up to lead the entire third estate in a great social revolution, a revolution that destroyed feudal privileges and established a capitalist order based on individualism and a market economy.

In recent years, a flood of new research has challenged these accepted views. Above all, revisionist historians have questioned the existence of a growing social conflict between a progressive capitalistic bourgeoisie and a reactionary feudal nobility in eighteenth-century France. Instead, these historians see both bourgeoisie and nobility as highly fragmented, riddled with internal rivalries. The great nobility, for example, was profoundly separated from the lesser nobility by differences in wealth, education, and world-view. Differences within the bourgeoisie—between wealthy financiers and local lawyers, for example—were no less profound. Rather than standing as unified blocs against each other, nobility and bourgeoisie formed two parallel social ladders increasingly linked together at the top by wealth, marriage, and Enlightenment culture.

Revisionist historians stress three developments in particular. First, the nobility remained a fluid and relatively open order. Throughout the eighteenth century, substantial numbers of successful commoners continued to seek and obtain noble status through government service and purchase of expensive positions conferring nobility. Second, key sections of the nobility were no less liberal than the middle class, and until revolution actually be-

gan, both groups generally supported the judicial opposition to the government led by the Parlement of Paris. Third, the nobility and the bourgeoisie were not really at odds in the economic sphere. Both looked to investment in land and government service as their preferred activities, and the ideal of the merchant capitalist was to gain enough wealth to retire from trade, purchase estates, and live nobly as a large landowner. At the same time, wealthy nobles often acted as aggressive capitalists, investing especially in mining, metallurgy, and foreign trade.

The revisionists have clearly shaken the belief that the bourgeoisie and the nobility were inevitably locked in growing conflict before the Revolution. But in stressing the similarities between the two groups, especially at the top, revisionists have also reinforced the view, long maintained by historians, that the Old Regime had ceased to correspond with social reality by the 1780s. Legally, society was still based on rigid orders inherited from the Middle Ages. In reality, France had already moved far toward being a society based on wealth and education, where an emerging elite that included both aristocratic and bourgeois notables was frustrated by a bureaucratic monarchy that continued to claim the right to absolute power.

The Formation of the National Assembly

The Revolution was under way by 1787, though no one could have realized what was to follow. Spurred by a depressed economy and falling tax receipts, Louis XVI's minister of finance revived old proposals to impose a general tax on all landed property as well as to form provincial assemblies to help administer the tax, and he convinced the king to call an assembly of notables to gain support for the idea. The assembled notables, who were mainly important noblemen and high-ranking clergy, were not in favor of it. In return for their support, they demanded that control over all government spending be given to the provincial assemblies. When the government refused, the notables responded that such sweeping tax changes required the approval of the Estates General, the representative body of all three estates, which had not met since 1614.

Facing imminent bankruptcy, the king tried to reassert his authority. He dismissed the notables and established new taxes by decree. In stirring language, the judges of the Parlement of Paris promptly declared the royal initiative null and void. When the king tried to exile the judges, a tremendous wave of protest swept the country. Frightened investors also refused to advance more loans to the state. Finally in July 1788, a beaten Louis XVI bowed to public opinion and called for a spring session of the Estates General. Absolute monarchy was collapsing.

What would replace it? Throughout the unprecedented election campaign of 1788 and 1789, that question excited France. All across the country, clergy, nobles, and commoners came together in their respective orders to draft petitions for change and to elect their respective delegates to the Estates General. The local assemblies of the clergy showed considerable dissatisfaction with the church hierarchy, and two-thirds of the delegates were chosen from among the poorer parish priests, who were commoners by birth. The nobles were politically divided. A conservative majority was drawn from the poorer and more numerous provincial nobility, but fully one-third of the nobility's representatives were liberals committed to major changes.

As for the third estate, there was great popular participation in the elections. Almost all male commoners twenty-five years of age or older had the right to vote. However, voting required two stages, which meant that most of the representatives finally selected by the third estate were well-educated, prosperous members of the middle class. Most of them were not businessmen but lawyers and government officials. Social status and prestige were matters of particular concern to this economic elite. There were no delegates elected from the great mass of laboring poor—the peasants and urban artisans.

The petitions for change coming from the three estates showed a surprising degree of consensus on most issues. There was general agreement that royal absolutism should give way to constitutional monarchy, in which laws and taxes would require the consent of the Estates General meeting regularly. All agreed that individual liberties would have to be guaranteed by law, that the economic position of the parish clergy would have to be improved, and that economic development required reforms. The striking similarities in the grievance petitions of the clergy, nobility, and third estate reflected the broad commitment of France's educated elite to liberalism.

Yet an increasingly bitter quarrel undermined this consensus during the intense electoral campaign: *how* would the Estates General vote, and precisely *who* would lead in the political reorganization that was generally desired? The Estates General of 1614 had sat as three separate houses. Any action had required the agreement of at least two branches, a requirement that had virtually guaranteed control by the nobility and the clergy. Immediately after the victory over the king, the aristocratic Parlement of Paris, mainly out of respect for tradition but partly out of a desire to enhance the nobility's political position, ruled that the Estates General should once again sit separately. The ruling was quickly denounced by some middle-class intellectuals, who demanded instead a single assembly dominated by the third estate to ensure fundamental reforms. Reflecting increased political competition

and a growing hostility toward aristocratic aspirations, the abbé Emmanuel Joseph Sieyès argued in 1789 in his famous pamphlet *What Is the Third Estate?* that the nobility was a tiny, overprivileged minority and that the neglected third estate constituted the true strength of the French nation. When the government agreed that the third estate should have as many delegates as the clergy and the nobility combined, but then rendered this act meaningless by upholding voting by separate order, middle-class leaders saw fresh evidence of an aristocratic conspiracy.

In May 1789, the twelve hundred delegates of the three estates paraded in medieval pageantry through the streets of Versailles to an opening session resplendent with feudal magnificence. The estates were almost immediately deadlocked. Delegates of the third estate refused to transact any business until the king ordered the clergy and nobility to sit with them in a single body. Finally, after a six-week war of nerves, a few parish priests began to go over to the third estate, which on June 17 voted to call itself the "National Assembly." On June 20, the delegates of the third estate, excluded from their hall because of "repairs," moved to a large indoor tennis court. There they swore the famous Oath of the Tennis Court, pledging not to disband until they had written a new constitution.

The king's actions were then somewhat contradictory. On June 23, he made a conciliatory speech urging reforms to a joint session, and four days later he ordered the three estates to meet together. At the same time, the vacillating and indecisive monarch apparently followed the advice of relatives and court nobles, who urged him to dissolve the Estates General by force. The king called an army of eighteen thousand troops toward Versailles, and on July 11 he dismissed his finance minister and his other more liberal ministers. Faced with growing opposition since 1787, Louis XVI had resigned himself to bankruptcy. Now he belatedly sought to reassert his historic "divine right" to rule. The middle-class delegates and their allies from the liberal nobility had done their best, but they were resigned to being disbanded at bayonet point. One third-estate delegate reassured a worried colleague, "You won't hang—you'll only have to go back home."[2]

The Revolt of the Poor and the Oppressed

While the educated delegates of the third estate pressed for symbolic equality with the nobility and clergy in a single legislative body at Versailles, economic hardship gripped the common people of France in a tightening vise. Grain was the basis of the diet of ordinary people in the eighteenth century, and in 1788 the harvest had been extremely poor. The price of bread began to soar.

The Oath of the Tennis Court   This painting, based on an unfinished work by Jacques-Louis David (1748–1825), enthusiastically celebrates the revolutionary rupture of June 20, 1789. Locked out of their assembly hall at Versailles and joined by some sympathetic priests, the delegates of the third estate have moved to an indoor tennis court and are swearing never to disband until they have written a new constitution and put France on a firm foundation. (*Réunion des Musées Nationaux/Art Resource, NY*)

In Paris, where bread was regularly subsidized by the government in an attempt to prevent popular unrest, the price rose to 4 sous. The poor could scarcely afford to pay 2 sous per pound, for even at that price a laborer with a wife and three children had to spend half of his wages to buy the family's bread.

Harvest failure and high bread prices unleashed a classic economic depression of the preindustrial age. With food so expensive and with so much uncertainty, the demand for manufactured goods collapsed. Thousands of artisans and small traders were thrown out of work. By the end of 1789, almost half of the French people would be in need of relief. One person in eight was a pauper living in extreme want. In Paris perhaps 150,000 of the city's 600,000 people were without work in July 1789.

Against this background of poverty and ongoing political crisis, the people of Paris entered decisively onto the revolutionary stage. They believed in a general, though ill-defined, way that the economic distress had human causes. They believed that they should have steady work and enough bread at fair prices to survive. Specifically, they feared that the dismissal of the king's moderate finance minister would put them at the mercy of aristocratic landowners and grain speculators. Rumors that the king's troops would sack the city began to fill the air. Angry crowds formed, and passionate voices urged action. On July 13, the people began to seize arms for the defense of the city as the king's armies moved toward Paris, and on July 14 several hundred people marched to the Bastille to search for weapons and gunpowder.

A medieval fortress with walls ten feet thick and eight great towers each one hundred feet high, the Bastille had long been used as a prison. It was guarded by eighty retired soldiers and thirty Swiss mercenaries. The governor of the fortress-prison refused to hand over the powder, panicked, and ordered his men to fire, killing ninety-eight people attempting to enter. Cannon were brought to batter the main gate, and fighting continued until the prison surrendered. The governor of the prison was later hacked to death, and his head and that of the mayor of Paris, who had been slow to give the crowd arms, were stuck on pikes and paraded through the streets. The next day a committee of citizens appointed the marquis de Lafayette commander of the city's armed forces. Paris was lost to the king, who was forced to recall the finance minister and disperse his troops. The popular uprising had broken the power monopoly of the royal army and thereby saved the National Assembly.

As the delegates resumed their long-winded and inconclusive debates at Versailles, the countryside sent them a radical and unmistakable message. Throughout France, peasants began to rise in spontaneous, violent, and effective insurrection against their lords, ransacking manor houses and burning feudal documents that recorded the peasants' obligations. Neither middle-class landowners, who often owned manors and village monopolies, nor the larger, more prosperous farmers were spared. In some areas, peasants reinstated traditional village practices, undoing recent enclosures and reoccupying old common lands. Peasants seized forests, and taxes went unpaid. Fear of vagabonds and outlaws—called the **Great Fear** by contemporaries— seized the countryside and fanned the flames of rebellion. The long-suffering peasants were doing their best to free themselves from manorial rights and exploitation.

Faced with chaos, yet afraid to call on the king to restore order, some liberal nobles and middle-class dele-

Storming the Bastille This representation by an untrained contemporary artist shows civilians and members of the Paris militia—the "conquerors of the Bastille"—on the attack. This successful action had enormous practical and symbolic significance, and July 14 has long been France's most important national holiday. *(Musée Carnavalet/Photo Hubert Josse—JLJ)*

gates at Versailles responded to peasant demands with a surprise maneuver on the night of August 4, 1789. The duke of Aiguillon, also notably one of France's greatest noble landowners, declared that

in several provinces the whole people forms a kind of league for the destruction of the manor houses, the ravaging of the lands, and especially for the seizure of the archives where the title deeds to feudal properties are kept. It seeks to throw off at last a yoke that has for many centuries weighted it down.[3]

He urged equality in taxation and the elimination of feudal dues. In the end, all the old exactions imposed on the peasants—serfdom where it still existed, exclusive hunting rights for nobles, fees for justice, village monopolies, the right to make peasants work on the roads, and a host of other dues—were abolished, generally without compensation. Though a clarifying law passed a week later was less generous, the peasants ignored the "fine print." They never paid feudal dues again. Thus the French peasantry, which already owned about 30 percent of all the land, achieved an unprecedented victory in the early days of revolutionary upheaval. Henceforth, the French peasants would seek mainly to protect and consolidate their revolutionary triumph. As the Great Fear subsided in the countryside, they became a force for order and stability.

A Limited Monarchy

The National Assembly moved forward. On August 27, 1789, it issued the Declaration of the Rights of Man, which stated, "Men are born and remain free and equal in rights." The declaration also maintained that mankind's natural rights are "liberty, property, security, and resistance to oppression" and that "every man is presumed innocent until he is proven guilty." As for law, "it is an expression of the general will; all citizens have the right to concur personally or through their representatives in its formation. . . . Free expression of thoughts and opinions is one of the most precious rights of mankind: every citizen may therefore speak, write, and publish freely." In short, this clarion call of the liberal revolutionary ideal guaranteed equality before the law, representative government for a sovereign people, and individual freedom. This revolutionary credo, only two pages long, was propagandized throughout France and Europe and around the world.

Moving beyond general principles to draft a constitution proved difficult. The questions of how much power the king should retain and whether he could permanently veto legislation led to another deadlock. Once again the decisive answer came from the poor—in this instance, the poor women of Paris.

Women customarily bought the food and managed the poor family's slender resources. In Paris great numbers of women also worked for wages, often within the putting-out system, making garments and luxury items destined for an aristocratic and international clientele. Immediately after the fall of the Bastille, many of France's great court nobles began to leave Versailles for foreign lands, so that a plummeting demand for luxuries intensified the general economic crisis; international markets also declined. The church was no longer able to give its traditional grants of food and money to the poor. Increasing unemployment and hunger put tremendous pressure on household managers, and the result was another popular explosion.

On October 5 some seven thousand desperate women marched the twelve miles from Paris to Versailles to demand action. A middle-class deputy looking out from the Assembly saw "multitudes arriving from Paris including fishwives and bullies from the market, and these people wanted nothing but bread." This great crowd invaded the Assembly, "armed with scythes, sticks and pikes." One tough old woman directing a large group of younger women defiantly shouted into the debate, "Who's that talking down there? Make the chatterbox shut up. That's not the point: the point is that we want bread."[4] Hers was the genuine voice of the people, essential to any understanding of the French Revolution.

The women invaded the royal apartments, slaughtered some of the royal bodyguards, and furiously searched for the queen, Marie Antoinette, who was widely despised for her frivolous and supposedly immoral behavior. "We are going to cut off her head, tear out her heart, fry her liver, and that won't be the end of it," they shouted, surging through the palace in a frenzy. It seems likely that only the intervention of Lafayette and the National Guard saved the royal family. But the only way to calm the disorder was for the king to go and live in Paris, as the crowd demanded.

The next day, the king, the queen, and their son left for Paris in the midst of a strange procession. The heads of two aristocrats, stuck on pikes, led the way. They were followed by the remaining members of the royal bodyguard, unarmed and mocked by fierce men holding sabers and pikes. A mixed and victorious multitude surrounded the carriage of the captured royal family, hurling crude insults at the queen. There was drinking and eating among the women, who had clearly emerged as a major element in the Parisian revolutionary crowd.[5]

The National Assembly followed the king to Paris, and the next two years, until September 1791, saw the consolidation of the liberal revolution. Under middle-class leadership, the National Assembly abolished the French nobility as a legal order and pushed forward with the creation of a

constitutional monarchy, which Louis XVI reluctantly agreed to accept in July 1790. In the final constitution, the king remained the head of state, but all lawmaking power was placed in the hands of the National Assembly, elected by the economic upper half of French males.

New laws broadened women's rights to seek divorce, to inherit property, and to obtain financial support from fathers for illegitimate children. But women were not allowed to vote or hold political office for at least two reasons. First, the great majority of comfortable, well-educated males in the National Assembly believed that women should be limited to child rearing and domestic duties and should leave politics and most public activities to men, as Rousseau had advocated in his influential *Emile* (see pages 686–687). Second, the delegates to the National Assembly were convinced that political life in absolutist France had been profoundly corrupt and that a prime example of this corruption was the way that some talented but immoral aristocratic women had used their sexual charms to manipulate weak rulers and their ministers. Thus delegates argued that excluding women from politics would help create the civic virtue that had been missing: pure, home-focused wives would raise the high-minded sons needed to govern the nation.

The National Assembly replaced the complicated patchwork of historic provinces with eighty-three departments of approximately equal size. The jumble of weights and measures that varied from province to province was reformed, leading to the introduction of the simple, uniform metric system in 1793. The National Assembly promoted the liberal concept of economic freedom. Monopolies, guilds, and workers combinations were prohibited, and barriers to trade within France were abolished in the name of economic liberty. Thus the National Assembly applied the critical spirit of the Enlightenment to reform France's laws and institutions completely.

The Assembly also imposed a radical reorganization on the country's religious life. It granted religious freedom to the tiny minority of French Jews and Protestants. Of greater impact, it then nationalized the Catholic church's property and abolished monasteries as useless relics of a distant past. The government used all former church property as collateral to guarantee a new paper currency, the *assignats,* and then sold these properties in an attempt to put the state's finances on a solid footing. Although the church's land was sold in large blocks, peasants eventually purchased much when it was subdivided. These purchases strengthened their attachment to the new revolutionary order in the countryside.

The religious reorganization of France brought the new government into conflict with the Catholic church and many sincere Christians, especially in the countryside. Many delegates to the National Assembly, imbued with the rationalism and skepticism of the eighteenth-century philosophes, harbored a deep distrust of popular piety and "superstitious religion." Thus they established a national church, with priests chosen by voters. In the face of widespread resistance, the National Assembly then required the Catholic clergy to take a loyalty oath to the new government and become just so many more employees of the state. The pope formally condemned this attempt to subjugate the church, and only half the priests of France took the oath of allegiance. The result was a deep division within both the country and the clergy on the religious question; confusion and hostility among French Catholics were pervasive. The attempt to remake the Catholic church, like the Assembly's abolition of guilds and workers combinations, sharpened the conflict between the educated classes and the common people that had been emerging in the eighteenth century. This policy toward the church was the revolutionary government's first important failure.

World War and Republican France, 1791–1799

When Louis XVI accepted the final version of the completed constitution in September 1791, a young and still obscure provincial lawyer and member of the National Assembly named Maximilien Robespierre (1758–1794) evaluated the work of two years and concluded, "The Revolution is over." Robespierre was both right and wrong. He was right in the sense that the most constructive and lasting reforms were in place. Nothing substantial in the way of liberty and useful reform would be gained in the next generation. He was wrong in the sense that a much more radical stage lay ahead. New heroes and new ideologies were to emerge in revolutionary wars and international conflict.

Foreign Reactions and the Beginning of War

The outbreak and progress of revolution in France produced great excitement and a sharp division of opinion in Europe and the United States. Liberals and radicals saw a mighty triumph of liberty over despotism. In Great Britain especially, they hoped that the French example would lead to a fundamental reordering of Parliament, which was in the hands of the aristocracy and a few wealthy merchants. After the French Revolution began, conservative leaders

FRENCH DEMOCRATS surprizing the Royal Runaways.

The Capture of Louis XVI, June 1791 This English cartoon satirizes the royal family's disastrous attempt to sneak out of France. Recognized and arrested only a few miles from safety across the Belgian border, Louis XVI appeared guilty of treason to many of the French. The radicalization of the Revolution accelerated. *(Courtesy of the Trustees of the British Museum)*

such as Edmund Burke (1729–1797) were deeply troubled by the aroused spirit of reform. In 1790 Burke published *Reflections on the Revolution in France,* one of the great intellectual defenses of European conservatism. He defended inherited privileges in general and those of the English monarchy and aristocracy. He glorified the unrepresentative Parliament and predicted that thoroughgoing reform like that occurring in France would lead only to chaos and tyranny. Burke's work sparked much debate.

One passionate rebuttal came from a young writer in London, Mary Wollstonecraft (1759–1797). Born into the middle class, Wollstonecraft was schooled in adversity by a mean-spirited father who beat his wife and squandered his inherited fortune. Determined to be independent in a society that generally expected women of her class to become homebodies and obedient wives, she struggled for years to earn her living as a governess and teacher—practically the only acceptable careers for single, educated women—before attaining success as a translator and author. Incensed by Burke's book, Wollstonecraft immediately wrote a blistering, widely read attack, *A Vindication of the Rights of Man* (1790).

Then she made a daring intellectual leap. She developed for the first time the logical implications of natural-law philosophy in her masterpiece, *A Vindication of the Rights of Woman* (1792). To fulfill the still-unrealized potential of the French Revolution and to eliminate the sexual inequality she had felt so keenly, she demanded that

the Rights of Women be respected . . . [and] JUSTICE for one-half of the human race. . . . It is time to effect a revolution in female manners, time to restore to them their lost

dignity, and make them, as part of the human species, labor, by reforming themselves, to reform the world.

Setting high standards for women—"I wish to persuade women to endeavor to acquire strength, both of mind and body"—Wollstonecraft broke with those who had a low opinion of women's intellectual potential. She advocated rigorous coeducation, which would make women better wives and mothers, good citizens, and even economically independent people. Women could manage businesses and enter politics if only men would give them the chance. Men themselves would benefit from women's rights, for Wollstonecraft believed that "the two sexes mutually corrupt and improve each other."[6] Wollstonecraft's analysis testified to the power of the Revolution to excite and inspire outside of France. Paralleling ideas put forth independently in France by Olympe de Gouges (1748–1793), a self-taught writer and woman of the people (see the feature "Listening to the Past: Revolution and Women's Rights" on pages 722–723), Wollstonecraft's work marked the birth of the modern women's movement for equal rights, and it was ultimately very influential.

The kings and nobles of continental Europe, who had at first welcomed the revolution in France as weakening a competing power, began to feel no less threatened than Burke and his supporters. When Louis XVI and Marie Antoinette were arrested and returned to Paris after trying unsuccessfully to slip out of France in June 1791, the monarchs of Austria and Prussia issued the Declaration of Pillnitz. This carefully worded statement declared their willingness to intervene in France in certain circumstances and was expected to have a sobering effect on revolutionary France without causing war.

But the crowned heads of Europe misjudged the revolutionary spirit in France. When the National Assembly disbanded, it sought popular support by decreeing that none of its members would be eligible for election to the new Legislative Assembly. This meant that when the new representative body convened in October 1791, it had a different character. The great majority of the legislators were still prosperous, well-educated, middle-class men, but they were younger and less cautious than their predecessors. Many of the deputies were loosely allied and called **Jacobins,** after the name of their political club.

The new representatives to the Assembly were passionately committed to liberal revolution and distrustful of monarchy after Louis's attempted flight. They increasingly lumped "useless aristocrats" and "despotic monarchs" together, and they easily whipped themselves into a patriotic fury with bombastic oratory. If the courts of Europe were attempting to incite a war of kings against France, then "we will incite a war of people against kings. . . . Ten million Frenchmen, kindled by the fire of liberty, armed with the sword, with reason, with eloquence would be able to change the face of the world and make the tyrants tremble on their thrones."[7] Only Robespierre and a very few others argued that people would not welcome liberation at the point of a gun. Such warnings were brushed aside. France would "rise to the full height of her mission," as one deputy urged. In April 1792, France declared war on Francis II, the Habsburg monarch.

France's crusade against tyranny went poorly at first. Prussia joined Austria in the Austrian Netherlands (present-day Belgium), and French forces broke and fled at their first encounter with armies of this First Coalition. The road to Paris lay open, and it is possible that only conflict between the eastern monarchs over the division of Poland saved France from defeat.

Military reversals and patriotic fervor led the Legislative Assembly to declare the country in danger. Volunteer armies from the provinces streamed through Paris, fraternizing with the people and singing patriotic songs like the stirring "Marseillaise," later the French national anthem.

In this supercharged wartime atmosphere, rumors of treason by the king and queen spread in Paris. On August 10, 1792, a revolutionary crowd attacked the royal palace at the Tuileries, capturing it after heavy fighting with the Swiss Guards. The king and his family fled for their lives to the nearby Legislative Assembly, which suspended the king from all his functions, imprisoned him, and called for a new National Convention to be elected by universal male suffrage. Monarchy in France was on its deathbed, mortally wounded by war and popular upheaval.

The Second Revolution

The fall of the monarchy marked a rapid radicalization of the Revolution, a phase that historians often call the **second revolution.** Louis's imprisonment was followed by the September Massacres. Wild stories seized the city that imprisoned counter-revolutionary aristocrats and priests were plotting with the allied invaders. As a result, angry crowds invaded the prisons of Paris and summarily slaughtered half the men and women they found. In late September 1792, the new, popularly elected National Convention proclaimed France a republic.

The republic sought to create a new popular culture, fashioning compelling symbols that broke with the past and glorified the new order. It adopted a brand-new revolutionary calendar, which eliminated saints' days and renamed the days and the months after the seasons of the year. Citizens were expected to address each other with the friendly "thou" of the people rather than with the formal "you" of the rich and powerful. The republic energetically promoted broad, open-air, democratic festivals. These spectacles brought the entire population together and sought to redirect the people's traditional enthusiasm for Catholic religious celebrations to secular holidays instilling republican virtue and a love of nation. These spectacles were less successful in villages than in cities, where popular interest in politics was greater and Catholicism was weaker.

All of the members of the National Convention were republicans, and at the beginning almost all belonged to the Jacobin club of Paris. But control of the Convention was increasingly contested by two bitterly competitive groups—the **Girondists,** named after a department in southwestern France, and **the Mountain,** led by Robespierre and another young lawyer, Georges Jacques Danton. The Mountain was so called because its members sat on the uppermost left-hand benches of the assembly hall. A majority of the indecisive Convention members, seated in the "Plain" below, floated back and forth between the rival factions.

This division was clearly apparent after the National Convention overwhelmingly convicted Louis XVI of treason. By a narrow majority, the Convention then sentenced him to death in January 1793. Louis died with tranquil dignity on the newly invented guillotine. One of his last statements was "I am innocent and shall die without fear. I would that my death might bring happiness to the French, and ward off the dangers which I foresee."[8]

Both the Girondists and the Mountain were determined to continue the "war against tyranny." The Prussians had been stopped at the Battle of Valmy on September 20, 1792, one day before the republic was proclaimed. French armies then invaded Savoy and captured Nice, moved into the German Rhineland, and by November 1792 were occupying the entire Austrian Netherlands. Everywhere they went, French armies of occupation chased the princes, "abolished feudalism," and found support among some peasants and middle-class people.

But the French armies also lived off the land, requisitioning food and supplies and plundering local treasures. The liberators looked increasingly like foreign invaders. International tensions mounted. In February 1793, the National Convention, at war with Austria and Prussia, declared war on Britain, Holland, and Spain as well. Republican France was now at war with almost all of Europe, a great war that would last almost without interruption until 1815.

As the forces of the First Coalition drove the French from the Austrian Netherlands, peasants in western France revolted against being drafted into the army. They were supported and encouraged in their resistance by devout Catholics, royalists, and foreign agents.

In Paris the quarrelsome National Convention found itself locked in a life-and-death political struggle between the Girondists and the Mountain. Both groups were sincere republicans, hating privilege and wanting to temper economic liberalism with social concern. Yet personal hatreds ran deep. The Girondists feared a bloody dictatorship by the Mountain, and the Mountain was no less convinced that the more moderate Girondists would turn to conservatives and even royalists in order to retain power. With the middle-class delegates so bitterly divided, the laboring poor of Paris emerged as the decisive political factor.

The laboring men and women of Paris always constituted—along with the peasantry in the summer of 1789—the elemental force that drove the Revolution forward. It was the artisans, day laborers, market women, and garment workers who had stormed the Bastille, marched on Versailles, driven the king from the Tuileries, and carried out the September Massacres. The laboring poor and the petty traders were often known as the **sans-culottes,** "without breeches," because sans-culottes men wore trousers instead of the knee breeches of the aristocracy and the solid middle class. The immediate interests of the sans-culottes were mainly economic, and in the

Contrasting Visions of the Sans-Culottes   The woman on the left, with her playful cat and calm simplicity, suggests how the French sans-culottes saw themselves as democrats and virtuous citizens. The ferocious sans-culotte harpy on the right, a creation of wartime England's vivid counter-revolutionary imagination, screams for more blood, more death: "I am the Goddess of Liberty! Long live the guillotine!" *(Bibliothèque Nationale, Paris)*

spring of 1793 rapid inflation, unemployment, and food shortages were again weighing heavily on poor families.

Moreover, by the spring of 1793, the sans-culottes had become keenly interested in politics. Encouraged by the so-called angry men, such as the passionate young ex-priest and journalist Jacques Roux, sans-culottes men and women were demanding radical political action to guarantee them their daily bread. At first the Mountain joined the Girondists in rejecting these demands. But in the face of military defeat, peasant revolt, and hatred of the Girondists, the Mountain and especially Robespierre became more sympathetic. The Mountain joined with sans-culottes activists in the city government to engineer a popular uprising, which forced the Convention to arrest thirty-one Girondist deputies for treason on June 2. All power passed to the Mountain.

Robespierre and others from the Mountain joined the recently formed Committee of Public Safety, to which the Convention had given dictatorial power to deal with the national emergency. These developments in Paris triggered revolt in leading provincial cities, such as Lyons and Marseilles, where moderates denounced Paris and demanded a decentralized government. The peasant revolt spread, and the republic's armies were driven back on all fronts. By July 1793, only the areas around Paris and on the eastern frontier were firmly held by the central government. Defeat seemed imminent.

Total War and the Terror

A year later, in July 1794, the Austrian Netherlands and the Rhineland were once again in the hands of conquering French armies, and the First Coalition was falling apart. This remarkable change of fortune was due to the revolutionary government's success in harnessing, for perhaps the first time in history, the explosive forces of a planned economy, revolutionary terror, and modern nationalism in a total war effort.

Robespierre and the Committee of Public Safety advanced with implacable resolution on several fronts in 1793 and 1794. First, they collaborated with the fiercely patriotic and democratic sans-culottes, who retained the common people's traditional faith in fair prices and a moral economic order and who distrusted most wealthy capitalists and all aristocrats. Thus Robespierre and his coworkers established, as best they could, a **planned economy** with egalitarian social overtones. Rather than let supply and demand determine prices, the government set maximum allowable prices for key products. Though the state was too weak to enforce all its price regulations, it did fix the price of bread in Paris at levels the poor

could afford. Rationing was introduced, and bakers were permitted to make only the "bread of equality"—a brown bread made of a mixture of all available flours. White bread and pastries were outlawed as luxuries. The poor of Paris may not have eaten well, but at least they ate.

They also worked, mainly to produce arms and munitions for the war effort. The government told craftsmen what to produce, nationalized many small workshops, and requisitioned raw materials and grain from the peasants. Sometimes planning and control did not go beyond orders to meet the latest emergency: "Ten thousand soldiers lack shoes. You will take the shoes of all the aristocrats in Strasbourg and deliver them ready for transport to headquarters at 10 A.M. tomorrow." But failures to control and coordinate were failures of means and not of desire. The second revolution and the ascendancy of the sans-culottes had produced an embryonic emergency socialism, which thoroughly frightened Europe's propertied classes and had great influence on the subsequent development of socialist ideology.

Second, while radical economic measures supplied the poor with bread and the armies with weapons, the **Reign of Terror** (1793–1794) used revolutionary terror to solidify the home front. Special revolutionary courts responsible only to Robespierre's Committee of Public Safety tried rebels and "enemies of the nation" for political crimes. Drawing on popular, sans-culottes support centered in the local Jacobin clubs, these local courts ignored normal legal procedures and judged severely. Some 40,000 French men and women were executed or died in prison. Another 300,000 suspects crowded the prisons and often brushed close to death in a revolutionary court.

Robespierre's Reign of Terror was one of the most controversial phases of the French Revolution. Most historians now believe that the Reign of Terror was not directed against any single class. Rather, it was a political weapon directed impartially against all who might oppose the revolutionary government. For many Europeans of the time, however, the Reign of Terror represented a frightening perversion of the generous ideals of 1789. It strengthened the belief that France had foolishly replaced a weak king with a bloody dictatorship.

The third and perhaps most decisive element in the French republic's victory over the First Coalition was its ability to draw on the explosive power of patriotic dedication to a national state and a national mission. An essential part of modern **nationalism**, this commitment was something new in history. With a common language and a common tradition newly reinforced by the ideas of popular sovereignty and democracy, large numbers of French people were stirred by a common loyalty. They developed

The French Revolution

May 5, 1789	Estates General convene at Versailles.
June 17, 1789	Third estate declares itself the National Assembly.
June 20, 1789	Oath of the Tennis Court is sworn.
July 14, 1789	Storming of the Bastille occurs.
July–August 1789	Great Fear ravages the countryside.
August 4, 1789	National Assembly abolishes feudal privileges.
August 27, 1789	National Assembly issues Declaration of the Rights of Man.
October 5, 1789	Women march on Versailles and force royal family to return to Paris.
November 1789	National Assembly confiscates church lands.
July 1790	Civil Constitution of the Clergy establishes a national church. Louis XVI reluctantly agrees to accept a constitutional monarchy.
June 1791	Royal family is arrested while attempting to flee France.
August 1791	Austria and Prussia issue the Declaration of Pillnitz.
April 1792	France declares war on Austria.
August 1792	Parisian mob attacks the palace and takes Louis XVI prisoner.
September 1792	September Massacres occur. National Convention declares France a republic and abolishes monarchy.
January 1793	Louis XVI is executed.
February 1793	France declares war on Britain, Holland, and Spain. Revolts take place in some provincial cities.
March 1793	Bitter struggle occurs in the National Convention between Girondists and the Mountain.
April–June 1793	Robespierre and the Mountain organize the Committee of Public Safety and arrest Girondist leaders.
September 1793	Price controls are instituted to aid the sans-culottes and mobilize the war effort.
1793–1794	Reign of Terror darkens Paris and the provinces.
Spring 1794	French armies are victorious on all fronts.
July 1794	Robespierre is executed. Thermidorian reaction begins.
1795–1799	Directory rules.
1795	Economic controls are abolished, and suppression of the sans-culottes begins.
1797	Napoleon defeats Austrian armies in Italy and returns triumphant to Paris.
1798	Austria, Great Britain, and Russia form the Second Coalition against France.
1799	Napoleon overthrows the Directory and seizes power.

The Last Roll Call   Prisoners sentenced to death by revolutionary courts listen to an official solemnly reading the names of those selected for immediate execution. After being bound, the prisoners will ride standing up in a small cart through the streets of Paris to the nearby guillotine. As this painting highlights, both women and men were executed for political crimes under the Terror. *(Mansell/TimePix)*

an intense emotional commitment to the defense of the nation, and they imagined the nation as a great loving family that included all right-thinking patriots.

In such circumstances, war was no longer the gentlemanly game of the eighteenth century, but rather total war, a life-and-death struggle between good and evil. Everyone had to participate in the national effort. According to a famous decree of August 23, 1793:

The young men shall go to battle and the married men shall forge arms. The women shall make tents and clothes, and shall serve in the hospitals; children shall tear rags into lint. The old men will be guided to the public places of the cities to kindle the courage of the young warriors and to preach the unity of the Republic and the hatred of kings.

Like the wars of religion, war in 1793 was a crusade. This war, however, was fought for a secular, rather than a religious, ideology.

The all-out mobilization of French resources under the Terror combined with the fervor of modern nationalism to create an awesome fighting machine. After August 1793, all unmarried young men were subject to the draft, and by January 1794 the French had about 800,000 soldiers on active duty in fourteen armies. A force of this size was unprecedented in the history of European warfare, and recent research concludes that the French armed forces outnumbered their enemies almost four to one.[9] Well trained, well equipped, and constantly indoctrinated, the enormous armies of the republic were led by young, impetuous generals. These generals often had risen from the ranks, and they personified the opportunities the Revolution seemed to offer gifted sons of the people. Following orders from Paris to attack relentlessly, French generals used mass assaults at bayonet point to overwhelm the enemy. "No maneuvering, nothing elaborate," declared the fearless

General Hoche. "Just cold steel, passion and patriotism."[10] By the spring of 1794, French armies were victorious on all fronts. The republic was saved.

The Thermidorian Reaction and the Directory, 1794–1799

The success of the French armies led Robespierre and the Committee of Public Safety to relax the emergency economic controls, but they extended the political Reign of Terror. Their lofty goal was increasingly an ideal democratic republic where justice would reign and there would be neither rich nor poor. Their lowly means were unrestrained despotism and the guillotine, which struck down any who might seriously question the new order. In March 1794, to the horror of many sans-culottes, Robespierre's Terror wiped out many of the angry men who had been criticizing Robespierre for being soft on the wealthy and who were led by the radical social democrat Jacques Hébert. Two weeks later, several of Robespierre's long-standing collaborators, led by the famous orator Danton, marched up the steps to the guillotine. A strange assortment of radicals and moderates in the Convention, knowing that they might be next, organized a conspiracy. They howled down Robespierre when he tried to speak to the National Convention on 9 Thermidor (July 27, 1794). On the following day, it was Robespierre's turn to be shaved by the revolutionary razor.

As Robespierre's closest supporters followed their leader, France unexpectedly experienced a thorough reaction to the despotism of the Reign of Terror. In a general way, this **Thermidorian reaction** recalled the early days of the Revolution. The respectable middle-class lawyers and professionals who had led the liberal revolution of 1789 reasserted their authority, drawing support from their own class, the provincial cities, and the better-off peasants. The National Convention abolished many economic controls, let prices rise sharply, and severely restricted the local political organizations where the sans-culottes had their strength. And all the while, wealthy bankers and newly rich speculators celebrated the sudden end of the Terror with an orgy of self-indulgence and ostentatious luxury, an orgy symbolized by the shockingly low-cut gowns that quickly became the rage among their wives and mistresses.

The collapse of economic controls, coupled with runaway inflation, hit the working poor very hard. The gaudy extravagance of the rich wounded their pride. The sans-culottes accepted private property, but they believed passionately in small business, decent wages, and economic

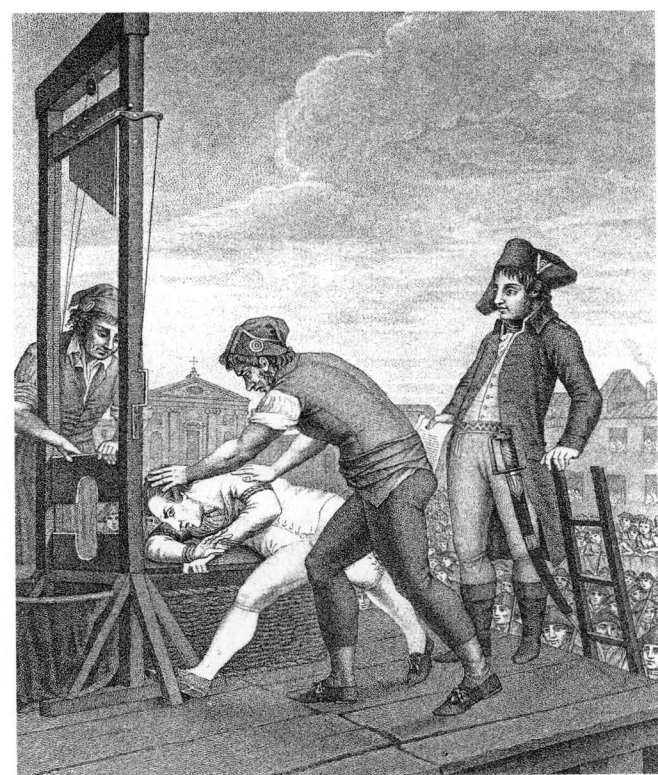

The Execution of Robespierre   The guillotine was painted red and completely wooden except for the heavy iron blade. Large crowds witnessed the executions in a majestic public square in central Paris, then known as the Place de la Revolution and now called the Place de la Concorde (Harmony Square). (*Musée Carnavalet/Edimedia*)

justice. Increasingly disorganized after Robespierre purged radical leaders, the common people of Paris finally revolted against the emerging new order in early 1795. The Convention quickly used the army to suppress these insurrections and made no concessions to the poor. In the face of all these reversals, the revolutionary fervor of the laboring poor in Paris finally subsided. Excluded and disillusioned, the urban poor would have little interest in and influence on politics until 1830.

In villages and small towns there arose a great cry for peace and a turning toward religion, especially from women, who had seldom experienced the political radicalization of sans-culottes women in the big cities. Instead, these women had tenaciously defended their culture and religious beliefs against the often heavy-handed attacks of antireligious revolutionary officials after 1789. As the government began to retreat on the religious question from 1796 to 1801, the women of rural France brought back the Catholic church and the open worship of God. In the words of a leading historian, these women worked for a return to a normal and structured lifestyle:

Peacefully but purposefully, they sought to re-establish a pattern of life punctuated by a pealing bell and one in which the rites of passage—birth, marriage, and death—were respected and hallowed. The state had intruded too far and women entered the public arena to push it back and won. It was one of the most resounding political statements made by the populace in the entire history of the Revolution.[11]

As for the middle-class members of the National Convention, in 1795 they wrote yet another constitution, which they believed would guarantee their economic position and political supremacy. As in previous elections, the mass of the population voted only for electors, whose number was cut back to men of substantial means. Electors then elected the members of a reorganized legislative assembly, as well as key officials throughout France. The new assembly also chose a five-man executive—the Directory.

The Directory continued to support French military expansion abroad. War was no longer so much a crusade as a means to meet ever-present, ever-unsolved economic problems. Large, victorious French armies reduced unemployment at home and were able to live off the territories they conquered and plundered.

The unprincipled action of the Directory reinforced widespread disgust with war and starvation. This general dissatisfaction revealed itself clearly in the national elections of 1797, which returned a large number of conservative and even monarchist deputies who favored peace at almost any price. The members of the Directory, fearing for their skins, used the army to nullify the elections and began to govern dictatorially. Two years later, Napoleon Bonaparte ended the Directory in a *coup d'état* and substituted a strong dictatorship for a weak one. The effort to establish stable representative government had failed.

The Napoleonic Era, 1799–1815

For almost fifteen years, from 1799 to 1814, France was in the hands of a keen-minded military dictator of exceptional ability. One of history's most fascinating leaders, Napoleon Bonaparte (1769–1821) realized the need to put an end to civil strife in France, in order to create unity and consolidate his rule. And he did. But Napoleon saw himself as a man of destiny, and the glory of war and the dream of universal empire proved irresistible. For

years he spiraled from victory to victory, but in the end he was destroyed by a mighty coalition united in fear of his restless ambition.

Napoleon's Rule of France

In 1799 when he seized power, young General Napoleon Bonaparte was a national hero. Born in Corsica into an impoverished noble family in 1769, Napoleon left home and became a lieutenant in the French artillery in 1785. After a brief and unsuccessful adventure fighting for Corsican independence in 1789, he returned to France as a French patriot and a dedicated revolutionary. Rising rapidly in the new army, Napoleon was placed in command of French forces in Italy and won brilliant victories there in 1796 and 1797. His next campaign, in Egypt, was a failure, but Napoleon returned to France before the fiasco was generally known. His reputation remained intact.

Napoleon soon learned that some prominent members of the legislature were plotting against the Directory. The dissatisfaction of these plotters stemmed not so much from the fact that the Directory was a dictatorship as from the fact that it was a weak dictatorship. Ten years of upheaval and uncertainty had made firm rule much more appealing than liberty and popular politics to these disillusioned revolutionaries. The abbé Sieyès personified this evolution in thinking. In 1789 he had written that the nobility was grossly overprivileged and that the entire people should rule the French nation. Now Sieyès's motto was "Confidence from below, authority from above."

Like the other members of his group, Sieyès wanted a strong military ruler. The flamboyant thirty-year-old Napoleon was ideal. Thus the conspirators and Napoleon organized a takeover. On November 9, 1799, they ousted the Directors, and the following day soldiers disbanded the legislature at bayonet point. Napoleon was named first consul of the republic, and a new constitution consolidating his position was overwhelmingly approved in a plebiscite in December 1799. Republican appearances were maintained, but Napoleon was already the real ruler of France.

The essence of Napoleon's domestic policy was to use his great and highly personal powers to maintain order and end civil strife. He did so by working out unwritten agreements with powerful groups in France whereby these groups received favors in return for loyal service. Napoleon's bargain with the solid middle class was codified in the famous Civil Code of 1804, which reasserted two of the fundamental principles of the liberal and essentially moderate revolution of 1789: equality of all male citizens before the law and absolute security of

The Napoleonic Era

November 1799	Napoleon overthrows the Directory.
December 1799	French voters overwhelmingly approve Napoleon's new constitution.
1800	Napoleon founds the Bank of France.
1801	France defeats Austria and acquires Italian and German territories in the Treaty of Lunéville. Napoleon signs the Concordat with the pope.
1802	France signs the Treaty of Amiens with Britain.
December 1804	Napoleon crowns himself emperor.
October 1805	Britain defeats the French and Spanish fleet at the Battle of Trafalgar.
December 1805	Napoleon defeats Austria and Russia at the Battle of Austerlitz.
1807	Napoleon redraws the map of Europe in the treaties of Tilsit.
1810	The Grand Empire is at its height.
June 1812	Napoleon invades Russia with 600,000 men.
Fall–Winter 1812	Napoleon makes a disastrous retreat from Russia.
March 1814	Russia, Prussia, Austria, and Britain form the Quadruple Alliance to defeat France.
April 1814	Napoleon abdicates and is exiled to Elba.
February–June 1815	Napoleon escapes from Elba and rules France until he is defeated at the Battle of Waterloo.

wealth and private property. Napoleon and the leading bankers of Paris established the privately owned Bank of France, which loyally served the interests of both the state and the financial oligarchy. Napoleon's defense of the new economic order also appealed successfully to the peasants, who had gained both land and status from the revolutionary changes. Thus Napoleon reconfirmed the gains of the peasantry and reassured the solid middle class, which had lost a large number of its revolutionary illusions in the face of social upheaval.

At the same time, Napoleon accepted and strengthened the position of the French bureaucracy. Building on the solid foundations that revolutionary governments had inherited from the Old Regime, he perfected a thoroughly centralized state. A network of prefects, subprefects, and centrally appointed mayors depended on Napoleon and served him well. Nor were members of the old nobility slighted. In 1800 and again in 1802, Napoleon granted amnesty to 100,000 émigrés on the condition that they return to France and take a loyalty oath. Members of this returning elite soon ably occupied many high posts in the expanding centralized state. Only one thousand die-hard monarchists were exempted and remained abroad. Napoleon also created a new imperial nobility in order to reward his most talented generals and officials.

Napoleon's skill in gaining support from important and potentially hostile groups is illustrated by his treatment of the Catholic church in France. In 1800 the French clergy was still divided into two groups: those who had taken an oath of allegiance to the revolutionary government and those in exile or hiding who had refused to do so. Personally uninterested in religion, Napoleon wanted to heal the religious division so that a united Catholic church in France could serve as a bulwark of order and social peace. After arduous negotiations, Napoleon and Pope Pius VII (1800–1823) signed the Concordat of 1801. The pope gained for French Catholics the precious right to practice their religion freely, but Napoleon gained political power: his government now nominated bishops, paid the clergy, and exerted great influence over the church in France.

The domestic reforms of Napoleon's early years were his greatest achievement. Much of his legal and administrative reorganization has survived in France to this day. More generally, Napoleon's domestic initiatives gave the great majority of French people a welcome sense of stability and national unity.

Order and unity had their price: Napoleon's authoritarian rule. Women, who had often participated in revolutionary politics without having legal equality, lost many of the gains they had made in the 1790s. Under the law of the new Napoleonic Code, women were dependents of either their fathers or their husbands, and they could not make contracts or even have bank accounts in their own names. Indeed, Napoleon and his advisers aimed at reestablishing a **family monarchy,** where the power of the husband and father was as absolute over the wife and the children as that of Napoleon was over his subjects.

Free speech and freedom of the press were continually violated. By 1811 only four newspapers were left, and they were little more than organs of government propaganda. The occasional elections were a farce. Later laws prescribed harsh penalties for political offenses.

These changes in the law were part of the creation of a police state in France. Since Napoleon was usually busy making war, this task was largely left to Joseph Fouché, an unscrupulous opportunist who had earned a reputation for brutality during the Reign of Terror. As minister of police, Fouché organized a ruthlessly efficient spy system, which kept thousands of citizens under continual police surveillance. People suspected of subversive activities were arbitrarily detained, placed under house arrest, or consigned to insane asylums. After 1810 political suspects were held in state prisons, as they had been during the Terror. There were about twenty-five hundred such political prisoners in 1814.

Napoleon's Wars and Foreign Policy

Napoleon was above all a military man, and a great one. After coming to power in 1799, he sent peace feelers to Austria and Great Britain, the two remaining members of the Second Coalition, which had been formed against France in 1798. When these overtures were rejected, French armies led by Napoleon decisively defeated the Austrians. In the Treaty of Lunéville (1801), Austria accepted the loss of almost all its Italian possessions, and German territory on the west bank of the Rhine was incorporated into France. Once more, as in 1797, the British were alone, and war-weary, like the French.

Still seeking to consolidate his regime domestically, Napoleon concluded the Treaty of Amiens with Great Britain in 1802. France remained in control of Holland, the Austrian Netherlands, the west bank of the Rhine, and most of the Italian peninsula. Napoleon was free to reshape the German states as he wished. The Treaty of Amiens was clearly a diplomatic triumph for Napoleon, and peace with honor and profit increased his popularity at home.

In 1802 Napoleon was secure but unsatisfied. Ever a romantic gambler as well as a brilliant administrator, he could not contain his power drive. Aggressively redrawing the map of Germany so as to weaken Austria and attract the secondary states of southwestern Germany toward France, Napoleon tried to restrict British trade with all of Europe. Deciding to renew war with Britain in May 1803, Napoleon concentrated his armies in the French ports on the Channel in the fall of 1803 and began making preparations to invade England. Yet Great Britain remained dominant on the seas. When Napoleon tried to bring his Mediterranean fleet around Gibraltar to northern France, a combined French and Spanish fleet was, after a series of mishaps, virtually annihilated by Lord Nelson at the Battle of Trafalgar on October 21, 1805. Invasion of England was henceforth impossible. Renewed fighting had its advantages, however, for the first consul used the wartime atmosphere to have himself proclaimed emperor in late 1804.

Austria, Russia, and Sweden joined with Britain to form the Third Coalition against France shortly before the Battle of Trafalgar. Actions such as Napoleon's assumption of the Italian crown had convinced both Alexander I of Russia and Francis II of Austria that Napoleon was a threat to their interests and to the European balance of power. Yet the Austrians and the Russians were no match for Napoleon, who scored a brilliant victory over them at the Battle of Austerlitz in December 1805. Alexander I decided to pull back, and Austria accepted large territorial losses in return for peace as the Third Coalition collapsed.

Victorious at Austerlitz, Napoleon proceeded to reorganize the German states to his liking. In 1806 he abolished many of the tiny German states as well as the ancient Holy Roman Empire. Napoleon established by decree the German Confederation of the Rhine, a union of fifteen German states minus Austria, Prussia, and Saxony.

The Coronation of Napoleon, 1804 (detail)   In this grandiose painting by Jacques-Louis David, Napoleon prepares to crown his beautiful wife, Josephine, in an elaborate ceremony in Notre Dame Cathedral. Napoleon, the ultimate upstart, also crowned himself. Pope Pius VII, seated glumly behind the emperor, is reduced to being a spectator. *(Louvre/Réunion des Musées Nationaux/Art Resource, NY)*

Naming himself "protector" of the confederation, Napoleon firmly controlled western Germany.

Napoleon's intervention in German affairs alarmed the Prussians, who mobilized their armies after more than a decade of peace with France. Napoleon attacked and won two more brilliant victories in October 1806 at Jena and Auerstädt, where the Prussians were outnumbered two to one. The war with Prussia, now joined by Russia, continued into the following spring, and after Napoleon's larger armies won another victory, Alexander I of Russia wanted peace.

For several days in June 1807, the young tsar and the French emperor negotiated face to face on a raft anchored in the middle of the Niemen River. All the while, the helpless Frederick William III of Prussia rode back and forth

on the shore anxiously awaiting the results. As the German poet Heinrich Heine said later, Napoleon had but to whistle and Prussia would have ceased to exist. In the subsequent treaties of Tilsit, Prussia lost half of its population, while Russia accepted Napoleon's reorganization of western and central Europe and promised to enforce Napoleon's economic blockade against British goods.

Increasingly Napoleon saw himself as the emperor of Europe and not just of France. The so-called Grand Empire he built had three parts. The core, or first part, was an ever-expanding France, which by 1810 included Belgium, Holland, parts of northern Italy, and much German territory on the east bank of the Rhine. Beyond French borders Napoleon established the second part: a number of dependent satellite kingdoms, on the thrones

716

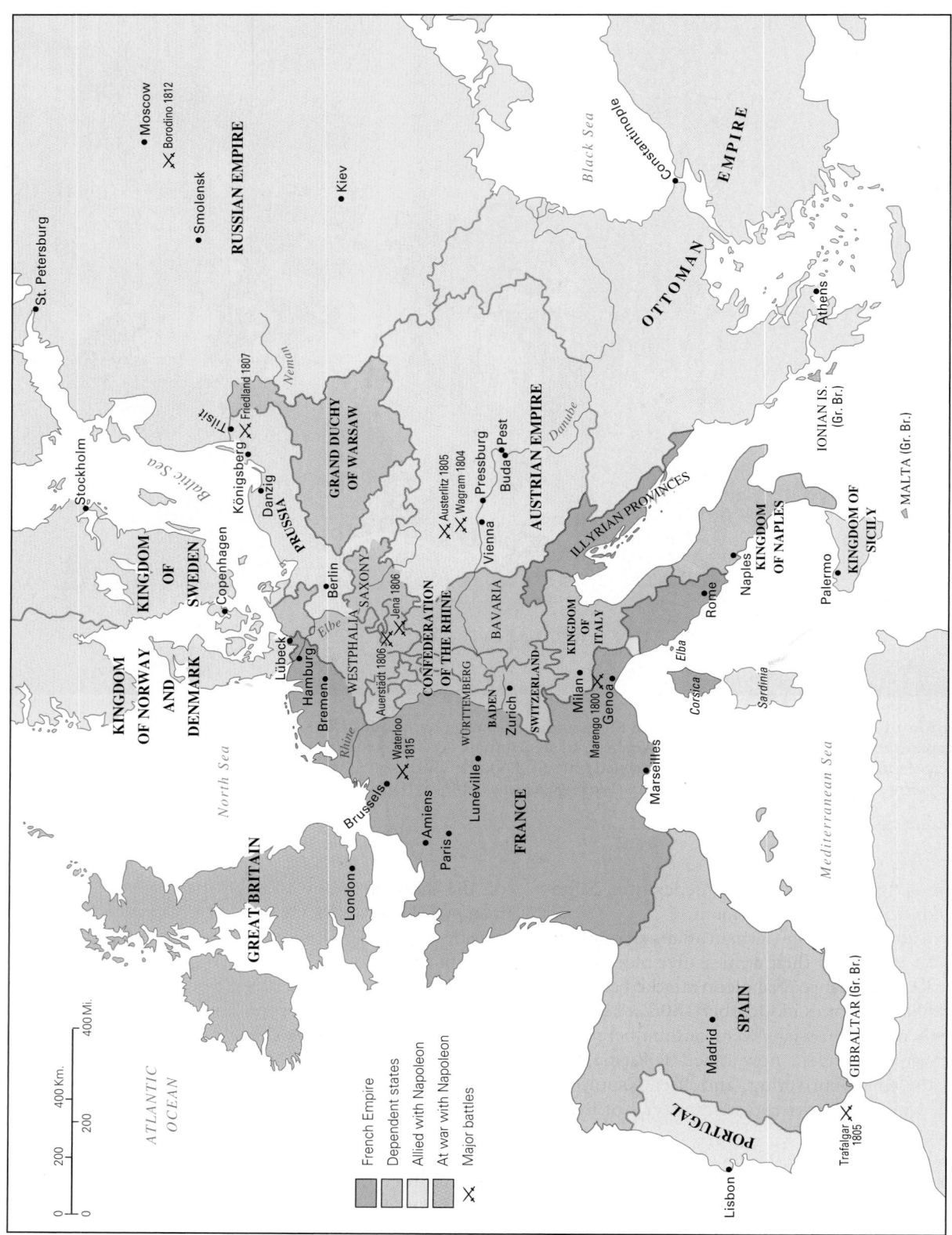

MAP 21.1 Napoleonic Europe in 1810 Only Great Britain remained at war with Napoleon at the height of the Grand Empire. Many British goods were smuggled through Helgoland, a tiny but strategic British possession off the German coast.

of which he placed (and replaced) the members of his large family. The third part comprised the independent but allied states of Austria, Prussia, and Russia. Both satellites and allies were expected after 1806 to support Napoleon's continental system and cease trade with Britain.

The impact of the Grand Empire on the peoples of Europe was considerable. In the areas incorporated into France and in the satellites (see Map 21.1), Napoleon introduced many French laws, abolishing feudal dues and serfdom where French revolutionary armies had not already done so. Some of the peasants and middle class benefited from these reforms. Yet Napoleon had to put the prosperity and special interests of France first in order to safeguard his power base. Levying heavy taxes in money and men for his armies, Napoleon came to be regarded more as a conquering tyrant than as an enlightened liberator. Thus French rule sparked patriotic upheavals and encouraged the growth of reactive nationalisms, for individuals in different lands learned to identify emotionally with their own embattled national families, as the French had done earlier.

The first great revolt occurred in Spain. In 1808 a coalition of Catholics, monarchists, and patriots rebelled against Napoleon's attempts to make Spain a French satellite with a Bonaparte as its king. French armies occupied Madrid, but the foes of Napoleon fled to the hills and waged uncompromising guerrilla warfare. Spain was a clear warning: resistance to French imperialism was growing.

Yet Napoleon pushed on, determined to hold his complex and far-flung empire together. In 1810, when the Grand Empire was at its height, Britain still remained at war with France, helping the guerrillas in Spain and Portugal. The continental system, organized to exclude British goods from the continent and force that "nation of shopkeepers" to its knees, was a failure. Instead, it was France that suffered from Britain's counter-blockade,

The War in Spain   This unforgettable etching by the Spanish painter Francisco Goya (1746–1828) comes from his famous collection "The Disasters of the War." A French firing squad executes captured Spanish rebels almost as soon as they are captured, an everyday event in a war of atrocities on both sides. Do you think these rebels are "terrorists," or "freedom fighters"? *(Foto Marburg/Art Resource, NY)*

which created hard times for French artisans and the middle class. Perhaps looking for a scapegoat, Napoleon turned on Alexander I of Russia, who in 1811 openly repudiated Napoleon's war of prohibitions against British goods.

Napoleon's invasion of Russia began in June 1812 with a force that eventually numbered 600,000, probably the largest force yet assembled in a single army. Only one-third of this Great Army was French, however; nationals of all the satellites and allies were drafted into the operation. (See the feature "Individuals in Society: Jakob Walter, German Draftee with Napoleon.") Originally planning to winter in the Russian city of Smolensk if Alexander did not sue for peace, Napoleon reached Smolensk and recklessly pressed on toward Moscow. The great Battle of Borodino that followed was a draw, and the Russians retreated in good order. Alexander ordered the evacuation of Moscow, which then burned in part, and he refused to negotiate. Finally, after five weeks in the abandoned city, Napoleon ordered a retreat. That retreat was one of the great military disasters in history. The Russian army, the Russian winter, and starvation cut Napoleon's army to pieces. When the frozen remnants staggered into Poland and Prussia in December, 370,000 men had died and another 200,000 had been taken prisoner.[12]

Leaving his troops to their fate, Napoleon raced to Paris to raise yet another army. Possibly he might still have saved his throne if he had been willing to accept a France reduced to its historical size—the proposal offered by Austria's foreign minister, Prince Klemens von Metternich. But Napoleon refused. Austria and Prussia deserted Napoleon and joined Russia and Great Britain in the Fourth Coalition. All across Europe, patriots called for a "war of liberation" against Napoleon's oppression, and the well-disciplined regular armies of Napoleon's enemies closed in for the kill. This time the coalition held together, cemented by the Treaty of Chaumont, which created a Quadruple Alliance intended to last for twenty years. Less than a month later, on April 4, 1814, a defeated Napoleon abdicated his throne. After this unconditional abdication, the victorious allies granted Napoleon the island of Elba off the coast of Italy as his own tiny state. Napoleon was even allowed to keep his imperial title, and France was required to pay him a yearly income of 2 million francs.

The allies also agreed to the restoration of the Bourbon dynasty, in part because demonstrations led by a few dedicated French monarchists indicated some support among the French people for that course of action. The new monarch, Louis XVIII (r. 1814–1824), tried to consolidate that support by issuing the Constitutional Char-

ter, which accepted many of France's revolutionary changes and guaranteed civil liberties. Indeed, the charter gave France a constitutional monarchy roughly similar to that established in 1791, although far fewer people had the right to vote for representatives to the resurrected Chamber of Deputies. Moreover, in an attempt to strengthen popular support for Louis XVIII's new government, France was treated leniently by the allies, which agreed to meet in Vienna to work out a general peace settlement.

Yet Louis XVIII—old, ugly, and crippled by gout—totally lacked the glory and magic of Napoleon. Hearing of political unrest in France and diplomatic tensions in Vienna, Napoleon staged a daring escape from Elba in February 1815. Landing in France, he issued appeals for support and marched on Paris with a small band of followers. French officers and soldiers who had fought so long for their emperor responded to the call. Louis XVIII fled, and once more Napoleon took command. But Napoleon's gamble was a desperate long shot, for the allies were united against him. At the end of a frantic period known as the Hundred Days, they crushed his forces at Waterloo on June 18, 1815, and imprisoned him on the rocky island of St. Helena, far off the western coast of Africa. Old Louis XVIII returned again—this time "in the baggage of the allies," as his detractors scornfully put it—and recommenced his reign. The allies now dealt more harshly with the apparently incorrigible French. As for Napoleon, he took revenge by writing his memoirs, skillfully nurturing the myth that he had been Europe's revolutionary liberator, a romantic hero whose lofty work had been undone by oppressive reactionaries. An era had ended.

Summary

The French Revolution left a compelling and many-sided political legacy. This legacy included, most notably, liberalism, assertive nationalism, radical democratic republicanism, embryonic socialism, and self-conscious conservatism. It also left a rich and turbulent history of electoral competition, legislative assemblies, and even mass politics. Thus the French Revolution and conflicting interpretations of its significance presented a whole range of political options and alternative visions of the future. For this reason, it was truly the revolution in modern European politics.

The revolution that began in America and spread to France was a liberal revolution. Revolutionaries on both sides of the Atlantic wanted to establish civil liberties and equality before the law within the framework of representative government, and they succeeded. In France liberal nobles and an increasingly class-conscious middle

Individuals in Society

Jakob Walter, German Draftee with Napoleon

In January 1812, a young German named Jakob Walter (1788–1864) was recalled to active duty in the army of Württemberg, a Napoleonic satellite in the Confederation of the Rhine. Stonemason and common draftee, Walter later wrote a rare enlisted man's account of the Russian campaign, a personal history that testified to the terrible price paid by the common people for a generation of war.

Napoleon's invasion of Russia was a desperate gamble from the beginning. French armies were accustomed to living off well-developed local economies, but this strategy did not work well in poor, sparsely populated eastern Europe. Scrounging for food dominated Walter's recollection of earlier fighting in Poland, and now, in 1812, the food situation was much worse. Crossing into Russia, Walter and his buddies found the nearby villages half-burned and stripped of food. Running down an occasional hog, they greedily tore it to pieces and ate it raw. Strangled by dust and thirst and then pelted for days by cold rain, the Great Army raced to catch the retreating Russians and force them into battle. When the famished troops stopped, the desperate search for food began.

In mid-August Walter's company helped storm the city of Smolensk in heavy fighting. From there onward, the road was littered with men, horses, and wagons, and all the towns and villages had been burned by the Russians to deprive the enemy of supplies. Surrounded by all these horrors, Walter almost lost his nerve, but he drew on his Catholic faith and found the courage "to go on trustingly to meet my fate."* Fighting at the great Battle of Borodino, "where the death cries and the shattering gunfire seemed a hell," he and the allied troops entered a deserted and fire-damaged Moscow in mid-September. But food, liquor, and fancy silks were there for the taking, and the weather was warm.

On October 18, the reprieve was over, and the retreating allied infantrymen re-entered Hell. Yet Walter, "still alert and spirited," was asked by an officer to be his attendant and received for his services a horse to ride. The horse proved a lifesaver. It allowed Walter to forage for food farther off the highway, to flee from approaching Cossacks, and to conserve his strength as vicious freezing winter weather set in. Yet food found at great peril could be quickly lost. Once Walter fought off some French soldiers with the help

The retreat from Moscow; detail of an engraving by G. Küstler. Soldiers strip the sick of their blankets and boots, leaving them to die in the cold.
(New York Public Library, Slavonic Division)

of some nearby Germans, who then robbed him of his bread. But what, he reflected later, could one expect? The starving men had simply lost their humanity. "I myself could look cold-bloodedly into the lamenting faces of the wounded, the freezing, and the burned," he wrote. When his horse was stolen as he slept, he silently stole someone else's. Struggling on in this brutal every-man-for-himself environment, Walter reached Poland in late December and hobbled home, a rare survivor. He went on to recover, marry, and have ten children.

Why did Jakob Walter survive? Pure chance surely played a large part. So did his robust constitution and street smarts. His faith in God also provided strength to meet each day's challenges. The beautiful vision of returning home and seeing his family offered equal encouragement. Finally, he lacked hatred and animosity, whether toward the Russians, the French, or whomever. He accepted the things he could not change and concentrated on those he could.

Questions for Analysis

1. Why was obtaining food such a problem for Jakob Walter and his fellow soldiers?
2. What impresses you most about Walter's account of the Russian campaign?

*Jakob Walter, *The Diary of a Napoleonic Foot Soldier*, ed. with an introduction by M. Raeff (New York: Penguin Books, 1993), p. 53. Also pp. 54, 66.

class overwhelmed declining monarchical absolutism and feudal privilege, thanks to the intervention of the common people—the sans-culottes and the peasants. Featuring electoral competition and civil equality, the government established by the Declaration of the Rights of Man and the French constitution of 1791 was remarkably similar to that created in America by the federal Constitution and the Bill of Rights. France's new political system reflected a social structure based increasingly on wealth and achievement rather than on tradition and legal privileges.

After the establishment of the republic, the radical phase of the Revolution during the Terror, and the fall of Robespierre, the educated elites and the solid middle class reasserted themselves under the Directory. And though Napoleon sharply curtailed representative institutions and individual rights, he effectively promoted the reconciliation of old and new, of centralized bureaucracy and careers open to talent, of noble and bourgeois in a restructured property-owning elite. Louis XVIII had to accept the commanding position of this restructured elite, and in granting representative government and civil liberties to facilitate his restoration to the throne in 1814, he submitted to the rest of the liberal triumph of 1789 to 1791. The liberal core of the French Revolution had successfully survived a generation of war and dictatorship.

Revolution in France, as opposed to in the United States, also left a multiplicity of legacies that extended well beyond the triumphant liberalism of 1789. Indeed, the lived experience of the French Revolution and the wars that went with it exercised a pervasive influence on politics and the political imagination in the nineteenth century, not only in France but throughout Europe and even the rest of the world. First, there was the radical legacy of the embattled republic of 1793 and 1794, with its sans-culottes democratic republicanism and its egalitarian ideology and embryonic socialism. This legacy would inspire republicans, democrats, and early socialists. Second, there was the legacy of a powerful and continuing reaction to the French Revolution and to aggressive French nationalism. Monarchists and traditionalists now believed that 1789 had been a tragic mistake. They concluded that democratic republicanism and sans-culottes activism led only to war, class conflict, and savage dictatorship. And even though revolutionary upheaval encouraged generations of radicals to believe that political revolution might remake society and even create a new humanity, conservatives and many comfortable moderates were profoundly disillusioned by the revolutionary era. They looked with nostalgia toward the supposedly ordered world of benevolent monarchy, firm government, and respectful common people.

Key Terms

liberty and equality	Jacobins
sovereignty	second revolution
bourgeoisie	Girondists
representative government	the Mountain
checks and balances	sans-culottes
classical liberalism	planned economy
estates	Reign of Terror
manorial rights	nationalism
Great Fear	Thermidorian reaction
constitutional monarchy	family monarchy

Notes

1. Quoted in R. R. Palmer, *The Age of the Democratic Revolution,* vol. 1 (Princeton, N.J.: Princeton University Press, 1959), p. 239.
2. G. Lefebvre, *The Coming of the French Revolution* (New York: Vintage Books, 1947), p. 81.
3. P. H. Beik, ed., *The French Revolution* (New York: Walker, 1970), p. 89.
4. G. Pernoud and S. Flaisser, eds., *The French Revolution* (Greenwich, Conn.: Fawcett, 1960), p. 61.
5. O. Hufton, *Women and the Limits of Citizenship in the French Revolution* (Toronto: University of Toronto Press, 1992), pp. 3–22.
6. Quotations from Wollstonecraft are drawn from E. W. Sunstein, *A Different Face: The Life of Mary Wollstonecraft* (New York: Harper & Row, 1975), pp. 208, 211; and H. R. James, *Mary Wollstonecraft: A Sketch* (London: Oxford University Press, 1932), pp. 60, 62, 69.
7. Quoted in L. Gershoy, *The Era of the French Revolution, 1789–1799* (New York: Van Nostrand, 1957), p. 150.
8. Pernoud and Flaisser, *The French Revolution,* pp. 193–194.
9. T. Blanning, *The French Revolutionary Wars, 1787–1802* (London: Arnold, 1996), pp. 116–128.
10. Quoted ibid., p. 123.
11. Hufton, *Women and the Limits of Citizenship,* p. 130.
12. D. Sutherland, *France, 1789–1815: Revolution and Counterrevolution* (New York: Oxford University Press, 1986), p. 420.

Suggested Reading

For fascinating eyewitness reports on the French Revolution, see the edited works by Beik and by Pernoud and Flaisser mentioned in the Notes. In addition, A. Young, *Travels in France During the Years 1787, 1788 and 1789* (1969), offers an engrossing contemporary description of France and Paris on the eve of revolution. E. Burke, *Reflections on the Revolution in France,* first published in 1790, is the classic conservative indictment. The intense passions the French Revolution has generated may be seen in nineteenth-century French historians, notably the enthusiastic J. Michelet, *History of the French Revolution;* the hostile H. Taine; and the judicious A. de Tocqueville, whose masterpiece, *The Old Regime and the French Revolution,* was first published in 1856. Important general studies on the entire period include the work by

Palmer, cited in the Notes, which paints a comparative international picture; E. J. Hobsbawm, *The Age of Revolution, 1789–1848* (1962); and O. Connelly, *French Revolution—Napoleonic Era* (1979). P. Schroeder, *The Transformation of European Politics, 1763–1848* (1994), is a masterful synthesis and reinterpretation, which may be compared with L. Dehio, *The Precarious Balance: Four Centuries of the European Power Struggle* (1962).

Revisionist scholarship has created a wealth of new scholarship and interpretation. A. Cobban, *The Social Interpretation of the French Revolution* (1964), and F. Furet, *Interpreting the French Revolution* (1981), are major reassessments of long-dominant ideas, which are admirably presented in N. Hampson, *A Social History of the French Revolution* (1963), and in the volume by Lefebvre listed in the Notes. F. Furet, *Revolutionary France, 1770–1880* (1995), is an extended development of the author's revisionist interpretations. E. Kennedy, *A Cultural History of the French Revolution* (1989), beautifully written and handsomely illustrated, and W. Doyle, *Origins of the French Revolution*, 3d ed. (1988), are excellent on long-term developments. Among valuable studies, which generally are often quite critical of revolutionary developments, several are noteworthy: J. Bosher, *The French Revolution* (1988); S. Schama, *Citizens: A Chronicle of the French Revolution* (1989); W. Doyle, *The Oxford History of the French Revolution* (1989); and D. Sutherland, *France, 1789–1815: Revolution and Counterrevolution* (1986).

Two excellent anthologies concisely presenting a range of interpretations are F. Kafker and J. Laux, eds., *The French Revolutions: Conflicting Interpretations,* 4th ed. (1989), and G. Best, ed., *The Permanent Revolution: The French Revolution and Its Legacy, 1789–1989* (1988). G. Rudé makes the men and women of the great days of upheaval come alive in *The Crowd in the French Revolution* (1959), whereas R. R. Palmer studies sympathetically the leaders of the Terror in *Twelve Who Ruled* (1941). Four other particularly interesting, detailed works are B. Shapiro, *Revolutionary Justice in Paris, 1789–1790* (1993); D. Jordan, *The Revolutionary Career of Maximilien Robespierre* (1985); J. P. Bertaud, *The Army of the French Revolution: From Citizen-Soldier to Instrument of Power* (1988); and C. L. R. James, *The Black Jacobins* (1938, 1980), on black slave revolt in Haiti. Other significant studies on aspects of revolutionary France include P. Jones's pathbreaking *The Peasantry in the French Revolution* (1988);

W. Sewell, Jr.'s imaginative *Work and Revolution in France: The Language of Labor from the Old Regime to 1848* (1980); and L. Hunt's innovative *The Family Romance of the French Revolution* (1992). M. Ozouf, *Festivals and the French Revolution* (1988), is a pioneering cultural study focusing on revolutionary symbols. Two major studies on the era's continuous wars are Blanning, cited in the Notes, and O. Connelly, *Blundering to Glory: Napoleon's Military Campaigns* (1987).

Studies on women in the French Revolution present conflicting interpretations. This may be seen by comparing two particularly important works: J. Landes, *Women and the Public Sphere in the Age of the French Revolution* (1988), and Hufton, listed in the Notes. D. Outram, *The Body and the French Revolution: Sex, Class and Political Culture* (1989), and L. Hunt, *The Family Romance of the French Revolution* (1992), provide innovative analyses of the gender-related aspects of revolutionary politics and are highly recommended. H. Applewhite and D. Levy, eds., *Women and Politics in the Age of Democratic Revolution* (1990), compares developments in leading countries. Mary Wollstonecraft's dramatic life is the subject of several good biographies, including those by Sunstein and James, cited in the Notes.

Two important works placing political developments in a comparative perspective are P. Higonnet, *Sister Republics: The Origins of French and American Republicanism* (1988), and E. Morgan, *Inventing the People: The Rise of Popular Sovereignty in England and America* (1988). B. Bailyn, *The Ideological Origins of the American Revolution* (1967), is also noteworthy.

The best synthesis on Napoleonic France is L. Bergeron, *France Under Napoleon* (1981). E. Arnold, Jr., ed., *A Documentary Survey of Napoleonic France* (1994), includes political and cultural selections. K. Kafker and J. Laux, eds., *Napoleon and His Times: Selected Interpretations* (1989), is an interesting collection of articles, which may be compared with R. Jones, *Napoleon: Man and Myth* (1977). Good biographies are J. Thompson, *Napoleon Bonaparte: His Rise and Fall* (1952); F. Markham, *Napoleon* (1964); and V. Cronin, *Napoleon Bonaparte* (1972). Wonderful novels inspired by the period include Raphael Sabatini's *Scaramouche,* a swashbuckler of revolutionary intrigue with accurate historical details; Charles Dickens's fanciful *A Tale of Two Cities;* and Leo Tolstoy's monumental saga of Napoleon's invasion of Russia (and much more), *War and Peace.*

Listening to the Past

Revolution and Women's Rights

The 1789 Declaration of the Rights of Man was a revolutionary call for legal equality, representative government, and individual freedom. But the new rights were strictly limited to men; Napoleon tightened further the subordination of French women.

Among those who saw the contradiction in granting supposedly universal rights to only half the population was Marie Gouze (1748–1793), known to history as Olympe de Gouges. The daughter of a provincial butcher and peddler, she pursued a literary career in Paris after the death of her husband. Between 1790 and 1793, she wrote more than two dozen political pamphlets under her new name. De Gouges's great work was her "Declaration of the Rights of Woman" (1791). Excerpted here, de Gouges's manifesto went beyond the 1789 Rights of Man. It called on males to end their oppression of women and give women equal rights. A radical on women's issues, de Gouges sympathized with the monarchy and criticized Robespierre in print. Convicted of sedition, she was guillotined in November 1793.

. . . Man, are you capable of being just? . . . Tell me, what gives you sovereign empire to oppress my sex? Your strength? Your talents? Observe the Creator in his wisdom . . . and give me, if you dare, an example of this tyrannical empire. Go back to animals, consult the elements, study plants . . . and distinguish, if you can, the sexes in the administration of nature. Everywhere you will find them mingled; everywhere they cooperate in harmonious togetherness in this immortal masterpiece.

Man alone has raised his exceptional circumstances to a principle. . . . [H]e wants to command as a despot a sex which is in full possession of its intellectual faculties; he pretends to enjoy the Revolution and to claim his rights to equality in order to say nothing more about it.

DECLARATION OF THE RIGHTS OF WOMAN AND THE FEMALE CITIZEN

For the National Assembly to decree in its last sessions, or in those of the next legislature:

Preamble

Mothers, daughters, sisters and representatives of the nation demand to be constituted into a national assembly. Believing that ignorance, omission, or scorn for the rights of woman are the only causes of public misfortunes and of the corruption of governments, [the women] have resolved to set forth in a solemn declaration the natural, inalienable, and sacred rights of woman. . . .

. . . the sex that is as superior in beauty as it is in courage during the sufferings of maternity recognizes and declares in the presence and under the auspices of the Supreme Being, the following Rights of Woman and of Female Citizens:

I. Woman is born free and lives equal to man in her rights. Social distinctions can be based only on the common utility.

II. The purpose of any political association is the conservation of the natural and imprescriptible rights of woman and man; these rights are liberty, property, security, and especially resistance to oppression.

III. The principle of all sovereignty rests essentially with the nation, which is nothing but the union of woman and man. . . .

IV. Liberty and justice consist of restoring all that belongs to others; thus, the only limits on the exercise of the natural rights of woman are perpetual male tyranny; these limits are to be reformed by the laws of nature and reason.

V. Laws of nature and reason proscribe all acts harmful to society. . . .

VI. The law must be the expression of the general will; all female and male citizens must contribute either personally or through their representatives to its formation; it must be the same for all: male and female citizens, being equal in the eyes of the law, must be equally admitted to all honors, positions, and public employment according to their capacity and without other distinctions besides those of their virtues and talents.

VII. No woman is an exception; she is accused, arrested, and detained in cases determined by law. Women, like men, obey this rigorous law.

VIII. The law must establish only those penalties that are strictly and obviously necessary. . . .

IX. Once any woman is declared guilty, complete rigor is [to be] exercised by the law.

X. No one is to be disquieted for his very basic opinions; woman has the right to mount the scaffold; she must equally have the right to mount the rostrum, provided that her demonstrations do not disturb the legally established public order.

XI. The free communication of thoughts and opinions is one of the most precious rights of woman, since that liberty assures the recognition of children by their fathers. Any female citizen thus may say freely, I am the mother of a child which belongs to you, without being forced by a barbarous prejudice to hide the truth. . . .

XIII. For the support of the public force and the expenses of administration, the contributions of woman and man are equal; she shares all the duties . . . and all the painful tasks; therefore, she must have the same share in the distribution of positions, employment, offices, honors, and jobs. . . .

XIV. Female and male citizens have the right to verify, either by themselves or through their representatives, the necessity of the public contribution. This can only apply to women if they are granted an equal share, not only of wealth, but also of public administration. . . .

XV. The collectivity of women, joined for tax purposes to the aggregate of men, has the right to demand an accounting of his administration from any public agent.

XVI. No society has a constitution without the guarantee of rights and the separation of powers; the constitution is null if the majority of individuals comprising the nation have not cooperated in drafting it.

XVII. Property belongs to both sexes whether united or separate; for each it is an inviolable and sacred right. . . .

The late-eighteenth-century French painting *La Liberté*. *(Bibliothèque Nationale, Paris/Art Resource, NY)*

Postscript

Women, wake up. . . . Discover your rights. . . . Oh, women, women! When will you cease to be blind? What advantage have you received from the Revolution? A more pronounced scorn, a more marked disdain. . . . [If men persist in contradicting their revolutionary principles,] courageously oppose the force of reason to the empty pretensions of superiority . . . and you will soon see these haughty men, not groveling at your feet as servile adorers, but proud to share with you the treasure of the Supreme Being. Regardless of what barriers confront you; it is in your power to free yourselves; you have only to want to. . . .

Questions for Analysis

1. On what basis did de Gouges argue for gender equality? Did she believe in natural law?

2. What consequences did "scorn for the rights of woman" have for France, according to de Gouges?

3. Did de Gouges stress political rights at the expense of social and economic rights? If so, why?

Source: Olympe de Gouges, "Declaration of the Rights of Woman," in Darline G. Levy, Harriet B. Applewhite, and Mary D. Johnson, eds., *Women in Revolutionary Paris, 1789–1795* (Urbana: University of Illinois Press, 1979), pp. 87–96. Copyright © 1979 by the Board of Trustees, University of Illinois. Used with permission.

A colored engraving by J. C. Bourne of the Great Western Railway emerging from a tunnel. *(Science & Society Picture Library, London)*

22 The Revolution in Energy and Industry

chapter outline

- The Industrial Revolution in Britain

- Industrialization in Continental Europe

- Capital and Labor

*W*hile the revolution in France was opening a new political era, another revolution was beginning to transform economic and social life. This was the Industrial Revolution, which began in Great Britain around the 1780s and started to influence continental Europe after 1815. Because the Industrial Revolution was less dramatic than the French Revolution, some historians see industrial development as basically moderate and evolutionary. But from a longer perspective, it was rapid and brought about numerous radical changes. Quite possibly only the development of agriculture during Neolithic times had a comparable impact and significance.

The Industrial Revolution profoundly modified much of human experience. It changed patterns of work, transformed the social class structure and the way people thought about class, and eventually even altered the international balance of political power. The Industrial Revolution also helped ordinary people gain a higher standard of living as the widespread poverty of the preindustrial world was gradually reduced.

Unfortunately, the improvement in the European standard of living was quite limited until about 1850 for at least two reasons. First, even in Britain, only a few key industries experienced a technological revolution. Many more industries continued to use old methods, especially on the continent, and this held down the increase in total production. Second, the increase in total population, which began in the eighteenth century (see page 638), continued all across Europe as the era of the Industrial Revolution unfolded. As a result, the rapid growth in population threatened to eat up the growth in production and to leave most individuals poorer than ever. As a consequence, rapid population growth provided a somber background for European industrialization and made the wrenching transformation all the more difficult.

- What, then, characterized the Industrial Revolution?
- What were its origins, and how did it develop?
- How did the changes it brought affect people and society in an era of continued rapid population growth?

These are some of the questions this chapter will seek to answer.

The Industrial Revolution in Britain

The Industrial Revolution began in Great Britain, that historic union of Scotland, Wales, and England—the wealthiest and the dominant part of the country. It was something new in history, and it was quite unplanned. With no models to copy and no idea of what to expect, Britain had to pioneer not only in industrial technology but also in social relations and urban living. Between 1793 and 1815, these formidable tasks were complicated by almost constant war with France. As the trailblazer in economic development, as France was in political change, Britain must command special attention.

MAP 22.1 Cottage Industry and Transportation in Eighteenth-Century England England had an unusually good system of navigable rivers. From about 1770 to 1800 a canal-building boom linked these rivers together and greatly improved inland transportation.

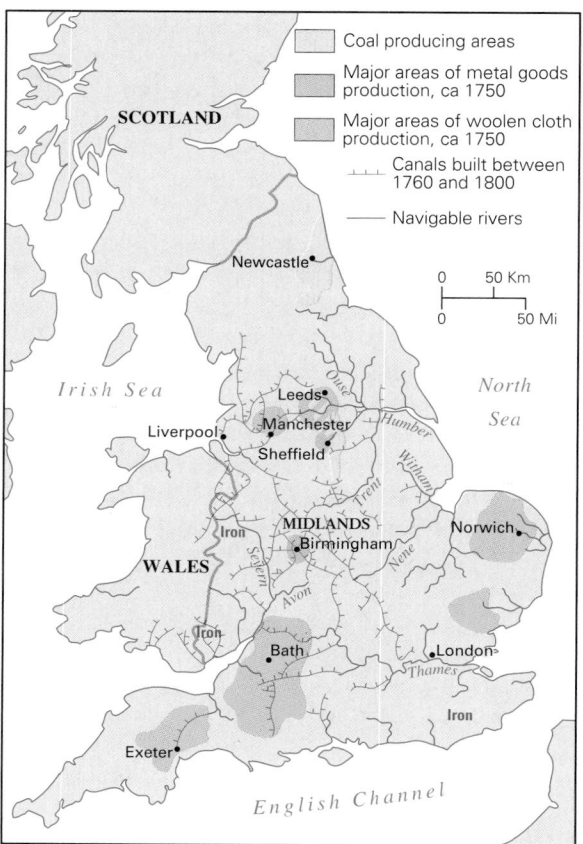

Eighteenth-Century Origins

Although many aspects of the British Industrial Revolution are still matters for scholarly debate, it is generally agreed that the industrial changes that did occur grew out of a long process of development. First, the expanding Atlantic economy of the eighteenth century served mercantilist Britain remarkably well. The colonial empire that Britain aggressively built, augmented by a strong position in Latin America and in the African slave trade, provided a growing market for British manufactured goods. So did the domestic market. In an age when it was much cheaper to ship goods by water than by land, no part of England was more than twenty miles from navigable water. Beginning in the 1770s, a canal-building boom greatly enhanced this natural advantage (see Map 22.1). Rivers and canals provided easy movement of England's and Wales's enormous deposits of iron and coal, resources that would be critical raw materials in Europe's early industrial age. Nor were there any tariffs within the country to hinder trade, as there were in France before 1789 and in politically fragmented Germany.

Second, agriculture played a central role in bringing about the Industrial Revolution in Britain. English farmers in particular were second only to the Dutch in productivity in 1700, and they were continually adopting new methods of farming as the century went on. The result, especially before 1760, was a period of bountiful crops and low food prices. The ordinary English family did not have to spend almost everything it earned just to buy bread. It could spend more on, for example, manufactured goods—leather shoes or a razor for the man, a bonnet or a shawl for the woman, toy soldiers for the son, and a doll for the daughter. Thus demand for goods within the country complemented the demand from the colonies.

Third, Britain had other assets that helped give rise to industrial leadership. Unlike eighteenth-century France, Britain had an effective central bank and well-developed credit markets. The monarchy and the aristocratic oligarchy, which had jointly ruled the country since 1688, provided stable and predictable government. At the same time, the government let the domestic economy operate with few controls, encouraging personal initiative, technical change, and a free market. Finally, Britain had long had a large class of hired agricultural laborers, rural proletarians whose numbers were further increased by the second great round of enclosures in the late eighteenth century. These rural wage earners were relatively mobile—compared to village-bound peasants in France and western Germany, for example—and along with cottage workers they formed a potential industrial labor force for capitalist entrepreneurs.

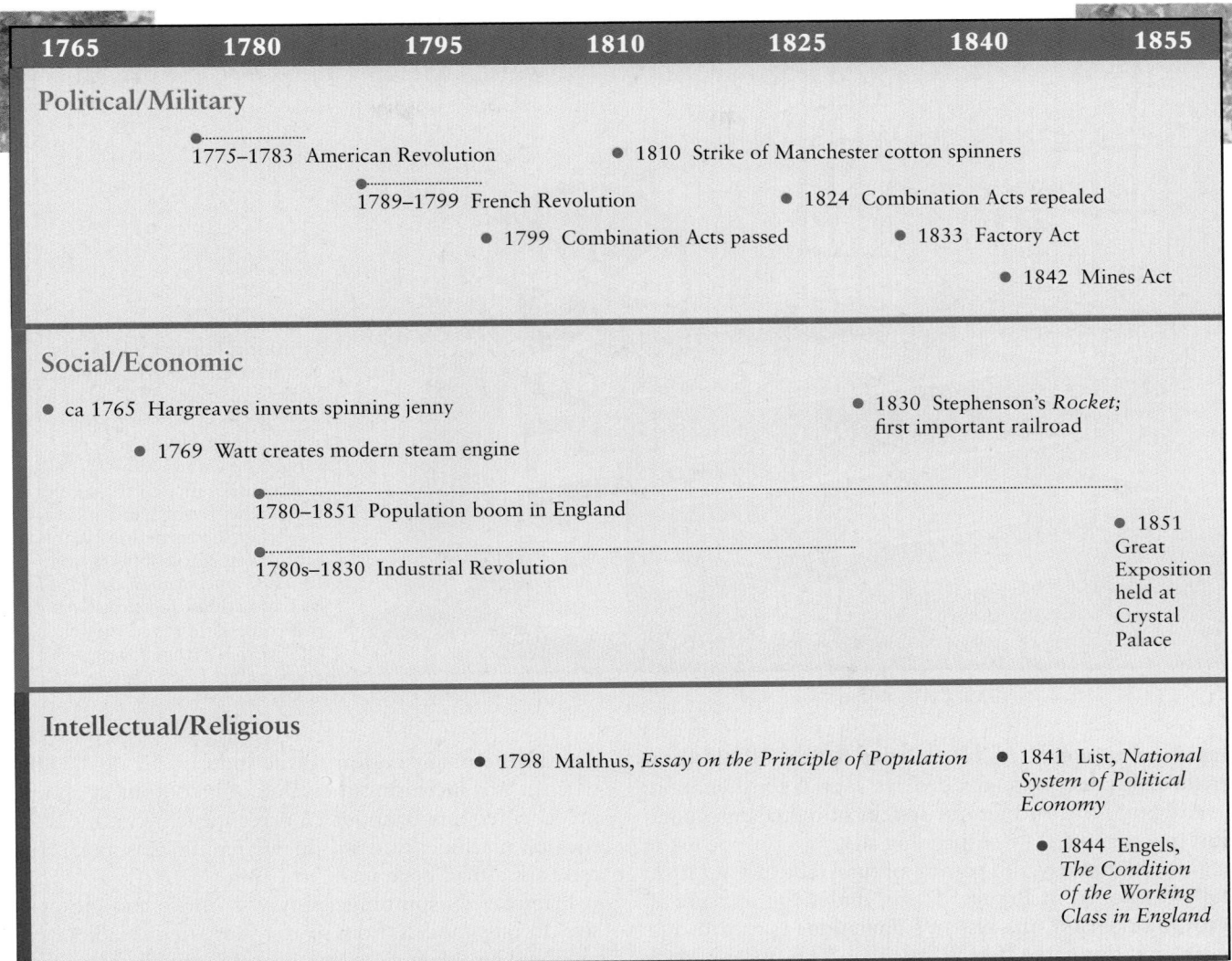

1765	1780	1795	1810	1825	1840	1855

Political/Military

1775–1783 American Revolution   • 1810 Strike of Manchester cotton spinners

1789–1799 French Revolution   • 1824 Combination Acts repealed

• 1799 Combination Acts passed   • 1833 Factory Act

• 1842 Mines Act

Social/Economic

• ca 1765 Hargreaves invents spinning jenny   • 1830 Stephenson's *Rocket;* first important railroad

• 1769 Watt creates modern steam engine

1780–1851 Population boom in England   • 1851 Great Exposition held at Crystal Palace

1780s–1830 Industrial Revolution

Intellectual/Religious

• 1798 Malthus, *Essay on the Principle of Population*   • 1841 List, *National System of Political Economy*

• 1844 Engels, *The Condition of the Working Class in England*

All these factors combined to initiate the **Industrial Revolution,** a term first coined by awed contemporaries in the 1830s to describe the burst of major inventions and technical changes they had witnessed in certain industries. This technical revolution went hand in hand with an impressive quickening in the annual rate of industrial growth in Britain. Whereas industry had grown at only 0.7 percent between 1700 and 1760 (before the Industrial Revolution), it grew at the much higher rate of 3 percent between 1801 and 1831 (when industrial transformation was in full swing).[1] The decisive quickening of growth probably came in the 1780s, after the American War of Independence and just before the French Revolution.

Therefore, the great economic and political revolutions that shaped the modern world occurred almost simulta- neously, though they began in different countries. The Industrial Revolution was, however, a longer process than the political upheavals. It was not complete in Britain until 1850, and it had no real impact on continental countries until after 1815.

The First Factories

The pressure to produce more goods for a growing market was directly related to the first decisive breakthrough of the Industrial Revolution—the creation of the world's first large factories in the British cotton textile industry. Technological innovations in the manufacture of cotton cloth led to a new system of production and social relationships. Since no other industry experienced such a

Woman Working a Hargreaves's Spinning Jenny The loose cotton strands on the slanted bobbins passed up to the sliding carriage and then on to the spindles in back for fine spinning. The worker, almost always a woman, regulated the sliding carriage with one hand and with the other she turned the crank on the wheel to supply power. By 1783 one woman could spin by hand a hundred threads at a time on an improved model. *(Mary Evans Picture Library)*

rapid or complete transformation before 1830, these trailblazing developments deserve special consideration.

Although the putting-out system of merchant capitalism (see page 642) was expanding all across Europe in the eighteenth century, this pattern of rural industry was most fully developed in Britain. There, under the pressure of growing demand, the system's limitations began to outweigh its advantages for the first time. This was especially true in the British textile industry after about 1760.

A constant shortage of thread in the textile industry focused attention on ways of improving spinning. Many a tinkering worker knew that a better spinning wheel promised rich rewards. It proved hard to spin the traditional raw materials—wool and flax—with improved machines, but cotton was different. Cotton textiles had first been imported into Britain from India by the East India Company, and by 1760 there was a tiny domestic industry in northern England. After many experiments over a generation, a gifted carpenter and jack-of-all-trades, James Hargreaves, invented his cotton-spinning jenny about 1765. At almost the same moment, a barber-turned-manufacturer named Richard Arkwright invented (or possibly pirated) another kind of spinning machine, the water frame. These breakthroughs produced an explo-

sion in the infant cotton textile industry in the 1780s, when it was increasing the value of its output at an unprecedented rate of about 13 percent each year. By 1790 the new machines were producing ten times as much cotton yarn as had been made in 1770.

Hargreaves's **spinning jenny** was simple and inexpensive. In early models, from six to twenty-four spindles were mounted on a sliding carriage, and each spindle spun a fine, slender thread. The woman moved the carriage back and forth with one hand and turned a wheel to supply power with the other. Now it was the male weaver who could not keep up with the vastly more efficient female spinner.

Arkwright's **water frame** employed a different principle. It quickly acquired a capacity of several hundred spindles and demanded much more power—waterpower. The water frame thus required large specialized mills, factories that employed as many as one thousand workers from the very beginning. The water frame could spin only coarse, strong thread, which was then put out for respinning on hand-powered cottage jennies. Around 1790 an alternative technique invented by Samuel Crompton also began to require more power than the human arm could supply. After that time, all cotton spinning was gradually concentrated in factories.

The first consequences of these revolutionary developments were more beneficial than is generally believed. Cotton goods became much cheaper, and they were bought and treasured by all classes. In the past, only the wealthy could afford the comfort and cleanliness of underwear, which was called **body linen** because it was made from expensive linen cloth. Now millions of poor people, who had earlier worn nothing underneath their coarse, filthy outer garments, could afford to wear cotton slips and underpants as well as cotton dresses and shirts.

Families using cotton in cottage industry were freed from their constant search for adequate yarn from scattered, part-time spinners, since all the thread needed could be spun in the cottage on the jenny or obtained from a nearby factory. The wages of weavers, now hard-pressed to keep up with the spinners, rose markedly until about 1792. Weavers were among the best-paid workers in England. They were known to walk proudly through the streets with 5-pound notes stuck in their hatbands, and they dressed like the middle class. As a result, large numbers of agricultural laborers became hand-loom weavers, while mechanics and capitalists sought to invent a power loom to save on labor costs. This Edmund Cartwright achieved in 1785. But the power looms of the factories worked poorly at first, and hand-loom weavers continued to receive good wages until at least 1800.

Working conditions in the early factories were less satisfactory than those of cottage weavers and spinners, and people were reluctant to work in them. Therefore, factory owners often turned to young children who had been abandoned by their parents and put in the care of local parishes. Parish officers often "apprenticed" such unfortunate foundlings to factory owners. The parish thus saved money, and the factory owners gained workers over whom they exercised almost the authority of slave owners.

Apprenticed as young as five or six years of age, boy and girl workers were forced by law to labor for their "masters" for as many as fourteen years. Housed, fed, and locked up nightly in factory dormitories, the young workers received little or no pay. Hours were appalling—commonly thirteen or fourteen hours a day, six days a week. Harsh physical punishment maintained brutal discipline. To be sure, poor children typically worked long hours and frequently outside the home for brutal masters. But the wholesale coercion of orphans as factory apprentices constituted exploitation on a truly unprecedented scale. This exploitation ultimately piqued the conscience of reformers and reinforced more humanitarian attitudes toward children and their labor in the early nineteenth century.

The creation of the world's first modern factories in the British cotton textile industry in the 1770s and 1780s, which grew out of the putting-out system of cottage production, was a major historical development. Both symbolically and substantially, the big new cotton mills marked the beginning of the Industrial Revolution in Britain. By 1831 the largely mechanized cotton textile industry towered above all others, accounting for fully 22 percent of the country's entire industrial production.

The Problem of Energy

The growth of the cotton textile industry might have been stunted or cut short, however, if water from rivers and streams had remained the primary source of power for the new factories. But this did not occur. Instead, an epoch-making solution was found to the age-old problem of energy and power. This solution permitted continued rapid development in cotton textiles, the gradual generalization of the factory system, and the triumph of the Industrial Revolution in Britain.

Human beings, like all living organisms, require energy. Adult men and women need two thousand to four thousand calories (units of energy) daily simply to fuel their bodies, work, and survive. Prehistoric people relied on plants and plant-eating animals as their sources of energy. With the development of agriculture, early civilizations were able to increase the number of useful plants and thus the supply of energy. Some plants could be fed to domesticated animals, such as the horse. Stronger than human beings, these animals converted the energy in the plants into work.

Human beings have long used their toolmaking abilities to construct machines that convert one form of energy into another for their own benefit. In the medieval period, people began to develop water mills to grind their grain and windmills to pump water and drain swamps. More efficient use of water and wind in the sixteenth and seventeenth centuries enabled human beings to accomplish more; intercontinental sailing ships were a prime example. Nevertheless, even into the eighteenth century, society continued to rely for energy mainly on plants, and human beings and animals continued to perform most work. This dependence meant that Western civilization remained poor in energy and power.

Lack of power lay at the heart of the poverty that afflicted the large majority of people. The man behind the plow and the woman at the spinning wheel could employ only horsepower and human muscle in their labor. No matter how hard they worked, they could not produce

Manchester, England, 1851 The development of the steam engine enabled industry to concentrate in towns and cities. Manchester mushroomed from a town of 20,000 in 1750 into "Cottonopolis," cotton city, with 400,000 inhabitants in 1850. In this painting the artist contrasts the smoky city and its awesome power with the idealized beauty of the suburbs, where the new rich settled and built their mansions. (*The Royal Collection, © 2002 Her Majesty Queen Elizabeth II*)

very much. What people needed were new sources of energy and more power at their disposal.

The shortage of energy had become particularly severe in Britain by the eighteenth century. Because of the growth of population, most of the great forests of medieval Britain had long ago been replaced by fields of grain and hay. Wood was in ever-shorter supply, yet it remained tremendously important. It served as the primary source of heat for all homes and industries and as a basic raw material. Processed wood (charcoal) was the fuel that was mixed with iron ore in the blast furnace to produce pig iron. The iron industry's appetite for wood was enormous, and by 1740 the British iron industry was stagnating. Vast forests enabled Russia to become the world's leading producer of iron, much of which was exported to Britain. But Russia's potential for growth was limited, too, and in a few decades Russia would reach the barrier of inadequate energy that was already holding England back.

The Steam Engine Breakthrough

As this early energy crisis grew worse, Britain looked toward its abundant and widely scattered reserves of coal as an alternative to its vanishing wood. Coal was first used in Britain in the late Middle Ages as a source of heat. By 1640 most homes in London were heated with it, and it also provided heat for making beer, glass, soap, and other products. Coal was not used, however, to produce mechanical energy or to power machinery. It was there that coal's potential was enormous, as a simple example shows.

A hard-working miner can dig out 500 pounds of coal a day using hand tools. Even an extremely inefficient converter, which transforms only 1 percent of the heat energy in coal into mechanical energy, will produce 27 horsepower-hours of work from that 500 pounds of coal. The miner, by contrast, produces only about 1 horsepower-hour in the course of a day. Early steam engines were powerful but still inefficient converters of energy.

As more coal was produced, mines were dug deeper and deeper and were constantly filling with water. Mechanical pumps, usually powered by animals walking in circles at the surface, had to be installed. At one mine, fully five hundred horses were used in pumping. Such power was expensive and bothersome. In an attempt to overcome these disadvantages, Thomas Savery in 1698 and Thomas Newcomen in 1705 invented the first primitive **steam engines.** Both engines were extremely inefficient. Both burned coal to produce steam, which was then used to operate a pump. However, by the early 1770s, many of the Savery engines and hundreds of the Newcomen engines were operating successfully, though inefficiently, in English and Scottish mines.

In the early 1760s, a gifted young Scot named James Watt (1736–1819) was drawn to a critical study of the steam engine. Watt was employed at the time by the University of Glasgow as a skilled craftsman making scientific instruments. The Scottish universities were pioneers in practical technical education, and in 1763 Watt was called on to repair a Newcomen engine being used in a physics course. After a series of observations, Watt saw that the Newcomen engine's waste of energy could be

reduced by adding a separate condenser. This splendid invention, patented in 1769, greatly increased the efficiency of the steam engine.

To invent something in a laboratory is one thing; to make it a practical success is quite another. Watt needed skilled workers, precision parts, and capital, and the relatively advanced nature of the British economy proved essential. A partnership with a wealthy English toymaker provided risk capital and a manufacturing plant. In the craft tradition of locksmiths, tinsmiths, and millwrights, Watt found skilled mechanics who could install, regulate, and repair his sophisticated engines. From ingenious manufacturers such as the cannonmaker John Wilkinson, Watt was gradually able to purchase precision parts. This support allowed him to create an effective vacuum and regulate a complex engine. In more than twenty years of constant effort, Watt made many further improvements. By the late 1780s, the steam engine had become a practical and commercial success in Britain.

The steam engine of Watt and his followers was the Industrial Revolution's most fundamental advance in technology. For the first time in history, humanity had, at least for a few generations, almost unlimited power at its disposal. For the first time, inventors and engineers could devise and implement all kinds of power equipment to

James Nasmyth's Mighty Steam Hammer Nasmyth's invention was the forerunner of the modern pile driver, and its successful introduction in 1832 epitomized the rapid development of steam power technology in Britain. In this painting by the inventor himself, workers manipulate a massive iron shaft being hammered into shape at Nasmyth's foundry near Manchester. *(Science & Society Picture Library, London)*

aid people in their work. For the first time, abundance was at least a possibility for ordinary men and women.

The steam engine was quickly put to use in several industries in Britain. It drained mines and made possible the production of ever more coal to feed steam engines elsewhere. The steam-power plant began to replace waterpower in the cotton-spinning mills during the 1780s, contributing greatly to that industry's phenomenal rise. Steam also took the place of waterpower in flour mills, in the malt mills used in breweries, in the flint mills supplying the china industry, and in the mills exported by Britain to the West Indies to crush sugar cane.

Steam power promoted important breakthroughs in other industries. The British iron industry was radically transformed. The use of powerful, steam-driven bellows in blast furnaces helped ironmakers switch over rapidly from limited charcoal to unlimited **coke** (which is made from coal) in the smelting of pig iron after 1770. In the 1780s, Henry Cort developed the puddling furnace, which allowed pig iron to be refined in turn with coke. Strong, skilled ironworkers—the puddlers—"cooked" molten pig iron in a great vat, raking off globs of refined iron for further processing. Cort also developed heavy-duty, steam-powered rolling mills, which were capable of spewing out finished iron in every shape and form.

The economic consequence of these technical innovations was a great boom in the British iron industry. In 1740 annual British iron production was only 17,000 tons. With the spread of coke smelting and the first impact of Cort's inventions, production reached 68,000 tons in 1788, 125,000 tons in 1796, and 260,000 tons in 1806. In 1844 Britain produced 3 million tons of iron. This was a truly amazing expansion. Once scarce and expensive, iron became the cheap, basic, indispensable building block of the economy.

The Coming of the Railroads

The second half of the eighteenth century saw extensive construction of hard and relatively smooth roads, particularly in France before the Revolution. Yet it was passenger traffic that benefited most from this construction. Overland shipment of freight, relying solely on horsepower, was still quite limited and frightfully expensive; shippers used rivers and canals for heavy freight whenever possible. It was logical, therefore, that inventors would try to use steam power.

As early as 1800, an American ran a "steamer on wheels" through city streets. Other experiments followed. In the 1820s, English engineers created steam cars capable of carrying fourteen passengers at ten miles an hour—as fast as the mail coach. But the noisy, heavy steam automobiles frightened passing horses and damaged themselves as well as the roads with their vibrations. For the rest of the century, horses continued to reign on highways and city streets.

The coal industry had long been using plank roads and rails to move coal wagons within mines and at the surface. Rails reduced friction and allowed a horse or a human being to pull a heavier load. Thus once a rail capable of supporting a heavy locomotive was developed in 1816, all sorts of experiments with steam engines on rails went forward. In 1825 after ten years of work, George Stephenson built an effective locomotive. In 1830 his *Rocket* sped down the track of the just-completed Liverpool and Manchester Railway at sixteen miles per hour. This was the world's first important railroad, fittingly steaming in the heart of industrial England. The line from Liverpool to Manchester was a financial as well as a technical success, and many private companies were quickly organized to build more rail lines. Within twenty years, they had completed the main trunk lines of Great Britain. Other countries were quick to follow.

The significance of the railroad was tremendous. The railroad dramatically reduced the cost and uncertainty of shipping freight overland. This advance had many economic consequences. Previously, markets had tended to be small and local; as the barrier of high transportation costs was lowered, markets became larger and even nationwide. Larger markets encouraged larger factories with more sophisticated machinery in a growing number of industries. Such factories could make goods more cheaply and gradually subjected most cottage workers and many urban artisans to severe competitive pressures.

In all countries, the construction of railroads created a strong demand for unskilled labor and contributed to the growth of a class of urban workers. Hard work on construction gangs was done in the open air with animals and hand tools. Many landless farm laborers and poor peasants, long accustomed to leaving their villages for temporary employment, went to build railroads. By the time the work was finished, life back home in the village often seemed dull and unappealing, and many men drifted to towns in search of work. By the time they sent for their wives and sweethearts to join them, they had become urban workers.

The railroad changed the outlook and values of the entire society. The last and culminating invention of the Industrial Revolution, the railroad dramatically revealed the power and increased the speed of the new age. Racing

The Saltash Bridge   Railroad construction presented innumerable challenges, such as the building of bridges to span rivers and gorges. Civil engineers responded with impressive feats, and their profession bounded ahead. This painting portrays the inauguration of I. K. Brunel's Saltash Bridge, where the railroad crosses the Tamar River into Cornwall in southwest England. The high spans allow large ships to pass underneath. *(Elton Collection, Ironbridge Gorge Museum Trust)*

down a track at sixteen miles per hour or, by 1850, at a phenomenal fifty miles per hour was a new and awesome experience. As a French economist put it after a ride on the Liverpool and Manchester in 1833, "There are certain impressions that one cannot put into words!"

Some great painters, notably Joseph M. W. Turner (1775–1851) and Claude Monet (1840–1926), succeeded in expressing this sense of power and awe. So did the massive new train stations, the cathedrals of the industrial age. Leading railway engineers such as Isambard Kingdom Brunel and Thomas Brassey, whose tunnels pierced mountains and whose bridges spanned valleys, became public idols—the astronauts of their day. Everyday speech absorbed the images of railroading. After you got up a "full head of steam," you "highballed" along. And if you didn't "go off the track," you might "toot your own whistle." The railroad fired the imagination.

Industry and Population

In 1851 London was the site of a famous industrial fair. This Great Exhibition was held in the newly built **Crystal Palace,** an architectural masterpiece made entirely of glass and iron, both of which were now cheap and abundant. For the millions who visited, one fact stood out: the little island of Britain was the "workshop of the world." It alone produced two-thirds of the world's coal and more than one-half of its iron and cotton cloth. More generally, it has been carefully estimated that in 1860 Britain produced a truly remarkable 20 percent of the entire world's output of industrial goods, whereas it had produced only about 2 percent of the world total in 1750.[2] Experiencing revolutionary industrial change, Britain became the first industrial nation (see Map 22.2).

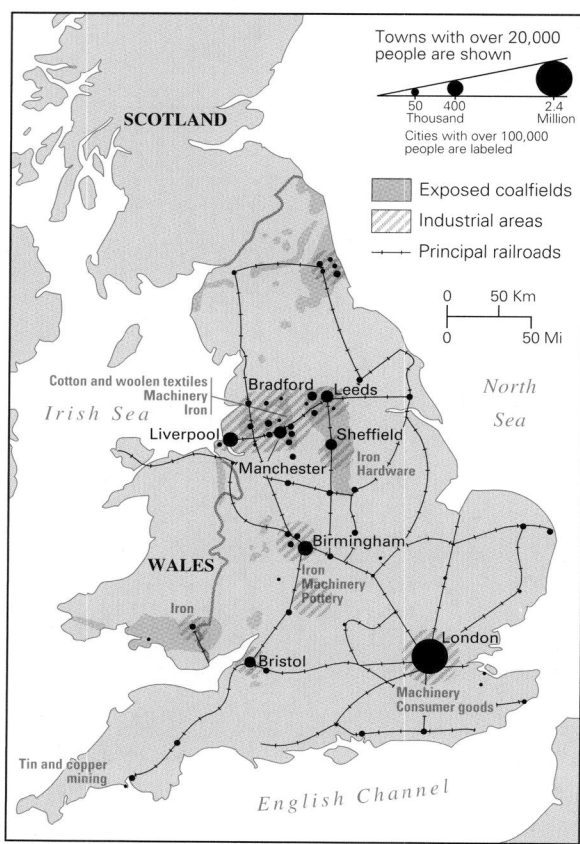

MAP 22.2 The Industrial Revolution in England, ca 1850 Industry concentrated in the rapidly growing cities of the north and the Midlands, where rich coal and iron deposits were in close proximity.

As the British economy significantly increased its production of manufactured goods, the gross national product (GNP) rose roughly fourfold at constant prices between 1780 and 1851. In other words, the British people as a whole increased their wealth and their national income dramatically. At the same time, the population of Britain boomed, growing from about 9 million in 1780 to almost 21 million in 1851. Thus growing numbers consumed much of the increase in total production. According to one important study, average consumption per person increased by only 75 percent between 1780 and 1851, as the growth in the total population ate up a large part of the fourfold increase in GNP in those years.[3]

Although the question is still debated, many economic historians now believe that rapid population growth in Great Britain was not harmful because it facilitated industrial expansion. More people meant a more mobile labor force, with a wealth of young workers in need of employment and ready to go where the jobs were. Contemporaries were much less optimistic. In his famous and influential *Essay on the Principle of Population* (1798), Thomas Malthus (1766–1834) argued that population would always tend to grow faster than the food supply. In Malthus's opinion, the only hope of warding off such "positive checks" to population growth as war, famine, and disease was "prudential restraint." That is, young men and women had to limit the growth of population by the old tried-and-true means of marrying late in life. But Malthus was not optimistic about this possibility. The powerful attraction of the sexes would cause most people to marry early and have many children.

Wealthy English stockbroker and leading economist David Ricardo (1772–1823) coldly spelled out the pessimistic implications of Malthus's thought. Ricardo's depressing **iron law of wages** posited that because of the pressure of population growth, wages would always sink to subsistence level. That is, wages would be just high enough to keep workers from starving. With Malthus and Ricardo setting the tone, economics was soon dubbed "the dismal science."

Malthus, Ricardo, and their many followers were proved wrong—in the long run. However, as the great economist John Maynard Keynes quipped during the Great Depression of the 1930s, "we are all dead in the long run." Those who lived through the Industrial Revolution could not see the long run in advance. As modern quantitative studies show, until the 1820s, or even the 1840s, contemporary observers might reasonably have concluded that the economy and the total population were racing neck and neck, with the outcome very much in doubt. The closeness of the race added to the difficulties inherent in the journey toward industrial civilization.

There was another problem as well. Perhaps workers, farmers, and ordinary people did not get their rightful share of the new wealth. Perhaps only the rich got richer, while the poor got poorer or made no progress. We will turn to this great issue after looking at the process of industrialization in continental countries.

Industrialization in Continental Europe

The new technologies developed in the British Industrial Revolution were adopted rather slowly by businesses in continental Europe. Yet by the end of the nineteenth century, several European countries as well as the United States had also industrialized their economies to a con-

The Crystal Palace   The Great Exhibition of 1851 attracted more than six million visitors, many of whom journeyed to London on the newly built railroads. Companies and countries displayed their products and juries awarded prizes in the strikingly modern Crystal Palace. Are today's malls really that different? *(Guildhall Library, Corporation of London/The Bridgeman Art Library International Ltd)*

siderable but variable degree. This meant that the process of Western industrialization proceeded gradually, with uneven jerks and national (and regional) variations.

Scholars are still struggling to explain these variations, especially since good answers may offer valuable lessons in our own time for poor countries seeking to improve their material condition through industrialization and economic development. The latest findings on the Western experience are encouraging. They suggest that there were alternative paths to the industrial world in the nineteenth century and that, today as then, there was no need to follow a rigid, predetermined British model.

National Variations

European industrialization, like most economic developments, requires some statistical analysis as part of the effort to understand it. Comparative data on industrial production in different countries over time help give us an overview of what happened. One set of data, the work of a Swiss scholar, compares the level of industrialization on a per capita basis in several countries from 1750 to 1913. These data are far from perfect because there are gaps in the underlying records. But they reflect basic trends and are presented in Table 22.1 for closer study.

As the heading of Table 22.1 makes clear, this is a per capita comparison of levels of industrialization—a comparison of how much industrial product was available, on average, to each person in a given country in a given year. Therefore, all the numbers in Table 22.1 are expressed in terms of a single index number of 100, which equals the per capita level of industrial goods in Great Britain (and Ireland) in 1900. Every number is thus a percentage of the 1900 level in Britain and is directly comparable. The countries are listed in roughly the order that they began to use large-scale, power-driven technology.

Table 22.1 Per Capita Levels of Industrialization, 1750–1913

	1750	1800	1830	1860	1880	1900	1913
Great Britain	10	16	25	64	87	100	115
Belgium	9	10	14	28	43	56	88
United States	4	9	14	21	38	69	126
France	9	9	12	20	28	39	59
Germany	8	8	9	15	25	52	85
Austria-Hungary	7	7	8	11	15	23	32
Italy	8	8	8	10	12	17	26
Russia	6	6	7	8	10	15	20
China	8	6	6	4	4	3	3
India	7	6	6	3	2	1	2

Note: All entries are based on an index value of 100, equal to the per capita level of industrialization in Great Britain in 1900. Data for Great Britain are actually for the United Kingdom, thereby including Ireland with England, Wales, and Scotland.

Source: P. Bairoch, "International Industrialization Levels from 1750 to 1980," *Journal of European Economic History* 11 (Fall 1982): 294. Reprinted with permission.

What does this overview of European industrialization tell us? First, and very significantly, one sees that in 1750 all countries were fairly close together and that Britain was only slightly ahead of its archenemy, France. Second, Britain had opened up a noticeable lead over all continental countries by 1800, and that gap progressively widened as the British Industrial Revolution accelerated to 1830 and reached full maturity by 1860. The British level of per capita industrialization was twice the French level in 1830, for example, and more than three times the French level in 1860. All other large countries (except the United States) had fallen even further behind Britain than France had at both dates. Sophisticated quantitative history confirms the primacy and relative rapidity of Britain's Industrial Revolution.

Third, variations in the timing and in the extent of industrialization in the continental powers and the United States are also apparent. Belgium, independent in 1831 and rich in iron and coal, led in adopting Britain's new technology. France developed factory production more gradually, and most historians now detect no burst in French mechanization and no acceleration in the growth of overall industrial output that may accurately be called revolutionary. They stress instead France's relatively good pattern of early industrial growth, which was unjustly tarnished by the spectacular rise of Germany and the United States after 1860. By 1913 Germany was rapidly closing in on Britain, while the United States had already passed the first industrial nation in per capita production.

Finally, all European states (as well as the United States, Canada, and Japan) managed to raise per capita industrial levels in the nineteenth century. These continent-wide increases stood in stark contrast to the large and tragic decreases that occurred at the same time in most non-Western countries, most notably in China and India. European countries industrialized to a greater or lesser extent even as most of the non-Western world *de*-industrialized. Thus differential rates of wealth- and power-creating industrial development, which heightened disparities within Europe, also greatly magnified existing inequalities between Europe and the rest of the world. We shall return to this momentous change in Chapter 26.

The Challenge of Industrialization

The different patterns of industrial development suggest that the process of industrialization was far from automatic. Indeed, building modern industry was an awesome challenge. To be sure, throughout Europe the eighteenth century was an era of agricultural improvement, population increase, expanding foreign trade, and growing cottage industry. Thus when the pace of British industry began to accelerate in the 1780s, continental businesses began to adopt the new methods as they

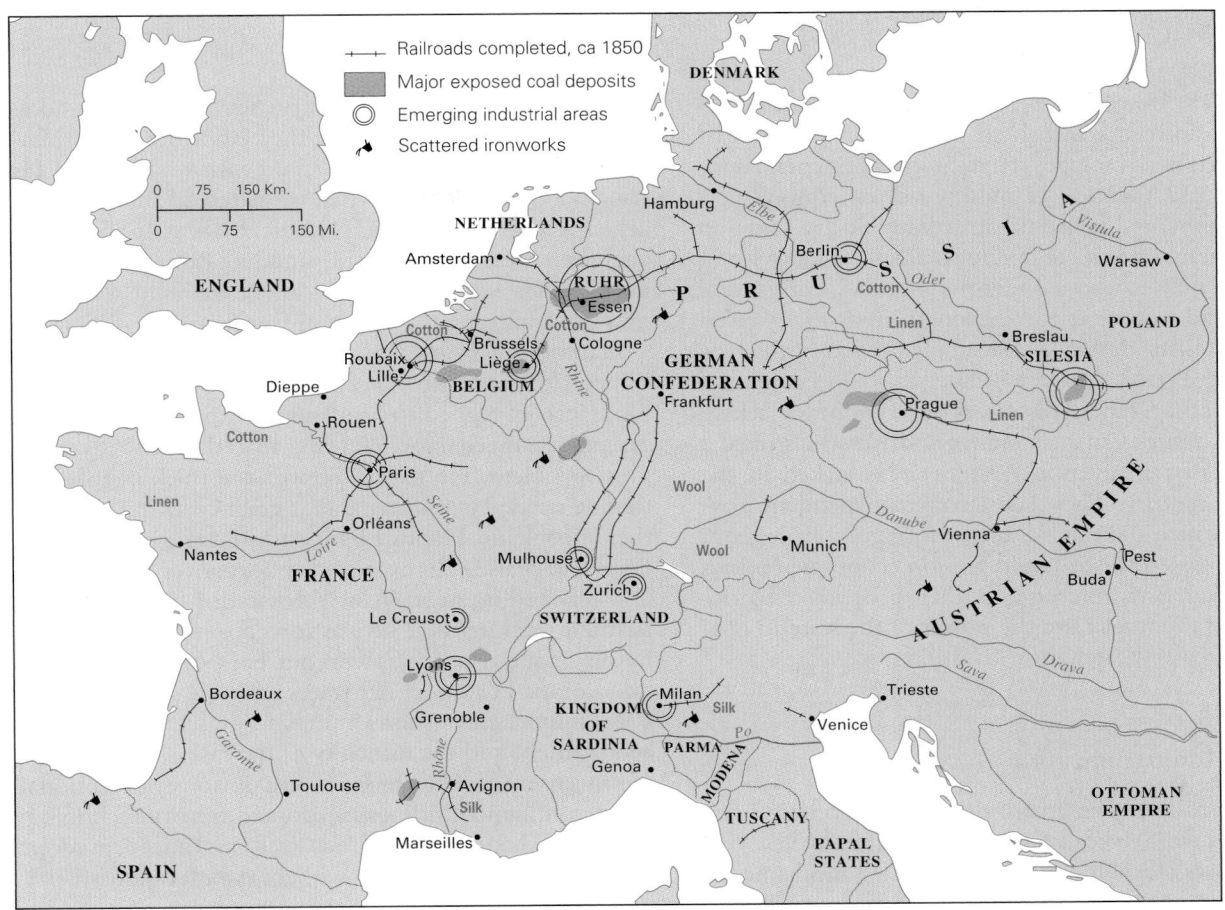

MAP 22.3 Continental Industrialization, ca 1850 Although continental countries were beginning to make progress by 1850, they still lagged far behind Britain. For example, continental railroad building was still in an early stage, whereas the British rail system was essentially complete.

proved their profitability. British industry enjoyed clear superiority, but at first the continent was close behind.

By 1815, however, the situation was quite different. In spite of wartime difficulties, British industry maintained the momentum of the 1780s and continued to grow and improve between 1789 and 1815. On the continent, the upheavals that began with the French Revolution had another effect: they disrupted trade, created runaway inflation, and fostered social anxiety. War severed normal communications between Britain and the continent, severely handicapping continental efforts to use new British machinery and technology. Moreover, the years from 1789 to 1815 were, even for the privileged French economy receiving special favors from Napoleon, a time of "national catastrophe"—in the graphic words of a leading French scholar.[4] Thus France and the rest of Europe were further behind Britain in 1815 than in 1789.

This widening gap made it more difficult, if not impossible, for other countries to follow the British pattern in en-

ergy and industry after peace was restored in 1815. Above all, in the newly mechanized industries, British goods were being produced very economically, and these goods had come to dominate world markets completely while the continental states were absorbed in war between 1792 and 1815. In addition, British technology had become so advanced and complicated that very few engineers or skilled technicians outside England understood it. Moreover, the technology of steam power had grown much more expensive. It involved large investments in the iron and coal industries and, after 1830, required the existence of railroads, which were very costly. Continental business people had great difficulty finding the large sums of money the new methods demanded, and there was a shortage of laborers accustomed to working in factories. Landowners and government officials were often so suspicious of the new form of industry and the changes it brought that they did little at first to encourage it. All these disadvantages slowed the spread of modern industry (see Map 22.3).

After 1815, however, when continental countries began to face up to the British challenge, they had at least three important advantages. First, most continental countries had a rich tradition of putting-out enterprise, merchant capitalists, and skilled urban artisans. Such a tradition gave continental firms the ability to adapt and survive in the face of new market conditions. Second, continental capitalists did not need to develop their own advanced technology. Instead, they could simply "borrow" the new methods developed in Great Britain, as well as engineers and some of the financial resources these countries lacked. European countries such as France and Russia also had a third asset that many non-Western areas lacked in the nineteenth century. They had strong independent governments, which did not fall under foreign political control. These governments could fashion economic policies to serve their own interests, as they proceeded to do. They would eventually use the power of the state to promote industry and catch up with Britain.

Agents of Industrialization

The British realized the great value of their technical discoveries and tried to keep their secrets to themselves. Until 1825 it was illegal for artisans and skilled mechanics to leave Britain; until 1843 the export of textile machinery and other equipment was forbidden. Many talented, ambitious workers, however, slipped out of the country illegally and introduced the new methods abroad.

One such man was William Cockerill, a Lancashire carpenter. He and his sons began building cotton-spinning equipment in French-occupied Belgium in 1799. In 1817 the most famous son, John Cockerill, purchased the old summer palace of the deposed bishops of Liège in southern Belgium. Cockerill converted the palace into a large industrial enterprise, which produced machinery, steam engines, and then railway locomotives. He also established modern ironworks and coal mines.

Cockerill's plants in the Liège area became an industrial nerve center, continually gathering new information and transmitting it across Europe. Many skilled British workers came illegally to work for Cockerill, and some went on to found their own companies throughout Europe. Newcomers brought the latest plans and secrets, so Cockerill could boast that ten days after an industrial advance occurred in Britain, he knew all about it in Belgium. Thus British technicians and skilled workers were a powerful force in the spread of early industrialization.

A second agent of industrialization were talented entrepreneurs such as Fritz Harkort, a business pioneer in the German machinery industry. Serving in England as a Prussian army officer during the Napoleonic wars, Harkort was impressed and enchanted with what he saw. He concluded that Germany had to match all these English achievements as quickly as possible. Setting up shop in an abandoned castle in the still-tranquil Ruhr Valley, Harkort felt an almost religious calling to build steam engines and become the "Watt of Germany."

Harkort's basic idea was simple, but it was enormously difficult to carry out. Lacking skilled laborers to do the job, Harkort turned to England for experienced, though expensive, mechanics. Getting materials also posed a great problem. He had to import the thick iron boilers that he needed from England at great cost. In spite of all these problems, Harkort built and sold engines, winning fame and praise. His ambitious efforts over sixteen years also resulted in large financial losses for himself and his partners, and in 1832 he was forced out of his company by his financial backers, who cut back operations to reduce losses. His career illustrates both the great efforts of a few important business leaders to duplicate the British achievement and the difficulty of the task.

Entrepreneurs like Harkort were obviously exceptional. Most continental businesses adopted factory technology slowly, and handicraft methods lived on. Indeed, as recent research on France has shown, continental industrialization usually brought substantial but uneven expansion of handicraft industry in both rural and urban areas for a time. Artisan production of luxury items grew in France as the rising income of the international middle class created foreign demand for silk scarfs, embroidered needlework, perfumes, and fine wines.

A third force for industrialization was government, which often helped business people in continental countries to overcome some of their difficulties. **Tariff protection** was one such support. For example, after Napoleon's wars ended in 1815, France was suddenly flooded with cheaper and better British goods. The French government responded by laying high tariffs on many British imports in order to protect the French economy. After 1815 continental governments bore the cost of building roads and canals to improve transportation.

They also bore to a significant extent the cost of building railroads. Belgium led the way in the 1830s and 1840s. In an effort to tie the newly independent nation together, the Belgian government decided to construct a state-owned system. Built rapidly as a unified network, Belgium's state-owned railroads stimulated the development of heavy industry and made the country an early industrial leader. Several of the smaller German states also built state systems.

The Prussian government provided another kind of invaluable support. It guaranteed that the state treasury would pay the interest and principal on railroad bonds if the closely regulated private companies in Prussia were unable to do so. Thus railroad investors in Prussia ran little risk, and capital was quickly raised. In France the state shouldered all the expense of acquiring and laying roadbed, including bridges and tunnels. Finished roadbed was leased to a carefully supervised private company, which usually benefited from a state guarantee of its debts and which needed to provide only the rails, cars, and management. In short, governments helped pay for railroads, the all-important leading sector in continental industrialization.

The career of German journalist and thinker Friedrich List (1789–1846) reflects government's greater role in industrialization on the continent than in England. List considered the growth of modern industry of the utmost importance because manufacturing was a primary means of increasing people's well-being and relieving their poverty. Moreover, List was a dedicated nationalist. He wrote that the "wider the gap between the backward and advanced nations becomes, the more dangerous it is to remain behind." For an agricultural nation was not only poor but also weak, increasingly unable to defend itself and maintain its political independence. To promote industry was to defend the nation.

The practical policies that List focused on in articles and in his influential *National System of Political Economy* (1841) were railroad building and the tariff. List supported the formation of a customs union, or *Zollverein,* among the separate German states. Such a tariff union came into being in 1834, allowing goods to move between the German member states without tariffs, while erecting a single uniform tariff against other nations. List

A German Ironworks, 1850 This big business enterprise has mastered the new British method of smelting iron with coke. Germany, and especially the state of Prussia, was well endowed with both iron and coal, and the rapid exploitation of these resources after 1840 transformed a poor agricultural country into an industrial powerhouse. *(Deutsches Museum Munich)*

wanted a high protective tariff, which would encourage infant industries, allowing them to develop and eventually hold their own against their more advanced British counterparts. List denounced the British doctrine of free trade as little more than Britain's attempt "to make the rest of the world, like the Hindus, its serfs in all industrial and commercial relations." By the 1840s List's **economic nationalism** had become increasingly popular in Germany and elsewhere.

Finally, banks, like governments, also played a larger and more creative role on the continent than in Britain. Previously, almost all banks in Europe had been private, organized as secretive partnerships. Because of the possibility of unlimited financial loss, the partners of private banks tended to be quite conservative and were content to deal with a few rich clients and a few big merchants. They generally avoided industrial investment as being too risky.

In the 1830s, two important Belgian banks pioneered in a new direction. They received permission from the growth-oriented government to establish themselves as corporations enjoying limited liability. That is, a stockholder could lose only his or her original investment in the bank's common stock and could not be assessed for any additional losses. Publicizing the risk-reducing advantage of limited liability, these Belgian banks were able to attract many shareholders, large and small. They mobilized impressive resources for investment in big companies, became industrial banks, and successfully promoted industrial development.

Similar corporate banks became important in France and Germany in the 1850s and 1860s. Usually working in collaboration with governments, they established and developed many railroads and many companies working in heavy industry, which were increasingly organized as limited liability corporations. The most famous such bank was the Crédit Mobilier of Paris, founded by Isaac and Emile Pereire, two young Jewish journalists from Bordeaux. The Crédit Mobilier advertised extensively. It used the savings of thousands of small investors as well as the resources of big ones. The activities of the bank were far-reaching; it built railroads all over France and Europe. As Emile Pereire had said in 1835, "It is not enough to outline gigantic programs on paper. I must write my ideas on the earth."

The combined efforts of skilled workers, entrepreneurs, governments, and industrial banks meshed successfully between 1850 and the financial crash of 1873. This was a period of unprecedentedly rapid economic growth on the continent. In Belgium, Germany, and France, key indicators of modern industrial development—such as railway mileage, iron and coal production, and steam-engine capacity—increased at average annual rates of 5 to 10 percent. As a result, rail networks were completed in western and much of central Europe, and the leading continental countries mastered the industrial technologies that had first been developed in Great Britain. In the early 1870s, Britain was still Europe's most industrial nation, but a select handful of countries were closing the gap that had been opened up by the Industrial Revolution.

Capital and Labor

Industrial development brought new social relations and intensified long-standing problems between capital and labor in both urban workshops and cottage industry (see pages 641–645). A new group of factory owners and industrial capitalists arose. These men and women and their families strengthened the wealth and size of the middle class, which had previously been made up mainly of merchants and professional people. The nineteenth century became the golden age of the middle class. Modern industry also created a much larger group, the factory workers. For the first time, large numbers of men, women, and children came together under one roof to work with complicated machinery for a single owner or a few partners in large companies.

The growth of new occupational groups in industry stimulated new thinking about social relations. Often combined with reflections on the French Revolution, this thinking led to the development of a new overarching interpretation—a new paradigm—regarding social relationships (see Chapter 23). Briefly, this paradigm argued, with considerable success, that individuals were members of economically determined classes, which had conflicting interests. Accordingly, the comfortable, well-educated "public" of the eighteenth century came increasingly to see itself as the backbone of the middle class (or the middle classes), and the "people" gradually transformed themselves into the modern working class (or working classes). And if the new class interpretation was more of a deceptive simplification than a fundamental truth for some critics, it appealed to many because it seemed to explain what was happening. Therefore, conflicting classes existed, in part, because many individuals came to believe they existed and developed an appropriate sense of class feeling—what Marxists call **class-consciousness.**

What, then, was the relationship between capital and labor in the early Industrial Revolution? Did the new industrial middle class ruthlessly exploit the workers, as Karl Marx and others have charged?

Ford Maddox Brown: Work This mid-century painting provides a rich visual representation of the new concepts of social class that became common by 1850. The central figures are the colorful laborers, endowed by the artist with strength and nobility. Close by, a poor girl minds her brother and sister for her working mother. On the right, a middle-class minister and a social critic observe and do intellectual work. What work does the couple on horseback perform? *(Birmingham Museums and Art Gallery/The Bridgeman Art Library International Ltd)*

The New Class of Factory Owners

Early industrialists operated in a highly competitive economic system. As the careers of Watt and Harkort illustrate, there were countless production problems, and success and large profits were by no means certain. Manufacturers therefore waged a constant battle to cut their production costs and stay afloat. Much of the profit had to go back into the business for new and better machinery. "Dragged on by the frenzy of this terrible life," according to one of the dismayed critics, the struggling manufacturer had "no time for niceties. He must conquer or die, make a fortune or drown himself."[5]

Most early industrialists drew upon their families and friends for labor and capital, but they came from a variety of backgrounds. Many, such as Harkort, were from well-established merchant families, which provided a rich network of contacts and support. Others, such as Watt and Cockerill, were of modest means, especially in the early days. Artisans and skilled workers of exceptional ability had unparalleled opportunities. Members of ethnic and religious groups who had been discriminated against in the traditional occupations controlled by the landed aristocracy jumped at the new chances and often helped each other. Scots, Quakers, and other Protestant dissenters were tremendously important in Britain; Protestants and Jews dominated banking in Catholic France. Many of the industrialists were newly rich, and, not surprisingly, they were very proud and self-satisfied.

As factories and firms grew larger, opportunities declined, at least in well-developed industries. It became considerably harder for a gifted but poor young mechanic to start a small enterprise and end up as a wealthy manufacturer. Formal education (for sons and males) became more important as a means of success and advancement, and formal education at the advanced level was expensive. In Britain by 1830 and in France and Germany by 1860, leading industrialists were more likely to have inherited their well-established enterprises, and they were financially much more secure than their struggling fathers and mothers had been. They also had a greater sense of class-consciousness, fully aware that ongoing industrial development had widened the gap between themselves and their workers.

The wives and daughters of successful businessmen also found fewer opportunities for active participation in Europe's increasingly complex business world. Rather than contributing as vital partners in a family-owned enterprise, as so many middle-class women such as Elizabeth Strutt had done (see the feature "Individuals in Society: The Strutt Family"), these women were increasingly valued for their ladylike gentility. By 1850 some influential women writers and most businessmen assumed that middle-class wives and daughters should steer clear of undignified work in offices and factories. Rather, a middle-class lady should protect and enhance her femininity. She should concentrate on her proper role as wife and mother, preferably in an elegant residential area far removed from ruthless commerce and the volatile working class.

The New Factory Workers

The social consequences of the Industrial Revolution have long been hotly debated. The condition of British workers during the transformation has always generated the most controversy among historians because Britain was the first country to industrialize and because the social consequences seemed harshest there. Before 1850 other countries had not proceeded very far with industrialization, and almost everyone agrees that the economic conditions of European workers improved after 1850. Thus the experience of British workers to about 1850 deserves special attention. (Industrial growth also promoted rapid urbanization, with its own awesome problems, as will be shown in Chapter 24.)

From the beginning, the Industrial Revolution in Britain had its critics. Among the first were the romantic poets. William Blake (1757–1827) called the early factories "satanic mills" and protested against the hard life of the London poor. William Wordsworth (1770–1850) lamented the destruction of the rural way of life and the pollution of the land and water. Some handicraft workers—notably the **Luddites,** who attacked whole factories in northern England in 1812 and after—smashed the new machines, which they believed were putting them out of work. Doctors and reformers wrote eloquently of problems in the factories and new towns, while Malthus and Ricardo concluded that workers would earn only enough to stay alive.

This pessimistic view was accepted and reinforced by Friedrich Engels (1820–1895), the future revolutionary and colleague of Karl Marx. After studying conditions in northern England, this young middle-class German published in 1844 *The Condition of the Working Class in England,* a blistering indictment of the middle classes. "At the bar of world opinion," he wrote, "I charge the English middle classes with mass murder, wholesale robbery, and all the other crimes in the calendar."[6] The new poverty of industrial workers was worse than the old poverty of cottage workers and agricultural laborers, according to Engels. The culprit was industrial capitalism, with its relentless competition and constant technical change. Engels's extremely influential charge of middle-class exploitation and increasing worker poverty was embellished by Marx and later socialists.

Meanwhile, other observers believed that conditions were improving for the working people. Andrew Ure wrote in 1835 in his study of the cotton industry that conditions in most factories were not harsh and were even quite good. Edwin Chadwick, a great and conscientious government official well acquainted with the problems of the working population, concluded that the "whole mass of the laboring community" was increasingly able "to buy more of the necessities and minor luxuries of life."[7] Nevertheless, if all the contemporary assessments had been counted up, those who thought conditions were getting worse for working people would probably have been the majority.

In an attempt to go beyond the contradictory judgments of contemporaries, some historians have looked at different kinds of sources. Statistical evidence is one such source. If working people suffered a great economic decline, as Engels and later socialists asserted, then the purchasing power of the working person's wages must have declined drastically.

Scholarly statistical studies have weakened the idea that the condition of the working class got much worse with industrialization. But the most recent studies also confirm the view that the early years of the Industrial Revolution were hard ones for British workers. There

Individuals in Society

The Strutt Family

For centuries economic life in Europe revolved around hundreds of thousands of small family enterprises. These family enterprises worked farms, crafted products, and traded goods. They built and operated the firms and factories of the early industrial era, with the notable exceptions of the capital-hungry railroads and a few big banks. Indeed, until late in the nineteenth century, close-knit family groups continued to control most successful businesses, including those organized as corporations.

One successful and fairly well-documented family enterprise began with the marriage of Jedediah Strutt (1726–1797) and Elizabeth Woollat (1729–1774) in Derbyshire in northern England in 1755. The son of a farmer, Jedediah fell in love with Elizabeth when he was apprenticed away from home as a wheelwright and lodged with her parents. Both young people grew up in the close-knit dissenting Protestant community, which did not accept the doctrines of the state-sponsored Church of England, and the well-educated Elizabeth worked in a local school for dissenters and then for a dissenter minister in London. Indecisive and self-absorbed, Jedediah inherited in 1754 a small stock of animals from an uncle and finally married Elizabeth the following year.

Aided by Elizabeth, who was "obviously a very capable woman" and who supplied some of the drive her husband had previously lacked, Jedediah embarked on a new career.* He invented a machine to make handsome, neat-fitting ribbed silk stockings, which had previously been made by hand. He secured a patent, despite strong opposition from competitors, and went into production. Elizabeth helped constantly in the enterprise, which was nothing less than an informal partnership between husband and wife.[†]

In 1757, for example, when Jedediah was fighting to uphold his patent in the local court, Elizabeth left her son of nine months and journeyed to London to seek a badly needed loan from her former employer. She also canvassed her London relatives and dissenter friends for orders for stockings and looked for sales agents and sources of capital. Elizabeth's letters reveal a detailed knowledge of ribbed stockings and the prices and quality of different kinds of thread. The family biographers, old-line economic historians writing without a trace of feminist concerns, conclude that her husband "owed much of his success to her energy and counsel." Elizabeth was always "active in

the business—a partner in herself."[‡] Historians have often overlooked such invaluable contributions from wives like Elizabeth, partly because the legal rights and consequences of partnership were denied to married women in Britain and Europe in the eighteenth and nineteenth centuries.

The Strutt enterprise grew and gradually prospered, but it always retained its family character. The firm built a large silk mill and then went into cotton spinning in partnership with Richard Arkwright, the inventor of the water frame (see page 728). The brothers of both Jedediah and Elizabeth worked for the firm, and their eldest daughter worked long hours in the warehouse. Bearing three sons, Elizabeth fulfilled yet another vital task because the typical family firm looked to its own members for managers and continued success. All three sons entered the business and became cotton textile magnates. Elizabeth never saw these triumphs. The loyal and talented wife in the family partnership died suddenly at age forty-five while in London with Jedediah on a business trip.

Jedediah Strutt (ca 1790), by Joseph Wright of Derby. (Derby Museum & Art Gallery/ The Bridgeman Art Library International Ltd)

Questions for Analysis

1. How and why did the Strutts succeed?
2. What does Elizabeth's life tell us about the role of British women in the early Industrial Revolution?

---

*R. Fitton and A. Wadsworth, *The Strutts and the Arkwrights, 1758–1830: A Study of the Early Factory System* (Manchester, England: Manchester University Press, 1958), p. 23.

[†] See the excellent discussion by C. Hall, "Strains in the 'Firm of Wife, Children and Friends'? Middle-Class Women and Employment in Early Nineteenth-Century England," in P. Hudson and W. Lee, eds., *Women's Work and the Family Economy in Historical Perspective* (Manchester, England: Manchester University Press, 1990), pp. 106–132.

[‡] Fitton and Wadsworth, *The Strutts,* pp. 110–111.

was little or no increase in the purchasing power of the average British worker from about 1780 to about 1820. The years from 1792 to 1815, a period of almost constant warfare with France, were particularly difficult. Food prices rose faster than wages, and the living conditions of the laboring poor declined. Only after 1820, and especially after 1840, did real wages rise substantially, so that the average worker earned and consumed roughly 50 percent more in real terms in 1850 than in 1770.[8] In short, there was considerable economic improvement for workers throughout Great Britain by 1850, but that improvement was hard won and slow in coming.

This important conclusion must be qualified, however. Increased purchasing power meant more goods, but not necessarily greater happiness. More goods may have provided meager compensation for work that was dangerous and monotonous, for example. Also, statistical studies do not say anything about how the level of unemployment may have risen, for there are no good unemployment statistics from this period. Furthermore, the hours in the average workweek increased; to an unknown extent, workers earned more simply because they worked more. Finally, the wartime decline was of great importance. The difficult war years were formative years for the new factory labor force, and they colored the early experience of modern industrial life in somber tones.

Another way to consider the workers' standard of living is to look at the goods that they purchased. Again the evidence is somewhat contradictory. Speaking generally, workers ate somewhat more food of higher nutritional quality as the Industrial Revolution progressed, except during wartime. Diets became more varied; people ate more potatoes, dairy products, fruits, and vegetables. Clothing improved, but housing for working people probably deteriorated somewhat. In short, per capita use of specific goods supports the position that the standard of living of the working classes rose, at least moderately, after the long wars with France.

Conditions of Work

What about working conditions? Did workers eventually earn more only at the cost of working longer and harder? Were workers exploited harshly by the new factory owners?

The first factories were cotton mills, which began functioning along rivers and streams in the 1770s. Cottage workers, accustomed to the putting-out system, were reluctant to work in the new factories even when they received relatively good wages because factory work was unappealing. In the factory, workers had to keep up with the machine and follow its tempo. They had to show up every day and work long, monotonous hours. Factory workers had to adjust their daily lives to the shrill call of the factory whistle.

Cottage workers were not used to that kind of life and discipline. All members of the family worked hard and long, but in spurts, setting their own pace. They could interrupt their work when they wanted to. Women and children could break up their long hours of spinning with other tasks. On Saturday afternoon the head of the family delivered the week's work to the merchant manufacturer and got paid. Saturday night was a time of relaxation and drinking, especially for the men. Recovering from his hangover on Tuesday, the weaver bent to his task on Wednesday and then worked frantically to meet his deadline on Saturday. Like some students today, he might "pull an all-nighter" on Thursday or Friday in order to get his work in.

Also, early factories resembled English poorhouses, where totally destitute people went to live at public expense. Some poorhouses were industrial prisons, where the inmates had to work in order to receive their food and lodging. The similarity between large brick factories and large stone poorhouses increased the cottage workers' fear of factories and their hatred of factory discipline.

It was cottage workers' reluctance to work in factories that prompted the early cotton mill owners to turn to abandoned and pauper children for their labor. As we have seen, these owners contracted with local officials to employ large numbers of these children, who had no say in the matter. Pauper children were often badly treated and terribly overworked in the mills, as they were when they were apprenticed as chimney sweeps, market girls, shoemakers, and so forth. In the eighteenth century, semiforced child labor seemed necessary and was socially accepted. From our modern point of view, it was cruel exploitation and a blot on the record of the new industrial system.

By 1790 the early pattern was rapidly changing. The use of pauper apprentices was in decline, and in 1802 it was forbidden by Parliament. Many more factories were being built, mainly in urban areas, where they could use steam power rather than waterpower and attract a workforce more easily than in the countryside. The need for workers was great. Indeed, people came from near and far to work in the cities, both as factory workers and as laborers, builders, and domestic servants. Yet as they took these new jobs, working people did not simply give in to a system of labor that had formerly repelled them. Rather, they helped modify the system by carrying over old, familiar working traditions.

Cotton Mill Workers   Family members often worked side by side in early British factories, and the child on the left is quite possibly the daughter of the woman nearby. They are combing raw cotton and drawing it into loose strands called rovings, which will be spun into fine thread on the machines to the right. *(Mary Evans Picture Library)*

For one thing, they often came to the mills and the mines as family units. This was how they had worked on farms and in the putting-out system. The mill or mine owner bargained with the head of the family and paid him or her for the work of the whole family. In the cotton mills, children worked for their mothers or fathers, collecting scraps and "piecing" broken threads together. In the mines, children sorted coal and worked the ventilation equipment. Their mothers hauled coal in the tunnels below the surface, while their fathers hewed with pick and shovel at the face of the seam.

The preservation of the family as an economic unit in the factories from the 1790s on made the new surroundings more tolerable, both in Great Britain and in other countries, during the early stages of industrialization. Parents disciplined their children, making firm measures socially acceptable, and directed their upbringing. The presence of the whole family meant that children and adults worked the same long hours (twelve-hour shifts were normal in cotton mills in 1800). In the early years, some very young children were employed solely to keep the family together. For example, Jedediah Strutt (see page 743) believed children should be at least ten years old to work in his mills, but he reluctantly employed seven-year-olds to satisfy their parents. Adult workers were not particularly interested in limiting the minimum working age or hours of their children as long as family members worked side by side. Only when technical changes threatened to place control and discipline in the hands of impersonal managers and overseers did adult workers protest against inhuman conditions in the name of their children.

Some enlightened employers and social reformers in Parliament definitely felt otherwise. They argued that more humane standards were necessary, and they used widely circulated parliamentary reports to influence public opinion. For example, Robert Owen (1771–1858), a very successful manufacturer in Scotland, testified in 1816 before an investigating committee on the basis of his experience. He stated that "very strong facts" demonstrated that employing children under ten years of age as factory workers was "injurious to the children, and not beneficial to the proprietors." The parliamentary committee asked him to explain, and the testimony proceeded as follows:

"Seventeen years ago, a number of individuals, with myself, purchased the New Lanark establishment from the late Mr Dale, of Glasgow. At that period I find that there were 500 children, who had been taken from poor-houses, chiefly in Edinburgh. . . . The hours of work at that time were thirteen, inclusive of meal times, and an hour and a half was allowed for meals. I very soon discovered that although those children were very well fed, well clothed, well lodged, and very great care taken of them when out of the mills, their growth and their minds were materially injured by being employed at those ages within the cotton mills for eleven and a half hours per day. . . . Their limbs were generally deformed, their growth was stunted, and although one of the best school-masters upon the old plan was engaged to instruct those children every night, in general they made but a very slow progress, even in learning the common alphabet. . . ."

"Do you think the age of ten the best period for the admission of children into full and constant employment for ten or eleven hours per day, within woollen, cotton, and other mills or manufactories?"

"I do not."

"What other period would you recommend for their full admission to full work?"

"Twelve years."[9]

Owen's testimony rang true because he had already raised the age of employment in his mills and was promoting education for young children. Workers also provided graphic testimony at such hearings as the reformers pressed Parliament to pass corrective laws. They scored some important successes.

Their most significant early accomplishment was the **Factory Act of 1833.** It limited the factory workday for children between nine and thirteen to eight hours and that of adolescents between fourteen and eighteen to twelve hours, although the act made no effort to regulate the hours of work for children at home or in small businesses. Children under nine were to be enrolled in the elementary schools that factory owners were required to establish. The employment of children declined rapidly. Thus the Factory Act broke the pattern of whole families working together in the factory because efficiency required standardized shifts for all workers.

Ties of blood and kinship were important in other ways in Great Britain in the formative years between about 1790 and 1840. Many manufacturers and builders hired workers through subcontractors. They paid the subcontractors on the basis of what the subcontractors and their crews produced—for smelting so many tons of pig iron or moving so much dirt or gravel for a canal or roadbed. Subcontractors in turn hired and fired their own workers, many of whom were friends and relations. The subcontractor might be as harsh as the greediest capitalist, but the relationship between subcontractor and work crew was close and personal. This kind of personal relationship had traditionally existed in cottage industry and in urban crafts, and it was more acceptable to many workers than impersonal factory discipline. This system also provided people with an easy way to find a job. Even today, a friend or relative who is a supervisor is frequently worth a host of formal application forms.

Ties of kinship were particularly important for newcomers, who often traveled great distances to find work. Many urban workers in Great Britain were from Ireland. Forced out of rural Ireland by population growth and deteriorating economic conditions from 1817 on, Irish in search of jobs could not be choosy; they took what they could get. As early as 1824, most of the workers in the Glasgow cotton mills were Irish; in 1851 one-sixth of the population of Liverpool was Irish. Like many other immigrant groups held together by ethnic and religious ties, the Irish worked together, formed their own neighborhoods, and not only survived but also thrived.

The Sexual Division of Labor

The era of the Industrial Revolution witnessed major changes in the sexual division of labor. In preindustrial Europe most people generally worked in family units. By tradition, certain jobs were defined by gender—women and girls for milking and spinning, men and boys for plowing and weaving—but many tasks might go to either sex. Family employment carried over into early factories and subcontracting, but it collapsed as child labor was restricted and new attitudes emerged. A different sexual division of labor gradually arose to take its place. The man emerged as the family's primary wage earner, while the woman found only limited job opportunities. Generally denied good jobs at good wages in the growing urban economy, women were expected to concentrate on unpaid housework, child care, and craftwork at home.

This new pattern of "separate spheres" had several aspects. First, all studies agree that married women from the working classes were much less likely to work full-time for wages outside the house after the first child arrived, although they often earned small amounts doing putting-out handicrafts at home and taking in boarders. Second, when married women did work for wages outside the house, they usually came from the poorest families, where the husbands were poorly paid, sick, unemployed, or missing. Third, these poor married (or widowed) women were joined by legions of young unmarried women, who worked full-time but only in certain jobs. Fourth, all women were generally confined to low-paying, dead-end jobs. Virtually no occupation open to women paid a wage sufficient for a person to live independently. Men predominated in the better-paying, more promising employments. Evolving gradually, but largely in place by 1850, the new sexual division of labor in Britain constituted a major development in the history of women and of the family.

If the reorganization of paid work along gender lines is widely recognized, there is no agreement on its causes. One school of scholars sees little connection with industrialization and finds the answer in the deeply ingrained sexist attitudes of a "patriarchal tradition," which predated the economic transformation. These scholars stress the role of male-dominated craft unions in denying working women access to good jobs and relegating them to unpaid housework. Other scholars, stressing that the gender roles of women and men can vary enormously with time and culture, look more to a combination of economic and biological factors in order to explain the emergence of a sex-segregated division of labor.

Three ideas stand out in this more recent interpretation. First, the new and unfamiliar discipline of the clock and the machine was especially hard on married women of the laboring classes. Above all, relentless factory discipline conflicted with child care in a way that labor on the farm or in the cottage had not. A woman operating earsplitting spinning machinery could mind a child of seven or eight working beside her (until such work was outlawed), but she could no longer pace herself through pregnancy or breast-feed her baby on the job. Thus a working-class woman had strong incentives to concentrate on child care within her home if her family could afford it.

Second, running a household in conditions of primitive urban poverty was an extremely demanding job in its own right. There were no supermarkets or public transportation. Everything had to be done on foot. Shopping and feeding the family constituted a never-ending challenge. The woman marched from one tiny shop to another, dragging her tired children (for who was to watch them?) and struggling valiantly with heavy sacks and tricky shopkeepers. Yet another brutal job outside the house—a "second shift"—had limited appeal for the average married woman. Thus women might well have accepted the emerging division of labor as the best available strategy for family survival in the industrializing society.[10]

Third, why were the women who did work for wages outside the home segregated and confined to certain "women's jobs"? No doubt the desire of males to monopolize the best opportunities and hold women down provides part of the answer. Yet as some feminist scholars have argued, sex-segregated employment was also a collective response to the new industrial system. Previously, at least in theory, young people worked under a watchful parental eye. The growth of factories and mines brought unheard-of opportunities for girls and boys to mix on the job, free of familial supervision. Continuing to mix after work, they were "more likely to form liaisons, initiate courtships, and respond to advances."[11] Such intimacy also led to more unplanned pregnancies and fueled the illegitimacy explosion that had begun in the late eighteenth century and that gathered force until at least 1850 (see pages 665–666). Thus segregation of jobs by gender was partly an effort by older people to help control the sexuality of working-class youths.

Investigations into the British coal industry before 1842 provide a graphic example of this concern. (See the feature "Listening to the Past: The Testimony of Young Mine Workers" on pages 752–753.) The middle-class men leading the inquiry, who expected their daughters and wives to pursue ladylike activities, often failed to appreciate the physical effort of the girls and women who dragged with belt and chain the unwheeled carts of coal along narrow underground passages. But they professed horror at the sight of girls and women working without shirts, which was a common practice because of the heat, and they quickly assumed the prevalence of licentious sex with the male miners, who also wore very little clothing. In fact, most girls and married women worked for related males in a family unit that provided considerable protection and restraint. Yet many witnesses from the working class also believed that "blackguardism and debauchery" were common and that "they are best out of the pits, the lasses." Some miners stressed particularly the danger of sexual aggression for girls working past puberty. As one explained:

I consider it a scandal for girls to work in the pits. Till they are 12 or 14 they may work very well but after that it's an abomination. . . . The work of the pit does not hurt them, it is the effect on their morals that I complain of, and after 14 they should not be allowed to go. . . . After that age it is dreadful for them.[12]

The **Mines Act of 1842** prohibited underground work for all women as well as for boys under ten.

Some women who had to support themselves protested against being excluded from coal mining, which paid higher wages than most other jobs open to working-class women. But provided they were part of families that could manage economically, the girls and the women who had worked underground were generally pleased with the law. In explaining her satisfaction in 1844, one mother of four provided a real insight into why many women accepted the emerging sexual division of labor:

While working in the pit I was worth to my [miner] husband seven shillings a week, out of which we had to pay 2½ shillings to a woman for looking after the younger children. I used to take them to her house at 4 o'clock in the morning, out of their own beds, to put them into hers. Then there was one shilling a week for washing; besides, there was mending to pay for, and other things. The house was not guided. The other children broke things; they did not go to school when they were sent; they would be playing about, and get ill-used by other children, and their clothes torn. Then when I came home in the evening, everything was to do after the day's labor, and I was so tired I had no heart for it; no fire lit, nothing cooked, no water fetched, the house dirty, and nothing comfortable for my husband. It is all far better now, and I wouldn't go down again.[13]

The Early Labor Movement in Britain

Many kinds of employment changed slowly during and after the Industrial Revolution in Great Britain. In 1850 more British people still worked on farms than in any other occupation. The second-largest occupation was domestic service, with more than one million household servants, 90 percent of whom were women. Thus many old, familiar jobs outside industry lived on and provided alternatives for individual workers. This helped ease the transition to industrial civilization.

Within industry itself, the pattern of artisans working with hand tools in small shops remained unchanged in many trades, even as some others were revolutionized by technological change. For example, as in the case of cotton and coal, the British iron industry was completely dominated by large-scale capitalist firms by 1850. Many large ironworks had more than one thousand people on their payrolls. Yet the firms that fashioned iron into small metal goods, such as tools, tableware, and toys, employed on average fewer than ten wage workers, who used time-honored handicraft skills. Only gradually after 1850 did some owners find ways to reorganize some handicraft industries with new machines and new patterns of work. The survival of small workshops gave many workers an alternative to factory employment.

Working-class solidarity and class-consciousness developed in small workshops as well as in large factories. In the northern factory districts, where thousands of "hired hands" looked across at a tiny minority of managers and owners, anticapitalist sentiments were frequent by the 1820s. Commenting in 1825 on a strike in the woolen center of Bradford and the support it had gathered from other regions, one paper claimed with pride that "it is all the workers of England against a few masters of Bradford."[14] Modern technology had created a few versus a many.

The transformation of some traditional trades by organizational changes, rather than technological innovations, could also create ill will and class feeling. The liberal concept of economic freedom gathered strength in the late eighteenth and early nineteenth centuries. As in France during the French Revolution, the British government attacked monopolies, guilds, and workers combinations in the name of individual liberty. In 1799 Parliament passed the **Combination Acts,** which outlawed unions and strikes. In 1813 and 1814, Parliament repealed the old and often disregarded law of 1563 regulating the wages of artisans and the conditions of apprenticeship. As a result of these and other measures, certain skilled artisan workers, such as bootmakers and high-quality tailors, found aggressive capitalists ignoring traditional work rules and flooding their trades with unorganized women workers and children to beat down wages.

The liberal capitalist attack on artisan guilds and work rules was bitterly resented by many craftworkers, who subsequently played an important part in Great Britain and in other countries in gradually building a modern labor movement to improve working conditions and to serve worker needs. The Combination Acts were widely disregarded by workers. Printers, papermakers, carpenters, tailors, and other such craftsmen continued to take collective action, and societies of skilled factory workers also organized unions. Unions sought to control the number of skilled workers, limit apprenticeship to mem-

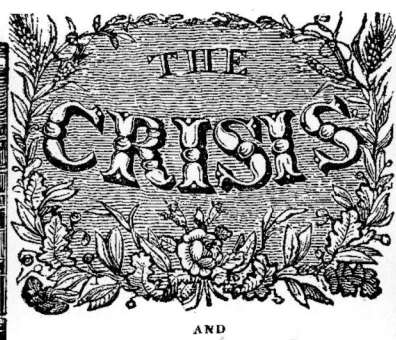

No. 11. Vol. III.] SATURDAY,   **THE CRISIS**   NOVEMBER 9, 1833. [Price 1½*d.*

AND

NATIONAL CO-OPERATIVE TRADES' UNION AND EQUITABLE LABOUR EXCHANGE GAZETTE

"THE CHARACTER OF EVERY HUMAN BEING IS FORMED FOR, AND NOT BY, THE INDIVIDUAL."—*Owen.*

Weekly Proceedings.

INSTITUTION, CHARLOTTE-STREET.
SUNDAY EVENING.

Mr. *Smith* lectured on "CIRCUMSTANCES—INFLUENCE OF CLIMATE ON RELIGION."

In hot climates men have always considered themselves entitled to as many wives as they chose. The Jews were not restricted to any number. Solomon had a thousand, and the chaste and more just than those of Moses himself, who by the authority of God went much further, in respect to women at least, than either Owen or St. Simon. These changes are entirely to be accounted for by a change of circumstances; there is no particular system or form of manners or customs either good or bad in themselves; but those which conduce to the greatest amount of happiness to the public at large, and the individual in particular, ought other replies,—"Every day as soon as they have dressed themselves they take up their arms, and, entering the lists, they fight till they cut each other in pieces. This is their diversion. But no sooner does the hour of repast approach, than they remount their steeds, all safe and whole again, and return to drink in the palace of Odin." But the hell of these cold climates is the very opposite of the hells that come from the tropics. The hell of these northern

The Working-Class Press *The Crisis,* an influential newspaper inspired by the teachings of Robert Owen, summed up its analysis of Britain's problems with two images at the top of the first page. Degrading poverty for the many and superfluous wealth for the few equaled national crisis. Newspapers helped to strengthen and channel the British labor movement. *(Private Collection/The Bridgeman Art Library International Ltd)*

bers' own children, and bargain with owners over wages. They were not afraid to strike; there was, for example, a general strike of adult cotton spinners in Manchester in 1810. In the face of widespread union activity, Parliament repealed the Combination Acts in 1824, and unions were tolerated, though not fully accepted, after 1825.

The next stage in the development of the British trade-union movement was the attempt to create a single large national union. This effort was led not so much by working people as by social reformers such as Robert Owen. Owen, a self-made cotton manufacturer (see page 746), had pioneered in industrial relations by combining firm discipline with concern for the health, safety, and hours of his workers. After 1815 he experimented with cooperative and socialist communities, including one at New Harmony, Indiana. Then in 1834 Owen organized one of the largest and most visionary of the early national unions, the **Grand National Consolidated Trades Union.** When this and other grandiose schemes collapsed, the British labor move-

ment moved once again after 1851 in the direction of craft unions. The most famous of these "new model unions" was the Amalgamated Society of Engineers, which represented skilled machinists. These unions won real benefits for members by fairly conservative means and thus became an accepted part of the industrial scene.

British workers also engaged in direct political activity in defense of their own interests. After the collapse of Owen's national trade union, many working people went into the Chartist movement, which sought political democracy. The key Chartist demand—that all men be given the right to vote—became the great hope of millions of aroused people. Workers were also active in campaigns to limit the workday in factories to ten hours and to permit duty-free importation of wheat into Great Britain to secure cheap bread. Thus working people developed a sense of their own identity and played an active role in shaping the new industrial system. They were neither helpless victims nor passive beneficiaries.

Summary

Western society's industrial breakthrough grew out of a long process of economic and social change in which the rise of capitalism, overseas expansion, and the growth of rural industry stood out as critical preparatory developments. Eventually taking the lead in all of these developments, and also profiting from stable government, abundant natural resources, and a flexible labor force, Britain experienced between the 1780s and the 1850s an epoch-making transformation, one that is still aptly termed the Industrial Revolution.

Building on technical breakthroughs, power-driven equipment, and large-scale enterprise, the Industrial Revolution in England greatly increased output in certain radically altered industries, stimulated the large handicraft and commercial sectors, and speeded up overall economic growth. Rugged Scotland industrialized at least as fast as England, and Great Britain became the first industrial nation. By 1850 the level of British per capita industrial production was surpassing continental levels by a growing margin, and Britain savored a near monopoly in world markets for mass-produced goods.

Continental countries inevitably took rather different paths to the urban industrial society. They relied more on handicraft production in both towns and villages. Only in the 1840s did railroad construction begin to create the strong demand for iron, coal, and railway equipment that speeded up the process of industrialization in the 1850s and 1860s.

The rise of modern industry had a profound impact on people and their lives. In the early stages, Britain again led the way, experiencing in a striking manner the long-term social changes accompanying the economic transformation. Factory discipline and Britain's stern capitalist economy weighed heavily on working people, who, however, actively fashioned their destinies and refused to be passive victims. Improvements in the standard of living came slowly, but they were substantial by 1850. The era of industrialization fostered new attitudes toward child labor, encouraged protective factory legislation, and called forth a new sense of class feeling and an assertive labor movement. It also promoted a more rigid division of roles and responsibilities within the family that was detrimental to women, another gradual but profound change of revolutionary proportions.

Key Terms

Industrial Revolution	tariff protection
spinning jenny	economic nationalism
water frame	class-consciousness
body linen	Luddites
steam engine	Factory Act of 1833
coke	Mines Act of 1842
Rocket	Combination Acts
Crystal Palace	Grand National Consoli-
iron law of wages	dated Trades Union

Notes

1. N. F. R. Crafts, *British Economic Growth During the Industrial Revolution* (Oxford: Oxford University Press, 1985), p. 32.
2. P. Bairoch, "International Industrialization Levels from 1750 to 1980," *Journal of European Economic History* 11 (Spring 1982): 269–333.
3. Crafts, *British Economic Growth*, pp. 45, 95–102.
4. M. Lévy-Leboyer, *Les banques européennes et l'industrialisation dans la première moitié du XIXe siècle* (Paris: Presses Universitaires de France, 1964), p. 29.
5. J. Michelet, *The People*, trans. with an introduction by J. P. McKay (Urbana: University of Illinois Press, 1973; original publication, 1846), p. 64.
6. F. Engels, *The Condition of the Working Class in England*, trans. and ed. W. O. Henderson and W. H. Chaloner (Stanford, Calif.: Stanford University Press, 1968), p. xxiii.
7. Quoted in W. A. Hayek, ed., *Capitalism and the Historians* (Chicago: University of Chicago Press, 1954), p. 126.
8. Crafts, *British Economic Growth*, p. 95.
9. Quoted in E. R. Pike, *"Hard Times": Human Documents of the Industrial Revolution* (New York: Praeger, 1966), p. 109.
10. See especially J. Brenner and M. Rama, "Rethinking Women's Oppression," *New Left Review* 144 (March–April 1984): 33–71, and sources cited there.
11. J. Humphries, ". . . 'The Most Free from Objection' . . . : The Sexual Division of Labor and Women's Work in Nineteenth-Century England," *Journal of Economic History* 47 (December 1987): 948.
12. Ibid., p. 941; Pike, *"Hard Times,"* p. 266.
13. Pike, *"Hard Times,"* p. 208.
14. Quoted in D. Geary, ed., *Labour and Socialist Movements in Europe Before 1914* (Oxford: Berg, 1989), p. 29.

Suggested Reading

There is a vast and exciting literature on the Industrial Revolution. R. Cameron, *A Concise Economic History of the World* (1989), provides an introduction to the issues and has a carefully annotated bibliography. J. Goodman and K. Honeyman, *Gainful Pursuits: The Making of Industrial Europe, 1600–1914* (1988); D. S. Landes, *The Unbound Prometheus:*

Technological Change and Industrial Development in Western Europe from 1750 to the Present (1969); and S. Pollard, *Peaceful Conquest: The Industrialization of Europe* (1981), are excellent general treatments of European industrial growth. These studies also suggest the range of issues and interpretations. R. Sylla and G. Toniolo, eds., *Patterns of European Industrialization* (1991), is an important collection by specialists. T. Kemp, *Industrialization in Europe,* 2d ed. (1985), is also useful. P. Hudson, *The Industrial Revolution* (1992); M. Berg, *The Age of Manufactures: Industry, Innovation and Work in Britain, 1700–1820* (1985); and P. Mathias, *The First Industrial Nation: An Economic History of Britain, 1700–1914* (1969), admirably discuss the various aspects of the British breakthrough and offer good bibliographies, as does the work by Crafts mentioned in the Notes. K. Pomeranz, *The Great Divergence: China, Europe, and the Making of the Modern World Economy* (2000), is a sophisticated reconsideration of why western Europe achieved this industrial breakthrough and China did not. W. Rostow, *The Stages of Economic Growth: A Non-Communist Manifesto* (1960), still stands as a popular, provocative study of global patterns.

W. Walton, *France and the Crystal Palace: Bourgeois Taste and Artisan Manufacture in the 19th Century* (1992), and H. Kirsh, *From Domestic Manufacturing to Industrial Revolution: The Case of the Rhineland Textile Districts* (1989), examine the gradual transformation of handicraft techniques and their persistent importance in the international economy. R. Cameron, *France and the Economic Development of Europe, 1800–1914* (1961), traces the spread of railroads and industry across Europe. A. S. Milward and S. B. Saul, *The Economic Development of Continental Europe, 1780–1870* (1973) and *The Development of the Economies of Continental Europe, 1850–1914* (1977), may be compared with J. Clapham's old-fashioned classic, *Economic Development of France and Germany* (1963). P. O'Brien, "Path Dependency, or Why Britain Became an Industrialized and Urbanized National Economy Long Before France," *Economic History Review* 49 (May 1966): 213–249, is a stimulating comparative essay, and C. Heywood, *The Economic Development of France, 1750–1914* (1992), introduces the main issues and provides an up-to-date bibliography. Other important works on industrial developments are C. Tilly and E. Shorter, *Strikes in France, 1830–1848* (1974); G. Tortella, *The Development of Modern Spain* (2000); L. Schofer, *The Formation of a Modern Labor Force* (1975), which focuses on the Silesian part of Germany; and W. Blackwell, *The Industrialization of Russia,* 2d ed. (1982). M. Wintle, *An Economic and Social History of the Netherlands: Demographic, Economic and Social Transitions* (2000), and L. Magnusson, *An Economic History of Sweden* (2000), are excellent surveys of developments in two smaller countries. L. Moch, *Paths to the City: Regional Migration in Nineteenth-Century France* (1983), and W. Schivelbusch, *Disenchanted Night: The Industrialization of Light in the Nineteenth Century* (1983), imaginatively analyze quite different aspects of industrialization's many consequences.

The debate between "optimists" and "pessimists" about the consequences of industrialization in Britain goes on. Two excellent studies with a gender perspective revitalize the debate: D. Valenze, *The First Industrial Woman* (1995); P. Hudson and W. Lee, eds., *Women's Work and the Family Economy in Historical Perspective* (1990). P. Taylor, ed., *The Industrial Revolution: Triumph or Disaster?* (1970), is a useful introduction to older studies. Hayek's collection of essays, cited in the Notes, stresses positive aspects. It is also fascinating to compare Engels's classic condemnation, cited in the Notes, with Andrew Ure's optimistic defense, *The Philosophy of Manufactures,* first published in 1835 and often reprinted. J. Rule, *The Labouring Classes in Early Industrial England, 1750–1850* (1987), is a recommended synthesis. E. P. Thompson continues and enriches the Engels tradition in *The Making of the English Working Class* (1963), an exciting book rich in detail and early working-class lore. Pike's documentary collection, cited in the Notes, provides fascinating insights into the lives of working people, as does the detailed investigation by C. Tuttle, *Hard Work in Factories and Mines: The Economics of Child Labor During the Industrial Revolution* (1999). An unorthodox but moving account of a doomed group is D. Bythell, *The Handloom Weavers* (1969). L. Davidoff and C. Hall, *Family Fortunes: Men and Women of the English Middle Class, 1750–1850* (1987), examines both economic activities and cultural beliefs with great skill. F. Klingender, *Art and the Industrial Revolution,* rev. ed. (1968), is justly famous, and M. Ignatieff, *A Just Measure of Pain* (1980), is an engrossing study of prisons during British industrialization. D. S. Landes, *Revolution in Time: Clocks and the Making of the Modern World* (1983), is a brilliant integration of industrial and cultural history.

Among general studies, G. S. R. Kitson Clark, *The Making of Victorian England* (1967), is particularly imaginative. A. Briggs, *Victorian People* (1955), provides an engrossing series of brief biographies. H. Ausubel discusses a major reformer in *John Bright* (1966), and B. Harrison skillfully illuminates the problem of heavy drinking in *Drink and the Victorians* (1971). The most famous contemporary novel dealing with the new industrial society is Charles Dickens's *Hard Times,* an entertaining but exaggerated story. *Mary Barton* and *North and South* by Elizabeth Gaskell are more realistic portrayals, and both are highly recommended.

The Testimony of Young Mine Workers

*T*he use of child labor in British *industrialization quickly attracted the attention of humanitarians and social reformers. This interest led to investigations by parliamentary commissions, which resulted in laws limiting the hours and the ages of children working in large factories. Designed to build a case for remedial legislation, parliamentary inquiries gave large numbers of workers a rare chance to speak directly to contemporaries and to historians.*

The moving passages that follow are taken from testimony gathered in 1841 and 1842 by the Ashley Mines Commission. Interviewing employers and many male and female workers, the commissioners focused on the physical condition of the youth and on the sexual behavior of workers far underground. The subsequent Mines Act of 1842 sought to reduce immoral behavior and sexual bullying by prohibiting underground work for all women (and for boys younger than ten).

Mr. Payne, coal master:

That children are employed generally at nine years old in the coal pits and sometimes at eight. In fact, the smaller the vein of coal is in height, the younger and smaller are the children required; the work occupies from six to seven hours per day in the pits; they are not ill-used or worked beyond their strength; a good deal of depravity exists but they are certainly not worse in morals than in other branches of the Sheffield trade, but upon the whole superior; the morals of this district are materially improving; Mr. Bruce, the clergyman, has been zealous and active in endeavoring to ameliorate their moral and religious education. . . .

Ann Eggley, hurrier, 18 years old:

I'm sure I don't know how to spell my name. We go at four in the morning, and sometimes at half-past four. We begin to work as soon as we get down. We get out after four, sometimes at five, in the evening. We work the whole time except an hour for dinner, and sometimes we haven't time to eat. I hurry [move coal wagons underground] by myself, and have done so for long. I know the corves [small coal wagons] are very heavy, they are the biggest corves anywhere about. The work is far too hard for me; the sweat runs off me all over sometimes. I am very tired at night. Sometimes when we get home at night we have not power to wash us, and then we go to bed. Sometimes we fall asleep in the chair. Father said last night it was both a shame and a disgrace for girls to work as we do, but there was naught else for us to do. I began to hurry when I was seven and I have been hurrying ever since. I have been 11 years in the pits. The girls are always tired. I was poorly twice this winter; it was with headache. I hurry for Robert Wiggins; he is not akin to me. . . . We don't always get enough to eat and drink, but we get a good supper. I have known my father go at two in the morning to work . . . and he didn't come out till four. I am quite sure that we work constantly 12 hours except on Saturdays. We wear trousers and our shifts in the pit and great big shoes clinkered and nailed. The girls never work naked to the waist in our pit. The men don't insult us in the pit. The conduct of the girls in the pit is good enough sometimes and sometimes bad enough. I never went to a day-school. I went a little to a Sunday-school, but I soon gave it over. I thought it too bad to be confined both Sundays and week-days. I walk about and get the fresh air on Sundays. I have not learnt to read. I don't know my letters. I never learnt naught. I never go to church or chapel; there is no church or chapel at Gawber, there is none nearer than a mile. . . . I have never heard that a good man came into the world who was God's son to save sinners. I never heard of Christ

This illustration of a girl dragging a coal wagon was one of several that shocked public opinion and contributed to the Mines Act of 1842. *(The British Library)*

at all. Nobody has ever told me about him, nor have my father and mother ever taught me to pray. I know no prayer; I never pray.

Patience Kershaw, aged 17:

My father has been dead about a year; my mother is living and has ten children, five lads and five lasses; the oldest is about thirty, the youngest is four; three lasses go to mill; all the lads are colliers, two getters and three hurriers; one lives at home and does nothing; mother does nought but look after home.

All my sisters have been hurriers, but three went to the mill. Alice went because her legs swelled from hurrying in cold water when she was hot. I never went to day-school; I go to Sunday-school, but I cannot read or write; I go to pit at five o'clock in the morning and come out at five in the evening; I get my breakfast of porridge and milk first; I take my dinner with me, a cake, and eat it as I go; I do not stop or rest any time for the purpose; I get nothing else until I get home, and then have potatoes and meat, not every day meat. I hurry in the clothes I have now got on, trousers and ragged jacket; the bald place upon my head is made by thrusting the corves; my legs have never swelled, but sisters' did when they went to mill; I hurry the corves a mile and more under ground and back; they weigh 300; I hurry 11 a day; I wear a belt and chain at the workings to get the corves out; the putters [miners] that I work for are *naked* except their caps; they pull off all their clothes; I see them at work when I go up; sometimes they beat me, if I am not quick enough, with their hands; they strike me upon my back; the boys take liberties with me, sometimes, they pull me about; I am the only girl in the pit; there are about 20 boys and 15 men; all the men are naked; I would rather work in mill than in coal-pit.

Isabel Wilson, 38 years old, coal putter:

When women have children thick [fast] they are compelled to take them down early. I have been married 19 years and have had 10 bairns [children]; seven are in life. When on Sir John's work was a carrier of coals, which caused me to miscarry five times from the strains, and was gai [very] ill after each. Putting is no so oppressive; last child was born on Saturday morning, and I was at work on the Friday night.

Once met with an accident; a coal brake my cheek-bone, which kept me idle some weeks.

I have wrought below 30 years, and so has the guid man; he is getting touched in the breath now.

None of the children read, as the work is no regular. I did read once, but no able to attend to it now; when I go below lassie 10 years of age keeps house and makes the broth or stir-about.

Questions for Analysis

1. To what extent are the testimonies of Ann Eggley and Patience Kershaw in harmony with that of Payne?

2. Describe the work of Eggley and Kershaw. What do you think of their work? Why?

3. What strikes you most about the lives of these workers?

4. The witnesses were responding to questions from middle-class commissioners. What did the commissioners seem interested in? Why?

Source: J. Bowditch and C. Ramsland, eds., *Voices of the Industrial Revolution.* Copyright © 1961, 1989 by the University of Michigan. Reprinted by permission.

Revolutionaries in Transylvania. Ana Ipatescu, of the first
group of revolutionaries in Transylvania against Russia,
1848. *(National Historical Museum, Bucharest/The Art Archive)*

23 Ideologies and Upheavals, 1815–1850

chapter outline

- The Peace Settlement

- Radical Ideas and Early Socialism

- The Romantic Movement

- Reforms and Revolutions

- The Revolutions of 1848

*T*he momentous economic and political transformation of modern times began in the late eighteenth century with the Industrial Revolution in England and then the French Revolution. Until about 1815, these economic and political revolutions were separate, involving different countries and activities and proceeding at very different paces. After peace returned in 1815, the situation changed. Economic and political changes tended to fuse, reinforcing each other and bringing about what historian Eric Hobsbawm has incisively called the **dual revolution.** For instance, the growth of the industrial middle class encouraged the drive for representative government, and the demands of the French sans-culottes in 1793 and 1794 inspired many socialist thinkers. Gathering strength, the dual revolution rushed on to alter completely first Europe and then the rest of the world. Much of world history in the past two centuries can be seen as the progressive unfolding of the dual revolution.

In Europe in the nineteenth century, as in Asia and Africa in more recent times, the interrelated economic and political transformation was built on complicated histories, strong traditions, and highly diverse cultures. Radical change was eventually a constant, but the particular results varied enormously. In central and eastern Europe especially, the traditional elites—the monarchs, noble landowners, and bureaucrats—proved capable of defending their privileges and eventually using nationalism as a way to respond to the dual revolution and to serve their interests, as we shall see in Chapter 25.

The dual revolution also posed a tremendous intellectual challenge. The meanings of the economic, political, and social changes that were occurring, as well as the ways they would be shaped by human action, were anything but clear. These changes fascinated observers and stimulated the growth of new ideas and powerful ideologies. The most important of these were conservatism, liberalism, nationalism, and socialism.

- How did thinkers develop these ideas to describe and shape the transformation going on before their eyes?
- How did the artists and writers of the romantic movement also reflect and influence changes in this era?

756

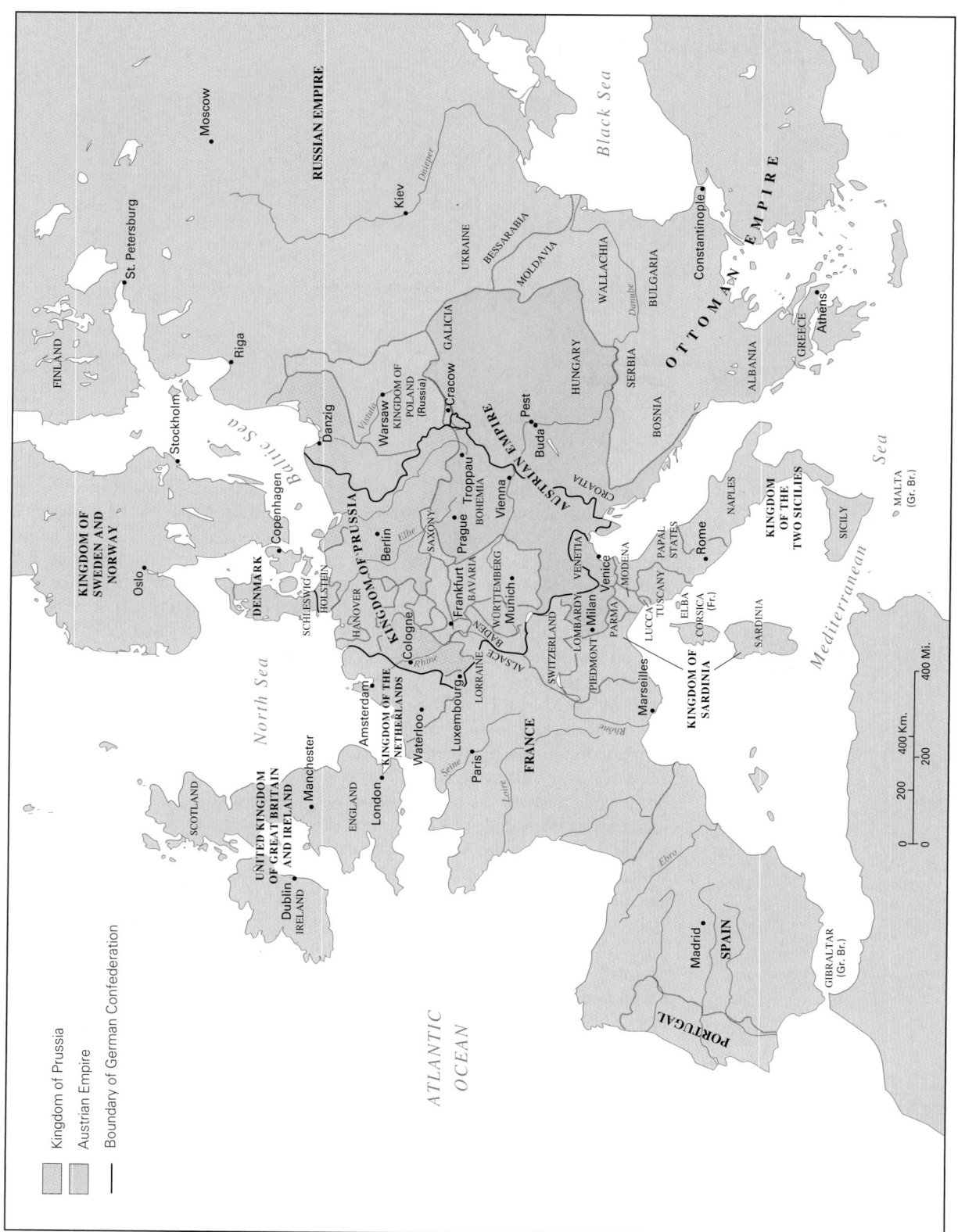

MAP 23.1 Europe in 1815 Europe's leaders re-established a balance of political power after the defeat of Napoleon. Prussia gained territory on the Rhine and in Saxony and consolidated its position as a Great Power.

Kingdom of Prussia

Austrian Empire

Boundary of German Confederation

1810	1820	1830	1840	1850	1860

Political/Military

1809–1848 Metternich serves as Austrian foreign minister

• 1815 Holy Alliance formed   • 1830 Greece wins independence from Turks

• 1819 Carlsbad Decrees issued by German Confederation

1830–1848 Reign of Louis Philippe in France

• 1832 Reform Bill in Britain   • 1848 Revolutions in France, Austria, and Prussia

Social/Economic

• 1815 Revision of Corn Laws in Britain

1845–1851 Great Famine in Ireland

• 1847 Ten Hours Act in Britain

Intellectual/Religious

1790s–1840s Romantic movement in literature and the arts

• 1810 Staël, *On Germany*   • 1839 Blanc, *Organization of Work*   • 1848 Marx and Engels, *The Communist Manifesto*

- How did the political revolution, derailed in France and resisted by European monarchs, eventually break out again after 1815?
- Why did the revolutionary surge triumph briefly in 1848 and then fail almost completely?

These are the questions this chapter will explore.

The Peace Settlement

The eventual triumph of revolutionary economic and political forces was by no means certain as the Napoleonic era ended. Quite the contrary. The conservative, aristocratic monarchies of Russia, Prussia, Austria, and Great Britain had finally defeated France and reaffirmed their determination to hold France in line. But many other international questions were outstanding, and the allies agreed to meet at the **Congress of Vienna** to fashion a general peace settlement.

Most people felt a profound longing for peace. The great challenge for political leaders in 1814 was to construct a settlement that would last and not sow the seeds of another war. Their efforts were largely successful and contributed to a century unmarred by destructive, generalized war (see Map 23.1).

The European Balance of Power

The allied powers were concerned first and foremost with the defeated enemy, France. Agreeing to the restoration of the Bourbon dynasty (see page 718), the allies were quite lenient toward France after Napoleon's abdication. France was given the boundaries it possessed in 1792, which were larger than those of 1789, and France did not have to pay any war reparations. Thus the victorious powers did not foment a spirit of injustice and revenge in the defeated country.

When the four allies of the Quadruple Alliance met together at the Congress of Vienna, assisted in a minor way

Adjusting the Balance The Englishman on the left uses his money to counterbalance the people that the Prussian and the fat Metternich are gaining in Saxony and Italy. Alexander I sits happily on his prize, Poland. This cartoon captures the essence of how most people thought about balance-of-power diplomacy at the Congress of Vienna. *(Bibliothèque Nationale, Paris)*

by a host of delegates from the smaller European states, they also agreed to raise a number of formidable barriers against renewed French aggression. The Low Countries—Belgium and Holland—were united under an enlarged Dutch monarchy capable of opposing France more effectively. Above all, Prussia received considerably more territory on France's eastern border so as to stand as the "sentinel on the Rhine" against France. In these ways, the Quadruple Alliance combined leniency toward France with strong defensive measures.

In their moderation toward France, the allies were motivated by self-interest and traditional ideas about the balance of power. To Klemens von Metternich and Robert Castlereagh, the foreign ministers of Austria and Great Britain, respectively, as well as their French counterpart, Charles Talleyrand, the balance of power meant an international equilibrium of political and military forces that would discourage aggression by any combina-

tion of states or, worse, the domination of Europe by any single state.

The Great Powers—Austria, Britain, Prussia, Russia, and France—used the balance of power to settle their own dangerous disputes at the Congress of Vienna. There was general agreement among the victors that each of them should receive compensation in the form of territory for their successful struggle against the French. Great Britain had already won colonies and strategic outposts during the long wars. Metternich's Austria gave up territories in Belgium and southern Germany but expanded greatly elsewhere, taking the rich provinces of Venetia and Lombardy in northern Italy as well as former Polish possessions and new lands on the eastern coast of the Adriatic (see Map 23.1). There was also agreement that Prussia and Russia should be compensated. But where and to what extent? That was the ticklish question that almost led to renewed war in January 1815.

The vaguely progressive, impetuous Tsar Alexander I of Russia wanted to restore the ancient kingdom of Poland, on which he expected to bestow the benefits of his rule. The Prussians agreed, provided they could swallow up the large and wealthy kingdom of Saxony, their German neighbor to the south. These demands were too much for Castlereagh and Metternich, who feared an unbalancing of forces in central Europe. In an astonishing about-face, they turned for diplomatic support to the wily Talleyrand and the defeated France he represented, signing a secret alliance directed against Russia and Prussia. War seemed imminent.

But the threat of war caused the rulers of Russia and Prussia to moderate their demands. Russia accepted a small Polish kingdom, and Prussia took only part of Saxony (see Map 23.1). This compromise was very much within the framework of balance-of-power ideology. And it enabled France to regain its Great Power status and end its diplomatic isolation.

Unfortunately for France, Napoleon suddenly escaped from his "comic kingdom" on the island of Elba. Yet the peace concluded after Napoleon's final defeat at Waterloo was still relatively moderate toward France. Fat old Louis XVIII was restored to his throne for a second time. France lost only a little territory, had to pay an indemnity of 700 million francs, and had to support a large army of occupation for five years.

The rest of the settlement already concluded at the Congress of Vienna was left intact. The members of the Quadruple Alliance, however, did agree to meet periodically to discuss their common interests and to consider appropriate measures for the maintenance of peace in Europe. This agreement marked the beginning of the European "congress system," which lasted long into the nineteenth century and settled many international crises through international conferences and balance-of-power diplomacy.

Intervention and Repression

There was also a domestic political side to the reestablishment of peace. Within their own countries, the leaders of the victorious states were much less flexible. In 1815 under Metternich's leadership, Austria, Prussia, and Russia embarked on a crusade against the ideas and politics of the dual revolution. This crusade lasted until 1848. The first step was the **Holy Alliance,** formed by Austria, Prussia, and Russia in September 1815. First proposed by Russia's Alexander I, the alliance soon became a symbol of the repression of liberal and revolutionary movements all over Europe.

In 1820 revolutionaries succeeded in forcing the monarchs of Spain and the southern Italian kingdom of the Two Sicilies to grant liberal constitutions against their wills. Metternich was horrified: revolution was rising once again. Calling a conference at Troppau in Austria under the provisions of the Quadruple Alliance, he and Alexander I proclaimed the principle of active intervention to maintain all autocratic regimes whenever they were threatened. Austrian forces then marched into Naples in 1821 and restored Ferdinand I to the throne of the Two Sicilies, while French armies likewise restored the Spanish regime.

In the following years, Metternich continued to battle against liberal political change. Sometimes he could do little, as in the case of the new Latin American republics that broke away from Spain. Nor could he undo the dynastic changes of 1830 and 1831 in France and Belgium. Nonetheless, until 1848 Metternich's system proved quite effective in central Europe, where his power was the greatest.

Metternich's policies dominated not only Austria and the Italian peninsula but also the entire German Confederation, which the peace settlement of Vienna had called into being. The confederation was composed of thirty-eight independent German states, including Prussia and Austria. These states met in complicated assemblies dominated by Austria, with Prussia a willing junior partner in the execution of repressive measures.

It was through the German Confederation that Metternich had the infamous **Carlsbad Decrees** issued in 1819. These decrees required the thirty-eight German member states to root out subversive ideas in their universities and newspapers. The decrees also established a permanent committee with spies and informers to investigate and punish any liberal or radical organizations.

Metternich and Conservatism

Metternich's determined defense of the status quo made him a villain in the eyes of most progressive, optimistic historians of the nineteenth century. Yet rather than denounce the man, we can try to understand him and the general conservatism he represented.

Born into the middle ranks of the landed nobility of the Rhineland, Prince Klemens von Metternich (1773–1859) was an internationally oriented aristocrat who made a brilliant diplomatic career in Austria. Austrian foreign minister from 1809 to 1848, the cosmopolitan Metternich always remained loyal to his class and jealously defended its rights and privileges to the day he died. Like most other conservatives of his time, he did so with a clear conscience. The nobility was one of Europe's most ancient institutions, and conservatives regarded tradition as the basic source of human institutions. In their view, the

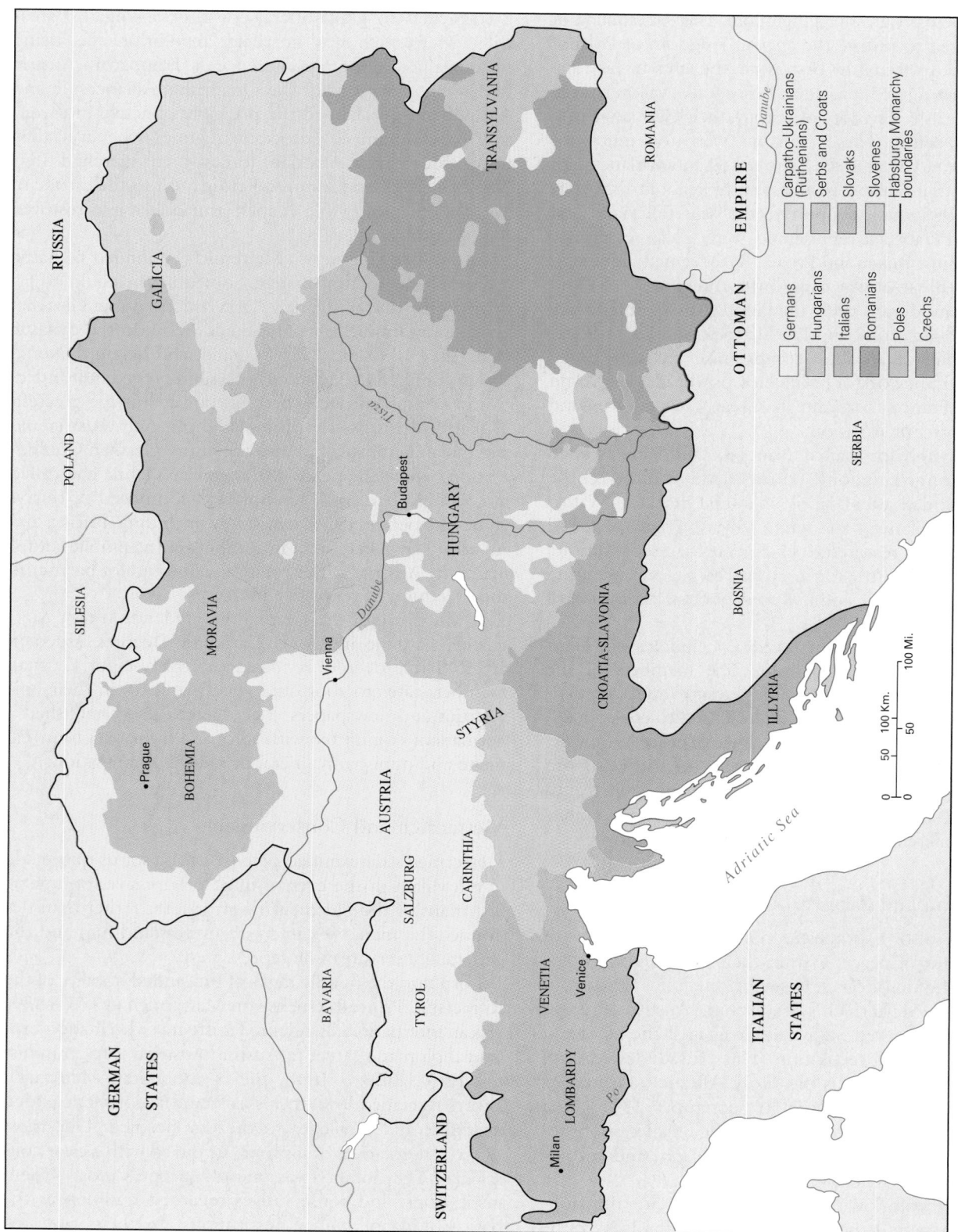

MAP 23.2 Peoples of the Habsburg Monarchy, 1815 The old dynastic state was a patchwork of nationalities. Note the widely scattered pockets of Germans and Hungarians.

Germans
Hungarians
Italians
Romanians
Poles
Czechs

Carpatho-Ukrainians (Ruthenians)
Serbs and Croats
Slovaks
Slovenes
Habsburg Monarchy boundaries

RUSSIA

POLAND

GALICIA

SILESIA

MORAVIA

BOHEMIA

• Prague

GERMAN STATES

BAVARIA

TYROL

SWITZERLAND

SALZBURG

AUSTRIA

Vienna •

Danube

CARINTHIA

STYRIA

Tisza

HUNGARY

Budapest •

Danube

TRANSYLVANIA

ROMANIA

OTTOMAN EMPIRE

CROATIA-SLAVONIA

SERBIA

BOSNIA

ILLYRIA

VENETIA

Venice •

LOMBARDY

Milan •

Po

ITALIAN STATES

Adriatic Sea

0   50   100 Km.
0   50   100 Mi.

proper state and society remained those of pre-1789 Europe, which rested on a judicious blend of monarchy, bureaucracy, aristocracy, and respectful commoners.

Metternich firmly believed that liberalism, as embodied in revolutionary America and France, had been responsible for a generation of war with untold bloodshed and suffering. Liberal demands for representative government and civil liberties had unfortunately captured the imaginations of some middle-class lawyers, business people, and intellectuals, who were engaged in a vast conspiracy to impose their beliefs on society and destroy the existing order. Like many other conservatives then and since, Metternich blamed liberal middle-class revolutionaries for stirring up the lower classes, which he believed desired nothing more than peace and quiet.

The threat of liberalism appeared doubly dangerous to Metternich because it generally went with national aspirations. Liberals believed that each people, each national group, had a right to establish its own independent government and seek to fulfill its own destiny. The idea of national self-determination was repellent to Metternich. It not only threatened the primacy of the aristocracy but also threatened to destroy the Austrian Empire and revolutionize central Europe.

The vast Austrian Empire of the Habsburgs was a great dynastic state. Formed over centuries by war, marriage, and luck, it was made up of many peoples (see Map 23.2). The Germans had long dominated the empire, yet they accounted for only one-fourth of the population. The Magyars (Hungarians), a substantially smaller group, dominated the kingdom of Hungary, though they did not account for a majority of the population in that part of the Austrian Empire.

The Czechs, the third major group, were concentrated in Bohemia and Moravia. There were also large numbers of Italians, Poles, and Ukrainians as well as smaller groups of Slovenes, Croats, Serbs, Ruthenians, and Romanians. The various Slavic peoples, together with the Italians and the Romanians, represented a widely scattered and completely divided majority in an empire dominated by Germans and Hungarians. Different ethnic groups often lived in the same provinces and even in the same villages. Thus the different parts and provinces of the empire differed in languages, customs, and institutions.

The multiethnic state Metternich served was both strong and weak. It was strong because of its large population and vast territories; it was weak because of its many and potentially dissatisfied nationalities. In these circumstances, Metternich virtually had to oppose liberalism and nationalism, for Austria was simply unable to accommodate these ideologies of the dual revolution.

Metternich   This portrait by Sir Thomas Lawrence reveals much about Metternich the man. Handsome, refined, and intelligent, Metternich was a great aristocrat who was passionately devoted to the defense of his class and its interests. *(The Royal Collection © Her Majesty Queen Elizabeth II)*

Radical Ideas and Early Socialism

In the years following the peace settlement of 1815 intellectuals and social observers sought to understand the revolutionary changes that had occurred and were still taking place. These efforts led to ideas that still motivate the world.

Almost all of these basic ideas were radical. In one way or another, they rejected the old, deeply felt conservatism, with its stress on tradition, a hereditary monarchy, a strong and privileged landowning aristocracy, and an official church. Instead, they developed and refined alternative visions—alternative ideologies—and tried to convince society to act on them. With time, they were very successful.

Liberalism

The principal ideas of **liberalism**—liberty and equality—were by no means defeated in 1815. First realized successfully in the American Revolution and then achieved in part in the French Revolution, this political and social philosophy continued to pose a radical challenge to revived conservatism. Liberalism demanded representative government as opposed to autocratic monarchy, equality before the law as opposed to legally separate classes. The idea of liberty also meant specific individual freedoms: freedom of the press, freedom of speech, freedom of assembly, and freedom from arbitrary arrest. In Europe only France with Louis XVIII's Constitutional Charter and Great Britain with its Parliament and historic rights of English men and women had realized much of the liberal program in 1815. Even in those countries, liberalism had not fully succeeded.

Although liberalism retained its cutting edge, it was seen by many as being a somewhat duller tool than it had been. The reasons for this were that liberalism faced more radical ideological competitors in the early nineteenth century. Opponents of liberalism especially criticized its economic principles, which called for unrestricted private enterprise and no government interference in the economy. This philosophy was popularly known as the doctrine of **laissez faire.** (This form of liberalism is often called "classical" liberalism in the United States in order to distinguish it sharply from modern American liberalism, which usually favors more government programs to meet social needs and to regulate the economy.)

The idea of a free economy had first been persuasively formulated by Scottish philosophy professor Adam Smith, whose *Inquiry into the Nature and Causes of the Wealth of Nations* (1776) founded modern economics. Smith was highly critical of eighteenth-century mercantilism and its attempt to regulate trade and economic activity. Far preferable were free competition and the "invisible hand" of the self-regulating market, which would give all citizens a fair and equal opportunity to do what they did best. Smith argued effectively that freely competitive private enterprise would result in greater income for everyone, not just the rich.

In early-nineteenth-century Britain this economic liberalism, which promoted continued economic growth in the Industrial Revolution, was embraced most enthusiastically by business groups and became a doctrine associated with business interests. Businessmen used the doctrine to defend their right to do as they wished in their factories. Labor unions were outlawed because they supposedly restricted free competition and the individual's "right to work."

In the early nineteenth century, liberal political ideals also became more closely associated with narrow class interests. Early nineteenth-century liberals favored representative government, but they generally wanted property qualifications attached to the right to vote. In practice, this meant limiting the vote to well-to-do aristocratic landowners, substantial businessmen, and successful members of the professions. Workers and peasants, as well as the lower middle class of shopkeepers, clerks, and artisans, did not own the necessary property and thus could not vote.

As liberalism became increasingly identified with the middle class after 1815, some intellectuals and foes of conservatism felt that liberalism did not go nearly far enough. Inspired by memories of the French Revolution and the example of Jacksonian democracy in the young American republic, they called for universal voting rights, at least for males, and for democracy. These democrats and republicans were more radical than the liberals, and they were more willing than most liberals to endorse violent upheaval to achieve goals. All of this meant that liberals and radical, democratic republicans could join forces against conservatives only up to a point.

Nationalism

Nationalism was a second radical idea in the years after 1815—an idea destined to have an enormous influence in the modern world. Nationalism had its immediate origins in the French Revolution and the Napoleonic wars, and there were already hints of its remarkable ability to spread and develop.

Early advocates of the "national idea" argued that each people had its own genius and its own *cultural* unity. For nationalists this cultural unity was basically self-evident, manifesting itself especially in a common language, history, and territory. In fact, in the early nineteenth century such cultural unity was more a dream than a reality as far as most nationalities were concerned. Within each ethnic grouping only an elite spoke a standardized written language. Local dialects abounded, and peasants from nearby villages often failed to understand each other. As for historical memory, it divided the inhabitants of the different German or Italian states as much as it unified them. Moreover, a variety of ethnic groups shared the territory of most states.

Despite these basic realities, sooner or later European nationalists usually sought to turn the cultural unity that they perceived into a *political* reality. They sought to make the territory of each people coincide with well-defined boundaries in an independent nation-state. It was this political goal that made nationalism so explosive in central and eastern Europe after 1815, when there were either too few states (Austria, Russia, and the Ottoman

Empire) or too many (the Italian peninsula and the German Confederation) and when different peoples overlapped and intermingled.

In recent years scholars have been trying to understand how the nationalist vision, often fitting so poorly with existing conditions and promising so much upheaval, was so successful in the long run. Certain interrelated ideas stand out.

Of fundamental importance in the rise of nationalism was the epoch-making development of complex industrial and urban society, which required much better communication between individuals and groups.[1] These communication needs promoted the use of a standardized national language within many countries, creating at least a superficial cultural unity as it eventually encompassed the entire population through mass education. When a minority population was large and concentrated, the nationalist campaign for a standardized language often led to a push for a separate nation-state.

Many scholars also argue that nations are recent creations, the product of the new, self-conscious nationalist ideology. Thus nation-states emerged in the nineteenth century as "imagined communities," communities seeking to bind millions of strangers together around the abstract concept of an all-embracing national identity. This meant bringing citizens together with emotionally charged symbols and ceremonies, such as independence holidays and patriotic parades. On such fleeting occasions the imagined nation of spiritual equals might celebrate its most hallowed traditions, which were often recent inventions.[2]

Creating Nationalism   Festivals and patriotic celebrations helped build a feeling of belonging to a large invisible community. This illustration from May 1848 depicts "the Solemn Entry of Archduke Johann of Austria into Frankfurt," when cannon sounded and dignitaries proclaimed the opening of a new era. The revolutionary assembly in Frankfurt had named Johann regent of the unified Germany that it was hoping to establish. In May 1849 the assembly offered the imperial crown to the king of Prussia. *(Germanisches Nationalmuseum, Nürnberg)*

Historians also stress the dynamic, ever-changing character of nationalism. Industrialism and mass education, so important in the later nineteenth century, played only a minor role before 1850. In those years the faith in nationhood was fresh, idealistic, and progressive.

Between 1815 and 1850 most people who believed in nationalism also believed in either liberalism or radical, democratic republicanism. A common faith in the creativity and nobility of the people was perhaps the single most important reason for the linking of these two concepts. Liberals and especially democrats saw the people as the ultimate source of all government. Yet liberals and nationalists agreed that the benefits of self-government would be possible only if the people were united by common traditions that transcended local interests and even class differences.

Early nationalists usually believed that every nation, like every citizen, had the right to exist in freedom and to develop its character and spirit. They were confident that a symphony of nations would promote the harmony and ultimate unity of all peoples. As the French historian Jules Michelet put it in *The People* in 1846, each citizen "learns to recognize his country . . . as a note in the grand concert; through it he himself participates and loves the world." Similarly, the great Italian patriot Giuseppe Mazzini believed that "in laboring according to the true principles of our country we are laboring for Humanity." (See the feature "Listening to the Past: Faith in Democratic Nationalism" on pages 784–785.) Thus the liberty of the individual and the love of a free nation overlapped greatly in the early nineteenth century.

Yet early nationalists also stressed the differences among peoples. Even early nationalism developed a strong sense of "we" and "they." To this "we-they" outlook, it was all too easy for nationalists to add two highly volatile ingredients: a sense of national mission and a sense of national superiority. Even Michelet, so alive to the aspirations of other peoples, could not help speaking in 1846 of the "superiority of France"; the principles espoused in the French Revolution had made France the "salvation of mankind."

German and Spanish nationalists had a very different opinion of France. In the narratives they constructed, the French often seemed oppressive, as the Germans did to the Czechs and as the Russians did to the Poles. Thus "they" often emerged as the enemy.

Early nationalism was ambiguous. Its main thrust was liberal and democratic. But below the surface lurked ideas of national superiority and national mission that could lead to aggression and conflict.

French Utopian Socialism

Socialism, the new radical doctrine after 1815, began in France, despite the fact that France lagged far behind Great Britain in developing modern industry. Early French socialist thinkers were acutely aware that the political revolution in France, the rise of laissez faire, and the emergence of modern industry in Britain were transforming society. They were disturbed because they saw these developments as fomenting selfish individualism and splitting the community into isolated fragments. There was, they believed, an urgent need for a further reorganization of society to establish cooperation and a new sense of community.

Early French socialists believed in economic planning. Inspired by the emergency measures of 1793 and 1794 in France, they argued that the government should rationally organize the economy and not depend on destructive competition to do the job. Early socialists also shared an intense desire to help the poor, and they preached that the rich and the poor should be more nearly equal economically. Finally, socialists believed that private property should be strictly regulated by the government or that it should be abolished and replaced by state or community ownership. Planning, greater economic equality, and state regulation of property—these were the key ideas of early French socialism and of all socialism since.

One of the most influential early socialist thinkers was a nobleman, Count Henri de Saint-Simon (1760–1825). Saint-Simon optimistically proclaimed the tremendous possibilities of industrial development: "The age of gold is before us!" The key to progress was proper social organization. Such an arrangement of society required the **parasites**—the court, the aristocracy, lawyers, and churchmen—to give way, once and for all, to the **doers**—the leading scientists, engineers, and industrialists. The doers would carefully plan the economy and guide it forward by undertaking vast public works projects and establishing investment banks. Saint-Simon also stressed in highly moralistic terms that every social institution ought to have as its main goal improved conditions for the poor.

After 1830 the socialist critique of capitalism became sharper. Charles Fourier (1772–1837), a lonely, saintly man with a tenuous hold on reality, described a socialist utopia in lavish mathematical detail. Hating the urban wage system, Fourier envisaged self-sufficient communities of 1,620 people living communally on 5,000 acres devoted to a combination of agriculture and industry.

Fourier was also an early proponent of the total emancipation of women. Extremely critical of middle-class family life, Fourier believed that most marriages were only another kind of prostitution. According to Fourier, young single women were shamelessly "sold" to their future husbands for dowries and other financial considerations. Therefore, Fourier called for the abolition of marriage, free unions based only on love, and sexual freedom. Many middle-class men and women found these ideas, which were shared and even practiced by some followers of Saint-Simon, shocking and immoral. The socialist program for the liberation of women as well as workers appeared to them as doubly dangerous and revolutionary.

Louis Blanc (1811–1882), a sharp-eyed, intelligent journalist, focused on practical improvements. In his *Organization of Work* (1839), he urged workers to agitate for universal voting rights and to take control of the state peacefully. Blanc believed that the state should set up government-backed workshops and factories to guarantee full employment. The right to work had to become as sacred as any other right.

Finally, there was Pierre Joseph Proudhon (1809–1865), a self-educated printer who wrote a pamphlet in 1840 titled *What Is Property?* His answer was that it was nothing but theft. Property was profit that was stolen from the worker, who was the source of all wealth. Unlike most socialists, Proudhon feared the power of the state and was often considered an anarchist.

Of great importance, the message of French utopian socialists interacted with the experiences of French urban workers. Workers cherished the memory of the radical phase of the French Revolution and its efforts to regulate economic life and protect the poor. Skilled artisans, with a long tradition of guilds, apprenticeship, and control of quality and wage rates, became violently opposed to laissez-faire laws that denied workers the right to organize and promoted brutal, unrestrained competition instead. Trying to maintain some control of their trades and conditions of work and developing a sense of class, workers favored collective action and government intervention in economic life. Thus the aspirations of workers and utopian theorists reinforced each other, and a genuine socialist movement emerged in Paris in the 1830s and 1840s. To Karl Marx was left the task of establishing firm foundations for modern socialism.

The Birth of Marxian Socialism

In 1848 the thirty-year-old Karl Marx (1818–1883) and the twenty-eight-year-old Friedrich Engels (1820–1895) published *The Communist Manifesto,* which became the bible of socialism. The son of a Jewish lawyer who had converted to Christianity, the atheistic young Marx had

Karl Marx   Active in the revolution of 1848, Marx fled from Germany in 1849 and settled in London. There he wrote *Capital,* the weighty exposition of his socialist theories, and worked to organize the working class. Marx earned a modest living as a journalist, supplemented by financial support from his coauthor, Friedrich Engels. *(The Granger Collection, New York)*

studied philosophy at the University of Berlin before turning to journalism and economics. He read widely in French socialist thought, and like Fourier he looked forward to the emancipation of women and the abolition of the family. By the time Marx was twenty-five, he was developing his own socialist ideas.

Early French socialists often appealed to the middle class and the state to help the poor. Marx ridiculed such appeals as naive. He argued that the interests of the middle class and those of the industrial working class were inevitably opposed to each other. Indeed, according to the *Manifesto,* the "history of all previously existing society is the history of class struggles." In Marx's view, one class had always exploited the other, and with the advent of modern industry, society was split more clearly than ever before: between the middle class (the **bourgeoisie**) and the modern working class (the **proletariat**).

Just as the bourgeoisie had triumphed over the feudal aristocracy, Marx predicted that the proletariat would conquer the bourgeoisie in a violent revolution. While a tiny minority owned the means of production and grew richer, the ever-poorer proletariat was constantly growing in size and in class-consciousness. In this process, the proletariat was aided, according to Marx, by a portion of the bourgeoisie who had gone over to the proletariat and who (like Marx and Engels) "had raised themselves to the level of comprehending theoretically the historical moment." The critical moment, Marx thought, was very near. "Let the ruling classes tremble at a Communist revolution. The proletarians have nothing to lose but their chains. They have a world to win. WORKING MEN OF ALL COUNTRIES, UNITE!" So ends *The Communist Manifesto.*

Marx's ideas united sociology, economics, and all human history in a vast and imposing edifice. He synthesized in his socialism not only French utopian schemes but also English classical economics and German philosophy—the major intellectual currents of his day.

Marx's debt to England was great. He was the last of the classical economists. Following David Ricardo, who had taught that labor was the source of all value, Marx went on to argue that profits were really wages stolen from the workers. Moreover, Marx incorporated Engels's charges of terrible oppression of the new class of factory workers in England; thus Marx's doctrines seemed to be based on hard facts.

Marx's theory of historical evolution was built on the philosophy of the German Georg Hegel (1770–1831). Hegel believed that each age is characterized by a dominant set of ideas, which produces opposing ideas and eventually a new synthesis. The idea of being had been dominant initially, for example, and it had produced its antithesis, the idea of nonbeing. This idea in turn had resulted in the synthesis of becoming. Thus history has pattern and purpose.

Marx retained Hegel's view of history as a dialectic process of change but made economic relationships between classes the driving force. This dialectic explained the decline of agrarian feudalism and the rise of industrial capitalism. Marx stressed repeatedly that the "bourgeoisie, historically, has played a most revolutionary part. . . . During its rule of scarcely one hundred years the bourgeoisie has created more massive and more colossal productive forces than have all preceding generations together." Marx's next idea, that it was now the bourgeoisie's turn to give way to the socialism of revolutionary workers, appeared to many the irrefutable capstone of a brilliant in-

terpretation of humanity's long development. Thus Marx pulled together powerful ideas and insights to create one of the great secular religions out of the intellectual ferment of the early nineteenth century.

The Romantic Movement

Radical concepts of politics and society were accompanied by comparable changes in literature and other arts during the dual revolution. The early nineteenth century marked the acme of the romantic movement, which profoundly influenced the arts and enriched European culture immeasurably.

The romantic movement was in part a revolt against classicism and the Enlightenment. Classicism was essentially a set of artistic rules and standards that went hand in glove with the Enlightenment's belief in rationality, order, and restraint. The classicists believed that the ancient Greeks and Romans had discovered eternally valid aesthetic rules and that playwrights and painters should continue to follow them. Classicists could enforce these rules in the eighteenth century because they dominated the courts and academies for which artists worked.

Forerunners of the romantic movement appeared from about 1750 on. Of these, Rousseau (see page 612)—the passionate advocate of feeling, freedom, and natural goodness—was the most influential. Romanticism then crystallized fully in the 1790s, primarily in England and Germany. The French Revolution kindled the belief that radical reconstruction was also possible in cultural and artistic life (even though many early English and German romantics became disillusioned with events in France and turned from liberalism to conservatism in politics). Romanticism gained strength until the 1840s.

Romanticism's Tenets

Romanticism was characterized by a belief in emotional exuberance, unrestrained imagination, and spontaneity in both art and personal life. In Germany early romantics of the 1770s and 1780s called themselves the **Sturm und Drang** ("Storm and Stress"), and many romantic artists of the early nineteenth century lived lives of tremendous emotional intensity. Suicide, duels to the death, madness, and strange illnesses were not uncommon among leading romantics. Romantic artists typically led bohemian lives, wearing their hair long and uncombed in preference to powdered wigs and living in cold garrets rather than frequenting stiff drawing rooms. They rejected materialism and sought to escape to lofty spiritual heights through

Nature and the Meaning of Life
Caspar David Friedrich (1774–1840) was Germany's greatest romantic painter, and his *Traveler Looking over a Sea of Fog* (1815) is a representative masterpiece. Friedrich's paintings often focus on dark silhouetted figures, silently contemplating an eerie landscape. Friedrich came to believe that humans were only an insignificant part of an all-embracing higher unity. *(Hamburger Kunsthalle)*

their art. Great individualists, the romantics believed the full development of one's unique human potential to be the supreme purpose in life. The romantics were driven by a sense of an unlimited universe and by a yearning for the unattained, the unknown, the unknowable.

Nowhere was the break with classicism more apparent than in romanticism's general conception of nature. Classicism was not particularly interested in nature. In the words of the eighteenth-century English author Samuel Johnson, "A blade of grass is always a blade of grass; men and women are my subjects of inquiry." Nature was portrayed by classicists as beautiful and chaste, like an eighteenth-century formal garden. The roman-

tics, in contrast, were enchanted by nature. For some it was awesome and tempestuous, while others saw nature as a source of spiritual inspiration. As the great English landscape artist John Constable declared, "Nature is Spirit visible."

Most romantics saw the growth of modern industry as an ugly, brutal attack on their beloved nature and on the human personality. They sought escape—in the unspoiled Lake District of northern England, in exotic North Africa, in an idealized Middle Ages.

Fascinated by color and diversity, the romantic imagination turned toward history with a passion. Beautiful, exciting, and important, history was the art of change over time—the key to a universe that was now perceived to be organic and dynamic, not mechanical and static as the Enlightenment had believed. Historical studies promoted the growth of national aspirations, fanning the embers of memory and encouraging entire peoples to seek in the past their special destinies.

Literature

Britain was the first country where romanticism flowered fully in poetry and prose, and the British romantic writers were among the most prominent in Europe. Wordsworth, Coleridge, and Scott were all active by 1800, to be followed shortly by Byron, Shelley, and Keats. All were poets: romanticism found its distinctive voice in poetry, as the Enlightenment had in prose.

A towering leader of English romanticism, William Wordsworth (1770–1850) traveled in France after his graduation from Cambridge. There he fell passionately in love with a Frenchwoman, who bore him a daughter. Deeply influenced by Rousseau and the spirit of the early French Revolution, Wordsworth returned to England and settled in the countryside with his sister, Dorothy, and Samuel Taylor Coleridge (1772–1834). In 1798 the two poets published their *Lyrical Ballads,* which abandoned flowery classical conventions for the language of ordinary speech and endowed simple subjects with the loftiest majesty.

One of the best examples of Wordsworth's romantic credo and genius is "Daffodils":

I wandered lonely as a cloud
That floats on high o'er vales and hills,
When all at once I saw a crowd,
A host, of golden daffodils;
Beside the lake, beneath the trees,
Fluttering and dancing in the breeze.

. . . .

The waves beside them danced, but they
Out-did the sparkling waves in glee:
A poet could not but be gay,
In such a jocund company:
I gazed—and gazed—but little thought
What wealth the show to me had brought:

For oft, when on my couch I lie
In vacant or in pensive mood,
They flash upon that inward eye
Which is the bliss of solitude;
And then my heart with pleasure fills,
And dances with the daffodils.

Here indeed are simplicity and love of nature in commonplace forms, which could be appreciated by everyone. Wordsworth's conception of poetry as the "spontaneous overflow of powerful feeling recollected in tranquility" is well illustrated by the last stanza.

Born in Edinburgh, Walter Scott (1771–1832) personified the romantic movement's fascination with history. Raised on his grandfather's farm, Scott fell under the spell of the old ballads and tales of the Scottish border. He was also deeply influenced by German romanticism, particularly by the immortal poet and dramatist Johann Wolfgang von Goethe (1749–1832). Scott translated Goethe's famous *Gotz von Berlichingen,* a play about a sixteenth-century knight who revolted against centralized authority and championed individual freedom—at least in Goethe's romantic drama. A natural storyteller, Scott composed long narrative poems and a series of historical novels. Scott excelled in re-creating the spirit of bygone ages and great historical events, especially those of Scotland.

Classicism remained strong in France under Napoleon and inhibited the growth of romanticism there. In 1813 Germaine de Staël (1766–1817), a Franco-Swiss writer living in exile, urged the French to throw away their worn-out classical models. Her study *On Germany* (1810) extolled the spontaneity and enthusiasm of German writers and thinkers, and it had a powerful impact on the post-1815 generation in France. (See the feature "Individuals in Society: Germaine de Staël.") Between 1820 and 1850, the romantic impulse broke through in the poetry and prose of Lamartine, de Vigny, Hugo, Dumas, and Sand. Of these, Victor Hugo (1802–1885) was the greatest in both poetry and prose.

Son of a Napoleonic general, Hugo achieved an amazing range of rhythm, language, and image in his lyric poetry. His powerful novels exemplified the romantic fascination with fantastic characters, exotic historical settings, and human emotions. The hero of Hugo's famous *Hunchback of Notre Dame* (1831) is the great cathedral's deformed bell-ringer, a "human gargoyle" overlooking the teeming life of fifteenth-century Paris. Renouncing his early conservatism, Hugo equated freedom in literature with liberty in politics and society. Hugo's political evolution was thus exactly the opposite of Wordsworth's, in whom youthful radicalism gave way to middle-aged caution. As the contrast between the two artists suggests, romanticism was a cultural movement compatible with many political beliefs.

Amandine Aurore Lucie Dupin (1804–1876), generally known by her pen name, George Sand, defied the narrow conventions of her time in an unending search

Individuals in Society

Germaine de Staël

Rich, intellectual, passionate, and assertive, Germaine Necker de Staël (1766–1817) astonished contemporaries and still fascinates historians. She was strongly influenced by her parents, poor Swiss Protestants who soared to the top of prerevolutionary Parisian society. Her brilliant but rigid mother filled Germaine's head with knowledge, and each week the precocious child listened, wide-eyed and attentive, to illustrious writers and philosophers performing at her mother's salon. At age twelve, she suffered a physical and mental breakdown. Only then was she allowed to have a playmate and romp and run on the family estate. Her adoring father was Jacques Necker, a banker who made an enormous fortune and became France's reform-minded minister of finance before the Revolution. Worshiping her father in adolescence, Germaine also came to love politics.

Accepting at nineteen an arranged marriage with Baron de Staël-Holstein, a womanizing Swedish diplomat bewitched by her dowry, Germaine began her life's work. She opened an intellectual salon and began to write and publish. Her wit and exuberance attracted foreigners and liberal French aristocrats, one of whom became the first of many lovers as her marriage soured and she searched unsuccessfully for the happiness of her parents' union. Fleeing Paris in 1792 and returning after the Thermidorian reaction, she subsequently angered Napoleon by criticizing his dictatorial rule. In 1803 he permanently banished her from Paris.

Retiring again to her isolated estate in Switzerland and skillfully managing her inherited wealth, Staël fought insomnia with opium and boredom with parties that attracted luminaries from all over Europe. Always seeking stimulation for her restless mind, she traveled widely in Italy and Germany and drew upon these experiences in her novel *Corinne* (1807) and her study *On Germany* (1810). Both works summed up her romantic faith and enjoyed enormous success.

Staël urged creative individuals to abandon traditional rules and classical models. She encouraged them to embrace experimentation, emotion, and enthusiasm. Enthusiasm, which she had in abundance, was the key, the royal road to creativity, personal fulfillment, and human improvement. Thrilling to music, for example, she felt that only an enthusiastic person could really appreciate this gift of God, this wordless message that "unifies our dual nature and blends senses and spirit in a common rapture."*

Yet a profound sadness runs through her writing. This sadness, so characteristic of the romantic temperament, grew in part out of disappointments in love and prolonged exile. But it also grew out of the insoluble predicament of being an enormously gifted woman in an age of intense male chauvinism.

Germaine de Staël, by J.-B. Isabey. (Réunion des Musées Nationaux/Art Resource, NY)

Little wonder that uneasy male competitors and literary critics took delight in ridiculing and defaming her as a neurotic and masculine woman, a mediocre and unnatural talent who had foolishly dared to enter the male world of serious thought and action. Even her supporters could not accept her for what she was. The admiring poet Lord Byron recognized her genius and called her "the most eminent woman author of this, or perhaps of any century." But he quickly added that "she should have been born a man."[†]

Buffeted and saddened by scorn and condescension because of her gender, Staël advocated equal rights for women throughout her life. Only with equal rights and duties—in education and careers, in love and marital relations—could an exceptional woman like herself, or indeed any woman, ever hope to realize her intellectual and emotional potential. Practicing what she preached as best she could, Germaine de Staël was a trailblazer in the struggle for women's rights.

Questions for Analysis

1. In what ways did Germaine de Staël's life and thought reflect basic elements of the romantic movement?
2. Why did male critics often attack Staël? What do these criticisms tell us about gender relations in the early nineteenth century?

---

*Quoted in G. R. Besser, *Germaine de Staël Revisited* (New York: Twayne Publishers, 1994), p. 106. Enhanced by a feminist perspective, this is the best recent study.
[†]Quoted ibid., p. 139.

for self-fulfillment. After eight years of unhappy marriage she abandoned her husband and took her two children to Paris to pursue a career as a writer. There Sand soon achieved fame and wealth, eventually writing over eighty novels on a variety of romantic and social themes. George Sand's striking individualism went far beyond her flamboyant preference for men's clothing and her notorious affairs. Her semi-autobiographical novel *Lélia* was shockingly modern, delving deeply into her tortuous quest for sexual and personal freedom.

In central and eastern Europe, literary romanticism and early nationalism often reinforced each other. Seeking a unique greatness in every people, well-educated romantics plumbed their own histories and cultures. Like modern anthropologists, they turned their attention to peasant life and transcribed the folk songs, tales, and proverbs that the cosmopolitan Enlightenment had disdained. The brothers Jacob and Wilhelm Grimm were particularly successful at rescuing German fairy tales from oblivion. In the Slavic lands, romantics played a decisive role in converting spoken peasant languages into modern written languages. The greatest of all Russian poets, Aleksander Pushkin (1799–1837), rejecting eighteenth-century attempts to force Russian poetry into a classical straitjacket, used his lyric genius to mold the modern literary language.

Art and Music

The greatest and most moving romantic painter in France was Eugène Delacroix (1798–1863), probably the illegitimate son of French foreign minister Talleyrand. Delacroix was a master of dramatic, colorful scenes that stirred the emotions. He was fascinated with remote and exotic subjects, whether lion hunts in Morocco or dreams of languishing, sensuous women in a sultan's harem. Yet he was also a passionate spokesman for freedom. His masterpiece, *Liberty Leading the People,* celebrated the nobility of popular revolution in general and revolution in France in particular.

In England the most notable romantic painters were Joseph M. W. Turner (1775–1851) and John Constable (1776–1837). Both were fascinated by nature, but their interpretations of it contrasted sharply, aptly symbolizing the tremendous emotional range of the romantic movement. Turner depicted nature's power and terror; wild storms and sinking ships were favorite subjects. Constable painted gentle Wordsworthian landscapes in which human beings were at one with their environment, the comforting countryside of unspoiled rural England.

It was in music that romanticism realized most fully and permanently its goals of free expression and emotional intensity. Abandoning well-defined structures, the great romantic composers used a wide range of forms to create a thousand musical landscapes and evoke a host of powerful emotions. Romantic composers also transformed the small classical orchestra, tripling its size by adding wind instruments, percussion, and more brass and strings. The crashing chords evoking the surge of the masses in Chopin's Revolutionary Etude, and the bottomless despair of the funeral march in Beethoven's Third Symphony—such were the modern orchestra's musical paintings that plumbed the depths of human feeling.

This range and intensity gave music and musicians much greater prestige than in the past. Music no longer simply complemented a church service or helped a nobleman digest his dinner. Music became a sublime end in itself, most perfectly realizing the endless yearning of the soul. The unbelievable one-in-a-million performer—the great virtuoso who could transport the listener to ecstasy and hysteria—became a cultural hero. People swooned for Franz Liszt (1811–1886), the greatest pianist of his age, as they scream for rock stars today.

Though romanticism dominated music until late in the nineteenth century, no composer ever surpassed its first great master, Ludwig van Beethoven (1770–1827). Extending and breaking open classical forms, Beethoven used contrasting themes and tones to produce dramatic conflict and inspiring resolutions. As one contemporary admirer wrote, "Beethoven's music sets in motion the lever of fear, of awe, of horror, of suffering, and awakens just that infinite longing which is the essence of Romanticism." Beethoven's range and output were tremendous. At the peak of his fame, he began to lose his hearing. He considered suicide but eventually overcame despair: "I will take fate by the throat; it will not bend me completely to its will."[3] Beethoven continued to pour out immortal music, although his last years were silent, spent in total deafness.

Reforms and Revolutions

While the romantic movement was developing, liberal, national, and socialist forces battered against the conservatism of 1815. In some countries, change occurred gradually and peacefully. Elsewhere, pressure built up like steam in a pressure cooker without a safety valve and eventually caused an explosion in 1848. Three important countries—Greece, Great Britain, and France—experienced variations on this basic theme.

Heroes of Romanticism Observed by a portrait of Byron and bust of Beethoven, Liszt plays for friends in this painting by Josef Danhauser. From left to right sit Alexander Dumas, George Sand (characteristically wearing men's garb), and Marie d'Agoult, Liszt's mistress. Standing are Victor Hugo, Niccolò Paganini, and Gioacchino Antonio Rossini. In fact, this gathering of geniuses was imaginary, part of an advertising campaign by a German piano manufacturer to sell pianos to the comfortable middle class. *(Bildarchiv Preussischer Kulturbesitz)*

National Liberation in Greece

National, liberal revolution, frustrated in Italy and Spain by conservative statesmen, succeeded first after 1815 in Greece. Since the fifteenth century, the Greeks had been living under the domination of the Ottoman Turks. In spite of centuries of foreign rule, the Greeks had survived as a people, united by their language and the Greek Orthodox religion. It was perfectly natural that the general growth of national aspirations and a desire for independence would inspire some Greeks in the early nineteenth century. This rising national movement led to the formation of secret societies and then to revolt in 1821, led by

Alexander Ypsilanti, a Greek patriot and a general in the Russian army.

The Great Powers, particularly Metternich, were opposed to all revolution, even revolution against the Islamic Turks. They refused to back Ypsilanti and supported the Ottoman Empire. Yet for many Europeans, the Greek cause became a holy one. Educated Americans and Europeans were in love with the culture of classical Greece; Russians were stirred by the piety of their Orthodox brethren. Writers and artists, moved by the romantic impulse, responded enthusiastically to the Greek national struggle.

The Greeks, though often quarreling among themselves, battled on against the Turks and hoped for the

Delacroix: Massacre at Chios The Greek struggle for freedom and independence won the enthusiastic support of liberals, nationalists, and romantics. The Ottoman Turks were portrayed as cruel oppressors who were holding back the course of history, as in this moving masterpiece by Delacroix. *(Réunion des Musées Nationaux/Art Resource, NY)*

eventual support of European governments. In 1827 Great Britain, France, and Russia responded to popular demands at home and directed Turkey to accept an armistice. When the Turks refused, the navies of these three powers trapped the Turkish fleet at Navarino and destroyed it. Russia then declared another of its periodic wars of expansion against the Turks. This led to the establishment of a Russian protectorate over much of present-day Romania, which had also been under Turkish rule. Great Britain, France, and Russia finally declared Greece independent in 1830 and installed a German prince as king of the new country in 1832. In the end, the Greeks had won: a small nation had gained its independence in a heroic war against a foreign empire.

Liberal Reform in Great Britain

Eighteenth-century British society had been both flexible and remarkably stable. It was dominated by the landowning aristocracy, but that class was neither closed nor rigidly defined. Successful business and professional people could buy land and become gentlefolk, while the common people had more than the usual opportunities of the preindustrial world. Basic civil rights for all were balanced by a tradition of deference to one's social superiors. Parliament was manipulated by the king and was thoroughly undemocratic. Only about 8 percent of the population could vote for representatives to Parliament, and by the 1780s there was growing interest in some kind of political reform.

But the French Revolution threw the British aristocracy into a panic for a generation, making it extremely hostile to any attempts to change the status quo. The Tory party, completely controlled by the landed aristocracy, was particularly fearful of radical movements at home and abroad. After 1815 the aristocracy defended its ruling position by repressing every kind of popular protest.

The first step in this direction began with revision of the **Corn Laws** in 1815. Corn Laws to regulate the foreign grain trade had long existed, but they were not needed during a generation of war with France because the British had been unable to import cheap grain from eastern Europe. As shortages occurred and agricultural prices skyrocketed, a great deal of marginal land had been brought under cultivation, fattening the landed aristocracy's rent rolls. Peace meant that grain could be imported again and that the price of wheat and bread would go down, benefiting almost everyone except the aristocracy. The aristocracy, however, rammed far-reaching changes in the Corn Laws through Parliament. The new regulation prohibited the importation of foreign grain unless the price at home rose to improbable levels. Seldom has a class legislated more selfishly for its own narrow economic advantage or done more to promote a class-based view of political action.

The change in the Corn Laws, coming as it did at a time of widespread unemployment and postwar economic distress, resulted in protests and demonstrations by urban laborers, who were supported by radical intellectuals. In 1817 the Tory government responded by temporarily suspending the traditional rights of peaceable assembly and habeas corpus. Two years later, Parliament passed the infamous Six Acts, which, among other things, placed controls on a heavily taxed press and practically eliminated all mass meetings. These acts followed an enormous but orderly protest, at Saint Peter's Fields in Manchester, that had been savagely broken up by armed cavalry. Nicknamed the **Battle of Peterloo,** in scornful reference to

the British victory at Waterloo, this incident demonstrated the government's determination to repress and stand fast.

Strengthened by ongoing industrial development, the new manufacturing and commercial groups insisted on a place for their new wealth alongside the landed wealth of the aristocracy in the framework of political power and social prestige. They called for many kinds of liberal reform: reform of town government, organization of a new police force, more rights for Catholics and dissenters, and reform of the Poor Laws that provided aid to some low-paid workers. In the 1820s, a less frightened Tory government moved in the direction of better urban administration, greater economic liberalism, and civil equality for Catholics. The prohibition on imports of foreign grain was replaced by a heavy tariff. These actions encouraged the middle classes to press on for reform of Parliament so they could have a larger say in government and perhaps repeal the latest revision of the Corn Laws, that symbol of aristocratic domination.

The Whig party, though led like the Tories by great aristocrats, had by tradition been more responsive to commercial and manufacturing interests. In 1830 a Whig ministry introduced "an act to amend the representation of the people of England and Wales." Defeated, then passed by the House of Commons, this reform bill was rejected by the House of Lords. But when in 1832 the Whigs got the king to promise to create enough new peers to pass the law, the House of Lords reluctantly gave in rather than see its snug little club ruined by upstart manufacturers and plutocrats. A mighty surge of popular protest had helped the king and lords make up their minds.

The Reform Bill of 1832 had profound significance. The House of Commons had emerged as the all-important legislative body. In the future, an obstructionist House of Lords could always be brought into line by the threat of creating new peers. The new industrial areas of the country gained representation in the Commons, and many old "rotten boroughs"—electoral districts that had very few voters and that the landed aristocracy had bought and sold—were eliminated.

The redistribution of seats reflected the shift in population to the northern manufacturing counties and the gradual emergence of an urban society. As a result of the Reform Bill of 1832, the number of voters increased by about 50 percent, giving about 12 percent of adult men in Britain and Ireland the right to vote. Comfortable middle-class groups in the urban population, as well as some substantial farmers who leased their land, received the vote. Thus the pressures building in Great Britain were successfully—though only temporarily—released. A major reform had been achieved peacefully, without revolution or civil war. More radical reforms within the system

The Prelude to 1848

March 1814	Russia, Prussia, Austria, and Britain form the Quadruple Alliance to defeat France.
April 1814	Napoleon abdicates.
May–June 1814	Bourbon monarchy is restored; Louis XVIII issues the Constitutional Charter providing for civil liberties and representative government. First Peace of Paris: allies combine leniency with a defensive posture toward France.
October 1814–June 1815	Congress of Vienna peace settlement establishes balance-of-power principle and creates the German Confederation.
February 1815	Napoleon escapes from Elba and marches on Paris.
June 1815	Napoleon defeated at the Battle of Waterloo.
September 1815	Austria, Prussia, and Russia form the Holy Alliance to repress liberal and revolutionary movements.
November 1815	Second Peace of Paris and renewal of Quadruple Alliance punish France and establish the European "congress system."
1819	In Carlsbad Decrees, Metternich imposes harsh measures throughout the German Confederation.
1820	Revolution occurs in Spain and the kingdom of the Two Sicilies. At the Congress of Troppau, Metternich and Alexander I of Russia proclaim the principle of intervention to maintain autocratic regimes.
1821	Austria crushes a liberal revolution in Naples and restores the Sicilian autocracy. Greeks revolt against the Ottoman Turks.
1823	French armies restore the Spanish regime. United States proclaims the Monroe Doctrine.
1824	Reactionary Charles X succeeds Louis XVIII in France.
1830	Charles X repudiates the Constitutional Charter; insurrection and collapse of the government follow. Louis Philippe succeeds to the throne and maintains a narrowly liberal regime until 1848. Greece wins independence from the Ottoman Empire.
1832	Reform Bill expands British electorate and encourages the middle class.
1839	Louis Blanc publishes *Organization of Work*.
1840	Pierre Joseph Proudhon publishes *What Is Property?*
1846	Jules Michelet publishes *The People*.
1848	Karl Marx and Friedrich Engels publish *The Communist Manifesto*.

Hayter: The House of Commons, 1833   This collective portrait of the first parliament elected after the Reform Bill of 1832 was painted over several years. The arrangement of the members reflects Britain's historic two-party system, with the majority on one side and the "loyal opposition" on the other. Most European countries developed multiparty systems and coalition politics, with competing groups seated in a large half circle. *(Trustees of the National Portrait Gallery, London)*

appeared difficult but not impossible. Legislation could solve problems and improve social conditions.

The principal radical program was embodied in the "People's Charter" of 1838 and the Chartist movement (see page 749). Partly inspired by the economic distress of the working class in the 1830s and 1840s, the Chartists' core demand was universal male (but not female) suffrage. They saw complete political democracy and rule by the common people as the means to a good and just society. Hundreds of thousands of people signed gigantic petitions calling on Parliament to grant all men the right to vote, first and most seriously in 1839, again in 1842, and yet again in 1848. Parliament rejected all three petitions. In the short run, the working poor failed with their Chartist demands, but they learned a valuable lesson in mass politics.

While calling for universal male suffrage, many working-class people joined with middle-class manufacturers in the Anti–Corn Law League, founded in Manchester in 1839. Mass participation made possible a popular crusade led by fighting liberals, who argued that lower food prices and more jobs in industry depended on repeal of the Corn Laws. Much of the working class agreed. When Ireland's potato crop failed in 1845, famine prices for food and even famine itself also seemed likely in England. To avert the impending catastrophe, Tory prime minister Robert Peel joined with the Whigs and a minority of his own party to repeal the Corn Laws in 1846 and allow free imports of grain. England escaped famine. Thereafter the liberal doctrine of free trade became almost sacred dogma in Great Britain.

The following year, the Tories passed a bill designed to help the working classes, but in a different way. The Ten Hours Act of 1847 limited the workday for women and young people in factories to ten hours. Tory aristocrats continued to champion legislation regulating factory conditions. They were competing vigorously with the middle class for the support of the working class. This healthy competition between a still-vigorous aristocracy and a strong middle class was a crucial factor in Great Britain's peaceful evolution. The working classes could make temporary alliances with either competitor to better their own conditions.

Ireland and the Great Famine

The people of Ireland did not benefit from the political competition in Britain. The great mass of the population (outside of the northern counties of Ulster, which were partly Presbyterian) were Irish Catholics, who rented their land from a tiny minority of Church of England Protestants, many of whom lived in England. These landlords lacked the improving zeal of their English counterparts and were content to use their power to grab as much as possible.

The result was that the condition of the Irish peasantry around 1800 was abominable. The typical peasant lived in a wretched cottage and could afford neither shoes nor stockings. Hundreds of shocking accounts describe hopeless poverty. Yet in spite of terrible conditions, population growth sped onward. The 3 million of 1725 reached 4 million in 1780 and doubled to 8 million by 1840. Between 1780 and 1840, 1.75 million people left Ireland for Britain and America.

The population grew so quickly for three reasons: extensive cultivation of the potato, early marriage, and exploitation of peasants by landlords. The cultivation of the potato, introduced into Ireland (and all of Europe) in the late sixteenth century, was originally a response to the pressure of numbers. Once peasants began to cultivate potatoes, many more people could exist. A single acre of land spaded and planted with potatoes could feed a family of six for a year, whereas two to four acres of grain and pasture were needed to feed the same number. The potato also could thrive on boggy wastelands.

Needing only a big potato patch to survive, Irish men and women married early. Setting up housekeeping was easy, for a cabin of mud and stone could be slapped together with the help of friends and relatives in a few days. A mat for a bed, chairs and a table, and an iron pot to boil potatoes were easily acquired. To be sure, the young couple was embracing a life of extreme poverty. They would literally live on potatoes—ten pounds a day for an average male—moistened at best with a cup of milk.

Yet the decision to marry and have large families made sense. Landlords only leased land for short periods. Peasants had no incentive to make permanent improvements because anything beyond what was needed for survival would quickly be taken by higher rent. Rural poverty was

Daniel McDonald: The Discovery of the Potato Blight Although the leaves of diseased plants usually shriveled and died, they could also look deceptively healthy. This Irish family has dug up its potato harvest and just discovered to its horror that the blight has rotted the crop. Like thousands of Irish families, this family now faces the starvation and the mass epidemics of the Great Famine. (*Department of Irish Folklore, University College, Dublin*)

inescapable and better shared with a spouse, while a dutiful son or a loving daughter was an old person's best hope of escaping destitution.

As population and potato dependency grew, conditions became more precarious. From 1820 onward deficiencies and diseases in the potato crop became more common. In 1845 and 1846, and again in 1848 and 1851, the potato crop failed in Ireland.

The result was unmitigated disaster—the **Great Famine.** Blight attacked the young plants, the leaves withered, and the tubers rotted. Widespread starvation and mass fever epidemics followed. Yet the British government, committed to rigid laissez-faire ideology and hoping that the repeal of the Corn Laws would alleviate the food shortage, was slow to act. When it did, its relief efforts were tragically inadequate. Moreover, the government continued to collect taxes, and landlords demanded their rents. Tenants who could not pay were evicted and their homes destroyed. Famine or no, Ireland remained the conquered jewel of foreign landowners.

The Great Famine shattered the pattern of Irish population growth. Fully 1 million emigrants fled the famine between 1845 and 1851, and at least 1.5 million died or went unborn because of the disaster. Alone among the countries of Europe, Ireland experienced a declining population in the nineteenth century, from about 8 million in 1845 to 4.4 million in 1911. Ireland became a land of continuous out-migration, late marriage, and widespread celibacy.

The Great Famine also intensified anti-British feeling and promoted Irish nationalism, for the bitter memory of starvation, exile, and British inaction was burned deeply into the popular consciousness. Patriots could call on powerful collective emotions in their campaigns for land reform, home rule, and, eventually, Irish independence.

The Revolution of 1830 in France

Louis XVIII's Constitutional Charter of 1814—theoretically a gift from the king but actually a response to political pressures—was basically a liberal constitution (see page 720). The economic and social gains made by sections of the middle class and the peasantry in the French Revolution were fully protected, great intellectual and artistic freedom was permitted, and a parliament with upper and lower houses was created. Immediately after Napoleon's abortive Hundred Days, the moderate, worldly king refused to bow to the wishes of die-hard aristocrats such as his brother Charles, who wished to sweep away all the revolutionary changes and return to a bygone age of royal absolutism and aristocratic pretension. Instead, Louis appointed as his ministers moderate royalists, who sought and obtained the support of a majority of the representatives elected to the lower Chamber of Deputies between 1816 and Louis's death in 1824.

Louis XVIII's charter was anything but democratic. Only about 100,000 of the wealthiest males out of a total population of 30 million had the right to vote for the deputies who, with the king and his ministers, made the laws of the nation. Nonetheless, the "notable people" who did vote came from very different backgrounds. There were wealthy businessmen, war profiteers, successful professionals, ex-revolutionaries, large landowners from the old aristocracy and the middle class, Bourbons, and Bonapartists.

The old aristocracy, with its pre-1789 mentality, was a minority within the voting population. It was this situation that Louis's successor, Charles X (r. 1824–1830), could not abide. Crowned in a lavish, utterly medieval, five-hour ceremony in the cathedral of Reims in 1824, Charles was a true reactionary. He wanted to re-establish the old order in France. Increasingly blocked by the opposition of the deputies, Charles finally repudiated the Constitutional Charter in an attempted coup in July 1830. He issued decrees stripping much of the wealthy middle class of its voting rights, and he censored the press. The immediate reaction, encouraged by journalists and lawyers, was an insurrection in the capital by printers, other artisans, and small traders. In "three glorious days," the government collapsed. Paris boiled with revolutionary excitement, and Charles fled. Then the upper middle class, which had fomented the revolt, skillfully seated Charles's cousin, Louis Philippe, duke of Orléans, on the vacant throne.

Louis Philippe (r. 1830–1848) accepted the Constitutional Charter of 1814; adopted the red, white, and blue flag of the French Revolution; and admitted that he was merely the "king of the French people." In spite of such symbolic actions, the situation in France remained fundamentally unchanged. Casimir Périer, a wealthy banker and Louis Philippe's new chief minister, bluntly told a deputy who complained when the vote was extended only from 100,000 to 170,000 citizens, "The trouble with this country is that there are too many people like you who imagine that there has been a revolution in France."[4] The wealthy notable elite actually tightened its control as the old aristocracy retreated to the provinces to sulk harmlessly. For the upper middle class, there had been a change in dynasty in order to protect the status quo and the narrowly liberal institutions of 1815. Republicans, democrats, social reformers, and the poor of Paris were bitterly disappointed. They had made a revolution, but it seemed for naught.

The Revolutions of 1848

In 1848 revolutionary political and social ideologies combined with severe economic crisis and the romantic impulse to produce a vast upheaval across Europe. Only the most advanced and the most backward major countries—reforming Great Britain and immobile Russia—escaped untouched. Governments toppled; monarchs and ministers bowed or fled. National independence, liberal-democratic constitutions, and social reform: the lofty aspirations of a generation seemed at hand. Yet in the end, the revolutions failed. Why was this so?

A Democratic Republic in France

The late 1840s in Europe were hard economically and tense politically. The potato famine in Ireland in 1845 and in 1846 had many echoes on the continent. Bad harvests jacked up food prices and caused misery and unemployment in the cities. "Prerevolutionary" outbreaks occurred all across Europe: an abortive Polish revolution in the northern part of Austria in 1846, a civil war between radicals and conservatives in Switzerland in 1847, and an armed uprising in Naples, Italy, in January 1848. Revolution was almost universally expected, but it took revolution in Paris—once again—to turn expectations into realities.

Louis Philippe's "bourgeois monarchy" had been characterized by stubborn inaction and complacency. There was a glaring lack of social legislation, and politics was dominated by corruption and selfish special interests. With only the rich voting for deputies, many of the deputies were docile government bureaucrats.

The government's stubborn refusal to consider electoral reform heightened a sense of class injustice among middle-class shopkeepers, skilled artisans, and unskilled working people, and it eventually touched off a popular revolt in Paris. Barricades went up on the night of February 22, 1848, and by February 24 Louis Philippe had abdicated in favor of his grandson. But the common people in arms would tolerate no more monarchy. This refusal led to the proclamation of a provisional republic, headed by a ten-man executive committee and certified by cries of approval from the revolutionary crowd.

A generation of historians and journalists had praised the First French Republic, and their work had borne fruit: the revolutionaries were firmly committed to a republic (as opposed to any form of constitutional monarchy), and they immediately set about drafting a constitution for France's Second Republic. Moreover, they wanted a truly popular and democratic republic so that the healthy, life-giving forces of the common people—the peasants, the artisans, and the unskilled workers—could reform society with wise legislation. In practice, building such a republic meant giving the right to vote to every adult male, and this was quickly done. Revolutionary compassion and sympathy for freedom were expressed in the freeing of all slaves in French colonies, the abolition of the death penalty, and the establishment of a ten-hour workday for Paris.

Yet there were profound differences within the revolutionary coalition in Paris. On the one hand, there were the moderate, liberal republicans of the middle class. They viewed universal male suffrage as the ultimate concession to be made to popular forces, and they strongly opposed any further radical social measures. On the other hand, there were radical republicans and hard-pressed artisans. Influenced by a generation of utopian socialists, and appalled by the poverty and misery of the urban poor, the radical republicans were committed to some kind of socialism. So were many artisans, who hated the unrestrained competition of cutthroat capitalism and who advocated a combination of strong craft unions and worker-owned businesses.

Worsening depression and rising unemployment brought these conflicting goals to the fore in 1848. Louis Blanc, who along with a worker named Albert represented the republican socialists in the provisional government, pressed for recognition of a socialist right to work. Blanc asserted that permanent government-sponsored cooperative workshops should be established for workers. Such workshops would be an alternative to capitalist employment and a decisive step toward a new, noncompetitive social order.

The moderate republicans wanted no such thing. They were willing to provide only temporary relief. The resulting compromise set up national workshops—soon to become little more than a vast program of pick-and-shovel public works—and established a special commission under Blanc to "study the question." This satisfied no one. The national workshops were, however, better than nothing. An army of desperate poor from the French provinces and even from foreign countries streamed into Paris to sign up. As the economic crisis worsened, the number enrolled in the workshops soared from 10,000 in March to 120,000 by June, and another 80,000 were trying unsuccessfully to join.

While the workshops in Paris grew, the French masses went to the election polls in late April. Voting in most cases for the first time, the people of France elected to the new Constituent Assembly about five hundred moderate republicans, three hundred monarchists, and one hundred radicals who professed various brands of socialism. One of the moderate republicans was the author of *Democracy in America,* Alexis de Tocqueville (1805–1859), who

The Triumph of Democratic Republics   This French illustration constructs a joyous, optimistic vision of the initial revolutionary breakthrough in 1848. The peoples of Europe, joined together around their respective national banners, are achieving republican freedom, which is symbolized by the statue of liberty and the discarded crowns. The woman wearing pants—very radical attire—represents feminist hopes for liberation. (*Archive of Arnoldo Mondadori Editore, Milan*)

had predicted the overthrow of Louis Philippe's government. To this brilliant observer, socialism was the most characteristic aspect of the revolution in Paris.

This socialist revolution was evoking a violent reaction not only among the frightened middle and upper classes but also among the bulk of the population—the peasants. The French peasants owned land, and according to Tocqueville, "private property had become with all those who owned it a sort of bond of fraternity."[5] The countryside, Tocqueville wrote, had been seized with a universal hatred of radical Paris. Returning from Normandy to take his seat in the new Constituent Assembly, Tocqueville saw that a majority of the members were firmly committed to the republic and strongly opposed to the socialists and their artisan allies, and he shared their sentiments.

This clash of ideologies—of liberal capitalism and socialism—became a clash of classes and arms after the elections. The new government's executive committee dropped Blanc and thereafter included no representative of the Parisian working class. Fearing that their socialist hopes were about to be dashed, artisans and unskilled workers invaded the Constituent Assembly on May 15 and tried to proclaim a new revolutionary state. But the government

was ready and used the middle-class National Guard to squelch this uprising. As the workshops continued to fill and grow more radical, the fearful but powerful propertied classes in the Assembly took the offensive. On June 22, the government dissolved the national workshops in Paris, giving the workers the choice of joining the army or going to workshops in the provinces.

The result was a spontaneous and violent uprising. Frustrated in attempts to create a socialist society, masses of desperate people were now losing even their life-sustaining relief. As a voice from the crowd cried out when the famous astronomer François Arago counseled patience, "Ah, Monsieur Arago, you have never been hungry!"[6] Barricades sprang up in the narrow streets of Paris, and a terrible class war began. Working people fought with the courage of utter desperation, but the government had the army and the support of peasant France. After three terrible "June Days" and the death or injury of more than ten thousand people, the republican army under General Louis Cavaignac stood triumphant in a sea of working-class blood and hatred.

The revolution in France thus ended in spectacular failure. The February coalition of the middle and working classes had in four short months become locked in mortal combat. In place of a generous democratic republic, the Constituent Assembly completed a constitution featuring a strong executive. This allowed Louis Napoleon, nephew of Napoleon Bonaparte, to win a landslide victory in the election of December 1848. The appeal of his great name as well as the desire of the propertied classes for order at any cost had produced a semi-authoritarian regime.

The Austrian Empire in 1848

Throughout central Europe, the first news of the upheaval in France evoked feverish excitement and eventually revolution. Liberals demanded written constitutions, representative government, and greater civil liberties from authoritarian regimes. When governments hesitated, popular revolts followed. Urban workers and students served as the shock troops, but they were allied with middle-class liberals and peasants. In the face of this united front, monarchs collapsed and granted almost everything. The popular revolutionary coalition, having secured great and easy victories, then broke down as it had in France. The traditional forces—the monarchy, the aristocracy, and the regular army—recovered their nerve, reasserted their authority, and took back many, though not all, of the concessions. Reaction was everywhere victorious.

The revolution in the Austrian Empire began in Hungary, where nationalistic Hungarians demanded national autonomy, full civil liberties, and universal suffrage. When the monarchy in Vienna hesitated, Viennese students and workers took to the streets, and peasant disorders broke out in parts of the empire. The Habsburg emperor Ferdinand I (r. 1835–1848) capitulated and promised reforms and a liberal constitution. Metternich fled in disguise toward London. The old absolutist order seemed to be collapsing with unbelievable rapidity.

The coalition of revolutionaries was not stable, however. The Austrian Empire was overwhelmingly agricultural, and serfdom still existed. On March 20, as part of its capitulation before upheaval, the monarchy abolished serfdom, with its degrading forced labor and feudal services. Feeling they had won a victory reminiscent of that in France in 1789, newly free men and women of the land then lost interest in the political and social questions agitating the cities. Meanwhile, the coalition of urban revolutionaries also broke down. When artisan workers and the urban poor rose in arms and presented their own demands for socialist workshops and universal voting rights for men, the prosperous middle classes recoiled in alarm.

The coalition of March was also weakened, and ultimately destroyed, by conflicting national aspirations. In March the Hungarian revolutionary leaders pushed through an extremely liberal, almost democratic, constitution. But the Hungarian revolutionaries also sought to transform the mosaic of provinces and peoples that was the kingdom of Hungary into a unified, centralized, Hungarian nation. To the minority groups that formed half of the population—the Croats, Serbs, and Romanians—such unification was completely unacceptable. Each felt entitled to political autonomy and cultural independence. The Habsburg monarchy in Vienna exploited the fears of the minority groups, and they were soon locked in armed combat with the new Hungarian government. In a somewhat similar way, Czech nationalists based in Bohemia and the city of Prague came into conflict with German nationalists. Thus conflicting national aspirations within the Austrian Empire enabled the monarchy to play off one group against the other.

Finally, the conservative aristocratic forces gathered around Emperor Ferdinand I regained their nerve and reasserted their great strength. The archduchess Sophia, a conservative but intelligent and courageous Bavarian princess married to the emperor's brother, provided a rallying point. Deeply ashamed of the emperor's collapse before a "mess of students," she insisted that Ferdinand, who had no heir, abdicate in favor of her son, Francis Joseph.[7] Powerful nobles who held high positions in the government, the army, and the church agreed completely. They organized around Sophia in a secret conspiracy to reverse and crush the revolution.

Their first breakthrough came when the army bombarded Prague and savagely crushed a working-class revolt there on June 17. Other Austrian officials and nobles began to lead the minority nationalities of Hungary against the revolutionary government proclaimed by the Hungarian patriots. At the end of October, the well-equipped, predominantly peasant troops of the regular Austrian army attacked the student and working-class radicals in Vienna and retook the city at the cost of more than four thousand casualties. Thus the determination of the Austrian aristocracy and the loyalty of its army were the final ingredients in the triumph of reaction and the defeat of revolution.

When Francis Joseph (r. 1848–1916) was crowned emperor of Austria immediately after his eighteenth birthday in December 1848, only Hungary had yet to be brought under control. But another determined conservative, Nicholas I of Russia (r. 1825–1855), obligingly lent his iron hand. On June 6, 1849, 130,000 Russian troops poured into Hungary and subdued the country after bitter fighting. For a number of years, the Habsburgs ruled Hungary as a conquered territory.

Prussia and the Frankfurt Assembly

After Austria, Prussia was the largest and most influential German kingdom. Prior to 1848, the goal of middle-class Prussian liberals had been to transform absolutist Prussia into a liberal constitutional monarchy, which would lead the thirty-eight states of the German Confederation into the liberal, unified nation desired by liberals throughout the German states. The agitation following the fall of Louis Philippe encouraged Prussian liberals to press their demands. When the artisans and factory workers in Berlin exploded in March and joined temporarily with the middle-class liberals in the struggle against the monarchy, the autocratic yet paternalistic Frederick William IV (r. 1840–1861) vacillated and finally caved in. On March 21, he promised to grant Prussia a liberal constitution and to merge Prussia into a new national German state that was to be created. But urban workers wanted much more and the Prussian aristocracy wanted much less than the moderate constitutional liberalism the

Street Fighting in Frankfurt, 1848   Workers and students could tear up the cobblestones, barricade a street, and make it into a fortress. But urban revolutionaries were untrained and poorly armed. They were no match for professional soldiers led by tough officers who were sent against them after frightened rulers had recovered their nerve. *(The Granger Collection, New York)*

king conceded. The workers issued a series of democratic and vaguely socialist demands that troubled their middle-class allies, and the conservative clique gathered around the king to urge counter-revolution.

As an elected Prussian Constituent Assembly met in Berlin to write a constitution for the Prussian state, a self-appointed committee of liberals from various German states successfully called for a national assembly to begin writing a federal constitution for a unified German state. Meeting in Frankfurt in May, the National Assembly was a curious revolutionary body. It was a really serious middle-class body of lawyers, professors, doctors, officials, and businessmen.

Convened to write a constitution, the learned body was soon absorbed in a battle with Denmark over the provinces of Schleswig and Holstein, an extremely complicated issue from a legal point of view. The provinces were inhabited primarily by Germans but were ruled by the king of Denmark, although Holstein was a member of the German Confederation. When Frederick VII, the new nationalistic king of Denmark, tried to integrate both provinces into the rest of his state, the Germans in these provinces revolted. Hypnotized by this conflict, the National Assembly at Frankfurt debated ponderously and finally called on the Prussian army to oppose Denmark in the name of the German nation. Prussia responded and began war with Denmark. As the Schleswig-Holstein issue demonstrated, the national ideal was a crucial factor motivating the German middle classes in 1848.

In March 1849, the National Assembly finally completed its drafting of a liberal constitution and elected King Frederick William of Prussia emperor of the new German national state (minus Austria and Schleswig-Holstein). By early 1849, however, reaction had been successful almost everywhere. Frederick William had reasserted his royal authority, disbanded the Prussian Constituent Assembly, and granted his subjects a limited, essentially conservative constitution. Reasserting that he ruled by divine right, Frederick William contemptuously refused to accept the "crown from the gutter." Bogged down by their preoccupation with nationalist issues, the reluctant revolutionaries in Frankfurt had waited too long and acted too timidly.

When Frederick William, who really wanted to be emperor but only on his own authoritarian terms, tried to get the small monarchs of Germany to elect him emperor, Austria balked. Supported by Russia, Austria forced Prussia to renounce all its schemes of unification in late 1850. The German Confederation was re-established. Attempts to unite the Germans—first in a liberal national state and then in a conservative Prussian empire—had failed completely.

Summary

In 1814 the victorious allied powers sought to restore peace and stability in Europe. Dealing moderately with France and wisely settling their own differences, the allies laid the foundations for beneficial international cooperation throughout much of the nineteenth century. Led by Metternich, the conservative powers also sought to prevent the spread of subversive ideas and radical changes in domestic politics. Yet European thought has seldom been more powerfully creative than after 1815, and ideologies of liberalism, nationalism, and socialism all developed to challenge the existing order in this period of early industrialization and rapid population growth. The romantic movement, breaking decisively with the dictates of classicism, reinforced the spirit of change and revolutionary anticipation.

All of these forces culminated in the liberal and nationalistic revolutions of 1848. Political, economic, and social pressures that had been building since 1815 exploded dramatically, but the upheavals of 1848 were abortive, and very few revolutionary goals were realized. The moderate, nationalistic middle classes were unable to consolidate their initial victories in France or elsewhere in Europe. Instead, they drew back when artisans, factory workers, and radical socialists rose up to present their own much more revolutionary demands. This retreat facilitated the efforts of dedicated aristocrats in central Europe and made possible the crushing of Parisian workers by a coalition of solid bourgeoisie and landowning peasantry in France. A host of fears, a sea of blood, and a torrent of disillusion had drowned the lofty ideals and utopian visions of a generation. The age of romantic revolution was over.

Key Terms

dual revolution	doers
Congress of Vienna	bourgeoisie
Holy Alliance	proletariat
Carlsbad Decrees	romanticism
liberalism	Sturm und Drang
laissez faire	Corn Laws
nationalism	Battle of Peterloo
socialism	Great Famine
parasites	

Notes

1. E. Gellner, *Nations and Nationalism* (Oxford: Basil Blackwell, 1983), especially pp. 19–39.
2. This paragraph draws on the influential views of B. Anderson, *Imagined Communities: Reflections on the Origins and Spread of*

Nationalism, rev. ed. (London/New York: Verso, 1991), and E. J. Hobsbawm and T. Ranger, eds., *The Invention of Tradition* (Cambridge: Cambridge University Press, 1983).

3. Quoted in F. B. Artz, *From the Renaissance to Romanticism: Trends in Style in Art, Literature, and Music, 1300–1830* (Chicago: University of Chicago Press, 1962), pp. 276, 278.

4. Quoted in G. Wright, *France in Modern Times,* 4th ed. (Chicago: Rand McNally, 1987), p. 145.

5. A. de Tocqueville, *Recollections* (New York: Columbia University Press, 1949), p. 94.

6. M. Agulhon, *1848* (Paris: Éditions du Seuil, 1973), pp. 68–69.

7. W. L. Langer, *Political and Social Upheaval, 1832–1852* (New York: Harper & Row, 1969), p. 361.

▌Suggested Reading

The works cited in the Notes are highly recommended. Wright's work is a lively introduction to French history with stimulating biographical discussions; Langer's is a balanced synthesis with an excellent bibliography. Among general studies, R. Gildea, *Barricades and Borders: Europe, 1800–1914,* 2d ed. (1996), is recommended. C. Morazé, *The Triumph of the Middle Classes* (1968), a wide-ranging procapitalist interpretation, may be compared with E. J. Hobsbawm's flexible Marxism in *The Age of Revolution, 1789–1848* (1962). For English history, E. Thompson, *The Rise of Respectable Society, 1830–1900* (1986), and A. Briggs's socially oriented *The Making of Modern England, 1784–1867* (1967), are excellent. C. Ó Gráda, *Black '47 and Beyond: The Irish Famine in History, Economy, and Memory* (1999), is an outstanding and imaginative treatment of the Great Famine. Restoration France is sympathetically portrayed by G. de Bertier de Sauvigny in *The Bourbon Restoration* (1967). R. Price, *A Social History of Nineteenth-Century France* (1987), is a fine synthesis. T. Hamerow studies the social implications of the dual revolution in Germany in *Restoration, Revolution, Reaction, 1815–1871* (1966). H. James, *A German Identity, 1770–1990* (1989), and J. Sheehan, *Germany, 1770–1866* (1989), are stimulating general histories that skillfully incorporate recent research. Two important reconsiderations of nationalism are B. Anderson, *Imagined Communities,* 2d ed. (1991); and E. Hobsbawm and T. Ranger, *The Invention of Tradition* (1990). R. Brubaker, *Citizenship and Nationhood in France and Germany* (1992), is an important comparative study. E. Kedourie, *Nationalism* (1960), is an influential historical critique of the new faith. H. Kissinger, *A World Restored* (1957), offers a provocative interpretation of the Congress of Vienna, which may be compared with H. Nicolson's entertaining *The Congress of Vienna* (1946). On 1848, J. Sperber, *The European Revolutions, 1848–1851* (1993), is a solid recent synthesis. M. Agulhon, *The Republican Experiment, 1848–1852* (1983), is outstanding. I. Deak, *The Lawful Revolution: Louis Kossuth and the Hungarians, 1848–49* (1979), is a noteworthy study of an interesting figure.

On early socialism and Marxism, see A. Lindemann's stimulating survey, *A History of European Socialism* (1983), and W. Sewell, Jr., *Work and Revolution in France: The Language of Labor from the Old Regime to 1848* (1980), as well as G. Lichtheim's high-powered *Marxism* (1961) and his *Short History of Socialism* (1970). J. Seigel, *Marx's Fate: The Shape of a Life* (1978), is a major biography. P. Stock-Morton, *The Life of Marie d'Agoult, Alias Daniel Stern* (2000), is a fascinating biography of the French romantic novelist, while Fourier is treated sympathetically in J. Beecher, *Charles Fourier* (1986). J. Schumpeter, *Capitalism, Socialism and Democracy* (1947), is magnificent but difficult, a real mind-stretcher. Also highly recommended are B. Taylor, *Eve and the New Jerusalem: Socialism and Feminism in the Nineteenth Century* (1983), which explores fascinating English attempts to emancipate workers and women at the same time, and B. Anderson, *Joyous Greetings: The First International Women's Movement* (2000), which stresses the importance of 1848. On liberalism, see R. Heilbroner's entertaining *The Worldly Philosophers* (1967) and G. de Ruggiero's classic *History of European Liberalism* (1959). M. Cranston, *The Romantic Movement* (1994), and J. Barzun, *Classic, Romantic and Modern* (1961), skillfully discuss romanticism. J. Seigel, *Bohemian Paris: Culture, Politics, and the Boundaries of Bourgeois Life* (1986), imaginatively places romantic aspirations in a broad cultural framework. R. Stromberg, *An Intellectual History of Modern Europe,* 3d ed. (1981), is a valuable survey. The important place of religion in nineteenth-century thought is considered from different perspectives in H. McLeod, *Religion and the People of Western Europe* (1981), and O. Chadwick, *The Secularization of the European Mind in the Nineteenth Century* (1976). Two good church histories with useful bibliographies are J. Altholz, *The Churches in the Nineteenth Century* (1967), and A. Vidler, *The Church in an Age of Revolution: 1789 to the Present Day* (1961).

The thoughtful reader is strongly advised to delve into the incredibly rich writing of contemporaries. J. Bowditch and C. Ramsland, eds., *Voices of the Industrial Revolution* (1961), is an excellent starting point, with well-chosen selections from leading economic thinkers and early socialists. H. Hugo, ed., *The Romantic Reader,* is another fine anthology. Mary Shelley's *Frankenstein,* a great romantic novel, draws an almost lovable picture of the famous monster and is highly recommended. Jules Michelet's compassionate masterpiece *The People,* a famous historian's anguished examination of French social divisions on the eve of 1848, draws one into the heart of the period and is highly recommended. Alexis de Tocqueville covers some of the same ground less romantically in his *Recollections,* which may be compared with Karl Marx's white-hot "instant history," *Class Struggles in France, 1848–1850.* Great novels that accurately portray aspects of the times are Victor Hugo, *Les Misérables,* an exciting story of crime and passion among France's poor; Honoré de Balzac, *La Cousine Bette* and *Le Père Goriot;* and Thomas Mann, *Buddenbrooks,* a wonderful historical novel that traces the rise and fall of a prosperous German family over three generations during the nineteenth century.

Faith in Democratic Nationalism

*Early advocates of the national ideal usually
believed that progress for one people would also
contribute to the progress of all humanity. They
believed that a Europe of independent nation-states
would provide the proper framework for securing
freedom, democracy, social justice, and even
international peace.*

*This optimistic faith guided Giuseppe Mazzini
(1805–1872), the leading prophet of Italian
nationalism and unification. Banished from Italy in
1830, the exiled Mazzini founded a secret society
called Young Italy to fight for Italian unification and
a democratic republic. Mazzini's group inspired
numerous local insurrections and then led Italy's
radicals in the unsuccessful revolutions of 1848. Italy
was united a decade later, but by other means.*

Mazzini's best-known work was The Duties of Man,
*a collection of essays. The following famous selection,
titled "Duties Towards Your Country," was written
in 1858 and addressed to Italian workingmen.*

Your first Duties . . . are to Humanity. . . . But
what can each of you, with his isolated powers,
do for the moral improvement, for the progress
of Humanity? . . .

God gave you the means of multiplying your
forces and your powers of action indefinitely when
he gave you a Country, when, like a wise overseer
of labor, who distributes the different parts of the
work according to the capacity of the workmen,
he divided Humanity into distinct groups upon
the face of our globe, and thus planted the seeds
of nations. Evil governments have disfigured the
design of God, which you may see clearly marked
out, as far, at least, as regards Europe, by the
courses of the great rivers, by the lines of the lofty
mountains, and by other geographical conditions;
they have disfigured it by conquest, by greed, by
jealousy of the just sovereignty of others;

disfigured it so much that today there is perhaps
no nation except England and France whose
confines correspond to this design.

[These evil governments] did not, and they do
not, recognize any country except their own
families and dynasties, the egoism of caste. But
the divine design will infallibly be fulfilled. Natural
divisions, the innate spontaneous tendencies of
the peoples will replace the arbitrary divisions
sanctioned by evil governments. The map of
Europe will be remade. The Countries of the
People will rise, defined by the voice of the free,
upon the ruins of the Countries of Kings and
privileged castes. Between these Countries there
will be harmony and brotherhood. And then the
work of Humanity for the general amelioration,
for the discovery and application of the real law of
life, carried on in association and distributed
according to local capacities, will be accomplished
by peaceful and progressive development.

Then each of you, strong in the affections and
in the aid of many millions of men speaking the
same language, endowed with the same
tendencies, and educated by the same historic
tradition, may hope by your personal effort to
benefit the whole of Humanity.

Without Country you have neither name, voice,
nor rights, no admission as brothers into the
fellowship of the Peoples. You are the bastards of
Humanity. Soldiers without a banner, . . . you will
find neither faith nor protection. . . . Do not
beguile yourselves with the hope of emancipation
from unjust social conditions if you do not first
conquer a Country for yourselves; where there is
no Country there is no common agreement to
which you can appeal; the egoism of self-interest
rules alone, and he who has the upper hand keeps
it, since there is no common safeguard for the
interests of all. . . .

O my Brothers! love your Country. Our
Country is our home, the home which God has

given us, placing therein a numerous family which we love and are loved by. . . . In labouring according to true principles for our Country we are labouring for Humanity; our Country is the fulcrum of the lever which we have to wield for the common good. If we give up this fulcrum we run the risk of becoming useless to our Country and to Humanity. . . .

There is no true Country without a uniform law. There is no true Country where the uniformity of that law is violated by the existence of caste, privilege, and inequality, where the powers and faculties of a large number of individuals are suppressed or dormant, where there is no common principle accepted, recognized, and developed by all. In such a state of things there can be no Nation, no People, but only a multitude, a fortuitous agglomeration of men whom circumstances have brought together and different circumstances will separate. In the name of your love for your Country you must combat without truce the existence of every privilege, every inequality, upon the soil which has given you birth. . . .

Your Country should be your Temple. God at the summit, a People of equals at the base. Do not accept any other formula, any other moral law, if you do not want to dishonour your Country and yourselves. Let the secondary laws for the gradual regulation of your existence be the progressive application of this supreme law.

And in order that they should be so, it is necessary that *all* should contribute to the making of them. The laws made by one fraction of the citizens only can never by the nature of things and men do otherwise than reflect the thoughts and aspirations and desires of that fraction; they represent, not the whole Country, but a third, a fourth part, a class, a zone of the Country. The law must express the general aspiration, promote the good of all, respond to a beat of the nation's heart. The whole nation therefore should be, directly or indirectly, the legislator. By yielding this mission to a few men, you put the egoism of one class in the place of the Country, which is the union of *all* the classes.

A Country is not a mere territory; the particular territory is only its foundation. The Country is the idea which rises upon that foundation; it is the sentiment of love, the sense of fellowship which binds together all the sons of that territory.

Portrait of Giuseppe Mazzini, from the Museo del Risorgimento, Milan. *(Museo del Risorgimento/ Scala/Art Resource, NY)*

So long as a single one of your brothers is not represented by his own vote in the development of the national life—so long as a single one vegetates uneducated among the educated—so long as a single one able and willing to work languishes in poverty for want of work—you have not got a Country such as it ought to be, the Country of all and for all.

Votes, education, work are the three main pillars of the nation; do not rest until your hands have solidly erected them.

Questions for Analysis

1. What did Mazzini mean by "evil governments"? Why are they evil?

2. What are the characteristics of the "true Country"?

3. What form of government is best? Why?

4. Why, according to Mazzini, should poor workingmen have been interested in the political unification of Italy?

5. How might a woman today criticize Mazzini's program? Debate how Mazzini might respond to such criticism.

Source: Slightly adapted from J. Mazzini, *The Duties of Man and Other Essays* (London: J. M. Dent and Sons, 1907), pp. 51–57.

John Perry, *A Bill-poster's Fantasy* (1855), explores the endless diversity of big-city entertainment. (*dunhill Museum & Archive, 48 Germyn Street, St. James's, London*)

chapter

24 Life in the Emerging Urban Society

chapter outline

- Taming the City

- Rich and Poor and Those in Between

- The Changing Family

- Science and Thought

*T*he era of intellectual and political upheaval that culminated in the revolutions of 1848 was also an era of rapid urbanization. After 1848 Western political development veered off in a novel and uncharted direction, but the growth of towns and cities rushed forward with undiminished force. Thus Western society was urban and industrial in 1900 as surely as it had been rural and agrarian in 1800. The urbanization of society was both a result of the Industrial Revolution and a reflection of its enormous long-term impact.

- What was life like in the cities, and how did it change?
- What did the emergence of urban industrial society mean for rich and poor and those in between?
- How did families change as they coped with the challenges and the opportunities of the developing urban civilization?
- What changes in science and thought reflected and influenced this new civilization?

These are the questions this chapter will investigate.

*T*aming the City

The growth of industry posed enormous challenges for all elements of Western society, from young factory workers confronting relentless discipline to aristocratic elites maneuvering to retain political power. As we saw in Chapter 22, the early consequences of economic transformation were mixed and far-reaching and by no means wholly negative. By 1850 at the latest, working conditions were improving and real wages were rising for the mass of the population, and they continued to do so until 1914. Thus given the poverty and uncertainty of preindustrial life, some historians maintain that the history of industrialization in the nineteenth century is probably better written in terms of increasing opportunities than in terms of greater hardships.

Critics of this relatively optimistic view of industrialization claim that it neglects the quality of life in urban areas. They stress that the new industrial

787

towns and cities were awful places where people, especially poor people, suffered from bad housing, lack of sanitation, and a sense of hopelessness. They ask if these drawbacks did not more than cancel out higher wages and greater opportunity. An examination of the development of cities in the nineteenth century provides some answers to this complex question.

Industry and the Growth of Cities

Since the Middle Ages, European cities had been centers of government, culture, and large-scale commerce. They had also been congested, dirty, and unhealthy. People were packed together almost as tightly as possible within the city limits. The typical city was a "walking city": for all but the wealthiest classes, walking was the only available form of transportation.

Infectious disease spread with deadly speed in cities, and people were always more likely to die in the city than in the countryside. In the larger towns, more people died each year than were born, on average, and urban populations were able to maintain their numbers only because newcomers were continually arriving from rural areas. Little could be done to improve these conditions, given the pervasive poverty, absence of urban transportation, lack of medical knowledge, and deadly overcrowding.

Clearly, deplorable urban conditions did not originate with the Industrial Revolution. What the Industrial Rev-

olution did was to reveal those conditions more nakedly than ever before. The steam engine freed industrialists from dependence on the energy of fast-flowing streams and rivers so that by 1800 there was every incentive to build new factories in urban areas. Cities had better shipping facilities than the countryside and thus better supplies of coal and raw materials. There were also many hands wanting work in the cities, for cities drew people like a magnet. And it was a great advantage for a manufacturer to have other factories nearby to supply the business's needs and buy its products. Therefore, as industry grew, there was also a rapid expansion of already overcrowded and unhealthy cities.

The challenge of the urban environment was felt first and most acutely in Great Britain. The number of people living in cities of 20,000 or more in England and Wales jumped from 1.5 million in 1801 to 6.3 million in 1851 and reached 15.6 million in 1891. Such cities accounted for 17 percent of the total English population in 1801, 35 percent as early as 1851, and fully 54 percent in 1891. Other countries duplicated the English pattern as they industrialized (see Map 24.1). An American observer was hardly exaggerating when he wrote in 1899 that "the most remarkable social phenomenon of the present century is the concentration of population in cities."[1]

In the 1820s and 1830s, people in Britain and France began to worry about the condition of their cities. In those years, the populations of a number of British cities

MAP 24.1 European Cities of 100,000 or More, 1800 and 1900   There were more large cities in Great Britain in 1900 than in all of Europe in 1800. Northwestern Europe was the most urbanized area.

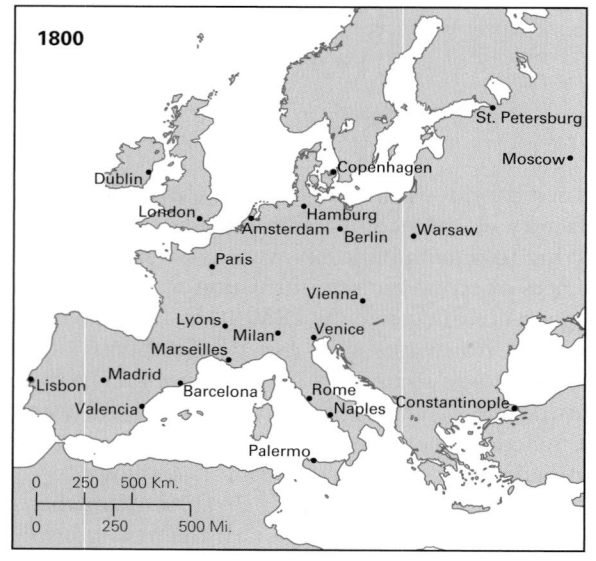
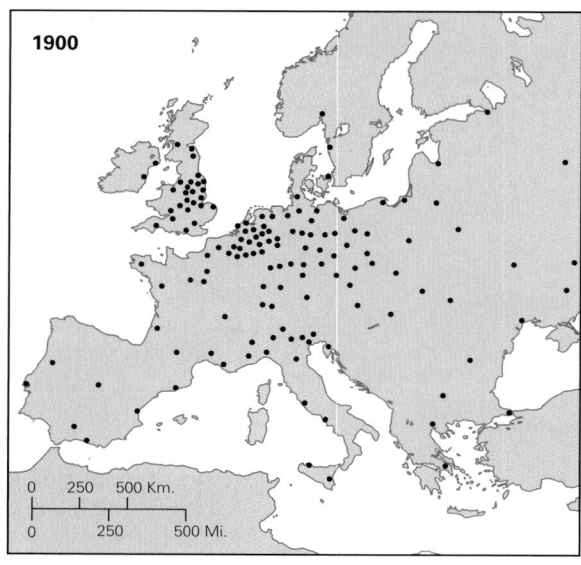

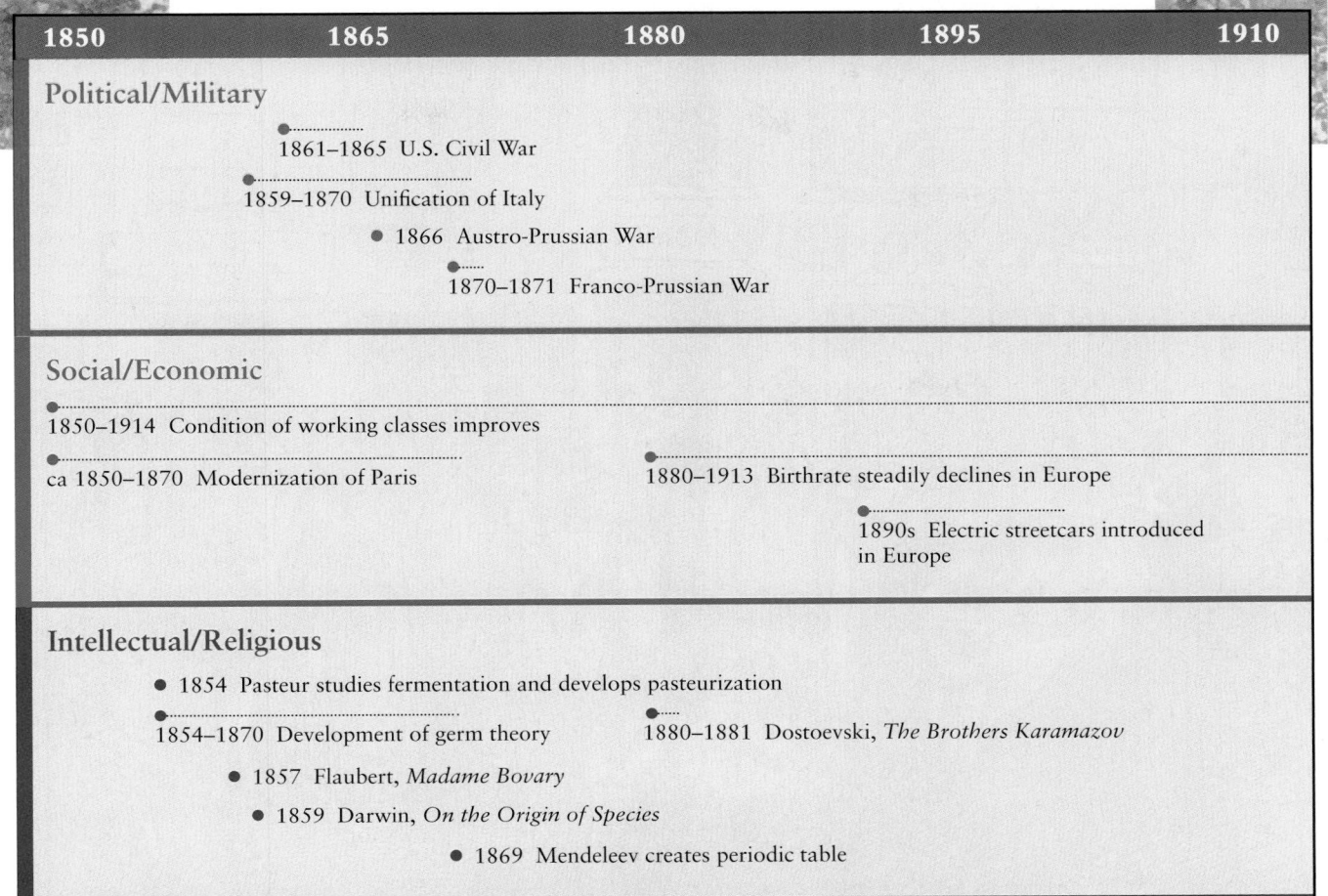

1850	1865	1880	1895	1910

Political/Military

1861–1865 U.S. Civil War

1859–1870 Unification of Italy

1866 Austro-Prussian War

1870–1871 Franco-Prussian War

Social/Economic

1850–1914 Condition of working classes improves

ca 1850–1870 Modernization of Paris

1880–1913 Birthrate steadily declines in Europe

1890s Electric streetcars introduced in Europe

Intellectual/Religious

1854 Pasteur studies fermentation and develops pasteurization

1854–1870 Development of germ theory

1880–1881 Dostoevski, *The Brothers Karamazov*

1857 Flaubert, *Madame Bovary*

1859 Darwin, *On the Origin of Species*

1869 Mendeleev creates periodic table

were increasing by 40 to 70 percent each decade. With urban areas expanding at such previously undreamed-of rates, people's fatalistic acceptance of overcrowded, unsanitary urban living conditions began to give way to active concern. Something urgently needed to be done.

On one point everyone could agree: except on the outskirts, each town or city was using every scrap of land to the fullest extent. Parks and open areas were almost nonexistent. Buildings were erected on the smallest possible lots in order to pack the maximum number of people into a given space. Narrow houses were built wall to wall in long rows. These row houses had neither front nor back yards, and only a narrow alley in back separated one row from the next. Or buildings were built around tiny courtyards completely enclosed on all four sides. Many people lived in extremely small, often overcrowded cellars or attics. "Six, eight, and even ten occupying one room is anything but uncommon," wrote a doctor from Aberdeen in Scotland for a government investigation in 1842.

These highly concentrated urban populations lived in extremely unsanitary and unhealthy conditions. Open drains and sewers flowed alongside or down the middle of unpaved streets. Toilet facilities were primitive in the extreme. In parts of Manchester, as many as two hundred people shared a single outhouse. Such privies filled up rapidly, and since they were infrequently emptied, sewage often overflowed and seeped into cellar dwellings. Moreover, some courtyards in poorer neighborhoods became dunghills, collecting excrement that was sometimes sold as fertilizer. By the 1840s there was among the better-off classes a growing, shocking "realization that, to put it as mildly as possible, millions of English men, women, and children were living in shit."[2]

Who or what was responsible for these awful conditions? The crucial factors were the tremendous pressure of more people and the *total* absence of public transportation. People simply had to jam themselves together if they were to be able to walk to shops and factories.

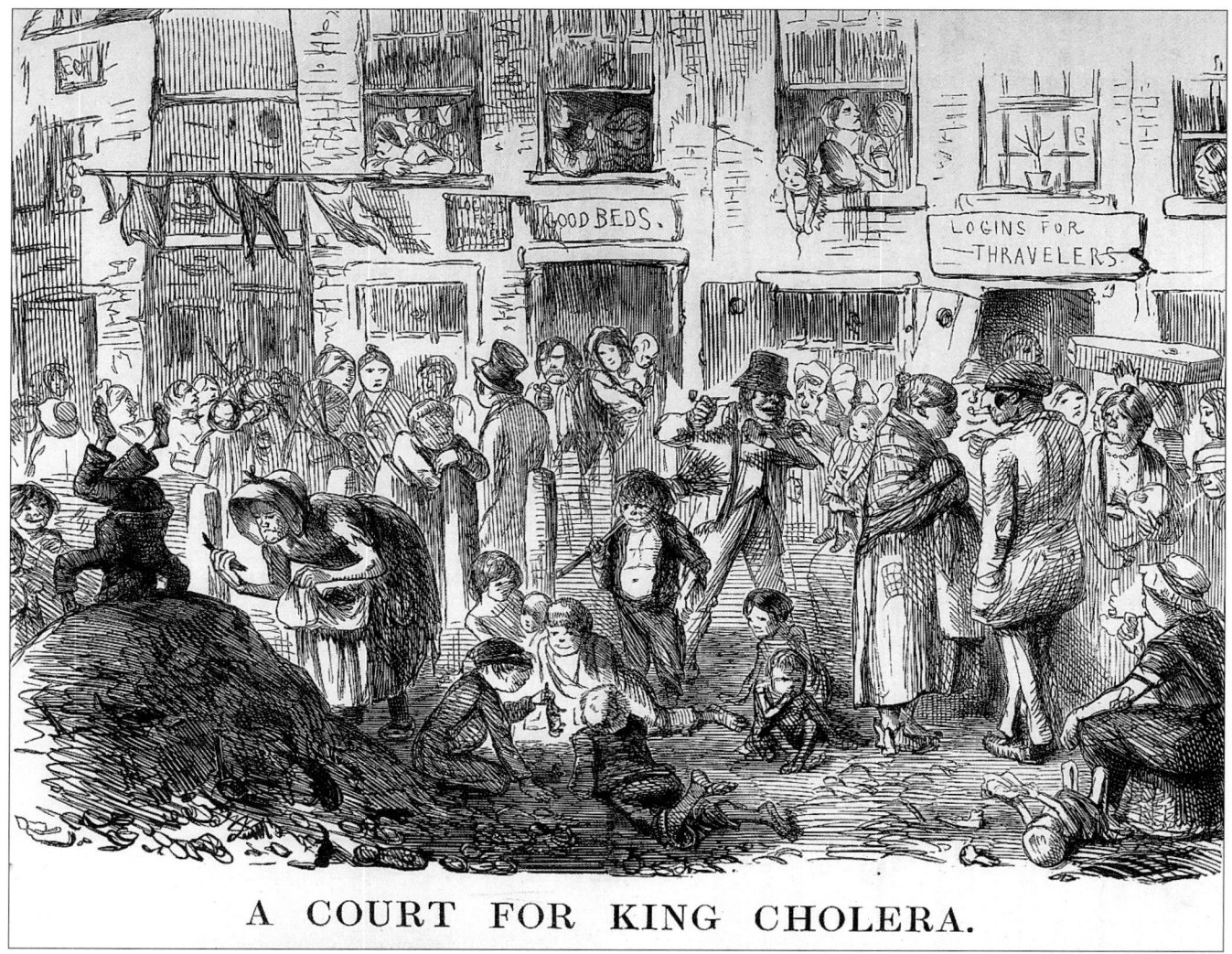

A COURT FOR KING CHOLERA.

Filth and Disease This 1852 drawing from *Punch* tells volumes about the unhealthy living conditions of the urban poor. In the foreground children play with a dead rat and a woman scavenges a dungheap. Cheap rooming houses provide shelter for the frightfully overcrowded population. *(The British Library)*

Another factor was that government in Great Britain, both local and national, was slow to provide sanitary facilities and establish adequate building codes. This slow pace was probably attributable more to a need to explore and identify what precisely should be done than to rigid middle-class opposition to government action. Certainly, Great Britain had no monopoly on overcrowded and unhealthy urban conditions; many continental cities with stronger traditions of municipal regulation were every bit as bad.

Most responsible of all was the sad legacy of rural housing conditions in preindustrial society combined with appalling ignorance. As one authority concludes, "the decent cottage was the exception, the hovel the rule."[3] Thus housing was far down on the newcomer's list of priorities, and ordinary people generally took dirt and filth for granted. One English miner told an investigator, "I do not think it usual for the lasses [in the coal mines] to wash their bodies; my sisters never wash themselves." As for the men, "their legs and bodies are as black as your hat."[4]

Public Health and the Bacterial Revolution

Although cleanliness was not next to godliness in most people's eyes, it was becoming so for some reformers. The most famous of these was Edwin Chadwick, one of the commissioners charged with the administration of relief to paupers under Britain's revised Poor Law of 1834. Chadwick was a good **Benthamite**—that is, a follower of radical philosopher Jeremy Bentham (1748–1832). Bentham had taught that public problems ought to be dealt with on a rational, scientific basis and according to the "greatest good for the greatest number." Applying these principles, Chadwick soon became convinced that disease and death actually caused poverty simply because a sick worker was an unemployed worker and orphaned children were poor children. Most important, Chadwick believed that disease could be prevented by cleaning up the urban environment. That was his "sanitary idea."

Chadwick collected detailed reports from local Poor Law officials on the "sanitary conditions of the laboring population" and published his hard-hitting findings in 1842. This mass of widely publicized evidence proved that disease was related to filthy environmental conditions, which were in turn caused largely by lack of drainage, sewers, and garbage collection.

Chadwick correctly believed that the stinking excrement of communal outhouses could be dependably carried off by water through sewers at less than one-twentieth the cost of removing it by hand. The cheap iron pipes and tile drains of the industrial age would provide running water and sewerage for all sections of town, not just the wealthy ones. In 1848, with the cause strengthened by the cholera epidemic of 1846, Chadwick's report became the basis of Great Britain's first public health law, which created a national health board and gave cities broad authority to build modern sanitary systems.

The public health movement won dedicated supporters in the United States, France, and Germany from the 1840s on. Governments accepted at least limited responsibility for the health of all citizens, and their programs broke decisively with the age-old fatalism of urban populations in the face of shockingly high mortality. By the 1860s and 1870s, European cities were making real progress toward adequate water supplies and sewerage systems, city dwellers were beginning to reap the reward of better health, and death rates began to decline (see Figure 24.1).

Still, effective control of communicable disease required a great leap forward in medical knowledge and biological theory. Early reformers such as Chadwick were seriously handicapped by the prevailing **miasmatic theory** of disease—the belief that people contract disease when they

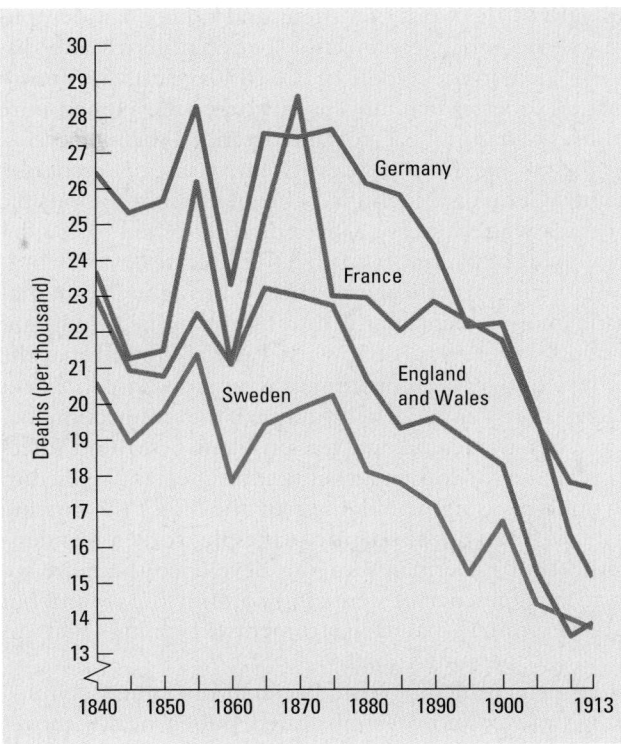

FIGURE 24.1 The Decline of Death Rates in England and Wales, Germany, France, and Sweden, 1840–1913 A rising standard of living, improvements in public health, and better medical knowledge all contributed to the dramatic decline of death rates in the nineteenth century.

breathe the bad odors of decay and putrefying excrement. Keen observation by doctors and public health officials in the 1840s and 1850s pinpointed the role of bad drinking water in the transmission of disease and suggested that contagion was *spread through* filth and not caused by it, thus weakening the miasmatic idea.

The breakthrough was the development of the **germ theory** of disease by Louis Pasteur (1822–1895), a French chemist who began studying fermentation in 1854 at the request of brewers. Using his microscope to develop a simple test that brewers could use to monitor the fermentation process and avoid spoilage, Pasteur found that fermentation depended on the growth of living organisms and that the activity of these organisms could be suppressed by heating the beverage—by **pasteurization.** The breathtaking implication was that specific diseases were caused by specific living organisms—germs—and that those organisms could be controlled in people as well as in beer, wine, and milk.

By 1870 the work of Pasteur and others had demonstrated the general connection between germs and disease. When, in the middle of the 1870s, German country doctor Robert Koch and his coworkers developed pure cultures of harmful bacteria and described their life cycles, the dam broke. Over the next twenty years, researchers—mainly Germans—identified the organisms responsible for disease after disease. These discoveries led to the development of a number of effective vaccines.

Acceptance of the germ theory brought about dramatic improvements in the deadly environment of hospitals and surgery. In 1865, when Pasteur showed that the air was full of bacteria, English surgeon Joseph Lister (1827–1912) immediately grasped the connection between aerial bacteria and the problem of wound infection. He reasoned that a chemical disinfectant applied to a wound dressing would "destroy the life of the floating particles." Lister's **antiseptic principle** worked wonders. In the 1880s, German surgeons developed the more sophisticated practice of sterilizing not only the wound but also everything—hands, instruments, clothing—that entered the operating room.

The achievements of the bacterial revolution coupled with the ever more sophisticated public health movement saved millions of lives, particularly after about 1880. Mortality rates began to decline dramatically in European countries (see Figure 24.1) as the awful death sentences of the past—diphtheria, typhoid, typhus, cholera, yellow fever—became vanishing diseases. City dwellers benefited especially from these developments. By 1910 a great silent revolution had occurred: the death rates for people of all ages in urban areas were generally no greater than those for people in rural areas, and sometimes they were less.

Urban Planning and Public Transportation

More effective urban planning was one of the keys to improving the quality of urban life. Urban planning was in decline by the early nineteenth century, but after 1850 its practice was revived and extended. France took the lead during the rule of Napoleon III (r. 1848–1870), who sought to stand above class conflict and promote the welfare of all his subjects through government action. He believed that rebuilding much of Paris would provide employment, improve living conditions, and testify to the power and glory of his empire. In the baron Georges Haussmann (1809–1884), an aggressive, impatient Alsatian whom he placed in charge of Paris, Napoleon III found an authoritarian planner capable of bulldozing

both buildings and opposition. In twenty years, Paris was transformed.

The Paris of 1850 was a labyrinth of narrow, dark streets, the results of desperate overcrowding. In a central city not twice the size of New York's Central Park lived more than one-third of the city's 1 million inhabitants. Terrible slum conditions and extremely high death rates were facts of life. There were few open spaces and only two public parks for the entire metropolis. Public transportation played a very small role in this enormous walking city.

Haussmann and his fellow planners proceeded on many interrelated fronts. With a bold energy that often shocked their contemporaries, they razed old buildings in order to cut broad, straight, tree-lined boulevards through the center of the city as well as in new quarters on the outskirts (see Map 24.2). These boulevards, designed in part to prevent the easy construction and defense of barricades by revolutionary crowds, permitted traffic to flow freely and afforded impressive vistas. Their creation also demolished some of the worst slums. New streets stimulated the construction of better housing, especially for the middle classes. Small neighborhood parks and open spaces were created throughout the city, and two very large parks suitable for all kinds of holiday activities were developed—one on the wealthy west side and one on the poor east side of the city. The city also improved its sewers, and a system of aqueducts more than doubled the city's supply of good fresh water.

Rebuilding Paris provided a new model for urban planning and stimulated modern urbanism throughout Europe, particularly after 1870. In city after city, public authorities mounted a coordinated attack on many of the interrelated problems of the urban environment. As in Paris, improvements in public health through better water supply and waste disposal often went hand in hand with new boulevard construction. Cities such as Vienna and Cologne followed the Parisian example of tearing down old walled fortifications and replacing them with broad, circular boulevards on which office buildings, town halls, theaters, opera houses, and museums were erected. These ring roads and the new boulevards that radiated out from them toward the outskirts eased movement and encouraged urban expansion (see Map 24.2). Zoning expropriation laws, which allowed a majority of the owners of land in a given quarter of the city to impose major street or sanitation improvements on a reluctant minority, were an important mechanism of the new urbanism.

The development of mass public transportation was also of great importance in the improvement of urban living conditions. In the 1870s, many European cities authorized private companies to operate horse-drawn street-

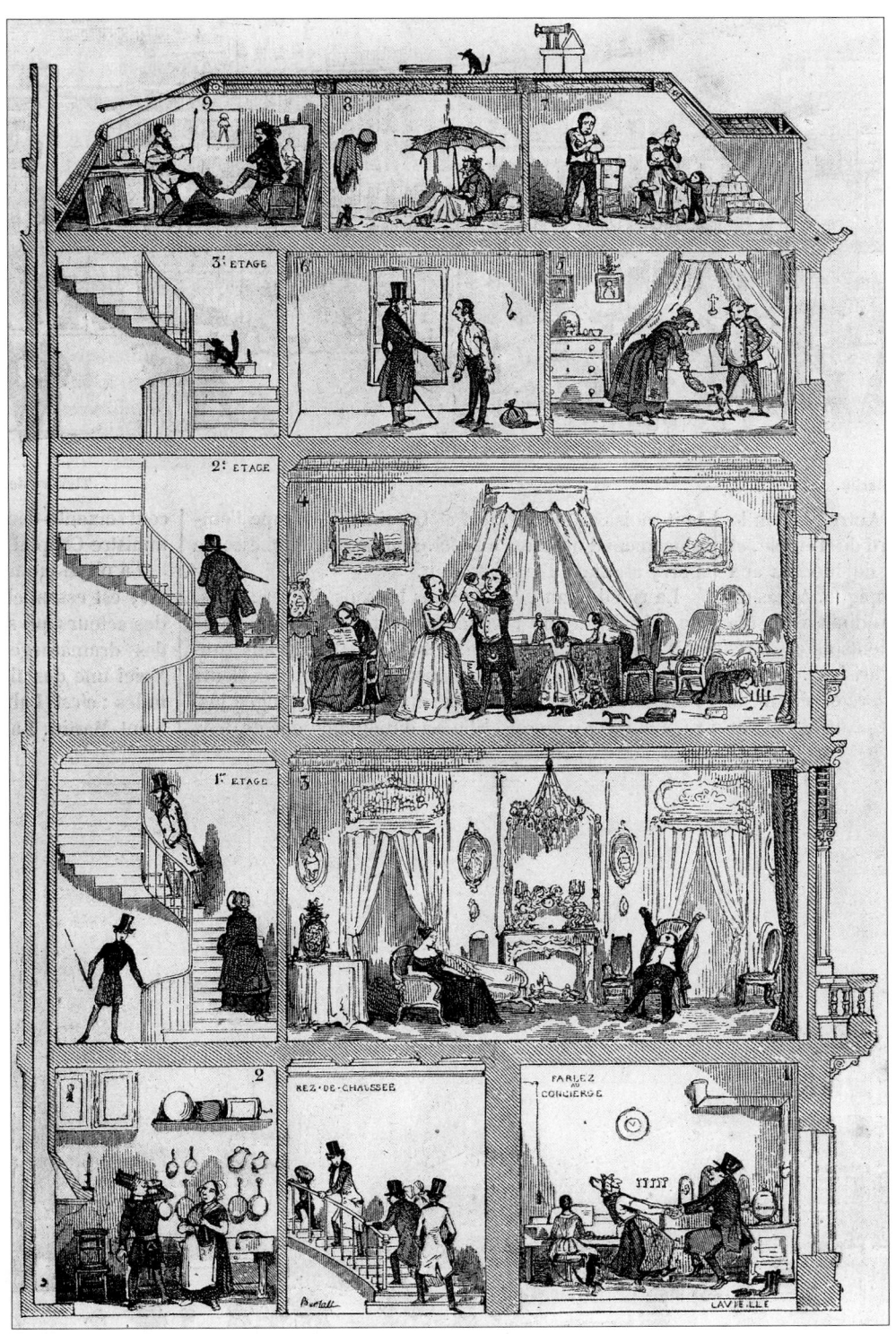

Apartment Living in Paris   This drawing shows how different social classes lived close together in European cities about 1850. Passing the middle-class family on the first floor (American second floor), the economic condition of the tenants declined until one reached abject poverty in the garret. (*Bibliothèque Nationale, Paris*)

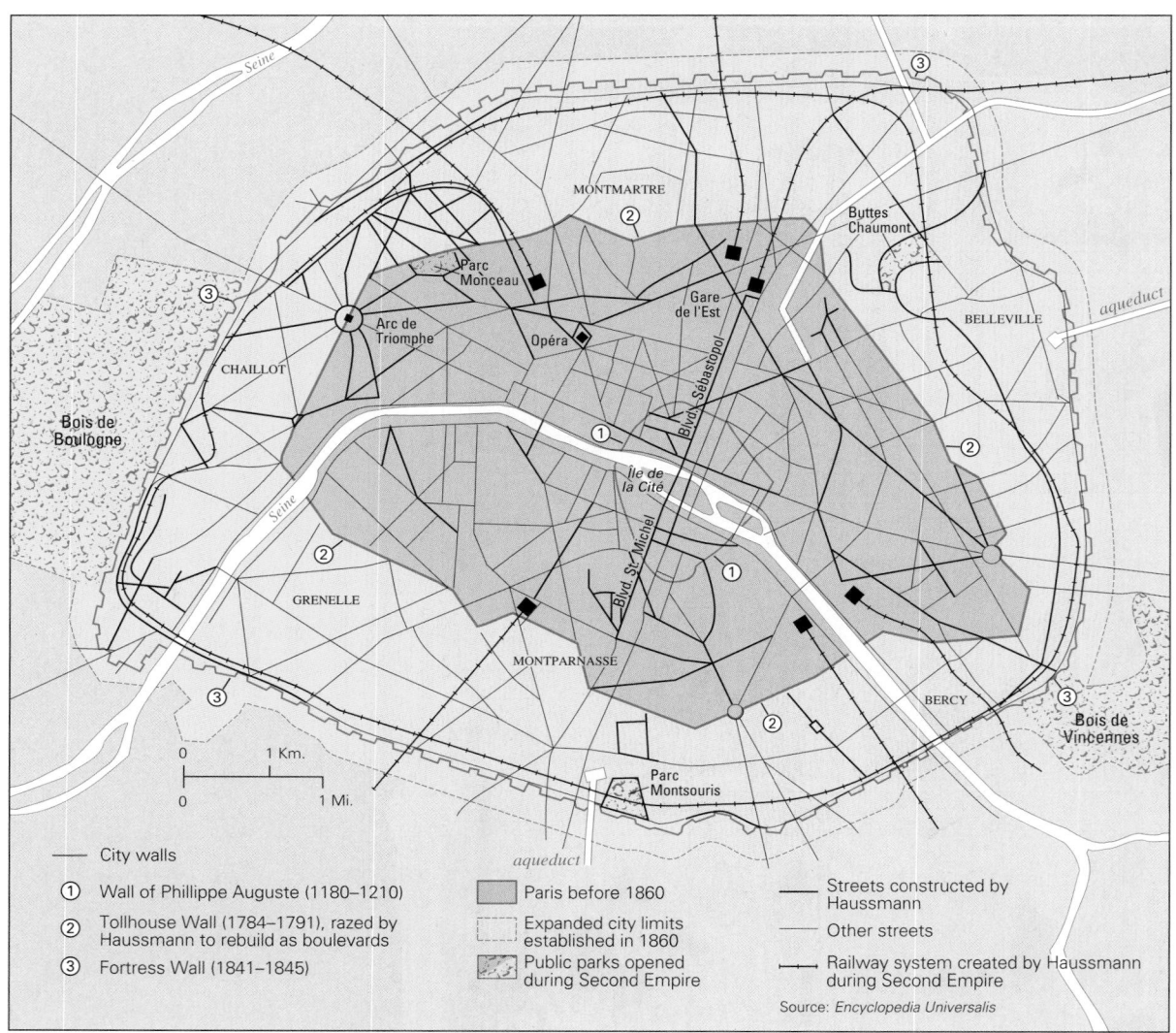

MAP 24.2 The Modernization of Paris, ca 1850–1870   Broad boulevards, large parks, and grandiose train stations transformed Paris. The cutting of the new north-south axis—known as the Boulevard Saint-Michel—was one of Haussmann's most controversial projects. It razed much of Paris's medieval core and filled the Île de la Cité with massive government buildings.

cars, which had been developed in the United States, to carry riders along the growing number of major thoroughfares. Then in the 1890s, the real revolution occurred: European countries adopted another American transit innovation, the electric streetcar.

Electric streetcars were cheaper, faster, more dependable, and more comfortable than their horse-drawn counterparts. Service improved dramatically. Millions of

Europeans—workers, shoppers, schoolchildren—hopped on board during the workweek. And on weekends and holidays, streetcars carried millions on happy outings to parks and countryside, racetracks and music halls. In 1886 the horse-drawn streetcars of Austria-Hungary, France, Germany, and Great Britain were carrying about 900 million riders. By 1910 electric streetcar systems in the four countries were carrying 6.7 billion riders.[5] Each man,

The Urban Landscape: Madrid in 1900 This wistful painting of a Spanish square on a rainy day, by Enrique Martinez Cubells y Ruiz (1874–1917), includes a revealing commentary on public transportation. Coachmen wait atop their expensive hackney cabs for a wealthy clientele, while modern electric streetcars that carry the masses converge on the square from all directions. *(Museo Municipal, Madrid/The Bridgeman Art Library International Ltd)*

woman, and child was using public transportation four times as often in 1910 as in 1886.

Good mass transit helped greatly in the struggle for decent housing. The new boulevards and horse-drawn streetcars had facilitated a middle-class move to better housing in the 1860s and 1870s; after 1890 electric streetcars gave people of modest means access to new, improved housing. The still-crowded city was able to ex-

pand and become less congested. In England in 1901, only 9 percent of the urban population was "overcrowded" in terms of the official definition of more than two persons per room. On the continent, many city governments in the early twentieth century were building electric streetcar systems that provided transportation to new public and private housing developments in outlying areas of the city for the working classes.

*R*ich and Poor and Those in Between

General improvements in health and in the urban environment had beneficial consequences for all kinds of people. Yet differences in living conditions among social classes remained gigantic.

Social Structure

How much did the almost-completed journey to an urban, industrialized world change the social framework of rich and poor and those in between? The first great change was a substantial and undeniable increase in the standard of living for the average person. The real wages of British workers, for example, which had already risen by 1850, almost doubled between 1850 and 1906. Similar increases occurred in continental countries as industrial development quickened after 1850. Ordinary people took a major step forward in the centuries-old battle against poverty, reinforcing efforts to improve many aspects of human existence.

There is another side to the income coin, however. Greater economic rewards for the average person did *not* eliminate hardship and poverty, nor did they make the wealth and income of the rich and the poor significantly more equal. In almost every advanced country around 1900, the richest 5 percent of all households in the population received 33 percent of all national income. The richest 20 percent of households received anywhere from 50 to 60 percent of all national income, while the entire bottom 80 percent received only 40 to 50 percent. Moreover, the bottom 30 percent of households received 10 percent or less of all income. These enormous differences are illustrated in Figure 24.2.

The middle classes, smaller than they are today, accounted for less than 20 percent of the population; thus the statistics show that the upper and middle classes alone received more than 50 percent of all income. The poorest 80 percent—the working classes, including peasants and agricultural laborers—received less altogether than the two richest classes. Moreover, income taxes on the wealthy were light or nonexistent. Thus the gap between rich and poor remained enormous at the beginning of the twentieth century. It was probably almost as great as it had been in the age of agriculture and aristocracy before the Industrial Revolution.

The great gap between rich and poor endured, in part, because industrial and urban development made society more diverse and less unified. By no means did society split into two sharply defined opposing classes, as Marx

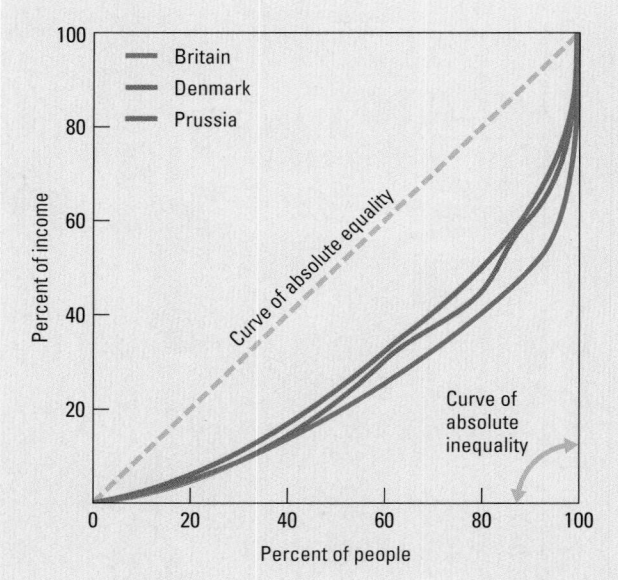

Distribution of Income

	Richest 5%	Richest 10%	Richest 20%	Poorest 60%
Britain	43%		59%	
Denmark	30%	39%	55%	31%
Prussia	30%		50%	33%

FIGURE 24.2 The Distribution of Income in Britain, Denmark, and Prussia in 1913   The so-called Lorenz curve is useful for showing the degree of economic inequality in a given society. The closer the actual distribution of income lies to the (theoretical) curve of absolute equality, where each 20 percent of the population receives 20 percent of all income, the more incomes are nearly equal. European society was very far from any such equality before World War I. Notice that incomes in Prussia were somewhat more equal than those in Britain. (*Source: S. Kuznets,* Modern Economic Growth, *pp. 208–209. Copyright © 1966 by Yale University Press. Reprinted by permission.*)

had predicted. Instead, economic specialization enabled society to produce more effectively and in the process created more new social groups than it destroyed. There developed an almost unlimited range of jobs, skills, and earnings; one group or subclass shaded off into another in a complex, confusing hierarchy. Thus the tiny elite of the very rich and the sizable mass of the dreadfully poor were separated from each other by a range of subclasses, each filled with individuals struggling to rise or at least to hold their own in the social order. In this atmosphere of competition and hierarchy, neither the middle classes nor the working classes acted as a unified force. This social and occupational hierarchy developed enormous variations, but the age-old pattern of great economic inequality remained firmly intact.

The Middle Classes

By the beginning of the twentieth century, the diversity and range within the urban middle class were striking. Indeed, it is more meaningful to think of a confederation of middle classes loosely united by occupations requiring mental, rather than physical, skill.

At the top stood the upper middle class, composed mainly of the most successful business families from banking, industry, and large-scale commerce. As people in the upper middle class gained in income and progressively lost all traces of radicalism after the trauma of 1848, they were almost irresistibly drawn toward the aristocratic lifestyle. And although the genuine hereditary aristocracy constituted only a tiny minority in every European country, it retained imposing wealth, unrivaled social prestige, and substantial political influence. This was especially true in central and eastern Europe, where the monarch—the highest-ranking noble of them all—continued to hold great political power.

As the aristocracy had long divided the year between palatial country estates and lavish townhouses during "the season," so the upper middle class purchased country places or built beach houses for weekend and summer use. The number of servants was an important indicator of wealth and standing for the middle class, as it had always been for the aristocracy. Private coaches and carriages, ever-expensive items in the city, were also signs of rising social status.

The topmost reaches of the upper middle class tended to shade off into the old aristocracy to form a new upper class of at most 5 percent of the population. Much of the aristocracy welcomed this development. Having experienced a sharp decline in its relative income in the course of industrialization, the landed aristocracy had met big business coming up the staircase and was often delighted to trade titles, country homes, and snobbish elegance for good hard cash. Some of the best bargains were made through marriages to American heiresses. Correspondingly, wealthy aristocrats tended increasingly to exploit their agricultural and mineral resources as if they were business people. Bismarck was not the only proud nobleman to make a fortune distilling brandy on his estates.

Below the wealthy upper middle class were much larger, much less wealthy, and increasingly diversified middle-class groups. Here one found the moderately successful industrialists and merchants as well as professionals in law and medicine. This was the middle middle class, solid and quite comfortable but lacking great wealth. Below it were independent shopkeepers, small traders, and tiny manufacturers—the lower middle class. Both of these traditional elements of the middle class expanded modestly in size with economic development.

Meanwhile, the traditional middle class was gaining two particularly important additions. The expansion of industry and technology created a growing demand for experts with specialized knowledge. The most valuable of the specialties became solid middle-class professions. Engineering, for example, emerged from the world of skilled labor as a full-fledged profession of great importance, considerable prestige, and many branches. Architects, chemists, accountants, and surveyors, to name only a few, first achieved professional standing in this period. They established criteria for advanced training and certification and banded together in organizations to promote and defend their interests.

Management of large public and private institutions also emerged as a kind of profession as governments provided more services and as very large corporations such as railroads came into being. Government officials and many private executives were not capitalists in the sense that they owned business enterprises. But public and private managers did have specialized knowledge and the capacity to earn a good living. And they shared most of the values of the business-owning entrepreneurs and the older professionals.

Industrialization also expanded and diversified the lower middle class. The number of independent, property-owning shopkeepers and small business people grew, and so did the number of white-collar employees—a mixed group of traveling salesmen, bookkeepers, store managers, and clerks who staffed the offices and branch stores of large corporations. White-collar employees were propertyless and often earned no more than the better-paid skilled or semiskilled workers did. Yet white-collar workers were fiercely committed to the middle class and to the ideal of moving up in society. In the Balkans, for example, clerks let their fingernails grow very long to distinguish themselves from people who worked with their hands. The tie, the suit, and soft, clean hands were no-less-subtle marks of class distinction than wages.

Relatively well educated but without complex technical skills, many white-collar groups aimed at achieving professional standing and the accompanying middle-class status. Elementary school teachers largely succeeded in this effort. From being miserably paid part-time workers

"The German Theater, Munich" This happy, vibrant poster advertisement calls the passerby to come and savor the treats of a popular music hall. Many music halls and vaudeville theaters attracted a mixed urban clientele, which included white-collar employees and better-paid workers. *(Barbara Singer/The Bridgeman Art Library International Ltd)*

in the early nineteenth century, teachers rode the wave of mass education to respectable middle-class status and income. Nurses also rose from the lower ranks of unskilled labor to precarious middle-class standing. Dentistry was taken out of the hands of working-class barbers and placed in the hands of highly trained (and middle-class) professionals.

Middle-Class Culture

In spite of growing occupational diversity and conflicting interests, the middle classes were loosely united by a certain style of life and culture. Food was the largest item in the household budget, for middle-class people liked to eat very well. The European middle classes consumed meat in

abundance, and a well-off family might spend 10 percent of its substantial earnings on meat and fully 25 percent of its income on food and drink. Spending on food was also great because the dinner party was this class's favored social occasion. A wealthy family might give a lavish party for eight to twelve almost every week, whereas more modest households would settle for once a month.

The middle-class wife could cope with this endless procession of meals, courses, and dishes because she had both servants and money at her disposal. Indeed, the employment of at least one enormously helpful full-time maid to cook and clean was the best single sign that a family had crossed the cultural divide separating the working classes from what some contemporary observers called the "servant-keeping classes." The greater a family's income, the greater the number of servants it employed. Food and servants together absorbed about 50 percent of income at all levels of the middle class.

Well fed and well served, the middle classes were also well housed by 1900. Many quite prosperous families rented, rather than owned, their homes. Apartment living, complete with tiny rooms for servants under the eaves of the top floor, was commonplace, and wealthy investors and speculative builders found good profits in middle-class housing. By 1900 the middle classes were also quite clothes-conscious. The factory, the sewing machine, and the department store had all helped reduce the cost and expand the variety of clothing. Middle-class women were particularly attentive to the fickle dictates of fashion. (See the feature "Images in Society: Class and Gender Boundaries in Women's Fashion, 1850–1914" on pages 800–801.)

Education was another growing expense, as middle-class parents tried to provide their children with ever more crucial advanced education. The keystones of culture and leisure were books, music, and travel. The long realistic novel, the heroics of composers Wagner and Verdi, the diligent striving of the dutiful daughter at the piano, and the packaged tour to a foreign country were all sources of middle-class pleasure.

Finally, the middle classes were loosely united by a shared code of expected behavior and morality. This code was strict and demanding. It laid great stress on hard work, self-discipline, and personal achievement. Men and women who fell into crime or poverty were generally assumed to be responsible for their own circumstances. Traditional Christian morality was reaffirmed by this code and was preached tirelessly by middle-class people. Drunkenness and gambling were denounced as vices; sexual purity and fidelity were celebrated as virtues. In short, the middle-class person was supposed to know right from wrong and was expected to act accordingly.

The Working Classes

About four out of five people belonged to the working classes at the turn of the century. Many members of the working classes—that is, people whose livelihoods depended on physical labor and who did not employ domestic servants—were still small landowning peasants and hired farm hands. This was especially true in eastern Europe. In western and central Europe, however, the typical worker had left the land. In Great Britain, less than 8 percent of the people worked in agriculture, and in rapidly industrializing Germany only 25 percent were employed in agriculture and forestry. Even in less industrialized France, less than 50 percent of the people depended on the land in 1900.

The urban working classes were even less unified and homogeneous than the middle classes. In the first place, economic development and increased specialization expanded the traditional range of working-class skills, earnings, and experiences. Meanwhile, the old sharp distinction between highly skilled artisans and unskilled manual workers gradually broke down. To be sure, highly skilled printers and masons as well as unskilled dockworkers and common laborers continued to exist. But between these extremes there appeared ever more semiskilled groups, many of which were composed of factory workers and machine tenders (see Figure 24.3).

In the second place, skilled, semiskilled, and unskilled workers developed widely divergent lifestyles and cultural values, and their differences contributed to a keen sense of social status and hierarchy within the working classes. The result was great variety and limited class unity.

Highly skilled workers, who made up about 15 percent of the working classes, became a real **labor aristocracy.** These workers earned only about two-thirds of the income of the bottom ranks of the servant-keeping classes, but that was fully twice as much as the earnings of unskilled workers. The most "aristocratic" of the highly skilled workers were construction bosses and factory foremen, men who had risen from the ranks and were fiercely proud of their achievement. The labor aristocracy also included members of the traditional highly skilled handicraft trades that had not been mechanized or placed in factories, like cabinetmakers, jewelers, and printers.

This group as a whole was under constant long-term pressure. Irregularly but inexorably, factory methods were being extended to more crafts, and many skilled artisans were being replaced by lower-paid semiskilled factory workers. Traditional woodcarvers and watchmakers virtually disappeared, for example, as the making of furniture and timepieces now took place in the factory. At the same time, the labor aristocracy was consistently being enlarged by new kinds of skilled workers such as shipbuilders and railway locomotive engineers. Thus the labor elite remained in a state of flux as individuals and whole crafts moved in and out of it.

To maintain this precarious standing, the upper working class adopted distinctive values and strait-laced, almost puritanical behavior. Like the middle classes, the labor aristocracy was strongly committed to the family and to economic improvement. Families in the upper working class saved money regularly, worried about their children's education, and valued good housing. Despite these similarities, skilled workers viewed themselves not as aspirants to the middle class but as the pacesetters and natural leaders of all the working classes. Well aware of the degradation not so far below them, they practiced self-discipline and stern morality.

The upper working class in general frowned on heavy drinking and sexual permissiveness. An organized temperance movement was strong in the countries of northern Europe. As one German labor aristocrat somberly warned, "The path to the brothel leads through the tavern" and from there quite possibly to drastic decline or total ruin for person and family.[6] Men and women of the labor aristocracy were also quick to find fault with those below them who failed to meet their standards. Finally, many members of the labor

---

FIGURE 24.3 The Urban Social Hierarchy

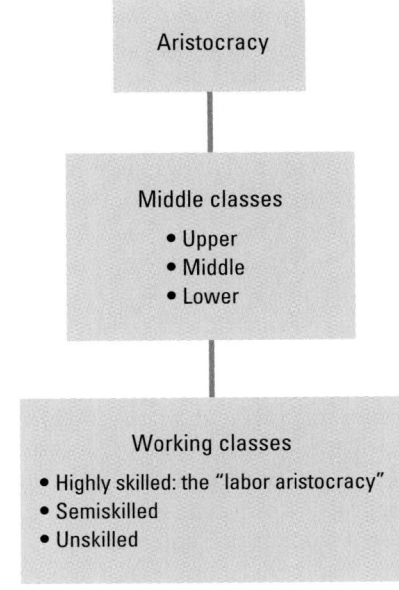

Class and Gender Boundaries in Women's Fashion, 1850–1914

Women's fashion was big business in the nineteenth century. Long the dominant industrial pursuit in human history, the production of textiles took off with the Industrial Revolution. In the later nineteenth century fashionable clothing, especially for middle-class women, became the first modern consumer industry as careful buyers snapped up the constantly changing ready-to-wear goods sold by large department stores.

In the nineteenth century, before society fragmented into many different groups expressing themselves in many dress styles, clothing patterns focused mainly on perceived differences in class and gender. The four illustrations presented here allow one to analyze the social information communicated through women's clothing. As you study these illustrations, note the principal characteristics and then try to draw out the larger implications. What does the impractical, restrictive clothing in these images reveal about society's view of women during this period? What is the significance of the emergence of alternative styles of well-groomed dress?

Most changes in women's fashion originated in Paris in the nineteenth century. Image 1 shows the attire worn by French aristocratic and wealthy middle-class women in the 1850s and 1860s. Note that these expensive dresses, flawlessly tailored by an army of skilled seamstresses, abound in elaborate embroidery, rich velvety materials, and fancy accessories. The circular spread of these floor-sweeping gowns is due to the crinoline, a slip with metal hoops that holds the skirt out on all sides. These women also are wearing the corset, the century's most characteristic women's undergarment, which was laced up tightly in back and pressed unmercifully from the breasts to the hips. What does this image tell you about the life of these women (their work, leisure activities, and so on)?

The intriguing 1875 painting by Atkinson Grimshaw, *Summer* (Image 2), shows a middle-class interior and the evolution of women's summer fashion two decades later. The corset still binds, but crinoline hoops have given way to the bustle, a cotton fan with steel reinforcement that pushes the dress out in back and exaggerates gender differences. The elaborate costume of the wealthy elite, available in cheaper ready-to-wear versions sold through department stores and mail-order catalogues throughout Europe, had become the standard for middle-class women. Emulating the elite in style, conventional middle-class women shopped carefully, scouting for sales, and drew a boundary separating themselves from working-class women in their simple cotton clothes. What implications, if any, do you see this having on class distinctions?

The young middle-class Englishwoman in an 1893 photo (Image 3) has chosen a woman's tailored suit, the only major English innovation in nineteenth-century women's fashion. This "alternative dress" combines the tie, suit jacket, vest, and straw hat—all initially items of male attire—with typical feminine elements,

Image 1 Crinoline Dresses, Paris, 1859. (*The Illustrated London News Picture Library*)

Image 2 Summer Dress with Bustle, England, 1875. *(Roy Miles, Esq./The Bridgeman Art Library International Ltd)*

Image 3 Alternative Fashion, England, 1893. *(Manchester City Art Galleries)*

Image 4 Loose-fitting Dress, France, 1910. *(© Corbis)*

such as the skirt and gloves. This practical, socially accepted alternative dress appealed to the growing number of women in paid employment in the 1890s. The historian Diana Crane has argued that this departure from the dominant style can be seen as a symbolic, nonverbal assertion of independence and equality with men.* Do you agree with this? If so, what was the significance of the pre-1914 turn from stifling corset to the more flexible brassiere and the mainstream embrace of loose-fitting garments, such as the 1910 dress in Image 4? Did the greater freedom of movement in clothing reflect the emerging emancipation of Western women? Or was the coquettish femininity of these loose, flowing dresses only a repackaging of the dominant culture's sharply defined gender boundaries?

*Diana Crane, *Fashion and Its Social Agendas: Class, Gender, and Identity in Clothing* (Chicago: University of Chicago Press, 2000), pp. 99–114.

The Labor Aristocracy   This group of British foremen is attending the International Exhibition in Paris in 1862. Their "Sunday best" includes the silk top hats and long morning coats of the propertied classes, but they definitely remain workers, the proud leaders of laboring people. *(© The Board of Trustees of the Victoria & Albert Museum)*

aristocracy had definite political and philosophical beliefs, which further strengthened their firm moral code.

Below the labor aristocracy stood semiskilled and unskilled urban workers. The enormous complexity of this sector of the world of labor is not easily summarized. Workers in the established crafts—carpenters, bricklayers, pipe fitters—stood near the top of the semiskilled hierarchy, often flirting with (or sliding back from) the labor elite. A large number of the semiskilled were factory workers who earned highly variable but relatively good wages and whose relative importance in the labor force was increasing.

Below the semiskilled workers was a larger group of unskilled workers that included day laborers such as longshoremen, wagon-driving teamsters, teenagers, and every kind of "helper." Many of these people had real skills and performed valuable services, but they were unorganized and divided, united only by the common fate of meager earnings. The same lack of unity characterized street vendors and market people—self-employed workers who

competed savagely with each other and with the established shopkeepers of the lower middle class.

One of the largest components of the unskilled group was domestic servants, whose numbers grew steadily in the nineteenth century. In advanced Great Britain, for example, one out of every seven employed persons was a domestic servant in 1911. The great majority were women; indeed, one out of every three girls in Britain between the ages of fifteen and twenty was a domestic servant. Throughout Europe and America, a great many female domestics in the cities were recent migrants from rural areas. As in earlier times, domestic service was still hard work at low pay with limited personal independence and the danger of sexual exploitation. For the full-time general maid in a lower-middle-class family, there was an unending routine of baby-sitting, shopping, cooking, and cleaning. In the great households, the girl was at the bottom of a rigid hierarchy of status-conscious butlers and housekeepers.

A School for Servants   Although domestic service was poorly paid, there was always plenty of competition for the available jobs. Schools sprang up to teach young women the manners and the household skills that employers in the "servant-keeping classes" demanded. *(Greater London Council Photograph Library)*

Nonetheless, domestic service had real attractions for "rough country girls" with strong hands and few specialized skills. Marriage prospects were better, or at least more varied, in the city. And though wages were low, they were higher and more regular than in hard agricultural work. Finally, as one London observer noted, young girls and other migrants were drawn to the city by

the contagion of numbers, the sense of something going on, the theaters and the music halls, the brightly lighted streets and busy crowds—all, in short, that makes the difference between the Mile End fair on a Saturday night, and a dark and muddy country lane, with no glimmer of gas and with nothing to do.[7]

Many young domestics from the countryside made a successful transition to working-class wife and mother. Yet with an unskilled or unemployed husband and a growing family, such a woman often had to join the broad ranks of workingwomen in the "sweated industries." These industries flowered after 1850 and resembled the old putting-out and cottage industries of earlier times. The women normally worked at home, paid by the piece and not by the hour. They and their young daughters, for whom organization and collective action were virtually impossible, earned pitiful wages and lacked any job security.

Some women did hand-decorating of every conceivable kind of object; the majority, however, made clothing, especially after the advent of the sewing machine. By 1900 only a few such tailors lingered on in high-priced "tailor-made" shops. An army of poor women accounted for the bulk of the inexpensive "ready-made" clothes displayed on department store racks and in tiny shops.

Working-Class Leisure and Religion

Notwithstanding the rise and fall of groups and individuals, the urban working classes sought fun and recreation, and they found both. Across the face of Europe, drinking remained unquestionably the favorite leisure-time activity of working people. For many middle-class moralists as well as moralizing historians since, love of drink has been a curse of the modern age—a sign of social dislocation and popular suffering. Certainly, drinking was deadly serious business. One English slum dweller recalled that "drunkenness was by far the commonest cause of dispute and misery in working class homes. On account of it one saw many a decent family drift down through poverty into total want."[8]

Generally, however, heavy "problem" drinking declined in the late nineteenth century as it became less and less socially acceptable. This decline reflected in part the moral leadership of the upper working class. At the same time, drinking became more public and social. Cafés and pubs became increasingly bright, friendly places. Working-class political activities, both moderate and radical, were also concentrated in taverns and pubs. Moreover, social drinking in public places by married couples and sweethearts became an accepted and widespread practice for the first time. This greater participation by women undoubtedly helped civilize the world of drink and hard liquor.

The two other leisure-time passions of the working classes were sports and music halls. A great decline in "cruel sports," such as bullbaiting and cockfighting, had occurred throughout Europe by the late nineteenth century. Their place was filled by modern spectator sports, of which racing and soccer were the most popular. There was a great deal of gambling on sports events, and for many a working person a desire to decipher racing forms provided a powerful incentive toward literacy. Music halls and vaudeville theaters, the working-class counterparts of middle-class opera and classical theater, were enormously popular throughout Europe. In 1900 there were more than fifty such halls and theaters in London alone. Music hall audiences were thoroughly mixed, which may account for the fact that drunkenness, sexual intercourse and pregnancy before marriage, marital difficulties, and problems with mothers-in-law were favorite themes of broad jokes and bittersweet songs.

In more serious moments, religion and Christian churches continued to provide working people with solace and meaning. The eighteenth-century vitality of popular religion in Catholic countries and the Protestant rejuvenation exemplified by German Pietism and English Methodism (see pages 681–682) carried over into the nineteenth century. Indeed, many historians see the early nineteenth century as an age of religious revival. Yet historians also recognize that by the last two or three decades of the nineteenth century, a considerable decline in both church attendance and church donations was occurring in most European countries. And it seems clear that this decline was greater for the urban working classes than for their rural counterparts or for the middle classes.

What did the decline in working-class church attendance really mean? Some have argued that it accurately reflected a general decline in faith and religious belief. Others disagree, noting correctly that most working-class families still baptized their children and considered themselves Christians. Although more research is necessary, it appears that the urban working classes in Europe did become more secular and less religious in the late nineteenth and early twentieth centuries. They rarely repudiated the Christian religion, but it tended to play a diminishing role in their daily lives.

Part of the reason for this change was that the construction of churches failed to keep up with the rapid growth of urban population, especially in new working-class neighborhoods. Thus the vibrant, materialistic urban environment undermined popular religious impulses, which were poorly served in the cities. Equally important, however, was the fact that throughout the nineteenth century both Catholic and Protestant churches were normally seen as they saw themselves—as conservative institutions defending social order and custom. Therefore, as the European working classes became more politically conscious, they tended to see the established (or quasi-established) "territorial church" as defending what they wished to change and as allied with their political opponents. Especially the men of the urban working classes developed vaguely antichurch attitudes, even though they remained neutral or positive toward religion. They tended to regard regular church attendance as "not our kind of thing"—not part of urban working-class culture.

The pattern was different in the United States. There, most churches also preached social conservatism in the nineteenth century. But because church and state had always been separate and because there was always a host of competing denominations and even different religions, working people identified churches much less with the political and social status quo. Instead, individual churches in the United States were often closely identified with an ethnic group rather than with a social class, and churches thrived, in part, as a means of asserting ethnic identity. This same process did occur in Europe if the church or synagogue had never been linked to the state and served as a focus for ethnic cohesion. Irish Catholic churches in Protestant Britain and Jewish synagogues in Russia were outstanding examples.

The Changing Family

Urban life wrought many fundamental changes in the family. Although much is still unknown, it seems clear that in the second half of the nineteenth century the family had stabilized considerably after the disruption of the late eighteenth and early nineteenth centuries. The home became more important for both men and women. The role of women and attitudes toward children underwent substantial change, and adolescence emerged as a distinct stage of life. These are but a few of the transformations that affected all social classes in varying degrees.

Premarital Sex and Marriage

By 1850 the preindustrial pattern of lengthy courtship and mercenary marriage was pretty well dead among the working classes. In its place, the ideal of romantic love had triumphed. Couples were ever more likely to come from different, even distant, towns and to be more nearly the same age, further indicating that romantic sentiment was replacing tradition and financial considerations.

Economic considerations in marriage remained more important to the middle classes than to the working classes after 1850. In France dowries and elaborate legal marriage contracts were common practice among the middle classes in the later nineteenth century, and marriage was for many families one of life's most crucial financial transactions. A popular author advised young Frenchmen that "marriage is in general a means of increasing one's credit and one's fortune and of insuring one's success in the world."[9] This preoccupation with money led many middle-class men in France and elsewhere to marry late, after they had been established economically, and to choose women considerably younger than themselves. These differences between husband and wife became a source of tension in many middle-class marriages.

A young woman of the middle class found her romantic life carefully supervised by her well-meaning mother, who schemed for a proper marriage and guarded her daughter's virginity like the family's credit. (See the feature "Listening to the Past: Middle-Class Youth and Sexuality" on pages 820–821.) After marriage, middle-class morality sternly demanded fidelity.

Middle-class boys were watched, too, but not as vigilantly. By the time they reached late adolescence, they had usually attained considerable sexual experience with maids or prostitutes.

In the early nineteenth century, sexual experimentation before marriage also triumphed, as did illegitimacy. There was an **illegitimacy explosion** between 1750 and 1850 (see page 665). By the 1840s, as many as one birth in three was occurring outside of wedlock in many large cities. Although poverty and economic uncertainty undoubtedly prevented many lovers from marrying, there were also many among the poor and propertyless who saw little wrong with having illegitimate offspring. One young Bavarian woman answered happily when asked why she kept having illegitimate children, "It's O.K. to make babies. . . . The king has o.k.'d it!"[10] Thus the pattern of romantic ideals, premarital sexual activity, and widespread illegitimacy was firmly established by midcentury among the urban working classes.

It is hard to know how European couples managed sex, pregnancy, and marriage after 1850 because such questions were considered improper both in polite conversation and in public opinion polls. Yet there are many telltale clues. In the second half of the century, the rising rate of illegitimacy was reversed: more babies were born to married mothers. Some observers have argued that this shift reflected the growth of puritanism and a lessening of sexual permissiveness among the unmarried. This explanation, however, is unconvincing.

The percentage of brides who were pregnant continued to be high and showed little or no tendency to decline after 1850. In many parts of urban Europe around 1900, as many as one woman in three was going to the altar an expectant mother. Moreover, unmarried people almost certainly used the cheap condoms and diaphragms the industrial age had made available to prevent pregnancy, at least in predominately Protestant countries.

Thus unmarried young people were probably engaging in just as much sexual activity as their parents and grandparents who had created the illegitimacy explosion of 1750 to 1850. But in the later nineteenth century, pregnancy for a young single woman led increasingly to marriage and the establishment of a two-parent household. This important development reflected the growing respectability of the working classes as well as their gradual economic improvement. Skipping out was less acceptable, and marriage was less of an economic challenge. Thus the urban working-class couple became more stable, and that stability strengthened the family as an institution.

Prostitution

In Paris alone, 155,000 women were registered as prostitutes between 1871 and 1903, and 750,000 others were suspected of prostitution in the same years. Men of all classes visited prostitutes, but the middle and upper classes supplied much of the motivating cash. Thus, though many middle-class men abided by the publicly professed code of stern puritanical morality, others indulged their appetites for prostitutes and sexual promiscuity.

My Secret Life, the anonymous eleven-volume autobiography of an English sexual adventurer from the servant-keeping classes, provides a remarkable picture of such a man. Beginning at an early age with a maid, the author becomes progressively obsessed with sex and devotes his life to living his sexual fantasies. In almost every one of his innumerable encounters all across Europe, this man of wealth simply buys his pleasure. Usually meetings are arranged in a businesslike manner: regular and part-time prostitutes quote their prices; working-class girls are corrupted by hot meals and baths.

At one point, he offers a young girl a sixpence for a kiss and gets it. Learning that the pretty, unskilled working girl earns nine pence a day, he offers her the equivalent of a week's salary for a few moments of fondling. When she finally agrees, he savagely exults that "*her* want was my opportunity." Later he offers more money for more gratification, and when she refuses, he tries unsuccessfully to rape her in a hackney cab. On another occasion he takes a farm worker by force.[11]

Obviously atypical in its excesses, *My Secret Life* does reveal the dark side of sex and class in urban society. Frequently thinking of their wives largely in terms of money, family, and social position, the men of the comfortable classes often purchased sex and even affection from poor girls both before and after marriage. Moreover, the great continuing differences between rich and poor made for every kind of debauchery and sexual exploitation. Brutal sexist behavior was part of life—a part the sternly moral women (and men) of the upper working class detested and tried to shield their daughters from. For many poor young women, prostitution, like domestic service, was a stage of life and not a permanent employment. Having done it for a while in their twenties, they went on to marry (or live with) men of their own class and establish homes and families.

Inside a Paris Brothel   In *The Reception Room in the Brothel on the Rue des Moulins,* a biting ironic painting by Henri de Toulouse-Lautrec (1864–1901), the aging madame maintains a prim and proper decorum while the women working for her lounge about on the couches. Wealthy nobleman by birth and tragically disabled by accident in childhood, Toulouse-Lautrec combined stupendous creativity and dedicated debauchery in his short life. His work focused on music halls, circuses, and the bizarre individuals who made Paris nightlife the scandal of Europe. *(The Bridgeman Art Library International Ltd)*

Kinship Ties

Within working-class homes, ties to relatives after marriage—kinship ties—were in general much stronger than many social observers have recognized. Most newlyweds tried to live near their parents, though not in the same house. Indeed, for many married couples in later-nineteenth-century cities, ties to mothers and fathers, uncles and aunts, were more important than ties to nonrelated acquaintances.

People turned to their families for help in coping with sickness, unemployment, death, and old age. Although governments were generally providing more welfare services by 1900, the average couple and its children inevitably faced crises. Funerals, for example, brought sudden demands, requiring a large outlay for special clothes, carriages, and burial services. Unexpected death or desertion could leave the bereaved or abandoned, especially widows and orphans, in need of financial aid or perhaps a foster home. Relatives responded hastily to such cries, knowing full well that their own time of need and repayment would undoubtedly come.

Relatives were also valuable at less tragic moments. If a couple was very poor, an aged relation often moved in to cook and mind the children so that the wife could earn badly needed income outside the home. Sunday dinners were often shared, as were outgrown clothing and useful information. Often the members of a large family group all lived in the same neighborhood.

Gender Roles and Family Life

Industrialization and the growth of modern cities brought great changes to the lives of European women. These changes were particularly consequential for married women, and most women did marry in the nineteenth century.

After 1850 the work of most wives became increasingly distinct and separate from that of their husbands. Husbands became wage earners in factories and offices, while wives tended to stay home and manage households and care for children. The preindustrial pattern among both peasants and cottage workers, in which husbands and wives worked together and divided up household duties and child rearing, declined. Only in a few occupations, such as retail trade, did married couples live where they worked and struggle together to make their mom-and-pop operations a success. Factory employment for married women also declined as the early practice of hiring entire families in the factory disappeared.

As economic conditions improved, most men expected married women to work outside the home only in poor families. One old English worker recalled that "the boy wanted to get into a position that would enable him to keep a wife and family, as it was considered a thoroughly unsatisfactory state of affairs if the wife had to work to help maintain the home."[12] The ideal became a strict division of labor by gender and rigidly constructed **separate spheres**: the wife as mother and homemaker, the husband as wage earner.

This rigid gender division of labor meant that married women faced great injustice when they needed—or wanted—to move into the man's world of employment outside the home. Husbands were unsympathetic or hostile. Well-paying jobs were off-limits to women, and a woman's wage was almost always less than a man's, even for the same work.

Moreover, married women were subordinated to their husbands by law and lacked many basic legal rights. In England the situation in the early nineteenth century was summed up in a famous line from jurist William Blackstone: "In law husband and wife are one person, and the husband is that person." Thus a wife in England had no legal identity and hence no right to own property in her own name. Even the wages she might earn belonged to her husband. In France the Napoleonic Code (see pages 712–714) also enshrined the principle of female subordination and gave the wife few legal rights regarding property, divorce, and custody of the children. Legal inferiority for women permeated Western society.

With all women facing discrimination in education and employment and with middle-class women suffering especially from a lack of legal rights, there is little wonder that some women rebelled and began the long-continuing fight for equality of the sexes and the rights of women. Their struggle proceeded on two main fronts. First, following in the steps of women such as Mary Wollstonecraft (see page 705), organizations founded by middle-class feminists campaigned for equal legal rights for women as well as access to higher education and professional employment. These middle-class feminists argued that unmarried women and middle-class widows with inadequate incomes simply had to have more opportunities to support themselves. Middle-class feminists also recognized that paid (as opposed to unpaid) work could relieve the monotony that some women found in their sheltered middle-class existence and put greater meaning into their lives.

In the later nineteenth century, these organizations scored some significant victories, such as the 1882 law giving English married women full property rights. More women found professional and white-collar employment, especially after about 1880. But progress was slow and hard won. For example, in Germany before

1900, women were not admitted as fully registered students at a single university, and it was virtually impossible for a woman to receive certification and practice as a lawyer or doctor. (See the feature "Individuals in Society: Franziska Tiburtius.") In the years before 1914, middle-class feminists increasingly focused their attention on political action and fought for the right to vote for women.

Women inspired by utopian and especially Marxian socialism blazed a second path. Often scorning the programs of middle-class feminists, socialist women leaders argued that the liberation of working-class women would come only with the liberation of the entire working class through revolution. In the meantime, they championed the cause of workingwomen and won some practical improvements, especially in Germany, where the socialist movement was most effectively organized. In a general way, these different approaches to women's issues reflected the diversity of classes in urban society.

If the ideology and practice of rigidly separate spheres undoubtedly narrowed women's horizons and caused some women to rebel, there was a brighter side to the same coin. As home and children became the typical wife's main concerns in the late nineteenth century, her control and influence there apparently became increasingly strong throughout Europe. Among the English working classes, it was the wife who generally determined how the family's money was spent. In many families, the husband gave all his earnings to his wife to manage, whatever the law might read. She returned to him only a small allowance for carfare, beer, tobacco, and union dues. All the major domestic decisions, from the children's schooling and religious instruction to the selection of new furniture or a new apartment, were hers. In France women had even greater power in their assigned domain. One English feminist noted in 1908 that "though legally women occupy a much inferior status than men [in France], in practice they constitute the superior sex. They are the power behind the throne."[13]

Women ruled at home partly because running the urban household was a complicated, demanding, and valuable task. Twice-a-day food shopping, penny-pinching, economizing, and the growing crusade against dirt—not to mention child rearing—were a full-time occupation. Nor were there any laborsaving appliances to help, and even when servants were present, they had to be carefully watched and supervised. Working yet another job for wages outside the home had limited appeal for most married women unless such earnings were essential for family survival. Many married women in the working classes did make a monetary contribution to family income by taking in boarders or doing piecework at home in the sweated industries (see page 803).

The wife also guided the home because a good deal of her effort was directed toward pampering her husband as he expected. In countless humble households, she saw that he had meat while she ate bread, that he relaxed by the fire while she did the dishes.

The woman's guidance of the household went hand in hand with the increased emotional importance of home and family. The home she ran was idealized as a warm shelter in a hard and impersonal urban world. For a child of the English slums in the early 1900s,

home, however poor, was the focus of all love and interests, a sure fortress against a hostile world. Songs about its beauties were ever on people's lips. "Home, sweet home," first heard in the 1870s, had become "almost a second national anthem." Few walls in lower-working-class houses lacked "mottoes"—colored strips of paper, about nine inches wide and eighteen inches in length, attesting to domestic joys: EAST, WEST, HOME'S BEST; BLESS OUR HOME; GOD IS MASTER OF THIS HOUSE; HOME IS THE NEST WHERE ALL IS BEST.[14]

By 1900 home and family were what life was all about for millions of people of all classes.

Married couples also developed stronger emotional ties to each other. Even in the comfortable classes, marriages in the late nineteenth century were based more on sentiment and sexual attraction than they had been earlier in the century, as money and financial calculation declined in importance. Affection and eroticism became more central to the couple after marriage. Gustave Droz, whose bestseller *Mr., Mrs., and Baby* went through 121 editions between 1866 and 1884, saw love within marriage as the key to human happiness. He condemned men who made marriage sound dull and practical, men who were exhausted by prostitutes and rheumatism and who wanted their young wives to be little angels. He urged women to follow their hearts and marry a man more nearly their own age:

A husband who is stately and a little bald is all right, but a young husband who loves you and who drinks out of your glass without ceremony, is better. Let him, if he ruffles your dress a little and places a kiss on your neck as he passes. Let him, if he undresses you after the ball, laughing like a fool. You have fine spiritual qualities, it is true, but your little body is not bad either and when one loves, one loves completely. Behind these follies lies happiness.[15]

Many French marriage manuals of the late 1800s stressed that women had legitimate sexual needs, such as

Individuals in Society

Franziska Tiburtius

Franziska Tiburtius, pioneering woman physician in Berlin. (Ullstein Bilderdienst)

Why did a small number of women in the late nineteenth century brave great odds and embark on a professional career? And how did a few of those manage to reach their objectives? The career and personal reflections of Franziska Tiburtius, a pioneer in German medicine, suggests that talent, determination, and economic necessity were critical ingredients.*

Like many women of her time who would study and pursue a professional career, Franziska Tiburtius (1843–1927) was born into a property-owning family of modest means. The youngest of nine children on a small estate in northeastern Germany, the sensitive child wilted with a harsh governess but flowered with a caring teacher and became an excellent student.

Graduating at sixteen and needing to support herself, Tiburtius had few opportunities. A young woman from a "proper" background could work as a governess or a teacher without losing her respectability and spoiling her matrimonial prospects, but that was about it. She tried both avenues. Working for six years as a governess in a noble family and no doubt learning that poverty was often one's fate in this genteel profession, she then turned to teaching. Called home from her studies in Britain in 1871 to care for her brother, who had contracted typhus as a field doctor in the Franco-Prussian War, she found her calling. She decided to become a medical doctor.

Supported by her family, Tiburtius's decision was truly audacious. In all Europe, only the University of Zurich in republican Switzerland accepted female students. Moreover, if it became known that she had studied medicine and failed, she would never get a job as a teacher. No parent would entrust a daughter to an "emancipated" radical who had carved up dead bodies!

Although the male students at the university sometimes harassed the women with crude pranks, Tiburtius thrived. The revolution of the microscope and the discovery of microorganisms was rocking Zurich, and she was fascinated by her studies. She became close friends with a fellow female medical student from Germany, Emilie Lehmus, with whom she would form a lifelong partnership in medicine. She did her internship with families of cottage workers around Zurich and loved her work.

Graduating at age thirty-three in 1876, Tiburtius went to stay with her brother the doctor in Berlin.

Though well qualified to practice, she ran into pervasive discrimination. She was not even permitted to take the state medical exams and could practice only as an unregulated (and unprofessional) "natural healer." But after persistent fighting with the bureaucrats, she was able to display her diploma and practice as "Franziska Tiburtius, M.D. University of Zurich." She and Lehmus were in business.

Soon the two women realized their dream and opened a clinic, subsidized by a wealthy industrialist, for women factory workers. The clinic filled a great need and was soon treating many patients. A room with beds for extremely sick women was later expanded into a second clinic.

Tiburtius and Lehmus became famous. For fifteen years, they were the only women doctors in all Berlin. An inspiration for a new generation of women, they added the wealthy to their thriving practice. But Tiburtius's clinics always concentrated on the poor, providing them with subsidized and up-to-date treatment. Talented, determined, and working with her partner, Tiburtius experienced the joys of personal achievement and useful service, joys that women and men share in equal measure.

Questions for Analysis

1. How does Franziska Tiburtius's life reflect both the challenges and the changing roles of middle-class women in the later nineteenth century?
2. In what ways was Tiburtius's career related to improvements in health in urban society and to the expansion of the professions?

*This portrait draws on Conradine Lück, *Frauen: Neun Lebens-schicksale* (Reutlingen: Ensslin & Laiblin, n.d.), pp. 153–185.

the "right to orgasm." Perhaps the French were a bit more enlightened in these matters than other nationalities. But the rise of public socializing by couples in cafés and music halls as well as franker affection within the family suggests a more erotic, pleasurable intimate life for women throughout Western society. This, too, helped make the woman's role as mother and homemaker acceptable and even satisfying.

Child Rearing

One striking sign of deepening emotional ties within the family was the growing love and concern that mothers gave their tiny infants. Because so many babies died so early in life, mothers in preindustrial Western society often avoided making a strong emotional commitment to a newborn in order to shield themselves from recurrent heartbreak. Early emotional bonding and a willingness to make real sacrifices for the welfare of the infant were beginning to spread among the comfortable classes by the end of the eighteenth century, but the ordinary mother of modest means adopted new attitudes only as the nineteenth century progressed. The baby became more important, and women became better mothers.

Mothers increasingly breast-fed their infants, for example, rather than paying wet nurses to do so. Breast-feeding involved sacrifice—a temporary loss of freedom, if nothing else. Yet in an age when there was no good alternative to mother's milk, it saved lives. This surge of maternal feeling also gave rise to a wave of specialized books on child rearing and infant hygiene, such as Droz's phenomenally successful book. Droz urged fathers to get into the act and pitied those "who do not know how to roll around on the carpet, play at being a horse and a great wolf, and undress their baby."[16] Another sign, from France, of increased affection is that fewer illegitimate babies were abandoned as foundlings after about 1850. Moreover, the practice of swaddling disappeared completely. Instead, ordinary mothers allowed their babies freedom of movement and delighted in their spontaneity.

A Working-Class Home, 1875 Emotional ties within ordinary families grew stronger in the nineteenth century. Parents gave their children more love and better care. *(Illustrated London News Library)*

The loving care lavished on infants was matched by greater concern for older children and adolescents. They, too, were wrapped in the strong emotional ties of a more intimate and protective family. For one thing, European women began to limit the number of children they bore in order to care adequately for those they had. It was evident by the end of the nineteenth century that the birthrate was declining across Europe, as Figure 24.4 shows, and it continued to do so until after World War II. The Englishwoman who married in the 1860s, for example, had an average of about six children; her daughter marrying in the 1890s had only four; and her granddaughter marrying in the 1920s had only two or possibly three.

The most important reason for this revolutionary reduction in family size, in which the comfortable and well-educated classes took the lead, was parents' desire to improve their economic and social position and that of their children. Children were no longer an economic asset in the later nineteenth century. By having fewer youngsters, parents could give those they had valuable advantages, from music lessons and summer vacations to long, expensive university educations and suitable dowries. A young German skilled worker with only one child spoke for many in his class when he said, "We want to get ahead, and our daughter should have things better than my wife and sisters did."[17] Thus the growing tendency of couples in the late nineteenth century to use a variety of contraceptive methods—rhythm method, withdrawal method, and mechanical devices—certainly reflected increased concern for children.

Indeed, many parents, especially in the middle classes, probably became *too* concerned about their children, unwittingly subjecting them to an emotional pressure cooker of almost unbearable intensity. The result was that many children and especially adolescents came to feel trapped and in need of greater independence.

Prevailing biological and medical theories led parents to believe in the possibility that their own emotional characteristics were passed on to their offspring and that they were thus directly responsible for any abnormality in a child. The moment the child was conceived was thought to be of enormous importance. "Never run the risk of conception when you are sick or over-tired or unhappy," wrote one influential American woman. "For the bodily condition of the child, its vigor and magnetic qualities, are much affected by conditions ruling this great moment."[18] So might the youthful "sexual excess" of the father curse future generations. Although this was true in the case of syphilis, which could be transmitted to unborn children, the rigid determinism of such views left little scope for the child's individual development.

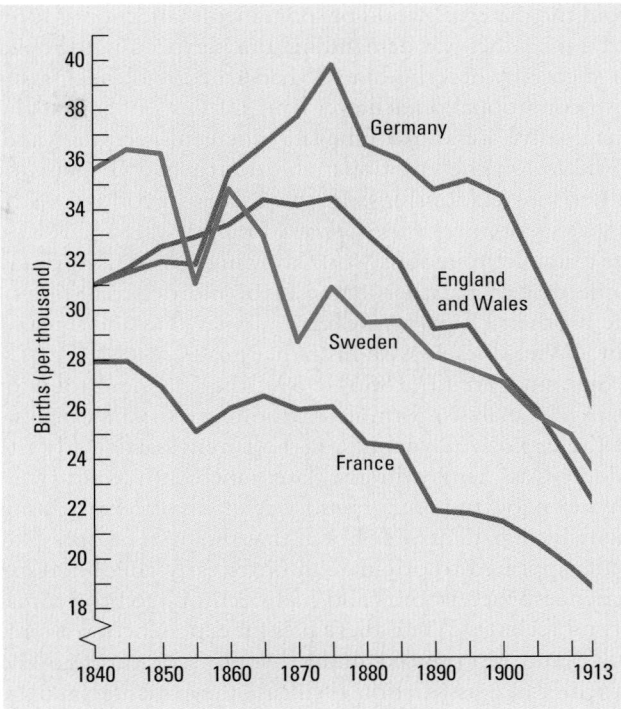

FIGURE 24.4 The Decline of Birthrates in England and Wales, France, Germany, and Sweden, 1840–1913 Women had fewer babies for a variety of reasons, including the fact that their children were increasingly less likely to die before reaching adulthood. Compare with Figure 24.1 on page 791.

Another area of excessive parental concern was the sexual behavior of the child. Masturbation was viewed with horror, for it represented an act of independence and even defiance. Diet, clothing, games, and sleeping were carefully regulated. Girls were discouraged from riding horses and bicycling because rhythmic friction simulated masturbation. Boys were dressed in trousers with shallow and widely separated pockets. Between 1850 and 1880, there were surgical operations for children who persisted in masturbating. Thereafter until about 1905, various restraining apparatuses were more often used.

These and less blatant attempts to repress the child's sexuality were a source of unhealthy tension, often made worse by the rigid division of gender roles within the family. It was widely believed that mother and child loved each other easily but that relations between father and child were necessarily difficult and often tragic. The father was a stranger; his world of business was far removed from the maternal world of spontaneous affection. More-over, the father was demanding, often expecting the child to succeed where he himself had failed and making his love conditional on achievement. Little wonder that the imaginative literature of the late nineteenth century came to deal with the emotional and destructive elements of father-son relationships. In the Russian Feodor Dosto-evski's great novel *The Brothers Karamazov* (1880–1881), for example, four sons work knowingly or unknowingly to destroy their father. Later at the murder trial, one of the brothers claims to speak for all mankind and screams out, "Who doesn't wish his father dead?"

Sigmund Freud (1856–1939), the Viennese founder of psychoanalysis, formulated the most striking analysis of the explosive dynamics of the family, particularly the middle-class family in the late nineteenth century. A physician by training, Freud began his career treating mentally ill patients. He noted that the hysteria of his pa-tients appeared to originate in bitter early-childhood ex-periences wherein the child had been obliged to repress strong feelings. When these painful experiences were re-called and reproduced under hypnosis or through the patient's free association of ideas, the patient could be brought to understand his or her unhappiness and even-tually deal with it.

One of Freud's most influential ideas concerned the Oedipal tensions resulting from the son's instinctive com-petition with the father for the mother's love and affection. More generally, Freud postulated that much of human be-havior is motivated by unconscious emotional needs whose nature and origins are kept from conscious awareness by various mental devices he called **defense mechanisms.** Freud concluded that much unconscious psychological energy is sexual energy, which is repressed and precariously controlled by rational thinking and moral rules. If Freud exaggerated the sexual and familial roots of adult be-havior, that exaggeration was itself a reflection of the tremendous emotional intensity of family life in the late nineteenth century.

The working classes probably had more avenues of escape from such tensions than did the middle classes. Unlike their middle-class counterparts, who remained economically dependent on their families until a long education was finished or a proper marriage secured, working-class boys and girls went to work when they reached adolescence. Earning wages on their own, they could bargain with their parents for greater independ-ence within the household by the time they were six-teen or seventeen. If they were unsuccessful, they could and did leave home to live cheaply as paying lodgers in other working-class homes. Thus the young person from the working classes broke away from the family more eas-ily when emotional ties became oppressive. In the twen-tieth century, middle-class youths would follow this lead.

Science and Thought

Major changes in Western science and thought accompa-nied the emergence of urban society. Two aspects of these complex intellectual developments stand out as especially significant. First, scientific knowledge expanded rapidly, influencing the Western world-view even more profoundly than ever before and spurring the creation of new prod-ucts and whole industries. Second, between about the 1840s and the 1890s, European literature underwent a shift from soaring romanticism to tough-minded realism.

The Triumph of Science

As the pace of scientific advance quickened and as theo-retical advances resulted in great practical benefits, science exercised growing influence on human thought. The in-tellectual achievements of the scientific revolution had resulted in few such benefits, and theoretical knowledge had also played a relatively small role in the Industrial Revolution in England. But breakthroughs in industrial technology enormously stimulated basic scientific inquiry, as researchers sought to explain theoretically how such things as steam engines and blast furnaces actually worked. The result was an explosive growth of fundamental scien-tific discoveries from the 1830s onward. And in contrast to earlier periods, these theoretical discoveries were in-creasingly transformed into material improvements for the general population.

A perfect example of the translation of better scientific knowledge into practical human benefits was the work of Louis Pasteur and his followers in biology and the med-ical sciences. Another was the development of the branch of physics known as **thermodynamics.** Building on Isaac Newton's laws of mechanics and on studies of steam en-gines, thermodynamics investigated the relationship between heat and mechanical energy. By midcentury, physicists had formulated the fundamental laws of ther-modynamics, which were then applied to mechanical en-gineering, chemical processes, and many other fields. The *law of conservation of energy* held that different forms of energy—such as heat, electricity, and magnetism—

could be converted but neither created nor destroyed. Nineteenth-century thermodynamics demonstrated that the physical world was governed by firm, unchanging laws.

Chemistry and electricity were two other fields characterized by extremely rapid scientific progress. And in both fields, "science was put in the service of industry," as the influential economist Alfred Marshall (1842–1924) argued at the time.

Chemists devised ways of measuring the atomic weight of different elements, and in 1869 the Russian chemist Dmitri Mendeleev (1834–1907) codified the rules of chemistry in the periodic law and the periodic table. Chemistry was subdivided into many specialized branches, such as **organic chemistry**—the study of the compounds of carbon. Applying theoretical insights gleaned from this new field, researchers in large German chemical companies discovered ways of transforming the dirty, useless coal tar that accumulated in coke ovens into beautiful, expensive synthetic dyes for the world of fashion. The basic discoveries of Michael Faraday (1791–1867) in electromagnetism in the 1830s and 1840s resulted in the first dynamo (generator) and opened the way for the subsequent development of the telegraph, electric motor, electric light, and electric streetcar.

The successful application of scientific research in the fast-growing electrical and organic chemical industries promoted solid economic growth between 1880 and 1913 and provided a model for other industries. Systematic "R & D"—research and development—was born in the late nineteenth century.

The triumph of science and technology had at least three more significant consequences. First, though ordinary citizens continued to lack detailed scientific knowledge, everyday experience and innumerable popularizers impressed the importance of science on the popular mind.

Second, as science became more prominent in popular thinking, the philosophical implications of science formulated in the Enlightenment spread to broad sections of the population. Natural processes appeared to be determined by rigid laws, leaving little room for either divine intervention or human will. Yet scientific and technical advances had also fed the Enlightenment's optimistic faith in human progress, which now appeared endless and automatic to many middle-class minds.

Third, the methods of science acquired unrivaled prestige after 1850. For many, the union of careful experiment and abstract theory was the only reliable route to truth and objective reality. The "unscientific" intuitions of poets and the revelations of saints seemed hopelessly inferior.

Social Science and Evolution

From the 1830s onward, many thinkers tried to apply the objective methods of science to the study of society. In some ways, these efforts simply perpetuated the critical thinking of the philosophes. Yet there were important differences. The new "social scientists" had access to the massive sets of numerical data that governments had begun to collect on everything from children to crime, from population to prostitution. In response, social scientists developed new statistical methods to analyze these facts "scientifically" and supposedly to test their theories. And the systems of the leading nineteenth-century social scientists were more unified, all-encompassing, and dogmatic than those of the philosophes. Marx was a prime example (see pages 765–766).

Another extremely influential system builder was French philosopher Auguste Comte (1798–1857). Initially a disciple of the utopian socialist Saint-Simon (see page 764), Comte wrote the six-volume *System of Positive Philosophy* (1830–1842), which was largely overlooked during the romantic era. But when the political failures of 1848 completed the swing to realism, Comte's philosophy came into its own. Its influence has remained great to this day.

Comte postulated that all intellectual activity progresses through predictable stages:

The great fundamental law . . . is this:—that each of our leading conceptions—each branch of our knowledge—passes successively through three different theoretical conditions: the Theological, or fictitious; the Metaphysical, or abstract; and the Scientific, or positive. . . . The first is the necessary point of departure of human understanding, and the third is the fixed and definitive state. The second is merely a transition.[19]

By way of example, Comte noted that the prevailing explanation of cosmic patterns had shifted, as knowledge of astronomy developed, from the will of God (the theological) to the will of an orderly nature (the metaphysical) to the rule of unchanging laws (the scientific). Later, this same intellectual progression took place in increasingly complex fields—physics, chemistry, and, finally, the study of society. Comte believed that by applying the scientific method, also called the **positivist method,** his new discipline of sociology would soon discover the eternal laws of human relations. This colossal achievement would in turn enable expert social scientists to impose a disciplined harmony and well-being on less enlightened citizens. Dismissing the "fictions" of traditional religions,

MR. BERGH TO THE RESCUE.

THE DEFRAUDED GORILLA. "That *Man* wants to claim my Pedigree. He says he is one of my Descendants."

Mr. BERGH. "Now, Mr. DARWIN, how could you insult him so?"

Satirizing Darwin's Ideas The heated controversies over Darwin's theory of evolution also spawned innumerable jokes and cartoons. This cartoon is by Darwin's contemporary, the American Thomas Nast. *(Culver Pictures)*

Comte became the chief priest of the religion of science and rule by experts.

Comte's stages of knowledge exemplify the nineteenth-century fascination with the idea of **evolution** and dynamic development. Thinkers in many fields, such as the romantic historians and "scientific" Marxists, shared and applied this basic concept. In geology, Charles Lyell (1797–1875) effectively discredited the long-standing view that the earth's surface had been formed by short-lived cataclysms, such as biblical floods and earthquakes. Instead, according to Lyell's principle of uniformitarianism, the same geological processes that are at work today slowly formed the earth's surface over an immensely long time. The evolutionary view of biological development,

first proposed by the Greek Anaximander in the sixth century B.C., re-emerged in a more modern form in the work of Jean Baptiste Lamarck (1744–1829). Lamarck asserted that all forms of life had arisen through a long process of continuous adjustment to the environment.

Lamarck's work was flawed—he believed that the characteristics parents acquired in the course of their lives could be inherited by their children—and was not accepted, but it helped prepare the way for Charles Darwin (1809–1882), the most influential of all nineteenth-century evolutionary thinkers. As the official naturalist on a five-year scientific cruise to Latin America and the South Pacific beginning in 1831, Darwin carefully collected specimens of the different animal species he encountered on the voyage. Back in England, convinced by fossil evidence and by his friend Lyell that the earth and life on it were immensely ancient, Darwin came to doubt the general belief in a special divine creation of each species of animal. Instead, he concluded, all life had gradually evolved from a common ancestral origin in an unending "struggle for survival." After long hesitation, Darwin published his research, which immediately attracted wide attention.

Darwin's great originality lay in suggesting precisely *how* biological evolution might have occurred. His theory is summarized in the title of his work *On the Origin of Species by the Means of Natural Selection* (1859). Decisively influenced by Thomas Malthus's gloomy theory that populations naturally grow faster than their food supplies (see page 734), Darwin argued that chance differences among the members of a given species help some survive while others die. Thus the variations that prove useful in the struggle for survival are selected naturally and gradually spread to the entire species through reproduction. Darwin did not explain why such variations occurred in the first place, and not until the early twentieth century did the study of genetics and the concept of mutation provide some answers.

As the capstone of already-widespread evolutionary thinking, Darwin's theory had a powerful and many-sided influence on European thought and the European middle classes. Darwin was hailed as the great scientist par excellence, the "Newton of biology," who had revealed once again the powers of objective science. Darwin's findings also reinforced the teachings of secularists such as Comte and Marx, who scornfully dismissed religious belief in favor of agnostic or atheistic materialism. In the great cities especially, religion was on the defensive. Finally, many writers applied the theory of biological evolution to human affairs. Herbert Spencer (1820–1903), an English disciple of Auguste Comte, saw the human race as driven forward to ever-greater specialization and progress by the brutal economic struggle. According to Spencer, this unending struggle efficiently determined the "survival of the fittest." The poor were the ill-fated weak; the prosperous were the chosen strong. Understandably, Spencer and other **Social Darwinists** were especially popular with the upper middle class.

Realism in Literature

In 1868 Emile Zola (1840–1902), the giant of the realist movement in literature, defended his violently criticized first novel against charges of pornography and corruption of morals. Such accusations were meaningless, Zola claimed: he was only a purely objective scientist using

the modern method, the universal instrument of inquiry of which this age makes such ardent use to open up the future. . . . I chose characters completely dominated by their nerves and their blood, deprived of free-will, pushed to each action of their lives by the fatality of their flesh. . . . I have simply done on living bodies the work of analysis which surgeons perform on corpses.[20]

Zola's literary manifesto articulated the key themes of **realism,** which had emerged in the 1840s and continued to dominate Western culture and style until the 1890s. Realist writers believed that literature should depict life exactly as it was. Forsaking poetry for prose and the personal, emotional viewpoint of the romantics for strict, scientific objectivity, the realists simply observed and recorded—content to let the facts speak for themselves.

The major realist writers focused their extraordinary powers of observation on contemporary everyday life. Emphatically rejecting the romantic search for the exotic and the sublime, they energetically pursued the typical and the commonplace. Beginning with a dissection of the middle classes, from which most of them sprang, many realists eventually focused on the working classes, especially the urban working classes, which had been neglected in imaginative literature before this time. The realists put a microscope to many unexplored and taboo subjects—sex, strikes, violence, alcoholism—and hastened to report that slums and factories teemed with savage behavior. Many shocked middle-class critics denounced realism as ugly sensationalism wrapped provocatively in pseudoscientific declarations and crude language.

The realists' claims of objectivity did not prevent the elaboration of a definite world-view. Unlike the romantics, who had gloried in individual freedom and an unlimited universe, realists such as Zola were strict determinists. Human beings, like atoms, were components of the physical world, and all human actions were caused by unalterable natural laws. Heredity and environment determined human behavior; good and evil were merely social conventions.

The realist movement began in France, where romanticism had never been completely dominant, and three of its greatest practitioners—Balzac, Flaubert, and Zola—were French. Honoré de Balzac (1799–1850) spent thirty years writing a vastly ambitious panorama of postrevolutionary French life. Known collectively as *The Human Comedy,* this series of nearly one hundred books vividly portrays more than two thousand characters from virtually all sectors of French society. Balzac pictures urban society as grasping, amoral, and brutal, characterized by a Darwinian struggle for wealth and power. In *Le Père Goriot*

"Life Is Everywhere"   The simple but profound joys of everyday life infuse this outstanding example of Russia's powerful realist tradition. Painted in 1888 by N. A. Yaroshenko, this representation of the mother and child and adoring men also draws on the classic theme of the infant Jesus and the holy family. *(Sovfoto)*

(1835), the hero, a poor student from the provinces, eventually surrenders his idealistic integrity to feverish ambition and society's pervasive greed.

Madame Bovary (1857), the masterpiece of Gustave Flaubert (1821–1880), is far narrower in scope than Balzac's work but unparalleled in its depth and accuracy of psychological insight. Unsuccessfully prosecuted as an outrage against public morality and religion, Flaubert's carefully crafted novel tells the ordinary, even banal, story of a frustrated middle-class housewife who has an adulterous love affair and is betrayed by her lover. Without moralizing, Flaubert portrays the provincial middle class as petty, smug, and hypocritical.

Zola was most famous for his seamy, animalistic view of working-class life. But he also wrote gripping, carefully researched stories featuring the stock exchange, the big department store, and the army, as well as urban slums and bloody coal strikes. Like many later realists, Zola sympathized with socialism, a sympathy evident in his overpowering novel *Germinal* (1885).

Realism quickly spread beyond France. In England, Mary Ann Evans (1819–1880), who wrote under the pen name George Eliot, brilliantly achieved a more deeply felt, less sensational kind of realism. "It is the habit of my imagination," George Eliot wrote, "to strive after as full a vision of the medium in which a character moves as one of the character itself." Her great novel *Middlemarch: A Study of Provincial Life* (1871–1872) examines masterfully the ways in which people are shaped by their social medium as well as their own inner strivings, conflicts, and moral choices. Thomas Hardy (1840–1928) was more in the Zola tradition. His novels, such as *Tess of the D'Urbervilles* (1891) and *The Return of the Native* (1878), depict men and women frustrated and crushed by fate and bad luck.

The greatest Russian realist, Count Leo Tolstoy (1828–1910), combined realism in description and character development with an atypical moralizing, which came to dominate his later work. Tolstoy's greatest work is *War and Peace* (1864–1869), a monumental novel set against the historical background of Napoleon's invasion of Russia in 1812. Tolstoy probed deeply into the lives of a multitude of unforgettable characters, such as the ill-fated Prince Andrei; the shy, fumbling Pierre; and the enchanting, level-headed Natasha. Tolstoy went to great pains to develop his fatalistic theory of history, which regards free will as an illusion and the achievements of even the greatest leaders as only the channeling of historical necessity. Yet Tolstoy's central message is one that most of the people discussed in this chapter would have readily accepted: human love, trust, and everyday family ties are life's enduring values.

Thoroughgoing realism (or "naturalism," as it was often called) arrived late in the United States, most arrestingly in the work of Theodore Dreiser (1871–1945). His first novel, *Sister Carrie* (1900), a story of an ordinary farm girl who does well going wrong in Chicago, so outraged conventional morality that the publisher withdrew the book. The United States subsequently became a bastion of literary realism in the twentieth century after the movement had faded away in Europe.

Summary

The revolution in industry had a decisive influence on the urban environment. The populations of towns and cities grew rapidly because it was economically advantageous to locate factories and offices in urban areas. This rapid growth worsened long-standing overcrowding and unhealthy living conditions and posed a frightening challenge for society. Eventually government leaders, city planners, reformers, scientists, and ordinary citizens responded. They took effective action in public health and provided themselves with other badly needed urban services. Gradually they tamed the ferocious savagery of the traditional city.

As urban civilization emerged, there were major changes in family life. Especially among the working classes, family life became more stable, more loving, and less mercenary. These improvements had a price, however. Gender roles for men and women became sharply defined and rigidly separate. Women especially tended to be locked into a subordinate and stereotypical role. Nonetheless, on balance, the quality of family life improved for all family members. Better, more stable family relations reinforced the benefits for the masses of higher real wages, increased social security, political participation, and education.

While the quality of urban and family life improved, the class structure became more complex and diversified than before. Urban society featured many distinct social groups, which existed in a state of constant flux and competition. The gap between rich and poor remained enormous and really quite traditional in mature urban society, although there were countless gradations between the extremes. Large numbers of poor women in particular continued to labor as workers in sweated industries, as domestic servants, and as prostitutes in order to satisfy the demands of their masters in the servant-keeping classes. Urban society in the late nineteenth century represented a long step forward for humanity, but it remained very unequal.

Inequality was a favorite theme of realist novelists such as Balzac and Zola. More generally, literary realism reflected Western society's growing faith in science, material progress, and evolutionary thinking. The emergence of urban, industrial civilization accelerated the secularization of the Western world-view.

Key Terms

Benthamite	defense mechanisms
miasmatic theory	thermodynamics
germ theory	organic chemistry
pasteurization	positivist method
antiseptic principle	evolution
labor aristocracy	Social Darwinists
illegitimacy explosion	realism
separate spheres	

Notes

1. A. Weber, *The Growth of Cities in the Nineteenth Century* (New York: Columbia University Press, 1899), p. 1.
2. S. Marcus, "Reading the Illegible," in *The Victorian City: Images and Realities,* ed. H. J. Dyos and Michael Wolff, vol. 1 (London: Routledge & Kegan Paul, 1973), p. 266.
3. E. Gauldie, *Cruel Habitations: A History of Working-Class Housing, 1780–1918* (London: George Allen & Unwin, 1974), p. 21.
4. Quoted in E. Chadwick, *Report on the Sanitary Condition of the Labouring Population of Great Britain,* ed. M. W. Flinn (Edinburgh: University of Edinburgh Press, 1965; original publication, 1842), pp. 315–316.
5. J. P. McKay, *Tramways and Trolleys: The Rise of Urban Mass Transport in Europe* (Princeton, N.J.: Princeton University Press, 1976), p. 81.
6. Quoted in R. P. Neuman, "The Sexual Question and Social Democracy in Imperial Germany," *Journal of Social History* 7 (Winter 1974): 276.
7. Quoted in J. A. Banks, "The Contagion of Numbers," in *The Victorian City: Images and Realities,* ed. H. J. Dyos and Michael Wolff, vol. 1 (London: Routledge & Kegan Paul, 1973), p. 112.
8. Quoted in R. Roberts, *The Classic Slum: Salford Life in the First Quarter of the Century* (Manchester, England: University of Manchester Press, 1971), p. 95.
9. Quoted in T. Zeldin, *France, 1848–1945,* vol. 1 (Oxford: Clarendon Press, 1973), p. 288.
10. Quoted in J. M. Phayer, "Lower-Class Morality: The Case of Bavaria," *Journal of Social History* 8 (Fall 1974): 89.
11. S. Marcus, *The Other Victorians: A Study of Sexuality and Pornography in Mid-Nineteenth-Century England* (New York: Basic Books, 1966), p. 142.
12. Quoted in G. S. Jones, "Working-Class Culture and Working-Class Politics in London, 1870–1900: Notes on the Remaking of a Working Class," *Journal of Social History* 7 (Summer 1974): 486.
13. Quoted in Zeldin, *France,* p. 346.
14. Roberts, *The Classic Slum,* p. 35.

15. Quoted in Zeldin, *France,* p. 295.
16. Quoted ibid., p. 328.
17. Quoted in Neuman, "The Sexual Question," p. 281.
18. Quoted in S. Kern, "Explosive Intimacy: Psychodynamics of the Victorian Family," *History of Childhood Quarterly* 1 (Winter 1974): 439.
19. A. Comte, *The Positive Philosophy of Auguste Comte,* trans. H. Martineau, vol. 1 (London: J. Chapman, 1853), pp. 1–2.
20. Quoted in G. J. Becker, ed., *Documents of Modern Literary Realism* (Princeton, N.J.: Princeton University Press, 1963), p. 159.

Suggested Reading

All of the books and articles cited in the Notes are highly recommended. T. Zeldin, *France, 1848–1945,* 2 vols. (1973, 1977), is a pioneering social history that opens many doors, as is the ambitious synthesis by T. Hamerow, *The Birth of a New Europe: State and Society in the Nineteenth Century* (1983). F. Thompson, *The Rise of Respectable Society: A Social History of Victorian Britain, 1830–1900* (1986), is a laudable survey.

On the European city, D. Harvey, *Consciousness and the Urban Experience* (1985), is provocative. D. Silverman, *Art Nouveau in Fin-de-Siècle France: Politics, Psychology, and Style* (1989), and D. Pickney, *Napoleon III and the Rebuilding of Paris* (1972), are major studies. Also recommended are P. Fritzsche, *Reading Berlin in 1900* (1996), an imaginative cultural investigation; O. Olsen, *The City as a Work of Art: London, Paris, and Vienna* (1986), an architectural feast; and M. Hamm, ed., *The City in Russian History* (1976), which still has no equal. T. Clark, *The Painting of Modern Life: Paris in the Age of Manet and His Followers* (1985), and J. Merriman, *Margins of City Life: Explorations on the French Urban Frontier* (1991), are important works on France. The outstanding study by J. Schmiechen, *Sweated Industries and Sweated Labor: The London Clothing Trades* (1984), complements H. Mayhew's wonderful contemporary study, *London Labour and the Labouring Poor* (1861), reprinted recently. D. Crane, *Fashion and Its Social Agendas: Class, Gender, and Identity* (2000), is an innovative and extremely helpful historical investigation. L. Tiersten, *Marianne in the Market: Envisioning Consumer Society in Fin-de-Siècle France* (2001), is a subtle treatment of women as consumers. E. Johnson, *Urbanization and Crime: Germany, 1871–1914* (1995), presents a portrait of a police state zealously defending property rights. J. P. Goubert, *The Conquest of Water: The Advent of Health in the Industrial Age* (1989), and A. Corbin, *The Foul and the Fragrant: Odor and the French Social Imagination of Public Health* (1986), are excellent introductions to sanitary developments and attitudes toward smells. For society as a whole, J. Burnett, *History of the Cost of Living* (1969), cleverly shows how different classes spent their money. B. Gottlieb, *The Family in the Western World* (1993), is a wide-ranging synthesis. L.

Pollock, *Forgotten Children: Parent-Child Relations from 1500 to 1900* (1983), explores long-term changes and patterns. J. Laver's handsomely illustrated *Manners and Morals in the Age of Optimism, 1848–1914* (1966) investigates the urban underworld and relations between the sexes. Sexual attitudes are also examined in J. Walkowitz, *Prostitution and Victorian Society: Women, Class and State* (1980), and L. Engelstein, *The Key to Happiness: Sex and the Search for Modernity in Fin-de-Siècle Russia* (1992). P. Allen, *The Wages of Sin: Sex and Disease, Past and Present* (2000), is the best history of sexually transmitted diseases. G. Alter, *Family and Female Life Course: The Women of Verviers, Belgium, 1849–1880* (1988), explores attitudes toward family planning.

Studies on women continue to expand rapidly. In addition to the general works by Shorter, Wrigley, Stone, and Tilly and Scott cited in Chapter 20, recommended recent surveys include U. Frevert, *Women in German History: From Bourgeois Emancipation to Sexual Liberation* (1990), and M. Perrot, ed., *A History of Private Life* (1990), a fascinating book. Eye-opening specialized investigations include L. Davidoff, *The Best Circles* (1973), and P. Jalland, *Women, Marriage and Politics, 1860–1914* (1986), on upper-class society types; B. Engel, *Between the Fields and the City: Women, Work and Family in Russia, 1861–1914* (1994); and P. Smith, *Feminism in the Third Republic* (1996). M. J. Peterson, *Love and Work in the Lives of Victorian Gentlewomen* (1989); J. Coffin, *The Politics of Women's Work: The Paris Garment Trades, 1750–1914* (1996); and M. Vicinus, *Independent Women: Work and Community for Single Women, 1850–1920* (1985), examine women at work. M. Vicinus, ed., *Suffer and Be Still* (1972) and *A Widening Sphere* (1981), are far-ranging collections of essays on women's history, as is R. Bridenthal, C. Koonz, and S. Stuard, eds., *Becoming Visible: Women in European History,* 2d ed. (1987). Feminism is treated perceptively in C. Moses, *French Feminism in the Nineteenth Century* (1984). L. Tickner, *The Spectacle of Women: Imagery of the Suffrage Campaign, 1907–1914* (1988), discusses Britain. J. Gillis, *Youth and History* (1974), is a good introduction.

Among studies on the working classes, M. Maynes, *Taking the Hard Road: Life Course in French and German Workers' Biographies in the Era of Industrialization* (1995), provides fascinating stories and shows how workers saw themselves. Everyday life in a great city comes wonderfully alive in W. S. Haine, *The World of the Paris Café: Sociability Among the French Working Class, 1789–1914* (1996). J. Wegs, *Growing Up Working Class: Continuity and Change Among Viennese Youth, 1890–1938* (1989), is recommended. Two good studies on the middle classes are P. Pillbeam, *The Middle Classes in Europe, 1789–1914: France, Germany, Italy, and Russia* (1990), a stimulating introduction, and J. Kocka and A. Mitchell, eds., *Bourgeois Society in Nineteenth-Century Europe* (1993), a collection by leading specialists. Two fine recent studies on the professions are A. Digby, *Making a*

Medical Living: Doctors and Patients in the English Market for Medicine, 1720–1922 (1994), and A. Quartaro, *Women Teachers and Popular Education in Nineteenth-Century France* (1995). Servants and their employers receive excellent treatment in T. McBride, *The Domestic Revolution: The Modernization of Household Service in England and France, 1820–1912* (1976), and B. Smith, *Ladies of the Leisure Class: The Bourgeoises of Northern France in the Nineteenth Century* (1981), which may be compared with the innovative study by M. Miller, *The Bon Marché: Bourgeois Culture and the Department Store, 1869–1920* (1981). J. Schmiechen and K. Carls, *The British Market Hall: A Social and Architectural History* (1999), is a fascinating and beautiful study of Britain's enclosed markets, which revolutionized the sale of food and proclaimed civic pride. T. Griffiths, *The Lancashire Working Classes, c. 1880–1930* (2001), reexamines both class and gender relationships, emphasizing the enduring centrality of family ties.

On Darwin and evolution, J. Weiner, *The Beak of the Finch: The Story of Evolution in Our Time* (1994), is a prizewinning, highly readable account. M. Ruse, *The Darwinian Revolution* (1979), and P. Bowler, *Evolution: The History of an Idea,* rev. ed. (1989), are also recommended. O. Chadwick, *The Secularization of the European Mind in the Nineteenth Century* (1976), analyzes the impact of science (and other factors) on religious belief. M. Teich and R. Porter, eds., *Fin de Siècle and Its Legacy* (1990), is a fascinating collection of essays, ranging widely from industry and cars to sports and painting. The masterpieces of the great realist social novelists remain among the best and most memorable introductions to nineteenth-century culture and thought. In addition to the novels discussed in this chapter and those cited in the Suggested Reading for Chapters 22 and 23, Ivan Turgenev's *Fathers and Sons* and Emile Zola's *The Dram-Shop* are especially recommended.

Middle-Class Youth and Sexuality

*G*rowing up in Vienna in a prosperous Jewish family, Stephan Zweig (1881–1942) became an influential voice calling for humanitarian values and international culture in early-twentieth-century Europe. Passionately opposed to the First World War, Zweig wrote poetry, plays, and novels. But he was most famous for many outstanding biographies, which featured shrewd psychological portraits of intriguing historical figures such as Magellan and Marie Antoinette. After Hitler came to power in Germany in 1933, Zweig lived in exile until his death in 1942.

Zweig's last work was The World of Yesterday *(1943), one of the truly fascinating autobiographies of the twentieth century. In the following passage taken from that work, Zweig recalls and also interprets the romantic experiences and the sexual separation of middle-class youth before the First World War.*

During the eight years of our higher schooling [beyond grade school], something had occurred which was of great importance to each one of us: we ten-year-olds had grown into virile young men of sixteen, seventeen, and eighteen, and Nature began to assert its rights. . . . It did not take us long to discover that those authorities in whom we had previously confided—school, family, and public morals—manifested an astonishing insincerity in this matter of sex. But what is more, they also demanded secrecy and reserve from us in this connection. . . .

This "social morality," which on the one hand privately presupposed the existence of sexuality and its natural course, but on the other would not recognize it openly at any price, was doubly deceitful. While it winked one eye at a young man and even encouraged him with the other "to sow his wild oats," as the kindly language of the home

put it, in the case of a woman it studiously shut both eyes and acted as if it were blind. That a man could experience desires, and was permitted to experience them, was silently admitted by custom. But to admit frankly that a woman could be subject to similar desires, or that creation for its eternal purposes also required a female polarity, would have transgressed the conception of the "sanctity of womanhood." In the pre-Freudian era, therefore, the axiom was agreed upon that a female person could have no physical desires as long as they had not been awakened by man, and that, obviously, was officially permitted only in marriage. But even in those moral times, in Vienna in particular, the air was full of dangerous erotic infection, and a girl of good family had to live in a completely sterilized atmosphere, from the day of her birth until the day when she left the altar on her husband's arm. In order to protect young girls, they were not left alone for a single moment. . . . Every book which they read was inspected, and above all else, young girls were constantly kept busy to divert their attention from any possible dangerous thoughts. They had to practise the piano, learn singing and drawing, foreign languages, and the history of literature and art. They were educated and overeducated. But while the aim was to make them as educated and as socially correct as possible, at the same time society anxiously took great pains that they should remain innocent of all natural things to a degree unthinkable today. A young girl of good family was not allowed to have any idea of how the male body was formed, or to know how children came into the world, for the angel was to enter into matrimony not only physically untouched, but completely "pure" spiritually as well. "Good breeding," for a young girl of that time, was identical with ignorance of life; and this ignorance ofttimes lasted for the rest of their lives. . . .

What possibilities actually existed for a young man of the middle-class world? In all the others, in the so-called lower classes, the problem was no problem at all. . . . In most of our Alpine villages the number of natural children greatly exceeded the legitimate ones. Among the proletariat, the worker, before he could get married, lived with another worker in free love. . . . It was only in our middle-class society that such a remedy as an early marriage was scorned. . . . And so there was an artificial interval of six, eight, or ten years between actual manhood and manhood as society accepted it; and in this interval the young man had to take care of his own "affairs" or adventures.

Those days did not give him too many opportunities. Only a very few particularly rich young men could afford the luxury of keeping a mistress, that is, taking an apartment and paying her expenses. And only a very few fortunate young men achieved the literary ideal of love of the times—the only one which it was permitted to describe in novels—an affair with a married woman. The others helped themselves for the most part with shopgirls and waitresses, and this offered little inner satisfaction. . . . But, generally speaking, prostitution was still the foundation of the erotic life outside of marriage; in a certain sense it constituted a dark underground vault over which rose the gorgeous structure of middle-class society with its faultless, radiant façade.

The present generation has hardly any idea of the gigantic extent of prostitution in Europe before the [First] World War. Whereas today it is as rare to meet a prostitute on the streets of a big city as it is to meet a wagon in the road, then the sidewalks were so sprinkled with women for sale that it was more difficult to avoid than to find them. To this was added the countless number of "closed houses," the night clubs, the cabarets, the dance parlours with their dancers and singers, and the bars with their "come-on" girls. At that time female wares were offered for sale at every hour and at every price. . . . And this was the same city, the same society, the same morality, that was indignant when young girls rode bicycles, and declared it a disgrace to the dignity of science when Freud in his calm, clear, and penetrating manner established truths that they did not wish to be true. The same world that so pathetically defended the purity of womanhood allowed this cruel sale of women, organized it, and even profited thereby.

We should not permit ourselves to be misled by sentimental novels or stories of that epoch. It was

Nineteenth-century illustration depicting socializing in Vienna. *(Österreichische Nationalbibliothek)*

a bad time for youth. The young girls were hermetically locked up under the control of the family, hindered in their free bodily as well as intellectual development. The young men were forced to secrecy and reticence by a morality which fundamentally no one believed or obeyed. Unhampered, honest relationships—in other words, all that could have made youth happy and joyous according to the laws of Nature—were permitted only to the very few.

Questions for Analysis

1. According to Zweig, how did the sex lives of young middle-class women and young middle-class men differ? What accounted for these differences?

2. Was there nonetheless a basic underlying unity in the way society treated both the young men and the young women of the comfortable middle class? If so, what was that unity?

3. Zweig ends this passage with a value judgment: "It was a bad time for youth." Do you agree or disagree? Why?

Source: The World of Yesterday by Stephan Zweig, translated by Helmut Ripperger. Translation copyright 1943 by the Viking Press, Inc. Used with permission of Viking Penguin, a division of Penguin Putnam Inc.

France's Napoleon III and Empress Eugénie greet Britain's
Queen Victoria and Prince Albert in a dazzling ceremony in Paris
in 1855. *(The Royal Collection © Her Majesty Queen Elizabeth II)*

chapter

25

The Age of Nationalism, 1850–1914

chapter outline

- Napoleon III in France

- Nation Building in Italy and Germany

- Nation Building in the United States

- The Modernization of Russia

- The Responsive National State, 1871–1914

- Marxism and the Socialist Movement

*T*he revolutions of 1848 closed one era and opened another. Urban industrial society began to take a strong hold on the continent and in the young United States, as it already had in Great Britain. Internationally, the repressive peace and diplomatic stability of Metternich's time were replaced by a period of war and rapid change. In thought and culture, exuberant romanticism gave way to hardheaded realism. In the Atlantic economy, the hard years of the 1840s were followed by good times and prosperity throughout most of the 1850s and 1860s. Perhaps most important of all, Western society progressively developed, for better or worse, a new and effective organizing principle capable of coping with the many-sided challenge of the dual revolution and the emerging urban civilization. That principle was nationalism—dedication to an identification with the nation-state.

The triumph of nationalism is an enormously significant historical development that was by no means completely predictable. After all, nationalism had been a powerful force since at least 1789. Yet it had repeatedly failed to realize its goals, most spectacularly so in 1848.

- Why, then, did nationalism become in one way or another an almost universal faith in Europe and in the United States between 1850 and 1914?
- More specifically, how did nationalism evolve so that it appealed not only to predominately middle-class liberals but also to the broad masses of society?

These are the questions this chapter will seek to answer.

*N*apoleon III in France

Early nationalism was generally liberal and idealistic and often democratic and radical as well. The ideas of nationhood and popular sovereignty posed a fearful revolutionary threat to conservatives like Metternich. Yet from the vantage point of the twentieth century, it is clear that nationalism wears many masks: it may be narrowly liberal or democratic and radical, as it was for Mazzini and Michelet, but it can also flourish in dictatorial states, which may be conservative, fascist, or communist. Napoleon I's France had already combined national feeling with authoritarian rule. Significantly, it was Napoleon's nephew, Louis Napoleon, who revived and extended this merger. He showed how governments could reconcile popular and conservative forces in an authoritarian nationalism. In doing so, he provided a model for political leaders elsewhere.

The Second Republic and Louis Napoleon

Although Louis Napoleon Bonaparte had played no part in French politics before 1848, universal male suffrage gave him three times as many votes as the four other presidential candidates combined in the French presidential election of December 1848. This outcome occurred for several reasons. First, Louis Napoleon had the great name of his uncle, whom romantics had transformed from a dictator into a demigod as they created a Napoleonic legend after 1820. Second, as Karl Marx stressed at the time, middle-class and peasant property owners feared the socialist challenge of urban workers, and they wanted a tough ruler to provide protection. Third, in late 1848 Louis Napoleon had a positive "program" for France, which was to guide him through most of his long reign. This program had been elaborated earlier in two pamphlets, *Napoleonic Ideas* and *The Elimination of Poverty,* which he had written while imprisoned for an attempt to overthrow Louis Philippe's government. Prior to the presidential election, these pamphlets had been widely circulated.

Above all, Louis Napoleon believed that the government should represent the people and that it should try hard to help them economically. But how were these tasks to be done? Parliaments and political parties were not the answer, according to Louis Napoleon. French politicians represented special-interest groups, particularly middle-class ones. The answer was a strong, even authoritarian, national leader, like the first Napoleon, who would serve all the people, rich and poor. This leader would be linked to each citizen by direct democracy, his sovereignty uncorrupted by politicians and legislative bodies. These political ideas went hand in hand with Louis Napoleon's vision of national unity and social progress. The state and its leader had a sacred duty to provide jobs and stimulate the economy. All classes would benefit by such action.

Louis Napoleon's political and social ideas were at least vaguely understood by large numbers of French peasants and workers in December 1848. To many common people, he

appeared to be a strong man *and* a forward-looking champion of their interests, and that is why they voted for him.

Elected to a four-year term, President Louis Napoleon had to share power with a conservative National Assembly. But in 1851, after the Assembly failed to change the constitution so he could run for a second term, Louis Napoleon began to conspire with key army officers. On December 2, 1851, he illegally dismissed the Assembly and seized power in a *coup d'état.* There was some armed resistance in Paris and widespread insurrection in the countryside in southern France, but these protests were crushed by the army. Restoring universal male suffrage, Louis Napoleon called on the French people, as his uncle had done, to legalize his actions. They did: 92 percent voted to make him president for ten years. A year later, 97 percent in a plebiscite made him hereditary emperor; for the third time, and by the greatest margin yet, the authoritarian Louis Napoleon was overwhelmingly elected to lead the French nation.

Napoleon III's Second Empire

Louis Napoleon—now proclaimed Emperor Napoleon III—experienced both success and failure between 1852 and 1870. His greatest success was with the economy, particularly in the 1850s. His government encouraged the new investment banks and massive railroad construction that were at the heart of the Industrial Revolution on the continent. The government also fostered general economic expansion through an ambitious program of public works, which included the rebuilding of Paris to improve the urban environment (see page 792). The profits of business people soared with prosperity, and unemployment declined greatly.

Louis Napoleon always hoped that economic progress would reduce social and political tensions. This hope was at least partially realized. Until the mid-1860s there was considerable support from France's most dissatisfied group, the urban workers. Napoleon III's regulation of pawnshops and his support of credit unions and better housing for the working classes were evidence of positive concern in the 1850s. In the 1860s, he granted workers the right to form unions and the right to strike—important economic rights denied by earlier governments.

At first, political power remained in the hands of the emperor. He alone chose his ministers, and they had great freedom of action. At the same time, Napoleon III restricted but did not abolish the Assembly. Members were elected by universal male suffrage every six years,

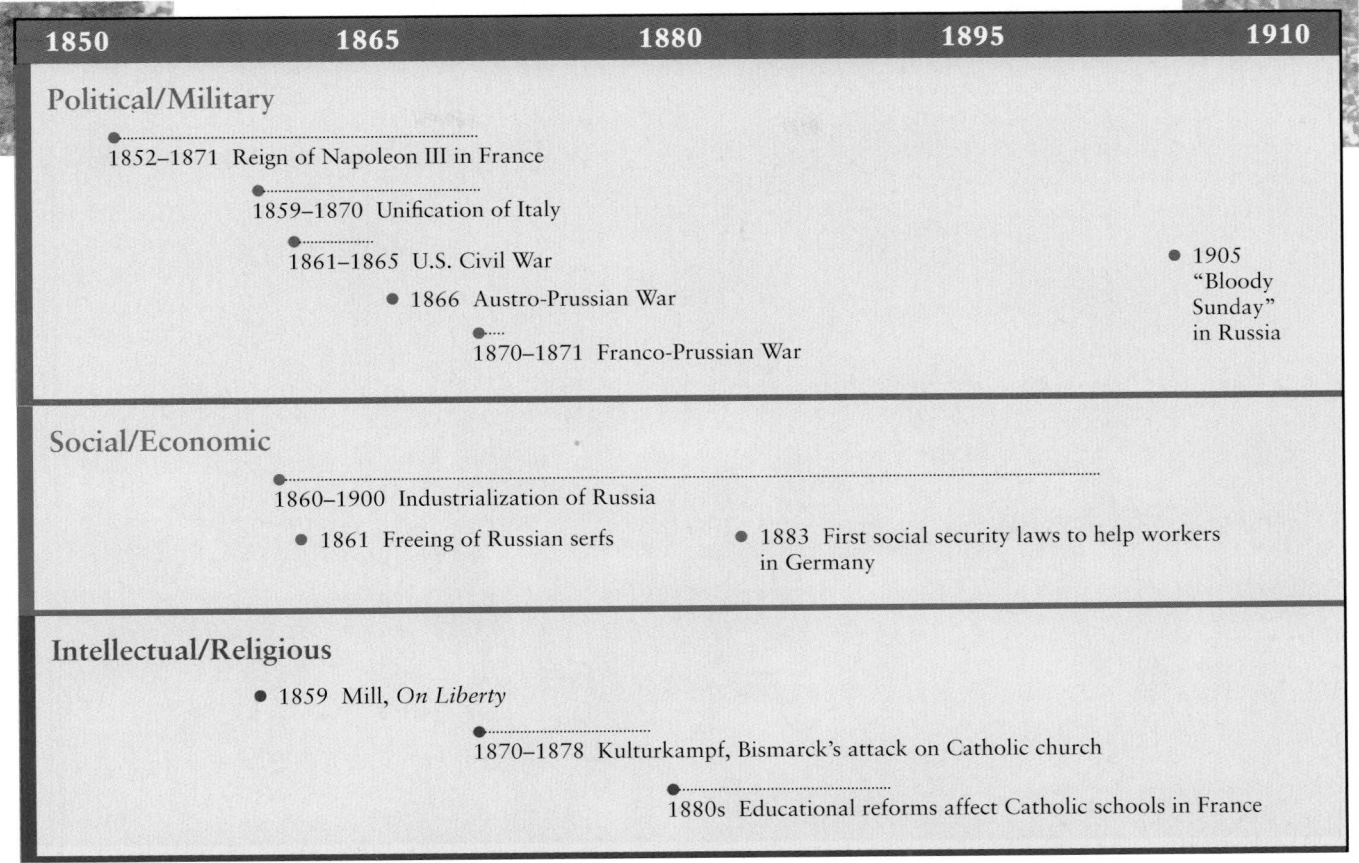

1850	1865	1880	1895	1910

Political/Military

1852–1871 Reign of Napoleon III in France

1859–1870 Unification of Italy

1861–1865 U.S. Civil War

1866 Austro-Prussian War

1870–1871 Franco-Prussian War

1905 "Bloody Sunday" in Russia

Social/Economic

1860–1900 Industrialization of Russia

1861 Freeing of Russian serfs

1883 First social security laws to help workers in Germany

Intellectual/Religious

1859 Mill, *On Liberty*

1870–1878 Kulturkampf, Bismarck's attack on Catholic church

1880s Educational reforms affect Catholic schools in France

and Louis Napoleon and his government took the parliamentary elections very seriously. They tried to entice notable people, even those who had opposed the regime, to stand as government candidates in order to expand the base of support. Moreover, the government used its officials and appointed mayors to spread the word that the election of the government's candidates—and the defeat of the opposition—was the key to roads, tax rebates, and a thousand other local concerns.

In 1857 and again in 1863, Louis Napoleon's system worked brilliantly and produced overwhelming electoral victories. Yet in the 1860s, Napoleon III's electoral system gradually disintegrated. A sincere nationalist, Napoleon had wanted to reorganize Europe on the principle of nationality and gain influence and territory for France and himself in the process. Instead, problems in Italy and the rising power of Prussia led to increasing criticism at home from his Catholic and nationalist supporters. With increasing effectiveness, the middle-class liberals who had always wanted a less authoritarian regime continued to denounce his rule.

Napoleon was always sensitive to the public mood. Public opinion, he once said, always wins the last victory. Thus in the 1860s, he progressively liberalized his empire. He gave the Assembly greater powers and the opposition candidates greater freedom, which they used to good advantage. In 1869 the opposition, consisting of republicans, monarchists, and liberals, polled almost 45 percent of the vote.

The next year, a sick and weary Louis Napoleon again granted France a new constitution, which combined a basically parliamentary regime with a hereditary emperor as chief of state. In a final great plebiscite on the eve of the disastrous war with Prussia, 7.5 million Frenchmen voted in favor of the new constitution, and only 1.5 million opposed it. Napoleon III's attempt to reconcile a strong national state with universal male suffrage was still evolving and was doing so in a democratic direction.

Paris in the Second Empire   This 1863 painting of the Tuileries Gardens by Edouard Manet (1832–1883) captures the brilliant colors of spring and the flashy glitter of unprecedented prosperity in the Second Empire. Manet, an early impressionist painter, shocked his contemporaries; one critic complained that this canvas "scorches the eyes." Manet's innovative interplay of light and shadow evokes the violent contrasts of modern life. *(National Gallery, London/The Bridgeman Art Library International Ltd)*

Nation Building in Italy and Germany

Louis Napoleon's triumph in 1848 and his authoritarian rule in the 1850s provided the old ruling classes of Europe with a new model in politics. To what extent might the expanding urban middle classes and even portions of the growing working classes rally to a strong and essentially conservative national state? This was one of the great political questions in the 1850s and 1860s. In central Europe, a resounding answer came with the national unification of Italy and Germany.

Italy to 1850

Italy had never been united prior to 1850. Part of Rome's great empire in ancient times, the Italian peninsula was divided in the Middle Ages into competing city-states, which led the commercial and cultural revival of the West with amazing creativity. A battleground for great powers after 1494, Italy was reorganized in 1815 at the Congress of Vienna. The rich northern provinces of Lombardy and Venetia were taken by Metternich's Austria. Sardinia and Piedmont were under the rule of an Italian monarch, and Tuscany, with its famous capital Florence,

MAP 25.1 The Unification of Italy, 1859–1870 The leadership of Sardinia-Piedmont and nationalist fervor were decisive factors in the unification of Italy.

shared north-central Italy with several smaller states. Central Italy and Rome were ruled by the papacy, which had always considered an independent political existence necessary to fulfill its spiritual mission. Naples and Sicily were ruled, as they had been for almost a hundred years, by a branch of the Bourbons. Metternich was not wrong in dismissing Italy as "a geographical expression" (see Map 25.1).

Between 1815 and 1848, the goal of a unified Italian nation captured the imaginations of many Italians. There were three basic approaches. The first was the radical program of the idealistic patriot Giuseppe Mazzini, who preached a centralized democratic republic based on universal male suffrage and the will of the people (see page 762). The second was that of Vincenzo Gioberti, a Catholic priest who called for a federation of existing states under the presidency of a progressive pope. The third was the program of those who looked for leadership to the autocratic kingdom of Sardinia-Piedmont, much as many Germans looked to Prussia.

The third alternative was strengthened by the failures of 1848, when Austria smashed Mazzini's republicanism. Almost by accident, Sardinia's monarch, Victor Emmanuel, retained the liberal constitution granted under duress in March 1848. This constitution provided for a fair degree of civil liberties and real parliamentary government, with deputies elected by a limited franchise based on income. To the Italian middle classes, Sardinia appeared to be a liberal, progressive state ideally suited to achieve the goal of national unification. By contrast, Mazzini's brand of democratic republicanism seemed quixotic and too radical.

As for the papacy, the initial cautious support by Pius IX (r. 1846–1878) for unification had given way to fear and hostility after he was temporarily driven from Rome during the upheavals of 1848. For a long generation, the papacy would stand resolutely opposed not only to national unification but also to most modern trends. In 1864 in the *Syllabus of Errors,* Pius IX strongly denounced rationalism, socialism, separation of church and state, and religious liberty, denying that "the Roman pontiff can and ought to reconcile and align himself with progress, liberalism, and modern civilization."

Cavour and Garibaldi in Italy

Sardinia had the good fortune of being led by a brilliant statesman, Count Camillo Benso di Cavour, the dominant figure in the Sardinian government from 1850 until his death in 1861. Indicative of the coming tacit alliance between the aristocracy and the solid middle class under the banner of the strong nation-state, Cavour came from a noble family and embraced the economic doctrines and business activities associated with the prosperous middle class. Before entering politics, he made a substantial fortune in sugar mills, steamships, banks, and railroads. Cavour's national goals were limited and realistic. Until 1859 he sought unity only for the states of northern and perhaps central Italy in a greatly expanded kingdom of Sardinia.

In the 1850s, Cavour worked to consolidate Sardinia as a liberal constitutional state capable of leading northern Italy. His program of highways and railroads, of civil liberties and opposition to clerical privilege, increased support for Sardinia throughout northern Italy. Yet

Cavour realized that Sardinia could not drive Austria out of Lombardy and Venetia and unify northern Italy under Victor Emmanuel without the help of a powerful ally. Accordingly, he worked for a secret diplomatic alliance with Napoleon III against Austria.

Finally, in July 1858 Cavour succeeded and goaded Austria into attacking Sardinia in 1859. Napoleon III came to Sardinia's defense. Then after the victory of the combined Franco-Sardinian forces, Napoleon III did a sudden about-face. Deciding it was not in his interest to have too strong a state on his southern border and criticized by French Catholics for supporting the pope's declared enemy, Napoleon III abandoned Cavour. He made a compromise peace with the Austrians at Villafranca in July 1859. Sardinia would receive only Lombardy, the area around Milan. The rest of the map of Italy would remain essentially unchanged. Cavour resigned in a rage.

Yet Cavour's plans were salvaged by the skillful maneuvers of his allies in the moderate nationalist movement. While the war against Austria had raged in the north, pro-Sardinian nationalists in central Italy had fanned popular revolts and driven out their easily toppled princes. Using and controlling the popular enthusiasm, the middle-class nationalist leaders in central Italy called for fusion with Sardinia. This was not at all what France and the other Great Powers wanted, but the nationalists held firm. Cavour returned to power in early 1860 and gained Napoleon III's support by ceding Savoy and Nice to France. The people of central Italy then voted overwhelmingly to join a greatly enlarged kingdom of Sardinia. Cavour had achieved his original goal of a northern Italian state (see Map 25.1).

For superpatriots such as Giuseppe Garibaldi (1807–1882), the job of unification was still only half done. The son of a poor sailor, Garibaldi personified the romantic, revolutionary nationalism and republicanism of Mazzini and 1848. Leading a corps of volunteers against Austria in 1859, Garibaldi emerged in 1860 as an independent force in Italian politics.

Partly to use him and partly to get rid of him, Cavour secretly supported Garibaldi's bold plan to "liberate" the kingdom of the Two Sicilies. Landing on the shores of Sicily in May 1860, Garibaldi's guerrilla band of a thousand **Red Shirts** captured the imagination of the Sicilian peasantry. Outwitting the twenty-thousand-man royal army, the guerrilla leader won battles, gained volunteers, and took Palermo. Then he and his men crossed to the mainland, marched triumphantly toward Naples, and prepared to attack Rome and the pope. But the wily Cavour quickly sent Sardinian forces to occupy most of the Papal States (but not Rome) and to intercept Garibaldi.

Garibaldi and Victor Emmanuel The historic meeting in Naples between the leader of Italy's revolutionary nationalists and the king of Sardinia sealed the unification of northern and southern Italy in a unitary state. With only the sleeve of his red shirt showing, Garibaldi offers his hand—and his conquests—to the uniformed king and his moderate monarchical government. *(Scala/Art Resource, NY)*

Cavour realized that an attack on Rome would bring about war with France, and he also feared Garibaldi's radicalism and popular appeal. Thus he immediately organized a plebiscite in the conquered territories. Despite the urging of some radical supporters, the patriotic Garibaldi did not oppose Cavour, and the people of the south voted to join Sardinia. When Garibaldi and Victor Emmanuel rode through Naples to cheering crowds, they symbolically sealed the union of north and south, of monarch and nation-state.

Cavour had succeeded. He had controlled Garibaldi and had turned popular nationalism in a conservative direction. The new kingdom of Italy, which expanded to include Venice in 1866 and Rome in 1870, was a parliamentary monarchy under Victor Emmanuel, neither radical nor democratic. Despite political unity, only a small minority of Italian males had the right to vote. The propertied classes and the common people were divided. A great and growing social and cultural gap separated the progressive, industrializing north from the stagnant, agrarian south. The new Italy was united on paper, but profound divisions remained.

Germany Before Bismarck

In the aftermath of 1848, the German states were locked in a political stalemate. After Austria and Russia blocked Frederick William's attempt to unify Germany "from above," tension grew between Austria and Prussia as each power sought to block the other within the German Confederation (see pages 759 and 781–782). Stalemate also prevailed in the domestic politics of the individual states in the 1850s.

At the same time, powerful economic forces were undermining the political status quo. Modern industry grew rapidly within the German customs union, or **Zollverein,** founded in 1834 to stimulate trade and increase the revenues of member states. The Zollverein had not included Austria, and after 1848 this exclusion became a crucial factor in the Austro-Prussian rivalry.

The Zollverein's tariff duties were substantially reduced so that Austria's highly protected industry could not bear to join. In retaliation, Austria tried to destroy the Zollverein, but without success. Indeed, by the end of 1853 all the German states except Austria had joined the customs union. A new Germany excluding Austria was becoming an economic reality. Middle-class and business groups in the Zollverein were enriching themselves and finding solid economic reasons to bolster their idealistic support of national unification. Prussia's leading role within the Zollverein gave it a valuable advantage in its struggle against Austria's supremacy in German political affairs.

The national uprising in Italy in 1859 made a profound impression in the German states. In Prussia great political change and war—perhaps with Austria, perhaps with France—seemed quite possible. Along with his top military advisers, the tough-minded William I of Prussia (r. 1861–1888), who had replaced the unstable Frederick William IV as regent in 1858 and become king himself in 1861, was convinced of the need for major army reforms. William I wanted to double the size of the highly disciplined regular army. Army reforms meant a bigger defense budget and higher taxes.

Prussia had emerged from 1848 with a parliament of sorts, which was in the hands of the liberal middle class by 1859. The wealthy middle class, like the landed aristocracy, was greatly overrepresented by the Prussian electoral system, and it wanted society to be less, not more, militaristic. Above all, middle-class representatives wanted to establish once and for all that the parliament, not the king, had the ultimate political power. They also wanted to ensure that the army was responsible to Prussia's elected representatives and was not a "state within a state." These demands were popular. The parliament rejected the military budget in 1862, and the liberals triumphed completely in new elections. King William then called on Count Otto von Bismarck to head a new ministry and defy the parliament. This was a momentous choice.

Bismarck and the Austro-Prussian War, 1866

The most important figure in German history between Luther and Hitler, Otto von Bismarck (1815–1898) has been the object of enormous interest and debate. A great hero to some, a great villain to others, Bismarck was above all a master of politics. Born into the Prussian landowning aristocracy, the young Bismarck was a wild and tempestuous student given to duels and drinking. Proud of his Junker heritage and always devoted to his Prussian sovereign, Bismarck had a strong personality and an unbounded desire for power. Yet in his drive to secure power for himself and for Prussia, Bismarck was extraordinarily flexible and pragmatic. "One must always have two irons in the fire," he once said. He kept his options open, pursuing one policy and then another as he moved with skill and cunning toward his goal.

Bismarck first honed his political skills as a high-ranking diplomat for the Prussian government. When he took office as chief minister in 1862, he made a strong but unfavorable impression. His speeches were a sensation and a scandal. Declaring that the government would rule without parliamentary consent, Bismarck lashed out at the middle-class opposition: "The great questions of the day will not be decided by speeches and resolutions—that was the blunder of 1848 and 1849—but by blood and iron." Denounced for this view that "might makes right," Bismarck had the Prussian bureaucracy go right on collecting taxes, even though the parliament refused to approve the budget. Bismarck reorganized the army. And for four years, from 1862 to 1866, the voters of Prussia continued to express their opposition by sending large liberal majorities to the parliament.

Opposition at home spurred the search for success abroad. The ever-knotty question of Schleswig-Holstein provided a welcome opportunity. In 1864, when the Danish king tried again, as in 1848, to bring the provinces into a more centralized Danish state against the will of the German Confederation, Prussia joined Austria in a short and successful war against Denmark. However, Bismarck was convinced that Prussia had to control completely the northern, predominately Protestant part of the German Confederation, which meant expelling Austria from German affairs. After the victory over Denmark, Bismarck's skillful maneuvering had Prussia in a position to force Austria out by war, if necessary. Bismarck knew that a war with Austria would have to be a localized one that would not provoke a mighty alliance against Prussia. By skillfully neutralizing Russia and France, he was in a position to engage in a war of his own making.

The Austro-Prussian War of 1866 lasted only seven weeks. Utilizing railroads to mass troops and the new breechloading needle gun to achieve maximum firepower, the reorganized Prussian army overran northern Germany and defeated Austria decisively at the Battle of Sadowa in Bohemia. Anticipating Prussia's future needs, Bismarck offered Austria realistic, even generous, peace terms. Austria paid no reparations and lost no territory to Prussia, although Venetia was ceded to Italy. But the German Confederation was dissolved, and Austria agreed to withdraw from German affairs. The states north of the Main River were grouped in the new North German Confederation, led by an expanded Prussia. The mainly Catholic states of the south remained independent while forming alliances with Prussia. Bismarck's fundamental goal of Prussian expansion was being realized (see Map 25.2).

The Taming of the Parliament

Bismarck had long been convinced that the old order he so ardently defended should make peace, on its own terms, with the liberal middle class and the nationalist movement. He realized that nationalism was not necessarily hostile to conservative, authoritarian government. Moreover, Bismarck believed that because of the events of 1848, the German middle class could be led to prefer the reality of national unity under conservative leadership to a long, uncertain battle for truly liberal institutions. During the constitutional struggle over army reform and parliamentary authority, he had delayed but not abandoned this goal. Thus during the attack on Austria in 1866, he increasingly identified Prussia's fate with the "national development of Germany."

In the aftermath of victory, Bismarck fashioned a federal constitution for the new North German Confederation. Each state retained its own local government, but the king of Prussia became president of the confederation, and the chancellor—Bismarck—was responsible only to the president. The federal government—William I and Bismarck—controlled the army and foreign affairs. There was also a legislature consisting of two houses that shared equally in the making of laws. Delegates to the upper house were appointed by the different states, but members of the lower house were elected by universal, single-class, male suffrage. With this radical innovation, Bismarck opened the door to popular participation and the possibility of going over the head of the middle class directly to the people, much as Napoleon III had done in France. All the while, however, ultimate power rested in the hands of Prussia and its king and army.

In Prussia itself, Bismarck held out an olive branch to the parliamentary opposition. Marshaling all his diplomatic skill, Bismarck asked the parliament to pass a special indemnity bill to approve after the fact all the government's spending between 1862 and 1866. Most of the liberals jumped at the chance to cooperate. For four long years, they had opposed and criticized Bismarck's "illegal" measures. Yet Bismarck, the king, and the army with its aristocratic leadership had succeeded beyond the wildest dreams of the liberal middle class. In 1866 German unity was in sight, and the people were to be allowed to participate actively in the new state.

Many liberals repented their "sins," and none repented more ardently than Hermann Baumgarten, a thoroughly decent history professor and member of the liberal opposition. In 1866 he confessed in an essay, "We thought that by agitation we could transform Germany. . . . Yet we have experienced a miracle almost without parallel. The victory of our principles would

Otto von Bismarck   The commanding presence and the haughty pride of the Prussian statesman are clearly evident in this photo taken shortly before he came to power. Dressed in formal diplomatic attire as Prussia's ambassador in Paris, Bismarck is perhaps on his way to see Emperor Louis Napoleon and size up his future adversary once again. *(AKG London)*

have brought us misery, whereas the defeat of our principles has brought boundless salvation."[1] The constitutional struggle was over. The German middle class was bowing respectfully before Bismarck and the monarchical authority and aristocratic superiority he represented. In the years before 1914, the values of the aristocratic Prussian army officer increasingly replaced those of the middle-class liberal in public esteem and set the social standard.[2]

MAP 25.2 The Unification of Germany, 1866–1871   This map deserves careful study. Note how Prussian expansion, Austrian expulsion from the old German Confederation, and the creation of a new German empire went hand in hand. Austria lost no territory, but Prussia's neighbors in the north suffered grievously or simply disappeared. The annexation of Alsace-Lorraine turned France into a lasting enemy of Germany before 1914.

The Franco-Prussian War, 1870–1871

The final act in the drama of German unification followed quickly. Bismarck realized that a patriotic war with France would drive the south German states into his

arms. The French obligingly played their part. The apparent issue—whether a distant relative of Prussia's William I (and France's Napoleon III) might become king of Spain—was only a diplomatic pretext. By 1870 the French leaders of the Second Empire, goaded by Bismarck and alarmed by their powerful new neighbor on the Rhine, had decided on a war to teach Prussia a lesson.

As soon as war against France began in 1870, Bismarck had the wholehearted support of the south German states. With other governments standing still—Bismarck's generosity to Austria in 1866 was paying big dividends—German forces under Prussian leadership decisively defeated the main French army at Sedan on September 1, 1870. Louis Napoleon himself was captured and humiliated. Three days later, French patriots in Paris proclaimed yet another French republic and vowed to continue fighting. But after five months, in January 1871, a starving Paris surrendered, and France went on to accept Bismarck's harsh peace terms. By this time, the south German states had agreed to join a new German empire. The victorious William I was proclaimed emperor of Germany in the Hall of Mirrors in the palace of Versailles. Europe had a nineteenth-century German "sun king." As in the 1866 constitution, the king of Prussia and his ministers had ultimate power in the new German Empire, and the lower house of the legislature was elected by universal male suffrage.

Bismarck and the German Empire imposed a harsh peace on France. France was forced to pay a colossal indemnity of 5 billion francs and to cede the rich eastern province of Alsace and part of Lorraine to Germany. The German general staff asserted that this annexation would enhance military security, and German nationalists claimed that the Alsacians, who spoke a German dialect as well as French, wanted to rejoin the fatherland after more than two hundred years. But both cases were weak, and revenge for France's real and imagined aggression in the past was probably the decisive factor. In any event, French men and women of all classes viewed the seizure of Alsace and Lorraine as a terrible crime. They could never forget and never forgive, and thus relations between France and Germany after 1871 were tragically poisoned.

The Franco-Prussian War, which Europeans generally saw as a test of nations in a pitiless Darwinian struggle for existence, released an enormous surge of patriotic feeling in Germany. Bismarck's genius, the invincible Prussian army, the solidarity of king and people in a unified nation—these and similar themes were trumpeted endlessly during and after the war. The weakest of the Great Powers in 1862 (after Austria, Britain, France, and Russia), Prussia had become, with fortification by the other German states, the most powerful state in Europe in less than a decade. Most Germans were enormously proud, blissfully imagining themselves the fittest and best of the European species. Semi-authoritarian nationalism and a "new conservatism," which was based on an alliance of the propertied classes and sought the active support of the working classes, had triumphed in Germany.

Nation Building in the United States

Closely linked to European developments in the nineteenth century, the United States experienced the full drama of separatist nationalism and bloody nation building. The "United" States was divided by slavery from its birth, as economic development in the young republic carried free and slaveholding states in very different directions. Northerners extended family farms westward and began building English-model factories in the Northeast. By 1850 an industrializing, urbanizing North was also building a system of canals and railroads and attracting most of the European immigrants. In the South, industry and cities did not develop, and newcomers avoided the region. And even though three-quarters of all Southern white families were small farmers and owned no slaves in 1850, plantation owners holding twenty or more slaves dominated the economy and the society. These profit-minded slave owners used gangs of black slaves to claim a vast new kingdom across the Deep South where cotton was king (see Map 25.3). By 1850, this kingdom produced 5 million bales a year and satisfied an apparently insatiable demand from textile mills in Europe and New England.

The rise of the cotton empire revitalized slave-based agriculture, spurred exports, and played a key role in igniting rapid U.S. economic growth. The large profits flowing from cotton also led influential Southerners to defend slavery, and Southern whites came to see themselves as a closely knit "we" distinct from the Northern "they." Northern whites viewed their free-labor system as being no less economically and morally superior. Thus regional antagonisms intensified.

These antagonisms came to a climax after 1848 when a defeated Mexico ceded to the United States a vast area stretching from west Texas to the Pacific Ocean. Debate over the extension of slavery in this new territory caused attitudes to harden on both sides. In Abraham Lincoln's famous words, the United States was a "house divided."

Lincoln's election as president in 1860 gave Southern "fire-eaters" the chance they had been waiting for. Eventually eleven states left the Union, determined to win their own independence and forming the Confederate States of America. When Southern troops fired on a Union fort in South Carolina's Charleston harbor, war began.

The long Civil War (1861–1865) was the bloodiest conflict in all of American history, but in the end the South was decisively defeated and the Union preserved. The vastly superior population, industry, and transportation of the North placed the South at a great, probably fatal, disadvantage. The enormous gap between the slave-owning elite and the poor whites also made it impossible for the South to build effectively on the patriotism of 1861. As the war ground on, many ordinary whites felt that the burden of war was falling mainly on their shoulders. Desertions from Southern armies mounted rapidly from 1863 on as soldiers became disillusioned.

In the North, by contrast, many people prospered during the war years. Enthusiasm remained high, and certain dominant characteristics of American life and national culture took shape. Powerful business corporations emerged, steadfastly supported by the Republican party during and after the war. The **Homestead Act** of 1862, which gave western land to settlers, and the Thirteenth Amendment of 1865, which ended slavery, reinforced the concept of free labor taking its chances in a market economy. Finally, the success of Lincoln and the North in holding the Union together seemed to confirm that the "manifest destiny" of the United States was indeed to straddle a continent as a great world power. Thus a new American nationalism grew out of the war aimed at preventing Southern nationhood.

Northern victory also led to a "national" policy of sorts toward American blacks. Congress at first guaranteed the legal freedom of blacks, but Northern whites lost interest in continued sectional struggle, and Southern whites regained control of the state governments. Moreover, freed blacks were generally forced to continue laboring for white landowners in the unfair arrangement called sharecropping. Thus as a result of

MAP 25.3 Slavery in the United States, 1860   This map illustrates the nation on the eve of the Civil War. Although many issues contributed to the developing opposition between North and South, slavery was the fundamental, enduring force that underlay all others. Lincoln's prediction, "I believe this government cannot endure permanently half slave and half free," tragically proved correct. *(Source: Carol Berkin et al., Making America: A History of the United States, 2nd ed., p. 322. Copyright © 1999 by Houghton Mifflin Company. Reprinted with permission.)*

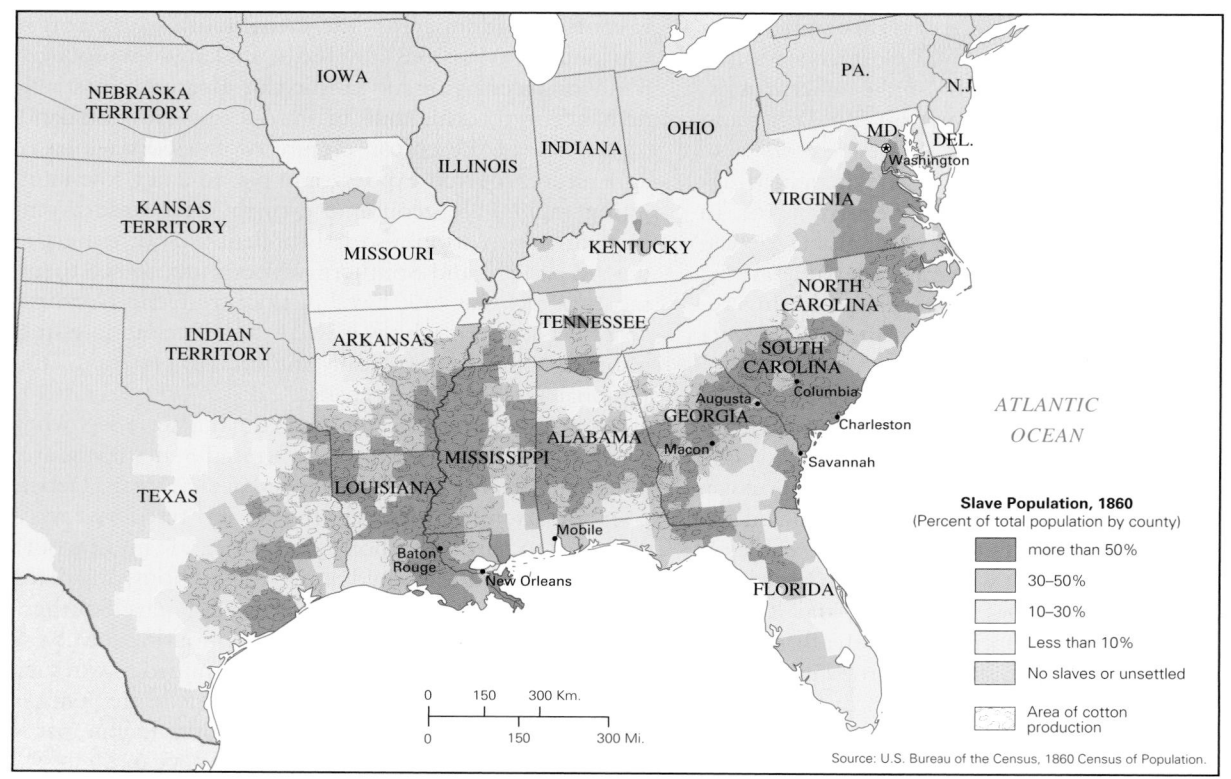

war and reunification, the life of blacks in the Southern states moved much closer to that of the small number of blacks in the North, who had long been free but unequal citizens.

The Modernization of Russia

Russia also experienced a profound midcentury crisis of nation building. This crisis was unlike those occurring in Italy and Germany, for Russia had no need to build a single state out of a jumble of principalities. The Russian empire was already an enormous multinational state that contained all the ethnic Russians and many other nationalities as well. Thus Russia's rulers saw national self-determination as a subversive ideology in the early nineteenth century, and they tried with some success to limit its development among their non-Russian subjects.

Then, after 1853, old autocratic Russia found itself in serious trouble. It became clear to Russia's leaders that the country had to embrace the process of **modernization,** defined narrowly and usefully as the changes that enable a country to compete effectively with the leading countries at a given time. This limited conception of modernization fits Russia after the Crimean War particularly well.

The "Great Reforms"

In the 1850s, Russia was a poor agrarian society. Industry was little developed, and almost 90 percent of the population lived on the land. Agricultural techniques were backward: the ancient open-field system reigned supreme. Serfdom was still the basic social institution. Bound to the lord on a hereditary basis, the peasant serf was little more than a slave. Individual serfs and serf families were regularly sold, with and without land, in the early nineteenth century. Serfs were obliged to furnish labor services or money payments as the lord saw fit. Moreover, the lord could choose freely among the serfs for army recruits, who had to serve for twenty-five years, and he could punish a serf with deportation to Siberia. Sexual exploitation of female serfs by their lords was common.

Serfdom had become the great moral and political issue for the government by the 1840s. Then the Crimean War of 1853 to 1856, arising out of a dispute with France over who should protect certain Christian shrines in the Ottoman Empire, brought crisis. Because the fighting was concentrated in the Crimean peninsula on the Black Sea, Russia's transportation network of rivers and wagons failed to supply the distant Russian armies adequately. France and Great Britain, aided by Sardinia and the Ottoman Empire, inflicted a humiliating defeat on Russia.

This military defeat marked a turning point in Russian history because it demonstrated that Russia had fallen behind the rapidly industrializing nations of western Europe in many areas. At the very least, Russia needed railroads, better armaments, and reorganization of the army if it was to maintain its international position. Moreover, the disastrous war had caused hardship and raised the specter of massive peasant rebellion. Reform of serfdom was imperative. And as the new tsar, Alexander II (r. 1855–1881), told the serf owners, it would be better if reform came from above. Military disaster thus forced Alexander II and his ministers along the path of rapid social change and general modernization.

The first and greatest of the reforms was the freeing of the serfs in 1861. Human bondage was abolished forever, and the emancipated peasants received, on average, about half of the land. Yet they had to pay fairly high prices for their land, and because the land was owned collectively, each peasant village was jointly responsible for the payments of all the families in the village. The government hoped that collective responsibility would strengthen the peasant village as a social unit and prevent the development of a class of landless peasants. In practice, collective ownership and responsibility made it very difficult for individual peasants to improve agricultural methods or leave their villages. Thus the effects of the reform were limited.

Most of the later reforms were also halfway measures. In 1864 the government established a new institution of local government, the **zemstvo.** Members of this local assembly were elected by a three-class system of towns, peasant villages, and noble landowners. A zemstvo executive council dealt with local problems. Russian liberals hoped that this reform would lead to an elected national parliament, but they were soon disappointed. The local zemstvo remained subordinate to the traditional bureaucracy and the local nobility. More successful was reform of the legal system, which established independent courts and equality before the law. Education and policies toward Russian Jews were also liberalized somewhat, and censorship was relaxed but not removed.

The Industrialization of Russia

Until the twentieth century, Russia's greatest strides toward modernization were economic rather than political. Industry and transport, both so vital to the military, were transformed in two industrial surges. The first of

The Fruits of Terrorism, 1881   In the late 1870s a small group of revolutionaries believed that killing the tsar could destroy the Russian state. Succeeding in blowing up the reforming Alexander II after several near misses, the five assassins, including one woman, were quickly caught and hung. Russia entered an era of reaction and harsh authoritarian rule. (Illustrated London News, *1881*)

these came after 1860. The government encouraged and subsidized private railway companies, and construction boomed. In 1860 the empire had only about 1,250 miles of railroads; by 1880 it had about 15,500 miles. The railroads enabled agricultural Russia to export grain and thus earn money for further industrialization. Industrial suburbs grew up around Moscow and St. Petersburg, and a class of modern factory workers began to take shape.

Industrial development strengthened Russia's military forces and gave rise to territorial expansion to the south and east. Imperial expansion greatly excited many ardent Russian nationalists and superpatriots, who became some of the government's most enthusiastic supporters. Industrial development also contributed mightily to the spread of Marxian thought and the transformation of the Russian revolutionary movement after 1890.

In 1881 Alexander II was assassinated by a small group of terrorists. The era of reform came to an abrupt end, for the new tsar, Alexander III (r. 1881–1894), was a determined reactionary. Russia, and indeed all of Europe, experienced hard times economically in the 1880s. Political modernization remained frozen until 1905, but economic modernization sped forward in the massive industrial surge of the 1890s. Nationalism played a decisive role, as it had after the Crimean War. The key leader was Sergei Witte, the tough, competent minister of finance from 1892 to 1903. Inspired by the writings of Friedrich List (see pages 739–740), Witte believed that the harsh reality of industrial backwardness was threatening Russia's power and greatness.

Therefore, under Witte's leadership the government built state-owned railroads rapidly, doubling the network to thirty-five thousand miles by the end of the century. The gigantic trans-Siberian line connecting Moscow with Vladivostok on the Pacific Ocean five thousand miles away was Witte's pride. Witte established high protective tariffs to build Russian industry, and he put the country on the gold standard of the "civilized world" in order to strengthen Russian finances.

Witte's greatest innovation, however, was to use the West to catch up with the West. He aggressively encouraged foreigners to use their abundant capital and advanced technology to build great factories in backward Russia. As he told the tsar, "The inflow of foreign capital is . . . the only way by which our industry will be able to supply our country quickly with abundant and cheap products."[3] This policy was brilliantly successful, especially in southern Russia. There, in eastern Ukraine, foreign capitalists and their engineers built an enormous and very modern steel and coal industry almost from scratch in little more than a decade. By 1900 only the United States, Germany, and Great Britain were producing more steel than Russia. The Russian petroleum industry had even pulled up alongside that of the United States and was producing and refining half the world's oil. A fiercely autocratic and independent Russia was catching up with the advanced nations of the West.

The Revolution of 1905

Catching up partly meant vigorous territorial expansion, for this was the age of Western imperialism. By 1903 Russia had established a sphere of influence in Chinese Manchuria and was casting greedy eyes on northern Korea. When the diplomatic protests of equally imperialistic Japan were ignored, the Japanese launched a surprise attack in February 1904. To the amazement of self-confident Europeans, Japan scored repeated victories, and Russia was forced in September 1905 to accept a humiliating defeat.

As is often the case, military disaster abroad brought political upheaval at home. The business and professional classes had long wanted to match economic with political modernization. Their minimal goal was to turn the last of Europe's absolutist monarchies into a liberal, representative regime. Factory workers, strategically concentrated in the large cities, had all the grievances of early industrialization and were organized in a radical and still illegal labor movement. Peasants had gained little from the era of reforms and were suffering from poverty and overpopulation. At the same time, nationalist sentiment was emerging among the empire's minorities. The politically and culturally dominant ethnic Russians were only about 45 percent of the population, and by 1900 some intellectuals among the subject nationalities were calling for self-rule and autonomy. Separatist nationalism was strongest among the Poles and Ukrainians. With the army pinned down in Manchuria, all these currents of discontent converged in the **revolution of 1905.**

The beginning of the revolution pointed up the incompetence of the government. On a Sunday in January 1905, a massive crowd of workers and their families converged

"Freedom!" So reads the red "socialist" banner of this peasant woman, who appears as the symbol of radical demands in the Russian countryside in the revolution of 1905. This vibrant drawing is on the first page of a new review featuring political cartoons from the rapidly growing popular press. *(New York Public Library)*

peacefully on the Winter Palace in St. Petersburg to present a petition to the tsar. The workers were led by a trade-unionist priest named Father Gapon, who had been secretly supported by the police as a preferable alternative to more radical unions. Carrying icons and respectfully singing "God save the tsar," the workers did not know Nicholas II had fled the city. Suddenly troops opened fire, killing and wounding hundreds. The **Bloody Sunday** massacre turned ordinary workers against the tsar and produced a wave of general indignation.

Outlawed political parties came out into the open, and by the summer of 1905 strikes, peasant uprisings, revolts among minority nationalities, and troop mutinies were sweeping the country. The revolutionary surge culminated in October 1905 in a great paralyzing general strike, which forced the government to capitulate. The tsar issued the **October Manifesto,** which granted full civil rights and promised a popularly elected duma (parliament) with real legislative power. The manifesto split the opposition. Frightened middle-class leaders helped the government repress the uprising and survive as a constitutional monarchy.

On the eve of the opening of the first **Duma** in May 1906, the government issued the new constitution, the Fundamental Laws. The tsar retained great powers. The Duma, elected indirectly by universal male suffrage, and a largely appointive upper house could debate and pass laws, but the tsar had an absolute veto. As in Bismarck's Germany, the emperor appointed his ministers, who did not need to command a majority in the Duma.

The disappointed, predominately middle-class liberals, the largest group in the newly elected Duma, saw the Fundamental Laws as a step backward. Efforts to cooperate with the tsar's ministers soon broke down. The tsar then dismissed the Duma, only to find that a more hostile and radical opposition was elected in 1907. After three months of deadlock, the tsar dismissed the second Duma. Thereupon he and his reactionary advisers unilaterally rewrote the electoral law so as to increase greatly the weight of the propertied classes at the expense of workers, peasants, and national minorities.

The new law had the intended effect. With landowners assured half the seats in the Duma, the government secured a loyal majority in 1907 and again in 1912. Thus armed, the tough, energetic chief minister, Peter Stolypin, pushed through important agrarian reforms designed to break down collective village ownership of land and encourage the more enterprising peasants—his "wager on the strong." In 1914, Russia was partially modernized, a conservative constitutional monarchy with a peasant-based but industrializing economy.

The Responsive National State, 1871–1914

For central and western Europe, the unification of Italy and Germany by "blood and iron" marked the end of a dramatic period of nation building. After 1871 the heartland of Europe was organized into strong national states. Only on the borders of Europe—in Ireland and Russia, in Austria-Hungary and the Balkans—did subject peoples still strive for political unity and independence. Despite national differences, European domestic politics after 1871 had a common framework, the firmly established national state. The common themes within that framework were the emergence of mass politics and growing mass loyalty toward the national state.

For good reason, ordinary people—the masses of an industrializing, urbanizing society—felt increasing loyalty to their governments. More people could vote. By 1914 universal male suffrage had become the rule rather than the exception. This development had as much psychological as political significance. Ordinary men were no longer denied the right to vote because they lacked wealth or education. They felt that they counted; they could influence the government to some extent. They were becoming "part of the system."

Women also began to demand the right to vote. The women's suffrage movement achieved its first success in the western United States, and by 1913 women could vote in twelve states. Europe, too, moved slowly in this direction. In 1914 Norway gave the vote to most women. Elsewhere, women such as the English Emmeline Pankhurst were very militant in their demands. They heckled politicians and held public demonstrations. These efforts generally failed before 1914, but they prepared the way for the triumph of the women's suffrage movement immediately after World War I.

As the right to vote spread, politicians and parties in national parliaments represented the people more responsively. The multiparty system prevailing in most countries meant that parliamentary majorities were built on shifting coalitions of different parties, and this gave individual parties leverage to obtain benefits for their supporters. Governments also passed laws to alleviate general problems, thereby acquiring greater legitimacy and appearing more worthy of support.

There was a less positive side to building support for strong nation-states after 1871. Governments found that they could manipulate national feeling to create a sense of unity and to divert attention away from underlying class conflicts. Conservative and moderate leaders found that workers who voted socialist would rally around the flag in a diplomatic crisis or cheer when distant territory of doubtful value was seized in Africa or Asia (see Chapter 26). Therefore, after 1871 governing elites frequently used antiliberal and militaristic policies to help manage domestic conflicts, but at the expense of increasing the international tensions that erupted in 1914 in cataclysmic war and revolution (see Chapter 27).

In these same years some fanatics and demagogic political leaders also sought to build extreme nationalist movements by whipping up popular animosity toward imaginary enemies, especially the Jews. The growth of modern anti-Semitism after 1880 epitomized the most negative aspects of European nationalism before the First World War.

The German Empire

Politics in Germany after 1871 reflected many of the general developments. The new German Empire was a federal union of Prussia and twenty-four smaller states. Much of the everyday business of government was conducted by the separate states, but there was a strong national government with a chancellor—until 1890, Bismarck—and a popularly elected lower house, called the **Reichstag.** Although Bismarck refused to be bound by a parliamentary majority, he tried nonetheless to maintain one. This situation gave the political parties opportunities. Until 1878 Bismarck relied mainly on the National Liberals, who had rallied to him after 1866. They supported legislation useful for further economic and legal unification of the country.

Less wisely, they backed Bismarck's attack on the Catholic church, the so-called **Kulturkampf,** or "struggle for civilization." Like Bismarck, the middle-class National Liberals were particularly alarmed by Pius IX's declaration of papal infallibility in 1870. That dogma seemed to ask German Catholics to put loyalty to their church above loyalty to their nation. Only in Protestant Prussia did the Kulturkampf have even limited success. Catholics throughout the country generally voted for the Catholic Center party, which blocked passage of national laws hostile to the church. Finally, in 1878 Bismarck abandoned his attack. Indeed, he and the Catholic Center party entered into an uneasy but mutually advantageous alliance. Their reasons for doing so were largely economic.

In 1873 there was a worldwide financial crash, which put European agriculture in an increasingly difficult position. Wheat prices plummeted as cheap grain poured in from the United States, Canada, and Russia, where new lands were opening up. More railroads and technical improvements in shipping cut freight rates for grain drastically. European peasants, with their smaller, less efficient farms, could not compete in cereal production, especially in western and southern Germany. The peasantry there was largely Catholic, and the Catholic Center party was thus converted to higher tariffs to protect the economic interests of its supporters.

The same competitive pressures caused the Protestant Junkers, who owned large estates in eastern Germany, to embrace the cause of higher tariffs. These noble landowners were joined by some of the iron and steel magnates of the Prussian Rhineland and Westphalia who had previously favored free trade. With three such influential groups lobbying energetically, Bismarck was happy to go along with a new protective tariff in 1879. In doing so, he won new supporters in the Reichstag—the Center party of the Catholics and the Conservative party of the Prussian landowners—and he held on to most of the National Liberals.

Bismarck had been looking for a way to increase taxes, and the solution he chose was higher tariffs. Many other governments acted similarly. The 1880s and 1890s saw a widespread return to protectionism. France, in particular, established very high tariffs to protect agriculture and industry, peasants and manufacturers, from foreign competition. Thus the German government and other governments responded effectively to a major economic problem and won greater loyalty. The general rise of protectionism in this period was also an outstanding example of the dangers of self-centered nationalism: new tariffs led to international name-calling and nasty trade wars.

As for socialism, Bismarck tried to stop its growth in Germany because he genuinely feared its revolutionary language and allegiance to a movement transcending the nation-state. In 1878, after two attempts on the life of William I by radicals (though not socialists), Bismarck used a carefully orchestrated national outcry to ram through the Reichstag a law that strictly controlled socialist meetings and publications and outlawed the Social Democratic party, which was thereby driven underground. However, German socialists displayed a discipline and organization worthy of the Prussian army itself. Bismarck decided to try another tack.

Thus Bismarck's essentially conservative nation-state pioneered with social measures designed to win the support of working-class people. In 1883 he pushed through the Reichstag the first of several modern social security laws to help wage earners. The laws of 1883 and 1884 established national sickness and accident insurance; the law of 1889 established old-age pensions and retirement benefits. Henceforth sick, injured, and retired workers

The Need for Social Security This dramatic painting of busy workers in an iron-rolling mill in Berlin highlights the many dangers of the industrial workplace. Industrial accidents that killed or maimed were a fact of life, as were work-related illnesses and periodic unemployment. Germany's pioneering social security laws were an influential response to these challenges. *(Alte Nationalgalerie, Berlin/AKG London)*

could look forward to some regular benefits from the state. This national social security system, paid for through compulsory contributions by wage earners and employers as well as grants from the state, was the first of its kind anywhere. Bismarck's social security system did not wean workers from voting socialist, but it did give them a small stake in the system and protect them from some of the uncertainties of the complex urban industrial world. This enormously significant development was a product of political competition and government efforts to win popular support.

Increasingly, the great issues in German domestic politics were socialism and the Marxian Social Democratic party. In 1890 the new emperor, the young, idealistic, and unstable William II (r. 1888–1918), opposed Bismarck's attempt to renew the law outlawing the Social Democratic party. Eager to rule in his own right and to earn the support of the workers, William II forced Bismarck to resign. After the "dropping of the pilot," German foreign policy changed profoundly and mostly for the worse, but the government did pass new laws to aid workers and to legalize socialist political activity.

Yet William II was no more successful than Bismarck in getting workers to renounce socialism. Indeed, socialist ideas spread rapidly, and more and more Social Democrats were elected to the Reichstag in the 1890s.

After opposing a colonial war in German Southwest Africa in 1906 that led to important losses in the general elections of 1907, the German Social Democratic party broadened its base and adopted a more patriotic tone. In 1912 the party scored a great electoral victory, becoming the largest single party in the Reichstag. This victory shocked aristocrats and their wealthy conservative middle-class allies, heightening the fears of an impending socialist upheaval in both groups. Yet the "revolutionary" socialists were actually becoming less radical in Germany. In the years before World War I, the strength of socialist opposition to greater military spending and imperialist expansion declined substantially, for example. German socialists identified increasingly with the German state, and they concentrated on gradual social and political reform.

Republican France

Although Napoleon III's reign made some progress in reducing antagonisms between classes, the war with Prussia undid these efforts, and in 1871 France seemed hopelessly divided once again. The patriotic republicans who proclaimed the Third Republic in Paris after the military disaster at Sedan refused to admit defeat. They defended Paris with great heroism for weeks, living off rats and zoo animals until they were starved into submission by German armies in January 1871. When national elections then sent a large majority of conservatives and monarchists to the National Assembly and France's new leaders decided they had no choice but to surrender Alsace and Lorraine to Germany, the traumatized Parisians exploded in patriotic frustration and proclaimed the Paris Commune in March 1871. Vaguely radical, the leaders of the Commune wanted to govern Paris without interference from the conservative French countryside. The National Assembly, led by aging politician Adolphe Thiers, would hear none of it. The Assembly ordered the French army into Paris and brutally crushed the Commune. Twenty thousand people died in the fighting. As in June 1848, it was Paris against the provinces, French against French.

Out of this tragedy, France slowly formed a new national unity, achieving considerable stability before 1914. How is one to account for this? Luck played a part. Until 1875 the monarchists in the "republican" National Assembly had a majority but could not agree who should be king. The compromise Bourbon candidate refused to rule except under the white flag of his ancestors—a completely unacceptable condition. In the meantime, Thiers's destruction of the radical Commune and his other firm measures showed the fearful provinces and the middle class that the Third Republic might be moderate and socially conservative. France therefore retained the republic, though reluctantly. As President Thiers cautiously said, this was "the government which divides us least."

Another stabilizing factor was the skill and determination of the moderate republican leaders in the early years. The most famous of these was Léon Gambetta, the son of an Italian grocer, a warm, easygoing, unsuccessful lawyer who had turned professional politician. A master of emerging mass politics, Gambetta combined eloquence with the personal touch as he preached a republic of truly equal opportunity. Gambetta was also instrumental in establishing absolute parliamentary supremacy between 1877 and 1879, when the deputies challenged Marshall MacMahon and forced the somewhat autocratic president of the republic to resign. By 1879 the great majority of members of both the upper and the lower houses of the National Assembly were republicans. Although these republicans were split among many parliamentary groups and later among several parties—a situation that led to constant coalition politics and the rapid turnover of ministers—the Third Republic had firm foundations after almost a decade.

The moderate republicans sought to preserve their creation by winning the hearts and minds of the next generation. Trade unions were fully legalized, and France acquired a colonial empire. More important, under the leadership of Jules Ferry, the moderate republicans of small towns and villages passed a series of laws between 1879 and 1886 establishing free compulsory elementary education for both girls and boys. At the same time, they greatly expanded the state system of public tax-supported schools. Thus France shared fully in the general expansion of public education, which served as a critical nation-building tool throughout the Western world in the late nineteenth century.

In France most elementary and much secondary education had traditionally been in the parochial schools of the Catholic church, which had long been hostile to republics and to much of secular life. Free compulsory elementary education in France became secular republican education. The pledge of allegiance and the national anthem replaced the catechism and the "Ave Maria." Young male and female teachers carried the ideology of patriotic republicanism into every corner of France and sought to win the loyalty of the young citizens to the republic.

Unlike most Western countries, which insisted on the total "purity" of their female teachers and would not hire married women, the Third Republic actively encouraged young teachers to marry and guaranteed that both partners would teach in the same location. There were three main reasons for this unusual policy. First, married female (and male) teachers with their own children provided a vivid contrast to celibate nuns (and priests), who had for generations stood for most primary education in the popular mind. Second, the republican leaders believed that married women (and men) would better cope with the potential loneliness and social isolation of unfamiliar towns and villages, especially where the local Catholic school was strong. Third, French politicians and opinion leaders worried continually about France's very low birthrate after 1870, and they believed that women combining teaching careers and motherhood would provide the country with a good example. Hiring married schoolteachers was part of an effort to create a whole new culture of universal, secular, and republican education. This illustrates a larger truth—that truly lasting political change must usually be supported by changes in the underlying culture.

Although the educational reforms of the 1880s disturbed French Catholics, many of them rallied to the republic in the 1890s. The limited acceptance of the modern world by the more liberal Pope Leo XIII (1878–1903) eased tensions between church and state. Unfortunately, the **Dreyfus affair** changed all that.

Alfred Dreyfus, a Jewish captain in the French army, was falsely accused and convicted of treason. His family never doubted his innocence and fought to reopen the case, enlisting the support of prominent republicans and intellectuals such as novelist Emile Zola. In 1898 and 1899, the case split France apart. On one side was the army, which had manufactured evidence against Dreyfus, joined by anti-Semites and most of the Catholic establishment. On the other side stood the civil libertarians and most of the more radical republicans.

This battle, which eventually led to Dreyfus's being declared innocent, revived republican feeling against the church. Between 1901 and 1905, the government severed all ties between the state and the Catholic church after centuries of close relations. The salaries of priests and bishops were no longer paid by the government, and all churches were given to local committees of lay Catholics. Catholic schools were put on their own financially and soon lost a third of their students. The state school system's power of indoctrination was greatly strengthened. In France only the growing socialist movement, with its very different and thoroughly secular ideology, stood in opposition to patriotic, republican nationalism.

Captain Alfred Dreyfus Leaving an 1899 reconsideration of his original court martial, Dreyfus receives an insulting "guard of dishonor" from soldiers whose backs are turned. Top army leaders were determined to brand Dreyfus as a traitor. *(Roger-Viollet/Getty Images)*

Great Britain and Ireland

Britain in the late nineteenth century has often been seen as a shining example of peaceful and successful political evolution. Germany was stuck with a manipulated parliament that gave an irresponsible emperor too much power; France had a quarrelsome parliament that gave its presidents too little power. Great Britain, in contrast, seemed to enjoy an effective two-party parliament that skillfully guided the country from classical liberalism to full-fledged democracy with hardly a misstep.

This view of Great Britain is not so much wrong as it is incomplete. After the right to vote was granted to males of the solid middle class in 1832, opinion leaders and politicians wrestled with the uncertainties of a further expansion of the franchise. In his famous essay *On Liberty,* published in 1859, philosopher John Stuart Mill (1806–1873), the leading heir to the Benthamite tradition (see page 791), probed the problem of how to protect the rights of individuals and minorities in the emerging age of mass electoral participation. Mill pleaded eloquently for the practical and moral value inherent in safeguarding individual differences and unpopular opinions. In 1867 Benjamin Disraeli and the Conservatives extended the vote to all middle-class males and the best-paid workers. The son of a Jewish stockbroker and himself a novelist and urban dandy, the ever-fascinating Disraeli (1804–1881) was willing to risk this "leap in the dark" in order to broaden the Conservative party's traditional base of aristocratic and landed support. After 1867 English political parties and electoral campaigns became more modern, and the "lower orders" appeared to vote as responsibly as their "betters." Hence the Third Reform Bill of 1884 gave the vote to almost every adult male.

While the House of Commons was drifting toward democracy, the House of Lords was content to slumber nobly. Between 1901 and 1910, however, that bastion of aristocratic conservatism tried to reassert itself. Acting as supreme court of the land, it ruled against labor unions in two important decisions. And after the Liberal party came to power in 1906, the Lords vetoed several measures passed by the Commons, including the so-called **People's Budget,** which was designed to increase spending on social welfare services. The Lords finally capitulated, as they had done in 1832, when the king threatened to create enough new peers to pass the bill.

Aristocratic conservatism yielded to popular democracy once and for all. The result was that extensive social welfare measures, slow to come to Great Britain, were passed in a spectacular rush between 1906 and 1914. During those years, the Liberal party, inspired by the fiery Welshman David Lloyd George (1863–1945), substantially raised taxes on the rich as part of the People's Budget. This income helped the government pay for national health insurance, unemployment benefits, old-age pensions, and a host of other social measures. The state was integrating the urban masses socially as well as politically.

This record of accomplishment was only part of the story, however. On the eve of World War I, the unanswered question of Ireland brought Great Britain to the brink of civil war. The terrible Irish famine fueled an Irish revolutionary movement. Thereafter, the English slowly granted concessions, such as the abolition of the privileges of the Anglican church and rights for Irish peasants. Liberal prime minister William Gladstone (1809–1898), who had proclaimed twenty years earlier that "my mission is to pacify Ireland," introduced bills to give Ireland self-government in 1886 and in 1893. They failed to pass. After two decades of relative quiet, Irish nationalists in the British Parliament saw their chance. They supported the Liberals in their battle for the People's Budget and received a home-rule bill for Ireland in return.

Thus Ireland, the emerald isle, was on the brink of achieving self-government. Yet Ireland was composed of two peoples. As much as the Irish Catholic majority in the southern counties wanted home rule, precisely that much did the Irish Protestants of the northern counties of Ulster come to oppose it. Motivated by the accumulated fears and hostilities of generations, the Protestants of Ulster refused to submerge themselves in a Catholic Ireland, just as Irish Catholics had refused to submit to a Protestant Britain.

The Ulsterites vowed to resist home rule in northern Ireland. By December 1913 they had raised 100,000 armed volunteers, and they were supported by much of English public opinion. Thus in 1914 the Liberals in the House of Lords introduced a compromise home-rule bill that did not apply to the northern counties. This bill, which openly betrayed promises made to Irish nationalists, was rejected, and in September the original home-rule bill was passed but simultaneously suspended for the duration of the hostilities—the momentous Irish question had been overtaken by an earth-shattering world war in August 1914.

Irish developments illustrated once again the power of national feeling and national movements in the nineteenth century. Moreover, they were proof that governments could not elicit greater loyalty unless they could capture and control that elemental current of national feeling. Though Great Britain had much going for it—power,

"No Home Rule"   Posters like this one helped to foment pro-British, anti-Catholic sentiment in the northern Irish counties of Ulster before the First World War. The rifle raised defiantly and the accompanying rhyme are a thinly veiled threat of armed rebellion and civil war. *(Reproduced with the kind permission of the Trustees of the National Museums & Galleries of Northern Ireland)*

Parliament, prosperity—none of these availed in the face of the conflicting nationalisms created by Catholics and Protestants in northern Ireland. Similarly, progressive Sweden was powerless to stop the growth of the Norwegian national movement, which culminated in Norway's breaking away from Sweden and becoming a fully independent nation in 1905. In this light, one can also see how hopeless was the case of the Ottoman Empire in Europe in the later nineteenth century. It was only a matter of time before the Serbs, Bulgarians, and Romanians would break away, and they did.

The Austro-Hungarian Empire

The dilemma of conflicting nationalisms in Ireland also helps one appreciate how desperate the situation in the Austro-Hungarian Empire had become by the early twentieth century. In 1849 Magyar nationalism had driven Hungarian patriots to declare an independent Hungarian republic, which was savagely crushed by Russian and Austrian armies (see page 780). Throughout the 1850s, Hungary was ruled as a conquered territory, and Emperor Francis Joseph and his bureaucracy tried hard to centralize the state and Germanize the language and culture of the different nationalities.

Then in the wake of defeat by Prussia in 1866, a weakened Austria was forced to strike a compromise and establish the so-called dual monarchy. The empire was divided in two, and the nationalistic Magyars gained virtual independence for Hungary. Henceforth each half of the empire agreed to deal with its own "barbarians"—its own minorities—as it saw fit. The two states were joined only by a shared monarch and common ministries for finance, defense, and foreign affairs.

In Austria ethnic Germans were only one-third of the population, and in 1895 many Germans saw their traditional dominance threatened by Czechs, Poles, and other Slavs. A particularly emotional issue in the Austrian parliament was the language used in government and elementary education at the local level. From 1900 to 1914 the parliament was so divided that ministries generally could not obtain a majority and ruled instead by decree. Efforts by both conservatives and socialists to defuse national antagonisms by stressing economic issues that cut across ethnic lines were largely unsuccessful.

In Hungary the Magyar nobility in 1867 restored the constitution of 1848 and used it to dominate both the Magyar peasantry and the minority populations until 1914. Only the wealthiest one-fourth of adult males had the right to vote, making the parliament the creature of the Magyar elite. Laws promoting the use of the Magyar (Hungarian) language in schools and government were rammed through and bitterly resented, especially by the Croatians and Romanians. While Magyar extremists campaigned loudly for total separation from Austria, the radical leaders of the subject nationalities dreamed in turn of independence from Hungary. Unlike most major countries, which harnessed nationalism to strengthen the state after 1871, the Austro-Hungarian Empire was progressively weakened and destroyed by it.

The Language Ordinances of 1897 The ordinances, which were intended to satisfy the Czechs by establishing equality between German and the local language in non-German districts of Austria, produced a powerful backlash among Germans. This wood engraving shows troops dispersing German protesters of the new law before the parliament building. *(Österreichische Nationalbibliothek)*

Jewish Emancipation and Modern Anti-Semitism

Revolutionary changes in political principles and the triumph of the nation-state brought equally revolutionary changes in Jewish life in western and central Europe. Beginning in France in 1791, Jews gradually gained their civil rights, although the process was slow and uneven. The decisive turning point came in 1848, when Jews formed part of the revolutionary vanguard in Vienna and Berlin and the Frankfurt Assembly endorsed full rights for German Jews. Important gains in 1848 survived the conservative reaction, and throughout the 1850s and 1860s liberals in Austria, Italy, and Prussia pressed successfully for legal equality. In 1871 the constitution of the new German Empire consolidated the process of Jewish emancipation in central Europe. It abolished all restrictions on Jewish marriage, choice of occupation, place of residence, and property ownership. Exclusion from government employment and discrimination in social relations remained. However, according to one leading historian, by 1871 "it was widely accepted in Central Europe that the gradual disappearance of anti-Jewish prejudice was inevitable."[4]

The process of emancipation presented Jews with challenges and opportunities. Traditional Jewish occupations, such as court financial agent, village moneylender, and peddler, were undermined by free-market reforms, but careers in business, the professions, and the arts were opening to Jewish talent. Many Jews responded energetically and successfully. Active in finance and railroad building, European Jews excelled in wholesale and retail trade, consumer industries, journalism, medicine, and law. By 1871 a majority of Jewish people in western and central Europe had improved their economic situation and entered the middle classes. Most Jewish people also identified strongly with their respective nation-states and with good reason saw themselves as patriotic citizens.

Vicious anti-Semitism reappeared after the stock market crash of 1873, beginning in central Europe. Drawing on long traditions of religious intolerance, ghetto exclusion, and periodic anti-Jewish riots and expulsions, this anti-Semitism was also a modern development. It built on the general reaction against liberalism and its economic and political policies. Modern anti-Semitism whipped up resentment against Jewish achievement and Jewish "financial control," while fanatics claimed that the

Jewish race (rather than the Jewish religion) posed a biological threat to the German people. Anti-Semitic beliefs were particularly popular among conservatives, extremist nationalists, and people who felt threatened by Jewish competition, such as small shopkeepers, officeworkers, and professionals.

Anti-Semites also created modern political parties to attack and degrade Jews. In 1893, the prewar electoral high point in Germany, small anti-Semitic parties secured 2.9 percent of the votes cast. However, in Austrian Vienna in the early 1890s, Karl Lueger and his "Christian socialists" won striking electoral victories, spurring Theodor Herzl to turn from German nationalism and advocate political **Zionism** and the creation of a Jewish state. (See the feature "Individuals in Society: Theodor Herzl.") Lueger, the popular mayor of Vienna from 1897 to 1910, combined fierce anti-Semitic rhetoric with municipal ownership of basic services, and he appealed especially to the German-speaking lower middle class—and an unsuccessful young artist named Adolf Hitler.

Before 1914 anti-Semitism was most oppressive in eastern Europe, where Jews also suffered from terrible poverty. In the Russian empire, where there was no Jewish emancipation and 4 million of Europe's 7 million Jewish people lived in 1880, officials used anti-Semitism to channel popular discontent away from the government and onto the Jewish minority. Russian Jews were denounced as foreign exploiters who corrupted national traditions, and in 1881–1882 a wave of violent pogroms commenced in southern Russia. The police and the army stood aside for days while peasants looted and destroyed Jewish property. Official harassment continued in the following decades, and quotas were placed on Jewish residency, education, and participation in the professions. As a result, some Russian Jews turned toward self-emancipation and the vision of a Zionist settlement in Palestine. Large numbers also emigrated to western Europe and the United States. About 2.75 million Jews left eastern Europe between 1881 and 1914.

Marxism and the Socialist Movement

Nationalism served, for better or worse, as a new unifying principle. But what about socialism? Did the rapid growth of socialist parties, which were generally Marxian parties dedicated to an international proletarian revolution, mean that national states had failed to gain the support of workers? Certainly, many prosperous and conservative citizens were greatly troubled by the socialist movement. And numerous historians have portrayed the years before 1914 as a time of increasing conflict between revolutionary socialism, on the one hand, and a nationalist alliance of the conservative aristocracy and the prosperous middle class, on the other. This question requires close examination.

The Socialist International

Socialism appealed to large numbers of workingmen and workingwomen in the late nineteenth century, and the growth of socialist parties after 1871 was phenomenal. (See the feature "Listening to the Past: The Making of a Socialist" on pages 852–853.) Neither Bismarck's antisocialist laws nor his extensive social security system checked the growth of the German Social Democratic party, which espoused the Marxian ideology. By 1912 it had millions of followers and was the largest party in the Reichstag. Socialist parties also grew in other countries, though nowhere else with such success. In 1883 Russian exiles in Switzerland founded the Russian Social Democratic party, which grew rapidly after 1890 despite internal disputes. In France various socialist parties re-emerged in the 1880s after the carnage of the Paris Commune. They were finally unified in 1905 in an increasingly powerful Marxian party called the French Section of the Workers International. Belgium and Austria-Hungary also had strong socialist parties.

As the name of the French party suggests, Marxian socialist parties were eventually linked together in an international organization. As early as 1848, Marx had laid out his intellectual system in *The Communist Manifesto* (see pages 765–766). He had declared that "the working men have no country," and he had urged proletarians of all nations to unite against their governments. Joining the flood of radicals and republicans who fled continental Europe for England and America after the unsuccessful revolutions of 1848, Marx settled in London. Poor and depressed, he lived on his meager earnings as a journalist and on the gifts of his friend Friedrich Engels. Marx never stopped thinking of revolution. Digging deeply into economics and history, he concluded that revolution follows economic crisis and tried to prove this in his greatest theoretical work, *Capital* (1867).

The bookish Marx also excelled as a practical organizer. In 1864 he played an important role in founding the First International of socialists—the International Working Men's Association. In the following years, he battled successfully to control the organization and used its annual meetings as a means of spreading his realistic, "scientific" doctrines of inevitable socialist revolution.

Individuals in Society

Theodor Herzl

In September 1897, only days after his vision and energy had called into being the First Zionist Congress in Basel, Switzerland, Theodor Herzl (1860–1904) assessed the results in his diary: "If I were to sum up the Congress in a word—which I shall take care not to publish—it would be this: At Basel I founded the Jewish state. If I said this out loud today I would be greeted by universal laughter. In five years perhaps, and certainly in fifty years, everyone will perceive it."* Herzl's buoyant optimism, which so often carried him forward, was prophetic. Leading the Zionist movement until his death at age forty-four in 1904, Herzl guided the first historic steps toward modern Jewish political nationhood and the creation of Israel in 1948.

Theodor Herzl was born in Budapest, Hungary, into an upper-middle-class, German-speaking Jewish family. When Herzl was eighteen, his family moved to Vienna, where he studied law. As a university student, he soaked up the liberal beliefs of most well-to-do Viennese Jews, who also championed the assimilation of German culture. Wrestling with his nonreligious Jewishness and his strong pro-German feeling, Herzl embraced German nationalism and joined a German dueling fraternity. There he discovered that full acceptance required openly anti-Semitic attitudes and a repudiation of all things Jewish. This Herzl could not tolerate, and he resigned. After receiving his law degree, he embarked on a literary career. In 1889 Herzl married into a wealthy Viennese Jewish family, but he and his socialite wife were mismatched and never happy together.

Herzl achieved considerable success as both a journalist and a playwright. His witty comedies focused on the bourgeoisie, including Jewish millionaires trying to live like aristocrats. Accepting many German stereotypes, Herzl sometimes depicted eastern Jews as uneducated and grasping. But as a dedicated, highly educated liberal, he mainly believed that the Jewish shortcomings he perceived were the results of age-old persecution and would disappear through education and assimilation. Herzl also took a growing pride in Jewish steadfastness in the face of victimization and suffering. He savored memories of his early Jewish education and going with his father to the synagogue.

The emergence of modern anti-Semitism shocked Herzl, as it did many acculturated Jewish Germans. Moving to Paris in 1891 as the correspondent for Vienna's leading liberal newspaper, Herzl studied politics and pondered recent historical developments. He then came to a bold conclusion, published in 1896 as *The Jewish State: An Attempt at a Modern Solution to the Jewish Question*. According to Herzl, Jewish assimilation had failed, and attempts to combat anti-Semitism would never succeed. Only by building an independent Jewish state could the Jewish people achieve dignity and renewal. As recent scholarship shows, Herzl developed his political nationalism, or Zionism, before the anti-Jewish agitation accompanying the Dreyfus affair, which only strengthened his faith in his analysis.

Theodor Herzl, ca 1900. (AKG London)

Generally rebuffed by skeptical Jewish elites in western and central Europe, Herzl turned for support to youthful idealists and the poor Jewish masses. He became an inspiring man of action, rallying the delegates to the annual Zionist congresses, directing the growth of the worldwide Zionist organization, and working himself to death. Herzl also understood that national consciousness required powerful emotions and symbols, such as a Jewish flag. Flags build nations, he said, because people "live and die for a flag."

Putting the Zionist vision before non-Jews and world public opinion, Herzl believed in international diplomacy and political agreements. He traveled constantly to negotiate with European rulers and top officials, seeking their support in securing territory for a Jewish state, usually in the Ottoman Empire. Aptly described by an admiring contemporary as "the first Jewish statesman since the destruction of Jerusalem," Herzl proved most successful in Britain. He paved the way for the 1917 Balfour Declaration, which solemnly pledged British support for a "Jewish homeland" in Palestine.

Questions for Analysis

1. Describe Theodor Herzl's background and early beliefs. Do you see a link between Herzl's early German nationalism and his later Zionism?
2. How did Herzl work as a leader to turn his Zionist vision into a reality?

*Quotes are from Theodor Herzl, *The Diaries of Theodor Herzl*, trans. and ed. with an introduction by Marvin Lowenthal (New York: Grosset & Dunlap, 1962), pp. 224, 22, xxi.

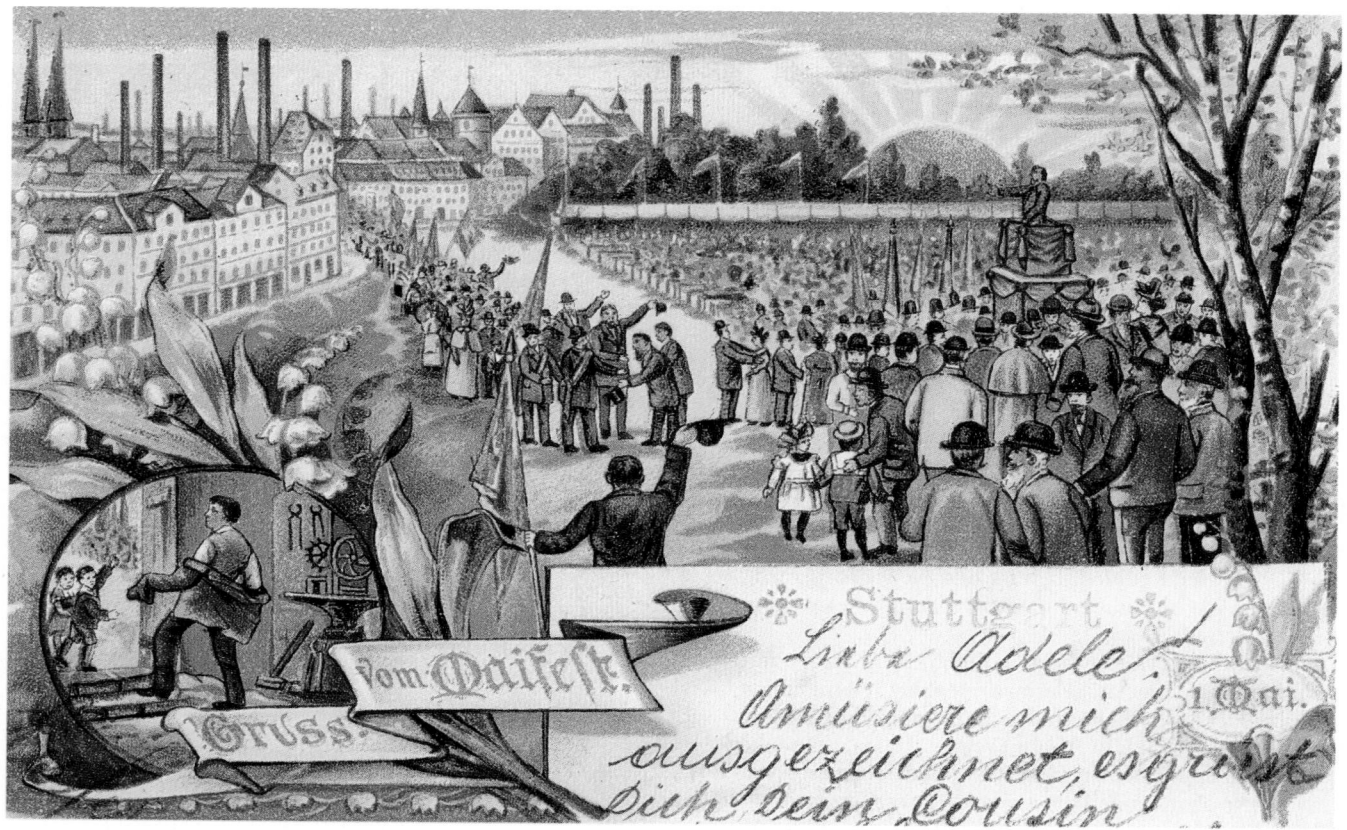

"Greetings from the May Day Festival"   Workers participated enthusiastically in the annual one-day strike on May 1 to honor internationalist socialist solidarity, as this postcard from a happy woman visitor to her cousin suggests. Speeches, picnics, and parades were the order of the day, and workers celebrated their respectability and independent culture. Picture postcards developed with railroads and mass travel. *(AKG London)*

Then Marx enthusiastically embraced the passionate, vaguely radical patriotism of the Paris Commune and its terrible conflict with the French National Assembly as a giant step toward socialist revolution. This impetuous action frightened many of his early supporters, especially the more moderate British labor leaders. The First International collapsed.

Yet international proletarian solidarity remained an important objective for Marxists. In 1889, as the individual parties in different countries grew stronger, socialist leaders came together to form the Second International, which lasted until 1914. The International was only a federation of national socialist parties, but it had a great psychological impact. Every three years, delegates from the different parties met to interpret Marxian doctrines and plan coordinated action. May 1 (May Day) was declared an annual international one-day strike, a day of marches and demonstrations. A permanent executive for the International was established. Many feared and many others rejoiced in the growing power of socialism and the Second International.

Unions and Revisionism

Was socialism really radical and revolutionary in these years? On the whole, it was not. Indeed, as socialist parties grew and attracted large numbers of members, they looked more and more toward gradual change and steady improvement for the working class and less and less toward revolution. The mainstream of European socialism became militantly moderate; that is, socialists increasingly combined radical rhetoric with sober action.

Workers themselves were progressively less inclined to follow radical programs. There were several reasons for this.

As workers gained the right to vote and to participate politically in the nation-state, they focused their attention more on elections than on revolutions. And as workers won real, tangible benefits, this furthered the process. Workers were also not immune to patriotic education and indoctrination during military service, and many responded positively to drum-beating parades and aggressive foreign policy as they loyally voted for socialists. Nor were workers a unified social group.

Perhaps most important of all, workers' standard of living rose gradually but substantially after 1850 as the promise of the Industrial Revolution was at least partially realized. In Great Britain, for example, workers could buy almost twice as much with their wages in 1906 as in 1850, and most of the increase came after 1870. Workers experienced similar gradual increases in most continental countries after 1850, though much less strikingly in late-developing Russia. Improvement in the standard of living was much more than merely a matter of higher wages. The quality of life improved dramatically in urban areas. For all these reasons, workers tended more and more to become militantly moderate: they demanded gains, but they were less likely to take to the barricades in pursuit of them.

The growth of labor unions reinforced this trend toward moderation. In the early stages of industrialization, modern unions were generally prohibited by law. A famous law of the French Revolution had declared all guilds and unions illegal in the name of "liberty" in 1791. In Great Britain, attempts by workers to unite were considered criminal conspiracies after 1799. Other countries had similar laws, and these obviously hampered union development. In France, for example, about two hundred workers were imprisoned each year between 1825 and 1847 for taking part in illegal combinations. Unions were considered subversive bodies, only to be hounded and crushed.

From this sad position workers struggled to escape. Great Britain led the way in 1824 and 1825 when unions won the right to exist but (generally) not the right to strike. After the collapse of Robert Owen's attempt to form one big union in the 1830s (see page 749), new and more practical kinds of unions appeared. Limited primarily to highly skilled workers such as machinists and carpenters, the "new model unions" avoided both radical politics and costly strikes. Instead, their sober, respectable leaders concentrated on winning better wages and hours for their members through collective bargaining and compromise. This approach helped pave the way to full acceptance in Britain in the 1870s, when unions won the right to strike without being held legally liable for the financial damage inflicted on employers. After 1890 unions for unskilled workers developed, and between 1901 and 1906 the legal position of British unions was further strengthened.

Germany was the most industrialized, socialized, and unionized continental country by 1914. German unions were not granted important rights until 1869, and until the antisocialist law was repealed in 1890, they were frequently harassed by the government as socialist fronts. Nor were socialist leaders particularly interested in union activity, believing as they did in the iron law of low wages and the need for political revolution. The result was that as late as 1895, there were only about 270,000 union members in a male industrial workforce of nearly 8 million. Then, with German industrialization still storming ahead and almost all legal harassment eliminated, union membership skyrocketed, reaching roughly 3 million in 1912.

This great expansion both reflected and influenced the changing character of German unions. Increasingly, unions in Germany focused on bread-and-butter issues—wages, hours, working conditions—rather than on the dissemination of pure socialist doctrine. Genuine collective bargaining, long opposed by socialist intellectuals as a "sellout," was officially recognized as desirable by the German Trade Union Congress in 1899. When employers proved unwilling to bargain, a series of strikes forced them to change their minds.

Between 1906 and 1913, successful collective bargaining gained a prominent place in German industrial relations. In 1913 alone, over ten thousand collective bargaining agreements affecting 1.25 million workers were signed. Gradual improvement, not revolution, was becoming the primary goal of the German trade-union movement.

The German trade unions and their leaders were in fact, if not in name, thoroughgoing revisionists. **Revisionism**—that most awful of sins in the eyes of militant Marxists in the twentieth century—was an effort by various socialists to update Marxian doctrines to reflect the realities of the time. Thus the socialist Edward Bernstein (1850–1932) argued in 1899 in his *Evolutionary Socialism* that Marx's predictions of ever-greater poverty for workers and ever-greater concentration of wealth in ever-fewer hands had been proved false. Therefore, Bernstein suggested, socialists should reform their doctrines and tactics. They should combine with other progressive forces to win gradual evolutionary gains for workers through legislation, unions, and further economic development. These views were denounced as heresy by the German Social Democratic party and later by the entire Second International. Yet the revisionist, gradualist approach continued to gain the tacit acceptance of many German socialists, particularly in the trade unions.

Moderation found followers elsewhere. In France the great socialist leader Jean Jaurès (1859–1914) formally repudiated revisionist doctrines in order to establish a unified socialist party, but he remained at heart a gradualist and optimistic secular humanist. Questions of revolution split Russian Marxists.

Socialist parties before 1914 had clear-cut national characteristics. Russians and socialists in the Austro-Hungarian Empire tended to be the most radical. The German party talked revolution and practiced reformism, greatly influenced by its enormous trade-union movement. The French party talked revolution and tried to practice it, unrestrained by a trade-union movement that was both very weak and very radical. In England the socialist but non-Marxian Labour party, reflecting the well-established union movement, was formally committed to gradual reform. In Spain and Italy, Marxian socialism was very weak. There anarchism, seeking to smash the state rather than the bourgeoisie, dominated radical thought and action.

In short, socialist policies and doctrines varied from country to country. Socialism itself was to a large extent "nationalized" behind the imposing façade of international unity. This helps explain why when war came in 1914, almost all socialist leaders supported their governments.

Summary

From the mid-nineteenth century on, Western society became nationalistic as well as urban and industrial. Nation-states gradually enlisted widespread popular support and gave men and women a greater sense of belonging. Even socialism became increasingly national in orientation, gathering strength as a champion of working-class interests in domestic politics. Yet even though nationalism served to unite peoples, it also drove them apart—obvious not only in the United States before the Civil War and in Austria-Hungary and Ireland, but also throughout Europe. There the universal national faith, which usually reduced social tensions within states, promoted a bitter, almost Darwinian, competition between states and thus threatened the progress and unity it had helped to build.

Key Terms

Red Shirts	Duma
Zollverein	Reichstag
Homestead Act	Kulturkampf
modernization	Dreyfus affair
zemstvo	People's Budget
revolution of 1905	Zionism
Bloody Sunday	revisionism
October Manifesto	

Notes

1. Quoted in H. Kohn, *The Mind of Germany: The Education of a Nation* (New York: Charles Scribner's Sons/Macmillan, 1960), p. 159.
2. H. Schulze, *States, Nations and Nationalism: From the Middle Ages to the Present* (Oxford: Blackwell, 1994), pp. 222–223, 246–247.
3. Quoted in J. McKay, *Pioneers for Profit: Foreign Entrepreneurship and Russian Industrialization, 1885–1913* (Chicago: University of Chicago Press, 1970), p. 11.
4. R. Seltzer, *Jewish People, Jewish Thought: The Jewish Experience in History* (New York: Macmillan, 1980), p. 533.

Suggested Reading

In addition to the general works mentioned in the Suggested Reading for Chapter 23, R. Gildea, *Barricades and Borders: Europe, 1800–1914,* 2d ed. (1996), and T. Blanning, *The Cambridge Illustrated History of Europe* (1996), provide useful and up-to-date surveys of the entire nineteenth century. G. Craig, *Germany, 1866–1945* (1980), and B. Moore, *Social Origins of Dictatorship and Democracy* (1966), are outstanding.

R. Tombs, *France, 1814–1914* (1996), is an impressive recent survey with an up-to-date bibliography, and R. Anderson, *France, 1870–1914* (1977), provides a clear introduction. D. Harvey, *Napoleon III and His Comic Empire* (1988), brings the world of Louis Napoleon vibrantly alive, whereas K. Marx, *The Eighteenth Brumaire of Louis Napoleon,* is a famous denunciation of the coup d'état. E. Weber, *France, Fin de Siècle* (1986), captures the spirit of Paris at the end of the century. G. Gullickson, *Unruly Women of Paris: Images of the Commune* (1996), is an exciting portrait of contested images of radical women in the Paris Commune, and E. Accampo, R. Fuchs, and M. Stewart, *Gender and the Politics of Social Reform in France, 1870–1914* (1995), shows how views of women influenced social legislation. E. Weber, *Peasants into Frenchmen* (1976), stresses the role of education and modern communications in the transformation of rural France after 1870. E. Cahm, *The Dreyfus Affair in French Society and Politics* (1996), and G. Chapman, *The Dreyfus Case: A Reassessment* (1955), are careful examinations of the famous case. In *Jean Barois,* Nobel Prize winner Roger Du Gard accurately re-creates in novel form the Dreyfus affair, and Emile Zola's novel *The Debacle* treats the Franco-Prussian War realistically.

The resurgence of European nationalism since the fall of communism has led to important new studies; particularly recommended are H. Schulze, *States, Nations and Nationalism: From the Middle Ages to the Present* (1996), and R. Brubaker, *Citizenship and Nationhood in France and Germany* (1992). D. M. Smith has written widely on Italy, and his *Garibaldi* (1956) and *Mazzini* (1994) are engaging biographies. In addition to the study on Germany by Kohn cited in the Notes, see O. Pflanze, *Bismarck and the Development in Germany: The Period of Unification, 1815–1871* (1963);

D. Williamson, *Bismarck and Germany, 1862–1890* (1994); and E. Eyck, *Bismarck and the German Empire* (1964). H. Wehler, *The German Empire, 1871–1918* (1985), stresses the strength of the landed nobility and the weakness of the middle class in an influential synthesis, which is challenged by D. Blackbourn and G. Eley, *The Peculiarities of German History: Bourgeois Society and Politics in Nineteenth-Century Germany* (1984). M. Kitchen, *The Cambridge Illustrated History of Germany* (1996), features handsome pictures and a readable text. F. Stern, *Gold and Iron* (1977), is a fascinating examination of relations between Bismarck and his financial adviser, the Jewish banker Bleichröder. L. Cecil, *Wilhelm II: Prince and Emperor, 1859–1900* (1989), probes the character and politics of Germany's ruler. K. McAleer, *Dueling: The Cult of Honor in Fin-de-Siècle Germany* (1994); K. D. Barkin, *The Controversy over German Industrialization, 1890–1902* (1970); and E. Spencer, *Management and Labor in Imperial Germany: Ruhr Industrialists as Employers* (1984), are valuable in-depth investigations. H. Glasser, ed., *The German Mind in the Nineteenth Century* (1981), is an outstanding anthology, as are R. E. Joeres and M. Maynes, eds., *German Women in the Eighteenth and Nineteenth Centuries* (1986), and P. Mendes-Flohr, ed., *The Jew in the Modern World: A Documentary History* (1980). C. Schorske, *Fin de Siècle Vienna: Politics and Culture* (1980), and P. Gay, *Freud, Jews, and Other Germans* (1978), are brilliant on aspects of modern culture. A. Sked, *The Decline and Fall of the Habsburg Empire, 1815–1918* (1989), and R. Kann, *The Multinational Empire*, 2 vols. (1950, 1964), probe the intricacies of the nationality problem in Austria-Hungary. Southern nationalism in the United States has been interpreted from different perspectives by P. Escott, *After Secession: Jefferson Davis and the Failure of Confederate Nationalism* (1974), and D. Faust, *The Creation of Confederate Nationalism* (1988). E. Foner, *A Short History of Reconstruction* (1989), is recommended.

In addition to the study on Russian industrial development by T. von Laue, *Sergei Witte and the Industrialization of Russia* (1963), McKay cited in the Notes, P. Gatrell, *The Tsarist Economy, 1850–1917* (1986), and A. Rieber, *Merchants and Entrepreneurs in Imperial Russia* (1982), are recommended. Among fine studies on Russian development, see especially H. Rogger, *Russia in the Age of Modernization and Revolution, 1881–1917* (1983), which has an excellent bibliography; T. Emmons, *The Russian Landed Gentry and the Peasant Emancipation of 1861* (1968); and H. Troyat, *Daily Life in Russia Under the Last Tsar* (1962). T. Friedgut, *Iuzovka and Revolution: Life and Work in Russia's Donbass, 1869–1924* (1989); R. Zelnik, *Labor and Society in Tsarist Russia, 1855–1870* (1971); and R. Johnson, *Peasant and Proletarian: The Working Class of Moscow at the End of the Nineteenth Century* (1979), skillfully treat different aspects of working-class life and politics. W. E. Mosse, *Alexander II and the Modernization of Russia* (1958), discusses midcentury reforms, whereas A. Geifman, *Thou Shalt Kill: Revolutionary Terrorism in Russia* (1993), probes the politics of violence in a pioneering study. J. Le Donne, *The Russian Empire and the World, 1700–1917: The Geopolitics of Expansion and Containment* (1996), reconsiders Russian foreign affairs.

G. Dangerfield, *The Strange Death of Liberal England* (1961), brilliantly examines social tensions in Ireland as well as Englishwomen's struggle for the vote before 1914. P. Gurney, *Co-operative Culture and the Politics of Consumption in England, 1870–1930* (1996), breaks new ground and is recommended. D. Boyce, *Nationalism in Ireland*, 2d ed. (1991), provides an excellent account of the Irish struggle for nationhood. The theme of aristocratic strength and survival is expanded in A. Mayer's provocative *Persistence of the Old Regime: Europe to the Great War* (1981). J. Seigel, *Marx's Fate: The Shape of a Life* (1978), is an outstanding biography. C. Schorske, *German Social Democracy, 1905–1917* (1955), is a modern classic. V. Lidtke, *The Alternative Culture: Socialist Labor in Imperial Germany* (1985), and J. Quataert, *Reluctant Feminists in German Social Democracy, 1885–1917* (1979), are also recommended for the study of the German socialists. H. Goldberg, *The Life of Jean Jaurès* (1962), is a sympathetic account of the great French socialist leader. Two excellent collections by specialists are L. Berlanstein, ed., *Rethinking Labor History* (1993), and D. Geary, ed., *Labour and Socialist Movements in Europe Before 1914* (1989), which examines several different countries.

Listening to the Past

The Making of a Socialist

Nationalism and socialism appeared locked in bitter competition in Europe before 1914, but they actually complemented each other in many ways. Both faiths were secular as opposed to religious, and both fostered political awareness. A working person who became interested in politics and developed nationalist beliefs might well convert to socialism at a later date.

This was the case for Adelheid Popp (1869–1939), a self-taught workingwoman who became an influential socialist leader. Born into a desperately poor working-class family in Vienna and remembering only a "hard and gloomy childhood," she was forced by her parents to quit school at age ten to begin full-time work. She struggled with low-paying piecework for years before she landed a solid factory job, as she recounts in the following selection from her widely read autobiography.

Always an avid reader, Popp became the editor of a major socialist newspaper for German working-women. She then told her life story so that all workingwomen might share her truth: "Socialism could change and strengthen others, as it did me."

[Finally] I found work again; I took everything that was offered me in order to show my willingness to work, and I passed through much. But at last things became better. [At age fifteen] I was recommended to a great factory which stood in the best repute. Three hundred girls and about fifty men were employed. I was put in a big room where sixty women and girls were at work. Against the windows stood twelve tables, and at each sat four girls. We had to sort the goods which had been manufactured, others had to count them, and a third set had to brand on them the mark of the firm. We worked from 7 A.M. to 7 P.M. We had an hour's rest at noon, half-an-hour

in the afternoon. . . . I had never yet been paid so much. . . .

I seemed to myself to be almost rich. . . . [Yet] from the women of this factory one can judge how sad and full of deprivation is the lot of a factory worker. In none of the neighbouring factories were the wages so high; we were envied everywhere. Parents considered themselves fortunate if they could get their daughters of fourteen in there on leaving school. . . . And even here, in this paradise, all were badly nourished. Those who stayed at the factory for the dinner hour would buy themselves for a few pennies a sausage or the leavings of a cheese shop. . . . In spite of all the diligence and economy, every one was poor, and trembled at the thought of losing her work. All humbled themselves, and suffered the worst injustice from the foremen, not to risk losing this good work, not to be without food. . . .

I did not only read novels and tales; I had begun . . . to read the classics and other good books. I also began to take an interest in public events. . . . I was not democratically inclined. I was full of enthusiasm then for emperors, and kings and highly placed personages played no small part in my fancies. . . . I bought myself a strict Catholic paper, that criticised very adversely the workers' movement, which was attracting notice. Its aim was to educate in a patriotic and religious direction. . . . I took the warmest interest in the events that occurred in the royal families, and I took the death of the Crown Prince of Austria so much to heart that I wept a whole day. . . . Political events [also] held me in suspense. The possibility of a war with Russia roused my patriotic enthusiasm. I saw my brother already returning from the battlefield covered with glory. . . .

When a particularly strong anti-Semitic feeling was noticeable in political life, I sympathised with it for a time. A broad sheet, "How Israel Attained Power and Sovereignty over all the Nations of the Earth," fascinated me. . . .

About this time an Anarchist group was active. Some mysterious murders which had taken place were ascribed to the Anarchists, and the police made use of them to oppress the rising workmen's movement. . . . I followed the trial of the Anarchists with passionate sympathy. I read all the speeches, and because, as always happens, Social Democrats, whom the authorities really wanted to attack, were among the accused, I learned their views. I became full of enthusiasm. Every single Social Democrat . . . seemed to me a hero. . . .

There was unrest among the workers . . . and demonstrations of protest followed. When these were repeated the military entered the "threatened" streets. . . . In the evenings I rushed in the greatest excitement from the factory to the scene of the disturbance. The military did not frighten me; I only left the place when it was "cleared."

Later on my mother and I lived with one of my brothers who had married. Friends came to him, among them some intelligent workmen. One of these workmen was particularly intelligent, and . . . could talk on many subjects. He was the first Social Democrat I knew. He brought me many books, and explained to me the difference between Anarchism and Socialism. I heard from him, also for the first time, what a republic was, and in spite of my former enthusiasm for royal dynasties, I also declared myself in favour of a republican form of government. I saw everything so near and so clearly, that I actually counted the weeks which must still elapse before the revolution of state and society would take place.

From this workman I received the first Social Democratic party organ. . . . I first learned from it to understand and judge of my own lot. I learned to see that all I had suffered was the result not of a divine ordinance, but of an unjust organization of society. . . .

In the factory I became another woman. . . . I told my [female] comrades all that I had read of the workers' movement. Formerly I had often told stories when they had begged me for them. But instead of narrating . . . the fate of some queen, I now held forth on oppression and

1890 engraving of a meeting of workers in Berlin. (*Bildarchiv Preussischer Kulturbesitz*)

exploitation. I told of accumulated wealth in the hands of a few, and introduced as a contrast the shoemakers who had no shoes and the tailors who had no clothes. On breaks I read aloud the articles in the Social Democratic paper and explained what Socialism was as far as I understood it. . . . [While I was reading] it often happened that one of the clerks passing by shook his head and said to another clerk: "The girl speaks like a man."

Questions for Analysis

1. How did Popp describe and interpret work in the factory?

2. To what extent did her socialist interpretation of factory life fit the facts she described?

3. What were Popp's political interests before she became a socialist?

4. How and why did she become a Social Democrat?

5. Was this account likely to lead other workingwomen to socialism? Why or why not?

Source: Slightly adapted from A. Popp, *The Autobiography of a Working Woman,* trans. E. C. Harvey (Chicago: F. G. Browne, 1913), pp. 29, 34–35, 39, 66–69, 71, 74, 82–90.

The Emigrant Ship by the British painter Charles J. Staniland,
1898. *(Bradford Art Galleries and Museums/The Bridgeman Art
Library International Ltd)*

26

The West and the World

chapter outline

- Industrialization and the World Economy

- The Great Migration

- Western Imperialism

- Responses to Western Imperialism

While industrialization and nationalism were transforming urban life and Western society, Western society itself was reshaping the world. At the peak of its power and pride, the West entered the third and most dynamic phase of the aggressive expansion that had begun with the Crusades and continued with the great discoveries and the rise of seaborne colonial empires. An ever-growing stream of products, people, and ideas flowed out of Europe in the nineteenth century. Hardly any corner of the globe was left untouched. The most spectacular manifestations of Western expansion came in the late nineteenth century when the leading European nations established or enlarged their far-flung political empires. The political annexation of territory in the 1880s—the "new imperialism," as it is often called by historians—was the capstone of a profound underlying economic and technological process.

- How and why did this many-sided, epoch-making expansion occur in the nineteenth century?
- What were some of its consequences for the West?
- How did Western expansion affect the rest of the world?

These are the questions this chapter will examine.

Industrialization and the World Economy

The Industrial Revolution created, first in Great Britain and then in continental Europe and North America, a growing and tremendously dynamic economic system. In the course of the nineteenth century, that system was extended across the face of the earth. Some of this extension into non-Western areas was peaceful and beneficial for all concerned, for the West had many products and techniques the rest of the world desired. If peaceful methods failed, however, Europeans did not stand on ceremony. They used their superior military power to force non-Western nations to open their doors to Western economic interests. In general, Westerners fashioned the global economic system so that the largest share of the ever-increasing gains from trade, technology, and migration flowed to the West and its propertied classes.

The Rise of Global Inequality

The Industrial Revolution in Europe marked a momentous turning point in human history. Indeed, only by placing Europe's economic breakthrough in a global perspective can one truly appreciate its revolutionary implications and consequences.

From such a global perspective, the ultimate significance of the Industrial Revolution was that it allowed those regions of the world that industrialized in the nineteenth century to increase their wealth and power enormously in comparison to those that did not. As a result, a gap between the industrializing regions (mainly Europe and North America) and the nonindustrializing ones (mainly Africa, Asia, and Latin America) opened up and grew steadily throughout the nineteenth century. Moreover, this pattern of uneven global development became institutionalized, or built into the structure of the world economy. Thus we evolved a "lopsided world," a world of rich lands and poor.

FIGURE 26.1 The Growth of Average Income per Person in the Third World, Developed Countries, and Great Britain, 1750–1970   Growth is given in 1960 U.S. dollars and prices. *(Source: P. Bairoch and M. Lévy-Leboyer, eds., Disparities in Economic Development Since the Industrial Revolution. Copyright © 1981 by P. Bairoch and M. Lévy-Leboyer. Reproduced with permission of Palgrave.)*

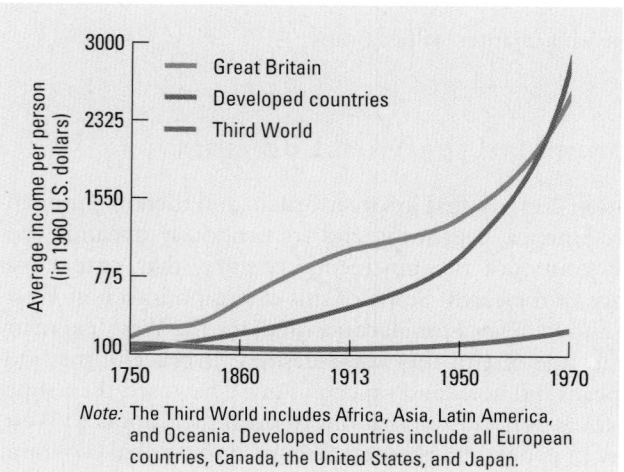

Note: The Third World includes Africa, Asia, Latin America, and Oceania. Developed countries include all European countries, Canada, the United States, and Japan.

Historians have long been aware of this gap, but it is only recently that historical economists have begun to chart its long-term evolution with some precision. Their findings are extremely revealing, although one must understand that they contain a margin of error and other limitations as well. The findings of one such study are summarized in Figure 26.1. This figure compares the long-term evolution of average income per person in today's "developed" (or industrialized) regions—defined as western and eastern Europe, North America, and Japan—with that found in the **Third World,** a term widely used by international organizations and by scholars to group Africa, Asia, and Latin America into a single unit. To get these individual income figures, researchers estimate a country's gross national product (GNP) at different points in time, convert those estimates to some common currency, and divide by the total population.

Figure 26.1 highlights three main points. First, in 1750 the average standard of living was no higher in Europe as a whole than in the rest of the world. In 1750 Europe was still a poor agricultural society. Moreover, the average per-person income in the wealthiest European country (Great Britain) was less than twice that in the poorest non-Western land. By 1970, however, the average person in the wealthiest countries had an income fully twenty-five times as great as that received by the average person in the poorest countries of Africa and Asia.

Second, it was industrialization that opened the gaps in average wealth and well-being among countries and regions. One sees that Great Britain had jumped well above the European average by 1830, when the first industrial nation was well in advance of its continental competitors. One also sees how Great Britain's lead gradually narrowed as other European countries and the United States successfully industrialized in the course of the nineteenth century.

Third, income per person stagnated in the Third World before 1913, in striking contrast to the industrializing regions. Only after 1945, in the era of political independence and decolonization, did Third World countries finally make some real economic progress, beginning in their turn the critical process of industrialization.

The rise of these enormous income disparities, which are poignant indicators of equal disparities in food and clothing, health and education, life expectancy and general material well-being, has generated a great deal of debate. One school of interpretation stresses that the West used science, technology, capitalist organization, and even its critical world-view to create its wealth and greater physical well-being. Another school argues that the West

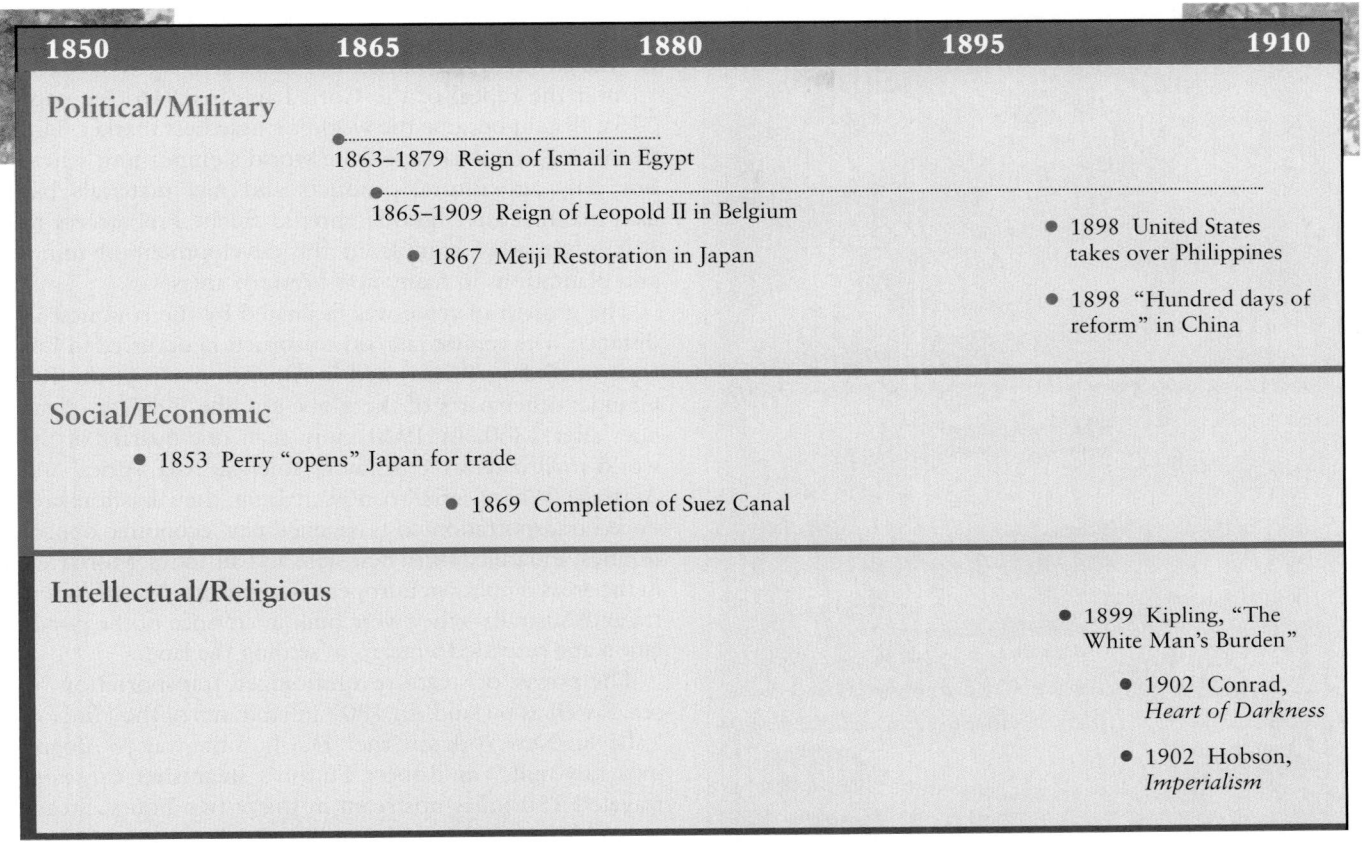

1850	1865	1880	1895	1910

Political/Military

1863–1879 Reign of Ismail in Egypt

1865–1909 Reign of Leopold II in Belgium

1867 Meiji Restoration in Japan

1898 United States takes over Philippines

1898 "Hundred days of reform" in China

Social/Economic

1853 Perry "opens" Japan for trade

1869 Completion of Suez Canal

Intellectual/Religious

1899 Kipling, "The White Man's Burden"

1902 Conrad, *Heart of Darkness*

1902 Hobson, *Imperialism*

used its political and economic power to steal much of its riches, continuing in the nineteenth (and twentieth) century the rapacious colonialism born of the era of expansion.

These issues are complex, and there are few simple answers. As noted in Chapter 22, the wealth-creating potential of technological improvement and more intensive capitalist organization was indeed great. At the same time, those breakthroughs rested, in part, on Great Britain's having already used political force to dominate part of the world economy by the late eighteenth century. In the nineteenth century other industrializing countries joined with Britain to extend Western domination over the entire world economy. Wealth—unprecedented wealth— was indeed created, but the lion's share of that new wealth flowed to the West and its propertied classes.

The World Market

Commerce between nations has always been a powerful stimulus to economic development. Never was this more true than in the nineteenth century, when world trade grew prodigiously. World trade grew modestly until about 1840, and then it took off. After a slowdown in the last years of the century, another surge lasted until World War I. In 1913 the value of world trade was roughly $38 billion, or about *twenty-five* times what it had been in 1800, even though prices of both manufactured goods and raw materials were lower in 1913 than in 1800. In a general way, the enormous increase in international commerce summed up the growth of an interlocking world economy centered in and directed by Europe.

Great Britain played a key role in using trade to tie the world together economically. In 1815 Britain already had a colonial empire, for India, Canada, Australia, and other scattered areas remained British possessions after American independence. The technological breakthroughs of the Industrial Revolution allowed Britain to manufacture cotton textiles, iron, and other goods more cheaply and to far outstrip domestic demand for such products. Thus British manufacturers sought export markets first in Europe and then around the world.

British Ships and Shipbuilders   The British continued to dominate international trade before the First World War. This handsome membership certificate of the British shipbuilders union features the vessels that drew the world together and were Britain's pride. Britain's thriving shipbuilding industry was concentrated in southern Scotland along the Clyde. *(Trade Union Congress, London/The Bridgeman Art Library International Ltd)*

Take the case of cotton textiles. By 1820 Britain was exporting 50 percent of its production. Europe bought 50 percent of these cotton textile exports, while India bought only 6 percent. Then as European nations and the United States erected protective tariff barriers and promoted domestic industry, British cotton textile manufacturers aggressively sought and found other foreign markets in non-Western areas. By 1850 India was buying 25 percent and Europe only 16 percent of a much larger total. As a British colony, India could not raise tariffs to protect its ancient cotton textile industry, and thousands of Indian weavers lost their livelihoods.

After the repeal of the Corn Laws in 1846 (see page 775), Britain became the world's single best market. Until 1914 Britain remained the world's emporium, where not only agricultural products and raw materials but also manufactured goods entered freely. Free access to Britain's market stimulated the development of mines and plantations in many non-Western areas.

The growth of trade was facilitated by the conquest of distance. The earliest railroad construction occurred in Europe (including Russia) and in America north of the Rio Grande; other parts of the globe saw the building of rail lines after 1860. By 1920 more than one-quarter of the world's railroads were in Latin America, Asia, Africa, and Australia. Wherever railroads were built, they drastically reduced transportation costs, opened new economic opportunities, and called forth new skills and attitudes. Moreover, in the areas of massive European settlement—North America and Australia—they were built in advance of the population and provided a means of settling the land.

The power of steam revolutionized transportation by sea as well as by land. In 1807 inhabitants of the Hudson Valley in New York saw the "Devil on the way to Albany in a saw-mill," as Robert Fulton's steamship *Clermont* traveled 150 miles upstream in thirty-two hours. Steam power, long used to drive paddle wheelers on rivers, particularly in Russia and North America, finally began to supplant sails on the oceans of the world in the late 1860s. Lighter, stronger, cheaper steel replaced iron, which had replaced wood. Screw propellers superseded paddle wheels, while mighty compound steam engines cut fuel consumption by half. Passenger and freight rates tumbled, and the intercontinental shipment of low-priced raw materials became feasible.

An account of an actual voyage by a typical tramp freighter highlights nineteenth-century developments in global trade. The ship left England in 1910 carrying rails and general freight to western Australia. From there it carried lumber to Melbourne in southeastern Australia, where it took on harvester combines for Argentina. In Buenos Aires it loaded wheat for Calcutta, and in Calcutta it took on jute for New York. From New York it carried a variety of industrial products to Australia before returning to England with lead, wool, and wheat after a voyage of approximately seventy-two thousand miles to six continents in seventeen months.

The revolution in land and sea transportation helped European pioneers open up vast new territories and produce agricultural products and raw materials there for sale in Europe. Moreover, the development of refriger-

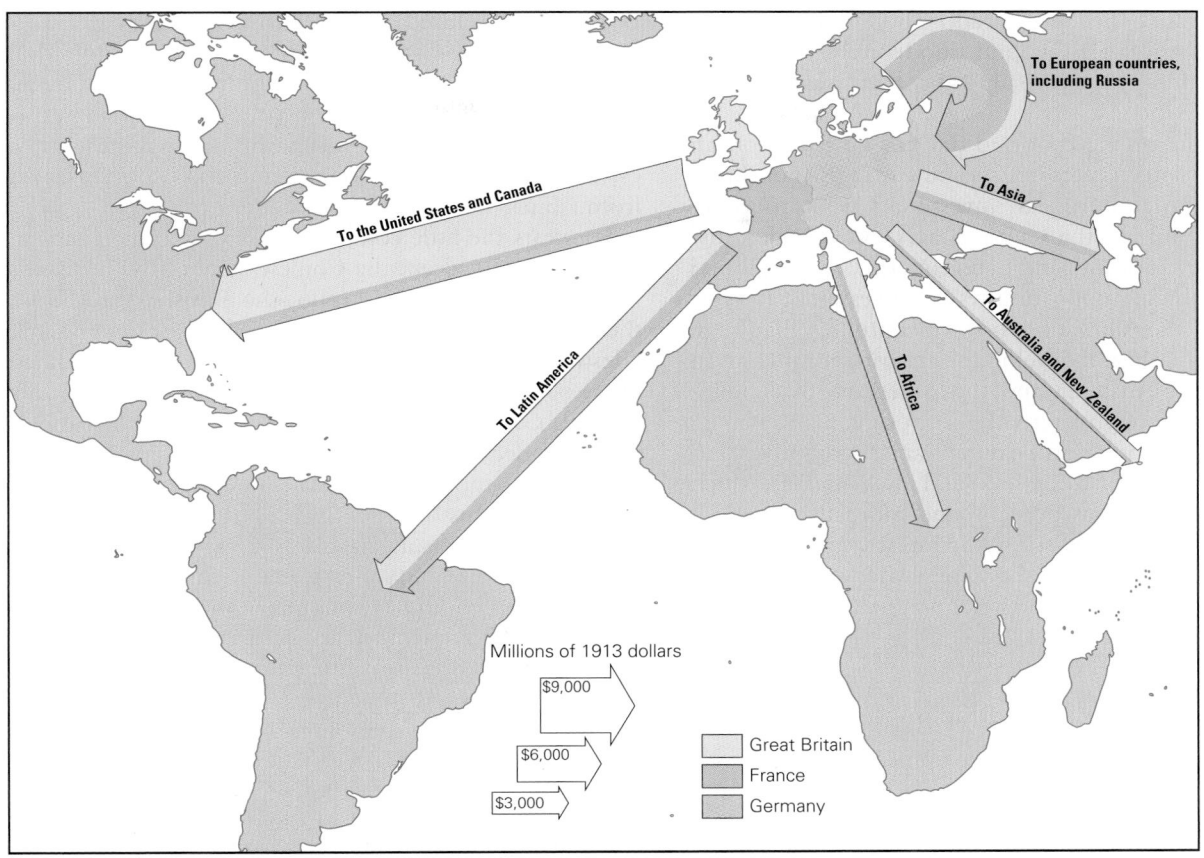

MAP 26.1 European Investment to 1914 Foreign investment grew rapidly after 1850, and Britain, France, and Germany were the major investing nations. As this map suggests, most European investment was not directed to the African and Asian areas seized by the "new imperialism" after 1880.

ated railway cars and, from the 1880s, refrigerator ships enabled first Argentina and then the United States, Australia, and New Zealand to ship mountains of chilled or frozen beef and mutton to European (mainly British) consumers. From Asia, Africa, and Latin America came not only the traditional tropical products—spices, tea, sugar, coffee—but also new raw materials for industry, such as jute, rubber, cotton, and coconut oil.

Intercontinental trade was enormously facilitated by the Suez and Panama Canals. Of great importance, too, was large and continual investment in modern port facilities, which made loading and unloading cheaper, faster, and more dependable. Finally, transoceanic telegraph cables inaugurated rapid communications among the financial centers of the world. While a British tramp freighter steamed from Calcutta to New York, a broker in London

was arranging by telegram for it to carry an American cargo to Australia. World commodity prices were also instantaneously conveyed by the same network of communications.

The growth of trade and the conquest of distance encouraged the expanding European economy to make massive foreign investments beginning about 1840. By the outbreak of World War I in 1914, Europeans had invested more than $40 billion abroad. Great Britain, France, and Germany were the principal investing countries, although by 1913 the United States was emerging as a substantial foreign investor. The sums involved were enormous (see Map 26.1). In the decade before 1914, Great Britain was investing 7 percent of its annual national income abroad, or slightly more than it was investing in its entire domestic economy.

The great gap between rich and poor within Europe meant that the wealthy and moderately well-to-do could and did send great sums abroad in search of interest and dividends.

Most of the capital exported did not go to European colonies or protectorates in Asia and Africa. About three-quarters of total European investment went to other European countries, the United States and Canada, Australia and New Zealand, and Latin America. Europe found its most profitable opportunities for investment in construction of the railroads, ports, and utilities that were necessary to settle and develop the almost-vacant lands in such places as Australia and the Americas. By lending money for a foreign railroad, Europeans also enabled white settlers to buy European rails and locomotives and developed sources of cheap food and raw materials. Much of this investment was peaceful and mutually beneficial for lenders and borrowers. The victims were native American Indians and Australian aborigines, who were decimated by the diseases, liquor, and weapons of an aggressively expanding Western society.

The Opening of China and Japan

Europe's relatively peaceful development of robust offshoots in sparsely populated North America, Australia, and much of Latin America absorbed huge quantities of goods, investments, and migrants. From a Western point of view, that was the most important aspect of Europe's global thrust. Yet Europe's economic and cultural penetration of old, densely populated civilizations was also profoundly significant, especially for the non-European peoples affected by it. With such civilizations Europeans also increased their trade and profit. Moreover, as had been the case ever since Vasco da Gama and Christopher Columbus, the expanding Western society was prepared to use force, if necessary, to attain its desires. This was what happened in China and Japan, two crucial examples of the general pattern of intrusion into non-Western lands.

Traditional Chinese civilization was self-sufficient. For centuries China had sent more goods and inventions to Europe than it had received, and this was still the case in the eighteenth century. Europeans and the English in particular had developed a taste for Chinese tea, but they had to pay for it with hard silver since China was uninterested in European wares. Trade with Europe was carefully regulated by the Chinese imperial government—the Qing (or Manchu) Dynasty—which was more interested in isolating and controlling the strange "sea barbarians" than in pursuing commercial exchange. The imperial government refused to establish diplomatic relations with the "inferior" European states, and it required all foreign merchants to live in the southern city of Canton and to buy from and sell to only the local merchant monopoly. Practices considered harmful to Chinese interests, such as the sale of opium and the export of silver from China, were strictly forbidden.

For years the little community of foreign merchants in Canton had to accept the Chinese system. By the 1820s, however, the dominant group, the British, were flexing their muscles. Moreover, in the smoking of opium—that "destructive and ensnaring vice" denounced by Chinese decrees—they had found something the Chinese really wanted. Grown legally in British-occupied India, opium was smuggled into China by means of fast ships and bribed officials. The more this rich trade developed, the greedier British merchants became. By 1836 the aggressive goal of the British merchants in Canton was an independent British colony in China and "safe and unrestricted liberty" in trade. Spurred on by economic motives, they pressured the British government to take decisive action and enlisted the support of British manufacturers with visions of vast Chinese markets to be opened.

At the same time, the Qing government decided that the **opium trade** had to be stamped out. It was ruining the people and stripping the empire of its silver, which was going to British merchants to pay for the opium. The government began to prosecute Chinese drug dealers vigorously and in 1839 sent special envoy Lin Tse-hsü to Canton. Lin Tse-hsü ordered the foreign merchants to obey China's laws, "for our great unified Manchu Empire regards itself as responsible for the habits and morals of its subjects and cannot rest content to see any of them become victims of a deadly poison."[1] The British merchants refused and were expelled, whereupon war soon broke out.

Using troops from India and being in control of the seas, the British occupied several coastal cities and forced China to surrender. In the Treaty of Nanking in 1842, the imperial government was forced to cede the island of Hong Kong to Britain forever, pay an indemnity of $100 million, and open up four large cities to foreign trade with low tariffs.

Thereafter the opium trade flourished, and Hong Kong developed rapidly as an Anglo-Chinese enclave. China continued to accept foreign diplomats in Beijing (Peking), the imperial capital. Finally, there was a second round of foreign attack between 1856 and 1860, culminating in the occupation of Beijing by seventeen thousand British and French troops and the intentional burning of the emperor's summer palace. Another round of harsh treaties gave European merchants and missionaries greater privileges and protection and forced the Chinese to accept trade and investment on unfavorable terms for several more cities. Thus did Europeans use military aggression to blow a hole in the wall of Chinese seclusion and open the country to foreign trade and foreign ideas.

China's neighbor Japan had its own highly distinctive civilization and even less use for Westerners. European traders and missionaries first arrived in Japan in the sixteenth century. By 1640 Japan had reacted quite negatively to their presence. The government decided to seal off the country from all European influences in order to preserve traditional Japanese culture and society. When American and British whaling ships began to appear off Japanese coasts almost two hundred years later, the policy of exclusion was still in effect. An order of 1825 commanded Japanese officials to "drive away foreign vessels without second thought."[2]

Japan's unbending isolation seemed hostile and barbaric to the West, particularly to the United States. It complicated the practical problems of shipwrecked American sailors and the provisioning of whaling ships and China traders sailing in the eastern Pacific. It also thwarted the hope of trade and profit. Moreover, Americans shared the self-confidence and dynamism of expanding Western society, and they felt destined to play a great role in the Pacific. To Americans it seemed the duty of the United States to force the Japanese to share their ports and behave as a "civilized" nation.

After several unsuccessful American attempts to establish commercial relations with Japan, Commodore Matthew Perry steamed into Edo (now Tokyo) Bay in 1853 and demanded diplomatic negotiations with the emperor. Japan entered a grave crisis. Some Japanese warriors urged resistance, but senior officials realized how defenseless their cities were against naval bombardment. Shocked and humiliated, they reluctantly signed a treaty with the United States that opened two ports and permitted trade. Over the next five years, more treaties spelled out the rights and privileges of the Western nations and their merchants in Japan. Japan was "opened." What the British had done in China with war, the Americans had done in Japan with only the threat of war.

East Meets West   This painting gives a Japanese view of the first audience of the American Consul and his staff with the shogun, Japan's hereditary military governor, in 1859. The Americans appear strange and ill at ease. (*Laurie Platt Winfrey, Inc.*)

Western Penetration of Egypt

Egypt's experience illustrates not only the explosive power of the expanding European economy and society but also their seductive appeal in non-Western lands. European involvement in Egypt also led to a new model of formal political control, which European powers applied widely in Africa and Asia after 1882.

Of great importance in African and Middle Eastern history, the ancient land of the pharaohs had since 525 B.C. been ruled by a succession of foreigners, most recently by the Ottoman Turks. In 1798 French armies under young General Napoleon Bonaparte invaded the Egyptian part of the Ottoman Empire and occupied the territory for three years. Into the power vacuum left by the French withdrawal stepped an extraordinary Albanian-born Turkish general, Muhammad Ali (1769–1849).

First appointed governor of Egypt by the Turkish sultan, Muhammad Ali soon disposed of his political rivals and set out to build his own state on the strength of a large, powerful army organized along European lines. He drafted for the first time the illiterate, despised peasant masses of Egypt, and he hired French and Italian army officers to train these raw recruits and their Turkish officers. The government was also reformed, new lands were cultivated, and communications were improved. By the time of his death in 1849, Muhammad Ali had established a strong and virtually independent Egyptian state, to be ruled by his family on a hereditary basis within the Turkish empire.

Muhammad Ali's policies of modernization attracted large numbers of Europeans to the banks of the Nile. As one Arab sheik of the Ottoman Empire remarked in the 1830s, "Englishmen are like ants; if one finds a bit of meat, hundreds follow."[3] The port city of Alexandria had more than fifty thousand Europeans by 1864. Europeans served not only as army officers but also as engineers, doctors, government officials, and police officers. Others found their "meat" in trade, finance, and shipping.

To pay for his ambitious plans, Muhammad Ali encouraged the development of commercial agriculture. This development had profound implications. Egyptian peasants were poor but largely self-sufficient, growing food for their own consumption on state-owned lands allotted to them by tradition. Faced with the possibility of export agriculture, high-ranking officials and members of Muhammad Ali's family began carving large private land-holdings out of the state domain. The new landlords made the peasants their tenants and forced them to grow cash crops geared to European markets. Thus Egyptian landowners "modernized" agriculture, but to the detriment of peasant well-being.

These trends continued under Muhammad Ali's grandson Ismail, who in 1863 began his sixteen-year rule as Egypt's **khedive,** or prince. Educated at France's leading military academy, Ismail was a westernizing autocrat. The large irrigation networks he promoted caused cotton production and exports to Europe to boom, and with his support the Suez Canal was completed by a French company in 1869. The Arabic of the masses replaced the Turkish of the conquerors as the official language. Young Egyptians educated in Europe spread new skills, and Cairo acquired modern boulevards and Western hotels. As Ismail proudly declared, "My country is no longer in Africa, we now form part of Europe."[4]

Yet Ismail was too impatient and reckless. His projects were enormously expensive, and the sale of his stock in the Suez Canal to the British government did not relieve the situation. By 1876 Egypt owed foreign bond-holders a colossal debt that it could not pay. Rather than let Egypt go bankrupt and repudiate its loans, the governments of France and Great Britain intervened politically to protect the European bondholders. They forced Ismail to appoint French and British commissioners to oversee Egyptian finances so that the Egyptian debt would be paid in full. This momentous decision implied direct European political control and was a sharp break with the previous pattern of trade and investment. Throughout most of the nineteenth century, Europeans had used military might and political force primarily to make sure that non-Western lands would accept European trade and investment. Now Europeans were going to determine the state budget and effectively rule Egypt.

Foreign financial control evoked a violent nationalistic reaction among Egyptian religious leaders, young intellectuals, and army officers. In 1879, under the leadership of Colonel Ahmed Arabi, they formed the Egyptian Nationalist party. Continuing diplomatic pressure, which forced Ismail to abdicate in favor of his weak son, Tewfiq (r. 1879–1892), resulted in bloody anti-European riots in Alexandria in 1882. A number of Europeans were killed, and Tewfiq and his court had to flee to British ships for safety. When the British fleet bombarded Alexandria, more riots swept the country, and Colonel Arabi led a revolt. But a British expeditionary force put down the rebellion and occupied all of Egypt.

The British said their occupation was temporary, but British armies remained in Egypt until 1956. They maintained the façade of the khedive's government as an autonomous province of the Ottoman Empire, but the khedive was a mere puppet. British rule did result in tax reforms and somewhat better conditions for peasants,

British Rule in Egypt   In this 1900 photo, a group of British soldiers enters Cairo's old fortress, the Citadel, with its graceful minarets and Ottoman military architecture. British armies occupied Egypt in 1882, and Egypt lost its political and economic independence. *(Billie Love)*

while foreign bondholders received their interest and Egyptian nationalists nursed their injured pride.

British rule in Egypt provided a new model for European expansion in densely populated lands. Such expansion was based on military force, political domination, and a self-justifying ideology of beneficial reform. This model was to predominate until 1914. Thus did Europe's Industrial Revolution lead to tremendous political as well as economic expansion throughout the world.

The Great Migration

A poignant human drama was interwoven with economic expansion: millions of people pulled up stakes and left their ancestral lands in the course of history's greatest migration. To millions of ordinary people, for whom the opening of China and the interest on the Egyptian debt had not the slightest significance, this great movement was the central experience in the saga of Western expansion. It was, in part, because of this **great migration** that the West's impact on the world in the nineteenth century was so powerful and many-sided.

The Pressure of Population

In the early eighteenth century, the growth of European population entered its third and decisive stage, which continued unabated until the twentieth century (see Chapter 19). Birthrates eventually declined in the nineteenth century, but so did death rates, mainly because of the rising standard of living and secondarily because of the medical revolution. Thus the population of Europe (including Asiatic Russia) more than doubled,

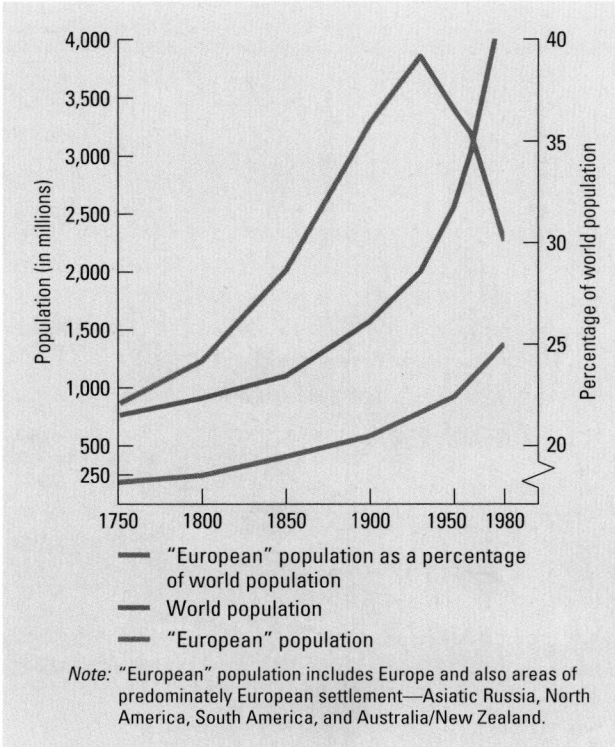

FIGURE 26.2 The Increase of European and World Populations, 1750–1980 *(Sources: W. Woodruff,* Impact of Western Man: A Study of Europe's Role in the World Economy. *St. Martin's Press, New York, 1967, p. 103; United Nations, Statistical Yearbook, 1982, 1985, pp. 2–3.)*

from approximately 188 million in 1800 to roughly 432 million in 1900.

These figures actually understate Europe's population explosion, for between 1815 and 1932 more than 60 million people left Europe. These migrants went primarily to the "areas of European settlement"—North and South America, Australia, New Zealand, and Siberia—where they contributed to a rapid growth in numbers. Since population grew more slowly in Africa and Asia than in Europe and the Americas, as Figure 26.2 shows, Europeans and people of predominately European origin jumped from about 22 percent of the world's total to about 38 percent on the eve of World War I.

The growing number of Europeans provided further impetus for Western expansion. It was a driving force behind emigration. As in the eighteenth century, the rapid

increase in numbers put pressure on the land and led to land hunger and relative overpopulation in area after area. In most countries, migration increased twenty years after a rapid growth in population, as many children of the baby boom grew up, saw little available land and few opportunities, and migrated. This pattern was especially prevalent when rapid population increase predated extensive industrial development, which offered the best long-term hope of creating jobs within the country and reducing poverty. Thus millions of country folk went abroad as well as to nearby cities in search of work and economic opportunity.

Before looking at the people who migrated, let us consider three facts. First, the number of men and women who left Europe increased rapidly before World War I. As Figure 26.3 shows, more than 11 million left in the first decade of the twentieth century, over five times the number departing in the 1850s. The outflow of migrants was clearly an enduring characteristic of European society for the entire period.

Second, different countries had very different patterns of movement. As Figure 26.3 also shows, people left Britain and Ireland (which are not distinguished in the British figures) in large numbers from the 1840s on. This emigration reflected not only rural poverty but also the movement of skilled, industrial technicians and the preferences shown to British migrants in the British Empire. Ultimately, about one-third of all European migrants between 1840 and 1920 came from the British Isles. German migration was quite different. It grew irregularly after about 1830, reaching a first peak in the early 1850s and another in the early 1880s. Thereafter it declined rapidly, for Germany's rapid industrialization was providing adequate jobs at home. This pattern contrasted sharply with that of Italy. More and more Italians left the country right up to 1914, reflecting severe problems in Italian villages and relatively slow industrial growth. Thus migration patterns mirrored social and economic conditions in the various European countries and provinces.

Third, although the United States absorbed the largest number of European migrants, less than half of all migrants went to the United States. Asiatic Russia, Canada, Argentina, Brazil, Australia, and New Zealand also attracted large numbers, as Figure 26.4 shows. Moreover, migrants accounted for a larger proportion of the total population in Argentina, Brazil, and Canada than in the United States. The common American assumption that European migration meant migration to the United States is quite inaccurate.

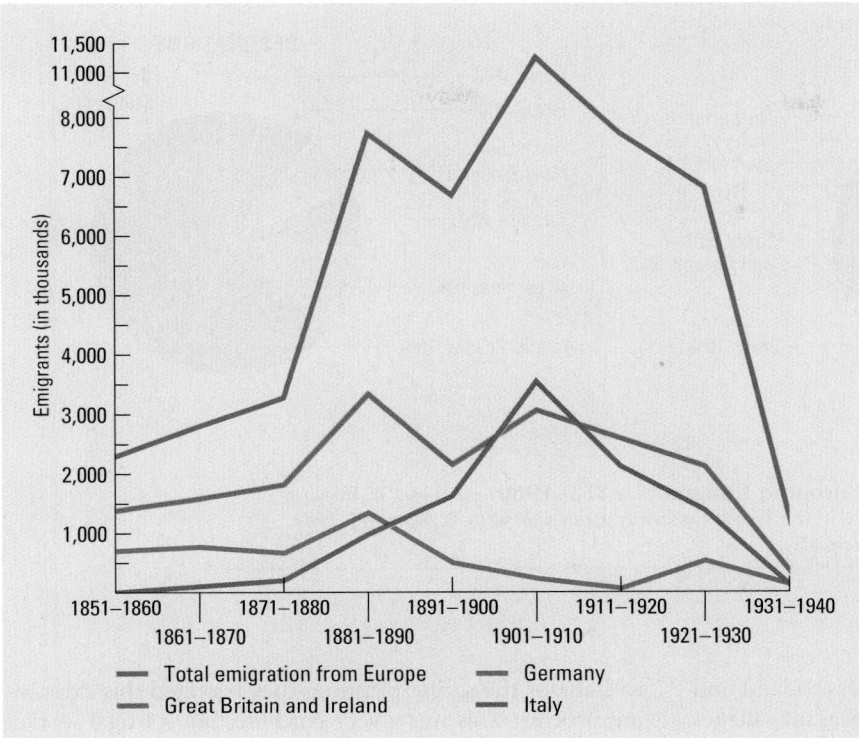

FIGURE 26.3 Emigration from Europe by Decades, 1851–1940 *(Source: W. Woodruff, ed.,* Impact of Western Man: A Study of Europe's Role in the World Economy. *Copyright © by W. Woodruff, 1982. Reprinted by permission of University Press of America.)*

European Migrants

What kind of people left Europe, and what were their reasons for doing so? The European migrant was most often a small peasant landowner or a village craftsman whose traditional way of life was threatened by too little land, estate agriculture, and cheap, factory-made goods. German peasants who left the Rhineland and southwestern Germany between 1830 and 1854, for example, felt trapped by what Friedrich List called the "dwarf economy," with its tiny landholdings and declining craft industries. Selling out and moving to buy much cheaper land in the American Midwest became a common response. Thus the European migrant was generally an energetic small farmer or skilled artisan trying hard to stay ahead of poverty, not a desperately impoverished landless peasant or urban proletarian.

Determined to maintain or improve their status, migrants were a great asset to the countries that received them. This was doubly so because the vast majority were young and very often unmarried. They came in the prime of life and were ready to work hard in the new land, at least for a time. Many Europeans moved but remained within Europe, settling temporarily or permanently in another European country. Jews from eastern Europe and peasants from Ireland migrated to Great Britain, Russians and Poles sought work in Germany, and Latin peoples from Spain, Portugal, and Italy entered France. Many Europeans were truly migrants as opposed to immigrants— that is, they returned home after some time abroad. One in two migrants to Argentina and probably one in three to the United States eventually returned to their native land.

The likelihood of repatriation varied greatly by nationality. People who migrated from the Balkans, for instance, were much more likely to return to their countries than people from Ireland and eastern European Jews. Once again, the possibility of buying land in the old country was of central importance. In Ireland (as well as in England and Scotland) land was tightly held by large, often absentee landowners, and little land was available for purchase. In Russia most land was held by non-Jews. Therefore, when Russian Jewish artisans began in the 1880s to escape both factory competition and oppression by migrating, it was basically a once-and-for-all departure.

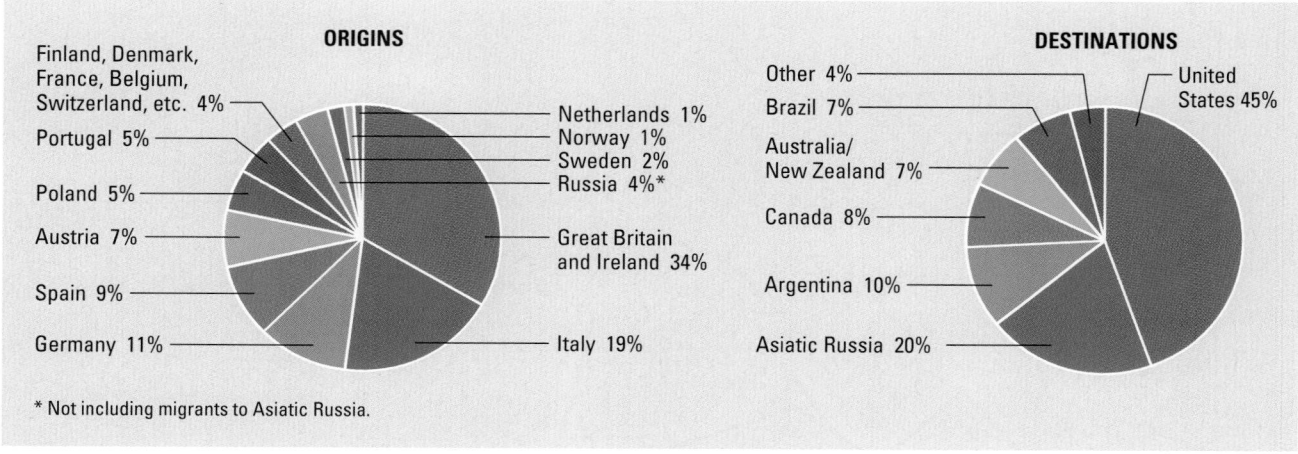

FIGURE 26.4 Origin and Destination of European Emigrants, 1851–1960 *(Source: W. Woodruff, Impact of Western Man: A Study of Europe's Role in the World Economy. Copyright © by W. Woodruff, 1982. Reprinted with permission of University Press of America.)*

Non-Jewish migrants from Russia had access to land and returned much more frequently to their peasant villages in central Russia, Poland, and Ukraine.

The mass movement of Italians illustrates many of the characteristics of European migration. As late as the 1880s, which was for Italians, as for Russian Jews, the first decade of substantial exodus, three of every four Italians depended on agriculture. With the influx of cheap North American wheat, the long-standing problems of the Italian village became more acute. With industry failing to provide enough jobs for the rapidly growing population, many small landowning peasants whose standard of living was falling began to leave their country. Migration provided them with an escape valve and possible income to buy more land. Landless laborers from areas dominated by large estates tended to stay in Italy and turned increasingly toward radical politics.

Many Italians went to the United States, but before 1900 more went to Argentina and Brazil. In Brazil the large coffee planters, faced with the collapse of black slavery, attracted Italians to their plantations with subsidized travel and promises of relatively high wages. France was also a favorite destination for Italians. In 1911 the Italian-born population of France was roughly a third as large as that in the United States.

Many Italians had no intention of settling abroad permanently. Some called themselves **swallows.** After harvesting their own wheat and flax in Italy, they "flew" to Argentina to harvest wheat between December and April. Returning to Italy for the spring planting, they repeated this exhausting process. This was a very hard life, but a frugal worker could save $250 to $300 in the course of a season.

Ties of family and friendship played a crucial role in the movement of peoples. Many people from a given province or village settled together in rural enclaves or tightly knit urban neighborhoods thousands of miles away. Very often a strong individual—a businessman, a religious leader—would blaze the way and others would follow, forming a "migration chain."

Many landless young European men and women were spurred to leave by a spirit of revolt and independence. In Sweden and in Norway, in Jewish Russia and in Italy, these young people felt frustrated by the small privileged classes, which often controlled both church and government and resisted demands for change and greater opportunity. Many a young Norwegian seconded the passionate cry of Norway's national poet, Martinius Bjørnson: "Forth will I! Forth! I will be crushed and consumed if I stay."[5]

Many young Jews wholeheartedly agreed with a spokesman of Kiev's Jewish community in 1882, who declared, "Our human dignity is being trampled upon, our wives and daughters are being dishonored, we are looted and pillaged: either we get decent human rights or else let us go wherever our eyes may lead us."[6] Thus for many, migration was a radical way to "get out from under." Migration slowed down when the people won basic political and social reforms, such as the right to vote and social security.

The Jewish Market, New York, 1900   The center of economic and social life in the Lower East Side
was the market. Jewish immigrants could usually find work with Jewish employers, and New York's Jewish
population soared from 73,000 in 1880 to 1.1 million in 1910. *(The Granger Collection, New York)*

Asian Migrants

Not all migration was from Europe. A substantial number of Chinese, Japanese, Indians, and Filipinos—to name
only four key groups—responded to rural hardship with
temporary or permanent migration. At least 3 million
Asians (as opposed to more than 60 million Europeans)
moved abroad before 1920. Most went as indentured laborers to work under incredibly difficult conditions on
the plantations or in the gold mines of Latin America,
southern Asia, Africa, California, Hawaii, and Australia.
White estate owners very often used Asians to replace or
supplement blacks after the suppression of the slave trade.

In the 1840s, for example, there was a strong demand
for field hands in Cuba, and the Spanish government actively recruited Chinese laborers. Between 1853 and
1873, when such migration was stopped, more than

130,000 Chinese laborers went to Cuba. The majority
spent their lives as virtual slaves. The great landlords of
Peru also brought in more than 100,000 workers from
China in the nineteenth century, and there were similar
movements of Asians elsewhere.

Such migration from Asia would undoubtedly have
grown to much greater proportions if planters and mine
owners in search of cheap labor had been able to hire
as many Asian workers as they wished. But they could
not. Asians fled the plantations and gold mines as soon as
possible, seeking greater opportunities in trade and
towns. There they came into conflict with local populations, whether in Malaya, East Africa, or areas settled by
Europeans.

These European settlers demanded a halt to Asian migration. One Australian brutally summed up the typical
view: "The Chinaman knows nothing about Caucasian

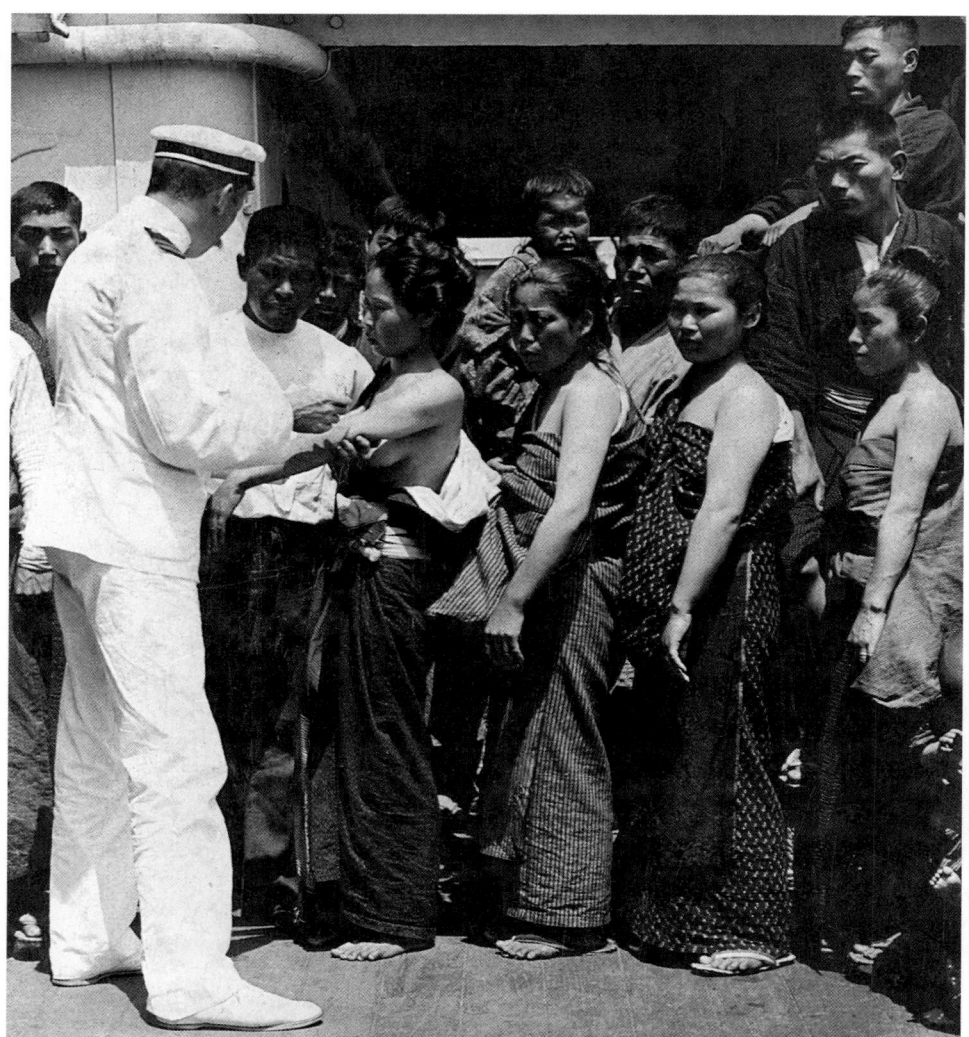

Vaccinating Migrants Bound for Hawaii, 1904   First Chinese, then Japanese, and finally Koreans and Filipinos went in large numbers across the Pacific to labor in Hawaii on American-owned sugar plantations in the late nineteenth century. The native Hawaiians had been decimated by disease, preparing the way for the annexation of Hawaii by the United States in 1898. *(Corbis)*

civilization. . . . It would be less objectionable to drive a flock of sheep to the poll than to allow Chinamen to vote."[7] By the 1880s, Americans and Australians were building **great white walls**—discriminatory laws designed to keep Asians out. Thus a final, crucial factor in the migrations before 1914 was the general policy of "whites only" in the open lands of possible permanent settlement. This, too, was part of Western dominance in the increasingly lopsided world. Largely successful in monopolizing the best overseas opportunities, Europeans and people of European ancestry reaped the main benefits from the great migration. By 1913 people in Australia, Canada, and the United States all had higher average incomes than people in Great Britain, still Europe's wealthiest nation.

Western Imperialism

The expansion of Western society reached its apex between about 1880 and 1914. In those years, the leading European nations not only continued to send massive streams of migrants, money, and manufactured goods around the world, but also rushed to create or enlarge vast *political* empires abroad. This political empire building contrasted sharply with the economic penetration of non-Western territories between 1816 and 1880, which had left a China or a Japan "opened" but politically independent. By contrast, the empires of the late nineteenth century recalled the old European colonial empires of the seventeenth and eighteenth centuries and led contemporaries to speak of the **new imperialism.**

Characterized by a frantic rush to plant the flag over as many people and as much territory as possible, the new imperialism had momentous consequences. It resulted in new tensions among competing European states, and it led to wars and rumors of war with non-European powers. The new imperialism was aimed primarily at Africa and Asia. It put millions of black, brown, and yellow peoples directly under the rule of whites. How and why did this happen?

The Scramble for Africa

The most spectacular manifestation of the new imperialism was the seizure of Africa, which broke sharply with previous patterns and fascinated contemporary Europeans and Americans. As late as 1880, European nations controlled only 10 percent of the African continent, and their possessions were hardly increasing. The French had begun conquering Algeria in 1830, and by 1880 substantial numbers of French, Italian, and Spanish colonists had settled among the overwhelming Arab majority.

At the other end of the continent, in South Africa, the British had taken possession of the Dutch settlements at Cape Town during the wars with Napoleon I. This takeover had led disgruntled Dutch cattle ranchers and farmers in 1835 to make their so-called Great Trek into the interior, where they fought the Zulu and Xhosa peoples for land. After 1853, while British colonies such as Canada and Australia were beginning to evolve toward self-government, the Boers, or **Afrikaners** (as the descendants of the Dutch in the Cape Colony were beginning to call themselves), proclaimed their political independence and defended it against British armies. By 1880 Afrikaner and British settlers, who detested each other, had wrested control of much of South Africa from the Zulu, Xhosa, and other African peoples.

European trading posts and forts dating back to the Age of Discovery and the slave trade dotted the coast of West Africa. The Portuguese proudly but ineffectively held their old possessions in Angola and Mozambique. Elsewhere over the great mass of the continent, Europeans did not rule.

Between 1880 and 1900, the situation changed drastically. Britain, France, Germany, and Italy scrambled for African possessions as if their national livelihoods depended on it. By 1900 nearly the whole continent had been carved up and placed under European rule: only Ethiopia in northeast Africa, which repulsed Italian invaders, and Liberia on the West African coast remained independent. In the years before 1914, the European powers tightened

their control and established colonial governments to rule their gigantic empires (see Map 26.2).

The Dutch settler republics also succumbed to imperialism, but the final outcome was quite different. The British, led by Cecil Rhodes in the Cape Colony, leapfrogged over the Afrikaner states in the early 1890s and established protectorates over Bechuanaland (now Botswana) and Rhodesia (now Zimbabwe and Zambia), named in honor of its freelance imperial founder. Trying unsuccessfully to undermine the stubborn Afrikaners in the Transvaal, where English-speaking capitalists like Rhodes were developing fabulously rich gold mines, the British conquered their white rivals in the bloody Boer War (1899–1902). In 1910 their territories were united with the old Cape Colony and the eastern province of Natal in a new Union of South Africa, established—unlike any other territory in Africa—as a largely "self-governing" colony. This enabled the defeated Afrikaners to use their numerical superiority over the British settlers to gradually take political power, as even the most educated nonwhites lost the right to vote outside the Cape Colony. (See the feature "Individuals in Society: Cecil Rhodes" on page 873.)

In the complexity of the European seizure of Africa, certain events and individuals stand out. Of enormous importance was the British occupation of Egypt in 1882, which established the new model of formal political control. There was also the role of Leopold II of Belgium (r. 1865–1909), an energetic, strong-willed monarch with a lust for distant territory. "The sea bathes our coast, the world lies before us," he had exclaimed in 1861. "Steam and electricity have annihilated distance, and all the non-appropriated lands on the surface of the globe can become the field of our operations and of our success."[8] By 1876 Leopold was focusing on central Africa. Subsequently, he formed a financial syndicate under his personal control to send Henry M. Stanley, a sensation-seeking journalist and part-time explorer, to the Congo basin. Stanley was able to establish trading stations, sign "treaties" with African chiefs, and plant Leopold's flag. Leopold's actions alarmed the French, who quickly sent out an expedition under Pierre de Brazza. In 1880 de Brazza signed a treaty of protection with the chief of the large Teke tribe and began to establish a French protectorate on the north bank of the Congo River.

Leopold's buccaneering intrusion into the Congo area raised the question of the political fate of Africa. By 1882 Europe had caught "African fever." There was a gold rush mentality, and the race for territory was on.

To lay down some basic rules for this new and dangerous game of imperialist competition in sub-Saharan Africa, Jules Ferry of France and Otto von Bismarck of Germany

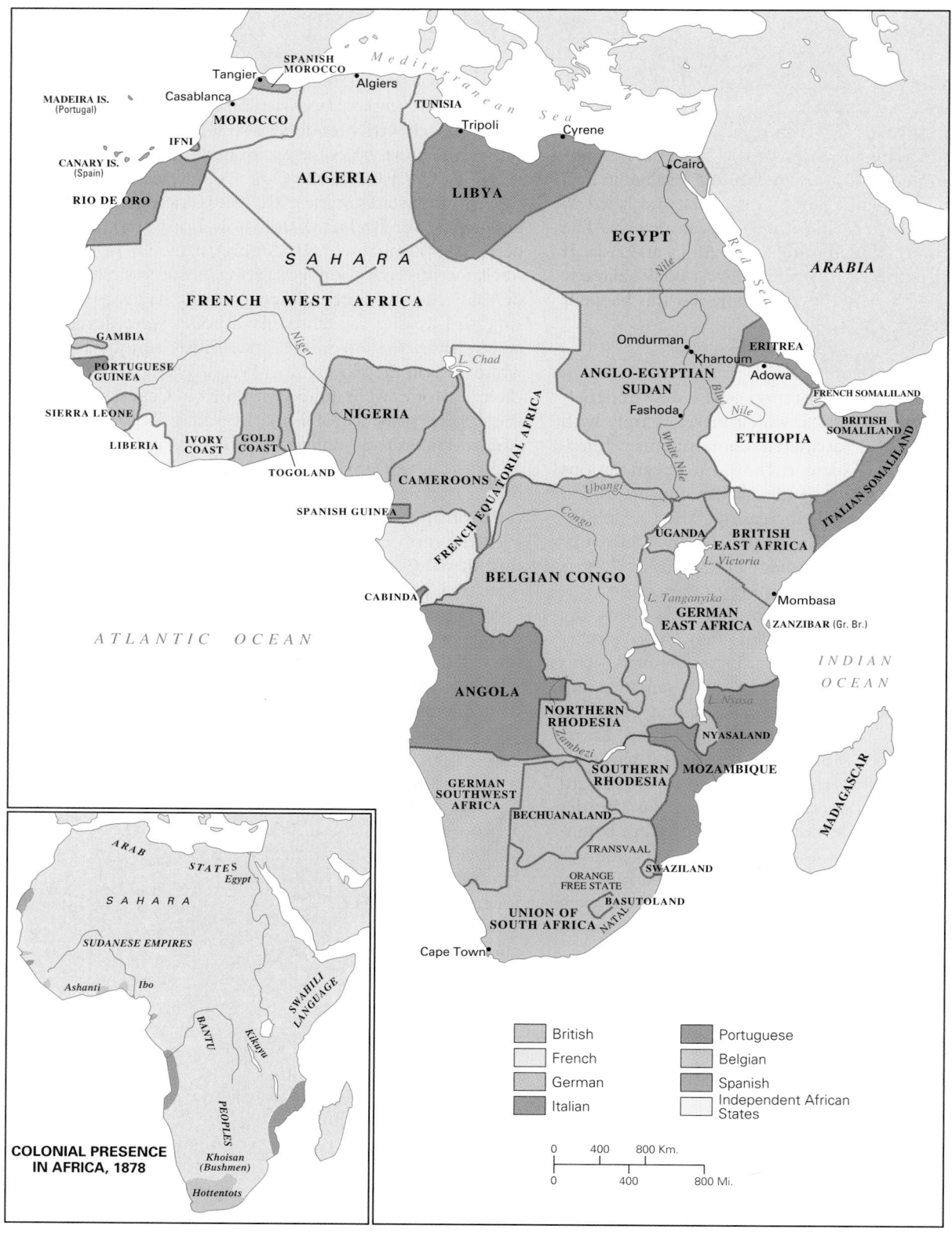

SPANISH MOROCCO
Tangier
Casablanca
Algiers
MADEIRA IS.
(Portugal)
TUNISIA
Tripoli
Cyrene
MOROCCO
IFNI
CANARY IS.
(Spain)
ALGERIA
LIBYA
Cairo
RIO DE ORO
EGYPT
Nile
ARABIA
Red Sea
SAHARA
FRENCH   WEST   AFRICA
Niger
L. Chad
Omdurman
Khartoum
ERITREA
Adowa
GAMBIA
PORTUGUESE
GUINEA
ANGLO-EGYPTIAN
SUDAN
FRENCH SOMALILAND
SIERRA LEONE
NIGERIA
Fashoda
BRITISH
SOMALILAND
LIBERIA
IVORY
COAST
GOLD
COAST
ETHIOPIA
White Nile
Blue Nile
TOGOLAND
CAMEROONS
Ubangi
ITALIAN SOMALILAND
SPANISH GUINEA
FRENCH EQUATORIAL AFRICA
Congo
UGANDA
BRITISH
EAST
AFRICA
BELGIAN CONGO
L. Victoria
CABINDA
L. Tanganyika
Mombasa
GERMAN
EAST AFRICA
ZANZIBAR (Gr. Br.)
ATLANTIC   OCEAN
INDIAN
OCEAN
ANGOLA
L. Nyasa
NORTHERN
RHODESIA
NYASALAND
Zambezi
GERMAN
SOUTHWEST
AFRICA
SOUTHERN
RHODESIA
MOZAMBIQUE
MADAGASCAR
BECHUANALAND
TRANSVAAL
SWAZILAND
ORANGE
FREE STATE
BASUTOLAND
UNION OF
SOUTH AFRICA
NATAL
Cape Town
Mediterranean Sea

COLONIAL PRESENCE
IN AFRICA, 1878

ARAB
STATES
Egypt
SAHARA
SUDANESE EMPIRES
Ashanti   Ibo
SWAHILI LANGUAGE
BANTU
Kikuyu
PEOPLES
Khoisan
(Bushmen)
Hottentots

British
French
German
Italian
Portuguese
Belgian
Spanish
Independent African
States

0   400   800 Km.
0   400   800 Mi.

MAP 26.2 The Partition of Africa   European nations carved up Africa after 1880 and built vast political empires. What African states remained independent?

arranged an international conference on Africa in Berlin in 1884 and 1885. The conference established the principle that European claims to African territory had to rest on "effective occupation" in order to be recognized by other states. This meant that Europeans would push relentlessly into interior regions from all sides and that no single European power would be able to claim the entire continent. The conference recognized Leopold's personal rule over a neutral Congo free state and agreed to work to stop slavery and the slave trade in Africa.

The **Berlin conference** coincided with Germany's sudden emergence as an imperial power. Prior to about 1880, Bismarck, like many other European leaders at the time, had seen little value in colonies. Colonies reminded him, he said, of a poor but proud nobleman who wore a fur coat when he could not afford a shirt underneath. Then in 1884 and 1885, as political agitation for expansion increased, Bismarck did an abrupt about-face, and Germany established protectorates over a number of small African kingdoms and tribes in Togo, Cameroons, southwest Africa, and, later, East Africa. In acquiring colonies, Bismarck cooperated against the British with France's Ferry, who was as ardent for empire as he was for education. (See the feature "Listening to the Past: A French Leader Defends Imperialism" on pages 884–885.) With Bismarck's tacit approval, the French pressed southward from Algeria, eastward from their old forts on the Senegal coast, and northward from their protectorate on the Congo River.

Meanwhile, the British began enlarging their West African enclaves and impatiently pushing northward from the Cape Colony and westward from Zanzibar. Their thrust southward from Egypt was blocked in the Sudan by fiercely independent Muslims, who massacred a British force at Khartoum in 1885.

A decade later, another British force, under General Horatio H. Kitchener, moved cautiously and more successfully up the Nile River, building a railroad to supply arms and reinforcements as it went. Finally, in 1898 these British troops met their foe at Omdurman (see Map 26.2), where Muslim tribesmen armed with spears charged time and time again only to be cut down by the recently invented machine gun. For one smug participant, the young British officer Winston Churchill, it was "like a pantomime scene" in a play. "These extraordinary foreign figures . . . march up one by one from the darkness of Barbarism to the footlights of civilization . . . and their conquerors, taking their possessions, forget even their names." For another, more somber English observer, "It was not a battle but an execution. The bodies were not in heaps . . . but they spread evenly over acres and acres."[9] In the end, eleven

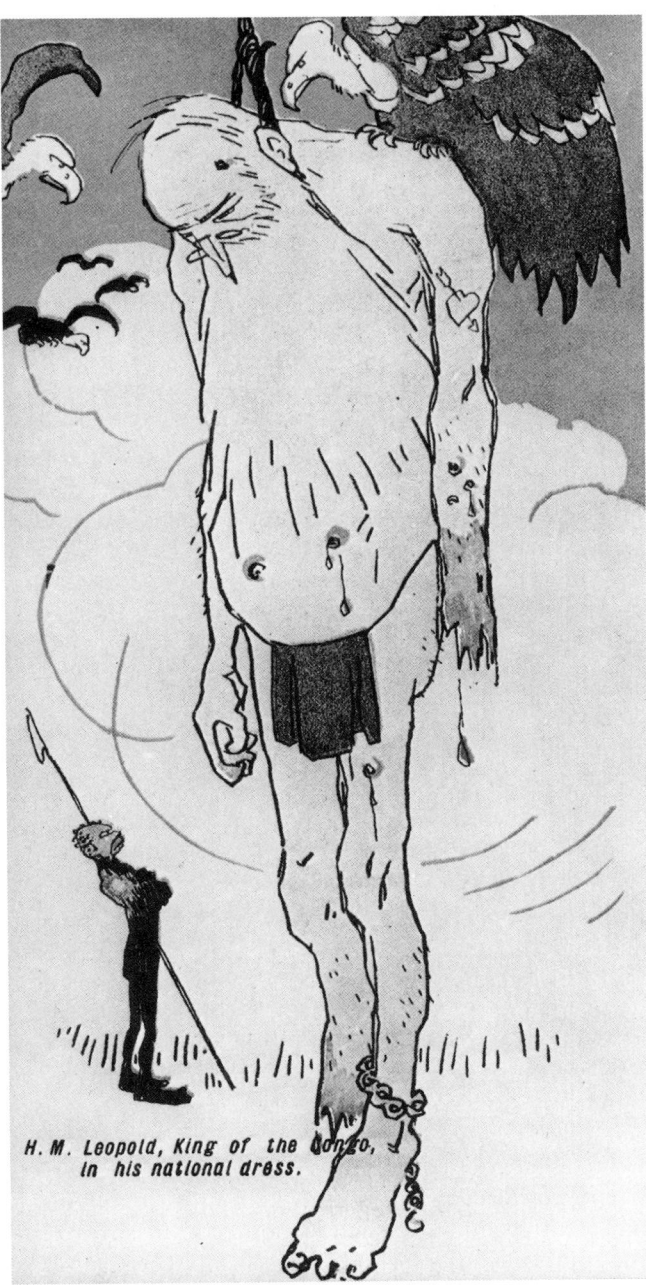

European Imperialism at its Worst   This 1908 English cartoon, "Leopold, King of the Congo, in his native dress," focuses on the barbaric practice of cutting off the hands and feet of Africans who refused to gather as much rubber as Leopold's company demanded. In 1908 an international human rights campaign forced the Belgian king to cede his personal fief to the Belgian state. *(Archive of Arnoldo Mondadori Editore, Milan)*

thousand brave Muslim tribesmen lay dead, while only twenty-eight Britons had been killed.

Continuing up the Nile after the Battle of Omdurman, Kitchener's armies found that a small French force had already occupied the village of Fashoda. Locked in imperial competition with Britain ever since the British occupation of Egypt, France had tried to beat the British to one of Africa's last unclaimed areas—the upper reaches of the Nile. The result was a serious diplomatic crisis and even the threat of war. Eventually, wracked by the Dreyfus affair (see page 842) and unwilling to fight, France backed down and withdrew its forces, allowing the British to take over.

The British conquest of the Sudan exemplifies the general process of empire building in Africa. The fate of the Muslim force at Omdurman was eventually inflicted on all native peoples who resisted European rule: they were blown away by vastly superior military force. But however much the European powers squabbled for territory and privilege around the world, they always had the sense to stop short of actually fighting each other. Imperial ambitions were not worth a great European war.

Imperialism in Asia

Although the sudden division of Africa was more spectacular, Europeans also extended their political control in Asia. In 1815 the Dutch ruled little more than the island of Java in the East Indies. Thereafter they gradually brought almost all of the three-thousand-mile archipelago under their political authority, though—in good imperialist fashion—they had to share some of the spoils with Britain and Germany. In the critical decade of the 1880s, the French under the leadership of Ferry took Indochina. India, Japan, and China also experienced a profound imperialist impact (see Map 26.3).

Two other great imperialist powers, Russia and the United States, also acquired rich territories in Asia. Russia moved steadily forward on two fronts throughout the nineteenth century. Russians conquered Muslim areas to the south in the Caucasus and in Central Asia and also proceeded to nibble greedily on China's outlying provinces in the Far East, especially in the 1890s.

The United States' great conquest was the Philippines, taken from Spain in 1898 after the Spanish-American War. When it quickly became clear that the United States had no intention of granting independence, Philippine patriots rose in revolt and were suppressed only after long, bitter fighting. Some Americans protested the taking of the Philippines, but to no avail. Thus another great Western power joined the imperialist ranks in Asia.

Causes of the New Imperialism

Many factors contributed to the late-nineteenth-century rush for territory and empire, which was in turn one aspect of Western society's generalized expansion in the age of industry and nationalism. It is little wonder that controversies have raged over interpretation of the new imperialism, especially since authors of every persuasion have often exaggerated particular aspects in an attempt to prove their own theories. Yet despite complexity and controversy, basic causes are clearly identifiable.

Economic motives played an important role in the extension of political empires, especially the British Empire. By the late 1870s, France, Germany, and the United States were industrializing rapidly behind rising tariff barriers. Great Britain was losing its early lead and facing increasingly tough competition in foreign markets. In this new economic situation, Britain came to value old possessions, such as India and Canada, more highly. The days when a leading free-trader such as Richard Cobden could denounce the "bloodstained fetish of Empire" and statesman Benjamin Disraeli could call colonies a "millstone round our necks" came to an abrupt end. When continental powers began to grab territory in the 1880s, the British followed suit immediately. They feared that France and Germany would seal off their empires with high tariffs and restrictions and that future economic opportunities would be lost forever.

Actually, the overall economic gains of the new imperialism proved quite limited before 1914. The new colonies were simply too poor to buy much, and they offered few immediately profitable investments. Nonetheless, even the poorest, most barren desert was jealously prized, and no territory was ever abandoned. Colonies became important for political and diplomatic reasons. Each leading country saw colonies as crucial to national security, military power, and international prestige. For instance, safeguarding the Suez Canal played a key role in the British occupation of Egypt, and protecting Egypt in turn led to the bloody conquest of the Sudan. Far-flung possessions guaranteed ever-growing navies the safe havens and the dependable coaling stations they needed in time of crisis or war.

Many people were convinced that colonies were essential to great nations. "There has never been a great power without great colonies," wrote one French publicist in 1877. "Every virile people has established colonial power," echoed the famous nationalist historian of Germany, Heinrich von Treitschke. "All great nations in the fullness of their strength have desired to set their mark upon barbarian lands and those who fail to participate in this great rivalry will play a pitiable role in time to come."[10]

Individuals in Society

Cecil Rhodes

Cecil Rhodes, after crushing the last African revolt in Rhodesia in 1896. (Brown Brothers)

Cecil Rhodes (1853–1902) epitomized the dynamism and the ruthlessness of the new imperialism. He built a corporate monopoly, claimed vast tracts in Africa, and established the famous Rhodes scholarships to develop colonial (and American) leaders who would love and strengthen the British Empire. But to Africans, he left a bitter legacy.

Rhodes came from a large middle-class family and at seventeen went to southern Africa to seek his fortune. He soon turned to diamonds, newly discovered at Kimberley, picked good partners, and was wealthy by 1876. But Rhodes, often called a dreamer, wanted more. He entered Oxford University, while returning periodically to Africa, and his musings crystallized in a belief in progress through racial competition and territorial expansion. "I contend," he wrote, "that we [English] are the finest race in the world and the more of the world we inhabit the better it is for the human race."*

Rhodes's belief in British expansion never wavered. In 1880 he formed the De Beers Mining Company, and by 1888 his firm monopolized southern Africa's diamond production and earned fabulous profits. Rhodes also entered the Cape Colony's legislature and became the all-powerful prime minister from 1890 to 1896. His main objective was to dominate the Afrikaner republics and to impose British rule on as much land as possible beyond their northern borders. Working through a state-approved private company financed in part by De Beers, Rhodes's agents forced and cajoled African kings to accept British "protection," then put down rebellions with Maxim machine guns. Britain thus obtained a great swath of empire on the cheap.

But Rhodes, like many high achievers obsessed with power and personal aggrandizement, went too far. He backed, and then in 1896 failed to call back, a failed invasion of the Transvaal, which was designed to topple the Dutch-speaking republic. Repudiated by top British leaders who had encouraged his plan, Rhodes had to resign as prime minister. In declining health, he continued to agitate against the Afrikaner republics. He died at age forty-nine as the Boer War (1899–1902) ended.

In accounting for Rhodes's remarkable but flawed achievements, both sympathetic and critical biographers stress his imposing size, enormous energy, and powerful personality. His ideas were commonplace, but he believed in them passionately, and he could persuade and inspire others to follow his lead. Rhodes the idealist was nonetheless a born negotiator, a crafty dealmaker who believed that everyone could be had for a price. According to his best biographer, Rhodes's homosexuality—discreet, partially repressed, and undeniable—was also "a major component of his magnetism and his success."[†] Never comfortable with women, he loved male companionship. He drew together a "band of brothers," both gay and straight, to share in the pursuit of power.

Rhodes cared nothing for the rights of blacks. Ever a combination of visionary and opportunist, he looked forward to an eventual reconciliation of Afrikaners and British in a united white front. Therefore, as prime minister of the Cape Colony, he broke with the colony's liberal tradition and supported Afrikaner demands to reduce drastically the number of black voters and limit black freedoms. This helped lay the foundation for the Union of South Africa's brutal policy of racial segregation known as *apartheid* after 1948.

Questions for Analysis

1. How did Rhodes relate to Afrikaners and to black Africans? How do you account for the differences and the similarities?
2. In what ways does Rhodes's career throw additional light on the debate over the causes of the new imperialism?

*Robert Rotberg, *The Founder: Cecil Rhodes and the Pursuit of Power* (New York: Oxford University Press, 1988), p. 150.
[†]Ibid., p. 408.

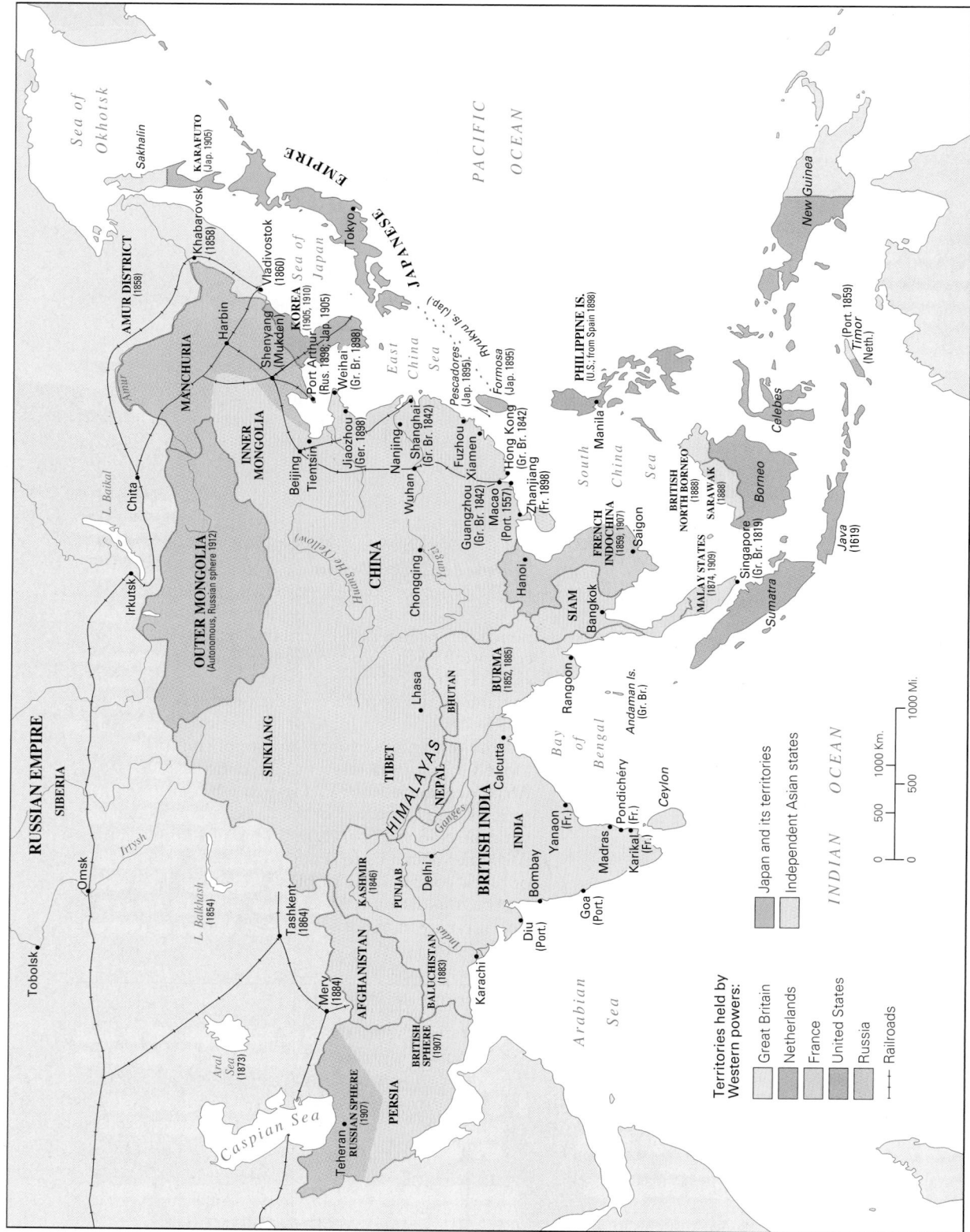

MAP 26.3 Asia in 1914 India remained under British rule, while China precariously preserved its political independence. The Dutch empire in modern-day Indonesia was old, but French control of Indochina was a product of the new imperialism.

Territories held by Western powers:
Great Britain
Netherlands
France
United States
Russia
━━━ Railroads

Japan and its territories
Independent Asian states

RUSSIAN EMPIRE

SIBERIA

Sea of Okhotsk

Sakhalin

KARAFUTO (Jap. 1905)

AMUR DISTRICT (1858)

Khabarovsk (1858)

Vladivostok (1860)

Harbin

MANCHURIA

Shenyang (Mukden)

Port Arthur (Rus. 1898, 1905)

Weihai (Gr. Br. 1898)

KOREA (1905, 1910) Jap. 1905

Sea of Japan

Tokyo

JAPANESE EMPIRE

PACIFIC OCEAN

New Guinea

(Port. 1859)
Timor (Neth.)

East China Sea

Ryukyu Is. (Jap.)

Pescadores (Jap. 1895)

Formosa (Jap. 1895)

INNER MONGOLIA

Beijing
Tientsin

Jiazhou (Ger. 1898)

Nanjing

Wuhan

Shanghai (Gr. Br. 1842)

Fuzhou

Guangzhou (Gr. Br. 1842)
Macao (Port. 1557)
Xiamen

Hong Kong (Gr. Br. 1842)

Zhanjiang (Fr. 1898)

PHILIPPINE IS. (U.S. from Spain 1898)

Manila

South China Sea

BRITISH NORTH BORNEO (1888)

SARAWAK (1888)

Borneo

Celebes

Java (1619)

Sumatra

OUTER MONGOLIA (Autonomous, Russian sphere 1912)

L. Baikal

Chita

Irkutsk

Amur

SINKIANG

CHINA

Huang He (Yellow)

Yangzi

Chongqing

Hanoi

FRENCH INDOCHINA (1859, 1907)

Saigon

SIAM

Bangkok

Singapore (Gr. Br. 1819)

MALAY STATES (1874, 1909)

Omsk

Tobolsk

Irtysh

L. Balkhash (1854)

Tashkent (1864)

Merv (1884)

Aral Sea (1873)

Caspian Sea

Teheran

PERSIA

RUSSIAN SPHERE (1907)

BRITISH SPHERE (1907)

BALUCHISTAN (1883)

AFGHANISTAN

Indus

KASHMIR (1846)

PUNJAB

Delhi

NEPAL

BHUTAN

TIBET

Lhasa

HIMALAYAS

BRITISH INDIA

Ganges

Calcutta

INDIA

Yanaon (Fr.)

BURMA (1852, 1885)

Rangoon

Andaman Is. (Gr. Br.)

Madras
Pondichéry (Fr.)
Karikal (Fr.)

Ceylon

Bay of Bengal

Bombay

Goa (Port.)

Diu (Port.)

Karachi

Arabian Sea

INDIAN OCEAN

0   500   1000 Km.

0   500   1000 Mi.

Treitschke's harsh statement reflects not only the increasing aggressiveness of European nationalism after Bismarck's wars of German unification but also Social Darwinian theories of brutal competition among races. As one prominent English economist argued, the "strongest nation has always been conquering the weaker . . . and the strongest tend to be best." Thus European nations, which were seen as racially distinct parts of the dominant white race, had to seize colonies to show they were strong and virile. Moreover, since racial struggle was nature's inescapable law, the conquest of "inferior" peoples was just. "The path of progress is strewn with the wreck . . . of inferior races," wrote one professor in 1900. "Yet these dead peoples are, in very truth, the stepping stones on which mankind has risen to the higher intellectual and deeper emotional life of today."[11] Social Darwinism and harsh racial doctrines fostered imperialist expansion.

So did the industrial world's unprecedented technological and military superiority. Three aspects were crucial. First, the rapidly firing machine gun, so lethal at Omdurman in the Sudan, was an ultimate weapon in many another unequal battle. Second, newly discovered quinine proved no less effective in controlling attacks of malaria, which had previously decimated whites in the tropics whenever they left breezy coastal enclaves and dared to venture into mosquito-infested interiors. Third, the combination of the steamship and the international telegraph permitted Western powers to quickly concentrate their firepower in a given area when it was needed. Never before—and never again after 1914—would the technological gap between the West and non-Western regions of the world be so great.

Social tensions and domestic political conflicts also contributed mightily to overseas expansion, according to a prominent interpretation of recent years. Certainly in Germany, in Russia, and in other countries to a lesser extent, contemporary critics of imperialism charged conservative political leaders with manipulating colonial issues in order to divert popular attention from the class struggle at home and to create a false sense of national unity. Thus imperial propagandists relentlessly stressed that colonies benefited workers as well as capitalists, providing jobs and cheap raw materials that raised workers' standard of living. Government leaders and their allies in the tabloid press successfully encouraged the masses to savor foreign triumphs and glory in the supposed increase in national prestige. In short, conservative leaders defined imperialist development as a national necessity, which they used to justify the status quo and their hold on power.

Finally, certain special-interest groups in each country were powerful agents of expansion. Shipping companies wanted lucrative subsidies. White settlers demanded more land and greater protection. Missionaries and humanitarians wanted to spread religion and stop the slave trade. Military men and colonial officials, whose role has often been overlooked, foresaw rapid advancement and high-paid positions in growing empires. The actions of such groups pushed the course of empire forward.

Western society did not rest the case for empire solely on naked conquest and a Darwinian racial struggle or on power politics and the need for naval bases on every ocean. Imperialists developed additional arguments in order to satisfy their consciences and answer their critics.

A favorite idea was that Europeans could and should "civilize" more primitive, nonwhite peoples. According to this view, nonwhites would eventually receive the benefits of modern economies, cities, advanced medicine, and higher standards of living. In time, they might be ready for self-government and Western democracy. Thus the French spoke of their sacred "civilizing mission." Rudyard Kipling (1865–1936), who wrote masterfully of Anglo-Indian life and was perhaps the most influential British writer of the 1890s, exhorted Europeans (and Americans in the United States) to unselfish service in distant lands:

Take up the White Man's Burden—
    Send forth the best ye breed—
Go bind your sons to exile
    To serve your captives' need,
To wait in heavy harness,
    On fluttered folk and wild—
Your new-caught, sullen peoples
    Half-devil and half-child.[12]

Many Americans accepted the ideology of the **white man's burden.** It was an important factor in the decision to rule, rather than liberate, the Philippines after the Spanish-American War. Like their European counterparts, these Americans sincerely believed that their civilization had reached unprecedented heights and that they had unique benefits to bestow on all "less advanced" peoples. Another argument was that imperial government protected natives from tribal warfare as well as cruder forms of exploitation by white settlers and business people.

Peace and stability under European control also facilitated the spread of Christianity. In Africa Catholic and Protestant missionaries competed with Islam south of the Sahara, seeking converts and building schools to spread the Gospel. Many Africans' first real contact with whites was in mission schools. Some peoples, such as the Ibo in Nigeria, became highly Christianized.

A Missionary School   A Swahili schoolboy leads his classmates in a reading lesson in Dar es Salaam in German East Africa before 1914, as portraits of Emperor William II and his wife look down on the classroom. Europeans argued that they were spreading the benefits of a superior civilization with schools like this one, which is unusually solid because of its strategic location in the capital city. *(Ullstein Bilderdienst)*

Such occasional successes in black Africa contrasted with the general failure of missionary efforts in India, China, and the Islamic world. There Christians often preached in vain to peoples with ancient, complex religious beliefs. Yet the number of Christian believers around the world did increase substantially in the nineteenth century, and missionary groups kept trying. Unfortunately, "many missionaries had drunk at the well of European racism," and this probably prevented them from doing better.[13]

Critics of Imperialism

The expansion of empire aroused sharp, even bitter, critics. A forceful attack was delivered in 1902, after the unpopular Boer War, by radical English economist J. A. Hobson (1858–1940) in his *Imperialism,* a work that in-

fluenced Lenin and others. Hobson contended that the rush to acquire colonies was due to the economic needs of unregulated capitalism, particularly the need of the rich to find outlets for their surplus capital. Yet, Hobson argued, imperial possessions did not pay off economically for the country as a whole. Only unscrupulous special-interest groups profited from them, at the expense of both the European taxpayer and the natives. Moreover, Hobson argued that the quest for empire diverted popular attention away from domestic reform and the need to reduce the great gap between rich and poor. These and similar arguments were not very persuasive, however. Most people then (and now) were sold on the idea that imperialism was economically profitable for the homeland, and a broad and genuine enthusiasm for empire developed among the masses.

Hobson and many other critics struck home, however, with their moral condemnation of whites imperiously ruling nonwhites. They rebelled against crude Social Darwinian thought. "O Evolution, what crimes are committed in thy name!" cried one foe. Another sardonically coined a new beatitude: "Blessed are the strong, for they shall prey on the weak."[14] Kipling and his kind were lampooned as racist bullies whose rule rested on brutality, racial contempt, and the Maxim machine gun. Henry Labouchère, a member of Parliament and prominent spokesman for this position, mocked Kipling's famous poem:

Pile on the Brown Man's burden!
And if ye rouse his hate,
Meet his old-fashioned reasons
With Maxims up to date,
With shells and Dum-Dum bullets
A hundred times plain
The Brown Man's loss must never
Imply the White Man's gain.[15]

Similarly, in *Heart of Darkness* Polish-born novelist Joseph Conrad (1857–1924) castigated the "pure selfishness" of Europeans in "civilizing" Africa; the main character, once a liberal scholar, turns into a savage brute.

Critics charged Europeans with applying a degrading double standard and failing to live up to their own noble ideals. At home Europeans had won or were winning representative government, individual liberties, and a certain equality of opportunity. In their empires, Europeans imposed military dictatorships on Africans and Asians; forced them to work involuntarily, almost like slaves; and discriminated against them shamelessly. Only by renouncing imperialism, its critics insisted, and giving captive peoples the freedoms Western society had struggled for since the French Revolution would Europeans be worthy of their traditions. Europeans who denounced the imperialist tide provided colonial peoples with a Western ideology of liberation.

Responses to Western Imperialism

To peoples in Africa and Asia, Western expansion represented a profoundly disruptive assault. Everywhere it threatened traditional ruling classes, traditional economies, and traditional ways of life. Christian missionaries and European secular ideologies challenged established beliefs and values. Non-Western peoples experienced a crisis of identity, one made all the more painful by the power and arrogance of the white intruders.

The initial response of African and Asian rulers was to try driving the unwelcome foreigners away. This was the case in China, Japan, and the upper Sudan, as we have seen. Violent antiforeign reactions exploded elsewhere again and again, but the superior military technology of the industrialized West almost invariably prevailed. Beaten in battle, many Africans and Asians concentrated on preserving their cultural traditions at all costs. Others found themselves forced to reconsider their initial hostility. Some (such as Ismail of Egypt) concluded that the West was indeed superior in some ways and that it was therefore necessary to reform their societies and copy European achievements. Thus it is possible to think of responses to the Western impact as a spectrum, with "traditionalists" at one end, "westernizers" or "modernizers" at the other, and many shades of opinion in between. Both before and after European domination, the struggle among these groups was often intense. With time, however, the modernizers tended to gain the upper hand.

When the power of both the traditionalists and the modernizers was thoroughly shattered by superior force, the great majority of Asians and Africans accepted imperial rule. Political participation in non-Western lands was historically limited to small elites, and the masses were used to doing what their rulers told them. In these circumstances Europeans, clothed in power and convinced of their righteousness, governed smoothly and effectively. They received considerable support from both traditionalists (local chiefs, landowners, religious leaders) and modernizers (Western-educated professional classes and civil servants).

Nevertheless, imperial rule was in many ways an imposing edifice built on sand. Support for European rule among the conforming and accepting millions was shallow and weak. Thus the conforming masses followed with greater or lesser enthusiasm a few determined personalities who came to oppose the Europeans. Such leaders always arose, both when Europeans ruled directly and when they manipulated native governments, for at least two basic reasons.

First, the nonconformists—the eventual anti-imperialist leaders—developed a burning desire for human dignity. They came to feel that such dignity was incompatible with foreign rule. Second, potential leaders found in the Western world the ideologies and justification for their protest. They discovered liberalism, with its credo of civil liberty and political self-determination. They echoed the demands of anti-imperialists in Europe and America that the West live up to its own ideals. Above all, they found themselves attracted to modern nationalism, which asserted that every people had the right to control its own destiny. After 1917 anti-imperialist revolt would find another weapon in Lenin's version of Marxian socialism. Thus the anti-imperialist search for dignity drew strength from Western culture, as is apparent in the development of three major Asian countries—India, Japan, and China.

Empire in India

India was the jewel of the British Empire, and no colonial area experienced a more profound British impact. Unlike Japan and China, which maintained a real or precarious independence, and unlike African territories, which were annexed by Europeans only at the end of the nineteenth century, India was ruled more or less absolutely by Britain for a very long time.

Arriving in India on the heels of the Portuguese in the seventeenth century, the British East India Company had conquered the last independent native state by 1848. The last "traditional" response to European rule—the attempt by the established ruling classes to drive the white man out by military force—was broken in India in 1857 and 1858. Those were the years of the **Great Rebellion** (which the British called a "mutiny"), when an insurrection by Muslim and Hindu mercenaries in the British army spread throughout northern and central India before it was finally crushed, primarily by loyal native troops from southern India. Thereafter Britain ruled India directly.

After 1858 India was ruled by the British Parliament in London and administered by a tiny, all-white civil service in India. In 1900 this elite consisted of fewer than 3,500 top officials, for a population of 300 million. The white elite, backed by white officers and native troops, was competent and generally well-disposed toward the welfare of the Indian peasant masses. Yet it practiced strict job discrimination and social segregation, and most of its members quite frankly considered the jumble of Indian peoples and castes to be racially inferior. As Lord Kitchener, one of the most distinguished top military commanders in India, stated:

It is this consciousness of the inherent superiority of the European which has won for us India. However well educated and clever a native may be, and however brave he may prove himself, I believe that no rank we can bestow on him would cause him to be considered an equal of the British officer.[16]

When, for example, the British Parliament in 1883 was considering a major bill to allow Indian judges to try white Europeans in India, the British community rose in protest and defeated the measure. The idea of being judged by Indians was inconceivable to the Europeans, who understood that the empire in India rested squarely on racial inequality.

In spite of (or perhaps even because of) their strong feelings of racial and cultural superiority, the British acted energetically and introduced many desirable changes to India. Realizing that they needed well-educated Indians to serve as skilled subordinates in the government and army, the British established a modern system of progressive secondary education in which all instruction was in English. Thus through education and government service, the British offered some Indians excellent opportunities for both economic and social advancement. High-caste Hindus, particularly quick to respond, emerged as skillful intermediaries between the British rulers and the Indian people, and soon they formed a new elite profoundly influenced by Western thought and culture.

This new bureaucratic elite played a crucial role in modern economic development, which was a second result of British rule. Irrigation projects for agriculture, the world's third-largest railroad network for good communications, and large tea and jute plantations geared to the world economy were all developed. Unfortunately, the lot of the Indian masses improved little, for the increase in production was eaten up by population increase.

Finally, with a well-educated, English-speaking Indian bureaucracy and modern communications, the British created a unified, powerful state. They placed under the same general system of law and administration the different Hindu and Muslim peoples and the vanquished kingdoms of the entire subcontinent—groups that had fought each other for centuries and had been repeatedly conquered by Muslim and Mongol invaders. It was as if Europe, with its many states and varieties of Christianity, had been conquered and united in a single great empire.

In spite of these achievements, the decisive reaction to European rule was the rise of nationalism among the Indian elite. No matter how anglicized and necessary a member of the educated classes became, he or she could never become the white ruler's equal. The top jobs, the best clubs, the modern hotels, and even certain railroad compartments were sealed off to brown-skinned Indians. The peasant masses might accept such inequality as the latest version of age-old oppression, but the well-educated, English-speaking elite eventually could not. For the elite, racial discrimination meant injured pride and bitter injustice. It flagrantly contradicted those cherished Western concepts of human rights and equality. Moreover, it was based on dictatorship, no matter how benign.

By 1885, when educated Indians came together to found the predominately Hindu Indian National Congress, demands were increasing for the equality and self-government that Britain had already granted white-settler colonies, such as Canada and Australia. By 1907, emboldened in part by Japan's success (see the next section), the radicals in the Indian National Congress were calling for complete independence. Even the moderates were demanding home rule for India through an elected parliament. Although there were sharp divisions between

Imperial Complexities in India   Britain permitted many native princes to continue their rule, if they accepted British domination. This photo shows a road-building project designed to facilitate famine relief in a southern native state. Officials of the local Muslim prince and their British "advisers" watch over workers drawn from the Hindu majority. *(Nizam's Good Works Project-Famine Relief: Road Building, Aurangabad 1895–1902, from Judith Mara Gutman,* Through Indian Eyes. *Courtesy, Private Collection)*

Hindus and Muslims, Indians were finding an answer to the foreign challenge. The common heritage of British rule and Western ideals, along with the reform and revitalization of the Hindu religion, had created a genuine movement for national independence.

The Example of Japan

When Commodore Matthew Perry arrived in Japan in 1853 with his crude but effective gunboat diplomacy, Japan was a complex feudal society. At the top stood a figurehead emperor, but real power was in the hands of a hereditary military governor, the **shogun.** With the help of a warrior nobility known as **samurai,** the shogun governed a country of hard-working, productive peasants and city dwellers. Often poor and restless, the intensely proud samurai were humiliated by the sudden American intrusion and the unequal treaties with Western countries.

When foreign diplomats and merchants began to settle in Yokohama, radical samurai reacted with a wave of antiforeign terrorism and antigovernment assassinations between 1858 and 1863. The imperialist response was swift and unambiguous. An allied fleet of American, British, Dutch, and French warships demolished key forts, further weakening the power and prestige of the shogun's government. Then in 1867, a coalition led by patriotic samurai seized control of the government with hardly any bloodshed and restored the political power of the emperor. This was the Meiji Restoration, a great turning point in Japanese development.

The immediate, all-important goal of the new government was to meet the foreign threat. The battle cry of the Meiji reformers was "Enrich the state and strengthen the armed forces." Yet how were these tasks to be done? In an about-face that was one of history's most remarkable chapters, the young but well-trained, idealistic but

The Rapid Modernization of the Japanese Army   This woodcut from about 1870 shows Japanese soldiers outfitted in Western uniforms and marching in Western formation. Japanese reformers, impressed by Prussian discipline and success on the battlefield, looked to Germany for their military models. *(Tsuneo Tamba Collection, Yokohama, Japan/Laurie Platt Winfrey, Inc.)*

flexible leaders of Meiji Japan dropped their antiforeign attacks. Convinced that Western civilization was indeed superior in its military and industrial aspects, they initiated from above a series of measures to reform Japan along modern lines. In the broadest sense, the Meiji leaders tried to harness the power inherent in Europe's dual revolution in order to protect their country and catch up with the West.

In 1871 the new leaders abolished the old feudal structure of aristocratic, decentralized government and formed a strong unified state. Following the example of the French Revolution, they dismantled the four-class legal system and declared social equality. They decreed freedom of movement in a country where traveling abroad had been a most serious crime. They created a free, competitive, government-stimulated economy. Japan began to build railroads and modern factories. Thus the new generation adopted many principles of a free, liberal society, and, as in Europe, such freedom resulted in a tremendously creative release of human energy.

Yet the overriding concern of Japan's political leadership was always a powerful state, and to achieve this, more than liberalism was borrowed from the West. A powerful modern navy was created, and the army was completely reorganized along European lines, with three-year military service for all males and a professional officer corps. This army of draftees effectively put down disturbances in the countryside, and in 1877 it was used to crush a major rebellion by feudal elements protesting the loss of their privileges. Japan also borrowed rapidly and adapted skillfully the West's science and modern technology, particularly in industry, medicine, and education. Many Japanese were encouraged to study abroad, and the government paid large salaries to attract foreign experts. These experts were always carefully controlled, however, and replaced by trained Japanese as soon as possible.

By 1890, when the new state was firmly established, the wholesale borrowing of the early restoration had given way to more selective emphasis on those things foreign that were in keeping with Japanese tradition. Following the model of the German Empire, Japan established an authoritarian constitution and rejected democracy. The power of the emperor and his ministers was vast; that of the legislature, limited.

Japan successfully copied the imperialism of Western society. Expansion not only proved that Japan was strong; it also cemented the nation together in a great mission. Having "opened" Korea with the gunboat diplomacy of imperialism in 1876, Japan decisively defeated China in a war over Korea in 1894 and 1895 and took Formosa (modern-day Taiwan). In the next years, Japan competed aggressively with the leading European powers for influence and territory in China, particularly Manchuria. There Japanese and Russian imperialism met and collided. In 1904 Japan attacked Russia without warning, and after a bloody war, Japan emerged with a valuable foothold in China, Russia's former protectorate over Port Arthur (see Map 26.3). By 1910, with the annexation of Korea, Japan had become a major imperialist power.

Japan became the first non-Western country to use an ancient love of country to transform itself and thereby meet the many-sided challenge of Western expansion. Moreover, Japan demonstrated convincingly that a modern Asian nation could defeat and humble a great Western power. Many Chinese nationalists were fascinated by Japan's achievement. A group of patriots in French-ruled southern Vietnam sent Vietnamese students to Japan to learn the island empire's secret of success. Japan provided patriots throughout Asia and Africa with an inspiring example of national recovery and liberation.

Toward Revolution in China

In 1860 the two-hundred-year-old Qing Dynasty in China appeared on the verge of collapse. Efforts to repel foreigners had failed, and rebellion and chaos wracked the country. Yet the government drew on its traditional strengths and made a surprising comeback that lasted more than thirty years.

Two factors were crucial in this reversal. First, the traditional ruling groups temporarily produced new and effective leadership. Loyal scholar-statesmen and generals quelled disturbances such as the great Tai Ping rebellion. The empress dowager Tzu Hsi, a truly remarkable woman, governed in the name of her young son and combined shrewd insight with vigorous action to revitalize the bureaucracy.

Second, destructive foreign aggression lessened, for the Europeans had obtained their primary goal of commercial and diplomatic relations. Indeed, some Europeans contributed to the dynasty's recovery. A talented Irishman effectively reorganized China's customs office and increased the government tax receipts, while a sympathetic Ameri-can diplomat represented China in foreign lands and helped strengthen the central government. Such efforts dovetailed with the dynasty's efforts to adopt some aspects of Western government and technology while maintaining traditional Chinese values and beliefs.

The parallel movement toward domestic reform and limited cooperation with the West collapsed under the blows of Japanese imperialism. The Sino-Japanese War of 1894 to 1895 and the subsequent harsh peace treaty revealed China's helplessness in the face of aggression, triggering a rush for foreign concessions and protectorates in China. At the high point of this rush in 1898, it appeared that the European powers might actually divide China among themselves, as they had recently divided Africa. Probably only the jealousy each nation felt toward its imperialist competitors saved China from partition, although the U.S. Open Door policy, which opposed formal annexation of Chinese territory, may have helped tip the balance. In any event, the tempo of foreign encroachment greatly accelerated after 1894.

So, too, did the intensity and radicalism of the Chinese reaction. Like the leaders of the Meiji Restoration, some

The Empress Dowager Tzu Hsi (1835–1908) Tzu Hsi drew on conservative forces, like the court eunuchs surrounding her here, to maintain her power. Three years after her death in 1908, a revolution broke out and forced the last Chinese emperor, a boy of six, to abdicate. *(Freer Gallery of Art and Arthur M. Sackler Gallery Archives, Smithsonian Institution. Photographer: Hsun-ling. Negative no. 261)*

modernizers saw salvation in Western institutions. In 1898 the government launched a desperate **hundred days of reform** in an attempt to meet the foreign challenge. More radical reformers, such as the revolutionary Sun Yat-sen (1866–1925), who came from the peasantry and was educated in Hawaii by Christian missionaries, sought to overthrow the dynasty altogether and establish a republic.

On the other side, some traditionalists turned back toward ancient practices, political conservatism, and fanatical hatred of the "foreign devils." "Protect the country, destroy the foreigner" was their simple motto. Such conservative, antiforeign patriots had often clashed with foreign missionaries, whom they charged with undermining reverence for ancestors and thereby threatening the Chinese family and the entire society. In the agony of defeat and unwanted reforms, secret societies such as the Boxers rebelled. In northeastern China, more than two hundred foreign missionaries and several thousand Chinese Christians were killed. Once again the imperialist response was swift and harsh. Peking was occupied and plundered by foreign armies. A heavy indemnity was imposed.

The years after the Boxer Rebellion (1900–1903) were ever more troubled. Anarchy and foreign influence spread as the power and prestige of the Qing Dynasty declined still further. Antiforeign, antigovernment revolutionary groups agitated and plotted. Finally in 1912, a spontaneous uprising toppled the Qing Dynasty. After thousands of years of emperors and empires, a loose coalition of revolutionaries proclaimed a Western-style republic and called for an elected parliament. The transformation of China under the impact of expanding Western society entered a new phase, and the end was not in sight.

Summary

In the nineteenth century, the industrializing West entered the third and most dynamic phase of its centuries-old expansion into non-Western lands. In so doing, Western nations profitably subordinated those lands to their economic interests, sent forth millions of emigrants, and established political influence in Asia and vast political empires in Africa. The reasons for this culminating surge were many, but the economic thrust of robust industrial capitalism, an ever-growing lead in technology, and the competitive pressures of European nationalism were particularly important.

Western expansion had far-reaching consequences. For the first time in human history, the world became in many ways a single unit. Moreover, European expansion diffused the ideas and techniques of a highly developed civilization. Yet the West relied on force to conquer and rule, and it treated non-Western peoples as racial inferiors. Thus non-Western elites, often armed with Western doctrines, gradually responded to the Western challenge. They launched a national, anti-imperialist struggle for dignity, genuine independence, and modernization. This struggle would emerge as a central drama of world history after the great European civil war of 1914 to 1918, which reduced the West's technological advantage and shattered its self-confidence and complacent moral superiority.

Key Terms

Third World	Afrikaners
opium trade	Berlin conference
khedive	white man's burden
great migration	Great Rebellion
swallows	shogun
great white walls	samurai
new imperialism	hundred days of reform

Notes

1. Quoted in A. Waley, *The Opium War Through Chinese Eyes* (New York: Macmillan, 1958), p. 29.
2. Quoted in J. W. Hall, *Japan, from Prehistory to Modern Times* (New York: Delacorte Press, 1970), p. 250.
3. Quoted in R. Hallett, *Africa to 1875* (Ann Arbor: University of Michigan Press, 1970), p. 109.
4. Quoted in Earl of Cromer, *Modern Egypt* (London, 1911), p. 48.
5. Quoted in T. Blegen, *Norwegian Migration to America,* vol. 2 (Northfield, Minn.: Norwegian-American Historical Association, 1940), p. 468.
6. Quoted in I. Howe, *World of Our Fathers* (New York: Harcourt Brace Jovanovich, 1976), p. 25.
7. Quoted in C. A. Price, *The Great White Walls Are Built: Restrictive Immigration to North America and Australia, 1836–1888* (Canberra: Australian National University Press, 1974), p. 175.
8. Quoted in W. L. Langer, *European Alliances and Alignments, 1871–1890* (New York: Vintage Books, 1931), p. 290.
9. Quoted in J. Ellis, *The Social History of the Machine Gun* (New York: Pantheon Books, 1975), pp. 86, 101.
10. Quoted in G. H. Nadel and P. Curtis, eds., *Imperialism and Colonialism* (New York: Macmillan, 1964), p. 94.
11. Quoted in W. L. Langer, *The Diplomacy of Imperialism,* 2d ed. (New York: Alfred A. Knopf, 1951), pp. 86, 88.
12. Rudyard Kipling, *The Five Nations* (London, 1903).
13. E. H. Berman, "African Responses to Christian Mission Education," *African Studies Review* 17 (1974): 530.
14. Quoted in Langer, *The Diplomacy of Imperialism,* p. 88.
15. Quoted in Ellis, *The Social History of the Machine Gun,* pp. 99–100.
16. Quoted in K. M. Panikkar, *Asia and Western Dominance: A Survey of the Vasco da Gama Epoch of Asian History* (London: George Allen & Unwin, 1959), p. 116.

Suggested Reading

General interpretations of European expansion in a broad perspective include K. Pomeranz, *The Great Divergence: China, Europe, and the Making of the Modern World Economy* (2000); A. Thornton, *Imperialism in the Twentieth Century* (1977); and T. Smith, *The Patterns of Imperialism* (1981). Valuable documentary collections include A. Conklin, ed., *European Imperialism, 1830–1930* (1999), and Bonnie Smith, ed., *Imperialism: A Collection of Documents* (2000). D. K. Field-house has written two fine surveys, *Economics and Empire, 1830–1914* (1970) and *Colonialism, 1870–1945* (1981). J. A. Hobson's classic *Imperialism* (1902) is readily available, and the Marxist-Leninist case is effectively presented in V. G. Kieran, *Marxism and Imperialism* (1975). Among the cultural studies probing the minds of imperialists and non-Europeans, E. Said, *Orientalism* (1978), is an influential and controversial interpretation, and B. Cohn, *Colonialism and Its Form of Knowledge: The British in India* (1966), is a culminating work by a leading anthropologist.

Britain's leading position in European imperialism is examined in a lively way by G. Goodlad, *British Foreign and Imperial Policy, 1865–1919* (2000); B. Porter, *The Lion's Share* (1976); and P. Cain and A. Hopkins, *British Imperialism: Innovation and Expansion, 1688–1914* (1993). P. Marshall, ed., *Cambridge Illustrated History of the British Empire* (1996), and D. Judd, *The Victorian Empire* (1970), are stunning pictorial histories. G. Stocking, *Victorian Anthropology* (1987), is a brilliant analysis of the cultural and racial implications of Western expansion. R. Robinson and J. Gallagher, *Africa and the Victorians: The Climax of Imperialism* (1961), is an influential interpretation. R. Aldrich, *Greater France: A History of French Overseas Expansion* (1996), and W. Baumgart, *Imperialism: The Idea and Reality of British and French Colonial Expansion* (1982), are well-balanced studies. A. Conklin, *A Mission to Civilize: The French Republican Ideal and West Africa, 1895–1930* (1997), is outstanding, and H. Brunschwig, *French Colonialism, 1871–1914* (1966), is a classic short study. A. Hochshild, *King Leopold's Ghost: A Story of Greed, Terror, and Heroism in Colonial Africa, 1895–1930* (1997), tells the chilling story of Belgian imperialism in the Congo and reaction to it. R. Rotberg, *The Founder: Cecil Rhodes and the Pursuit of Power* (1988), examines the imperialist's mind and times with great skill, and B. Roberts, *Cecil Rhodes: Flawed Colossus* (1987), is engaging and entertaining. A. Blunt, *Travel, Gender, and Imperialism: Mary Kingsley and West Africa* (1994), analyzes a complicated woman whose travels made her into a powerful critic of British expansion. D. Headrick looks at the diffusion of Western technology in *The Tentacles of Progress: Technology Transfer in the Age of Imperialism, 1850–1940* (1988), and P. Curtin, *Death by Migration: Europe's Encounter with the Tropical World in the Nineteenth Century* (1989), ably charts the medical revolution in the tropics. R. Vecoli and S. Sinke, eds., *A Century of European Migrations, 1830–1930* (1991), and L. Moch, *Moving Europeans: Migration in Europe Since 1650* (1993), are valuable general studies.

Howe and Blegen, cited in the Notes, provide dramatic accounts of Jewish and Norwegian migration to the United States. Most other migrant groups have also found their historians: M. Walker, *Germany and the Emigration, 1816–1885* (1964), and W. Adams, *Ireland and Irish Emigration to the New World* (reissued 1967), are outstanding. Ellis's well-illustrated study of the machine gun is fascinating, as is Price on the restriction of Asian migration to Australia. Both works are cited in the Notes.

E. Wolf, *Europe and the People Without History* (1982), considers, with skill and compassion, the impact of imperialism on non-Western peoples. Two classic studies on personal relations between European rulers and non-European subjects are D. Mannoni, *Prospero and Caliban: The Psychology of Colonialization* (1964), and F. Fanon, *Wretched of the Earth* (1965), a bitter attack on white racism by a black psychologist active in the Algerian revolution. B. Smith, *European Vision and the South Pacific* (1988), is an original and influential work combining art history and intellectual development. V. Ware, *Beyond the Pale: White Women, Racism and History* (1992), and C. Midgley, ed., *Gender and Imperialism* (1998), examine the complex role of European women in imperialism. Novels also bring the psychological and human dimensions of imperialism alive. H. Rider Haggard, *King Solomon's Mines,* portrays the powerful appeal of adventure in exotic lands; Rudyard Kipling, the greatest writer of European expansion, is at his stirring best in *Kim* and *Soldiers Three.* Joseph Conrad unforgettably probes European motives in *Heart of Darkness.* William Boyd, *An Ice-Cream War,* a good story of British and Germans fighting each other in Africa during the First World War, is a favorite with students.

P. Ebrey, *The Cambridge Illustrated History of China* (1996), is a lively and beautiful work by a leading specialist. J. Spence, *The Search for Modern China* (1990), is also recommended. I. Hsü, *The Rise of Modern China,* 5th ed. (1995), is a fine history with many suggestions for further reading. E. Reischauer's topical survey, *Japan: The Story of a Nation* (1981), is recommended, as are T. Huber, *The Revolutionary Origins of Modern Japan* (1981), and Y. Fukuzawa, *Autobiography* (1966), the account of a leading intellectual who saw the birth of modern Japan.

G. Perry, *The Middle East: Fourteen Islamic Centuries* (1983), concisely surveys nineteenth-century developments. B. Lewis, *The Middle East and the West* (1963), is a penetrating analysis of the impact of Western ideas on Middle Eastern thought. P. Curtin et al., *African History: From Earliest Times to Independence,* 2d ed. (1995), and R. July, *A History of the African People,* 4th ed. (1992), contain excellent brief introductions to Africa in the age of imperialism. J. D. Fage, *A History of Africa,* 3d ed. (1995), is also recommended. A classic study of Western expansion from an Indian viewpoint is Panikkar's volume mentioned in the Notes. S. Wolpert, *A New History of India,* 5th ed. (1997), incorporates recent scholarship in a wide-ranging study that is highly recommended.

A French Leader Defends Imperialism

*A*lthough Jules Ferry (1832–1893) first gained
political prominence as an ardent champion of
secular public education, he was most famous for his
empire building. While he was French premier in
1880–1881 and again in 1883–1885, France
occupied Tunisia, extended its rule in Indochina,
seized Madagascar, and penetrated the Congo.
Criticized by conservatives, socialists, and some left-
wing republicans for his colonial expansion, Ferry
defended his policies before the French National
Assembly and also elaborated a philosophy of
imperialism in his writings.

In a speech to the Assembly on July 28, 1883,
portions of which follow, Ferry answered his critics
and summarized his three main arguments with
brutal honesty. Note that Ferry adamantly insisted
that imperial expansion did not weaken France in its
European struggle with Germany, as some opponents
charged, but rather that it increased French grandeur
and power. Imperialists needed the language of
patriotic nationalism to be effective.

M. Jules Ferry: Gentlemen, . . . I believe that
there is some benefit in summarizing and
condensing, in the form of arguments, the
principles, the motives, and the various interests
by which a policy of colonial expansion may be
justified; it goes without saying that I will try to
remain reasonable, moderate, and never lose sight
of the major continental interests which are the
primary concern of this country. What I wish to
say, to support this proposition, is that in fact, just
as in word, the policy of colonial expansion is a
political and economic system; I wish to say that
one can relate this system to three orders of ideas:
economic ideas, ideas of civilization in its highest
sense, and ideas of politics and patriotism.

In the area of economics, I will allow myself to
place before you, with the support of some

figures, the considerations which justify a policy of
colonial expansion from the point of view of that
need, felt more and more strongly by the
industrial populations of Europe and particularly
those of our own rich and hard working country:
the need for export markets. Is this some kind of
chimera? Is this a view of the future or is it not
rather a pressing need, and, we could say, the cry
of our industrial population? I will formulate only
in a general way what each of you, in the different
parts of France, is in a position to confirm. Yes,
what is lacking for our great industry, drawn
irrevocably on to the path of exportation by the
[free trade] treaties of 1860, what it lacks more
and more is export markets. Why? Because next
door to us Germany is surrounded by barriers,
because beyond the ocean, the United States of
America has become protectionist, protectionist in
the most extreme sense. . . .

Gentlemen, there is a second point, . . . the
humanitarian and civilizing side of the question.
On this point the honorable M. Camille Pellatan
has jeered in his own refined and clever manner;
he jeers, he condemns, and he says "What is this
civilization which you impose with cannonballs?
What is it but another form of barbarism? Don't
these populations, these inferior races, have the
same rights as you? Aren't they masters of their
own houses? Have they called upon you? You
come to them against their will, you offer them
violence, but not civilization." There, gentlemen,
is the thesis; I do not hesitate to say that this is
not politics, nor is it history: it is political
metaphysics. ("Ah, Ah" *on far left.*)

. . . Gentlemen, I must speak from a higher and
more truthful plane. It must be stated openly that,
in effect, superior races have rights over inferior
races. *(Movement on many benches on the far left.)*

M. Jules Maigne: Oh! You dare to say this in the
country which has proclaimed the rights of man!

M. de Guilloutet: This is a justification of slavery
and the slave trade! . . .

M. Jules Ferry: I repeat that superior races have a right, because they have a duty. They have the duty to civilize inferior races. . . . *(Approval from the left. New interruptions from the extreme left and from the right.)*

. . . M. Pelletan . . . then touched upon a third point, more delicate, more serious, and upon which I ask your permission to express myself quite frankly. It is the political side of the question. The honorable M. Pelletan, who is a distinguished writer, always comes up with remarkably precise formulations. I will borrow from him the one which he applied the other day to this aspect of colonial policy.

"It is a system," he says, "which consists of seeking out compensations in the Orient with a circumspect and peaceful seclusion which is actually imposed upon us in Europe."

I would like to explain myself in regard to this. I do not like this word, "compensation," and, in effect, not here but elsewhere it has often been used in a treacherous way. If what is being said or insinuated is that any government in this country, any Republican minister could possibly believe that there are in any part of the world compensations for the disasters which we have experienced [in connection with our defeat in the Franco-Prussian War of 1870–1871], an injury is being inflicted . . . and an injury undeserved by that government. *(Applause at the center and left.)* I will ward off this injury with all the force of my patriotism! *(New applause and bravos from the same benches.)*

Gentlemen, there are certain considerations which merit the attention of all patriots. The conditions of naval warfare have been profoundly altered. ("Very true! Very true!")

At this time, as you know, a warship cannot carry more than fourteen days' worth of coal, no matter how perfectly it is organized, and a ship which is out of coal is a derelict on the surface of the sea, abandoned to the first person who comes along. Thence the necessity of having on the oceans provision stations, shelters, ports for defense and revictualling. *(Applause at the center and left. Various interruptions.)* And it is for this that we needed Tunisia, for this that we needed Saigon and the Mekong Delta, for this that we need Madagascar, that we are at Diégo-Suarez and Vohemar [two Madagascar ports] and will never leave them! *(Applause from a great number of benches.)* Gentlemen, in Europe as it is today, in this competition of so many rivals which we see growing around us, some by perfecting their military or maritime forces, others by the prodigious development of an ever growing

Jules Ferry, French politician and ardent imperialist. *(Corbis)*

population; in a Europe, or rather in a universe of this sort, a policy of peaceful seclusion or abstention is simply the highway to decadence! Nations are great in our times only by means of the activities which they develop; it is not simply "by the peaceful shining forth of institutions" *(interruptions on the extreme left and right)* that they are great at this hour.

. . . [The Republican Party] has shown that it is quite aware that one cannot impose upon France a political ideal conforming to that of nations like independent Belgium and the Swiss Republic; that something else is needed for France: that she cannot be merely a free country, that she must also be a great country, exercizing all of her rightful influence over the destiny of Europe, that she ought to propagate this influence throughout the world and carry everywhere that she can her language, her customs, her flag, her arms, and her genius. *(Applause at center and left.)*

Questions for Analysis

1. What was Jules Ferry's economic argument for imperial expansion? Why had colonies recently gained greater economic value?

2. How did Ferry's critics attack the morality of foreign expansion? How did Ferry try to claim the moral high ground in his response?

3. What political arguments did Ferry advance? How would you characterize his philosophy of politics and national development?

Source: Speech before the French National Assembly, July 28, 1883. Reprinted in R. A. Austen, ed., *Modern Imperialism: Western Overseas Expansion and Its Aftermath, 1776–1965* (Lexington, Mass.: D. C. Heath, 1969), pp. 70–73.

John Singer Sargent's World War I painting *Gassed* (detail).
(By courtesy of the Trustees of the Imperial War Museum)

27

The Great Break: War and Revolution

chapter outline

- The First World War

- The Home Front

- The Russian Revolution

- The Peace Settlement

*I*n the summer of 1914, the nations of Europe went willingly to war. They believed they had no other choice. Moreover, both peoples and governments confidently expected a short war leading to a decisive victory. Such a war, they believed, would "clear the air," and European society would be able to go on as before.

These expectations were almost totally mistaken. The First World War was long, indecisive, and tremendously destructive. To the shell-shocked generation of survivors, it was known simply as the Great War: the war of unprecedented scope and intensity. From today's perspective, it is clear that the First World War marked a great break in the course of Western historical development since the French and Industrial Revolutions. A noted British political scientist has gone so far as to say that even in victorious and relatively fortunate Great Britain, the First World War was *the* great turning point in government and society, "as in everything else in modern British history. . . . There's a much greater difference between the Britain of 1914 and, say, 1920, than between the Britain of 1920 and today."[1] This strong statement contains a great amount of truth, for all of Europe as well as for Britain.

- What caused the Great War?
- How did the war lead to revolution and the fall of empires?
- How and why did war and revolution have such enormous and destructive consequences?
- How did the years of trauma and bloodshed form elements of today's world, many of which people now accept and even cherish?

These are the questions this chapter will address and try to answer.

*T*he First World War

The First World War was so long and destructive because it involved all the Great Powers and because it quickly degenerated into a senseless military stalemate. Like evenly matched boxers in a championship bout, the two sides tried to wear each other down. But there was no referee to call a draw, only the blind hammering of a life-or-death struggle. What were the roots of this terrible ordeal?

The Bismarckian System of Alliances

The Franco-Prussian War and the founding of the German Empire opened a new era in international relations. France was decisively defeated in 1871 and forced to pay a large war indemnity and give up Alsace-Lorraine. In ten short years, from 1862 to 1871, Bismarck had made Prussia-Germany—traditionally the weakest of the Great Powers—the most powerful nation in Europe (see pages 829–833). Had Bismarck been a Napoleon or a Hitler, for whom no gain was ever sufficient, continued expansion would no doubt sooner or later have raised a powerful coalition against the new German Empire. Yet he was

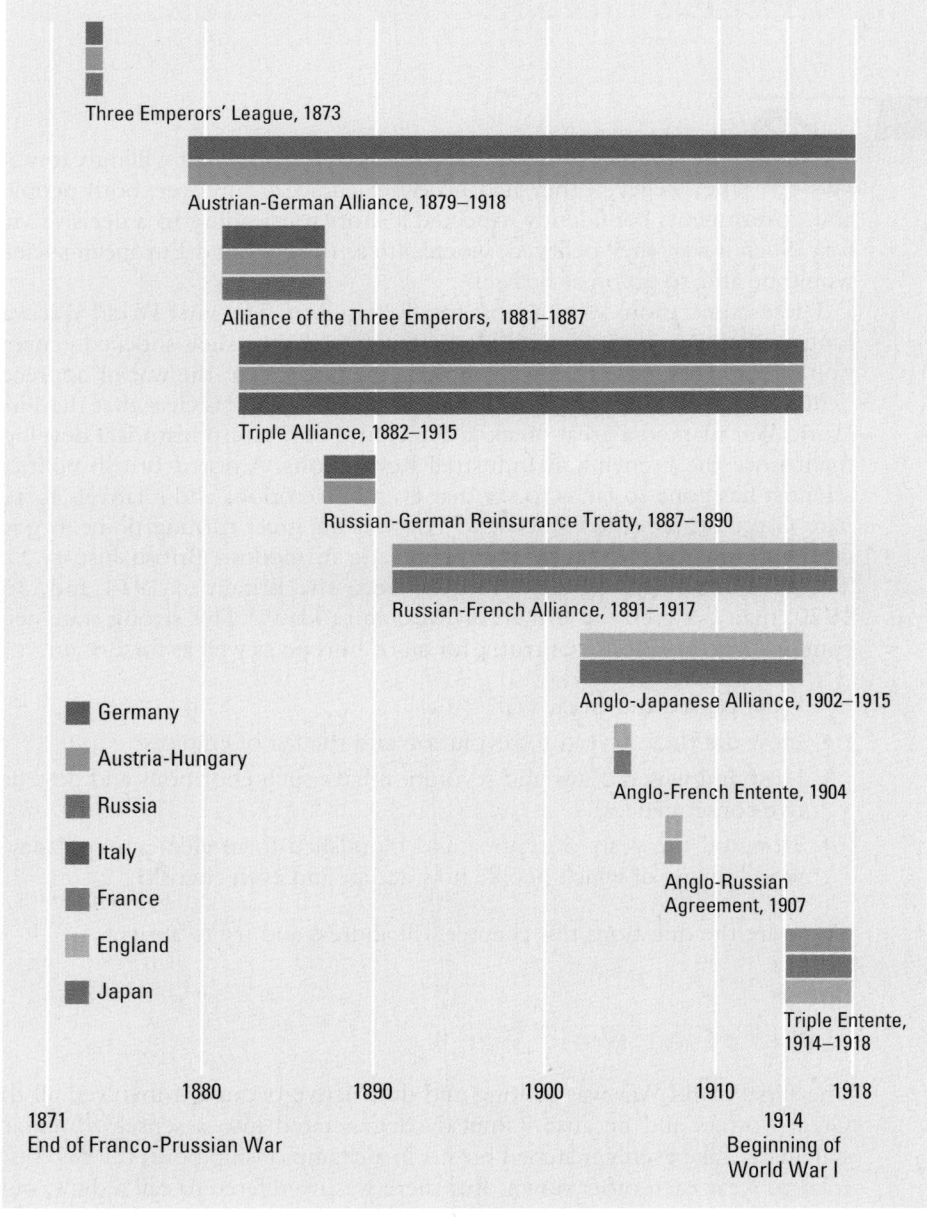

FIGURE 27.1 The Alliance System After 1871   Bismarck's subtle diplomacy maintained reasonably good relations among the eastern monarchies—Germany, Russia, and Austria-Hungary—and kept France isolated. The situation changed dramatically in 1891, when the Russian-French Alliance divided the Great Powers into two fairly equal military blocs.

Three Emperors' League, 1873

Austrian-German Alliance, 1879–1918

Alliance of the Three Emperors, 1881–1887

Triple Alliance, 1882–1915

Russian-German Reinsurance Treaty, 1887–1890

Russian-French Alliance, 1891–1917

Anglo-Japanese Alliance, 1902–1915

Anglo-French Entente, 1904

Anglo-Russian Agreement, 1907

Triple Entente, 1914–1918

Germany
Austria-Hungary
Russia
Italy
France
England
Japan

1880   1890   1900   1910   1918

1871
End of Franco-Prussian War

1914
Beginning of World War I

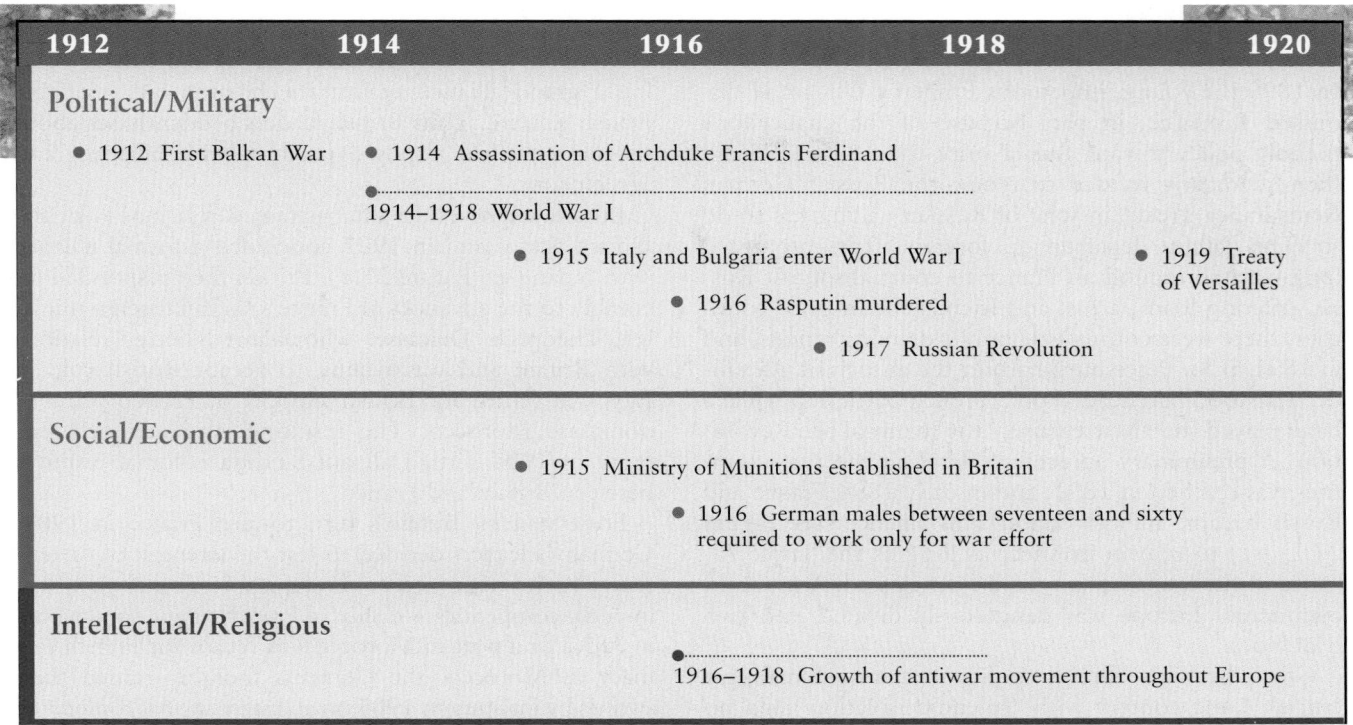

1912	1914	1916	1918	1920

Political/Military

- 1912 First Balkan War
- 1914 Assassination of Archduke Francis Ferdinand

1914–1918 World War I

- 1915 Italy and Bulgaria enter World War I
- 1916 Rasputin murdered
- 1917 Russian Revolution
- 1919 Treaty of Versailles

Social/Economic

- 1915 Ministry of Munitions established in Britain
- 1916 German males between seventeen and sixty required to work only for war effort

Intellectual/Religious

1916–1918 Growth of antiwar movement throughout Europe

not. As Bismarck never tired of repeating after 1871, Germany was a "satisfied" power. Within Europe, Germany had no territorial ambitions and wanted only peace.

But how was peace to be preserved? Bismarck's first concern was to keep an embittered France diplomatically isolated and without military allies. His second concern was the threat to peace posed from the east, from Austria-Hungary and from Russia. Those two enormous multinational empires had many conflicting interests, particularly in the Balkans, where the Ottoman Empire—the "sick man of Europe"—was ebbing fast. There was a real threat that Germany might be dragged into a great war between the two rival empires. Bismarck's solution was a system of alliances (see Figure 27.1) to restrain both Russia and Austria-Hungary, to prevent conflict between them, and to isolate a hostile France, which could never forget the loss of Alsace-Lorraine.

A first step was the creation in 1873 of the conservative **Three Emperors' League,** which linked the monarchs of Austria-Hungary, Germany, and Russia in an alliance against radical movements. In 1877 and 1878, when Russia's victories in a war with the Ottoman Empire threatened the balance of Austrian and Russian interests in the Balkans and the balance of British and Russian interests in the Middle East, Bismarck played the

role of sincere peacemaker. But his balancing efforts at the Congress of Berlin in 1878 infuriated Russian nationalists, and this led Bismarck to conclude a defensive military alliance with Austria against Russia in 1879. Motivated by tensions with France, Italy joined Germany and Austria in 1882, thereby forming what became known as the Triple Alliance.

Bismarck continued to work for peace in eastern Europe, seeking to neutralize tensions between Austria-Hungary and Russia. In 1881 he capitalized on their mutual fears and cajoled them both into a secret alliance with Germany. This Alliance of the Three Emperors lasted until 1887.

Bismarck also maintained good relations with Britain and Italy, while encouraging France in Africa but keeping France isolated in Europe. In 1887 Russia declined to renew the Alliance of the Three Emperors because of new tensions in the Balkans. Bismarck craftily substituted the Russian-German Reinsurance Treaty, by which both states promised neutrality if the other was attacked.

Bismarck's accomplishments in foreign policy after 1871 were great. For almost a generation, he maintained German leadership in international affairs, and he worked successfully for peace by managing conflicts and by restraining Austria-Hungary and Russia with defensive alliances.

The Rival Blocs

In 1890 the young, impetuous Emperor William II dismissed Bismarck, in part because of the chancellor's friendly policy toward Russia since the 1870s. William then adamantly refused to renew the Russian-German Reinsurance Treaty, in spite of Russian willingness to do so. This fateful departure in foreign affairs prompted long-isolated republican France to court absolutist Russia, offering loans, arms, and friendship. In both countries, there were enthusiastic public demonstrations, and in 1891 in St. Petersburg harbor, the autocratic Alexander III stood bareheaded on a French battleship while a band played the "Marseillaise," the hymn of the Revolution. A preliminary agreement between the two countries was reached in 1891, and in early 1894 France and Russia became military allies. This alliance (see Figure 27.1) was to remain in effect as long as the Triple Alliance of Austria, Germany, and Italy existed. As a result, continental Europe was dangerously divided into two rival blocs.

Great Britain's foreign policy became increasingly crucial. Long content with "splendid isolation" and no permanent alliances, Britain after 1891 was the only uncommitted Great Power. Could Britain afford to remain isolated, or would it feel compelled to take sides? Alliance with France or Russia certainly seemed highly unlikely. With a vast and rapidly expanding empire, Britain was often in serious conflict with these countries around the world.

Britain also squabbled with Germany, but many Germans and some Britons felt that a "natural alliance" united the advanced, racially related Germanic and Anglo-Saxon peoples. However, the generally good relations that had prevailed between Prussia and Great Britain ever since the mid-eighteenth century, and certainly under Bismarck, gave way to a bitter Anglo-German rivalry.

There were several reasons for this tragic development. Commercial rivalry in world markets between Germany and Great Britain increased sharply in the 1890s, and William II's tactless public statements and Germany's pursuit of world power unsettled the British. Above all, Germany's decision in 1900 to expand greatly its battle fleet posed a challenge to Britain's long-standing naval supremacy. This decision coincided with the hard-fought Boer War (1899–1902) between the British and the tiny Dutch republics of southern Africa, which had a major impact on British policy. British political leaders saw that Britain was overextended around the world. The Boer War also brought into the open widespread anti-British feeling, as editorial writers in many nations denounced this latest manifestation of British imperialism. There was even talk of Germany, Austria, France, and Russia forming a grand alliance against the bloated but insatiable British Empire. Thus British leaders prudently set about shoring up their exposed position with alliances and agreements.

Britain improved its often-strained relations with the United States and in 1902 concluded a formal alliance with Japan (see Figure 27.1). Britain then responded favorably to the advances of France's skillful foreign minister, Théophile Delcassé, who wanted better relations with Britain and was willing to accept British rule in Egypt in return for British support of French plans to dominate Morocco. The resulting Anglo-French Entente of 1904 settled all outstanding colonial disputes between Britain and France.

Frustrated by Britain's turn toward France in 1904, Germany's leaders decided to test the strength of the entente. Rather than accept the typical territorial payoff of imperial competition—a slice of French jungle somewhere in Africa or a port in Morocco—in return for French primacy in Morocco, the Germans foolishly rattled their swords by insisting in 1905 on an international conference on the whole Moroccan question. Germany's crude bullying forced France and Britain closer together, and Germany left the resulting Algeciras Conference of 1906 empty-handed and isolated (except for Austria-Hungary).

The result of the Moroccan crisis and the Algeciras Conference was something of a diplomatic revolution. Britain, France, Russia, and even the United States began to see Germany as a potential threat, a would-be intimidator that might seek to dominate all Europe. At the same time, German leaders began to see sinister plots to "encircle" Germany and block its development as a world power. In 1907 Russia, battered by its disastrous war with Japan and the revolution of 1905, agreed to settle its quarrels with Great Britain in Persia and Central Asia with the Anglo-Russian Agreement (see Figure 27.1). As a result of that agreement, Germany's blustering paranoia increased, as did Britain's thinly disguised hostility.

Germany's decision to add a large, enormously expensive fleet of big-gun battleships to its already expanding navy also heightened tensions after 1907. German nationalists, led by the extremely persuasive Admiral Alfred von Tirpitz, saw a large navy as the legitimate mark of a great world power and as a source of pride and patriotic unity. But British leaders such as David Lloyd George saw it as a detestable military challenge, which forced them to spend the "People's Budget" (see page 843) on battleships rather than social welfare. Ongoing economic rivalry also contributed to distrust and hostility between

German Warships Under Full Steam   As these impressive ships engaged in battle exercises in 1907 suggest, Germany did succeed in building a large modern navy. But Britain was equally determined to maintain its naval superiority, and the spiraling arms race helped poison relations between the two countries. *(Bibliothèque des Arts Décoratifs/Jean-Loup Charmet/The Bridgeman Art Library International Ltd)*

the two nations. Unscrupulous journalists and special-interest groups in both countries portrayed healthy competition in foreign trade and investment as a form of economic warfare.

Many educated shapers of public opinion and ordinary people in Britain and Germany were increasingly locked in a fateful "love-hate" relationship between the two countries. Proud nationalists in both countries simultaneously admired and feared the power and accomplishments of their nearly equal rival. In 1909 the mass-circulation London *Daily Mail* hysterically informed its readers in a series of reports that "Germany is deliberately preparing to destroy the British Empire."[2] By then Britain was psychologically, if not officially, in the Franco-Russian camp. The leading nations of Europe were divided into two hostile blocs, both ill-prepared to deal with upheaval on Europe's southeastern frontier.

The Outbreak of War

In the early years of the twentieth century, war in the Balkans was as inevitable as anything can be in human history. The reason was simple: nationalism was destroying the Ottoman Empire and threatening to break up the Austro-Hungarian Empire. The only questions were what kinds of wars would occur and where they would lead.

Greece had long before led the struggle for national liberation, winning its independence in 1832. In 1875 widespread nationalist rebellion in the Ottoman Empire had resulted in Turkish repression, Russian intervention, and Great Power tensions. Bismarck had helped resolve this crisis at the 1878 Congress of Berlin, which worked out the partial division of Turkish possessions in Europe. Austria-Hungary obtained the right to "occupy and administer" Bosnia and Herzegovina. Serbia and Romania

MAP 27.1 The Balkans After the Congress of Berlin, 1878   The Ottoman Empire suffered large territorial losses but remained a power in the Balkans.

MAP 27.2 The Balkans in 1914   Ethnic boundaries did not follow political boundaries, and Serbian national aspirations threatened Austria-Hungary.

won independence, and a part of Bulgaria won local autonomy. The Ottoman Empire retained important Balkan holdings, for Austria-Hungary and Russia each feared the other's domination of totally independent states in the area (see Map 27.1).

After 1878 the siren call of imperialism lured European energies, particularly Russian energies, away from the Balkans. This diversion helped preserve the fragile balance of interests in southeastern Europe. By 1903, however, Balkan nationalism was on the rise once again. Serbia led the way, becoming openly hostile toward both Austria-Hungary and the Ottoman Empire. The Serbs, a Slavic people, looked to Slavic Russia for support of their national aspirations. To block Serbian expansion and to take advantage of Russia's weakness after the revolution of 1905, Austria in 1908 formally annexed Bosnia and

Herzegovina, with their large Serbian, Croatian, and Muslim populations. The kingdom of Serbia erupted in rage but could do nothing without Russian support.

In 1912, in the First Balkan War, Serbia joined Greece and Bulgaria to attack the Ottoman Empire and then quarreled with Bulgaria over the spoils of victory—a dispute that led in 1913 to the Second Balkan War. Austria intervened in 1913 and forced Serbia to give up Albania. After centuries, nationalism had finally destroyed the Ottoman Empire in Europe (see Map 27.2). This sudden but long-awaited event elated the Balkan nationalists and dismayed the leaders of multinational Austria-Hungary. The former hoped and the latter feared that Austria might be next to be broken apart.

Within this tense context, Archduke Francis Ferdinand, heir to the Austrian and Hungarian thrones, and his wife, Sophie, were assassinated by Serbian revolutionaries living in Bosnia on June 28, 1914, during a state visit to the Bosnian capital of Sarajevo. The assassins were closely connected to the ultranationalist Serbian society the **Black Hand.** This revolutionary group was secretly supported by members of the Serbian government and was dedicated to uniting all Serbians in a single state. Although the leaders of Austria-Hungary did not and could not know all the details of Serbia's involvement in the assassination plot, they concluded after some hesitation that Serbia had to be severely punished once and for all. On July 23 Austria-Hungary finally presented Serbia with an unconditional ultimatum.

The Serbian government had just forty-eight hours in which to agree to demands that would amount to control of the Serbian state. When Serbia replied moderately but evasively, Austria began to mobilize and then declared war on Serbia on July 28. Thus a desperate multinational Austria-Hungary deliberately chose war in a last-ditch attempt to stem the rising tide of hostile nationalism within its borders and save the existing state. The "Third Balkan War" had begun.

Of prime importance in Austria-Hungary's fateful decision was Germany's unconditional support. Emperor William II and his chancellor, Theobald von Bethmann-Hollweg, gave Austria-Hungary a "blank check" and urged aggressive measures in early July, even though they realized that war between Austria and Russia was the most probable result. They knew Russian pan-Slavs saw Russia not only as the protector but also as the eventual liberator of southern Slavs. A resurgent Russia could not stand by, as in the Bosnian crisis, and simply watch the Serbs be crushed. Yet Bethmann-Hollweg apparently hoped that while Russia (and therefore France) would go

Nationalist Opposition in the Balkans   This band of well-armed and determined guerrillas from northern Albania was typical of groups fighting against Ottoman rule in the Balkans. Balkan nationalists succeeded in driving the Ottoman Turks out of most of Europe, but their victory increased tensions with Austria-Hungary and among the Great Powers. *(Roger-Viollet/Getty Images)*

"Never Forget!"   This 1915 French poster with its passionate headline dramatizes Germany's brutal invasion of Belgium in 1914. Neutral Belgium is personified as a traumatized mother, assaulted and ravished by savage outlaws. The "rape of Belgium" featured prominently—and effectively—in anti-German propaganda. *(Mary Evans Picture Library)*

without mobilizing against the other. Therefore, on July 29 Russia ordered full mobilization and in effect declared general war.

The same tragic subordination of political considerations to military strategy descended on Germany. The German general staff had also thought only in terms of a two-front war. The staff's plan for war—the Schlieffen plan, the work of Count Alfred von Schlieffen, chief of the German general staff from 1891 to 1906 and a professional military man—called for knocking out France first with a lightning attack through neutral Belgium before turning on Russia. Thus on August 2, 1914, General Helmuth von Moltke, "acting under a dictate of self-preservation," demanded that Belgium permit German armies to pass through its territory. Belgium, whose neutrality had been solemnly guaranteed in 1839 by all the great states including Prussia, refused. Germany attacked. Thus Germany's terrible, politically disastrous response to a war in the Balkans was an all-out invasion of France by way of the plains of neutral Belgium on August 3. In the face of this act of aggression, Great Britain joined France and declared war on Germany the following day. The First World War had begun.

Reflections on the Origins of the War

Although few events in history have aroused such interest and controversy as the coming of the First World War, the question of immediate causes and responsibilities can be answered with considerable certainty. Austria-Hungary deliberately started the Third Balkan War. A war for the right to survive was Austria-Hungary's desperate, though understandable, response to the aggressive, yet understandable, revolutionary drive of Serbian nationalists to unify their people in a single state. Moreover, in spite of Russian intervention in the quarrel, it is clear that from the beginning of the crisis, Germany not only pushed and goaded Austria-Hungary but also was responsible for turning a little war into the Great War by means of a sledgehammer attack on Belgium and France. Why Germany was so aggressive in 1914 is less certain.

Diplomatic historians stress that German leaders lost control of the international system after Bismarck's resignation in 1890. They felt increasingly that Germany's status as a world power was declining, while that of Britain, France, Russia, and the United States was growing. Indeed, the powers of what officially became in August 1914 the **Triple Entente**—Great Britain, France, and Russia—were checking Germany's vague but real aspirations as well as working to strangle Austria-Hungary,

to war, Great Britain would remain neutral, unwilling to fight for "Russian aggression" in the distant Balkans.

In fact, the diplomatic situation was already out of control. Military plans and timetables began to dictate policy. Russia, a vast country, would require much longer to mobilize its armies than Germany and Austria-Hungary. On July 28, as Austrian armies bombarded Belgrade, Tsar Nicholas II ordered a partial mobilization against Austria-Hungary. Almost immediately he found that this was impossible. All the complicated mobilization plans of the Russian general staff had assumed a war with both Austria and Germany: Russia could not mobilize against one

Germany's only real ally. Germany's aggression in 1914 reflected the failure of all European leaders, not just those in Germany, to incorporate Bismarck's mighty empire permanently and peacefully into the international system.

A more controversial interpretation argues that domestic conflicts and social tensions lay at the root of German aggression. Germany industrialized and urbanized rapidly after 1870 and established a popularly elected parliament. But German society was not democratized, and ultimate political power remained concentrated in the hands of the monarchy, the army, and the Prussian nobility. Determined to hold on to power and frightened by the rising socialist movement and a powerful wave of strikes in 1914, which were encouraged but never controlled by a few radical socialist intellectuals such as the fiery Rosa Luxemburg (see pages 912 and 913), the German ruling class was willing to take chances. It was willing to gamble on diplomatic victory and even on war as the means of rallying the masses to its side and preserving its privileged position. Historians have also discerned similar, if less clear-cut, behavior in Great Britain, where leaders faced civil war in northern Ireland, and in Russia, where the revolution of 1905 had brought tsardom to its knees.

This debate over social tensions and domestic political factors correctly suggests that the triumph of nationalism was a crucial underlying precondition of the Great War. Nationalism was at the heart of the Balkan wars, in the form of Serbian aspirations and the grandiose pan-German versus pan-Slavic racism of some fanatics. Nationalism also drove the spiraling arms race. Broad popular commitment to "my country right or wrong" weakened groups that thought in terms of international communities and consequences. Thus the big international bankers, who were frightened by the prospect of war in July 1914, and the extreme-left socialists, who believed that the enemy was at home and not abroad, were equally out of step with national feeling. In each country, the great majority of the population enthusiastically embraced the outbreak of war in August 1914. In each country, people believed that their country had been wronged, and they rallied to defend it. Patriotic nationalism brought unity in the short run.

In all of this, the wealthy governing classes certainly underestimated the risk of war to themselves in 1914. They had forgotten that great wars and great social revolutions very often go hand in hand. Metternich's alliance of conservative forces in support of international peace and the social status quo had become only a distant memory.

The First Battle of the Marne

When the Germans invaded Belgium in August 1914, they and everyone else believed that the war would be short, for urban society rested on the food and raw materials of the world economy: "The boys will be home by Christmas." The Belgian army heroically defended its homeland, however, and fell back in good order to join a rapidly landed British army corps near the Franco-Belgian border. This action complicated the original Schlieffen plan of concentrating German armies on the right wing and boldly capturing Paris in a vast encircling movement. Moreover, the German left wing in Lorraine failed to retreat, thwarting the plan to suck French armies into Germany and then annihilate them. Instead, by the end of August, dead-tired German soldiers were advancing along an enormous front in the scorching summer heat. The neatly designed prewar plan to surround Paris from the north and west had been thrown into confusion.

French armies totaling 1 million, reinforced by more than 100,000 British troops, had retreated in orderly fashion before Germany's 1.5 million men in the field. Under the leadership of the steel-nerved General Joseph Joffre, the French attacked a gap in the German line at the Battle of the Marne on September 6. For three days, France threw everything into the attack. At one point, the French government desperately requisitioned all the taxis of Paris to rush reserves to the troops at the front. Finally, the Germans fell back. Paris and France had been miraculously saved (see Map 27.3 on page 898).

Stalemate and Slaughter

The attempts of French and British armies to turn the German retreat into a rout were unsuccessful, however, and so were moves by both sides to outflank each other in northern France. As a result, both sides began to dig trenches to protect themselves from machine-gun fire. By November 1914, an unbroken line of trenches extended from the Belgian ports through northern France, past the fortress of Verdun, and on to the Swiss frontier.

In the face of this unexpected stalemate, slaughter on the western front began in earnest. The defenders on both sides dug in behind rows of trenches, mines, and barbed wire. For days and even weeks, ceaseless shelling by heavy artillery supposedly "softened up" the enemy in a given area (and also signaled the coming attack). Then young draftees and their junior officers went "over the top" of the trenches in frontal attacks on the enemy's line.

The cost in lives of this **trench warfare** was staggering, the gains in territory minuscule. The massive French and

The Tragic Absurdity of Trench Warfare   Soldiers charge across a scarred battlefield and overrun an enemy trench. The dead defender on the right will fire no more. But this is only another futile charge that will yield much blood and little land. A whole generation is being decimated by the slaughter. *(By courtesy of the Trustees of the Imperial War Museum)*

British offensives during 1915 never gained more than 3 miles of blood-soaked earth from the enemy. In the Battle of the Somme in the summer of 1916, the British and French gained an insignificant 125 square miles at the cost of 600,000 dead or wounded, while the Germans lost 500,000 men. In that same year the unsuccessful German campaign against Verdun cost 700,000 lives on both sides. British poet Siegfried Sassoon (1886–1967) wrote of the Somme offensive, "I am staring at a sunlit picture of Hell."

Terrible 1917 saw General Robert Nivelle's French army almost destroyed in a grand spring attack at Cham-

pagne. At Passchendaele in the fall, the British traded 400,000 casualties for 50 square miles of Belgian Flanders. The hero of Erich Remarque's great novel *All Quiet on the Western Front* (1929) describes one attack:

We see men living with their skulls blown open; we see soldiers run with their two feet cut off. . . . Still the little piece of convulsed earth in which we lie is held. We have yielded no more than a few hundred yards of it as a prize to the enemy. But on every yard there lies a dead man.

Such was war on the western front.

Otto Dix: War Returning to Germany after the war, Dix was haunted by the horrors he had seen. This vivid expressionist masterpiece, part of a triptych painted in 1929–1932, probes the tormented memory of endless days in muddy trenches and dugouts, living with rats and lice and the constant danger of exploding shells, snipers, and all-out attack. Many who escaped death or dismemberment were mentally wounded forever by their experiences. *(Staatliche Kunstsammlungen Dresden, © 2002 Artists Rights Society [ARS], New York/VG Bild-Kunst, Bunn)*

The war of the trenches shattered an entire generation of young men. Millions who could have provided political creativity and leadership after the war were forever missing. Moreover, those who lived through the slaughter were maimed, shell-shocked, embittered, and profoundly disillusioned. The young soldiers went to war believing in the world of their leaders and elders, the pre-1914 world of order, progress, and patriotism. Then, in Remarque's words, the "first bombardment showed us our mistake, and under it the world as they had taught it

to us broke in pieces." For many soldiers the battlefield struggle became life's crucial experience, which "soft" civilians could never understand. A chasm opened up between veterans and civilians, making the hard postwar reconstruction all the more difficult.

The Widening War

On the eastern front, slaughter did not degenerate into suicidal trench warfare. With the outbreak of the war, the

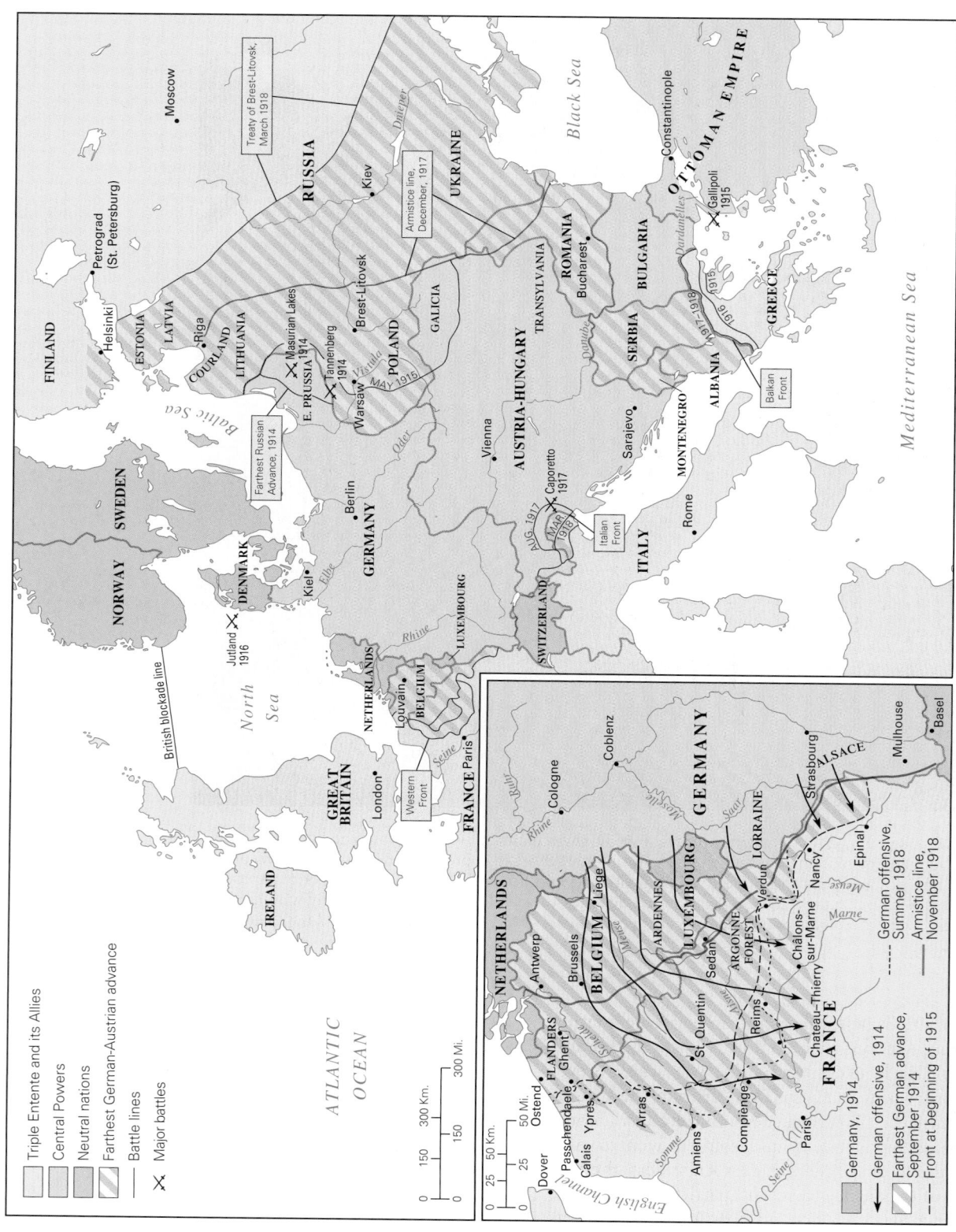

MAP 27.3 The First World War in Europe The trench war on the western front was concentrated in Belgium and northern France, while the war in the east encompassed an enormous territory.

Triple Entente and its Allies
Central Powers
Neutral nations
Farthest German-Austrian advance
— Battle lines
X Major battles

Germany, 1914
German offensive, 1914
Farthest German advance, September 1914
Front at beginning of 1915
German offensive, Summer 1918
Armistice line, November 1918

Indian Soldiers   from the so-called warrior castes had long been a critical factor in imperial Britain's global power. These Indian troops, preparing for the Battle of the Somme in 1916, ironically appear to be out for a pleasant bicycling excursion. Dispatched to France in October 1914, most Indian soldiers were moved to western Asia in 1915 to fight against the Ottoman Empire. *(By courtesy of the Trustees of the Imperial War Museum)*

"Russian steamroller" immediately moved into eastern Germany. Very badly damaged by the Germans under Generals Paul von Hindenburg and Erich Ludendorff at the Battles of Tannenberg and the Masurian Lakes in August and September 1914, Russia never threatened Germany again. On the Austrian front, enormous armies seesawed back and forth, suffering enormous losses. Austro-Hungarian armies were repulsed twice by Serbia in bitter fighting. But with the help of German forces, they reversed the Russian advances of 1914 and forced the Russians to retreat deep into their own territory in the eastern campaign of 1915. A staggering 2.5 million Russians were killed, wounded, or taken prisoner that year.

These changing tides of victory and defeat brought neutral countries into the war (see Map 27.3). Italy, a member of the Triple Alliance since 1882, had declared its neutrality in 1914 on the grounds that Austria had launched a war of aggression. Then in May 1915, Italy joined the Triple Entente of Great Britain, France, and Russia in return for promises of Austrian territory. Bulgaria allied with Austria and Germany, now known as the Central Powers, in September 1915 in order to settle old scores with Serbia.

The entry of Italy and Bulgaria in 1915 was part of a general widening of the war. The Balkans, with the exception of Greece, came to be occupied by the Central Powers, and British forces were badly defeated in 1915 trying to take the Dardanelles from Turkey, Germany's ally. More successful was the entente's attempt to incite Arab nationalists against their Turkish overlords. An enigmatic British colonel, soon known to millions as Lawrence of Arabia, aroused the Arab princes to revolt in early 1917. In 1918 British armies from Egypt smashed the Ottoman Empire once and for all. In the Middle East campaign, the British drew on forces from Australia, New Zealand, and India. Contrary to German hopes, the colonial subjects of the British (and French) did not revolt but loyally supported their foreign masters. The European war extended around the globe as Great Britain, France, and Japan seized Germany's colonies.

Another crucial development in the expanding conflict came in April 1917, when the United States declared war on Germany. American intervention grew out of the war at sea, sympathy for the Triple Entente, and the increasing desperation of total war. At the beginning of the war, Britain and France had established a total naval blockade to strangle the Central Powers. No neutral ship was permitted to sail to Germany with any cargo. The blockade annoyed Americans, but effective propaganda about German atrocities in occupied Belgium as well as lush profits from selling war supplies to Britain and France blunted American indignation.

Moreover, in early 1915 Germany launched a counterblockade using the murderously effective submarine, a new weapon that violated traditional niceties of fair warning under international law. In May 1915, after sinking about ninety ships in the British war zone, a German submarine sank the British passenger liner *Lusitania,* which was also carrying arms and munitions. More than 1,000 lives, among them 139 Americans, were lost. President Woodrow Wilson protested vigorously. Germany was forced to relax its submarine warfare for almost two years; the alternative was almost certain war with the United States.

Early in 1917, the German military command—confident that improved submarines could starve Britain into submission before the United States could come to its rescue—resumed unrestricted submarine warfare. Like the invasion of Belgium, this was a reckless gamble. "German submarine warfare against commerce," President Wilson had told a sympathetic Congress and people, "is a warfare against mankind." Thus the last uncommitted great nation, as fresh and enthusiastic as Europe had been in 1914, entered the world war in April 1917, almost three years after it began. Eventually the United States was to tip the balance in favor of the Triple Entente and its allies.

The Home Front

Before looking at the last year of the Great War, let us turn our attention to the people on the home front. They were tremendously involved in the titanic struggle. War's impact on them was no less massive than on the men crouched in the trenches. (See the feature "Listening to the Past: The Experience of War" on pages 918–919.)

Mobilizing for Total War

In August 1914, most people had greeted the outbreak of hostilities enthusiastically. In every country, the masses believed that their nation was in the right and defending itself from aggression. With the exception of a few extreme left-wingers, even socialists supported the war. In Germany, for example, the trade unions voted not to

strike, and socialists in the Reichstag voted money for war credits in order to counter the threat of Russian despotism. A German socialist volunteered for the front, explaining to fellow members of the Reichstag that "to shed one's blood for the fatherland is not difficult: it is enveloped in romantic heroism."[3] Everywhere the support of the masses and working class contributed to national unity and an energetic war effort.

By mid-October generals and politicians had begun to realize that more than patriotism would be needed to win the war, whose end was not in sight. Each country experienced a relentless, desperate demand for men and weapons. In France, for example, the generals found themselves needing 100,000 heavy artillery shells a day, as opposed to the 12,000 they had anticipated using. This enormous quantity had to come from a French steel industry that had lost three-fourths of its iron resources in the first days of the war, when Germany seized the mines of French Lorraine. Each belligerent quickly faced countless shortages, for prewar Europe had depended on foreign trade and a great international division of labor. In each country, economic life and organization had to change and change fast to keep the war machine from sputtering to a stop. And change they did.

In each country, a government of national unity began to plan and control economic and social life in order to wage **total war.** Free-market capitalism was abandoned, at least "for the duration." Instead, government planning boards established priorities and decided what was to be produced and consumed. Rationing, price and wage controls, and even restrictions on workers' freedom of movement were imposed by government. Only through such regimentation could a country make the greatest possible military effort. Thus, though there were national variations, the great nations all moved toward planned economies commanded by the established political leadership.

The economy of total war blurred the old distinction between soldiers on the battlefield and civilians at home. The war was a war of whole peoples and entire populations. Based on tremendously productive industrial economies not confined to a single nation, total war yielded an effective—and therefore destructive—war effort on all sides.

However awful the war was, the ability of governments to manage and control highly complicated economies strengthened the cause of socialism. With the First World War, state socialism became for the first time a realistic economic blueprint rather than a utopian program. Germany illustrates the general trend. It also went furthest in developing a planned economy to wage total war.

As soon as war began, Walter Rathenau, the talented, foresighted Jewish industrialist in charge of Germany's largest electric company, convinced the government to set up the **War Raw Materials Board** to ration and distribute raw materials. Under Rathenau's direction, every useful material from foreign oil to barnyard manure was inventoried and rationed. Moreover, the board launched successful attempts to produce substitutes, such as synthetic rubber and synthetic nitrates. Without the spectacular double achievement of discovering a way to "fix" nitrogen present in the air and then producing synthetic nitrates in enormous quantity to make explosives, the blockaded German war machine would have stalled in a matter of months. An aggressive recycling campaign, including everything from fruit peels to women's hair, augmented these efforts.

Food was also rationed in accordance with physical need. Men and women doing hard manual work were given extra rations. During the last two years of the war, only children and expectant mothers received milk rations. At the same time, Germany failed to tax the war profits of private firms heavily enough. This contributed to massive deficit financing, inflation, the growth of a black market, and the eventual re-emergence of class conflict.

Following the terrible Battles of Verdun and the Somme in 1916, Chancellor Bethmann-Hollweg was driven from office in 1917 by military leaders Hindenburg and Ludendorff, who became the real rulers of Germany. They decreed the ultimate mobilization for total war. Germany, said Hindenburg, could win only "if all the treasures of our soil that agriculture and industry can produce are used exclusively for the conduct of War. . . . All other considerations must come second."[4] Thus in December 1916, military leaders rammed through the Reichstag the Auxiliary Service Law, which required all males between seventeen and sixty to work only at jobs considered critical to the war effort.

Although women and children were not specifically mentioned, this forced-labor law was also aimed at them. Many women already worked in war factories, mines, and steel mills, where they labored, like men, at the heaviest and most dangerous jobs. With the passage of the Auxiliary Service Law, many more women followed. People averaged little more than one thousand calories a day. Thus in Germany total war led to the establishment of history's first "totalitarian" society, and war production increased while some people starved to death.

Rationing in Germany   This ration coupon shows a long line of hungry people waiting to buy half a pound of strictly rationed sausage, the sale of which the city government has just announced. Food rations were cut as the Allied blockade tightened, and rationing continued in Germany for some time after the war. *(AKG London)*

Great Britain mobilized for total war less rapidly and less completely than Germany, for it could import materials from its empire and from the United States. By 1915, however, a serious shortage of shells had led to the establishment of the Ministry of Munitions under David Lloyd George. The ministry organized private industry to produce for the war, controlled profits, allocated labor, fixed wage rates, and settled labor disputes. By December 1916, when Lloyd George became prime minister, the British economy was largely planned and regulated. More than two hundred factories and 90 percent of all imports were bought and allocated directly by the state. Subsequently, even food was strictly rationed, while war production continued to soar. Great Britain had followed successfully in Germany's footsteps.

The Social Impact

The social impact of total war was no less profound than the economic impact, though again there were important national variations. The millions of men at the front and the insatiable needs of the military created a tremendous demand for workers. Jobs were available for everyone. This situation—seldom, if ever, seen before 1914, when unemployment and poverty had been facts of urban life—brought about momentous changes.

One such change was greater power and prestige for labor unions. Having proved their loyalty in August 1914, labor unions became an indispensable partner of government and private industry in the planned war economy. Unions cooperated with war governments on work rules, wages, and production schedules in return for real participation in important decisions. This entry of labor leaders and unions into policy-making councils paralleled the entry of socialist leaders into the war governments.

The role of women changed dramatically. In every country, large numbers of women left home and domestic service to work in industry, transportation, and offices. By 1917 women formed fully 43 percent of the labor force in Russia. Moreover, women became highly visible—not only as munitions workers but as bank tellers, mail carriers, even police officers.

At first, the male-dominated unions were hostile to women moving into new occupations, believing that their presence would lower wages and change work rules. But government pressure and the principle of equal pay for equal work (at least until the end of the war) overcame these objections. Women also served as nurses and doctors at the front. In general, the war greatly expanded the range of women's activities and changed attitudes toward women. As a direct result of women's many-sided

war effort, Britain, Germany, and Austria granted women the right to vote immediately after the war. Women also showed a growing spirit of independence during the war, as they started to bob their hair, shorten their skirts, and smoke in public.

War promoted greater social equality, blurring class distinctions and lessening the gap between rich and poor. This blurring was most apparent in Great Britain, where wartime hardship was never extreme. In fact, the bottom third of the population generally lived *better* than they ever had, for the poorest gained most from the severe shortage of labor. English writer Robert Roberts recalled how his parents' tiny grocery store in the slums of Manchester thrived during the war as never before when people who had scrimped to buy bread and soup bones were able to afford fancy cakes and thick steaks. In 1924 a British government study revealed that only half as many families lived in severe poverty as in 1911, even though total production of goods had not increased. In continental countries, greater equality was reflected in full employment, rationing according to physical needs, and a sharing of hardships. There, too, society became more uniform and more egalitarian, in spite of some war profiteering.

Finally, death itself had no respect for traditional social distinctions. It savagely decimated the young aristocratic officers who led the charge, and it fell heavily on the mass of drafted peasants and unskilled workers who followed. Yet death often spared the aristocrats of labor, the skilled workers and foremen. Their lives were too valuable to squander at the front, for they were needed to train the newly recruited women and older unskilled men laboring valiantly in war plants at home.

Growing Political Tensions

During the first two years of war, most soldiers and civilians supported their governments. Even in Austria-Hungary—the most vulnerable of the belligerents, with its competing nationalities—loyalty to the state and monarchy remained astonishingly strong through 1916. Belief in a just cause, patriotic nationalism, the planned economy, and a sharing of burdens united peoples behind their various national leaders.

Each government employed rigorous censorship to control public opinion, and each used both crude and subtle propaganda to maintain popular support. German propaganda hysterically pictured black soldiers from France's African empire raping German women, while German atrocities in Belgium and elsewhere were ceaselessly recounted and exaggerated by the French and British. Patriotic posters and slogans, slanted news, and

Waging Total War A British war plant strains to meet the insatiable demand for trench-smashing heavy artillery shells. Quite typically, many of these defense workers are women. *(By courtesy of the Trustees of the Imperial War Museum)*

biased editorials inflamed national hatreds and helped sustain superhuman efforts.

By the spring of 1916, however, people were beginning to crack under the strain of total war. In April 1916, Irish nationalists in Dublin tried to take advantage of this situation and rose up against British rule in their great Easter Rebellion. A week of bitter fighting passed before the rebels were crushed and their leaders executed. On May 1, 1916, several thousand demonstrators in Berlin heard the radical socialist leader Karl Liebknecht (1871–1919) shout, "Down with the government! Down with the war!" Liebknecht was immediately arrested and imprisoned, but his daring action electrified Europe's far left. Strikes and protest marches over inadequate food began to flare up on every home front.

Soldiers' morale also began to decline. Italian troops mutinied. Numerous French units refused to fight after

General Nivelle's disastrous offensive of May 1917. Only tough military justice for leaders and a tacit agreement with the troops that there would be no more grand offensives enabled the new general in chief, Henri Philippe Pétain, to restore order. A rising tide of war-weariness and defeatism also swept France's civilian population before Georges Clemenceau emerged as a ruthless and effective wartime leader in November 1917. Clemenceau (1841–1929) established a virtual dictatorship, pouncing on strikers and jailing without trial journalists and politicians who dared to suggest a compromise peace with Germany.

The strains were worse for the Central Powers. In October 1916, the chief minister of Austria was assassinated by a young socialist crying, "Down with Absolutism! We want peace!"[5] The following month, when feeble old Emperor Francis Joseph died, a symbol of unity disappeared.

In spite of absolute censorship, political dissatisfaction and conflicts among nationalities grew. In April 1917, Austria's chief minister summed up the situation in the gloomiest possible terms. The country and army were exhausted. Another winter of war would bring revolution and disintegration. "If the monarchs of the Central Powers cannot make peace in the coming months," he wrote, "it will be made for them by their peoples."[6] Both Czech and Yugoslav leaders demanded autonomous democratic states for their peoples. The British blockade kept tightening; people were starving.

The strain of total war and of the Auxiliary Service Law was also evident in Germany. In the winter of 1916 to 1917, Germany's military position appeared increasingly desperate. Stalemates and losses in the west were matched by temporary Russian advances in the east: hence the military's insistence on an all-or-nothing gamble of unrestricted submarine warfare when the Triple Entente refused in December 1916 to consider peace on terms favorable to the Central Powers.

Also, the national political unity of the first two years of war was collapsing as the social conflict of prewar Germany re-emerged. A growing minority of moderate socialists in the Reichstag began to vote against war credits. With little taste for violent upheaval and civil war, they called for a compromise "peace without annexations or reparations." In July 1917, a coalition of socialists and Catholics passed a resolution in the Reichstag to that effect. Such a peace was unthinkable for conservatives and military leaders. So also was the surge in revolutionary agitation and strikes by war-weary workers that occurred in early 1917. When the bread ration was further reduced in April, more than 200,000 workers struck and demonstrated for a week in Berlin, returning to work only under the threat of prison and military discipline. Thus militaristic Germany, like its ally Austria-Hungary (and its enemy France), was beginning to crack in 1917. Yet it was Russia that collapsed first and saved the Central Powers—for a time.

The Russian Revolution

The Russian Revolution of 1917 was one of modern history's most momentous events. Directly related to the growing tensions of World War I, it had a significance far beyond the wartime agonies of a single European nation. The Russian Revolution opened a new era. For some, it was Marx's socialist vision come true; for others, it was the triumph of dictatorship. To all, it presented a radically new prototype of state and society.

The Fall of Imperial Russia

Like its allies and its enemies, Russia embraced war with patriotic enthusiasm in 1914. At the Winter Palace, while throngs of people knelt and sang, "God save the tsar," Tsar Nicholas II (r. 1894–1917) repeated the oath Alexander I had sworn in 1812 and vowed never to make peace as long as the enemy stood on Russian soil. Russia's lower house, the Duma, voted war credits. Conservatives anticipated expansion in the Balkans, while liberals and most socialists believed alliance with Britain and France would bring democratic reforms. For a moment, Russia was united.

Unprecedented artillery barrages used up Russia's supplies of shells and ammunition, and better-equipped German armies inflicted terrible losses. In 1915 substantial numbers of Russian soldiers were sent to the front without rifles; they were told to find their arms among the dead. There were 2 million Russian casualties in 1915 alone. Nevertheless, Russia's battered peasant army did not collapse but continued to fight courageously, and Russia moved toward full mobilization on the home front. The Duma and organs of local government took the lead, setting up special committees to coordinate defense, industry, transportation, and agriculture. These efforts improved the military situation. Yet there were many failures, and Russia mobilized less effectively for total war than the other warring nations.

The great problem was leadership. Under the constitution resulting from the revolution of 1905 (see pages 837–838), the tsar had retained complete control over the bureaucracy and the army. Legislation proposed by the Duma, which was weighted in favor of the wealthy and conservative classes, was subject to the tsar's veto. Moreover, Nicholas II fervently wished to maintain the sacred inheritance of supreme royal power, which, with the Orthodox church, was for him the key to Russia's greatness. A kindly, slightly stupid man, of whom a friend said he "would have been an ideal country gentleman, devoting his life to wife and children, his farms and his sport," Nicholas failed to form a close partnership with his citizens in order to fight the war more effectively. He came to rely instead on the old bureaucratic apparatus, distrusting the moderate Duma, rejecting popular involvement, and resisting calls to share power.

As a result, the Duma, the educated middle classes, and the masses became increasingly critical of the tsar's leadership. Following Nicholas's belated dismissal of the incompetent minister of war, demands for more democratic and responsive government exploded in the Duma in the summer of 1915. In September parties ranging from conservative to moderate socialist formed the Progressive bloc, which called for a completely new government responsible to the Duma instead of the tsar. In answer, Nicholas temporarily adjourned the Duma and announced that he was traveling to the front in order to lead and rally Russia's armies.

His departure was a fatal turning point. With the tsar in the field with the troops, control of the government was taken over by the hysterical empress, Tsarina Alexandra, and a debauched adventurer and self-proclaimed holy man, Rasputin. A minor German princess and granddaughter of England's Queen Victoria, Nicholas's wife was a devoted mother with a sick child, a strong-willed woman with a hatred of parliaments. Having constantly urged her husband to rule absolutely, Alexandra tried to do so herself in his absence. She seated and unseated the top ministers. Her most trusted adviser was "our Friend Grigori," an uneducated Siberian preacher who was appropriately nicknamed "Rasputin"—the "Degenerate."

Rasputin began his career with a sect noted for mixing sexual orgies with religious ecstasies, and his influence rested on mysterious healing powers. Alexis, Alexandra's fifth child and heir to the throne, suffered from the rare blood disease hemophilia. The tiniest cut meant uncontrollable bleeding, terrible pain, and possible death. Medical science could do nothing. Only Rasputin could miraculously stop the bleeding, perhaps through hypnosis. The empress's faith in Rasputin was limitless. "Believe more in our Friend," she wrote her husband in 1916. "He lives for you and Russia." In this atmosphere of unreality, the government slid steadily toward revolution.

In a desperate attempt to right the situation and end unfounded rumors that Rasputin was the empress's lover, three members of the high aristocracy murdered Rasputin in December 1916. The empress went into semipermanent shock, her mind haunted by the dead man's prophecy: "If I die or you desert me, in six months you will lose your son and your throne."[7] Food shortages in the cities worsened; morale declined. On March 8, women calling for bread in Petrograd (formerly St. Petersburg) started riots, which spontaneously spread to the factories and then elsewhere throughout the city. From the front, the tsar ordered troops to restore order, but discipline broke down, and the soldiers joined the revolutionary crowd. The Duma responded by declaring a provisional government on March 12, 1917. Three days later, Nicholas abdicated.

The Provisional Government

The March revolution was the result of an unplanned uprising of hungry, angry people in the capital, but it was joyfully accepted throughout the country. The patriotic upper

"The Russian Ruling House"   This wartime cartoon captures the ominous, spellbinding power of Rasputin over Tsar Nicholas II and his wife, Alexandra. Rasputin's manipulations disgusted Russian public opinion and contributed to the monarchy's collapse. *(Stock Montage)*

and middle classes rejoiced at the prospect of a more determined and effective war effort, while workers happily anticipated better wages and more food. All classes and political parties called for liberty and democracy. They were not disappointed. As Lenin said, Russia became the freest country in the world. After generations of arbitrary authoritarianism, the provisional government quickly established equality before the law; freedom of religion, speech, and assembly; the right of unions to organize and strike; and the rest of the classic liberal program.

Yet both the liberal and moderate socialist leaders of the provisional government rejected social revolution. The reorganized government formed in May 1917, which included the fiery agrarian socialist Alexander

Kerensky, who became prime minister in July. He refused to confiscate large landholdings and give them to peasants, fearing that such drastic action in the countryside would only complete the disintegration of Russia's peasant army. For the patriotic Kerensky, as for other moderate socialists, the continuation of war was still the all-important national duty. There would be plenty of time for land reform later, and thus all the government's efforts were directed toward a last offensive in July. Human suffering and war-weariness grew, sapping the limited strength of the provisional government.

From its first day, the provisional government had to share power with a formidable rival—the **Petrograd Soviet** (or council) of Workers' and Soldiers' Deputies. Modeled on the revolutionary soviets of 1905, the Petrograd Soviet was a huge, fluctuating mass meeting of two thousand to three thousand workers, soldiers, and socialist intellectuals. Seeing itself as a true grassroots revolutionary democracy, this counter- or half-government suspiciously watched the provisional government and issued its own radical orders, further weakening the provisional government. Most famous of these was **Army Order No. 1,** issued to all Russian military forces as the provisional government was forming.

Army Order No. 1 stripped officers of their authority and placed power in the hands of elected committees of common soldiers. Designed primarily to protect the revolution from some counter-revolutionary Bonaparte on horseback, the order instead led to a total collapse of army discipline. Many an officer was hanged for his sins. Meanwhile, following the foolhardy summer offensive, masses of peasant soldiers began "voting with their feet," to use Lenin's graphic phrase. That is, they began returning to their villages to help their families get a share of the land, which peasants were simply seizing as they settled old scores in a great agrarian upheaval. All across the country, liberty was turning into anarchy in the summer of 1917. It was an unparalleled opportunity for the most radical and most talented of Russia's many socialist leaders, Vladimir Ilyich Lenin (1870–1924).

Lenin and the Bolshevik Revolution

From his youth, Lenin's whole life had been dedicated to the cause of revolution. Born into the middle class, Lenin became an implacable enemy of imperial Russia when his older brother was executed for plotting to kill the tsar in 1887. As a law student, Lenin began searching for a revolutionary faith. He found it in Marxian socialism, which began to win converts among radical intellectuals as industrialization surged forward in Russia in the 1890s.

Exiled to Siberia for three years because of socialist agitation, Lenin studied Marxian doctrines with religious intensity. After his release, this young priest of socialism joined fellow believers in western Europe. There he lived for seventeen years and developed his own revolutionary interpretations of the body of Marxian thought.

Three interrelated ideas were central for Lenin. First, like other eastern European radical socialists after 1900, he turned to the early fire-breathing Marx of 1848 and *The Communist Manifesto* for inspiration. Thus Lenin stressed that capitalism could be destroyed only by violent revolution. He tirelessly denounced all revisionist theories of a peaceful evolution to socialism as betraying Marx's message of unending class conflict. Lenin's second, more original idea was that under certain conditions a socialist revolution was possible even in a relatively backward country like Russia. There the industrial working class was small, but peasants were poor and thus potential revolutionaries.

Lenin believed that at a given moment revolution was determined more by human leadership than by vast historical laws. Thus was born his third basic idea: the necessity of a highly disciplined workers' party, strictly controlled by a dedicated elite of intellectuals and full-time revolutionaries like Lenin himself. Unlike ordinary workers and trade-union officials, this elite would never be seduced by short-term gains. It would not stop until revolution brought it to power.

Lenin's theories and methods did not go unchallenged by other Russian Marxists. At meetings of the Russian Social Democratic Labor party in London in 1903, matters came to a head. Lenin demanded a small, disciplined, elitist party, while his opponents wanted a more democratic party with mass membership. The Russian party of Marxian socialism promptly split into two rival factions. Lenin's camp was called **Bolsheviks,** or "majority group"; his opponents were *Mensheviks,* or "minority group." Lenin's majority did not last, but Lenin did not care. He kept the fine-sounding name Bolshevik and developed the party he wanted: tough, disciplined, revolutionary.

Unlike most other socialists, Lenin did not rally round the national flag in 1914. Observing events from neutral Switzerland, he saw the war as a product of imperialistic rivalries and as a marvelous opportunity for class war and socialist upheaval. After the March revolution the German government provided the impatient Lenin, his wife, and about twenty trusted colleagues with safe passage across Germany and back into Russia in April 1917. The Germans hoped that Lenin would undermine the sagging war effort of the world's freest society. They were not disappointed.

The Russian Revolution

1914	Russia enthusiastically enters the First World War.
1915	Russia suffers 2 million casualties. Progressive bloc calls for a new government responsible to the Duma rather than to the tsar. Tsar Nicholas adjourns the Duma and departs for the front; Alexandra and Rasputin exert a strong influence on the government.
December 1916	Rasputin is murdered.
March 8, 1917	Bread riots take place in Petrograd (St. Petersburg).
March 12, 1917	Duma declares a provisional government.
March 15, 1917	Tsar Nicholas abdicates without protest.
April 3, 1917	Lenin returns from exile and denounces the provisional government.
May 1917	Reorganized provisional government, including Kerensky, continues the war. Petrograd Soviet issues Army Order No. 1, granting military power to committees of common soldiers.
Summer 1917	Agrarian upheavals: peasants seize estates; peasant soldiers desert the army to participate.
October 1917	Bolsheviks gain a majority in the Petrograd Soviet.
November 6, 1917	Bolsheviks seize power; Lenin heads the new "provisional workers' and peasants' government."
November 1917	Lenin accepts peasant seizure of land and worker control of factories; all banks are nationalized.
January 1918	Lenin permanently disbands the Constituent Assembly.
February 1918	Lenin convinces the Bolshevik Central Committee to accept a humiliating peace with Germany in order to safeguard the revolution.
March 1918	Treaty of Brest-Litovsk: Russia loses one-third of its population. Trotsky as war commissar begins to rebuild the Russian army. Government moves from Petrograd to Moscow.
1918–1920	Great civil war takes place.
Summer 1918	Eighteen regional governments compete for power. White armies oppose the Bolshevik Revolution.
1919	White armies are on the offensive but divided politically; they receive little benefit from Allied intervention.
1920	Lenin and the Red Army are victorious, retaking Belorussia and Ukraine.

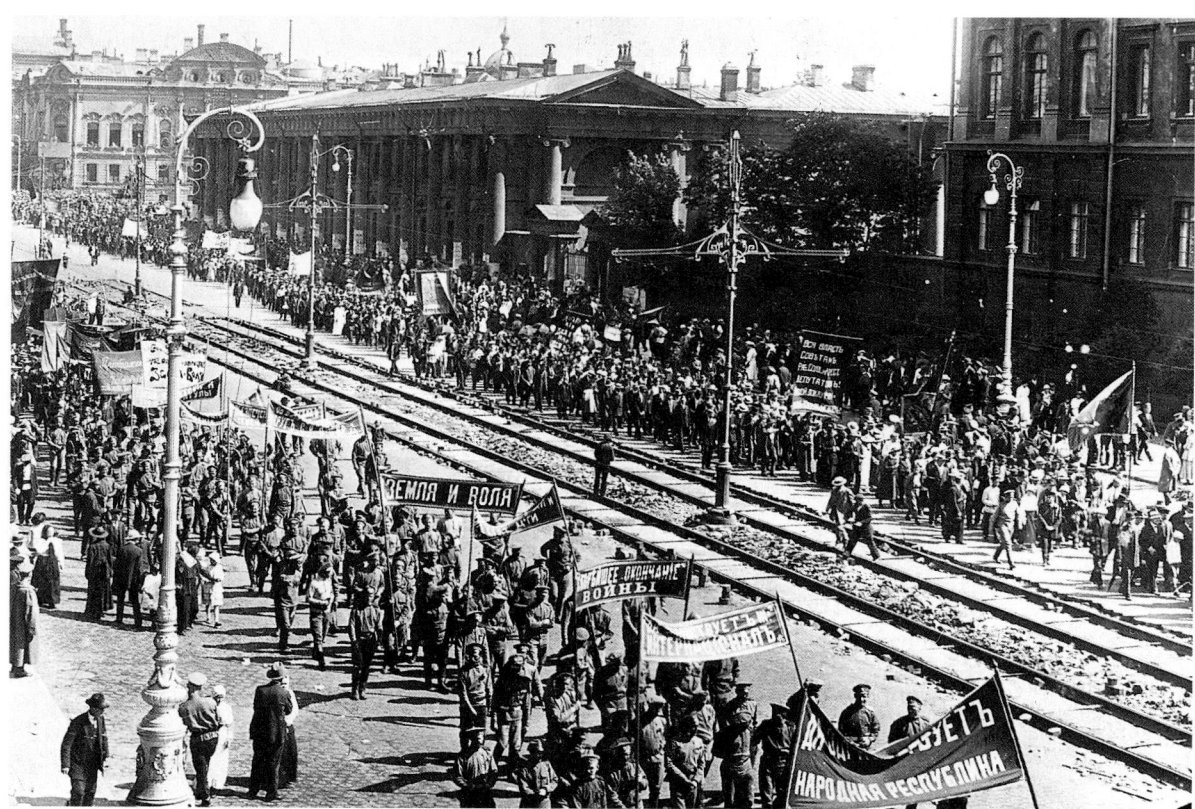

Mass Demonstrations in Petrograd, June 1917　The protests showed a surge of working-class support for the Bolsheviks. In this photo a few banners of the Mensheviks and other moderate socialists are drowned in a sea of Bolshevik slogans. *(Sovfoto)*

Arriving triumphantly at Petrograd's Finland Station on April 3, Lenin attacked at once. To the great astonishment of the local Bolsheviks, he rejected all cooperation with the "bourgeois" provisional government of the liberals and moderate socialists. His slogans were radical in the extreme: "All power to the soviets"; "All land to the peasants"; "Stop the war now." Never a slave to Marxian determinism, the brilliant but not unduly intellectual Lenin was a superb tactician. The moment was now.

Yet Lenin almost overplayed his hand. An attempt by the Bolsheviks to seize power in July collapsed, and Lenin fled and went into hiding. He was charged with being a German agent, and indeed he and the Bolsheviks were getting money from Germany.[8] But no matter. Intrigue between Kerensky, who became prime minister in July, and his commander in chief, General Lavr Kornilov, a popular war hero "with the heart of a lion and the brains of a sheep," resulted in Kornilov's leading a feeble attack against the provisional government in September. In the face of this rightist "counter-revolutionary" threat,

the Bolsheviks were rearmed and redeemed. Kornilov's forces disintegrated, but Kerensky lost all credit with the army, the only force that might have saved him and democratic government in Russia.

Trotsky and the Seizure of Power

Throughout the summer, the Bolsheviks had appealed very effectively to the workers and soldiers of Petrograd, markedly increasing their popular support. Party membership had soared from 50,000 to 240,000, and in October the Bolsheviks gained a fragile majority in the Petrograd Soviet. It was now Lenin's supporter Leon Trotsky (1879–1940), a spellbinding revolutionary orator and independent radical Marxist, who brilliantly executed the Bolshevik seizure of power.

Painting a vivid but untruthful picture of German and counter-revolutionary plots, Trotsky first convinced the Petrograd Soviet to form a special military-revolutionary committee in October and make him its leader. Military power in the capital passed into Bolshevik hands. Trotsky's second master stroke was to insist that the Bolsheviks reduce opposition to their coup by taking power in the name not of the Bolsheviks, but of the more popular and democratic soviets, which were meeting in Petrograd from all over Russia in early November. On the night of November 6, militants from Trotsky's committee joined with trusty Bolshevik soldiers to seize government buildings and pounce on members of the provisional government. Then they went on to the congress of soviets. There a Bolshevik majority—roughly 390 of 650 turbulent delegates—declared that all power had passed to the soviets and named Lenin head of the new government.

The Bolsheviks came to power for three key reasons. First, by late 1917 democracy had given way to anarchy: power was there for those who would take it. Second, in Lenin and Trotsky the Bolsheviks had an utterly determined and truly superior leadership, which both the tsarist government and the provisional government lacked. Third, in 1917 the Bolsheviks succeeded in appealing to many soldiers and urban workers, people who were exhausted by war and eager for socialism. With time, many workers would become bitterly disappointed, but for the moment they had good reason to believe that they had won what they wanted.

Dictatorship and Civil War

History is full of short-lived coups and unsuccessful revolutions. The truly monumental accomplishment of Lenin, Trotsky, and the rest of the Bolsheviks was not taking power but keeping it. In the next four years, the Bolsheviks went on to conquer the chaos they had helped create, and they began to build their kind of dictatorial socialist society. The conspirators became conquerors. How was this done?

Lenin had the genius to profit from developments over which he and the Bolsheviks had no control. Since summer, a peasant revolution had been sweeping across Russia as the tillers of the soil invaded and divided among themselves the estates of the landlords and the church. Peasant seizure of the land—a Russian 1789—was not very Marxian, but it was quite unstoppable in 1917. Thus Lenin's first law, which supposedly gave land to the peasants, actually merely approved what peasants were already doing. Urban workers' great demand in November was direct control of individual factories by local workers committees. This, too, Lenin ratified with a decree in November.

Unlike many of his colleagues, Lenin acknowledged that Russia had lost the war with Germany and that the only realistic goal was peace at any price. That price was very high. Germany demanded in December 1917 that

Lenin Rallies Worker and Soldier Delegates At a midnight meeting of the Petrograd Soviet, the Bolsheviks rise up and seize power on November 6, 1917. This painting from the 1940s idealizes Lenin, but his great talents as a revolutionary leader are undeniable. In this re-creation Stalin, who actually played only a small role in the uprising, is standing behind Lenin, already his trusty right-hand man. *(Sovfoto)*

the Soviet government give up all its western territories. These areas were inhabited by Poles, Finns, Lithuanians, and other non-Russians—all those people who had been conquered by the tsars over three centuries and put into the "prisonhouse of nationalities," as Lenin had earlier called the Russian empire.

At first, Lenin's fellow Bolsheviks would not accept such great territorial losses. But when German armies resumed their unopposed march into Russia in February 1918, Lenin had his way in a very close vote in the Central Committee of the party. "Not even his greatest enemy can deny that at this moment Lenin towered like a giant over his Bolshevik colleagues."[9] A third of old Russia's population was sliced away by the German meat ax in the Treaty of Brest-Litovsk in March 1918. With peace, Lenin had escaped the certain disaster of continued war and could pursue his goal of absolute political power for the Bolsheviks —now renamed Communists—within Russia.

In November 1917, the Bolsheviks had cleverly proclaimed their regime only a "provisional workers' and peasants' government," promising that a freely elected **Constituent Assembly** would draw up a new constitution. But free elections produced a stunning setback for the Bolsheviks, who won less than one-fourth of the elected delegates. The Socialist Revolutionaries—the peasants' party—had a clear majority. The Constituent Assembly met for only one day, on January 18, 1918. It was then permanently disbanded by Bolshevik soldiers acting under Lenin's orders. Thus even before the peace with Germany, Lenin was forming a one-party government.

The destruction of the democratically elected Constituent Assembly helped feed the flames of civil war. People who had risen up for self-rule in November saw that once again they were getting dictatorship from the capital. For the next three years, "Long live the [democratic] soviets; down with the Bolsheviks" was to be a popular slogan. The officers of the old army took the lead in organizing the so-called White opposition to the Bolsheviks in southern Russia, Ukraine, Siberia, and west of Petrograd. The Whites came from many social groups and were united only by their hatred of the Bolsheviks—the Reds.

By the summer of 1918, fully eighteen self-proclaimed regional governments—several of which represented minority nationalities—were competing with Lenin's Bolsheviks in Moscow. By the end of the year, White armies were on the attack. In October 1919, it appeared they might triumph, as they closed in on Lenin's government from three sides. Yet they did not. By the spring of 1920, the White armies had been almost completely defeated, and the Bolshevik Red Army had retaken Belorussia and Ukraine. The following year, the Communists also reconquered the independent nationalist governments of the Caucasus. The civil war was over; Lenin had won.

Lenin and the Bolsheviks won for several reasons. Strategically, they controlled the center, while the Whites were always on the fringes and disunited. Moreover, the poorly defined political program of the Whites was vaguely conservative, and it did not unite all the foes of the Bolsheviks under a progressive, democratic banner. Most important, the Communists quickly developed a better army, an army for which the divided Whites were no match.

Once again, Trotsky's leadership was decisive. The Bolsheviks had preached democracy in the army and elected officers in 1917. But beginning in March 1918, Trotsky as war commissar re-established the draft and the most drastic discipline for the newly formed Red Army. Soldiers deserting or disobeying an order were summarily shot. Moreover, Trotsky made effective use of former tsarist army officers, who were actively recruited and given unprecedented powers of discipline over their troops. In short, Trotsky formed a disciplined and effective fighting force.

The Bolsheviks also mobilized the home front. Establishing **war communism**—the application of the total war concept to a civil conflict—they seized grain from peasants, introduced rationing, nationalized all banks and industry, and required everyone to work. Although these measures contributed to a breakdown of normal economic activity, they also served to maintain labor discipline and to keep the Red Army supplied.

"Revolutionary terror" also contributed to the Communist victory. The old tsarist secret police was re-established as the **Cheka,** which hunted down and executed thousands of real or supposed foes, such as the tsar and his family and other "class enemies." At one point shortly after the government moved from Petrograd to Moscow in March 1918, a circus clown in Moscow was making fun of the Bolsheviks to an appreciative audience. Chekists in the crowd quickly pulled out their guns and shot several laughing people. Moreover, people were shot or threatened with being shot for minor nonpolitical failures. The terror caused by the secret police became a tool of the government. The Cheka sowed fear, and fear silenced opposition.

Finally, foreign military intervention in the civil war ended up helping the Communists. After Lenin made peace with Germany, the Allies (U.S., Britain, Japan) sent troops to Archangel and Vladivostok to prevent war materiel they had sent the provisional government from being captured by the Germans. After the Soviet government nationalized all foreign-owned factories without compensation and refused to pay all of Russia's foreign debts, Western governments, particularly France, began to support White armies in the south and west. Yet these efforts were small and halfhearted. In 1919 Western peoples were sick of war, and few Western politicians believed in a military crusade against the Bolsheviks. Thus Allied intervention in the civil war did not aid the Whites effectively, though it did permit the Communists to appeal to the patriotic nationalism of ethnic Russians, in particular former tsarist army officers. Allied intervention was both too little and too much.

Together, the Russian Revolution and the Bolshevik triumph were one of the reasons the First World War was such a great turning point in modern history. A radically new government, based on socialism and one-party dictatorship, came to power in a great European state, maintained power, and eagerly encouraged worldwide revolution. Although halfheartedly constitutional monarchy in Russia was undoubtedly headed for some kind of political crisis before 1914, it is hard to imagine the triumph of the most radical proponents of change and reform except in a situation of total collapse. That was precisely what happened to Russia in the First World War.

The Peace Settlement

Victory over revolutionary Russia boosted sagging German morale, and in the spring of 1918 the Germans launched their last major attack against France. Yet this offensive failed, just as those before it had. With breathtaking rapidity, the United States, Great Britain, and France decisively defeated Germany militarily. The guns of world war finally fell silent. Then as civil war spread in Russia and as chaos engulfed much of eastern Europe, the victorious Western Allies came together in Paris to establish a lasting peace.

Expectations were high; optimism was almost unlimited. The Allies labored intensively and soon worked out terms for peace with Germany and for the creation of the peacekeeping League of Nations. Nevertheless, the hopes of peoples and politicians were soon disappointed, for the peace settlement of 1919 turned out to be a failure. Rather than creating conditions for peace, it sowed the seeds of another war. Surely this was the ultimate tragedy of the Great War, a war that directly and indirectly cost $332 billion and left 10 million dead and another 20 million wounded. How did this tragedy happen? Why was the peace settlement unsuccessful?

The End of the War

In early 1917, the strain of total war was showing everywhere. After the Russian Revolution in March, there were major strikes in Germany. In July a coalition of moderates passed a "peace resolution" in the Reichstag, calling for peace without territorial annexations. To counter this moderation born of war-weariness, the German military established a virtual dictatorship. The military also aggressively exploited the collapse of Russian armies, winning great concessions in the Treaty of Brest-Litovsk in March 1918.

With victory in the east quieting German moderates, General Ludendorff and company fell on France once more in the great spring offensive of 1918. For a time, German armies pushed forward, coming within thirty-five miles of Paris. But Ludendorff's exhausted, overextended forces never broke through. They were decisively stopped in July at the second Battle of the Marne, where 140,000 fresh American soldiers saw action. Adding 2 million men in arms to the war effort by August, the late but massive American intervention decisively tipped the scales in favor of Allied victory.

By September British, French, and American armies were advancing steadily on all fronts, and a panicky General Ludendorff realized that Germany had lost the war.

Yet he insolently insisted that moderate politicians shoulder the shame of defeat, and on October 4 the emperor formed a new, more liberal German government to sue for peace. As negotiations over an armistice dragged on, an angry and frustrated German people finally rose up. On November 3, sailors in Kiel mutinied, and throughout northern Germany soldiers and workers began to establish revolutionary councils on the Russian soviet model. The same day, Austria-Hungary surrendered to the Allies and began breaking apart. Revolution broke out in Germany, and masses of workers demonstrated for peace in Berlin. With army discipline collapsing, the emperor abdicated and fled to Holland. Socialist leaders in Berlin proclaimed a German republic on November 9 and simultaneously agreed to tough Allied terms of surrender. The armistice went into effect on November 11, 1918. The war was over.

Revolution in Germany

Military defeat brought political revolution to Germany and Austria-Hungary, as it had to Russia. In Austria-Hungary the revolution was primarily nationalistic and republican in character. Having started the war to preserve an antinationalistic dynastic state, the Habsburg empire had perished in the attempt. In its place, independent Austrian, Hungarian, and Czechoslovakian republics were proclaimed, while a greatly expanded Serbian monarchy united the South Slavs and took the name Yugoslavia. The prospect of firmly establishing the new national states overrode class considerations for most people in east-central Europe.

The German Revolution of November 1918 resembled the Russian Revolution of March 1917. In both cases, a genuine popular uprising welled up from below, toppled an authoritarian monarchy, and brought the establishment of a liberal provisional republic. In both countries, liberals and moderate socialists took control of the central government, while workers' and soldiers' councils formed a counter-government. In Germany, however, the moderate socialists and their liberal allies won, and the Lenin-like radical revolutionaries in the councils lost. In communist terms, the liberal, republican revolution in Germany in 1918 was only half a revolution: a bourgeois political revolution without a communist second installment. It was Russia without Lenin's Bolshevik triumph.

There were several reasons for the German outcome. The great majority of Marxian socialist leaders in the Social Democratic party were, as before the war, really pink and not red. They wanted to establish real political democracy and civil liberties, and they favored the gradual

The Allied Leaders at Versailles The old tiger, Clemenceau of France, gestures with his walking stick to the scholarly Woodrow Wilson, as the strong-willed Lloyd George strides forward on the left. The negotiations at Versailles were difficult and often bitter, but the Allies reached a compromise agreement and imposed it on Germany. *(Corbis)*

elimination of capitalism. They were also German nationalists, appalled by the prospect of civil war and revolutionary terror. Moreover, there was less popular support among workers, soldiers, and peasants.

Of crucial importance was the fact that the moderate German Social Democrats, unlike Kerensky and company, accepted defeat and ended the war the day they took power. This act ended the decline in morale among soldiers and prevented the regular army, with its conservative officer corps, from disintegrating. When radicals headed by Karl Liebknecht and Rosa Luxemburg and their supporters in the councils tried to seize control of the government in Berlin in January, the moderate socialists called on the army to crush the uprising. Liebknecht and Luxemburg were arrested and then brutally murdered by army leaders. Their murders, widely believed to have had government support, caused many working-class activists in the Social Democratic party to break away in anger and join the pro-Lenin German Communist party that Liebknecht's group had just founded. Finally, even if the moderate socialists had followed Liebknecht and Luxemburg on the Leninist path,

it is very unlikely they would have succeeded. Civil war in Germany would certainly have followed. And the Allies, who were already occupying western Germany according to the terms of the armistice, would have marched on to Berlin and ruled Germany directly. Historians have often been unduly hard on Germany's moderate socialists. (See the feature "Individuals in Society: Rosa Luxemburg.")

The Treaty of Versailles

The peace conference opened in Paris in January 1919 with seventy delegates representing twenty-seven victorious nations. There were great expectations. A young British diplomat later wrote that the victors "were convinced that they would never commit the blunders and iniquities of the Congress of Vienna [of 1815]." Then the "misguided, reactionary, pathetic aristocrats" had cynically shuffled populations; now "we believed in nationalism, we believed in the self-determination of peoples." Indeed, "we were journeying to Paris . . . to found a new order in Europe. We were preparing not Peace only, but Eternal Peace."[10] This general optimism and idealism had been greatly strengthened by President Wilson's January 1918 peace proposal, the Fourteen Points, which stressed national self-determination and the rights of small countries.

The real powers at the conference were the United States, Great Britain, and France, for Germany was not allowed to participate and Russia was locked in civil war and did not attend. Italy was considered part of the Big Four, but its role was quite limited. Almost immediately the three great Allies began to quarrel. President Wilson, who was wildly cheered by European crowds as the spokesman for a new idealistic and democratic international cooperation, was almost obsessed with creating the **League of Nations.** Wilson insisted that this question come first, for he passionately believed that only a permanent international organization could protect member states from aggression and avert future wars. Wilson had his way, although Lloyd George of Great Britain and especially Clemenceau of France were unenthusiastic. They were primarily concerned with punishing Germany.

Playing on British nationalism, Lloyd George had already won a smashing electoral victory in December on the popular platform of making Germany pay for the war. "We shall," he promised, "squeeze the orange until the pips squeak." Personally inclined to make a somewhat moderate peace with Germany, Lloyd George was to a considerable extent a captive of demands for a total victory worthy of the sacrifices of total war against a totally depraved enemy. As Kipling summed up the general

Individuals in Society

Rosa Luxemburg

When Rosa Luxemburg (1870–1919) was arrested and then clubbed down and murdered by soldiers while being taken to jail, the left wing of European socialism lost a leading thinker and a passionate activist. But it gained an icon, a revolutionary saint.

Luxemburg grew up in Warsaw, the fifth child in a loving, nonreligious Jewish family. Speaking Polish and German at home, the mature Luxemburg identified "indignantly with Polish victims of linguistic oppression far more easily than with her fellow Jews."* But recent research also suggests that she was profoundly affected by the 1881 anti-Jewish riots and massacres in Russia and tsarist Poland, when middle-class Jewish families like hers huddled in terror until the Russian government decided the riots had gone far enough. These pogroms of 1881 led many Jewish intellectuals to turn to socialism. So it was with Luxemburg. She found in Marxism the promise of liberation for *all* oppressed groups and thus an end to terrible ethnic hatreds.

Smuggled out of Poland in 1889 and studying economics and socialism in Zurich with like-minded Polish exiles, one of whom became her lover and lifelong companion in revolution, Luxemburg settled in 1898 in Germany, the heartland of Marxian socialism. Small, foreign-born, and walking with a limp because of a childhood accident, she relentlessly attacked all revisions of Marxism (see page 849) and emerged in Germany as the "most prominent and influential of the party's radicals." She denounced any compromise with capitalism and stressed the absolute necessity of revolution.

Luxemburg also played a leading role in the outlawed Polish Socialist party. She thrilled to the revolution of 1905 in the tsarist empire and worked feverishly for the cause in Warsaw—"the happiest months of my life." Strengthened in her revolutionary convictions, she fought to radicalize Germany's socialists. When senior party and trade-union leaders opposed her ideas and tried to marginalize her, she went over their heads to the rank and file. A popular speaker who lectured tirelessly to enthusiastic working-class audiences, "Red Rosa" even challenged army discipline and the emperor as she condemned militarism as well as capitalism. In 1913 she told a large meeting, "If they think we are going to lift the weapons of murder against our French and other

brethren, then we shall shout: 'We will not do it!'"[†] Arrested and tried for sedition, she was sentenced to prison.

The outbreak of war put existing trends in fast-forward. Luxemburg was heartbroken when the Second International stood by impotently in all countries and Germany's Social Democrats rallied to the government. From prison she denounced her former coworkers as working-class traitors and cheered on Karl Liebknecht's tiny group of radical socialists (see page 912). After her release in November 1918, she embraced the Bolshevik Revolution and worked with heart and soul for a replay of radical revolution in Germany until her martyr's death two months later.

Rosa Luxemburg's legacy is complex, but two points seem clear. First, she personified brilliantly the resurgent radical minority in Marxian socialism after 1905, which eventually triumphed in Russia and was rejected in Germany. Second, brave and ever multinational, Luxemburg embodied the strongest element in prewar socialism's hostility toward militarism and national hatreds, an idealistic vision tragically shattered in the great break of World War I.

Rosa Luxemburg, addressing a meeting of the Socialist International in 1907. (AKG London)

Questions for Analysis

1. In what ways did Rosa Luxemburg's career reflect tensions and divisions in the Marxian socialist movement in Germany and throughout Europe before and during the First World War?
2. Evaluate Luxemburg's life. Was she a success or a failure? Or was she both? Defend your conclusions in a class debate.

---

*Richard Abraham, *Rosa Luxemburg: A Life for the International* (Oxford and New York: Berg, 1989), p. 20; also pp. 75, 80. This brief study is excellent.

[†] J. P. Nettl, *Rosa Luxemburg,* abr. ed. (New York: Schocken Books, 1969), p. 321.

British feeling at the end of the war, the Germans were "a people with the heart of beasts."[11]

France's Georges Clemenceau, "the Tiger" who had broken wartime defeatism and led his country to victory, wholeheartedly agreed. Like most French people, Clemenceau wanted old-fashioned revenge. He also wanted lasting security for France. This, he believed, required the creation of a buffer state between France and Germany, the permanent demilitarization of Germany, and vast German reparations. He feared that sooner or later Germany with its 60 million people would attack France with its 40 million unless the Germans were permanently weakened. Moreover, France had no English Channel (or Atlantic Ocean) as a reassuring barrier against German aggression. Wilson, supported by Lloyd George, would hear none of this. Clemenceau's demands seemed vindictive, violating morality and the principle of national self-determination. By April the countries attending the conference were deadlocked on the German question, and Wilson packed his bags to go home.

In the end, convinced that France could not afford to face Germany alone in the future, Clemenceau agreed to a compromise. He gave up the French demand for a Rhineland buffer state in return for a formal defensive alliance with the United States and Great Britain. Under the terms of this alliance, both Wilson and Lloyd George promised that their countries would come to France's aid in the event of a German attack. Thus Clemenceau appeared to win his goal of French security, as Wilson had won his of a permanent international organization. The Allies moved quickly to finish the settlement, believing that any adjustments would later be possible within the dual framework of a strong Western alliance and the League of Nations (see Map 27.4).

The **Treaty of Versailles** between the Allies and Germany was the key to the settlement, and the terms were not unreasonable as a first step toward re-establishing international order. Had Germany won, it seems certain that France and Belgium would have been treated with greater severity, as Russia had been at Brest-Litovsk. Germany's colonies were given to France, Britain, and Japan as League of Nations mandates. Germany's territorial losses within Europe were minor, thanks to Wilson. Alsace-Lorraine was returned to France. Parts of Germany inhabited primarily by Poles were ceded to the new Polish state, in keeping with the principle of national self-determination. Predominately German Danzig was also placed within the Polish tariff lines, but as a self-governing city under League of Nations protection. Germany had to limit its army to 100,000 men and agree to build no military fortifications in the Rhineland.

More harshly, the Allies declared that Germany (with Austria) was responsible for the war and had therefore to pay reparations equal to all civilian damages caused by the war. This unfortunate and much-criticized clause expressed inescapable popular demands for German blood, but the actual figure was not set, and there was the clear possibility that reparations might be set at a reasonable level in the future when tempers had cooled.

When presented with the treaty, the German government protested vigorously. But there was no alternative, especially considering that Germany was still starving because the Allies had not yet lifted their naval blockade. On June 28, 1919, German representatives of the ruling moderate Social Democrats and the Catholic party signed the treaty in the Sun King's Hall of Mirrors at Versailles, where Bismarck's empire had been joyously proclaimed almost fifty years before.

Separate peace treaties were concluded with the other defeated powers—Austria, Hungary, Bulgaria, and Turkey. For the most part, these treaties merely ratified the existing situation in east-central Europe following the breakup of the Austro-Hungarian Empire. Like Austria, Hungary was a particularly big loser, as its "captive" nationalities (and some interspersed Hungarians) were ceded to Romania, Czechoslovakia, Poland, and Yugoslavia. Italy got some Austrian territory. The Turkish empire was broken up. France received Lebanon and Syria, while Britain took Iraq and Palestine, which was to include a Jewish national home first promised by Britain in 1917. Officially League of Nations mandates, these acquisitions of the Western powers were one of the more imperialistic elements of the peace settlement. Another was mandating Germany's holdings in China to Japan. The age of Western imperialism lived on. National self-determination remained a reality only for Europeans and their offspring.

American Rejection of the Versailles Treaty

The rapidly concluded peace settlement of early 1919 was not perfect, but within the context of war-shattered Europe it was an acceptable beginning. The principle of national self-determination, which had played such a large role in starting the war, was accepted and served as an organizing framework. Germany had been punished but not dismembered. A new world organization complemented a traditional defensive alliance of satisfied powers. The serious remaining problems could be worked out in the future. Moreover, Allied leaders had seen speed as essential for another reason: they detested Lenin and feared that his Bolshevik Revolution might spread. They realized that their best answer to Lenin's

MAP 27.4 Shattered Empires and Territorial Changes After World War I The Great War brought tremendous changes in eastern Europe. New nations were established, and a dangerous power vacuum was created between Germany and Soviet Russia.

unending calls for worldwide upheaval was peace and tranquillity for war-weary peoples.

There were, however, two great interrelated obstacles to such peace: Germany and the United States. Plagued by communist uprisings, reactionary plots, and popular disillusionment with losing the war at the last minute, Germany's moderate socialists and their liberal and Catholic supporters faced an enormous challenge. Like French republicans after 1871, they needed time (and luck) if they were to establish firmly a peaceful and democratic republic. Progress in this direction required understanding, yet firm treatment of Germany by the victorious Western Allies, particularly by the United States.

However, the U.S. Senate and, to a lesser extent, the American people rejected Wilson's handiwork. Republican senators led by Henry Cabot Lodge refused to ratify the Treaty of Versailles without changes in the articles creating the League of Nations. The key issue was the League's power—more apparent than real—to require member states to take collective action against aggression.

Lodge and others believed that this requirement gave away Congress's constitutional right to declare war. No doubt Wilson would have been wise to accept some reservations. In failing health, Wilson, with narrow-minded self-righteousness, rejected all attempts at compromise. In doing so, Wilson ensured that the treaty would never be ratified by the United States in any form and that the United States would never join the League of Nations. Moreover, the Senate refused to ratify Wilson's treaties forming a defensive alliance with France and Great Britain. America turned its back on Europe.

Perhaps understandable in the light of American traditions and the volatility of mass politics, the Wilson-Lodge fiasco and the newfound gospel of isolationism nevertheless represented a tragic and cowardly renunciation of America's responsibility. Using America's action as an excuse, Great Britain, too, refused to ratify its defensive alliance with France. Bitterly betrayed by its allies, France stood alone. Very shortly France was to take actions against Germany that would feed the fires of German resentment and seriously undermine democratic forces in the new republic. The great hopes of early 1919 had turned to ashes by the end of the year. The Western alliance had collapsed, and a grandiose plan for permanent peace had given way to a fragile truce. For this and for what came later, the United States must share a large part of the guilt.

More subtle but quite universal in its impact was an administrative revolution. This revolution, born of the need to mobilize entire societies and economies for total war, greatly increased the power of government. And after the guns grew still, government planning and wholesale involvement in economic and social life did not disappear in Europe. Liberal market capitalism and a well-integrated world economy were among the many casualties of the administrative revolution, and greater social equality was everywhere one of its results. Thus even in European countries where a communist takeover never came close to occurring, society still experienced a great revolution.

Finally, the "war to end war" did not bring peace—only a fragile truce. In the West, the Allies failed to maintain their wartime solidarity. Germany remained unrepentant and would soon have more grievances to nurse. Moreover, the victory of national self-determination in eastern Europe created small, weak states and thus a power vacuum between a still-powerful Germany and a potentially mighty communist Russia. A vast area lay open to military aggression from two sides.

Summary

Why did World War I have such revolutionary consequences? Why was it such a great break with the past? World War I was, first of all, a war of committed peoples. In France, Britain, and Germany in particular, governments drew on genuine popular support. This support reflected not only the diplomatic origins of the war but also the way western European society had been unified under the nationalist banner in the later nineteenth century, despite the fears that the growing socialist movement aroused in conservatives. The relentlessness of total war helps explain why so many died, why so many were crippled physically and psychologically, and why Western civilization would in so many ways never be the same again. More concretely, the war swept away monarchs and multinational empires. National self-determination apparently triumphed across Europe, not only in Austria-Hungary but also in many of Russia's western borderlands. Except in Ireland and parts of Soviet Russia, the revolutionary dream of national unity, born of the French Revolution, had finally come true.

Two other revolutions were products of the war. In Russia the Bolsheviks established a radical regime, smashed existing capitalist institutions, and stayed in power with a new kind of authoritarian rule. Whether the new Russian regime was truly Marxian or socialist was questionable, but it indisputably posed a powerful, ongoing revolutionary challenge to Europe and its colonial empires.

Key Terms

Three Emperors' League	Army Order No. 1
Black Hand	Bolsheviks
Triple Entente	Constituent Assembly
trench warfare	war communism
Lusitania	Cheka
total war	League of Nations
War Raw Materials Board	Treaty of Versailles
Petrograd Soviet	

Notes

1. M. Beloff, quoted in *U.S. News & World Report,* March 8, 1976, p. 53.
2. Quoted in J. Remak, *The Origins of World War I* (New York: Holt, Rinehart & Winston, 1967), p. 84.
3. Quoted in J. E. Rodes, *The Quest for Unity: Modern Germany, 1848–1970* (New York: Holt, Rinehart & Winston, 1971), p. 178.
4. Quoted in F. P. Chambers, *The War Behind the War, 1914–1918* (London: Faber & Faber, 1939), p. 168.
5. Quoted in R. O. Paxton, *Europe in the Twentieth Century* (New York: Harcourt Brace Jovanovich, 1975), p. 109.
6. Quoted in Chambers, *The War Behind the War,* p. 378.
7. Quoted ibid., pp. 302, 304.
8. A. B. Ulam, *The Bolsheviks* (New York: Collier Books, 1968), p. 349.
9. Ibid., p. 405.
10. H. Nicolson, *Peacemaking 1919* (New York: Grosset & Dunlap Universal Library, 1965), pp. 8, 31–32.
11. Quoted ibid., p. 24.

Suggested Reading

E. Hobsbawm, *The Age of Extremes: A History of the World, 1914–1991* (1996), is a provocative interpretation by a famous historian, with a good discussion of war and revolution. O. Hale, *The Great Illusion, 1900–1914* (1971), is a thorough account of the prewar era. Remak's volume cited in the Notes, J. Joll, *The Origins of the First World War* (1992), and L. Lafore, *The Long Fuse* (1971), are recommended studies of the causes of the First World War. V. Steiner, *Britain and the Origins of the First World War* (1978), and E. Brose, *The Kaiser's Army, 1870–1914: Technological, Tactical, and Operational Dilemmas in Germany During the Machine Age* (2001), are also major contributions. K. Jarausch, *The Enigmatic Chancellor* (1973), is an important study on Bethmann-Hollweg and German policy in 1914. M. Gilbert, *The First World War: A Complete History* (1994), is comprehensive, while C. Falls, *The Great War* (1961), is a fine brief introduction to military aspects of the war. B. Tuchman, *The Guns of August* (1962), is a marvelous account of the dramatic first month of the war and the beginning of military stalemate. J. Winter, *The Experience of World War I* (1988), is a strikingly illustrated history of the war, and A. Horne, *The Price of Glory: Verdun 1916* (1979), is a moving account of the famous siege. J. Ellis, *Eye-Deep in Hell* (1976), is a vivid account of trench warfare, whereas J. Keegan's fascinating *Face of Battle* (1976) examines soldiers and warfare in a long-term perspective. V. Brittain's *Testament of Youth* (1933), the moving autobiography of an English nurse in wartime, shows lives buffeted by new ideas and personal tragedies, and D. Gorham, *Vera Brittain: A Feminist Life* (1996), is a major study of Brittain's life. A. Marwick, *War and Change in Twentieth-Century Europe* (1990), is a useful synthesis.

F. L. Carsten, *War Against War* (1982), considers radical movements in Britain and Germany. The comprehensive and exciting study by Chambers mentioned in the Notes is still very useful. M. Higonnet, J. Jensen, and M. Weitz, eds., *Behind the Lines: Gender and the Two World Wars* (1987), examines the changes that the war brought for women and for relations between the sexes. S. Hynes, *A War Imagined: The First World War and English Culture* (1990), examines intellectual and cultural reactions. Two important studies on France are M. Hanna, *The Mobilization of Intellect: French Scholars and Writers in the Great War* (1996), and J. Keiger, *Raymond Poincaré* (1997), an excellent reconsideration of one of France's most important leaders before, during, and after the First World War. G. Feldman, *Army, Industry, and Labor in Germany, 1914–1918* (1966), shows the impact of total war and military dictatorship on Germany. Two excellent collections of essays, R. Wall and J. Winter, eds., *The Upheaval of War: Family, Work, and Welfare in Europe, 1914–1918* (1988), and J. Roth, ed., *World War I* (1967), probe the enormous consequences of the war for people and society. In addition to F. Fischer's influential interpretation, *Germany's Aims in the First World War* (1967), the debate over Germany's guilt and aggression may be approached through G. Feldman, ed., *German Imperialism, 1914–1918* (1972),

and A. Hillgruber, *Germany and the Two World Wars* (1981). Two excellent biographies on Rosa Luxemburg—R. Abraham, *Rosa Luxemburg: A Life for the International* (1989), an excellent introduction, and J. Nettl, *Rosa Luxemburg* (2 vols., 1966; abr. ed., 1966), a pioneering and sympathetic study—also discuss the splits between radical and moderate socialists during the war. In addition to Erich Maria Remarque's great novel *All Quiet on the Western Front* (1928), Henri Barbusse, *Under Fire* (1917), and Jules Romains, *Verdun* (1939), are highly recommended for their fictional yet realistic re-creations of the war. P. Fussell, *The Great War and Modern Memory* (1975), probes all the powerful literature inspired by the war. M. Eksteins, *Rites of Spring: The Great War and the Birth of the Modern Age* (1989), is an imaginative cultural investigation that has won critical acclaim.

C. Read, *From Tsar to Soviets: The Russian People and Their Revolution, 1917–1921* (1996), is highly recommended. S. Fitzpatrick, *The Russian Revolution* (1982), is an older provocative interpretation. R. Suny and A. Adams, eds., *The Russian Revolution and Bolshevik Victory* (1990), presents a wide range of old and new interpretations. Ulam's work cited in the Notes, which focuses on Lenin, is a classic introduction to the Russian Revolution, whereas D. Volkogonov, *Lenin: A New Biography* (1994), is a lively study with some new revelations by a well-known post-Communist Russian historian. B. Wolfe, *Three Who Made a Revolution* (1955), an old but good collective biography of Lenin, Trotsky, and Stalin, and R. Conquest, *V. I. Lenin* (1972), are recommended. L. Trotsky himself wrote the colorful and exciting *History of the Russian Revolution* (1932), which may be compared with the classic eyewitness account of the young, pro-Bolshevik American J. Reed, *Ten Days That Shook the World* (1919). A. Geifman, *Thou Shalt Kill: Revolutionary Terrorism in Russia, 1894–1917* (1994), is an important pioneering work on the cultural impact of political assassination. R. Pipes, *The Formation of the Soviet Union* (1968), is recommended for its excellent treatment of the nationality problem during the revolution. D. Koenker, W. Rosenberg, and R. Suny, eds., *Party, State and Society in the Russian Civil War* (1989), probes the social foundations of Bolshevik victory. A. Wildman, *The End of the Russian Imperial Army* (1980), is a fine account of the soldiers' revolt, and G. Leggett, *The Cheka: Lenin's Secret Police* (1981), shows revolutionary terror in action. S. Volkov, *St. Petersburg: A Cultural History* (1997), is particularly moving on the great city's tragic moments in the twentieth century. Boris Pasternak's justly celebrated *Doctor Zhivago* is a great historical novel of the revolutionary era. R. Massie, *Nicholas and Alexandra* (1971), is a moving popular biography of Russia's last royal family and the terrible health problem of the heir to the throne. Nicolson's study listed in the Notes captures the spirit of the Versailles settlement. T. Bailey, *Woodrow Wilson and the Lost Peace* (1963), and W. Widenor, *Henry Cabot Lodge and the Search for an American Foreign Policy* (1981), are also recommended. A. Mayer, *The Politics and Diplomacy of Peacemaking* (1969), stresses the influence of domestic social tensions and widespread fear of further communist revolt.

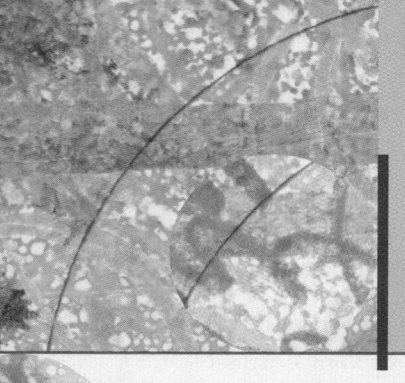

The Experience of War

World War I was a "total" war: it enlisted the efforts of men, women, and children, both at home and on the battlefield. It was a terrifying and painful experience for all those involved. To be sure, it was not the romantic endeavor it was purported to be. The documents below offer two different wartime experiences. The first excerpt is from a letter written by a German soldier fighting in the trenches. The second is from the diary of a Viennese woman. As you read both passages, think about the different ways war and its consequences were made real for these two people.

A German Soldier Writes from the Trenches, March 1915

Souchez, March 11th, 1915

"So fare you well, for we must now be parting," so run the first lines of a soldier-song which we often sang through the streets of the capital. These words are truer than ever now, and these lines are to bid farewell to you, to all my nearest and dearest, to all who wish me well or ill, and to all that I value and prize.

Our regiment has been transferred to this dangerous spot, Souchez. No end of blood has already flowed down this hill. A week ago the 142nd attacked and took four trenches from the French. It is to hold these trenches that we have been brought here. There is something uncanny about this hill-position. Already, times without number, other battalions of our regiment have been ordered here in support, and each time the company came back with a loss of twenty, thirty or more men. In the days when we had to stick it out here before, we had 22 killed and 27 wounded. Shells roar, bullets whistle; no dug-outs, or very bad ones; mud, clay, filth, shell-holes so deep that one could bathe in them.

This letter has been interrupted no end of times. Shells began to pitch close to us—great English

12-inch ones—and we had to take refuge in a cellar. One such shell struck the next house and buried four men, who were got out from the ruins horribly mutilated. I saw them and it was ghastly!

Everybody must be prepared now for death in some form or other. Two cemeteries have been made up here, the losses have been so great. I ought not to write that to you, but I do so all the same, because the newspapers have probably given you quite a different impression. They tell only of our gains and say nothing about the blood that has been shed, of the cries of agony that never cease. The newspaper doesn't give any description either of *how* the "heroes" are laid to rest, though it talks about "heroes' graves" and writes poems and such-like about them. Certainly in Lens I have attended funeral-parades where a number of dead were buried in one large grave with pomp and circumstance. But up here it is pitiful the way one throws the dead bodies out of the trench and lets them lie there, or scatters dirt over the remains of those which have been torn to pieces by shells.

I look upon death and call upon life. I have not accomplished much in my short life, which has been chiefly occupied with study. I have commended my soul to the Lord God. It bears His seal and is altogether His. Now I am free to dare anything. My future life belongs to God, my present one to the Fatherland, and I myself still possess happiness and strength.

A Viennese Woman Remembers Home Front Life

Ten dekagrammes [3½ ounces] of horse-flesh per head are to be given out to-day for the week. The cavalry horses held in reserve by the military authorities are being slaughtered for lack of fodder, and the people of Vienna are for a change to get a few mouthfuls of meat of which they have so long been deprived. Horse-flesh! I should like to know whether my instinctive repugnance to horse-flesh as food is personal, or whether my dislike is shared by many other housewives. My loathing of it is based, I believe, not on a physical but on a psychological prejudice.

I overcame my repugnance, rebuked myself for being sentimental, and left the house. A soft, steady rain was falling, from which I tried to protect myself with galoshes, waterproof, and umbrella. As I left the house before seven o'clock and the meat distribution did not begin until nine o'clock, I hoped to get well to the front of the queue.

No sooner had I reached the neighbourhood of the big market hall than I was instructed by the police to take a certain direction. I estimated the crowd waiting here for a meagre midday meal at two thousand at least. Hundreds of women had spent the night here in order to be among the first and make sure of getting their bit of meat. Many had brought with them improvised seats—a little box or a bucket turned upside down. No one seemed to mind the rain, although many were already wet through. They passed the time chattering, and the theme was the familiar one: What have you had to eat? What are you going to eat? One could scent an atmosphere of mistrust in these conversations: they were all careful not to say too much or to betray anything that might get them into trouble.

At length the sale began. Slowly, infinitely slowly, we moved forward. The most determined, who had spent the night outside the gates of the hall, displayed their booty to the waiting crowd: a ragged, quite freshly slaughtered piece of meat with the characteristic yellow fat. [Others] alarmed those standing at the back by telling them that there was only a very small supply of meat and that not half the people waiting would get a share of it. The crowd became very uneasy and impatient, and before the police on guard could prevent it, those standing in front organized an attack on the hall which the salesmen inside were powerless to repel. Everyone seized whatever he could lay his hands on, and in a few moments all the eatables had vanished. In the confusion stands were overturned, and the police forced back the aggressors and closed the gates. The crowds waiting outside, many of whom had been there all night and were soaked through, angrily demanded their due, whereupon the mounted police made a little charge, provoking a wild panic and much screaming and cursing. At length I reached home, depressed and disgusted, with a broken umbrella and only one galosh.

We housewives have during the last four years grown accustomed to standing in queues; we have

Germans wait in line for their meager rations in Berlin in 1916. *(Corbis)*

also grown accustomed to being obliged to go home with empty hands and still emptier stomachs. Only very rarely do those who are sent away disappointed give cause for police intervention. On the other hand, it happens more and more frequently that one of the pale, tired women who have been waiting for hours collapses from exhaustion. The turbulent scenes which occurred to-day inside and outside the large market hall seemed to me perfectly natural. In my dejected mood the patient apathy with which we housewives endure seemed to me blameworthy and incomprehensible.

Questions for Analysis

1. How did the soldier see the war he was in? Was it a grand patriotic effort? Or was it a story of senseless bloodshed and loss of life?

2. How did the soldiers cope with the reality of war in the trenches?

3. How did the experience of the Viennese woman differ from the soldier's?

4. Were the women who pillaged the food hall "blameworthy" or "reprehensible," as the Viennese woman says?

Sources: Alfons Ankenbrand, in *German Students' War Letters*, ed. A. F. Wedd (London: Methuen, 1929), pp. 72–73; *Blockade: The Diary of an Austrian Middle-Class Woman, 1914–1924,* trans. Winifred Ray (New York: Ray Long & Richard Smith, 1932), pp. 63–68.

This detail of George Grosz's *Draussen und Drinnen* (Outside and Inside)
captures the uncertainty and anxiety of the 1920s. *(AKG London)*

chapter

28

The Age of Anxiety

chapter outline

- Uncertainty in Modern Thought

- Modern Art and Music

- Movies and Radio

- The Search for Peace and Political Stability

- The Great Depression, 1929–1939

*W*hen Allied diplomats met in Paris in early 1919 with their optimistic plans for building a lasting peace, most people looked forward to happier times. They hoped that life would return to normal after the terrible trauma of total war. They hoped that once again life would make sense in the familiar prewar terms of peace, prosperity, and progress. These hopes were in vain. The Great Break—the First World War and the Russian Revolution—had mangled too many things beyond repair. Life would no longer fit neatly into the old molds.

Instead, great numbers of men and women felt themselves increasingly adrift in a strange, uncertain, and uncontrollable world. They saw themselves living in an age of anxiety, an age of continual crisis (this age lasted until at least the early 1950s). In almost every area of human experience, people went searching for ways to put meaning back into life.

- What did such doubts and searching mean for Western thought, art, and culture?
- How did leaders deal with the political dimensions of uncertainty and try to re-establish real peace and prosperity between 1919 and 1939?
- Why did those leaders fail?

These are the questions this chapter will explore.

Uncertainty in Modern Thought

A complex revolution in thought and ideas was under way before the First World War, but only small, unusual groups were aware of it. After the war, these new and upsetting ideas began to spread through the entire population. Western society as a whole began to question and even abandon many cherished values and beliefs that had guided it since the eighteenth-century Enlightenment and the nineteenth-century triumph of industrial development, scientific advances, and evolutionary thought.

Before 1914 most people still believed in progress, reason, and the rights of the individual. Progress was a daily reality, apparent in the rising standard

"The War, As I Saw It"   This was the title of a series of grotesque drawings that appeared in 1920 in *Simplicissimus,* Germany's leading satirical magazine. Nothing shows better the terrible impact of World War I than this profoundly disturbing example of expressionist art. *(Caroline Buckler)*

of living, the taming of the city, and the steady increase in popular education. Such developments also encouraged the comforting belief in the logical universe of New-tonian physics as well as faith in the ability of a rational human mind to understand that universe through intel-lectual investigation. And just as there were laws of sci-ence, so were there laws of society that rational human beings could discover and then wisely act on. At the same time, the rights of the individual were not just taken for granted; they were actually increasing. Well-established political rights were gradually spreading to women and workers, and new "social rights," such as old-age pen-

sions, were emerging. In short, before World War I most Europeans had a moderately optimistic view of the world, and with good reason.

Nevertheless, since the 1880s, a small band of serious thinkers and creative writers had been attacking these well-worn optimistic ideas. These critics rejected the general faith in progress and the power of the rational human mind. An expanding chorus of thinkers echoed and enlarged their views after the experience of history's most destructive war—a war that suggested to many that human beings were a pack of violent, irrational animals quite capable of tearing the individual and his or her

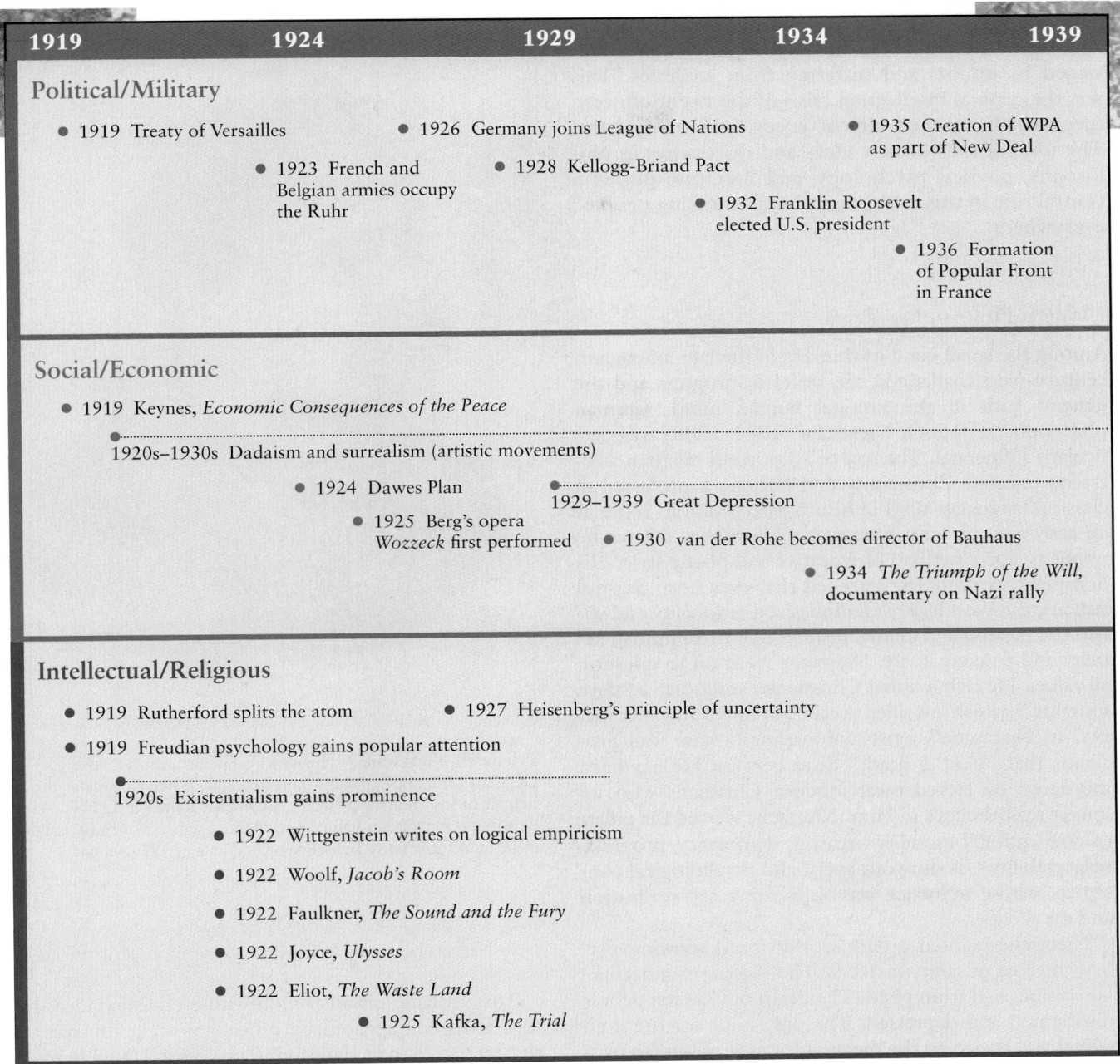

| 1919 | 1924 | 1929 | 1934 | 1939 |

Political/Military

- 1919 Treaty of Versailles
- 1923 French and Belgian armies occupy the Ruhr
- 1926 Germany joins League of Nations
- 1928 Kellogg-Briand Pact
- 1932 Franklin Roosevelt elected U.S. president
- 1935 Creation of WPA as part of New Deal
- 1936 Formation of Popular Front in France

Social/Economic

- 1919 Keynes, *Economic Consequences of the Peace*
- 1920s–1930s Dadaism and surrealism (artistic movements)
- 1924 Dawes Plan
- 1925 Berg's opera *Wozzeck* first performed
- 1929–1939 Great Depression
- 1930 van der Rohe becomes director of Bauhaus
- 1934 *The Triumph of the Will*, documentary on Nazi rally

Intellectual/Religious

- 1919 Rutherford splits the atom
- 1919 Freudian psychology gains popular attention
- 1927 Heisenberg's principle of uncertainty
- 1920s Existentialism gains prominence
- 1922 Wittgenstein writes on logical empiricism
- 1922 Woolf, *Jacob's Room*
- 1922 Faulkner, *The Sound and the Fury*
- 1922 Joyce, *Ulysses*
- 1922 Eliot, *The Waste Land*
- 1925 Kafka, *The Trial*

rights to shreds. Disorientation and pessimism were particularly acute in the 1930s, when the rapid rise of harsh dictatorships and the Great Depression transformed old certainties into bitter illusions.

No one expressed this state of uncertainty better than French poet and critic Paul Valéry (1871–1945) in the early 1920s. Speaking of the "crisis of the mind," Valéry noted that Europe was looking at its future with dark foreboding:

The storm has died away, and still we are restless, uneasy, as if the storm were about to break. Almost all the affairs of men remain in a terrible uncertainty. We think of what has disappeared, and we are almost destroyed by what has been destroyed; we do not know what will be born, and we fear the future, not without reason. . . . Doubt and disorder are in us and with us. There is no thinking man, however shrewd or learned he may be, who can hope to dominate this anxiety, to escape from this impression of darkness.[1]

In the midst of economic, political, and social disruptions, Valéry saw the "cruelly injured mind," besieged by doubts and suffering from anxieties. This was the general intellectual crisis of the twentieth century, which touched almost every field of thought. The implications of new ideas and discoveries in philosophy, physics, psychology, and literature played a central role in this crisis, disturbing "thinking people" everywhere.

Modern Philosophy

Among the small band of thinkers in the late nineteenth century who challenged the belief in progress and the general faith in the rational human mind, German philosopher Friedrich Nietzsche (1844–1900) was particularly influential. The son of a Lutheran minister, Nietzsche rejected Christianity and became a professor of classical languages until ill health forced him to retire at an early age. Never a systematic philosopher, Nietzsche wrote as a prophet in a provocative and poetic style. His first great work in 1872 argued that ever since classical Athens, the West had overemphasized rationality and stifled the passion and animal instinct that drive human activity and true creativity. Nietzsche went on to question all values. He claimed that Christianity embodied a "slave morality," which glorified weakness, envy, and mediocrity. In Nietzsche's most famous line, a wise fool proclaims that "God is dead," dead because He has been murdered by lackadaisical modern Christians who no longer really believe in Him. Nietzsche viewed the pillars of conventional morality—reason, democracy, progress, respectability—as outworn social and psychological constructs whose influence was suffocating self-realization and excellence.

Nietzsche painted a dark world, foreshadowing perhaps his loss of sanity in 1889. The West was in decline; false values had triumphed. The death of God left people disoriented and depressed. The only hope for the individual was to accept the meaninglessness of human existence and then make that very meaninglessness a source of self-defined personal integrity and hence liberation. This would at least be possible for a few superior individuals, who could free themselves from the humdrum thinking of the masses and become true heroes. Little read during his active years, Nietzsche attracted growing attention in the early twentieth century, especially from German radicals who found inspiration in Nietzsche's ferocious assault on the conventions of pre-1914 imperial Germany. Subsequent generations have each discovered

Friedrich Nietzsche   This colored photograph of the German philosopher was taken in 1882, when he was at the height of his creative powers. A brilliant iconoclast, Nietzsche debunked European values and challenged the optimistic faith in human rationality before World War I. *(AKG London)*

new Nietzsches, and his influence remains enormous to this day.

This growing dissatisfaction with established ideas before 1914 was apparent in other important thinkers. In the 1890s, French philosophy professor Henri Bergson (1859–1941) convinced many young people through his writing that immediate experience and intuition were as important as rational and scientific thinking for understanding reality. Indeed, according to Bergson, a religious experience or a mystical poem was often more accessible to human comprehension than a scientific law or a mathematical equation.

Another thinker who agreed about the limits of rational thinking was French socialist Georges Sorel (1847–1922). Sorel frankly characterized Marxian socialism as an inspiring but unprovable religion rather than a rational scientific truth. Socialism would come to power, he believed, through a great, general strike of all working people, which would shatter capitalist society. Sorel rejected democracy and believed that the masses of the new socialist society would have to be tightly controlled by a small revolutionary elite.

The First World War accelerated the revolt against established certainties in philosophy, but that revolt went in two very different directions. In English-speaking countries, the main development was the acceptance of logical empiricism (or logical positivism) in university circles. In continental countries, the primary development in philosophy was existentialism.

Logical empiricism was truly revolutionary. It quite simply rejected most of the concerns of traditional philosophy, from the existence of God to the meaning of happiness, as nonsense and hot air. This outlook began primarily with Austrian philosopher Ludwig Wittgenstein (1889–1951), who later immigrated to England, where he trained numerous disciples.

Wittgenstein argued in his pugnacious *Tractatus Logico-Philosophicus* (Essay on Logical Philosophy) in 1922 that philosophy is only the logical clarification of thoughts, and therefore it becomes the study of language, which expresses thoughts. The great philosophical issues of the ages—God, freedom, morality, and so on—are quite literally senseless, a great waste of time, for statements about them can be neither tested by scientific experiments nor demonstrated by the logic of mathematics. Statements about such matters reflect only the personal preferences of a given individual. As Wittgenstein put it in the famous last sentence of his work, "Of what one cannot speak, of that one must keep silent." Logical empiricism, which has remained dominant in England and the United States to this day, drastically reduced the scope of philosophical inquiry. Anxious people could find few, if any, answers in this direction.

Some looked for answers in **existentialism.** Highly diverse and even contradictory, existential thinkers were loosely united in a courageous search for moral values in a world of terror and uncertainty. Theirs were true voices of the age of anxiety.

Most existential thinkers in the twentieth century were atheists. Often inspired by Nietzsche, who had already proclaimed the death of God and called for new values, they did not believe a supreme being had established humanity's fundamental nature and given life its meaning. In the words of the famous French existentialist Jean-Paul Sartre (1905–1980), human beings simply exist: "They turn up, appear on the scene." Only after they "turn up" do they seek to define themselves. Honest human beings are terribly alone, for there is no God to help them. They are hounded by despair and the meaninglessness of life. The crisis of the existential thinker epitomized the modern intellectual crisis—the shattering of beliefs in God, reason, and progress.

Existentialists did recognize that human beings, unless they kill themselves, must act. Indeed, in the words of Sartre, "man is condemned to be free." There is therefore the possibility—indeed, the necessity—of giving meaning to life through actions, of defining oneself through choices. To do so, individuals must become "engaged" and choose their own actions courageously and consistently and in full awareness of their inescapable responsibility for their own behavior. In the end, existentialists argued, human beings can overcome life's absurdity.

Modern existentialism first attained prominence in Germany in the 1920s when philosophers Martin Heidegger and Karl Jaspers found a sympathetic audience among disillusioned postwar university students. But it was in France during and immediately after World War II that existentialism came of age. The terrible conditions of the war reinforced the existential view of and approach to life. On the one hand, the armies of the German dictator Hitler had conquered most of Europe and unleashed a hideous reign of barbarism. On the other, men and women had more than ever to define themselves by their actions. Specifically, each individual had to choose whether to join the resistance against Hitler or accept and even abet tyranny. The writings of Sartre, who along with Albert Camus (1913–1960) was the leading French existentialist, became enormously influential. Himself active in the French resistance, Sartre and his colleagues offered a powerful answer to profound moral issues and the contemporary crisis.

The Revival of Christianity

The loss of faith in human reason and in continual progress also led to a renewed interest in the Christian view of the world. Christianity and religion in general had been on the defensive in intellectual circles since the Enlightenment. In the years before 1914, some theologians, especially Protestant ones, had felt the need to interpret Christian doctrine and the Bible so that they did not seem to contradict science, evolution, and common sense. Christ was therefore seen primarily as the greatest moral teacher, and the "supernatural" aspects of his divinity were strenuously played down. Indeed, some modern theologians were embarrassed by the miraculous, unscientific aspects of Christianity and turned away from them.

Especially after World War I, a number of thinkers and theologians began to revitalize the fundamentals of Christianity. Sometimes described as Christian existentialists because they shared the loneliness and despair of atheistic existentialists, they stressed human beings' sinful nature, the need for faith, and the mystery of God's forgiveness. The revival of fundamental Christian belief after World War I was fed by rediscovery of the work of nineteenth-century Danish religious philosopher Søren Kierkegaard (1813–1855), whose ideas became extremely influential. Having rejected formalistic religion, Kierkegaard had eventually resolved his personal anguish over his imperfect nature by making a total religious commitment to a remote and majestic God.

Similar ideas were brilliantly developed by Swiss Protestant theologian Karl Barth (1886–1968), whose many influential writings after 1920 sought to re-create the religious intensity of the Reformation. For Barth, the basic fact about human beings is that they are imperfect, sinful creatures whose reason and will are hopelessly flawed. Religious truth is therefore made known to human beings only through God's grace. People have to accept God's word and the supernatural revelation of Jesus Christ with awe, trust, and obedience. Lowly mortals should not expect to "reason out" God and his ways.

Among Catholics, the leading existential Christian thinker was Gabriel Marcel (1887–1973). Born into a cultivated French family, where his atheistic father was "gratefully aware of all that . . . art owed to Catholicism but regarded Catholic thought itself as obsolete and tainted with absurd superstitions,"[2] Marcel found in the Catholic church an answer to what he called the postwar "broken world." Catholicism and religious belief provided the hope, humanity, honesty, and piety for which he hungered. Flexible and gentle, Marcel and his countryman Jacques Maritain (1882–1973) denounced anti-Semitism and supported closer ties with non-Catholics.

After 1914 religion became much more relevant and meaningful to thinking people than it had been before the war. In addition to Marcel and Maritain, many other illustrious individuals turned to religion between about 1920 and 1950. Poets T. S. Eliot and W. H. Auden, novelists Evelyn Waugh and Aldous Huxley, historian Arnold Toynbee, Oxford professor C. S. Lewis, psychoanalyst Karl Stern, physicist Max Planck, and philosopher Cyril Joad were all either converted to religion or attracted to it for the first time. Religion, often of a despairing, existential variety, was one meaningful answer to terror and anxiety. In the words of a famous Roman Catholic convert, English novelist Graham Greene, "One began to believe in heaven because one believed in hell."[3]

The New Physics

Ever since the scientific revolution of the seventeenth century, scientific advances and their implications had greatly influenced the beliefs of thinking people. By the late nineteenth century, science was one of the main pillars supporting Western society's optimistic and rationalistic view of the world. The Darwinian concept of evolution had been accepted and assimilated in most intellectual circles. Progressive minds believed that science, unlike religion and philosophical speculation, was based on hard facts and controlled experiments. Science seemed to have achieved an unerring and almost complete picture of reality. Unchanging natural laws seemed to determine physical processes and permit useful solutions to more and more problems. All this was comforting, especially to people who were no longer committed to traditional religious beliefs. And all this was challenged by the new physics.

An important first step toward the new physics was the discovery at the end of the nineteenth century that atoms were not like hard, permanent little billiard balls. They were actually composed of many far-smaller, fast-moving particles, such as electrons and protons. Polish-born physicist Marie Curie (1867–1934) and her French husband discovered that radium constantly emits subatomic particles and thus does not have a constant atomic weight. Building on this and other work in radiation, German physicist Max Planck (1858–1947) showed in 1900 that subatomic energy is emitted in uneven little spurts, which Planck called "quanta," and not in a steady stream, as previously believed. Planck's discovery called into question the old sharp distinction between matter and energy; the implication was that matter and energy might be different forms of the same thing. The old view of atoms as the stable, basic building blocks of nature, with a different kind of unbreakable atom for each of the ninety-two chemical elements, was badly shaken.

In 1905 the German-Jewish genius Albert Einstein (1879–1955) went further than the Curies and Planck in undermining Newtonian physics. His famous theory of special relativity postulated that time and space are relative to the viewpoint of the observer and that only the speed of light is constant for all frames of reference in the universe. In order to make his revolutionary and paradoxical idea somewhat comprehensible to the nonmathematical layperson, Einstein later used analogies involving moving trains. For example, if a woman in the middle of a moving car got up and walked forward to the door, she had gone, relative to the train, a half car length. But relative to an observer on the embankment, she had gone farther. The closed framework of Newtonian physics was quite limited compared to that of Einsteinian physics, which unified an apparently infinite universe with the incredibly small, fast-moving subatomic world. Moreover, Einstein's theory stated clearly that matter and energy are interchangeable and that even a particle of matter contains enormous levels of potential energy.

The 1920s opened the "heroic age of physics," in the apt words of one of its leading pioneers, Ernest Rutherford (1871–1937). Breakthrough followed breakthrough. In 1919 Rutherford showed that the atom could be split. By 1944 seven subatomic particles had been identified, of which the most important was the **neutron.** The neutron's capacity to pass through other atoms allowed for even more intense experimental bombardment of matter, leading to chain reactions of unbelievable force. This was the road to the atomic bomb.

Although few nonscientists understood this revolution in physics, the implications of the new theories and discoveries, as presented by newspapers and popular writers, were disturbing to millions of men and women in the 1920s and 1930s. The new universe was strange and troubling. It lacked any absolute objective reality. Everything was "relative," that is, dependent on the observer's

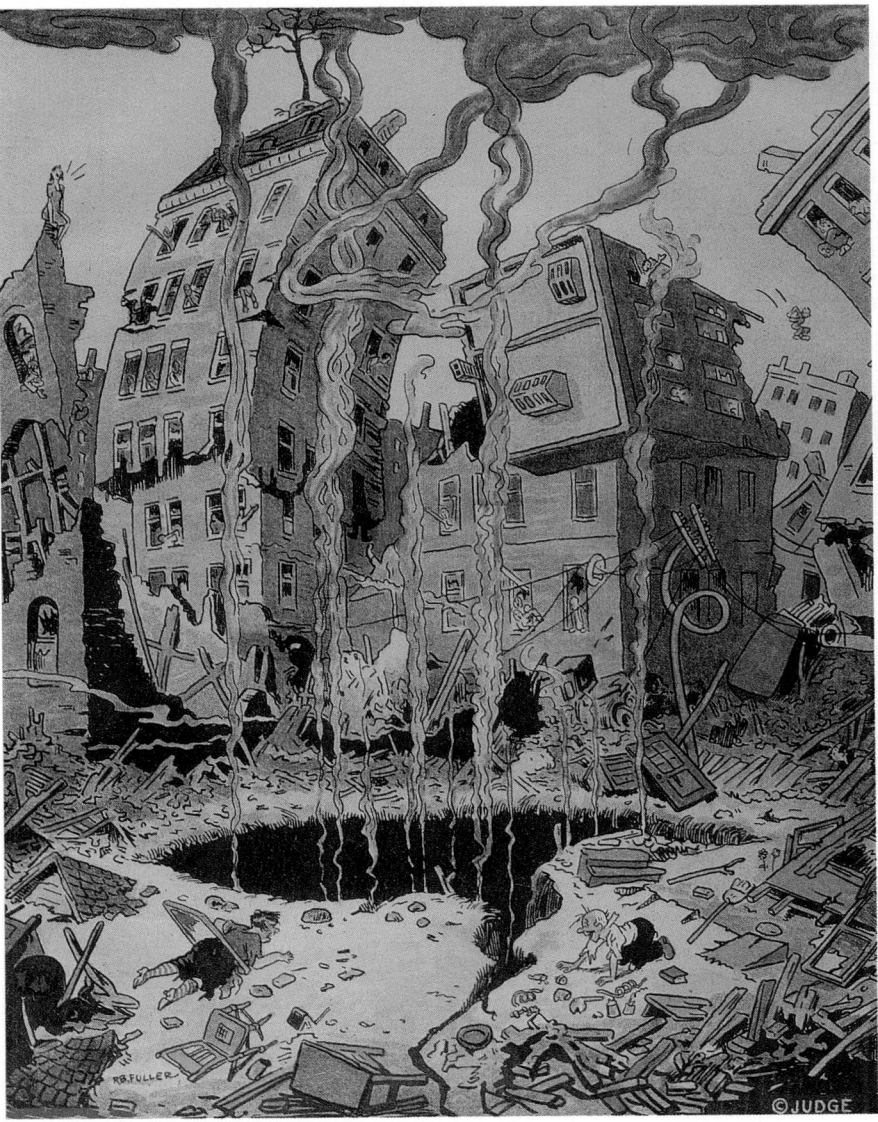

Unlocking the Power of the Atom
Many of the fanciful visions of science fiction came true in the twentieth century, although not exactly as first imagined. This 1927 cartoon satirizes a professor who has split the atom and unwittingly destroyed his building and neighborhood in the process. In the Second World War the professors harnessed the atom in bombs and decimated faraway cities and foreign civilians. *(Mary Evans Picture Library)*

frame of reference. Moreover, the universe was uncertain and undetermined, without stable building blocks. In 1927 German physicist Werner Heisenberg (1901–1976) formulated the "principle of uncertainty," which postulates that because it is impossible to know the position and speed of an individual electron, it is therefore impossible to predict its behavior. Instead of Newton's dependable, rational laws, there seemed to be only tendencies and probabilities in an extraordinarily complex and uncertain universe.

Moreover, a universe described by abstract mathematical symbols seemed to have little to do with human experience and human problems. When, for example, Planck was asked what science could contribute to resolving conflicts of values, his response was simple: "Science is not qualified to speak to this question." Physics, the queen of the sciences, no longer provided people easy, optimistic answers—for that matter, it did not provide any answers at all.

Freudian Psychology

With physics presenting an uncertain universe so unrelated to ordinary human experience, questions regarding the power and potential of the human mind assumed special significance. The findings and speculations of leading psychologist Sigmund Freud (see page 812) were particularly disturbing.

Before Freud, poets and mystics had probed the unconscious and irrational aspects of human behavior. But most professional, "scientific" psychologists assumed that a single, unified conscious mind processed sense experiences in a rational and logical way. Human behavior in turn was the result of rational calculation—of "thinking"—by the conscious mind. Basing his insights on the analysis of dreams and of hysteria, Freud developed a very different view of the human psyche beginning in the late 1880s.

Munch: The Dance of Life Like his contemporary Sigmund Freud, the expressionist painter Edvard Munch studied the turmoil and fragility of human thought and action. Solitary figures struggling with fear and uncertainty dominate his work. Here the girl in white represents innocence, the tense woman in black stands for mourning and rejection, and the woman in red evokes the joy of passing pleasure. *(National Gallery, Oslo, Norway/Scala/Art Resource, NY)*

According to Freud, human behavior is basically irrational. The key to understanding the mind is the primitive, irrational unconscious, which he called the **id.** The unconscious is driven by sexual, aggressive, and pleasure-seeking desires and is locked in a constant battle with the other parts of the mind: the rationalizing conscious (the **ego**), which mediates what a person *can* do, and ingrained moral values (the **superego**), which specify what a person *should* do. Human behavior is a product of a fragile compromise between instinctual drives and the controls of rational thinking and moral values. Since the instinctual drives are extremely powerful, the ever-present danger for individuals and whole societies is that unacknowledged drives will overwhelm the control mechanisms in a violent, distorted way. Yet Freud also agreed with Nietzsche that the mechanisms of rational thinking and traditional moral values can be too strong. They can repress sexual desires too effectively, crippling individuals and entire peoples with guilt and neurotic fears.

Freudian psychology and clinical psychiatry had become an international movement by 1910, but only after 1918 did they receive popular attention, especially in the Protestant countries of northern Europe and in the United States. Many opponents and even some enthusiasts interpreted Freud as saying that the first requirement for mental health is an uninhibited sex life. Thus after the First World War, the popular interpretation of Freud reflected and encouraged growing sexual experimentation, particularly among middle-class women. For more serious students, the psychology of Freud and his followers drastically undermined the old, easy optimism about the rational and progressive nature of the human mind.

Twentieth-Century Literature

The general intellectual climate of pessimism, relativism, and alienation was also articulated in literature. Novelists developed new techniques to express new realities. The great nineteenth-century novelists had typically written as all-knowing narrators, describing realistic characters and their relationship to an understandable, if sometimes harsh, society. In the twentieth century, most major writers adopted the limited, often confused viewpoint of a single individual. Like Freud, these novelists focused their attention on the complexity and irrationality of the human mind, where feelings, memories, and desires are forever scrambled. The great French novelist Marcel Proust (1871–1922), in his semi-autobiographical *Remembrance of Things Past* (1913–1927), recalled bittersweet memories of childhood and youthful love and tried

Virginia Woolf Her novels captured sensations like impressionist paintings, and her home attracted a circle of artists and writers known as the Bloomsbury Group. Many of Woolf's essays dealt with women's issues and urged greater opportunity for women's creativity. *(Gisèle Freund/Photo Researchers, Inc.)*

to discover their innermost meaning. To do so, Proust lived like a hermit in a soundproof Paris apartment for ten years, withdrawing from the present to dwell on the past.

Serious novelists also used the **stream-of-consciousness technique** to explore the psyche. In *Jacob's Room* (1922), Virginia Woolf (1882–1941) created a novel made up of a series of internal monologues, in which ideas and emotions from different periods of time bubble up as randomly as from a patient on a psychoanalyst's couch. William Faulkner (1897–1962), perhaps America's greatest twentieth-century novelist, used the same technique in *The Sound and the Fury* (1922), much of whose intense drama is confusedly seen through the eyes of an idiot. The most famous stream-of-consciousness novel—and surely the most disturbing novel of its generation—is *Ulysses,* which Irish novelist James Joyce (1882–1941) published in 1922. Into an account of an ordinary day in the life of an ordinary man, Joyce weaves an extended ironic parallel between his hero's aimless wanderings through the streets and pubs of Dublin and the adventures of Homer's hero Ulysses on his way home from Troy. Abandoning conventional grammar and blending foreign words, puns, bits of knowledge, and scraps of memory together in bewildering confusion, the language of *Ulysses* is intended to mirror modern life itself: a gigantic riddle waiting to be unraveled.

As creative writers turned their attention from society to the individual and from realism to psychological relativity, they rejected the idea of progress. Some even described "anti-utopias," nightmare visions of things to come. In 1918 an obscure German high school teacher named Oswald Spengler (1880–1936) published *The Decline of the West,* which quickly became an international sensation. According to Spengler, every culture experiences a life cycle of growth and decline. Western civilization, in Spengler's opinion, was in its old age, and death was approaching in the form of conquest by the yellow race. T. S. Eliot (1888–1965), in his famous poem *The Waste Land* (1922), depicts a world of growing desolation, although after his conversion to Anglo-Catholicism in 1927, Eliot came to hope cautiously for humanity's salvation. No such hope appears in the work of Franz Kafka (1883–1924), whose novels *The Trial* (1925) and *The Castle* (1926), as well as several of his greatest short stories, portray helpless individuals crushed by inexplicably hostile forces. The German-Jewish Kafka died young, at forty-one, and so did not see the world of his nightmares materialize in the Nazi state.

Englishman George Orwell (1903–1950), however, had seen both that reality and its Stalinist counterpart by 1949, when he wrote perhaps the ultimate in anti-utopian literature: *1984.* Orwell set the action in the future, in 1984. Big Brother—the dictator—and his totalitarian state use a new kind of language, sophisticated technology, and psychological terror to strip a weak individual of his last shred of human dignity. The supremely self-confident chief of the Thought Police tells the tortured, broken, and framed Winston Smith, "If you want a picture of the future, imagine a boot stamping on a human face—forever."[4] A phenomenal best-seller, *1984* spoke to millions of people in the closing years of the age of anxiety.

Modern Art and Music

Throughout the twentieth century, there has been considerable unity in the arts. The "modernism" of the immediate prewar years and the 1920s is still strikingly modern. Like the scientists and creative artists who were partaking of the same culture, creative artists rejected old forms and old values. Modernism in art and music meant constant experimentation and a search for new kinds of expression. And though many people find the numerous and varied modern visions of the arts strange, disturbing, and even ugly, the twentieth century, so dismal in many respects, will probably stand as one of Western civilization's great artistic eras.

Architecture and Design

Modernism in the arts was loosely unified by a revolution in architecture. This revolution intended nothing less than a transformation of the physical framework of urban society according to a new principle: **functionalism.** Buildings, like industrial products, should be useful and "functional"—that is, they should serve, as well as possible, the purpose for which they were made. Thus architects and designers had to work with engineers, town planners, and even sanitation experts. Moreover, they had to throw away useless ornamentation and find beauty and aesthetic pleasure in the clean lines of practical constructions and efficient machinery. Franco-Swiss genius Le Corbusier (1887–1965) insisted that "a house is a machine for living in."[5]

The United States, with its rapid urban growth and lack of rigid building traditions, pioneered in the new architecture. In the 1890s, the Chicago school of architects, led by Louis H. Sullivan (1856–1924), used cheap steel, reinforced concrete, and electric elevators to build skyscrapers and office buildings lacking almost any exterior ornamentation. In the first decade of the twentieth century, Sullivan's student Frank Lloyd Wright (1869–1959) built a series of radically new and truly modern houses featuring low lines, open interiors, and mass-produced building materials. Europeans were inspired by these and other American examples of functional construction, like the massive, unadorned grain elevators of the Midwest.

In Europe architectural leadership centered in German-speaking countries until Hitler took power in 1933. In 1911 twenty-eight-year-old Walter Gropius (1883–1969) broke sharply with the past in his design of the

Frank Lloyd Wright: The "Falling Water" House   Often considered Wright's masterpiece, Falling Water combines modern architectural concepts with close attention to a spectacular site. Anchored to a high rock ledge by means of reinforced concrete, the house soars out over a cascading waterfall at Bear Run in western Pennsylvania. Built in 1937 for a Pittsburgh businessman, Falling Water is now open to the public and attracts 70,000 visitors each year. *(Western Pennsylvania Conservancy/Art Resource, NY)*

Fagus shoe factory at Alfeld, Germany—a clean, light, elegant building of glass and iron. After the First World War, Gropius merged the schools of fine and applied arts at Weimar into a single, interdisciplinary school, the **Bauhaus.** The Bauhaus brought together many leading modern architects, designers, and theatrical innovators. Working as an effective, inspired team, they combined the study of fine art, such as painting and sculpture, with the study of applied art in the crafts of printing, weaving, and furniture making. Throughout the 1920s, the Bau-

haus, with its stress on functionalism and good design for everyday life, attracted enthusiastic students from all over the world. It had a great and continuing impact.

Another leader in the "international" style, Ludwig Mies van der Rohe (1886–1969), followed Gropius as director of the Bauhaus in 1930 and immigrated to the United States in 1937. His classic Lake Shore Apartments in Chicago, built between 1948 and 1951, symbolized the triumph of steel-frame and glass-wall modern architecture in the great building boom after the Second World War.

Modern Painting

Modern painting grew out of a revolt against French impressionism. The *impressionism* of such French painters as Claude Monet (1840–1926), Pierre Auguste Renoir (1841–1919), and Camille Pissarro (1830–1903) was, in part, a kind of "superrealism." Leaving exact copying of objects to photography, these artists sought to capture the momentary overall feeling, or impression, of light falling on a real-life scene before their eyes. By 1890, when impressionism was finally established, a few artists known as *postimpressionists,* or sometimes as *expressionists,* were already striking out in new directions. After 1905 art increasingly took on a nonrepresentational, abstract character, a development that reached its high point after World War II.

Though individualistic in their styles, postimpressionists were united in their desire to know and depict worlds other than the visible world of fact. Like the early-nineteenth-century romantics, they wanted to portray unseen, inner worlds of emotion and imagination. Like modern novelists, they wanted to express a complicated psychological view of reality as well as an overwhelming emotional intensity. In *The Starry Night* (1889), for example, the great Dutch expressionist Vincent van Gogh (1853–1890) painted the moving vision of his mind's

Van Gogh: The Starry Night   Van Gogh absorbed impressionism in Paris, but under the burning sun of southern France he went beyond the portrayal of external reality. In *The Starry Night* (1889) flaming cypress trees, exploding stars, and a comet-like Milky Way swirl together in one great cosmic rhythm. Painting an inner world of intense emotion and wild imagination, van Gogh contributed greatly to the rise of expressionism in modern art. *(© MoMA/Scala/Art Resource, NY. © 2002 Artists Rights Society [ARS], New York/ADAGP, Paris)*

eye (see the illustration). Paul Gauguin (1848–1903), the French stockbroker-turned-painter, pioneered in expressionist techniques, though he used them to infuse his work with tranquillity and mysticism. In 1891 he fled to the South Pacific in search of unspoiled beauty and a primitive way of life. Gauguin believed that the form and design of a picture were important in themselves and that the painter need not try to represent objects on canvas as the eye actually saw them.

Fascination with form, as opposed to light, was characteristic of postimpressionism and expressionism. Paul Cézanne (1839–1906), who had a profound influence on twentieth-century painting, was particularly committed to form and ordered design. He told a young painter, "You must see in nature the cylinder, the sphere, and the cone."[6] As Cézanne's later work became increasingly abstract and nonrepresentational, it also moved away from the traditional three-dimensional perspective toward the two-dimensional plane, which has characterized so much of modern art. The expressionism of a group of painters led by Henri Matisse (1869–1954) was so extreme that an exhibition of their work in Paris in 1905 prompted shocked critics to call them *les fauves*—"the wild beasts." Matisse and his followers still painted real objects, but their primary concern was the arrangement of color, line, and form as an end in itself.

In 1907 a young Spaniard in Paris, Pablo Picasso (1881–1973), founded another movement—*cubism.* (See the feature "Images in Society: Pablo Picasso and Modern Art" on pages 934–935.) Cubism concentrated on a complex geometry of zigzagging lines and sharply angled, overlapping planes. About three years later came the ultimate stage in the development of abstract, nonrepresentational art. Artists such as the Russian-born Wassily Kandinsky (1866–1944) turned away from nature completely. "The observer," said Kandinsky, "must learn to look at [my] pictures . . . as form and color combinations . . . as a representation of mood and not as a representation of *objects.*"[7] On the eve of the First World War, extreme expressionism and abstract painting were developing rapidly not only in Paris but also in Russia and Germany. Modern art had become international.

In the 1920s and 1930s, the artistic movements of the prewar years were extended and consolidated. The most notable new developments were *dadaism* and *surrealism.* **Dadaism** attacked all accepted standards of art and behavior, delighting in outrageous conduct. Its name, from the French word *dada,* meaning "hobbyhorse," is deliberately nonsensical. A famous example of dadaism is a reproduction of Leonardo da Vinci's *Mona Lisa* in which the famous woman with the mysterious smile sports a mustache and is ridiculed with an obscene inscription. After 1924 many dadaists were attracted to surrealism, which became very influential in art in the late 1920s and 1930s. Surrealists painted a fantastic world of wild dreams and complex symbols, where watches melted and giant metronomes beat time in precisely drawn but impossible alien landscapes. Refusing to depict ordinary visual reality, surrealist painters made powerful statements about the age of anxiety.

Modern Music

Developments in modern music were strikingly parallel to those in painting. Composers, too, were attracted by the emotional intensity of expressionism. The ballet *The Rite of Spring* by composer Igor Stravinsky (1882–1971) practically caused a riot when it was first performed in Paris in 1913 by Sergei Diaghilev's famous Russian dance company. The combination of pulsating, dissonant rhythms from the orchestra pit and an earthy representation of lovemaking by the dancers on the stage seemed a shocking, almost pornographic enactment of a primitive fertility rite.

After the experience of the First World War, when irrationality and violence seemed to pervade the human experience, expressionism in opera and ballet flourished. One of the most famous and powerful examples was the opera *Wozzeck,* by Alban Berg (1885–1935), first performed in Berlin in 1925. Blending a half-sung, half-spoken kind of dialogue with harsh, atonal music, *Wozzeck* is a gruesome tale of a soldier driven by Kafka-like inner terrors and vague suspicions of unfaithfulness to murder his mistress.

Some composers turned their backs on long-established musical conventions. As abstract painters arranged lines and color but did not draw identifiable objects, so modern composers arranged sounds without creating recognizable harmonies. Led by Viennese composer Arnold Schönberg (1874–1951), they abandoned traditional harmony and tonality. The musical notes in a given piece were no longer united and organized by a key; instead they were independent and unrelated. Schönberg's twelve-tone music of the 1920s arranged all twelve notes of the scale in an abstract, mathematical pattern, or "tone row." This pattern sounded like no pattern at all to the ordinary listener and could be detected only by a highly trained eye studying the musical score. Accustomed to the harmonies of classical and romantic music, audiences generally resisted modern atonal music. Only after the Second World War did it begin to win acceptance.

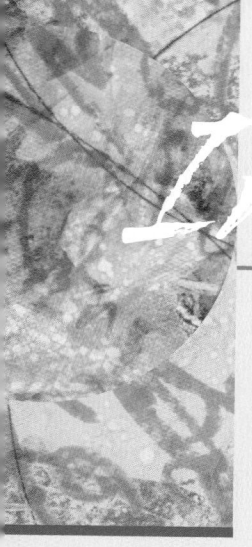

Pablo Picasso and Modern Art

Pablo Picasso (1881–1973) was probably the most significant artist of the early twentieth century. For more than seventy years, he personified the individuality, freedom, and revolutionary creativity of the modern artist.

Born at Málaga in southern Spain, Picasso quickly demonstrated a precocious talent. At nineteen he headed for Paris, Europe's art capital. Suffering from poverty and falling into depression, he painted the weak and the poor in somber blue and purple tones. These pessimistic paintings of Picasso's "Blue Period" (1901–1904) are masterpieces in the tradition of Spanish realism.

Yet the young Picasso soon sought a new visual reality. In 1907 his arduous struggle to create a new style resulted in *Les Demoiselles d'Avignon* (Image 1), a painting originating in memories of a brothel scene in Barcelona. This work was considered a revolutionary upheaval in art. Since the Renaissance, artists had been expected to follow well-established rules, seeing objects in an orderly perspective from a single viewpoint and creating "beauty" and unified human forms. Do the faces of the central figures in this work conform to these rules? Regard the figures on either side, who were painted later. Notice how the light fails to combine with the shadow to create bodies with continuous, three-dimensional contours. The figures appear broken into large, flat planes with heads that are twisted, fractured dislocations. Do you see the magical violence of a pictorial breakthrough or a grotesque, ugly departure?

Picasso extended his revolutionary experiments, and after 1910 he was joined by others. A critic called the new school cubism because these artists used many geometric forms in intersecting planes. Objects, viewed from many shifting viewpoints, often emerged as purely abstract designs.

Three Musicians (Image 2), painted in 1921, represents mature cubism. Many people believe that it marks the culmination of Picasso's cubist style. What similarities and differences do you see between this picture and Image 1? Notice the limited number of viewpoints, with

Image 1 Les Demoiselles d'Avignon (1907). (© MoMA/Scala/Art Resource, NY. © 2002 Artists Rights Society [ARS], New York/ADAGP, Paris)

Image 2 **Three Musicians** (1921).
(© MoMA/Scala/Art Resource, NY.
© 2002 Artists Rights Society [ARS],
New York/ADAGP, Paris)

and the dissonant, syncopated rhythm of modern music. Picasso always drew back from pure abstraction because he began with real objects and used models.

Picasso's passionate involvement in his times infuses his immense painting *Guernica* (Image 3), often considered his greatest work. Painted for the Spanish pavilion at the Paris International Exhibition in 1937, this mural, with its mournful white, black, and blue colors, was inspired by the Spanish civil war and the deadly terror bombing of Guernica by fascist planes in a single night. In this complex work, a shrieking woman falls from a burning house on the far right. On the left, a woman holds a dead child, while toward the center are fragments of a warrior and a screaming horse pierced by a spear. Do cubist techniques heighten the effect? Picasso also draws on other aspects of the modernist revolution here. Compare *Guernica* with the expressionist works on pages 897 and 922. Surrealists were fascinated with grotesque subject matter and apparently unrelated objects in surprising situations. Are these elements also present here? Picasso wanted his painting to be an unforgettable attack on "brutality and darkness." Did he succeed? How do the works presented here enhance your understanding of modern art?

the white clown, the harlequin, the monk, their instruments, and the table in front cut up into rectangular shapes and reassembled in recognizable form on a shallow series of planes. What is the effect of the bright primary colors and the harmonious, decorative order? Picasso had been making the sets for Sergei Diaghilev's famous Russian dance company in Paris, and these three jagged figures from traditional Italian comedy seem to convey the atmosphere of the theater

Image 3 **Guernica** (1937). *(Museo del Prado/Giraudon/Art Resource, NY. © Artists Rights Society [ARS], New York/ADAGP, Paris)*

The Great Dictator In 1940 the renowned actor and director Charlie Chaplin abandoned the little tramp to satirize the "great dictator," Adolf Hitler. Chaplin had strong political views and made a number of films with political themes as the escapist fare of the Great Depression gave way to the reality of the Second World War. *(The Museum of Modern Art/ Still Film Archives)*

Movies and Radio

Until after World War II at the earliest, these revolutionary changes in art and music appealed mainly to a minority of "highbrows" and not to the general public. That public was primarily and enthusiastically wrapped up in movies and radio. The long-declining traditional arts and amusements of people in villages and small towns almost vanished, replaced by standardized, commercial entertainment.

Moving pictures were first shown as a popular novelty in naughty peepshows—"What the Butler Saw"—and penny arcades in the 1890s, especially in Paris. The first movie houses date from an experiment in Los Angeles in

1902. They quickly attracted large audiences and led to the production of short, silent action films such as the eight-minute *Great Train Robbery* of 1903. American directors and business people then set up "movie factories," at first in the New York area and then after 1910 in Los Angeles. These factories churned out two short films each week. On the eve of the First World War, full-length feature films such as the Italian *Quo Vadis* and the American *Birth of a Nation,* coupled with improvements in the quality of pictures, suggested the screen's vast possibilities.

During the First World War, the United States became the dominant force in the rapidly expanding silent-film industry. In the 1920s, Mack Sennett (1884–1960) and his zany Keystone Kops specialized in short, slapstick comedies noted for frantic automobile chases, custard-pie battles, and gorgeous bathing beauties. Screen stars such as Mary Pickford and Lillian Gish, Douglas Fairbanks and Rudolf Valentino, became household names, with their own "fan clubs." Yet Charlie Chaplin (1889–1978), a funny little Englishman working in Hollywood, was unquestionably the king of the "silver screen" in the 1920s. In his enormously popular role as a lonely tramp, complete with baggy trousers, battered derby, and an awkward, shuffling walk, Chaplin symbolized the "gay spirit of laughter in a cruel, crazy world."[8] Chaplin also demonstrated that in the hands of a genius, the new medium could combine mass entertainment and artistic accomplishment.

The early 1920s were also the great age of German films. Protected and developed during the war, the large German studios excelled in bizarre expressionist dramas, beginning with *The Cabinet of Dr. Caligari* in 1919. Unfortunately, their period of creativity was short-lived. By 1926 American money was drawing the leading German talents to Hollywood and consolidating America's international domination. Film making was big business, and European theater owners were forced to book whole blocks of American films to get the few pictures they really wanted. This system put European producers at a great disadvantage until "talkies" permitted a revival of national film industries in the 1930s, particularly in France.

Whether foreign or domestic, motion pictures became the main entertainment of the masses until after the Second World War. In Great Britain one in every four adults went to the movies twice a week in the late 1930s, and two in five went at least once a week. Continental countries had similar figures. The greatest appeal of motion pictures was that they offered ordinary people a temporary escape from the hard realities of everyday life. The appeal of escapist entertainment was especially strong during the Great Depression. Millions flocked to musical comedies featuring glittering stars such as Ginger Rogers and Fred Astaire and to the fanciful cartoons of Mickey Mouse and his friends.

Radio became possible with the transatlantic "wireless" communication of Guglielmo Marconi (1874–1937) in 1901 and the development of the vacuum tube in 1904, which permitted the transmission of speech and music. But only in 1920 were the first major public broadcasts of special events made in Great Britain and the United States. Lord Northcliffe, who had pioneered in journalism with the inexpensive, mass-circulation *Daily Mail,* sponsored a broadcast of "only one artist . . . the world's very best, the soprano Nellie Melba."[9] Singing from London in English, Italian, and French, Melba was heard simultaneously all over Europe on June 16, 1920. This historic event captured the public's imagination. The meteoric career of radio was launched.

Every major country quickly established national broadcasting networks. In the United States such networks were privately owned and financed by advertising. In Great Britain Parliament set up an independent, public corporation, the British Broadcasting Corporation (BBC), supported by licensing fees. Elsewhere in Europe the typical pattern was direct control by the government.

Whatever the institutional framework, radio became popular and influential. By the late 1930s, more than three out of every four households in both democratic Great Britain and dictatorial Germany had at least one cheap, mass-produced radio.

Radio in unscrupulous hands was particularly well suited for political propaganda. Dictators such as Mussolini and Hitler controlled the airwaves and could reach enormous national audiences with their frequent, dramatic speeches. In democratic countries, politicians such as President Franklin Roosevelt and Prime Minister Stanley Baldwin effectively used informal "fireside chats" to bolster their support.

Motion pictures also became powerful tools of indoctrination, especially in countries with dictatorial regimes. Lenin himself encouraged the development of Soviet film making, believing that the new medium was essential to the social and ideological transformation of the country. Beginning in the mid-1920s, a series of epic films, the most famous of which were directed by Sergei Eisenstein (1898–1948), brilliantly dramatized the communist view of Russian history.

In Germany Hitler turned to a young and immensely talented woman film maker, Leni Riefenstahl (b. 1902), for a masterpiece of documentary propaganda, *The Triumph of the Will,* based on the Nazi party rally at Nuremberg in 1934. Riefenstahl combined stunning aerial photography, joyful crowds welcoming Hitler, and mass processions of young Nazi fanatics. Her film was a brilliant and all-too-powerful documentary of Germany's "Nazi rebirth." The new media of mass culture were potentially dangerous instruments of political manipulation.

The Search for Peace and Political Stability

As established patterns of thought and culture were challenged and mangled by the ferocious impact of World War I, so also was the political fabric stretched and torn by the consequences of the great conflict. The Versailles settlement had established a shaky truce, not a solid peace. Thus national leaders faced a gigantic task as they struggled with uncertainty and sought to create a stable international order within the general context of intellectual crisis and revolutionary artistic experimentation.

The pursuit of real and lasting peace proved difficult for many reasons. Germany hated the Treaty of Versailles. France was fearful and isolated. Britain was undependable, and the United States had turned its back on European problems. Eastern Europe was in ferment, and no one could predict the future of communist Russia. Moreover, the international economic situation was poor and greatly complicated by war debts and disrupted patterns of trade. Yet for a time, from 1925 to late 1929, it appeared that peace and stability were within reach. When the subsequent collapse of the 1930s mocked these hopes, the disillusionment of liberals in the democracies was intensified.

Germany and the Western Powers

Germany was the key to lasting peace. Yet to Germans of all political parties, the Treaty of Versailles represented a harsh, dictated peace, to be revised or repudiated as soon as possible. The treaty had neither broken nor reduced Germany, which was potentially still the strongest country in Europe. Thus the treaty had fallen between two stools: too harsh for a peace of reconciliation, too soft for a peace of conquest.

Moreover, with ominous implications for the future, France and Great Britain did not see eye to eye on Germany. By the end of 1919, France wanted to stress the harsh elements in the Treaty of Versailles. Most of the war in the west had been fought on French soil, and the expected costs of reconstruction, as well as repaying war debts to the United States, were staggering. Thus French politicians believed that massive reparations from Germany were a vital economic necessity. Also, having compromised with President Wilson only to be betrayed by America's failure to ratify the treaty, many French leaders saw strict implementation of all provisions of the Treaty of Versailles as France's last best hope. Large reparation payments could hold Germany down indefinitely, and France would realize its goal of security.

The British soon felt differently. Prewar Germany had been Great Britain's second-best market in the entire world, and after the war a healthy, prosperous Germany appeared to be essential to the British economy. Indeed, many English people agreed with the analysis of the young English economist John Maynard Keynes (1883–1946), who eloquently denounced the Treaty of Versailles in his famous *Economic Consequences of the Peace* (1919). According to Keynes's interpretation, astronomical reparations and harsh economic measures would impoverish Germany and also increase economic hardship in all countries. Only a complete revision of the foolish treaty could save Germany—and Europe. Keynes's attack exploded like a bombshell and became very influential. It stirred deep guilt feelings about Germany in the English-speaking world, feelings that often paralyzed English and American leaders in their relations with Germany and its leaders between the First and Second World Wars.

The British were also suspicious of France's army—the largest in Europe, and authorized at Versailles to occupy the German Rhineland until 1935—and France's foreign policy. Ever since 1890, France had looked to Russia as a powerful ally against Germany. But with Russia hostile and communist, and with Britain and the United States unwilling to make any firm commitments, France turned to the newly formed states of eastern Europe for diplomatic support. In 1921 France signed a mutual defense pact with Poland and associated itself closely with the so-called Little Entente, an alliance that joined Czechoslovakia, Romania, and Yugoslavia against defeated and bitter Hungary.

While French and British leaders drifted in different directions, the Allied reparations commission completed its work. In April 1921, it announced that Germany had to pay the enormous sum of 132 billion gold marks ($33 billion) in annual installments of 2.5 billion gold marks. Facing possible occupation of more of its territory, the young German republic—generally known as the Weimar Republic—made its first payment in 1921. Then in 1922, wracked by rapid inflation and political assassinations and motivated by hostility and arrogance as well, the Weimar Republic announced its inability to pay more. It proposed a moratorium on reparations for three years, with the clear implication that thereafter reparations would be either drastically reduced or eliminated entirely.

The British were willing to accept a moratorium on reparations, but the French were not. Led by their tough-minded prime minister, Raymond Poincaré (1860–1934), they decided they had to either call Germany's bluff or see the entire peace settlement dissolve to France's great disadvantage. So, despite strong British protests, in early January 1923, armies of France and its ally Belgium moved out of the Rhineland and began to occupy the Ruhr district, the heartland of industrial Germany, creating the most serious international crisis of the 1920s. If forcible collection proved impossible, France would use occupation to paralyze Germany and force it to accept the Treaty of Versailles.

Strengthened by a wave of patriotism, the German government ordered the people of the Ruhr to stop working and start passively resisting the French occupation. The coal mines and steel mills of the Ruhr grew silent, leaving 10 percent of Germany's total population in need of relief. The French answer to passive resistance was to seal off the Ruhr and the entire Rhineland from the rest of Germany, letting in only enough food to prevent starvation.

By the summer of 1923, France and Germany were engaged in a great test of wills. French armies could not collect reparations from striking workers at gunpoint. But French occupation was indeed paralyzing Germany and its economy and had turned rapid German inflation into runaway inflation. Faced with the need to support the striking Ruhr workers and their employers, the German government began to print money to pay its bills. Prices soared. People went to the store with a big bag of paper money; they returned home with a handful of groceries. German money rapidly lost all value.

Runaway inflation brought about a social revolution. The accumulated savings of many retired and middle-class people were wiped out. Catastrophic inflation cruelly mocked the old middle-class virtues of thrift, caution, and self-reliance. Many Germans felt betrayed. They hated and blamed the Western governments, their own government, big business, the Jews, the workers, and the communists for their misfortune. They were psychologically prepared to follow radical leaders in a crisis.

In August 1923, as the mark fell and political unrest grew throughout Germany, Gustav Stresemann (1878–1929) assumed leadership of the government. Stresemann adopted a compromising attitude. He called off passive resistance in the Ruhr and in October agreed in principle to pay reparations but asked for a re-examination of Germany's ability to pay. Poincaré accepted. His hard line was becoming increasingly unpopular with French citizens,

"Hands Off the Ruhr"   The French occupation of the Ruhr to collect reparations payments raised a storm of patriotic protest in Germany. This anti-French poster of 1923 turns Marianne, the personification of French republican virtue, into a vicious harpy. *(International Instituut voor Sociale Geschiedenis)*

and it was hated in Britain and the United States. (See the feature "Individuals in Society: Gustav Stresemann.")

More generally, in both Germany and France, power was finally passing to the moderates, who realized that continued confrontation was a destructive, no-win situation. Thus after five long years of hostility and tension, culminating in a kind of undeclared war in the Ruhr in 1923, Germany and France decided to give compromise and cooperation a try. The British, and even the Americans, were willing to help. The first step was a reasonable agreement on the reparations question.

Hope in Foreign Affairs, 1924–1929

The reparations commission appointed an international committee of financial experts headed by American banker Charles G. Dawes to re-examine reparations from a broad perspective. The resulting **Dawes Plan** (1924) was accepted by France, Germany, and Britain. Germany's yearly reparations were reduced and depended on the level of German economic prosperity. Germany would also receive large loans from the United States to promote German recovery. In short, Germany would get private loans from the United States and pay reparations to France and Britain, thus enabling those countries to repay the large sums they owed the United States.

This circular flow of international payments was complicated and risky, but for a while it worked. The German republic experienced a spectacular economic recovery. With prosperity and large, continual inflows of American capital, Germany easily paid about $1.3 billion in reparations in 1927 and 1928, enabling France and Britain to pay the United States. In this way the Americans belatedly played a part in the general economic settlement that, though far from ideal, facilitated the worldwide recovery of the late 1920s.

This economic settlement was matched by a political settlement. In 1925 the leaders of Europe signed a number of agreements at Locarno, Switzerland. Germany and France solemnly pledged to accept their common border, and both Britain and Italy agreed to fight either France or Germany if one invaded the other. Stresemann also agreed to settle boundary disputes with Poland and Czechoslovakia by peaceful means, and France promised those countries military aid if Germany attacked them. For years, a "spirit of Locarno" gave Europeans a sense of growing security and stability in international affairs.

Other developments also strengthened hopes. In 1926 Germany joined the League of Nations, where Stresemann continued his "peace offensive." In 1928 fifteen countries signed the Kellogg-Briand Pact, initiated by French prime minister Aristide Briand and U.S. secretary of state Frank B. Kellogg. This multinational pact "condemned and renounced war as an instrument of national policy." The signing states agreed to settle international disputes peacefully. Often seen as idealistic nonsense because it made no provisions for action in case war actually occurred, the pact was still a positive step. It fostered the cautious optimism of the late 1920s and also encouraged the hope that the United States would accept its responsibilities as a great world power and contribute to European stability.

Hope in Democratic Government

Domestic politics also offered reason to hope. During the occupation of the Ruhr and the great inflation, republican government in Germany had appeared on the verge of collapse. In 1923 communists momentarily entered provincial governments, and in November an obscure nobody named Adolf Hitler leaped onto a table in a beer hall in Munich and proclaimed a "national socialist revolution." But Hitler's plot to seize control of the government was poorly organized and easily crushed, and Hitler was sentenced to prison, where he outlined his theories and program in his book *Mein Kampf* (My Struggle). Throughout the 1920s, Hitler's National Socialist party attracted support only from a few fanatical anti-Semites, ultranationalists, and disgruntled ex-servicemen. In 1928 his party had an insignificant twelve seats in the Reichstag. Indeed, after 1923 democracy seemed to take root in Weimar Germany. A new currency was established, and the economy boomed.

The moderate businessmen who tended to dominate the various German coalition governments were convinced that economic prosperity demanded good relations with the Western powers, and they supported parliamentary government at home. Stresemann himself was a man of this class, and he was the key figure in every government until his death in 1929. Elections were held regularly, and republican democracy appeared to have growing support among a majority of the Germans.

There were, however, sharp political divisions in the country. Many unrepentant nationalists and monarchists populated the right and the army. Members of Germany's recently formed Communist party were noisy and active on the left. The Communists, directed from Moscow, reserved their greatest hatred and sharpest barbs for their cousins the Social Democrats, whom they endlessly accused of betraying the revolution. The working classes were divided politically, but a majority supported the nonrevolutionary but socialist Social Democrats.

The situation in France had numerous similarities to that in Germany. Communists and Socialists battled for the support of the workers. After 1924 the democratically elected government rested mainly in the hands of coalitions of moderates, and business interests were well represented. France's great accomplishment was rapid rebuilding of its war-torn northern region. The expense of this undertaking led, however, to a large deficit and substantial inflation. By early 1926, the franc had fallen to 10 percent of its prewar value, causing a severe crisis. Poincaré was recalled to office, while Briand remained minister for foreign affairs. The Poincaré government proceeded to slash spending and raise taxes, restoring confidence in the economy. The franc was "saved," stabilized at about one-fifth of its prewar value. Good times prevailed until 1930.

Despite political shortcomings, France attracted artists and writers from all over the world in the 1920s. Much of the intellectual and artistic ferment of the times flourished in Paris. As writer Gertrude Stein (1874–1946), a leader of the large colony of American expatriates living in Paris, later recalled, "Paris was where the twentieth century was."[10] More generally, France appealed to foreigners and the French as a harmonious combination of small businesses and family farms, of bold innovation and solid traditions.

Britain, too, faced challenges after 1920. The wartime trend toward greater social equality continued, however,

American Jazz in Paris This woodcut from a 1928 French book on cafés and nightclubs suggests how black musicians took Europe by storm, although the blacks are represented stereotypically. One French critic concluded that American blacks had attained a "pre-eminent" place in music since the war, "for they have impressed the entire world with their vibrating or melancholy rhythms." *(AKG London)*

Individuals in Society

Gustav Stresemann

The German foreign minister Gustav Stresemann (1878–1929) is a controversial historical figure. Hailed by many as a hero of peace, he was denounced as a traitor by radical German nationalists and then by Hitler's Nazis. After World War II, revisionist historians stressed Stresemann's persistent nationalism and cast doubt on his peaceful intentions. Weimar Germany's most renowned leader is a fascinating example of the restless quest for convincing historical interpretation.

Stresemann's origins were modest. His parents were Berlin innkeepers and retailers of bottled beer, and only Gustav of their five children was able to attend high school. Attracted first to literature and history, Stresemann later turned to economics, earned a doctoral degree, and quickly reached the top as a manager and director of German trade associations. A highly intelligent extrovert with a knack for negotiation, Stresemann entered the Reichstag in 1907 as a business-oriented liberal and nationalist. When World War I erupted, he believed, like most Germans, that Germany had acted defensively and was not at fault. He emerged as a strident nationalist and urged German annexation of conquered foreign territories. Germany's collapse in defeat and revolution devastated Stresemann. He seemed a prime candidate for the hateful extremism of the far right.

Yet although Stresemann opposed the Treaty of Versailles as an unjust and unrealistic imposition, he turned back toward the center. He accepted the new Weimar Republic and played a growing role in the Reichstag as the leader of his own small probusiness party. His hour came in the Ruhr crisis, when French and Belgian troops occupied the district. Named chancellor in August 1923, he called off passive resistance and began talks with the French. His government also quelled communist uprisings; put down rebellions in Bavaria, including Hitler's attempted coup; and ended runaway inflation with a new currency. Stresemann fought to preserve German unity, and he succeeded.

Voted out as chancellor in November 1923, Stresemann remained as foreign minister in every government until his death in 1929. Proclaiming a policy of peace and agreeing to pay reparations, he achieved his greatest triumph in the Locarno agreements of 1925 (see page 939). But the interlocking guarantees of existing French and German borders (and the related agreements to resolve peacefully all disputes with Poland and Czechoslovakia) did not lead the French to make any further concessions that might have disarmed Stresemann's extremist foes. Working himself to death, he made little additional progress in achieving international reconciliation and sovereign equality for Germany.

Foreign Minister Gustav Stresemann of Germany (right) *leaves a meeting with Aristide Briand, his French counterpart.* (Corbis)

Stresemann was no fuzzy pacifist. Historians debunking his "legend" are right in seeing an enduring love of nation in his defense of German interests. But Stresemann, like his French counterpart Aristide Briand, was a statesman of goodwill who wanted peace through mutually advantageous compromise. A realist trained by business and politics in the art of the possible, Stresemann also reasoned that Germany had to be a satisfied and equal partner if peace was to be secure. His unwillingness to guarantee Germany's eastern borders (see Map 27.4 on page 915), which is often criticized, reflects his conviction that keeping some Germans under Polish and Czechoslovak rule created a ticking time bomb in Europe. Stresemann was no less convinced that war on Poland would almost certainly re-create the Allied coalition that had crushed Germany in 1918.* His insistence on the necessity of peace in the east as well as the west was prophetic. Hitler's 1939 invasion of Poland resulted in an even mightier coalition that almost annihilated Germany in 1945.

Questions for Analysis

1. What did Gustav Stresemann do to promote reconciliation in Europe? How did his policy toward France differ from that toward Poland and Czechoslovakia?
2. What is your interpretation of Stresemann? Does he arouse your sympathy or your suspicion and hostility? Why?

*Robert Grathwol, "Stresemann: Reflections on His Foreign Policy," *Journal of Modern History* 45 (March 1973): 52–70.

helping maintain social harmony. The great problem was unemployment. Many of Britain's best markets had been lost during the war. In June 1921, almost 2.2 million people—23 percent of the labor force—were out of work, and throughout the 1920s unemployment hovered around 12 percent. Yet the state provided unemployment benefits of equal size to all those without jobs and supplemented those payments with subsidized housing, medical aid, and increased old-age pensions. These and other measures kept living standards from seriously declining, defused class tensions, and pointed the way toward the welfare state Britain established after World War II.

Relative social harmony was accompanied by the rise of the Labour party as a determined champion of the working classes and of greater social equality. Committed to the kind of moderate, "revisionist" socialism that had emerged before World War I (see pages 848–849), the Labour party replaced the Liberal party as the main opposition to the Conservatives. The new prominence of the Labour party reflected the decline of old liberal ideals of competitive capitalism, limited government control, and individual responsibility. In 1924 and 1929, the Labour party under Ramsay MacDonald (1866–1937) governed the country with the support of the smaller Liberal party. Yet Labour moved toward socialism gradually and democratically, so that the middle classes were not overly frightened as the working classes won new benefits.

The Conservatives under Stanley Baldwin (1867–1947) showed the same compromising spirit on social issues. The last line of Baldwin's greatest speech in March 1925 summarized his international and domestic programs: "Give us peace in our time, O Lord." In spite of such conflicts as the 1926 strike by hard-pressed coal miners, which ended in an unsuccessful general strike, social unrest in Britain was limited in the 1920s and in the 1930s as well. In 1922 Britain granted southern, Catholic Ireland full autonomy after a bitter guerrilla war, thereby removing another source of prewar friction. Thus developments in both international relations and the domestic politics of the leading democracies gave cause for optimism in the late 1920s.

The Great Depression, 1929–1939

Like the Great War, the **Great Depression** must be spelled with capital letters. Economic depression was nothing new. Depressions occurred throughout the nineteenth century with predictable regularity, as they recur in the form of recessions and slumps to this day. What was new about this depression was its severity and dura-

tion. It struck the entire world with ever-greater intensity from 1929 to 1933, and recovery was uneven and slow. Only with the Second World War did the depression disappear in much of the world.

The social and political consequences of prolonged economic collapse were enormous. The depression shattered the fragile optimism of political leaders in the late 1920s. Mass unemployment and failing farms made insecurity a reality for millions of ordinary people, who had paid little attention to the intellectual crisis or to new directions in art and ideas (see Map 28.1). In desperation, people looked for leaders who would "do something." They were willing to support radical attempts to deal with the crisis by both democratic leaders and dictators.

The Economic Crisis

There is no agreement among historians and economists about why the Great Depression was so deep and lasted so long. Thus it is best to trace the course of the great collapse before trying to identify what caused it.

Though economic activity was already declining moderately in many countries by early 1929, the crash of the stock market in the United States in October of that year triggered the collapse into the Great Depression. The American economy had prospered in the late 1920s, but there were large inequalities in income and a serious imbalance between "real" investment and stock market speculation. Thus net investment—in factories, farms, equipment, and the like—actually fell from $3.5 billion in 1925 to $3.2 billion in 1929. In the same years, as money flooded into stocks, the value of shares traded on the exchanges soared from $27 billion to $87 billion. As a financial historian concludes in an important new study, "It should have been clear to everybody concerned that a crash was inevitable under such conditions."[11] Of course it was not. Irving Fisher, one of America's most brilliant economists, was highly optimistic in 1929 and fully invested in stocks. He then lost his entire fortune and would have been forced from his house if his university had not bought it and rented it to him.

The American stock market boom was built on borrowed money. Many wealthy investors, speculators, and people of modest means had bought stocks by paying only a small fraction of the total purchase price and borrowing the remainder from their stockbrokers. Such buying "on margin" was extremely dangerous. When prices started falling, the hard-pressed margin buyers either had to put up more money, which was often impossible, or sell their shares to pay off their brokers. Thus thousands of people started selling all at once. The result was a financial

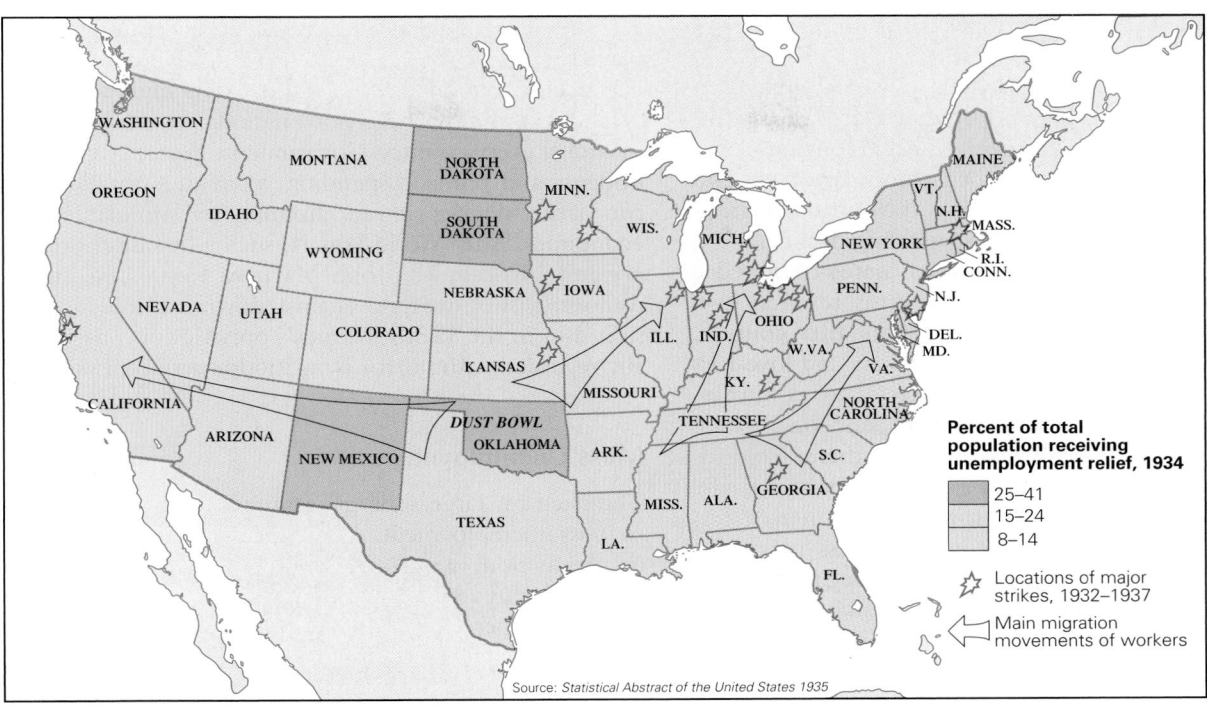

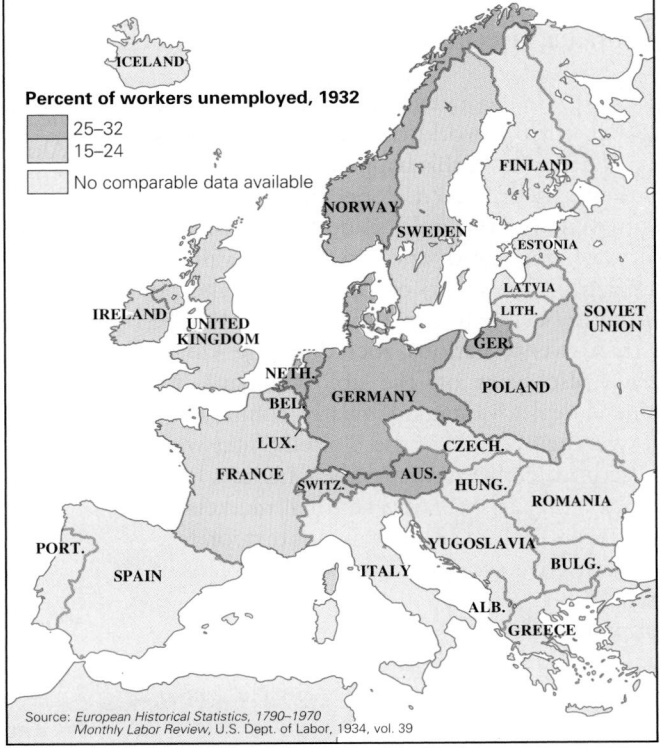

MAP 28.1 The Great Depression in the United States, Britain, and Europe National and regional differences were substantial. Germany, industrial northern Britain, and the American Midwest were particularly hard hit.

panic. Countless investors and speculators were wiped out in a matter of days or weeks.

The general economic consequences were swift and severe. Stripped of wealth and confidence, battered investors and their fellow citizens started buying fewer goods. Prices fell, production began to slow down, and unemployment began to rise. Soon the entire American economy was caught in a vicious, spiraling decline.

The financial panic in the United States triggered a worldwide financial crisis, and that crisis resulted in a drastic decline in production in country after country. Throughout the 1920s, American bankers and investors had lent large amounts of capital to many countries. Many of these loans were short-term, and once panic broke, New York bankers began recalling them. Gold reserves thus began to flow out of European countries, particularly Germany and Austria, toward the United States. It became very hard for European business people to borrow money, and the panicky public began to withdraw its savings from the banks. These banking problems eventually led to the crash of the largest bank in Austria in 1931 and then to general financial chaos. The recall of private loans by American bankers also accelerated the collapse in world prices, as business people around the world dumped industrial goods and agricultural commodities in a frantic attempt to get cash to pay what they owed.

The financial crisis led to a general crisis of production: between 1929 and 1933, world output of goods fell by an estimated 38 percent. As this happened, each country turned inward and tried to go it alone. In 1931, for example, Britain went off the gold standard, refusing to convert bank notes into gold, and reduced the value of its money. Britain's goal was to make its goods cheaper and therefore more salable in the world market. But because more than twenty nations, including the United States in 1934, also went off the gold standard, few countries gained a real advantage. Similarly, country after country followed the example of the United States when in 1930 it raised protective tariffs to their highest levels ever and tried to seal off shrinking national markets for American producers only. Within this context of fragmented and destructive economic nationalism, recovery finally began in 1933.

Although opinions differ, two factors probably best explain the relentless slide to the bottom from 1929 to early 1933. First, the international economy lacked a leadership able to maintain stability when the crisis came. Specifically, as a noted American economic historian concludes, the seriously weakened British, the traditional leaders of the world economy, "couldn't and the United States wouldn't" stabilize the international economic system in 1929.[12] The United States, which had momentarily played a positive role after the occupation of the Ruhr, cut back its international lending and erected high tariffs.

The second factor was poor national economic policy in almost every country. Governments generally cut their budgets and reduced spending when they should have run large deficits in an attempt to stimulate their economies. After World War II, such a "counter-cyclical policy," advocated by John Maynard Keynes, became a well-established weapon against downturn and depression. But in the 1930s, Keynes's prescription was generally regarded with horror by orthodox economists.

Mass Unemployment

The need for large-scale government spending was tied to mass unemployment. As the financial crisis led to cuts in production, workers lost their jobs and had little money to buy goods. In Britain unemployment had averaged 12 percent in the 1920s; between 1930 and 1935, it averaged more than 18 percent. Far worse was the case of the United States, where unemployment had averaged only 5 percent in the 1920s. In 1932 unemployment soared to about 33 percent of the entire labor force: 14 million people were out of work (see Map 28.1). Only by pumping new money into the economy could the government increase demand and break the vicious cycle of decline.

Along with economic effects, mass unemployment posed a great social problem. Poverty increased dramatically, although in most countries unemployed workers generally received some kind of meager unemployment benefits or public aid that prevented starvation. (See the feature "Listening to the Past: Life on the Dole in Great Britain" on pages 950–951.) Millions of people lost their spirit, condemned to an apparently hopeless search for work or to idle boredom. Homes and ways of life were disrupted in millions of personal tragedies. Young people postponed marriages, and birthrates fell sharply. There was an increase in suicide and mental illness. Poverty or the threat of poverty became a grinding reality. In 1932 the workers of Manchester, England, appealed to their city officials—a typical plea echoed throughout the Western world:

We tell you that thousands of people . . . are in desperate straits. We tell you that men, women, and children are going hungry. . . . We tell you that great numbers are being rendered distraught through the stress and worry of trying to exist without work. . . .

If you do not do this—if you do not provide useful work for the unemployed—what, we ask, is your alternative? Do not

Isaac Soyer: Employment Agency (1937)   The frustration and agony of looking for work against long odds are painfully evident in this American masterpiece. The time-killing, pensive resignation, and dejection seen in the three figures are only aspects of the larger problem. One of three talented brothers born in Russia and trained as artists in New York, Isaac Soyer worked in the tradition of American realism and concentrated on people and the influence of their environment. *(Oil on canvas, 34¼ × 45 in. Collection of Whitney Museum of American Art, Purchase 37.44)*

imagine that this colossal tragedy of unemployment is going on endlessly without some fateful catastrophe. Hungry men are angry men.[13]

Only strong government action could deal with mass unemployment, a social powder keg preparing to explode.

The New Deal in the United States

Of all the major industrial countries, only Germany was harder hit by the Great Depression, or reacted more radically to it, than the United States. Depression was so traumatic in the United States because the 1920s had

been a period of complacent optimism. The Great Depression and the response to it marked a major turning point in American history.

President Herbert Hoover (1895–1972) and his administration initially reacted to the stock market crash and economic decline with dogged optimism and limited action. But when the full force of the financial crisis struck Europe in the summer of 1931 and boomeranged back to the United States, people's worst fears became reality. Banks failed; unemployment soared. Between 1929 and 1932, industrial production fell by about 50 percent.

In these tragic circumstances, Franklin Delano Roosevelt (1882–1945), an inspiring wheelchair-bound aristocrat previously crippled by polio, won a landslide electoral victory in 1932 with grand but vague promises of a "**New Deal** for the forgotten man."

Roosevelt's basic goal was to reform capitalism in order to preserve it. Roosevelt rejected socialism and government ownership of industry in 1933. To right the situation, he chose forceful government intervention in the economy.

In this choice, Roosevelt was flexible, pragmatic, and willing to experiment. He and his "brain trust" of advisers adopted policies echoing the American experience in World War I, when the American economy had been thoroughly planned and regulated.

Innovative programs promoted agricultural recovery, a top priority. Almost half of the American population still lived in rural areas, and American farmers were hard hit by the depression. Roosevelt's decision to leave the gold standard and devalue the dollar was designed to raise American prices and rescue farmers. The Agricultural Adjustment Act of 1933 also aimed at raising prices and farm income by limiting production. These planning measures worked for a while, and farmers repaid Roosevelt in 1936 with overwhelming support.

The most ambitious attempt to control and plan the economy was the National Recovery Administration (NRA). Intended to reduce competition and fix prices and wages for everyone's benefit, the NRA broke with the cherished American tradition of free competition and aroused conflicts among business people, consumers, and bureaucrats. It did not work well and was declared unconstitutional in 1935.

Roosevelt and his advisers then attacked the key problem of mass unemployment directly. The federal government accepted the responsibility of employing directly as many people as financially possible. New agencies were created to undertake a vast range of projects. The most famous of these was the Works Progress Administration (**WPA**), set up in 1935. One-fifth of the entire labor force worked for the WPA at some point in the 1930s, constructing public buildings, bridges, and highways. The WPA was enormously popular, and the hope of a government job helped check the threat of social revolution in the United States.

Relief programs like the WPA were part of the New Deal's most fundamental commitment, the commitment to use the federal government to provide for the welfare of all Americans. This commitment marked a profound shift from the traditional stress on family support and community responsibility. Embraced by a large majority in the 1930s, this shift in attitudes proved to be one of the New Deal's most enduring legacies.

Other social measures aimed in the same direction. Following the path blazed by Germany's Bismarck in the 1880s, the U.S. government in 1935 established a national social security system, with old-age pensions and unemployment benefits, to protect many workers against some of life's uncertainties. The National Labor Relations Act of 1935 gave union organizers the green light by declaring collective bargaining to be the policy of the United States. Union membership more than doubled, from 4 million in 1935 to 9 million in 1940. In general, between 1935 and 1938 government rulings and social reforms chipped away at the privileges of the wealthy and tried to help ordinary people.

Yet despite undeniable accomplishments in social reform, the New Deal was only partly successful as a response to the Great Depression. At the height of the recovery in May 1937, 7 million workers were still unemployed, as opposed to a high of 15 million in 1933. The economic situation then worsened seriously in the recession of 1937 and 1938, and unemployment was still a staggering 10 million when war broke out in Europe in September 1939. The New Deal never did pull the United States out of the depression.

The Scandinavian Response to the Depression

Of all the Western democracies, the Scandinavian countries under Social Democratic leadership responded most successfully to the challenge of the Great Depression. Having grown steadily in number in the late nineteenth century, the **Social Democrats** became the largest political party in Sweden and then in Norway after the First World War. In the 1920s, they passed important social reform legislation for both peasants and workers, gained practical administrative experience, and developed a unique kind of socialism. Flexible and nonrevolutionary, Scandinavian socialism grew out of a strong tradition of cooperative community action. Even before 1900, Scandinavian agricultural cooperatives had shown how individual peasant families could join together for everyone's benefit. Labor leaders and capitalists were also inclined to work together.

When the economic crisis struck in 1929, socialist governments in Scandinavia built on this pattern of cooperative social action. Sweden in particular pioneered in the use of large-scale deficits to finance public works and thereby maintain production and employment. Scandinavian governments also increased social welfare benefits, from old-age pensions and unemployment insurance to subsidized housing and maternity allowances. All this spending required a large bureaucracy and high taxes,

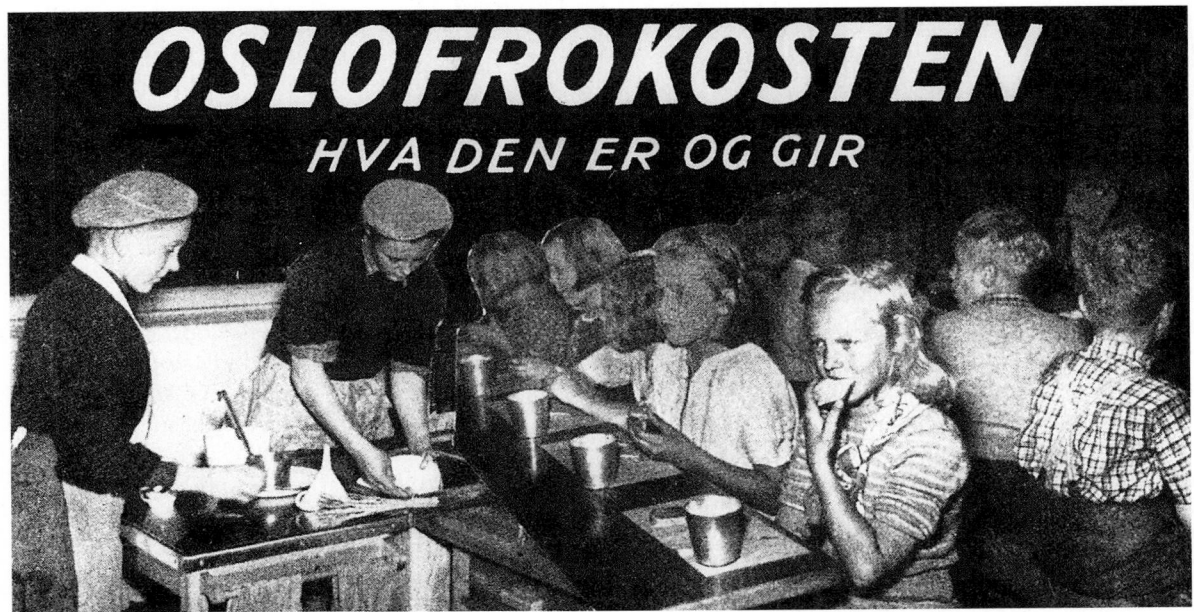

Oslo Breakfast   Scandinavian socialism championed cooperation and practical welfare measures, playing down strident rhetoric and theories of class conflict. The Oslo Breakfast exemplified the Scandinavian approach. It provided every schoolchild in the Norwegian capital with a good breakfast free of charge. *(Universitets-biblioteket i Oslo)*

first on the rich and then on practically everyone. Yet both private and cooperative enterprise thrived, as did democracy. Some observers saw Scandinavia's welfare socialism as an appealing "middle way" between sick capitalism and cruel communism or fascism.

Recovery and Reform in Britain and France

In Britain MacDonald's Labour government and then, after 1931, the Conservative-dominated coalition government followed orthodox economic theory. The budget was balanced, but unemployed workers received barely enough welfare to live. Despite government lethargy, the economy recovered considerably after 1932. By 1937 total production was about 20 percent higher than in 1929. In fact, for Britain the years after 1932 were actually somewhat better than the 1920s had been, quite the opposite of the situation in the United States and France.

This good but by no means brilliant performance reflected the gradual reorientation of the British economy. After going off the gold standard in 1931 and establishing protective tariffs in 1932, Britain concentrated increasingly on the national, rather than the international, market. The old export industries of the Industrial Revo-lution, such as textiles and coal, continued to decline, but new industries, such as automobiles and electrical appliances, grew in response to British home demand. Moreover, low interest rates encouraged a housing boom. By the end of the decade, there were highly visible differences between the old, depressed industrial areas of the north and the new, growing areas of the south. These developments encouraged Britain to look inward and avoid unpleasant foreign questions.

Because France was relatively less industrialized and more isolated from the world economy, the Great Depression came late. But once the depression hit France, it stayed and stayed. Decline was steady until 1935, and a short-lived recovery never brought production or employment back up to predepression levels. Economic stagnation both reflected and heightened an ongoing political crisis. There was no stability in government. As before 1914, the French parliament was made up of many political parties, which could never cooperate for very long. In 1933, for example, five coalition cabinets formed and fell in rapid succession.

The French lost the underlying unity that had made government instability bearable before 1914. Fascist-type organizations agitated against parliamentary democracy and looked to Mussolini's Italy and Hitler's Germany for inspiration. In February 1934, French fascists and semifascists rioted and threatened to overturn the republic. At the same time, the Communist party and many workers opposed to the existing system were looking to Stalin's Russia for guidance. The vital center of moderate republicanism was sapped from both sides.

Frightened by the growing strength of the fascists at home and abroad, the Communists, the Socialists, and the Radicals formed an alliance—the **Popular Front**—for the national elections of May 1936. Their clear victory reflected the trend toward polarization. The number of Communists in the parliament jumped dramatically from 10 to 72, while the Socialists, led by Léon Blum, became the strongest party in France, with 146 seats. The really quite moderate Radicals slipped badly, and the conservatives lost ground to the semifascists.

In the next few months, Blum's Popular Front government made the first and only real attempt to deal with the social and economic problems of the 1930s in France. Inspired by Roosevelt's New Deal, the Popular Front encouraged the union movement and launched a far-reaching program of social reform, complete with paid vacations and a forty-hour workweek. Popular with workers and the lower middle class, these measures were quickly sabotaged by rapid inflation and cries of revolution from fascists and frightened conservatives. Wealthy people sneaked their money out of the country, labor unrest grew, and France entered a severe financial crisis. Blum was forced to announce a "breathing spell" in social reform.

The fires of political dissension were also fanned by civil war in Spain. Communists demanded that France support the Spanish republicans, while many French conservatives would gladly have joined Hitler and Mussolini in aiding the attack of Spanish fascists. Extremism grew, and France itself was within sight of civil war. Blum was forced to resign in June 1937, and the Popular Front quickly collapsed. An anxious and divided France drifted aimlessly once again, preoccupied by Hitler and German rearmament.

Summary

After the First World War, Western society entered a complex and difficult era—truly an age of anxiety. Intellectual life underwent a crisis marked by pessimism, uncertainty, and fascination with irrational forces. Ceaseless experimentation and rejection of old forms characterized art and music, while motion pictures and radio provided a new, standardized entertainment for the masses. Intellectual and artistic developments that had been confined to small avant-garde groups before 1914, along with the insecure state of mind they expressed, gained wider currency.

Politics and economics were similarly disrupted. In the 1920s, political leaders groped to create an enduring peace and rebuild the prewar prosperity, and for a brief period late in the decade, they even seemed to have succeeded. Then the Great Depression shattered that fragile stability. Uncertainty returned with redoubled force in the 1930s. The international economy collapsed, and unemployment struck millions worldwide. The democracies turned inward as they sought to cope with massive domestic problems and widespread disillusionment. Generally speaking, they were not very successful, although relief measures and social concern eased distress and prevented revolutions in the leading Western nations. The old liberal ideals of individual rights and responsibilities, elected government, and economic freedom declined and seemed outmoded to many. And in many countries of central and eastern Europe, these ideas were abandoned completely, as we shall see in the next chapter.

Key Terms

logical empiricism	dadaism
existentialism	Dawes Plan
neutron	*Mein Kampf*
id, ego, and superego	Great Depression
stream-of-consciousness	New Deal
technique	WPA
functionalism	Social Democrats
Bauhaus	Popular Front

Notes

1. P. Valéry, *Variety,* trans. M. Cowley (New York: Harcourt Brace, 1927), pp. 27–28.
2. Quoted in S. Hughes, *The Obstructed Path: French Social Thought in the Years of Desperation, 1930–1960* (New York: Harper & Row, 1967), p. 82.
3. G. Greene, *Another Mexico* (New York: Viking Press, 1939), p. 3.
4. G. Orwell, *1984* (New York: New American Library, 1950), p. 220.
5. C. E. Jeanneret-Gris (Le Corbusier), *Towards a New Architecture* (London: J. Rodker, 1931), p. 15.
6. Quoted in A. H. Barr, Jr., *What Is Modern Painting?* 9th ed. (New York: Museum of Modern Art, 1966), p. 27.
7. Quoted ibid., p. 25.
8. R. Graves and A. Hodge, *The Long Week End: A Social History of Great Britain, 1918–1939* (New York: Macmillan, 1941), p. 131.
9. Quoted in A. Briggs, *The Birth of Broadcasting,* vol. 1 (London: Oxford University Press, 1961), p. 47.
10. Quoted in R. J. Sontag, *A Broken World, 1919–1939* (New York: Harper & Row, 1971), p. 129.
11. Dietmar Rothermund, *The Global Impact of the Great Depression, 1929–1939* (London and New York: Routledge, 1996), p. 50.

12. C. P. Kindleberger, *The World in Depression, 1929–1939* (Berkeley and Los Angeles: University of California Press, 1973), p. 292.
13. Quoted in S. B. Clough et al., eds., *Economic History of Europe: Twentieth Century* (New York: Harper & Row, 1968), pp. 243–245.

▌Suggested Reading

A. Bullock, ed., *The Twentieth Century* (1971), is particularly noteworthy because it is a lavish visual feast combined with penetrating essays on major developments. Two excellent accounts of contemporary history—one with a liberal and the other with a conservative point of view—are R. Paxton, *Europe in the Twentieth Century,* 3d ed. (1997), and P. Johnson, *Modern Times: The World from the Twenties to the Eighties* (1983). R. Clark, *Hope and Glory: Britain, 1900–1990* (1996), and J. McMillan, *Twentieth-Century France: Politics and Society, 1898–1991* (1992), are two recommended national surveys. Crucial changes in thought before and after World War I are discussed in three rewarding intellectual histories: S. Kern, *The Culture of Time and Space, 1880–1918* (1983); M. Berman, *All That Is Solid Melts into Air: The Experience of Modernity* (1982); and G. Masur, *Prophets of Yesterday* (1961). M. Biddiss, *Age of the Masses: Ideas and Society Since 1870* (1977), is stimulating and useful. R. Stromberg, *European Intellectual History Since 1789* (1986), is a clear general account. W. Kaufmann, *Nietzsche* (1974), is a sympathetic and justly famous older study, and S. Aschheim, *The Nietzsche Legacy in Germany, 1890–1990* (1992), considers the range of responses to the pioneering philosopher.

N. Cantor, *The American Century: Varieties of Culture in Modern Times* (1997), is a pugnacious and stimulating survey. J. Rewald, *The History of Impressionism* (1961), and R. Golan, *Modernity and Nostalgia: Art and Politics in France Between the Wars* (1995), are excellent and also reflect changing tastes in art history. H. Jaffé, *Pablo Picasso* (1982), is a visual feast and highly recommended. Barr, cited in the Notes, is helpful. P. Collaer, *A History of Modern Music* (1961), and H. R. Hitchcock, *Architecture: Nineteenth and Twentieth Centuries* (1958), are good introductions, whereas T. Wolfe, *From Bauhaus to My House* (1981), is a lively critique of modern architecture. L. Barnett, *The Universe and Dr. Einstein* (1952), is a fascinating study of the new physics. A. Storr, *Freud* (1989), and P. Rieff, *Freud* (1956), consider the man and how his theories have stood the test of time. S. Freud, *Civilization and Its Discontents* (1930), which is highly recommended, explores Freud's theory of instinct and repression, arguing that society's necessary repression of instinctual drives will always leave people unhappy. M. White, ed., *The Age of Analysis* (1955), opens up basic questions of twentieth-century psychology and philosophy. T. Judt, *The Burden of Responsibility: Blum, Camus, Aron, and the French Twentieth Century* (1998), probes the moral and intellectual issues of the modern age. H. Liebersohn, *Fate and Utopia in German Sociology* (1988), analyzes developments in German social science. J. Willett, *The New Sobriety: Art and Politics in the Weimar Period, 1917–1933* (1978), considers the artistic renaissance and the political culture in Germany in the 1920s. M. Marrus, ed., *Emergence of Leisure* (1974), is a pioneering inquiry into an important aspect of mass culture. H. Daniels-Rops, *A Fight for God,* 2 vols. (1966), is a sympathetic history of the Catholic church between 1870 and 1939.

G. Ambrosius and W. Hibbard, *A Social and Economic History of Twentieth-Century Europe* (1989), and F. Tipton and R. Aldrich, *An Economic and Social History of Europe, 1890–1939* (1987), are recommended and interesting to compare. P. Fritzsche, *Rehearsals for Fascism: Populism and Political Mobilization in Weimar Germany* (1990), R. Wohl, *The Generation of 1914* (1979), and R. Kuisel, *Capital and State in Modern France: Renovation and Economic Management* (1982), are three important studies on aspects of the postwar challenge. J. Jacobson, *Locarno Diplomacy: Germany and the West, 1925–1929* (1972), is a superb study of Stresemann and enduring tensions after the Locarno breakthrough. B. Martin, *France and the Après Guerre: Illusions and Disillusionments* (1999), is a solid work with masterful portraits of key figures. S. Reynolds, *France Between the Wars: Gender and Politics* (1996), and J. Keiger, *Raymond Poincaré* (1996), are major reconsiderations of French politics from different perspectives. H. James, *The German Slump: Politics and Economics, 1924–1936* (1986), is an excellent analysis of economic recovery and subsequent collapse. M. Childs, *Sweden: The Middle Way* (1961), applauds Sweden's efforts at social reform. O. and L. Handlin, *Liberty in America Since 1600,* vol. 4 (1994), argues that the United States has erred in moving from equality of opportunity to equality of results since 1920. In addition to the contemporary works discussed in the text, the crisis of the interwar period comes alive in R. Crossman, ed., *The God That Failed* (1950), in which famous Western writers tell why they were attracted to and later repelled by communism; J. Ortega y Gasset's renowned *The Revolt of the Masses* (1932); and F. A. Hayek's *The Road to Serfdom* (1944), a famous warning of the dangers to democratic freedoms.

In addition to Rothermund's and Kindleberger's excellent studies of the Great Depression cited in the Notes, P. Temin, *Lessons from the Great Depression* (1987), is a judicious evaluation by an outstanding economic historian. J. Garraty, *Unemployment in History* (1978), is noteworthy, though novels best portray the human tragedy of economic decline. W. Holtby, *South Riding* (1936), and W. Greenwood, *Love on the Dole* (1933), are moving stories of the Great Depression in England. Hans Fallada, *Little Man, What Now?* (1932), is the classic counterpart for Germany. Also highly recommended as commentaries on English life between the wars are N. Gray, *The Worst of Times: An Oral History of the Great Depression in Britain* (1985), and George Orwell, *The Road to Wigan Pier* (1972). Among French novelists, André Gide painstakingly examines the French middle class and its values in *The Counterfeiters;* Albert Camus, the greatest of the existential novelists, is at his unforgettable best in *The Stranger* (1942) and *The Plague* (1947).

Life on the Dole in Great Britain

*P*eriodic surges in unemployment were an old
story in capitalist economies, but the long-term
joblessness of millions in the Great Depression was
something new and unexpected. In Britain especially,
where the depression followed a weak postwar
recovery, large numbers suffered involuntary idleness
for years at a time. Whole families lived "on the dole,"
the weekly welfare benefits paid by the government.

*One of the most insightful accounts of unemployed
workers was written by the British journalist and
novelist George Orwell (1903–1950), who studied
the conditions in northern England and wrote* The
Road to Wigan Pier *(1937). An independent
socialist who distrusted rigid Marxism, Orwell
believed that socialism could triumph in Britain
if it came to mean "justice and liberty" for a
commonsense majority. Orwell's disillusionment with
authoritarian socialism and communism pervades his
most famous work,* 1984 *(1949).*

When you see the unemployment figures quoted
at two millions, it is fatally easy to take this as
meaning that two million people are out of work
and the rest of the population is comparatively
comfortable. . . . [Adding in the destitute,] you
might take the number of underfed people in England (for *everyone* on the dole or thereabouts is
underfed) as being, at the very most, five millions.

This is an enormous under-estimate, because, in
the first place, the only people shown on
unemployment figures are those actually drawing
the dole—that is, in general, heads of families. An
unemployed man's dependants do not figure on
the list unless they too are drawing a separate
allowance. . . . In addition there are great
numbers of people who are in work but who,
from a financial point of view, might equally be
unemployed, because they are not drawing
anything that can be described as a living wage.
Allow for these and their dependants, throw in as

before the old-age pensioners, the destitute and
other nondescripts, and you get an *underfed*
population of well over ten millions. . . .

Take the figures for Wigan, which is typical
enough of the industrial and mining districts. . . .
The total population of Wigan is a little under
87,000; so that at any moment more than one
person in three out of the whole population—not
merely the registered workers—is either drawing
or living on the dole. . . .

Nevertheless, in spite of the frightful extent of
unemployment, it is a fact that poverty—extreme
poverty—is less in evidence in the industrial North
than it is in London. Everything is poorer and
shabbier, there are fewer motor-cars and fewer
well-dressed people; but also there are fewer
people who are obviously destitute. . . . In the
industrial towns the old communal way of life has
not yet broken up, tradition is still strong and
almost everyone has a family—potentially,
therefore, a home. In a town of 50,000 or
100,000 inhabitants there is no casual and as it
were unaccounted-for population; nobody
sleeping in the streets, for instance. Moreover,
there is just this to be said for the unemployment
regulations, that they do not discourage people
from marrying. A man and wife on twenty-three
shillings a week are not far from the starvation line,
but they can make a home of sorts; they are vastly
better off than a single man on fifteen shillings. . . .

But there is no doubt about the deadening,
debilitating effect of unemployment upon
everybody, married or single, and upon men more
than upon women. . . . Everyone who saw
Greenwood's play *Love on the Dole* must remember
that dreadful moment when the poor, good, stupid
working man beats on the table and cries out, "O
God, send me some work!" This was not dramatic
exaggeration, it was a touch from life. That cry
must have been uttered, in almost those words, in
tens of thousands, perhaps hundreds of thousands
of English homes, during the past fifteen years.

But, I think not again—or at least, not so often. . . . When people live on the dole for years at a time they grow used to it, and drawing the dole, though it remains unpleasant, ceases to be shameful. Thus the old, independent, workhouse-fearing tradition is undermined. . . .

So you have whole populations settling down, as it were, to a lifetime of the P.A.C. . . . Take, for instance, the fact that the working class think nothing of getting married on the dole. . . . Life is still fairly normal, more normal than one really has the right to expect. Families are impoverished, but the family-system has not broken up. The people are in effect living a reduced version of their former lives. Instead of raging against their destiny they have made things tolerable by lowering their standards.

But they don't necessarily lower their standards by cutting out luxuries and concentrating on necessities; more often it is the other way about—the more natural way, if you come to think of it. Hence the fact that in a decade of unparalleled depression, the consumption of all cheap luxuries has increased. The two things that have probably made the greatest difference of all are the movies and the mass-production of cheap smart clothes since the war. The youth who leaves school at fourteen and gets a blind-alley job is out of work at twenty, probably for life; but for two pounds ten on the hire-purchase system he can buy himself a suit which, for a little while and at a little distance, looks as though it had been tailored in Savile Row. The girl can look like a fashion plate at an even lower price. . . . You can stand on the street corner, indulging in a private daydream of yourself as Clark Gable or Greta Garbo, which compensates you for a great deal. . . .

Trade since the war has had to adjust itself to meet the demands of underpaid, underfed people, with the result that a luxury is nowadays almost always cheaper than a necessity. One pair of plain solid shoes costs as much as two ultra-smart pairs. . . . And above all there is gambling, the cheapest of all luxuries. Even people on the verge of starvation can buy a few days' hope ("Something to live for," as they call it) by having a penny on a sweepstake. . . . Twenty million people are underfed but literally everyone in England has access to a radio. What we have lost in food we have gained in electricity. Whole sections of the working class who have been plundered of all they really need are being compensated, in part, by cheap luxuries which mitigate the surface of life.

Do you consider all this desirable? No, I don't. But it may be that the psychological adjustment

Poster used in the election campaign of 1931, when unemployment rose to a new record high. (*Conservative Research Department/The Bridgeman Art Library International Ltd*)

which the working class are visibly making is the best they could make in the circumstances. They have neither turned revolutionary nor lost their self-respect; merely they have kept their tempers and settled down to make the best of things on a fish-and-chip standard. The alternative would be God knows what continued agonies of despair; or it might be attempted insurrections which, in a strongly governed country like England, could only lead to futile massacres and a régime of savage repression.

Questions for Analysis

1. According to Orwell, "extreme poverty" was less visible in the northern industrial towns than in London. Were family relations important in this regard?

2. What were the consequences of long-term unemployment for English workers? Were some of the consequences surprising?

3. Judging from Orwell's description, did radical revolution seem likely in England in the Great Depression? Why or why not?

Source: Excerpts from Chapter V in *The Road to Wigan Pier* by George Orwell, copyright © 1958 and renewed 1986 by the Estate of Sonia B. Orwell. Reprinted by permission of Harcourt, Inc.

Hugo Jager's photograph of a crowd of enthusiastic Hitler supporters.
(Hugo Jager, Life Magazine, © Time Inc.)

29 Dictatorships and the Second World War

chapter outline

- Authoritarian States

- Stalin's Soviet Union

- Mussolini and Fascism in Italy

- Hitler and Nazism in Germany

- Nazi Expansion and the Second World War

*T*he era of anxiety and economic depression was also a time of growing strength for political dictatorship. Popularly elected governments and basic civil liberties declined drastically in Europe. On the eve of the Second World War, liberal democratic governments were surviving only in Great Britain, France, the Low Countries, the Scandinavian nations, and Switzerland. Elsewhere in Europe, various kinds of "strongmen" ruled. Dictatorship seemed the wave of the future. Thus the intellectual and economic crisis discussed in Chapter 28 and the decline in liberal political institutions and rise of dictatorship to be considered in this chapter were interrelated elements in the general crisis of European civilization.

The era of dictatorship is a highly disturbing chapter in the history of Western civilization. The key development was not only the resurgence of authoritarian rule but also the rise of a particularly ruthless and dynamic tyranny. This new kind of tyranny reached its full realization in the Soviet Union and Nazi Germany in the 1930s. Stalin and Hitler mobilized their peoples for enormous undertakings and ruled with unprecedented severity. Hitler's mobilization was ultimately directed toward racial aggression and territorial expansion, and his sudden attack on Poland in 1939 started World War II.

Nazi armies were defeated by a great coalition, and today we want to believe that the era of totalitarian dictatorship was a terrible accident, that Stalin's slave-labor camps and Hitler's gas chambers "can't happen again." Yet the cruel truth is that horrible atrocities continue to plague the world in our time. The Khmer Rouge inflicted genocide on its people in Kampuchea, and civil war in Bosnia and in Rwanda led to racially motivated atrocities recalling the horrors of World War II. And there are other examples. Thus it is all the more vital that we understand Europe's era of brutal and aggressive dictatorship in order to guard against the possibility of its recurrence in the future.

- What was the nature of twentieth-century dictatorship and authoritarian rule?
- How did people live in the most extreme states—the Soviet Union and Nazi Germany?
- How did the rise of aggressive dictatorships result in another world war?

These are among the questions this chapter will seek to answer.

953

Authoritarian States

Both conservative and radical dictatorships swept through Europe in the 1920s and 1930s. Although these two types of dictatorship shared some characteristics and sometimes overlapped in practice, they were in essence profoundly different. Conservative authoritarian regimes were an old story in Europe. Radical, totalitarian dictatorships were a new and frightening development.

Conservative Authoritarianism

The traditional form of antidemocratic government in European history was conservative authoritarianism. Like Catherine the Great in Russia and Metternich in Austria, the leaders of such governments tried to prevent major changes that would undermine the existing social order. To do so, they relied on obedient bureaucracies, vigilant police departments, and trustworthy armies. Popular participation in government was forbidden or limited to such natural allies as landlords, bureaucrats, and high church officials. Liberals, democrats, and socialists were persecuted as subversive radicals, often finding themselves in jail or exile.

Yet old-fashioned authoritarian governments were limited in their power and in their objectives. They had neither the ability nor the desire to control many aspects of their subjects' lives. Nor did they wish to do so. Preoccupied with the goal of mere survival, these governments largely limited their demands to taxes, army recruits, and passive acceptance. As long as the people did not try to change the system, they often had considerable personal independence.

After the First World War, this kind of authoritarian government revived, especially in the less-developed eastern part of Europe. There the parliamentary regimes that had been founded on the wreckage of empires in 1918 fell one by one. By early 1938, only economically and socially advanced Czechoslovakia remained true to liberal political ideals. Conservative dictators also took over in Spain and Portugal.

There were several reasons for this development. These lands lacked a strong tradition of self-government, with its necessary restraint and compromise. Moreover, many of these new states, such as Yugoslavia, were torn by ethnic conflicts that threatened their very existence. Dictatorship appealed to nationalists and military leaders as a way to repress such tensions and preserve national unity. Large landowners and the church were still powerful forces in these largely agrarian areas, and they often looked to dictators to save them from progressive land reform or communist agrarian upheaval. So did some members of the middle class, which was small and weak in eastern Europe. Finally, though some kind of democracy managed to stagger through the 1920s in Austria, Bulgaria, Romania, Greece, Estonia, and Latvia, the Great Depression delivered the final blow to those countries by 1936.

Although some of the conservative authoritarian regimes adopted certain Hitlerian and fascist characteristics in the 1930s, their general aims were limited. They were concerned more with maintaining the status quo than with forcing society into rapid change or war. This tradition continued into the late twentieth century, especially in some of the military dictatorships that ruled in Latin America until the late 1980s.

Radical Totalitarian Dictatorships

Conservative authoritarianism predominated in the smaller states of central and eastern Europe by the mid-1930s, but a new kind of radical dictatorship emerged in the Soviet Union, Germany, and, to a lesser extent, Italy. Almost all scholars agree that the leaders of these radical dictatorships violently rejected parliamentary restraint and liberal values. Scholars also agree that these dictatorships exercised unprecedented control over the masses and sought to mobilize them for action. However, there has always been controversy over the interpretation of these regimes.

One extremely useful approach relates the radical dictatorships to the rise of modern totalitarianism. The concept of **totalitarianism** emerged in the 1920s and 1930s, although it is frequently and mistakenly seen as developing only after 1945 as part of anti-Soviet propaganda during the cold war. In 1924 Benito Mussolini spoke of the "fierce totalitarian will" of his movement in Italy. In the 1930s more and more British, American, and German exiled writers used the concept of totalitarianism to describe what they saw happening before their eyes. They linked Italian and especially German fascism with Soviet communism in "a 'new kind of state' that could be called totalitarian." With the alliance between Hitler and Stalin in 1939, "all doubts" about the totalitarian nature of both dictatorships "were swept away for most Americans."[1]

Early writers believed that modern totalitarian dictatorship burst on the scene with the revolutionary total war effort of 1914–1918. The war called forth a tendency to subordinate all institutions and all classes to the state in order to achieve one supreme objective: victory. As the French thinker Elie Halévy put it in 1936 in his

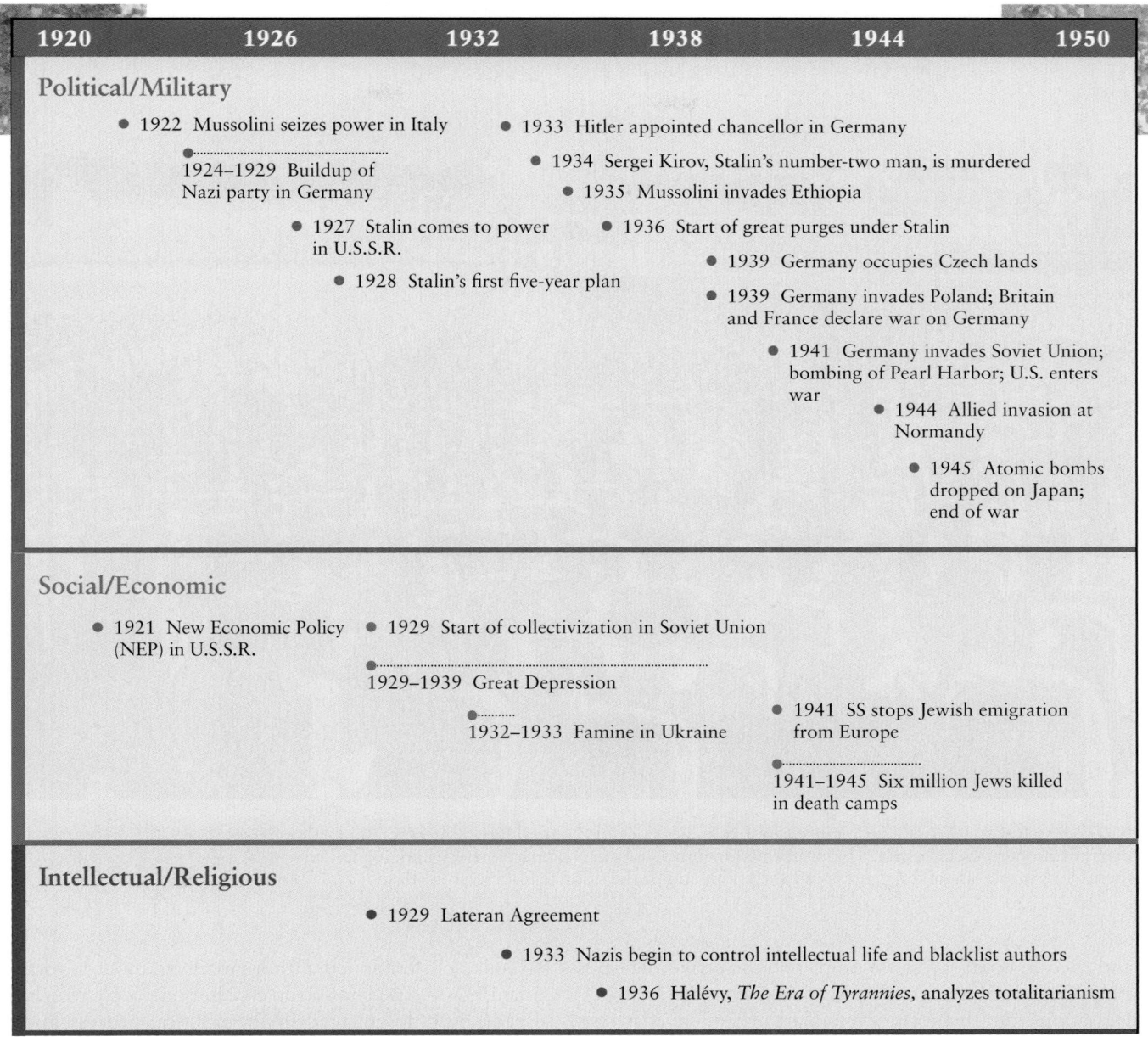

1920	1926	1932	1938	1944	1950

Political/Military

- 1922 Mussolini seizes power in Italy
- 1924–1929 Buildup of Nazi party in Germany
- 1927 Stalin comes to power in U.S.S.R.
- 1928 Stalin's first five-year plan
- 1933 Hitler appointed chancellor in Germany
- 1934 Sergei Kirov, Stalin's number-two man, is murdered
- 1935 Mussolini invades Ethiopia
- 1936 Start of great purges under Stalin
- 1939 Germany occupies Czech lands
- 1939 Germany invades Poland; Britain and France declare war on Germany
- 1941 Germany invades Soviet Union; bombing of Pearl Harbor; U.S. enters war
- 1944 Allied invasion at Normandy
- 1945 Atomic bombs dropped on Japan; end of war

Social/Economic

- 1921 New Economic Policy (NEP) in U.S.S.R.
- 1929 Start of collectivization in Soviet Union
- 1929–1939 Great Depression
- 1932–1933 Famine in Ukraine
- 1941 SS stops Jewish emigration from Europe
- 1941–1945 Six million Jews killed in death camps

Intellectual/Religious

- 1929 Lateran Agreement
- 1933 Nazis begin to control intellectual life and blacklist authors
- 1936 Halévy, *The Era of Tyrannies,* analyzes totalitarianism

influential *The Era of Tyrannies,* the varieties of modern totalitarian tyranny—fascism, Nazism, and communism—could be thought of as "feuding brothers" with a common father: the nature of modern war.[2]

Writers such as Halévy believed that the crucial experience of World War I was carried further by Lenin and the Bolsheviks during the Russian civil war. Lenin showed how a dedicated minority could achieve victory over a less determined majority and subordinate institutions and human rights to the needs of a single group—the

Communist party—and its leader. Providing a model for single-party dictatorship, Lenin inspired imitators, including Adolf Hitler. The modern totalitarian state reached maturity in the 1930s in the Stalinist U.S.S.R. and Nazi Germany.

Embellishing on early insights, numerous Western political scientists and historians argued in the 1950s and 1960s that the totalitarian state used modern technology and communications to exercise complete political power. But it did not stop there. Increasingly, the state took over

Nazi Mass Rally, 1936   This picture captures the essence of the totalitarian interpretation of dynamic modern dictatorship. The uniformed members of the Nazi party have willingly merged themselves into a single force and await the command of the godlike leader. *(Wide World Photos)*

and tried to control just as completely the economic, social, intellectual, and cultural aspects of people's lives. Deviation from the norm, even in art or family behavior, could become a crime. In theory, nothing was politically neutral; nothing was outside the scope of the state.

This vision of total state represented a radical revolt against liberalism. Classical liberalism (see page 762) sought to limit the power of the state and protect the rights of the individual. Moreover, liberals stood for rationality, peaceful progress, economic freedom, and a strong middle class. All of that disgusted totalitarians as sentimental slop. They believed in willpower, preached conflict, and worshiped violence. The individual was infinitely less valuable than the state, and there were no lasting rights, only temporary rewards for loyal and effective service.

Unlike old-fashioned authoritarianism, modern totalitarianism was based not on an elite but on people who had already become engaged in the political process, most notably through commitment to nationalism and socialism. Thus totalitarian societies were fully mobilized societies moving toward some goal and possessing boundless dynamism. As soon as one goal was achieved at the cost of enormous sacrifice, another arose at the leader's command to take its place. Thus totalitarianism was a *permanent* revolution, an *unfinished* revolution, in which rapid, profound change imposed from on high went on forever.

In developing the concept of totalitarianism, scholars recognized that there were major differences between Stalin's communist U.S.S.R. and Hitler's Nazi Germany. Soviet communism, growing out of Marxian socialism, seized all private property (except personal property) for the state and crushed the middle classes. Nazi Germany, growing out of extreme nationalism and racism, criticized big landowners and industrialists, but both private property and the middle classes survived. This difference in property and class relations led some scholars to speak of "totalitarianism of the left"—Stalinist Russia—and "totalitarianism of the right"—Nazi Germany.

A second group of writers in the 1930s approached radical dictatorships outside the Soviet Union through the concept of **fascism.** A term of pride for Mussolini and Hitler, who used it to describe the supposedly "total" and revolutionary character of their movements, fascism was severely criticized by these writers and linked to decaying capitalism and domestic class conflict. Orthodox Marxists, generally sympathetic to the Soviet Union and the socialism it established, argued that fascism was the way powerful capitalists sought to create a mass movement capable of destroying the revolutionary working class and thus protect their enormous profits.

Scholarly interest in fascism declined in the 1950s but revived thereafter. Comparative studies of fascist movements all across Europe showed that they shared many characteristics, including extreme, often expansionist nationalism; an antisocialism aimed at destroying working-class movements; alliances with powerful capitalists and landowners; a dynamic and violent leader; and glorification of war and the military. Yet these studies also highlighted how fascist movements generally failed to gain political power.

In recent years, many historians have tended to adopt a third approach, emphasizing the uniqueness of developments in each country. This is especially true for Hitler's Germany, where some elements of the totalitarian interpretation have been nuanced and revised, as we shall see. A similar revaluation of Stalin's U.S.S.R. is in progress now that the fall of communism has opened the former Soviet Union's archives to new research. For many of today's historians, the differences within broad historical patterns often seem more important than the similarities.

In summary, these conclusions seem appropriate. First, although the concept of totalitarianism has been questioned, it remains a valuable tool for historical understanding. It correctly highlights that both Hitler's Germany and Stalin's Soviet Union made an unprecedented "total claim" on the belief and behavior of their respective citizens, as a noted scholar has recently concluded.[3] Second, antidemocratic, antisocialist fascist movements sprang up all over Europe, but only in Italy

and Germany (and some would say Spain) were they able to take power. Studies of fascist movements seeking to gain power locate important common elements, but they do not explain what fascist governments in Italy and Germany actually did. Finally, it is important to remember that the problem of Europe's radical dictatorships is complex and that there are few easy answers.

Stalin's Soviet Union

Lenin's harshest critics claim that he established the basic outlines of a modern totalitarian dictatorship after the Bolshevik Revolution and during the Russian civil war. If this is so, then Joseph Stalin (1879–1953) certainly finished the job. A master of political infighting, Stalin cautiously consolidated his power and eliminated his enemies in the mid-1920s. Then in 1928, as undisputed leader of the ruling Communist party, he launched the first **five-year plan**—the "revolution from above," as he so aptly termed it.

The five-year plans were extremely ambitious. Often incorrectly considered a mere set of economic measures to speed up the Soviet Union's industrial development, the five-year plans actually marked the beginning of a renewed attempt to mobilize and transform Soviet society along socialist lines. The ultimate goal of the plans was to generate new attitudes, new loyalties, and a new socialist humanity. The means Stalin and the small Communist party elite chose in order to do so were constant propaganda, enormous sacrifice by the people, and the concentration of all power in party hands. Thus the Soviet Union in the 1930s became a dynamic, modern totalitarian state.

From Lenin to Stalin

By spring 1921, Lenin and the Bolsheviks had won the civil war, but they ruled a shattered and devastated land. Many farms were in ruins, and food supplies were exhausted. In southern Russia, drought combined with the ravages of war to produce the worst famine in generations. By 1920, according to the government, from 50 to 90 percent of the population in seventeen provinces was starving. Industrial production also broke down completely. In 1921, for example, output of steel and cotton textiles was only about 4 percent of what it had been in 1913. The Bolsheviks had destroyed the economy as well as their foes.

In the face of economic disintegration, riots by peasants and workers, and an open rebellion by previously pro-Bolshevik sailors at Kronstadt, the tough but ever-flexible Lenin changed course. In March 1921, he announced the **New Economic Policy (NEP),** which re-established limited economic freedom in an attempt to rebuild agriculture and industry. During the civil war, the Bolsheviks had simply seized grain without payment. Now peasant producers were permitted to sell their surpluses in free markets, and private traders and small handicraft manufacturers were allowed to reappear. Heavy industry, railroads, and banks, however, remained wholly nationalized.

The NEP was shrewd and successful both politically and economically. Politically, it was a necessary but temporary compromise with the Soviet Union's overwhelming peasant majority. Realizing that his government was not strong enough to take land from the peasants and turn them into state workers, Lenin made a deal with the only force capable of overturning his government. Economically, the NEP brought rapid recovery. In 1926 industrial output surpassed the level of 1913, and Soviet peasants were producing almost as much grain as before the war. Counting shorter hours and increased social benefits, urban workers as well as peasants were living somewhat better than they had in the past.

Abstract Art in Soviet Russia   The Russian Wassily Kandinsky, whose 1920 *Composition No. 224* is shown here, is generally considered the originator of abstract painting. Making his revolutionary breakthrough in prewar Germany, Kandinsky returned to Russia in World War I and led the adventuresome, highly creative Soviet avant-garde until he left again in 1922. Later, Stalin condemned modern art of all kinds and purged experimental creators. *(State Russian Museum, St. Petersburg/The Bridgeman Art Library International Ltd)*

As the economy recovered and the government partially relaxed its censorship and repression, an intense struggle for power began in the inner circles of the Communist party, for Lenin had left no chosen successor when he died in 1924. The principal contenders were the stolid Stalin and the flamboyant Trotsky.

The son of a shoemaker, Joseph Dzhugashvili—later known as Stalin—studied for the priesthood but was expelled from his theological seminary, probably for rude rebelliousness. By 1903 he had joined the Bolsheviks. In the years before the First World War, he engaged in many revolutionary activities in the southern Transcaucasian area of the multinational Russian empire, including a daring bank robbery to get money for the Bolsheviks. This raid gained Lenin's attention and approval.

Stalin was a good organizer but a poor speaker and writer, with no experience outside of Russia. Trotsky, a great and inspiring leader who had planned the 1917 takeover (see pages 908–909) and then created the victorious Red Army, appeared to have all the advantages. Yet it was Stalin who succeeded Lenin. Stalin won because he was more effective at gaining the all-important support of the party, the only genuine source of power in the one-party state. Rising to general secretary of the party's Central Committee just before Lenin's first stroke in 1922, Stalin used his office to win friends and allies with jobs and promises.

The practical Stalin also won because he appeared better able than the brilliant Trotsky to relate Marxian teaching to Soviet realities in the 1920s. Stalin developed a theory of "socialism in one country" that was more appealing to the majority of communists than Trotsky's doctrine of "permanent revolution." Stalin argued that the Russian-dominated Soviet Union had the ability to build socialism on its own. Trotsky maintained that socialism in the Soviet Union could succeed only if revolution occurred quickly throughout Europe. To many Russian communists, Trotsky's views seemed to sell their country short and to promise risky conflicts with capitalist countries by recklessly encouraging revolutionary movements around the world. Stalin's willingness to break with the NEP and "build socialism" at home appealed to young militants in the party, who detested the capitalist-appearing NEP.

With cunning skill, Stalin gradually achieved supreme power between 1922 and 1927. First, he allied with Trotsky's personal enemies to crush Trotsky, who was expelled from the Soviet Union in 1929 and eventually was murdered in Mexico in 1940, undoubtedly on Stalin's order. Second, Stalin aligned with the moderates, who wanted to go slow at home, to suppress Trotsky's radical followers. Third, having defeated all the radicals, he turned against his allies, the moderates, and destroyed them as well. Stalin's final triumph came at the party congress of December 1927, which condemned all "deviation from the general party line" formulated by Stalin. The dictator and his followers were then ready to launch the revolution from above—the real revolution for millions of ordinary citizens.

The Five-Year Plans

The party congress of 1927, which ratified Stalin's consolidation of power, marked the end of the NEP and the beginning of the era of socialist five-year plans. Building on planning models developed by Soviet economists in the 1920s, the first five-year plan had staggering economic objectives. In just five years, total industrial output was to increase by 250 percent. Heavy industry, the preferred sector, was to grow even faster. Agricultural production was slated to increase by 150 percent, and one-fifth of the peasants in the Soviet Union were scheduled to give up their private plots and join socialist collective farms. By 1930 economic and social change was sweeping the country.

Stalin unleashed his "second revolution" for a variety of interrelated reasons. There were, first of all, ideological considerations. Like Lenin, Stalin and his militant supporters were deeply committed to socialism as they understood it. They feared a gradual restoration of capitalism, and they burned to stamp out the NEP's private traders, independent artisans, and property-owning peasants. Purely economic motivations were also important. Although the economy had recovered, it seemed to have stalled in 1927 and 1928. A new socialist offensive seemed necessary if industry and agriculture were to grow rapidly.

Political considerations were most important. Internationally, there was the old problem, remaining from prerevolutionary times, of catching up with the advanced and presumably hostile capitalist nations of the West. Stalin said in 1931, when he pressed for ever-greater speed and sacrifice, "We are fifty or a hundred years behind the advanced countries. We must make good this distance in ten years. Either we do it, or we shall go under."[4]

Domestically, there was what communist writers of the 1920s called the "cursed problem"—the problem of the peasants. For centuries the peasants had wanted to own the land, and finally they had it. Sooner or later, the communists reasoned, the peasants would become conservative little capitalists and pose a threat to the regime. At the same time, the mainly urban communists believed that the feared and despised "class enemy" in the villages

Life in a Forced-Labor Camp This rare photo from about 1933 shows the reality of deported peasants and other political prisoners building the Stalin–White Sea Canal in far northern Russia, with their bare hands and under the most dehumanizing conditions. In books and plays Stalin's followers praised the project as a model for the regeneration of "reactionaries" and "kulak exploiters" through the joys of socialist work. *(David King Collection)*

could be squeezed to provide the enormous sums needed for all-out industrialization. Thus Stalin decided on a war against the peasantry in order to bring it under the control of the state and to make it pay the costs of the new socialist offensive.

That war was **collectivization**—the forcible consolidation of individual peasant farms into large, state-controlled enterprises. Beginning in 1929, peasants all over the Soviet Union were ordered to give up their land and animals and become members of collective farms, although they continued to live in their own homes. As for the **kulaks,** the better-off peasants, Stalin instructed party workers to "liquidate them as a class." Stripped of land and livestock, the kulaks were generally not even permitted to join the collective farms. Many starved or were deported to forced-labor camps for "re-education."

Since almost all peasants were in fact poor, the term *kulak* soon meant any peasant who opposed the new system.

Whole villages were often attacked. One conscience-stricken colonel in the secret police confessed to a foreign journalist,

I am an old Bolshevik. I worked in the underground against the Tsar and then I fought in the Civil War. Did I do all that in order that I should now surround villages with machine guns and order my men to fire indiscriminately into crowds of peasants? Oh, no, no![5]

Forced collectivization of the peasants led to economic and human disaster. Large numbers of peasants slaughtered their animals and burned their crops in sullen, hopeless protest. Between 1929 and 1933, the number of horses, cattle, sheep, and goats in the Soviet Union fell by at least half. Nor were the state-controlled collective farms more productive. The output of grain barely increased between 1928 and 1938, when it was almost identical to that of 1913. Moreover, the state had to invest heavily in agriculture, building thousands of tractors to replace slaughtered draft horses. Collectivized agriculture was unable to make any substantial financial contribution to Soviet industrial development in the first five-year plan.

The human dimension of the tragedy was absolutely staggering. As one leading historian writes in outrage, "The number dying in Stalin's war against the peasants was higher than the total deaths of all the countries in World War I." Yet, he notes, in Stalin's war only one side was armed and the other side bore almost all the casualties, many of whom were women, children, and the old.[6] Stalin himself confided to Winston Churchill at Yalta in 1945 that 10 million people had died in the course of collectivization.

In Ukraine the drive against peasants snowballed into a general assault on Ukrainians as reactionary nationalists and enemies of socialism. Thus in 1932, as collectivization and deportations continued, Stalin and his associates set levels of grain deliveries for the Ukrainian collective at excessively high levels, and they refused to relax those quotas or even allow food relief when Ukrainian communist leaders reported that starvation was occurring. The result was a terrible man-made famine in Ukraine in 1932 and 1933, which probably claimed 6 million lives. Stalin denied completely the existence of famine, and for years the party successfully suppressed much of the truth at home and abroad.

Collectivization, justly called the "second serfdom," was a cruel but real victory for communist ideologues. By the end of 1932, fully 60 percent of peasant families had been herded onto collective farms; by 1938, 93 percent. Regimented as employees of the state and dependent on the state-owned tractor stations, the collectivized peasants were no longer even a potential political threat to Stalin and the Communist party. Moreover, the state paid very low prices for grain to guarantee cheap bread for urban workers, who were much more important politically than the peasants.

Yet, as recent research shows, peasants fought back with indirect daily opposition and forced the supposedly all-powerful state to make modest compromises. Peasants secured the right to limit a family's labor on the state-run farms and to cultivate tiny family plots, which provided them with much of their food. In 1938 these family plots produced 22 percent of all Soviet agricultural produce on only 4 percent of all cultivated land, eloquent testimony to the inefficiency of collectivized agriculture and the quiet resistance of the weak in the countryside.

The industrial side of the five-year plans was more successful—indeed, quite spectacular. Soviet industry pro-duced about four times as much in 1937 as it had in 1928. No other major country had ever achieved such rapid industrial growth. Heavy industry led the way; consumer industry grew quite slowly. A new heavy industrial complex was built almost from scratch in western Siberia. Industrial growth also went hand in hand with urban development, and more than 25 million people migrated to cities during the 1930s.

The great industrialization drive, concentrated between 1928 and 1937, was an awe-inspiring achievement purchased at enormous sacrifice. The sudden creation of dozens of new factories required a great increase in total investment. Although few nations had ever invested more than one-sixth of their yearly net national income, Soviet planners decreed that more than one-third of net income go for investment. This meant that only two-thirds of everything being produced could be consumed by the people *and* the increasingly voracious military. The money for investment was collected from the people by means of heavy, hidden sales taxes.

Two other factors contributed importantly to rapid industrialization: firm labor discipline and foreign engineers. Between 1930 and 1932, trade unions lost most of their power. The government could assign workers to any job anywhere in the country, and individuals could not move without the permission of the police. When factory managers needed more hands, they called on their counterparts on the collective farms, who sent them millions of "unneeded" peasants over the years.

Foreign engineers were hired to plan and construct many of the new factories. Highly skilled American engineers, hungry for work in the depression years, were particularly important until newly trained Soviet experts began to replace them after 1932. The gigantic mills of the new Siberian steel industry were modeled on America's best. Thus Stalin's planners harnessed even the skill and technology of capitalist countries to promote the surge of socialist industry.

Life and Culture in Soviet Society

The aim of Stalin's five-year plans was to create a new kind of society and human personality as well as a strong industrial economy and a powerful army. Stalin and his helpers were good Marxian economic determinists. Once everything was owned by the state, they believed, a socialist society and a new kind of human being would inevitably emerge. Their utopian vision of a new humanity floundered, but they did build a new society, whose broad outlines existed into the mid-1980s. Life in this society had both good and bad aspects.

Because consumption was reduced to pay for investment, there was no improvement in the average standard of living. Indeed, the most careful studies show that the average nonfarm wage apparently purchased only about half as many goods in 1932 as in 1928. After 1932 real wages rose slowly, so that in 1937 workers could buy about 60 percent of what they had bought in 1928 and less than in 1913. Collectivized peasants experienced greater declines.

Life was hard in Stalin's Soviet Union. The masses of people lived primarily on black bread and wore old, shabby clothing. There were constant shortages in the stores, although very heavily taxed vodka was always readily available. A shortage of housing was a particularly serious problem. Millions were moving into the cities, but the government built few new apartments. In 1940 there were approximately 4 people per room in every urban dwelling, as opposed to 2.7 per room in 1926. A relatively lucky family received one room for all its members and shared both a kitchen and a toilet with others on the floor. Less fortunate workers, kulaks, and class enemies built scrap-lumber shacks or underground dugouts in shantytowns.

Life was hard but by no means hopeless. Idealism and ideology had real appeal for many communists, who saw themselves heroically building the world's first socialist society while capitalism crumbled in a worldwide depression and degenerated into fascism in the West. This optimistic belief in the future of the Soviet Union also attracted many disillusioned Westerners to communism in the 1930s.

On a more practical level, Soviet workers did receive some important social benefits, such as old-age pensions, free medical services, free education, and day-care centers for children. Unemployment was almost unknown. Finally, there was the possibility of personal advancement.

The keys to improving one's position were specialized skills and technical education. Rapid industrialization required massive numbers of trained experts, such as skilled workers, engineers, and plant managers. Thus the Stalinist state broke with the egalitarian policies of the 1920s and provided tremendous incentives to those who could serve its needs. It paid the mass of unskilled workers and collective farmers very low wages, but it dangled high salaries and many special privileges before its growing technical and managerial elite. This elite joined with the political and artistic elites in a new upper class, whose members were rich, powerful, and insecure. Thus millions struggled for an education. One young man summed it up: "In Soviet Russia there is no capital except education. If a person does not want to become a collective farmer or just a cleaning woman, the only means you have to get something is through education."[7]

Adult Education Illiteracy, especially among women, was a serious problem after the Russian Revolution. This early photo suggests how many adults successfully learned to read and write throughout the Soviet Union. *(Sovfoto)*

The radical transformation of Soviet society had a profound impact on women's lives. Marxists had traditionally believed that both capitalism and the middle-class husband exploited women. The Russian Revolution of 1917 immediately proclaimed complete equality of rights for women. In the 1920s, divorce and abortion were made easily available, and women were urged to work outside the home and liberate themselves sexually. The most prominent Bolshevik feminist, Alexandra Kollontai, went so far as to declare that the sex act had no more significance than "drinking a glass of water."[8] After Stalin came to power, sexual and familial liberation was played down, and the most lasting changes for women involved work and education.

Young women were constantly told that they had to be fully equal to men. Peasant women in Russia had long experienced the equality of backbreaking physical labor in the countryside, and with the advent of the five-year plans, millions of women also toiled in factories and in heavy construction, building dams, roads, and steel mills in summer heat and winter frost. Many of the opportunities open to men through education were also open to women. Determined women pursued their studies and entered the ranks of the better-paid specialists in industry and science. Medicine practically became a woman's profession. By 1950, 75 percent of all doctors in the Soviet Union were women.

Soviet society also demanded great sacrifices from women. The vast majority of women simply *had* to work outside the home. Wages were so low that it was almost impossible for a family or couple to live only on the husband's earnings. Men continued to dominate the very best jobs. Finally, rapid change and economic hardship led to many broken families, creating further physical and emotional strains for women. In any event, the massive mobilization of women was a striking characteristic of the Soviet state.

Culture lost its autonomy in the 1930s and became thoroughly politicized through constant propaganda and indoctrination. Party activists lectured workers in factories and peasants on collective farms, while newspapers, films, and radio broadcasts endlessly recounted socialist achievements and capitalist plots. Whereas the 1920s had seen considerable experimentation in modern art and theater, intellectuals were ordered by Stalin to become "engineers of human minds." Writers and artists who could effectively combine genuine creativity and political propaganda became the darlings of the regime. It became increasingly important for the successful writer and artist to glorify Russian nationalism. Russian history was rewritten so that early tsars such as Ivan the Terrible and Peter the Great became worthy forerunners of the greatest Russian leader of all—Stalin.

Stalin and Soviet Workers, Marching to Victory   Stalin appeared rarely in public, but posters singing his praises were everywhere. Here the mighty ruler is almost one of the boys. "Our program is realistic," Stalin proclaims on the poster, "because it is you and me working together." *(David King Collection)*

Stalin seldom appeared in public, but his presence was everywhere—in portraits, statues, books, and quotations from his "sacred" writings. Although the government persecuted religion and turned churches into "museums of atheism," the state had both an earthly religion and a high priest—Marxism-Leninism and Joseph Stalin.

Stalinist Terror and the Great Purges

In the mid-1930s, the great offensive to build socialism and a new socialist personality culminated in ruthless police terror and a massive purging of the Communist party. First used by the Bolsheviks in the civil war to maintain their power, terror as state policy was revived in the collectivization drive against the peasants. The top members of the party and government publicly supported Stalin's initiatives, but there was some grumbling in the party. At a small gathering in November 1932, even Stalin's wife complained bitterly about the misery of the people and the horrible famine in Ukraine. Stalin showered her with insults, and she died that same night, apparently by her own hand. In late 1934, Stalin's number-two man, Sergei Kirov, was suddenly and mysteriously murdered. Although Stalin himself probably ordered Kirov's murder, he used the incident to launch a reign of terror.

In August 1936, sixteen prominent Old Bolsheviks confessed to all manner of plots against Stalin in spectacular public trials in Moscow. Then in 1937 the secret police arrested a mass of lesser party officials and newer members, also torturing them and extracting more confessions for more show trials. In addition to the party faithful, union officials, managers, intellectuals, army officers, and countless ordinary citizens were struck down. In all, at least 8 million people were probably arrested, and millions of these were executed or never returned from prisons and forced-labor camps.

Stalin and the remaining party leadership recruited 1.5 million new members to take the place of those purged. Thus more than half of all Communist party members in 1941 had joined since the purges. "These new men were 'thirty-something' products of the Second Revolution of the 1930s, Stalin's upwardly mobile yuppies, so to speak."[9] Often sons (and daughters) of workers, they had usually studied in the new technical schools, and they soon proved capable of managing the government and large-scale production. A product of the great purges, this new generation of Stalin-formed communists would serve the leader effectively until his death in 1953, and they would govern the Soviet Union until the early 1980s.

Stalin's mass purges remain baffling, for almost all historians believe that those purged posed no threat and confessed to crimes they had not committed. Certainly the highly publicized purges sent a warning to the people: no one was secure; everyone had to serve the party and its leader with redoubled devotion. Some Western scholars have also argued that the terror reflected a fully developed totalitarian state, which must always be fighting real or imaginary enemies.

The long-standing Western interpretation that puts the blame for the great purges on Stalin, which became very popular in Russia after the fall of communism, has nevertheless been challenged in recent years. Some historians now argue that Stalin's fears were exaggerated but real. Moreover, these fears and suspicions were shared by many in the party and in the general population. Bombarded with ideology and political slogans, the population responded energetically to Stalin's directives. Investigations and trials snowballed into a mass hysteria, a new witch-hunt that claimed millions of victims.[10] In short, in this view of the 1930s, a deluded Stalin found large numbers of willing collaborators for crime as well as for achievement.

Mussolini and Fascism in Italy

Mussolini's movement and his seizure of power in 1922 were important steps in the rise of dictatorships in Europe between the two world wars. Like all the future dictators, the young Mussolini hated liberalism and wanted to destroy it in Italy. But although Mussolini began as a revolutionary socialist, like Stalin, he turned against the working class and successfully sought the support of conservatives. At the same time, Mussolini and his supporters were the first to call themselves "fascists"—revolutionaries determined to create a certain kind of totalitarian state. Yet few scholars today would argue that Mussolini succeeded. His dictatorship was brutal and theatrical, but it remained a halfway house between conservative authoritarianism and dynamic totalitarianism.

The Seizure of Power

In the early twentieth century, Italy was a liberal state with civil rights and a constitutional monarchy. On the eve of the First World War, the parliamentary regime finally granted universal male suffrage, and Italy appeared to be moving toward democracy. But there were serious problems. Much of the Italian population was still poor, and many peasants were more attached to their villages and local interests than to the national state. Moreover, the papacy, many devout Catholics, conservatives, and landowners remained strongly opposed to liberal institutions and to the heirs of Cavour and Garibaldi—the middle-class lawyers and politicians who ran the country largely for their own benefit. Relations between church and state were often tense. Class differences were also extreme, and a powerful revolutionary socialist movement had developed. Only in Italy among the main European countries did the radical left wing of the Socialist party gain the leadership as early as 1912, and only in Italy did the Socialist party unanimously oppose the war from the very beginning.[11]

The war worsened the political situation. Having fought on the side of the Allies almost exclusively for purposes of territorial expansion, the parliamentary government bitterly disappointed Italian nationalists with Italy's modest gains at Versailles. Workers and peasants also felt cheated: to win their support during the war, the government had promised social and land reform, which it did not deliver after the war.

The Russian Revolution inspired and energized Italy's revolutionary socialist movement. The Socialist party quickly lined up with the Bolsheviks, and radical workers and peasants began occupying factories and seizing land in 1920. These actions scared and mobilized the property-owning classes. Moreover, after the war the pope lifted his ban on participation by Catholics in Italian politics, and a strong Catholic party quickly emerged. Thus by 1921 revolutionary socialists, antiliberal conservatives, and frightened property owners were all opposed—though for different reasons—to the liberal parliamentary government.

Into these crosscurrents of unrest and fear stepped the blustering, bullying Benito Mussolini (1883–1945). Son of a village schoolteacher and a poor blacksmith, Mussolini began his political career as a Socialist party leader and radical newspaper editor before World War I. In 1914, powerfully influenced by antidemocratic cults of violent action, the young Mussolini urged that Italy join the Allies, a stand for which he was expelled from the Italian Socialist party. Later Mussolini fought at the front and was wounded in 1917. Returning home, he began organizing bitter war veterans like himself into a band of fascists—from the Italian word for "a union of forces."

At first Mussolini's program was a radical combination of nationalist and socialist demands, including territorial expansion, benefits for workers, and land reform for peasants. As such, it competed directly with the well-organized Socialist party and failed to get off the ground. When Mussolini saw that his violent verbal assaults on rival Socialists won him growing support from conservatives and the frightened middle classes, he shifted gears in 1920. In thought and action, Mussolini was a striking example of the turbulent uncertainty of the age of anxiety.

Mussolini and his growing private army of **Black Shirts** began to grow violent. Typically, a band of fascist toughs would roar off in trucks at night and swoop down on a few isolated Socialist organizers, beating them up and force-feeding them almost deadly doses of castor oil. Few people were killed, but socialist newspapers, union halls, and local Socialist party headquarters were destroyed. Mussolini's toughs pushed Socialists out of the city governments of northern Italy.

A skillful politician, Mussolini allowed his followers to convince themselves that they were not just opposing the "Reds" but also making a real revolution of their own, forging a strong, dynamic movement that would help the little people against the established interests. With the government breaking down in 1922, largely because of the chaos created by his direct-action bands, Mussolini stepped forward as the savior of order and property. Striking a conservative note in his speeches and gaining the sympathetic neutrality of army leaders, Mussolini demanded the resignation of the existing government and his own appointment by the king. In October 1922, to force matters, a large group of fascists marched on Rome to threaten the king and force him to call on Mussolini. The threat worked. Victor Emmanuel III (r. 1900–1946), who had no love for the old liberal politicians, asked Mussolini to form a new cabinet. Thus, after widespread violence and a threat of armed uprising, Mussolini seized power "legally." He was immediately granted dictatorial authority for one year by the king and the parliament.

The Regime in Action

Mussolini became dictator on the strength of Italians' rejection of parliamentary government coupled with fears of Soviet-style revolution. Yet what he intended to do with his power was by no means clear until 1924. Some of his dedicated supporters pressed for a "second revolution." Mussolini's ministers, however, included old conservatives, moderates, and even two reform-minded Socialists. A new electoral law was passed giving two-thirds of the representatives in the parliament to the party that won the most votes, a change that allowed the Fascist party and its allies to win an overwhelming majority in 1924. Shortly thereafter, five of Mussolini's thugs kidnapped and murdered Giacomo Matteotti, the leader of the Socialists in the parliament. In the face of this outrage, the opposition demanded that Mussolini's armed squads be dissolved and all violence be banned.

Although Mussolini may or may not have ordered Matteotti's murder, he stood at the crossroads of a severe political crisis. After some hesitation, he charged forward. Declaring his desire to "make the nation Fascist," he imposed a series of repressive measures. Freedom of the press was abolished, elections were fixed, and the government ruled by decree. Mussolini arrested his political opponents, disbanded all independent labor unions, and put dedicated Fascists in control of Italy's schools. Moreover, he created a fascist youth movement, fascist labor unions, and many other fascist organizations. Mussolini trumpeted his goal in a famous slogan of 1926: "Everything in the state, nothing outside the state, nothing against the state." By the end of that year, Italy was a one-party dictatorship under Mussolini's unquestioned leadership.

Mussolini   A charismatic orator with a sure touch for emotional propaganda, Mussolini loved settings that linked fascist Italy to the glories of imperial Rome. Poised to address a mass rally in Rome at the time of Matteotti's murder, Mussolini then called for 90,000 more volunteers to join his gun-toting fascist militia. Members of the militia stand as an honor guard in front of the podium. *(Popperfoto)*

Mussolini, however, did not complete the establishment of a modern totalitarian state. His Fascist party never became all-powerful. It never destroyed the old power structure, as the Communists did in the Soviet Union, or succeeded in dominating it, as the Nazis did in Germany. Membership in the Fascist party was more a sign of an Italian's respectability than a commitment to

radical change. Interested primarily in personal power, Mussolini was content to compromise with the old conservative classes that controlled the army, the economy, and the state. He never tried to purge these classes or even move very vigorously against them. He controlled and propagandized labor but left big business to regulate itself, profitably and securely. There was no land reform.

Mussolini also drew increasing support from the Catholic church. In the **Lateran Agreement** of 1929, he recognized the Vatican as a tiny independent state, and he agreed to give the church heavy financial support. The pope expressed his satisfaction and urged Italians to support Mussolini's government.

Nothing better illustrates Mussolini's unwillingness to harness everyone and everything for dynamic action than his treatment of women. He abolished divorce and told women to stay at home and produce children. To promote that goal, he decreed a special tax on bachelors in 1934. In 1938 women were limited by law to a maximum of 10 percent of the better-paying jobs in industry and government. Italian women appear not to have changed their attitudes or behavior in any important way under fascist rule.

Mussolini's government did not pass racial laws until 1938 and did not persecute Jews savagely until late in the Second World War, when Italy was under Nazi control. Nor did Mussolini establish a truly ruthless police state. Only twenty-three political prisoners were condemned to death between 1926 and 1944. In spite of much pompous posing by the chauvinist leader and in spite of mass meetings, salutes, and a certain copying of Hitler's aggression in foreign policy after 1933, Mussolini's fascist Italy, though repressive and undemocratic, was never really totalitarian.

Hitler and Nazism in Germany

The most frightening dictatorship developed in Nazi Germany. A product of Hitler's evil genius as well as of Germany's social and political situation and the general attack on liberalism and rationality in the age of anxiety, the Nazi movement shared some of the characteristics of Mussolini's Italian model and was a form of fascism. But Nazi dictatorship smashed or took over most independent organizations, mobilized the economy, and violently persecuted the Jewish population. Thus Nazism asserted an unlimited claim over German society and proclaimed the ultimate power of its endlessly aggressive leader—Adolf Hitler. The aspirations of Nazism were truly totalitarian.

The Roots of Nazism

Nazism grew out of many complex developments, of which the most influential were extreme nationalism and racism. These two ideas captured the mind of the young Hitler, and it was he who dominated Nazism for as long as it lasted.

Born the fourth child of a successful Austrian customs official and an indulgent mother, Adolf Hitler (1889–1945) spent his childhood in small towns in Austria. A good student in grade school, Hitler did poorly on reaching high school and dropped out at age fourteen following the death of his father. After four years of unfocused loafing, Hitler finally left for Vienna, where he lived a comfortable, lazy life on his generous orphan's pension and found most of the perverted beliefs that guided his life.

In Vienna Hitler soaked up extreme German nationalism, which was particularly strong there. Austro-German nationalists believed Germans to be a superior people and the natural rulers of central Europe. They often advocated union with Germany and violent expulsion of "inferior" peoples as the means of maintaining German domination of the Austro-Hungarian Empire.

Hitler was deeply impressed by Vienna's mayor, Karl Lueger (1844–1910). With the help of the Catholic trade unions, Lueger had succeeded in winning the support of the little people of Vienna, and he showed Hitler the enormous potential of anticapitalist and antiliberal propaganda.

From Lueger and others, Hitler eagerly absorbed virulent anti-Semitism, racism, and hatred of Slavs. He developed an unshakable belief in the crudest, most exaggerated distortions of the Darwinian theory of survival, the superiority of Germanic races, and the inevitability of racial conflict. Thus anti-Semitism and racism became Hitler's most passionate convictions, his explanation for everything. The Jews, he claimed, directed an international conspiracy of finance capitalism and Marxian socialism against German culture, German unity, and the German race. Hitler's belief was totally irrational, but he never doubted it.

Although he moved to Munich in 1913 to avoid being drafted in the Austrian army, the lonely Hitler greeted the outbreak of the First World War as a salvation. He later wrote in his autobiography, *Mein Kampf,* that, "overcome by passionate enthusiasm, I fell to my knees and thanked heaven out of an overflowing heart." The struggle and discipline of war gave life meaning, and Hitler served bravely as a dispatch carrier on the western front.

When Germany was suddenly defeated in 1918, Hitler's world was shattered. Not only was he a fanatical nationalist, but war was also his reason for living. Convinced that Jews and Marxists had "stabbed Germany in the back," he vowed to fight on.

In late 1919, Hitler joined a tiny extremist group in Munich called the German Workers' party. In addition to denouncing Jews, Marxists, and democrats, the German Workers' party promised unity under a uniquely German "national socialism" that would abolish the injustices of capitalism and create a mighty "people's community." By 1921 Hitler had gained absolute control of this small but growing party. He was already a master of mass propaganda and political showmanship. His most effective tool was the mass rally, where he often worked his audience into a frenzy with wild, demagogic attacks on the Versailles treaty, the Jews, the war profiteers, and Germany's Weimar Republic.

Party membership multiplied tenfold after early 1922. In late 1923, the Weimar Republic seemed on the verge of collapse, and Hitler, inspired by Mussolini's recent easy victory, decided on an armed uprising in Munich. Despite the failure of the poorly organized plot and Hitler's arrest, Nazism had been born.

Hitler's Road to Power

At his trial, Hitler violently denounced the Weimar Republic, and he gained enormous publicity and attention. Moreover, he learned from his unsuccessful revolt. Hitler concluded that he had to undermine, rather than overthrow, the government and come to power legally through electoral competition. He forced his more violent supporters to accept his new strategy. He also used his brief prison term to dictate *Mein Kampf*. There he expounded on his basic themes: "race," with a stress on anti-Semitism; "living space," with a sweeping vision of war and conquered territory; and the leader-dictator (**Führer**), with unlimited, arbitrary power.

In the years of prosperity and relative stability between 1924 and 1929, Hitler concentrated on building his National Socialist German Workers' party, or Nazi party. By 1928 the party had 100,000 highly disciplined members under Hitler's absolute control. To appeal to the middle-class voters, Hitler de-emphasized the anticapitalist elements of national socialism and vowed to fight Bolshevism.

Yet the Nazis remained a small splinter group in 1928, when they received only 2.6 percent of the vote in the general elections and twelve seats in the Reichstag. There the Nazi deputies pursued the legal strategy of using democracy to destroy democracy.

The Great Depression, shattering economic prosperity from 1929 on, presented Hitler with a fabulous opportunity. Unemployment jumped from 1.3 million in 1929

"The Officers of Tomorrow"   The Nazis tried hard to win the support of young people. After they came to power, the Nazis put boys in the uniform of the Hitler Youth, shown here in a German historical museum. The Hitler Youth preached Nazi values and militarism, the message of the poster and its caption. *(AKG London)*

to 5 million in 1930. By the end of 1932, an incredible 43 percent of the labor force was unemployed. Industrial production fell by one-half between 1929 and 1932. No factor contributed more to Hitler's success than the economic crisis. Never very interested in economics before, Hitler began promising German voters economic as well as political and international salvation.

Above all, Hitler rejected free-market capitalism and advocated government programs to bring recovery. Hitler pitched his speeches especially to middle- and lower-middle-class groups—small business people, officeworkers, artisans, and peasants—as well as to skilled workers striving for middle-class status. Seized by panic as bankruptcies increased, unemployment soared, and the Communists made dramatic election gains, great numbers of middle- and lower-middle-class people "voted their pocket-

books,"[12] as new research argues convincingly, and deserted the conservative and moderate parties for the Nazis. In the election of 1930, the Nazis won 6.5 million votes and 107 seats, and in July 1932 they gained 14.5 million votes—38 percent of the total—and became the largest party in the Reichstag.

The appeal to pocketbook interests was particularly effective in the early 1930s because Hitler appeared more mainstream, playing down his anti-Jewish hatred and racist nationalism. A master of mass propaganda and psychology, he had written in *Mein Kampf* that the masses were the "driving force of the most important changes in this world" and were themselves driven by fanaticism and not by knowledge. To arouse such hysterical fanaticism, he believed that all propaganda had to be limited to a few simple, endlessly repeated slogans. But now when he harangued vast audiences with wild oratory and simple slogans, he featured "national rebirth" and the "crimes" of the Versailles treaty. And many uncertain individuals, surrounded by thousands of enthralled listeners, found a sense of belonging as well as hope for better times.

Hitler and the Nazis also appealed strongly to German youth. Indeed, in some ways the Nazi movement was a mass movement of young Germans. Hitler himself was only forty in 1929, and he and most of his top aides were much younger than other leading German politicians. "National Socialism is the organized will of the youth," proclaimed the official Nazi slogan, and the battle cry of Gregor Strasser, a leading Nazi organizer, was "Make way, you old ones."[13] In 1931 almost 40 percent of Nazi party members were under thirty, compared with 20 percent of Social Democrats. National recovery, exciting and rapid change, and personal advancement were the appeals of Nazism to millions of German youths.

Another reason Hitler came to power was that normal democratic government broke down as early as May 1930. Unable to gain the support of a majority in the Reichstag, Chancellor (chief minister) Heinrich Brüning convinced the president, the aging war hero General Hindenburg, to authorize rule by decree. Intending to use this emergency measure indefinitely, Brüning was determined to overcome the economic crisis by cutting back government spending and ruthlessly forcing down prices and wages. Brüning's ultra-orthodox policies not only intensified the economic collapse in Germany but also convinced many voters that the country's republican leaders were stupid and corrupt, thereby adding to Hitler's appeal.

The continuation of the struggle between the Social Democrats and the Communists, right up until the moment Hitler took power, was another aspect of the breakdown of democratic government. The Communists refused to cooperate with the Social Democrats, even though the two parties together outnumbered the Nazis in the Reichstag, even after the elections of 1932. German Communists (and the still complacent Stalin) were blinded by hatred of socialists and by ideology: the Communists believed that Hitler's fascism represented the last agonies of monopoly capitalism and that a communist revolution would soon follow his taking power. Disunity on the left was undoubtedly another nail in the republic's coffin.

Finally, Hitler excelled in the dirty, backroom politics of the decaying Weimar Republic. That, in fact, brought him to power. In complicated infighting in 1932, he cleverly succeeded in gaining additional support from key people in the army and big business. These people thought they could use Hitler for their own advantage to get increased military spending, fat contracts, and tough measures against workers. Many conservative and nationalistic politicians thought similarly. They thus accepted Hitler's demand to join the government only if he became chancellor. There would be only two other National Socialists and nine solid conservatives as ministers, and in such a coalition government, they reasoned, Hitler could be used and controlled. On January 30, 1933, Adolf Hitler, leader of the largest party in Germany, was legally appointed chancellor by Hindenburg.

The Nazi State and Society

Hitler moved rapidly and skillfully to establish an unshakable dictatorship. Continuing to maintain legal appearances, he immediately called for new elections. In the midst of a violent electoral campaign, the Reichstag building was partly destroyed by fire. Hitler screamed that the Communist party was responsible, and he convinced President Hindenburg to sign dictatorial emergency acts that practically abolished freedom of speech and assembly as well as most personal liberties.

When the Nazis won only 44 percent of the vote in the elections, Hitler immediately outlawed the Communist party and arrested its parliamentary representatives. Then on March 23, 1933, the Nazis pushed through the Reichstag the so-called **Enabling Act,** which gave Hitler absolute dictatorial power for four years. Armed with the Enabling Act, Hitler and the Nazis moved to smash or control all independent organizations. Their deceitful stress on legality, coupled with divide-and-conquer techniques, disarmed the opposition until it was too late for effective resistance.

Germany soon became a one-party state. Only the Nazi party was legal. Elections were farces. The Reichstag was jokingly referred to as the most expensive glee club in the country, for its only function was to sing hymns of praise to the Führer. Hitler and the Nazis took over the government bureaucracy intact, installing many Nazis in top positions. At the same time, they created a series of overlapping Nazi party organizations responsible solely to Hitler.

As research in recent years shows, the resulting system of dual government was riddled with rivalries, contradictions, and inefficiencies. Thus the Nazi state was sloppy and often disorganized, lacking the all-encompassing unity that its propagandists claimed. Yet this fractured system suited Hitler and his purposes. He could play the established bureaucracy against his private, personal "party government" and maintain his freedom of action. Hitler could concentrate on general principles and the big decisions, which he always made.

In the economic sphere, one big decision outlawed strikes and abolished independent labor unions, which were replaced by the Nazi Labor Front. Professional people—doctors and lawyers, teachers and engineers—also saw their previously independent organizations swallowed up by Nazi associations. Publishing houses were put under Nazi control, and universities and writers were quickly brought into line. Democratic, socialist, and Jewish literature was put on ever-growing blacklists. Passionate students and pitiful professors burned forbidden books in public squares. Modern art and architecture were ruthlessly prohibited. Life became violently anti-intellectual. As the cynical Joseph Goebbels put it, "When I hear the word 'culture' I reach for my gun."[14] By 1934 a brutal dictatorship characterized by frightening dynamism and obedience to Hitler was already largely in place.

Only the army retained independence, and Hitler moved brutally and skillfully to establish his control there, too. The Nazi storm troopers (the SA), the quasi-military band of 3 million toughs in brown shirts who had fought communists and beaten up Jews before the Nazis took power, expected top positions in the army and even talked of a "second revolution" against capitalism. Hitler decided that the SA leaders had to be eliminated. Needing to preserve good relations with the army as well as with big business, he struck on the night of June 30, 1934. Hitler's elite personal guard—the SS—arrested and shot without trial roughly a thousand SA leaders and assorted political enemies. Shortly thereafter army leaders swore a binding oath of "unquestioning obedience . . . to the Leader of the German State and People, Adolf Hitler." The SS grew rapidly. Under its methodical, inhuman leader, Heinrich Himmler (1900–1945), the SS joined with the political police, the Gestapo, to expand its network of special courts and concentration camps. Nobody was safe.

From the beginning, Jews were a special object of Nazi persecution. By the end of 1934, most Jewish lawyers, doctors, professors, civil servants, and musicians had lost their jobs and the right to practice their professions. In 1935 the infamous Nuremberg Laws classified as Jewish anyone having one or more Jewish grandparents and deprived Jews of all rights of citizenship. By 1938 roughly 150,000 of Germany's half a million Jews had emigrated, sacrificing almost all their property in order to leave Germany.

In late 1938, the attack on the Jews accelerated. A well-organized wave of violence, known to history as "Kristallnacht," smashed windows, looted shops, and destroyed homes and synagogues. German Jews were then rounded up and made to pay for the damage. Another 150,000 Jews fled Germany. Some Germans privately opposed these outrages, but most went along or looked the other way. This lack of opposition reflected anti-Semitism to a degree still being debated by historians, but it certainly reflected the strong popular support Hitler's government enjoyed.

Hitler's Popularity

Hitler had promised the masses economic recovery—"work and bread"—and he delivered. Breaking with Brüning's do-nothing policies, Hitler launched a large public works program to help pull Germany out of the depression. Work began on superhighways, offices, gigantic sports stadiums, and public housing. Hitler also appointed as Germany's central banker a well-known conservative named Hjalmar Schacht, who skillfully restored credit and business. In 1936 an openly aggressive Hitler broke with Schacht, and Germany turned decisively toward rearmament and preparation for war. As a result of these policies (and plain good luck), unemployment dropped steadily, from 6 million in January 1933 to about 1 million in late 1936. By 1938 there was a shortage of workers, as unemployment fell to 2 percent, and women began to take jobs previously denied them by the antifeminist Nazis. Thus between 1932 and 1938, the standard of living for the average employed worker increased moderately. The profits of business rose sharply. For millions of people, economic recovery was tangible evidence that Nazi promises were more than show and propaganda.

For the masses of ordinary German citizens who were not Jews, Slavs, Gypsies, Jehovah's Witnesses, communists, or homosexuals, Hitler's government meant greater equality and more opportunities. In 1933 the position of the traditional German elites—the landed aristocracy, the wealthy capitalists, and the well-educated professional classes—was still very strong. Barriers between classes were generally high. Hitler's rule introduced changes that lowered these barriers. For example, stiff educational requirements, which favored the well-to-do, were relaxed. The new Nazi elite included many young and poorly educated dropouts, rootless lower-middle-class people like Hitler who rose to the top with breathtaking speed. More generally, the Nazis tolerated privilege and wealth only as long as they served the needs of the party. Even big business was constantly ordered around.

Yet few historians today believe that Hitler and the Nazis brought about a real social revolution, as an earlier generation of scholars often argued. Millions of modest middle-class and lower-middle-class people *felt* that Germany was becoming more open and equal, as Nazi propagandists constantly claimed. But quantitative studies show that the well-educated classes held on to most of their advantages and that only a modest social leveling occurred in the Nazi years. It is significant that the Nazis shared with the Italian fascists the stereotypic view of women as housewives and mothers. Only under the relentless pressure of war did they reluctantly mobilize large numbers of German women for work in offices and factories.

Hitler's rabid nationalism, which had helped him gain power, continued to appeal to Germans after 1933. Ever since the wars against Napoleon, many Germans had believed in a special mission for a superior German nation. The successes of Bismarck had furthered such feelings, and near-victory in World War I made nationalists eager for renewed expansion in the 1920s. Thus when Hitler went from one foreign triumph to another and a great German empire seemed within reach, the majority of the population was delighted and kept praising the Führer's actions well into the war.

Not all Germans supported Hitler, however, and a number of German groups actively resisted him after 1933. Tens of thousands of political enemies were imprisoned, and thousands were executed. But opponents of the Nazis pursued various goals, and they were never unified, a fact that helps account for their ultimate lack of success. In the first years of Hitler's rule, the principal resisters were the communists and the socialists in the trade unions. But the expansion of the SS system of terror after 1935 smashed most of these leftists. A second group of opponents arose in the Catholic and Protestant churches. However, their efforts were directed primarily at preserving genuine religious life, not at overthrowing Hitler. Finally in 1938 (and again in 1942–1944), some high-ranking army officers, who feared the consequences of Hitler's reckless aggression, plotted against him, unsuccessfully.

Nazi Expansion and the Second World War

Although economic recovery and somewhat greater opportunity for social advancement won Hitler support, they were only byproducts of the Nazi regime. The guiding and unique concepts of Nazism remained space and race—the territorial expansion of the superior German race. As Germany regained its economic strength and as independent organizations were brought under control, Hitler formed alliances with other dictators and began expanding. German expansion was facilitated by the un-

certain and divided Western democracies, which tried to buy off Hitler to avoid war.

Yet war inevitably broke out, in both the West and the East, for Hitler's ambitions were essentially unlimited. On both war fronts, Nazi soldiers scored enormous successes until late 1942, establishing a vast empire of death and destruction. Hitler's reckless aggression also raised a mighty coalition determined to smash the Nazi order. Led by Britain, the United States, and the Soviet Union, the Grand Alliance—to use Winston Churchill's favorite term—functioned quite effectively in military terms. By the summer of 1943, the tide of battle had turned. Two years later, Germany and its allies lay in ruins, utterly defeated. Thus the terrible Nazi empire proved short-lived.

Aggression and Appeasement, 1933–1939

Hitler's tactics in international politics after 1933 strikingly resembled those he had used in domestic politics between 1924 and 1933. When Hitler was weak, he righteously proclaimed that he intended to overturn the "unjust system" established by the Treaties of Versailles and Locarno—but only by legal means. As he grew stronger, and as other leaders showed their willingness to compromise, he increased his demands and finally began attacking his independent neighbors (see Map 29.1).

Hitler realized that his aggressive policies had to be carefully camouflaged at first, for Germany's army was limited by the Treaty of Versailles to only 100,000 men. As he told a group of army commanders in February 1933, the early stages of his policy of "conquest of new living space in the East and its ruthless Germanization" had serious dangers. If France had real leaders, Hitler said, it would "not give us time but attack us, presumably with its eastern satellites."[15] To avoid such threats to his plans, Hitler loudly proclaimed his peaceful intentions to all the world. Nevertheless, he felt strong enough to walk out of a sixty-nation disarmament conference and withdraw from the League of Nations in October 1933. Gustav Stresemann's policy of peaceful cooperation (see pages 938–939) was dead; the Nazi determination to rearm was out in the open.

Following this action, Hitler sought to incorporate independent Austria into a greater Germany. But a worried Mussolini, who had initially greeted Hitler as a fascist little brother, massed his troops on Brenner Pass and threatened to fight. When in March 1935 Hitler established a general military draft and declared the "unequal" disarmament clauses of the Treaty of Versailles null and void, other countries appeared to understand the danger. With France taking the lead, Italy and Great Britain protested strongly and warned against future aggressive actions.

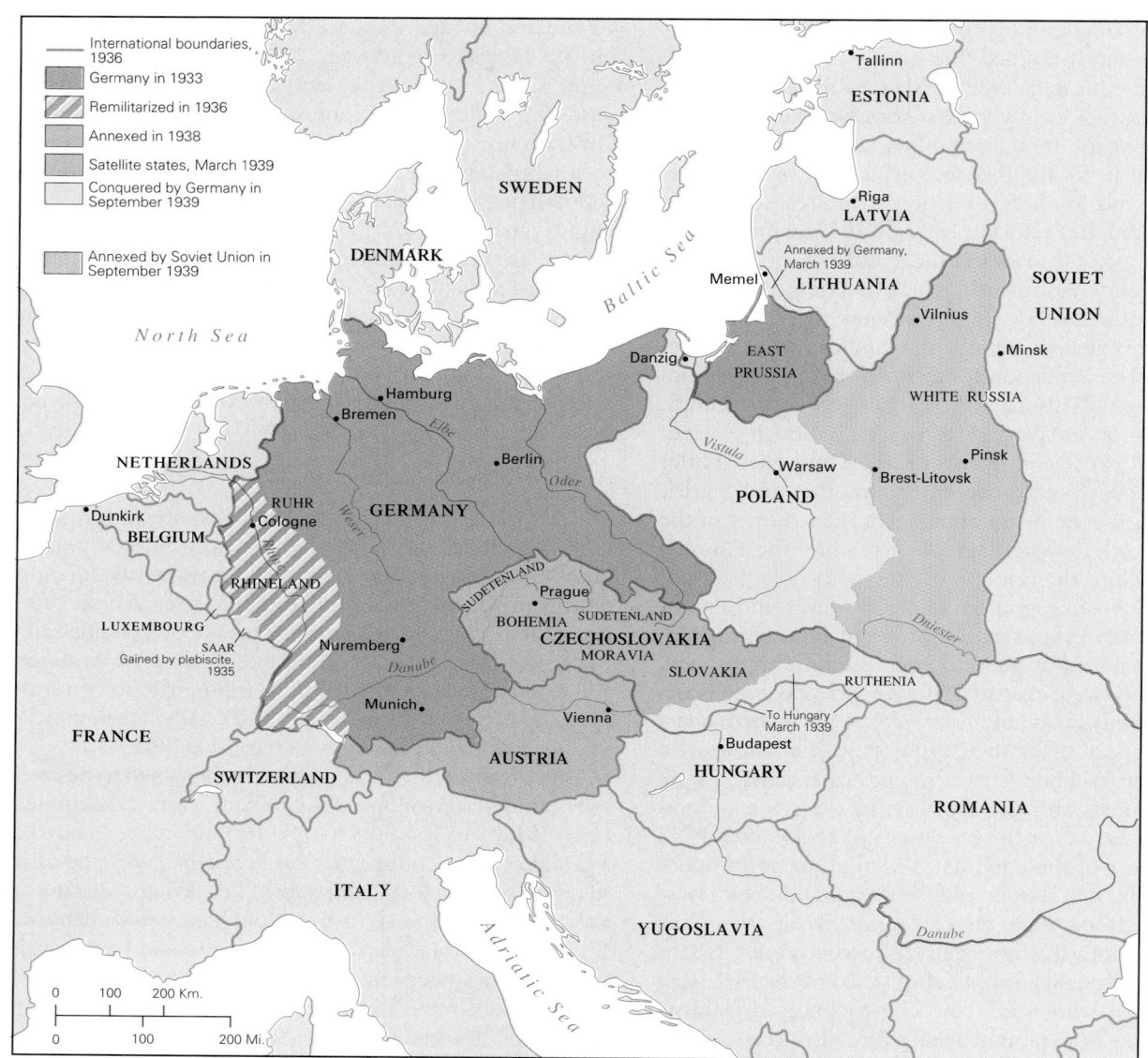

MAP 29.1 The Growth of Nazi Germany, 1933–1939   Until March 1939, Hitler brought ethnic Germans into the Nazi state; then he turned on the Slavic peoples he had always hated. He stripped Czechoslovakia of its independence and prepared for an attack on Poland in September 1939.

Yet the emerging united front against Hitler quickly collapsed. Of crucial importance, Britain adopted a policy of **appeasement,** granting Hitler everything he could reasonably want (and more) in order to avoid war. The first step was an Anglo-German naval agreement in June 1935 that broke Germany's isolation. The second step came in March 1936 when Hitler suddenly marched his armies into the demilitarized Rhineland, brazenly violat-ing the Treaties of Versailles and Locarno. This was the last good chance to stop the Nazis, for Hitler had or-dered his troops to retreat if France resisted militarily. But an uncertain France would not move without British support, and the occupation of German soil by German armies seemed right and just to Britain. With a greatly improved strategic position, Germany handed France a tremendous psychological defeat.

Events Leading to World War II

1919	Treaty of Versailles is signed; J. M. Keynes publishes *Economic Consequences of the Peace.*
1919–1920	U.S. Senate rejects the Treaty of Versailles.
1921	Germany is billed $33 billion in reparations.
1922	Mussolini seizes power in Italy; Germany proposes a moratorium on reparations.
January 1923	France and Belgium occupy the Ruhr; Germany orders passive resistance to the occupation.
October 1923	Stresemann agrees to reparations based on Germany's ability to pay.
1924	Dawes Plan: German reparations are reduced and put on a sliding scale. Large U.S. loans to Germany are recommended to promote German recovery; Adolf Hitler dictates *Mein Kampf.*
1924–1929	Spectacular German economic recovery occurs; circular flow of international funds enables sizable reparations payments.
1925	Treaties of Locarno promote European security and stability.
1926	Germany joins the League of Nations.
1928	Kellogg-Briand Pact renounces war as an instrument of international affairs.
1929	Young Plan further reduces German reparations; U.S. stock market crashes.
1929–1939	Great Depression rages.
1931	Japan invades Manchuria.
1932	Nazis become the largest party in the Reichstag.
January 1933	Hitler is appointed chancellor of Germany.
March 1933	Reichstag passes the Enabling Act, granting Hitler absolute dictatorial power.
October 1933	Germany withdraws from the League of Nations.
July 1934	Nazis murder the Austrian chancellor.
1935	Nuremberg Laws deprive Jews of all rights of citizenship.
March 1935	Hitler announces German rearmament.
June 1935	Anglo-German naval agreement is signed.
October 1935	Mussolini invades Ethiopia and receives Hitler's support.
March 1936	German armies move unopposed into the demilitarized Rhineland.
July 1936	Civil war breaks out in Spain.
1937	Japan invades China; Rome-Berlin Axis in effect.
March 1938	Germany annexes Austria.
September 1938	Munich Conference: Britain and France agree to German seizure of the Sudetenland from Czechoslovakia.
March 1939	Germany occupies the rest of Czechoslovakia; appeasement ends in Britain.
August 1939	Nazi-Soviet nonaggression pact is signed.
September 1, 1939	Germany invades Poland.
September 3, 1939	Britain and France declare war on Germany.

British appeasement, which practically dictated French policy, lasted far into 1939. It was motivated by British feelings of guilt toward Germany and the pacifism of a population still horrified by the memory of the First World War. As in Germany, many powerful conservatives in Britain underestimated Hitler. They believed that Soviet communism was the real danger and that Hitler could be used to stop it. A leading member of Britain's government personally told Hitler in November 1937 that it was his conviction that Hitler "not only had accomplished great things in Germany itself, but that through the total destruction of Communism in his own country . . . Germany rightly had to be considered as a Western bulwark against Communism."[16] Such rigid anticommunist feelings made an alliance between the Western powers and Stalin unlikely.

As Britain and France opted for appeasement and the Soviet Union watched all developments suspiciously, Hitler found powerful allies. In 1935 the bombastic Mussolini decided that imperial expansion was needed to revitalize Italian fascism. From Italian colonies on the east coast of Africa, he attacked the independent African kingdom of Ethiopia. The Western powers and the League of Nations piously condemned Italian aggression, but Hitler supported Italy energetically and overcame Mus-

solini's lingering doubts about the Nazis. The result in late 1936 was an agreement on close cooperation between Italy and Germany, the so-called Rome-Berlin Axis. Japan, which had been expanding into Manchuria since 1931, soon joined the Axis alliance.

At the same time, Germany and Italy intervened in the long, complicated Spanish civil war, where their support eventually helped General Francisco Franco's fascist movement defeat republican Spain. Only the Soviet Union gave aid to the leftist government that Franco fought, for public opinion in Britain and especially in France was hopelessly divided on the Spanish question.

In late 1937, while proclaiming peaceful intentions to the British and their gullible prime minister, Neville Chamberlain, Hitler told his generals his real plans. His "unshakable decision" was to crush Austria and Czechoslovakia at the earliest possible moment as the first step in his long-contemplated drive to the east for living space. By threatening Austria with invasion, Hitler forced the Austrian chancellor in March 1938 to put local Nazis in control of the government. The next day, German armies moved in unopposed, and Austria became two more provinces of Greater Germany (see Map 29.1).

Simultaneously, Hitler began demanding that the pro-Nazi, German-speaking minority of western Czechoslo-

Hitler's Success with Aggression This biting criticism of appeasing leaders by the cartoonist David Low appeared shortly after Hitler remilitarized the Rhineland. Appeasement also appealed to millions of ordinary citizens in Britain and France, who wanted to avoid at any cost another great war. *(Reproduced by permission of London Evening/Solo Standard)*

vakia—the Sudetenland—be turned over to Germany. Yet democratic Czechoslovakia was prepared to defend itself. Moreover, France had been Czechoslovakia's ally since 1924; and if France fought, the Soviet Union was pledged to help. War appeared inevitable, but appeasement triumphed again. In September 1938, Chamberlain flew to Germany three times in fourteen days. In these negotiations, to which the U.S.S.R. was deliberately not invited, Chamberlain and the French agreed with Hitler that the Sudetenland should be ceded to Germany immediately. Returning to London from the Munich Conference, Chamberlain told cheering crowds that he had secured "peace with honor . . . peace for our time." Sold out by the Western powers, Czechoslovakia gave in.

Confirmed once again in his opinion of the Western democracies as weak and racially degenerate, Hitler accelerated his aggression. In a shocking violation of his solemn assurances that the Sudetenland was his last territorial demand, Hitler's armies occupied the Czech lands in March 1939, while Slovakia became a puppet state. The effect on Western public opinion was electrifying. For the first time, there was no possible rationale of self-determination for Nazi aggression since Hitler was seizing Czechs and Slovaks as captive peoples. Thus when Hitler used the question of German minorities in Danzig as a pretext to confront Poland, a suddenly militant Chamberlain declared that Britain and France would fight if Hitler attacked his eastern neighbor. Hitler did not take these warnings seriously and decided to press on.

In an about-face that stunned the world, Hitler offered and Stalin signed a ten-year Nazi-Soviet nonaggression pact in August 1939. Each dictator promised to remain neutral if the other became involved in war. An attached secret protocol, which became known only after the war, ruthlessly divided eastern Europe into German and Soviet zones, "in the event of a political territorial reorganization." The nonaggression pact itself was enough to make Britain and France cry treachery, for they, too, had been negotiating with Stalin. But Stalin had remained distrustful of Western intentions, and Hitler had offered immediate territorial gain.

For Hitler, everything was set. He told his generals on the day of the nonaggression pact, "My only fear is that at the last moment some dirty dog will come up with a mediation plan." On September 1, 1939, German armies and warplanes smashed into Poland from three sides. Two days later, Britain and France, finally true to their word, declared war on Germany. The Second World War had begun.

Hitler's Empire, 1939–1942

Using planes, tanks, and trucks in the first example of a **blitzkrieg,** or "lightning war," Hitler's armies crushed Poland in four weeks. While the Soviet Union quickly took its part of the booty—the eastern half of Poland and the independent Baltic states of Lithuania, Estonia, and Latvia—French and British armies dug in in the west. They expected another war of attrition and economic blockade.

In spring 1940, the lightning war struck again. After occupying Denmark, Norway, and Holland, German motorized columns broke through southern Belgium, split the Franco-British forces, and trapped the entire British army on the beaches of Dunkirk. By heroic efforts, the British withdrew their troops but not their equipment.

France was taken by the Nazis. Aging marshal Henri-Philippe Pétain formed a new French government—the so-called Vichy government—to accept defeat, and German armies occupied most of France. By July 1940, Hitler ruled practically all of western continental Europe; Italy was an ally, and the Soviet Union and Spain were friendly neutrals. Only Britain, led by the uncompromising Winston Churchill (1874–1965), remained unconquered. Churchill proved to be one of history's greatest wartime leaders, rallying the British with stirring speeches, infectious confidence, and bulldog determination.

Germany sought to gain control of the air, the necessary first step toward an amphibious invasion of Britain. In the Battle of Britain, up to a thousand German planes attacked British airfields and key factories in a single day, dueling with British defenders high in the skies. Losses were heavy on both sides. Then in September Hitler angrily and foolishly changed his strategy, turning from military objectives to indiscriminate bombing of British cities in an attempt to break British morale. British aircraft factories increased production, anti-aircraft defense improved with the help of radar, and the heavily bombed people of London defiantly dug in. In September and October 1940, Britain was beating Germany three to one in the air war. There was no possibility of an immediate German invasion of Britain.

In these circumstances, the most reasonable German strategy would have been to attack Britain through the eastern Mediterranean, taking Egypt and the Suez Canal and pinching off Britain's supply of oil. By April 1941, Germany had already moved to the southeast, conquering Greece and Yugoslavia and forcing Hungary, Romania, and Bulgaria into alliances. But Hitler was not a reasonable person. His lifetime obsession with a vast eastern European empire for the "master race" dictated policy. So in June 1941, German armies suddenly attacked

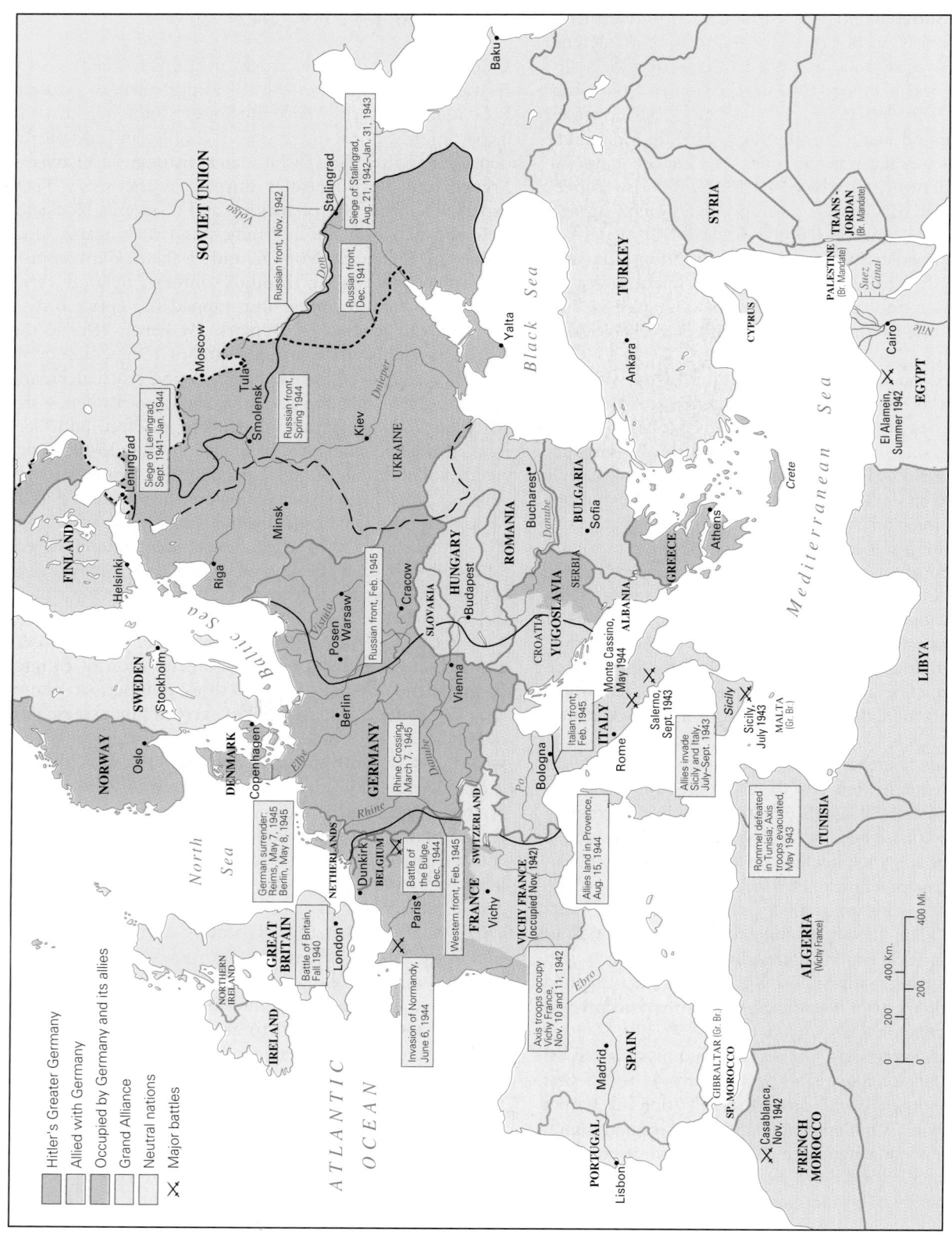

MAP 29.2 World War II in Europe The map shows the extent of Hitler's empire at its height, before the Battle of Stalingrad in late 1942 and the subsequent advances of the Allies until Germany surrendered on May 7, 1945.

Hitler's Greater Germany
Allied with Germany
Occupied by Germany and its allies
Grand Alliance
Neutral nations
X Major battles

SOVIET UNION

Baku

Siege of Stalingrad,
Aug. 21, 1942–Jan. 31, 1943

Stalingrad

Russian front, Nov. 1942

Volga

Don

Russian front,
Dec. 1941

Moscow

Tula

Smolensk

Russian front, Spring 1944

Kiev

Dnieper

UKRAINE

Siege of Leningrad,
Sept. 1941–Jan. 1944

Leningrad

Minsk

Black Sea

Yalta

TURKEY

Ankara

SYRIA

PALESTINE
(Br. Mandate)

TRANS-
JORDAN
(Br. Mandate)

Suez Canal

Nile

Cairo

El Alamein,
Summer 1942

EGYPT

FINLAND

Helsinki

Riga

Baltic Sea

Posen

Warsaw

Russian front, Feb. 1945

Vistula

Cracow

SLOVAKIA

HUNGARY

Budapest

Vienna

ROMANIA

Bucharest

Danube

BULGARIA

Sofia

SERBIA

CROATIA

YUGOSLAVIA

ALBANIA

GREECE

Athens

Crete

CYPRUS

Mediterranean Sea

SWEDEN

Stockholm

NORWAY

Oslo

DENMARK

Copenhagen

Elbe

Berlin

GERMANY

Rhine Crossing,
March 7, 1945

Danube

Po

Bologna

Italian front,
Feb. 1945

Monte Cassino,
May 1944

ITALY

Rome

Salerno,
Sept. 1943

Sicily,
July 1943

Sicily

MALTA
(Gr. Br.)

Allies invade
Sicily and Italy,
July–Sept. 1943

Rommel defeated
in Tunisia; Axis
troops evacuated,
May 1943

TUNISIA

LIBYA

German surrender:
Reims, May 7, 1945
Berlin, May 8, 1945

NETHERLANDS

Dunkirk

BELGIUM

Battle of
the Bulge,
Dec. 1944

SWITZERLAND

Western front, Feb. 1945

FRANCE

Paris

Vichy

VICHY FRANCE
(occupied Nov. 1942)

Axis troops occupy
Vichy France,
Nov. 10 and 11, 1942

Allies land in Provence,
Aug. 15, 1944

Rhine

GREAT
BRITAIN

Battle of Britain,
Fall 1940

London

NORTHERN
IRELAND

IRELAND

Invasion of Normandy,
June 6, 1944

*North
Sea*

Ebro

ALGERIA
(Vichy France)

SP. MOROCCO

GIBRALTAR (Gr. Br.)

SPAIN

Madrid

PORTUGAL

Lisbon

Casablanca,
Nov. 1942

FRENCH
MOROCCO

*ATLANTIC
OCEAN*

400 Mi.

400 Km.

200

200

0

0

London, 1940 Hitler believed that his relentless terror bombing of London—the "blitz"—could break the will of the British people. He was wrong. The blitz caused enormous destruction, but Londoners went about their business with courage and calm determination, as this unforgettable image of a milkman in the rubble suggests. *(Corbis)*

the Soviet Union along a vast front (see Map 29.2). By October 1941, Leningrad was practically surrounded, Moscow was besieged, and most of Ukraine had been overrun. But with Britain still unconquered, Hitler's decision was a wild, irrational gamble epitomizing the violent, unlimited, and ultimately self-destructive ambitions of Nazism. The Soviets did not collapse, and when a severe winter struck German armies outfitted in summer uniforms, the invaders were stopped.

While Hitler's armies dramatically expanded the war in Europe, his Japanese allies did the same in Asia. Engaged in a general but undeclared war against China since 1937, Japan's rulers had increasingly come into diplomatic conflict with the Pacific basin's other great power, the United States. When the Japanese occupied French Indochina in July 1941, the United States retaliated by cutting off sales of vital rubber, scrap iron, oil, and aviation fuel. Tension mounted further, and on December 7, 1941, Japan attacked the U.S. naval base at Pearl Harbor in Hawaii. Hitler immediately declared war on the United States, and Japanese forces advanced swiftly into Southeast Asia (see Map 29.3 on page 982).

Meanwhile, though stalled in Russia, Hitler ruled over a vast European empire stretching from the outskirts of Moscow to the English Channel. Hitler, the Nazi leadership, and the loyal German army were positioned to greatly accelerate construction of their "New Order" in Europe, and they continued their efforts until their final

collapse in 1945. In doing so, they showed what Nazi victory would have meant.

Hitler's **New Order** was based firmly on the guiding principle of Nazi totalitarianism: racial imperialism. Within this New Order, the Nordic peoples—the Dutch, Norwegians, and Danes—received preferential treatment, for they were racially related to the master race, the Germans. The French, an "inferior" Latin people, occupied a middle position. They were heavily taxed to support the Nazi war effort but were tolerated as a race. Once Nazi reverses began to mount in late 1942, however, all the occupied territories of western and northern Europe were exploited with increasing intensity. Material shortages and both mental and physical suffering afflicted millions of people.

Slavs in the conquered territories to the east were treated with harsh hatred as "subhumans." At the height of his success in 1941 and 1942, Hitler set the tone. He painted for his intimate circle the fantastic vision of a vast eastern colonial empire where Poles, Ukrainians, and Russians would be enslaved and forced to die out, while Germanic peasants resettled the resulting abandoned lands. But he needed countless helpers and many ambitious initiators to turn his dreams into reality. These accomplices came forth.

Himmler and the elite corps of SS volunteers, supported (or condoned) by military commanders and German policemen in the occupied territories, pressed relentlessly to implement this program of destruction even before victory was secured. In western Poland, the SS arrested and evacuated Polish peasants to cleanse the region and create a "mass settlement space" for Germans. Polish workers and Soviet prisoners of war were transported to Germany, where conditions of slave labor were so harsh that four out of five Soviet prisoners did not survive the war.

Finally, the Nazi state condemned all European Jews to extermination, along with many Gypsies, Jehovah's Witnesses, and captured communists. After the fall of Warsaw, the Nazis stepped up their expulsion campaign and began deporting all German Jews to occupied Poland. There they and Jews from all over Europe were concentrated in ghettos, compelled to wear the Jewish star, and turned into slave laborers.

In 1941, as part of the "war of annihilation" in the Soviet Union, expulsion spiraled into extermination. On the Russian front, Himmler's special SS killing squads and also regular army units forced Soviet Jews to dig giant pits, which became mass graves as the victims were lined up on the edge and cut down by machine guns. Then in late 1941, Hitler and the Nazi leadership, in some still-debated combination, ordered the SS to stop all Jewish emigration from Europe and speeded up planning for mass murder. As one German diplomat put it, "The Jewish Question must be resolved in the course of the war, for only so can it be solved without a worldwide outcry."[17] The "final solution of the Jewish question"— the murder of every single Jew—had begun. Jews were systematically arrested, packed like cattle onto freight trains, and dispatched to extermination camps. Many

Prelude to Murder   This photo captures the terrible inhumanity of Nazi racism. Frightened and bewildered families from the soon-to-be-destroyed Warsaw Ghetto are being forced out of their homes by German soldiers for deportation to concentration camps. There they face murder in the gas chambers. *(Hulton Archive/Getty Images)*

Jews could hardly imagine the enormity of the crime that lay before them. (See the feature "Listening to the Past: Witness to the Holocaust" on pages 986–987.)

At the camps, the victims were taken by force or deception to "shower rooms," which were actually gas chambers. These gas chambers, first perfected in the quiet, efficient execution of seventy thousand mentally ill Germans between 1938 and 1941, permitted rapid, hideous, and thoroughly bureaucratized mass murder. For fifteen to twenty minutes came the terrible screams and gasping sobs of men, women, and children choking to death on poison gas. Then, only silence. Special camp workers quickly yanked the victims' gold teeth from their jaws, and the bodies were then cremated, or sometimes boiled for oil to make soap. At Auschwitz-Birkenau, the most infamous of the Nazi death factories, as many as twelve thousand human beings were slaughtered each day. The extermination of European Jews was the ultimate monstrosity of Nazi racism and racial imperialism. By 1945, 6 million Jews had been murdered.

Who was responsible for this terrible crime? An older generation of historians usually laid most of the guilt on Hitler and the Nazi leadership. Ordinary Germans had little knowledge of the extermination camps, it was argued, and those who cooperated had no alternative given the brutality of Nazi terror and totalitarian control. But in recent years, many studies have revealed a much broader participation of German people in the Holocaust and popular indifference (or worse) to the fate of the Jews. Yet exactly why so many perpetrated or condoned Nazi crimes has remained unclear.

In a controversial work, the American historian Daniel Goldhagen has reignited discussion of Nazi crimes by arguing that, above all, the extreme anti-Semitism of "ordinary Germans" led them to respond to Hitler and to become his "willing executioners" in World War II.[18] Yet in most occupied countries, local non-German officials also cooperated in the arrest and deportation of Jews to a large extent. As in Germany, only a few exceptional bystanders, like those in the French village of Le Chambon, did not turn a blind eye. (See the feature "Individuals in Society: Le Chambon, a Refuge for the Persecuted.") Thus some scholars have concluded that the key for most Germans (and most people in occupied countries) was that they felt no personal responsibility for Jews, and therefore they were not prepared to help them. This meant that many individuals, conditioned by Nazi racist propaganda but also influenced by peer pressure and brutalizing wartime violence, were psychologically prepared to perpetrate ever-greater crimes. They were ready to plumb the depths of evil and to spiral downward from mistreatment to arrest to mass murder.

The Grand Alliance

While the Nazis built their savage empire, the Allies faced the hard fact that chance, rather than choice, had brought them together. Stalin had been cooperating fully with Hitler between August 1939 and June 1941, and only the Japanese attack on Pearl Harbor in December 1941 and Hitler's immediate declaration of war had overwhelmed powerful isolationism in the United States. The Allies' first task was to overcome their mutual suspicions and build an unshakable alliance on the quicksand of accident. By means of three interrelated policies, they succeeded.

First, President Roosevelt accepted Churchill's contention that the United States should concentrate first on defeating Hitler. Only after victory in Europe was achieved would the United States turn toward the Pacific for an all-out attack on Japan, the lesser threat. The promise of huge military aid under America's policy of **Europe first** helped solidify the anti-Hitler coalition.

Second, within the European framework, the Americans and the British put immediate military needs first. They consistently postponed tough political questions relating to the eventual peace settlement and thereby avoided conflicts that might have split the alliance until after the war.

Third, to further encourage mutual trust, the Allies adopted the principle of the "unconditional surrender" of Germany and Japan. This policy cemented the Grand Alliance because it denied Hitler any hope of dividing his foes. It probably also discouraged Germans and Japanese who might have tried to overthrow their dictators in order to make a compromise peace. Of great importance for the postwar shape of Europe, it meant that Soviet and Anglo-American armies would almost certainly come together to divide all of Germany, and most of the continent, among the victorious allies.

The military resources of the Grand Alliance were awesome. The strengths of the United States were its mighty industry, its large population, and its national unity. Even before Pearl Harbor, President Roosevelt had called America the "arsenal of democracy" and given military aid to Britain and the Soviet Union. Now the United States geared up rapidly for all-out war production and drew heavily on a generally cooperative Latin America for resources. It not only equipped its own armies but also eventually gave its allies about $50 billion in arms and equipment. Britain received by far the most, but about one-fifth of the total went to the Soviet Union in the form of badly needed trucks, planes, and munitions.

Too strong to lose and too weak to win standing alone, Britain continued to make a great contribution as well. The British economy was totally and effectively

The Normandy Invasion, Omaha Beach Airborne paratroopers landed behind German coastal fortifications around midnight, and American and British forces hit several beaches at daybreak as Allied ships and bombers provided cover. American troops secured full control of Omaha Beach by nightfall, but at a price of three thousand casualties. Allied air power prevented the Germans from bringing up reserves and counterattacking. *(Corbis)*

mobilized, and the sharing of burdens through rationing and heavy taxes on war profits maintained social harmony. Moreover, by early 1943 the Americans and the British were combining small aircraft carriers with radar-guided bombers to rid the Atlantic of German submarines. Britain, the impregnable floating fortress, became a gigantic frontline staging area for the decisive blow to the heart of Germany.

As for the Soviet Union, so great was its strength that it might well have defeated Germany without Western help. In the face of the German advance, whole factories and populations were successfully evacuated to eastern Russia and Siberia. There war production was reorganized and expanded, and the Red Army was increasingly well supplied. The Red Army was also well led, for a new generation of talented military leaders quickly arose to replace those so recently purged. Most important of all, Stalin drew on the massive support and heroic determination of the Soviet people, especially those in the central Russian heartland. Broad-based Russian nationalism, as opposed to narrow communist ideology, became the powerful unifying force in what was appropriately called the "Great Patriotic War of the Fatherland."

Finally, the United States, Britain, and the Soviet Union were not alone. They had the resources of much of the world at their command. And, to a greater or lesser extent, they were aided by a growing resistance movement against the Nazis throughout Europe, even in Germany. Thus although Ukrainian peasants sometimes welcomed the Germans as liberators, the barbaric occupation policies of the Nazis quickly drove them to join and support behind-the-lines guerrilla forces. More generally, after the U.S.S.R. was invaded in June 1941, communists throughout Europe took the lead in the underground resistance, joined by a growing number of patriots and Christians. Anti-Nazi leaders from occupied countries established governments-in-exile in London, like that of the "Free French" under the intensely proud General Charles de Gaulle. These governments gathered valuable secret information from resistance fighters and even organized armies to help defeat Hitler.

The Tide of Battle

Barely halted at the gates of Moscow and Leningrad in 1941, the Germans renewed their offensive against the Soviet Union in July 1942, driving toward the southern city of Stalingrad and occupying most of the city in a month of incredibly savage house-to-house fighting.

Then, in November 1942, Soviet armies counterattacked. They rolled over Romanian and Italian troops to the north and south of Stalingrad, quickly closing the

Individuals in Society

Le Chambon, a Refuge for the Persecuted

On a cold night in February 1943, French officials arrived in Le Chambon-sur-Lignon in southern France. Known as a "nest of Jews in Protestant country," Le Chambon was a mountainous town of three thousand people that hid Jews and openly said so to the government.* Now the officials had finally come to arrest the Protestant minister André Trocmé, the assistant minister Edouard Theis, and the local school principal—the leaders of this defiant cell. Watching silently, the villagers demonstrated their unmistakable solidarity. They lined the streets, sang "A Mighty Fortress Is Our God," and then fell in behind their friends as they passed. As on other occasions, the people of Le Chambon showed the moral courage that would cause others in the region to search their hearts and examine their own conduct toward Jews.

Imprisoned in a camp with communists and resistance fighters, the three men led religious services, discussion groups, and classes that attracted prisoners and even guards. The camp administration, perhaps fearing that its authority was being subverted, offered the three men freedom in return for a signed oath of obedience to the Vichy government, which ruled southern France in collaboration with the Nazi occupiers in the north. Trocmé and his companions refused, but they were mysteriously released the next day. Returning home, Trocmé believed that the village had influential friends in the government.

The strength of the villagers and the quality of their leadership, so clearly evident in these confrontations with the state in early 1943, help explain how Le Chambon became one of the safest places for Jews in Europe in the first two years of the Nazi occupation and how it and the surrounding area successfully sheltered about thirty-five hundred Jewish refugees. Pastors Trocmé and Theis were inspired rebels who wanted to live an active, dangerous Christian love. They conceived of Le Chambon as a city of refuge for the innocent and as a means of overcoming evil with good through nonviolence. Magda Trocmé, André's spirited wife and the mother of four young children, was equally important. Warm and practical, she instinctively aided those in need. She welcomed Jews arriving at the parsonage, housed them, and helped find families to shelter them. She carried on after André himself fled in late 1943 to escape arrest by the Gestapo. Within the village, prayer meetings became conspiracies of goodness. A Jewish refugee printer forged papers and ration cards for the guests, and Theis and the local network helped them escape to Switzerland.

If the how is clear, the why is less so. Certainly a collective memory of persecution helped the Protestants of Le Chambon and nearby villages to identify with the Jews and feel a moral responsibility for their fate. They, too, were a tiny minority in France, the descendants of Protestant refugees who had fled to the mountains and been hounded and executed. But non-Protestants also joined the cause. Above all, the Trocmés, Theis, and the villagers responded because they had a strong moral philosophy rooted in their Christian belief. They believed that they should not obey evil laws but rather abide by God's commandments. They considered it evil to harm anyone, for God had instructed them to love and care for each other. Finally, Le Chambon was broadly representative of other exceptional groups and individuals who worked to help Jews in Nazi Europe. The common experience showed that a sense of moral responsibility was crucial, and that goodness, like evil, is contagious in life-and-death ethical situations.

André and Magda Trocmé, resistance leaders at Le Chambon, in a family snapshot taken shortly before 1940. (Papers of André and Magda Trocmé, Swarthmore College Peace Collection)

Questions for Analysis

1. What did the people of Le Chambon-sur-Lignon do? Why did they do it?
2. What is the larger significance of the town's actions in terms of the Holocaust? Debate the idea that "goodness, like evil, is contagious."

*Philip Hallie, *Lest Innocent Blood Be Shed: The Story of the Village of Le Chambon and How Goodness Happened There* (New York: Harper & Row, 1979), p. 18. In addition to this moving study, see *Weapons of Spirit* (1986), a documentary film by Pierre Sauvage.

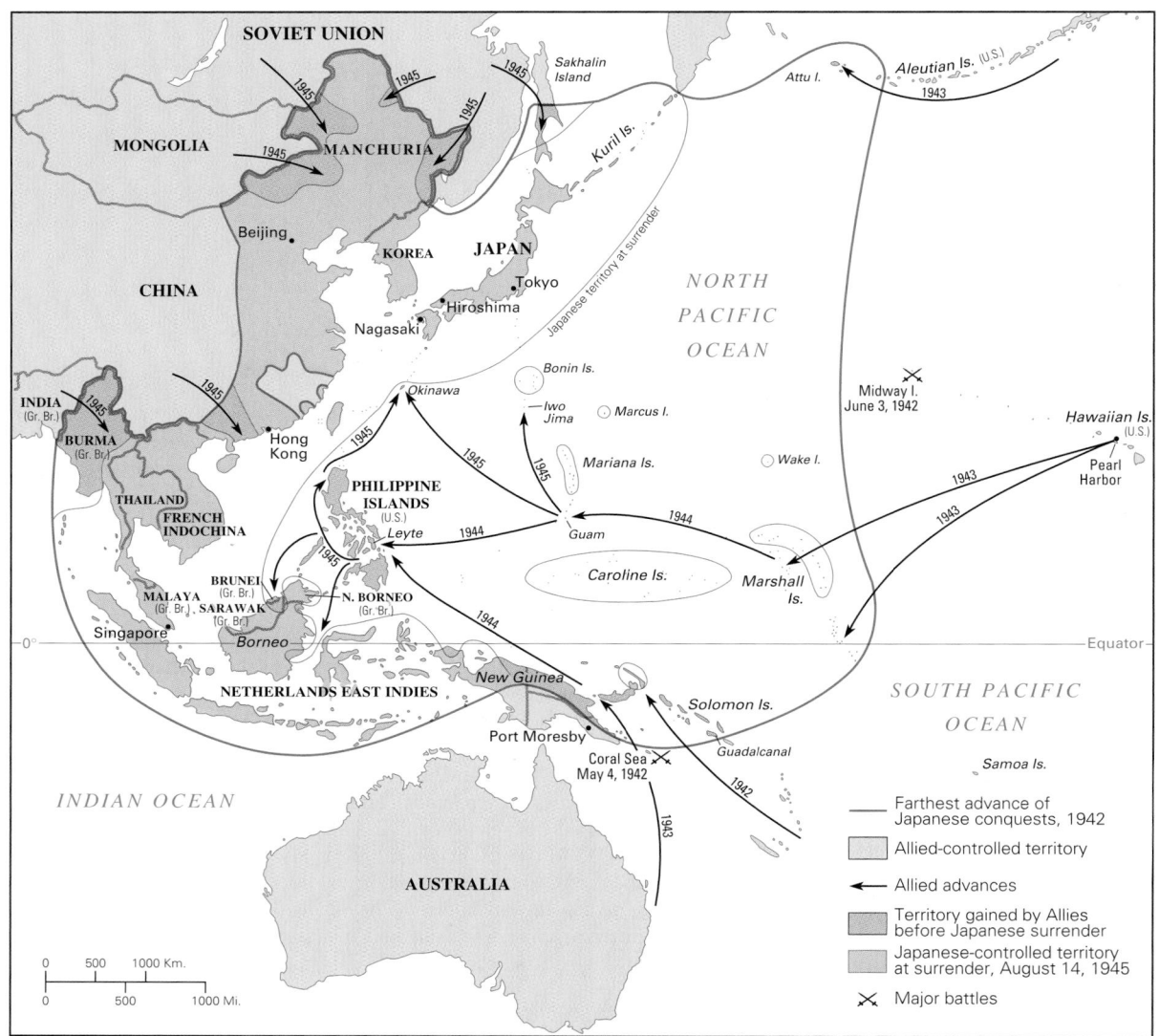

MAP 29.3 World War II in the Pacific   Japanese forces overran an enormous amount of territory in 1942, which the Allies slowly recaptured in a long, bitter struggle. As this map shows, Japan still held a large Asian empire in August 1945, when the unprecedented devastation of atomic warfare suddenly forced it to surrender.

trap and surrounding the entire German Sixth Army of 300,000 men. The surrounded Germans were systematically destroyed, until by the end of January 1943 only 123,000 soldiers were left to surrender. Hitler, who had refused to allow a retreat, had suffered a catastrophic defeat. In the summer of 1943, the larger, better-equipped Soviet armies took the offensive and began moving forward (see Map 29.2).

In late 1942, the tide also turned in the Pacific and in North Africa. By late spring 1942, Japan had established a

great empire in East Asia (see Map 29.3). Unlike the Nazis, the Japanese made clever appeals to local nationalists, who hated European imperial domination and preferred Japan's so-called Greater Asian Co-prosperity Sphere.

Then in the Battle of the Coral Sea in May 1942, Allied naval and air power stopped the Japanese advance and also relieved Australia from the threat of invasion. This victory was followed by the Battle of Midway Island, in which American pilots sank all four of the attacking Japanese aircraft carriers and established American naval superiority in the Pacific. In August 1942, American marines attacked Guadalcanal in the Solomon Islands. Badly hampered by the policy of "Europe first"—only 15 percent of Allied resources were going to fight the war in the Pacific in early 1943—the Americans and the Australians nevertheless began "island hopping" toward Japan. Japanese forces were on the defensive.

In North Africa the war had been seesawing back and forth since 1940 (see Map 29.2). In May 1942, combined German and Italian armies were finally defeated by British forces at the Battle of El Alamein, only seventy miles from Alexandria. In October the British counterattacked in Egypt, and almost immediately thereafter an Anglo-American force landed in Morocco and Algeria. These French possessions, which were under the control of Pétain's Vichy government, quickly went over to the side of the Allies.

Having driven the Axis powers from North Africa by the spring of 1943, Allied forces maintained the initiative by invading Sicily and then mainland Italy. Mussolini was deposed by a war-weary people, and the new Italian government publicly accepted unconditional surrender in September 1943. Italy, it seemed, was liberated. Yet German commandos rescued Mussolini in a daring raid and put him at the head of a puppet government. German armies seized Rome and all of northern Italy. Fighting continued in Italy.

Indeed, bitter fighting continued in Europe for almost two years. Germany, less fully mobilized for war than Britain in 1941, applied itself to total war in 1942 and enlisted millions of German women and millions of prisoners of war and slave laborers from all across occupied Europe in that effort. Between early 1942 and July 1944, German war production actually tripled. Although British and American bombing raids killed many German civilians, these raids were surprisingly ineffective from a military point of view. Also, German resistance against Hitler failed. After an unsuccessful attempt on Hitler's life in July 1944, SS fanatics brutally liquidated thousands of Germans. Terrorized at home and frightened by the prospect of unconditional surrender, the Germans fought on with suicidal stoicism.

On June 6, 1944, American and British forces under General Dwight Eisenhower landed on the beaches of Normandy, France, in history's greatest naval invasion. In a hundred dramatic days, more than 2 million men and almost half a million vehicles pushed inland and broke through German lines. Rejecting proposals to strike straight at Berlin in a massive attack, Eisenhower moved forward cautiously on a broad front. Not until March 1945 did American troops cross the Rhine and enter Germany.

A Hiroshima Survivor Remembers Yasuko Yamagata was seventeen when she saw the brilliant blue-white "lightning flash" that became a fiery orange ball consuming everything that would burn. Thirty years later Yamagata painted this scene, her most unforgettable memory of the atomic attack. An incinerated woman, poised as if running with her baby clutched to her breast, lies near a water tank piled high with charred corpses. *(From a public exhibition assembled by the Japan Broadcasting Corporation)*

The Soviets, who had been advancing steadily since July 1943, reached the outskirts of Warsaw by August 1944. For the next six months, they moved southward into Romania, Hungary, and Yugoslavia. In January 1945, the Red Army again moved westward through Poland, and on April 26 it met American forces on the Elbe River. The Allies had closed their vise on Nazi Germany and overrun Europe. As Soviet forces fought their way into Berlin, Hitler committed suicide in his bunker, and on May 7 the remaining German commanders capitulated.

Three months later, the United States dropped atomic bombs on Hiroshima and Nagasaki in Japan. Mass bombing of cities and civilians, one of the terrible new practices of World War II, had ended in the final nightmare—unprecedented human destruction in a single blinding flash. On August 14, 1945, the Japanese announced their surrender. The Second World War, which had claimed the lives of more than 50 million soldiers and civilians, was over.

Summary

The Second World War marked the climax of the tremendous practical and spiritual maladies of the age of anxiety, which led in many lands to the rise of dictatorships. Many of these dictatorships were variations on conservative authoritarianism, but there was also a fateful innovation—a new kind of dictatorship that was dynamic and theoretically unlimited in its actions.

When apprehensive middle-class liberals in the West faced the rise of these new dictatorships, they often focused on their perceived similarities. Liberals fastened on the violent, profoundly antiliberal, and apparently totalitarian character of these brutal challengers, linking the one-party socialism of Lenin and Stalin with the one-party fascism of Mussolini and Hitler. In contrast, the political left often insisted on the differences between the revolutionary socialist tradition—triumphing, however imperfectly, in the Bolsheviks' Soviet Union—and the reactionary and capitalist nature of European fascist movements and fascist governments in Italy and Germany.

As the dramatic struggles of the 1930s and the Second World War (and early cold war) fall into a longer perspective and as more historians concentrate on the specific developments in each regime, Hitler's Nazism appears increasingly as a uniquely evil and nihilistic system. Nazism had fascist origins, but German fascism in power ultimately presented only superficial similarities with fascism in Italy. As for Hitler's Germany and Stalin's U.S.S.R., both asserted a total claim on the lives of their citizens, posed ambitious goals, and found enthusiastic supporters. This combination gave both dictatorships their awesome power and dynamism. That dynamism was, however, channeled in quite different directions. Stalin and the Communist party aimed at building their kind of socialism and a new socialist personality at home. Hitler and the Nazi elite aimed at unlimited territorial and racial aggression on behalf of a master race; domestic recovery was only a means to that end.

Nazi racism and unlimited aggression made war inevitable, first with the western European democracies, then with hated eastern neighbors, and finally with the United States. Plunging Europe into the ultimate nightmare, unlimited aggression unwittingly forged a mighty coalition that smashed the racist Nazi empire and its leader. In the words of the ancient Greeks, he whom the gods would destroy, they first make mad.

Key Terms

totalitarianism	Lateran Agreement
fascism	Nazism
five-year plan	Führer
New Economic Policy (NEP)	Enabling Act
collectivization	appeasement
kulaks	blitzkrieg
Black Shirts	New Order
	Europe first

Notes

1. A. Gleason, *Totalitarianism: The Inner History of the World War* (New York: Oxford University Press, 1995), p. 50.
2. E. Halévy, *The Era of Tyrannies* (Garden City, N.Y.: Doubleday, 1965), pp. 265–316, esp. p. 300.
3. I. Kershaw, *The Nazi Dictatorship: Problems and Perspectives of Interpretation,* 2d ed. (London: Edward Arnold, 1989), p. 34.
4. Quoted in A. G. Mazour, *Soviet Economic Development: Operation Outstrip, 1921–1965* (Princeton, N.J.: Van Nostrand, 1967), p. 130.
5. Quoted in I. Deutscher, *Stalin: A Political Biography,* 2d ed. (New York: Oxford University Press, 1967), p. 325.
6. R. Conquest, *The Harvest of Sorrow: Soviet Collectivization and the Terror-Famine* (New York: Oxford University Press, 1986), pp. 4, 303.
7. Quoted in H. K. Geiger, *The Family in Soviet Russia* (Cambridge, Mass.: Harvard University Press, 1968), p. 156.
8. Quoted in B. Rosenthal, "Women in the Russian Revolution and After," in *Becoming Visible: Women in European History,* ed. R. Bridenthal and C. Koonz (Boston: Houghton Mifflin, 1976), p. 383.
9. M. Malia, *The Soviet Tragedy: A History of Socialism in Russia* (New York: Free Press, 1994), p. 248.
10. R. Thurston, *Life and Terror in Stalin's Russia, 1934–1941* (New Haven, Conn.: Yale University Press, 1996), esp. pp. 16–106; also Malia, *The Soviet Tragedy,* pp. 227–270.
11. R. Vivarelli, "Interpretations on the Origins of Fascism," *Journal of Modern History* 63 (March 1991): 41.
12. W. Brustein, *The Logic of Evil: The Social Origins of the Nazi Party, 1925–1933* (New Haven, Conn.: Yale University Press, 1996), pp. 52, 182.
13. Quoted in K. D. Bracher, *The German Dictatorship: The Origins, Structure and Effects of National Socialism* (New York: Praeger, 1970), pp. 146–147.
14. Quoted in R. Stromberg, *An Intellectual History of Modern Europe* (New York: Appleton-Century-Crofts, 1966), p. 393.
15. Quoted in Bracher, *The German Dictatorship,* p. 289.
16. Quoted ibid., p. 306.
17. Quoted in M. Marrus, *The Holocaust in History* (Hanover, N.H., and London: University Press of New England, 1987), p. 28.
18. D. Goldhagen, *Hitler's Willing Executioners: Ordinary Germans and the Holocaust* (New York: Vintage Books, 1997).

Suggested Reading

The historical literature on fascist and totalitarian dictatorships is rich and fascinating. Kershaw's work, cited in the Notes, provides an excellent survey of this literature, includes extensive bibliographical references, and is highly recommended. P. Brooker, *Twentieth-Century Dictatorships: The Ideological One-Party State* (1995), compares leading examples throughout the world, and Gleason, cited in the Notes, is an important recent study. H. Arendt, *The Origins of Totalitarianism* (1951), is a classic interpretation. F. L. Carsten, *The Rise of Fascism* (1982), and W. Laqueur, ed., *Fascism* (1976), are also recommended. Z. Sternhell, *Neither Right nor Left: Fascist Ideology in France* (1986), is important and stimulating, stressing the antiliberal and antisocialist origins of fascist thinking in France.

Malia's work, cited in the Notes, is a provocative reassessment of Soviet history and an excellent introduction to scholarly debates. It may be compared with the fine synthesis of M. Lewin, *The Making of the Soviet System* (1985). R. Stites, *The Women's Liberation Movement in Russia: Feminism, Nihilism, and Bolshevism, 1860–1930* (1978), and the works by Geiger and Deutscher, cited in the Notes, are highly recommended. D. Volkogonov, *Autopsy for an Empire: The Seven Leaders Who Built the Soviet Union* (1998), is an engrossing collective biography by a leading Russian historian. S. Cohen, *Bukharin and the Bolshevik Revolution* (1973), examines the leading spokesman of moderate communism, who was destroyed by Stalin. R. Conquest, *The Great Terror: A Reassessment* (1990), is an excellent account of Stalin's purges of the 1930s, and A. Solzhenitsyn, *The Gulag Archipelago* (1964), passionately condemns Soviet police terror. Three important reconsiderations of Soviet purges, women, and urban life are Thurston's revisionist work, cited in the Notes; S. Fitzpatrick and Y. Slezkine, eds., *In the Shadow of Revolution: Life Stories of Russian Women from 1917 to the Second World War* (2000); and S. Kotkin, *Magnetic Mountain: Stalinism as Civilization* (1995). Arthur Koestler, *Darkness at Noon* (1956), is a famous fictional account of Stalin's trials of the Old Bolsheviks. Conquest's work, cited in the Notes, authoritatively recounts Soviet collectivization and the human-made famine. J. Scott, *Behind the Urals* (1973), is a remarkable eyewitness account of an American steelworker in the Soviet Union in the 1930s.

A. De Grand, *Italian Fascism: Its Origins and Development* (1989), and A. Lyttelton, *The Seizure of Power: Fascism in Italy, 1919–1929,* 2d ed. (1987), are excellent studies of Italy under Mussolini. D. Mack Smith, *Mussolini* (1982), is authoritative. Ignazio Silone, *Bread and Wine* (1937), is a moving novel by a famous opponent of dictatorship in Italy. E. Morante, *History* (1978), a fictional account of one family's divergent reactions to Mussolini's rule, is recommended. Two excellent books on Spain are H. Thomas, *The Spanish Civil War* (1977), and E. Malefakis, *Agrarian Reform and Peasant Revolution in Spain* (1970). In the area of foreign relations, G. Kennan, *Russia and the West Under Lenin and Stalin* (1961), is justly famous. R. Paxton, *Vichy France* (1973), tells a controversial story extremely well.

On Germany, F. Stern, *The Politics of Cultural Despair* (1963), and W. Smith, *The Ideological Origins of Nazi Imperialism* (1986), are fine complementary studies on the origins of Nazism. Bracher's work, cited in the Notes, remains an outstanding account of Hitler's Germany. Two major studies by influential German historians are M. Brozat, *The Nazi State* (1981), and H. Mommsen, *From Weimar to Auschwitz* (1991). W. Shirer, *The Rise and Fall of the Third Reich* (1960), is a gripping popular account of an American journalist who experienced Nazi Germany firsthand. A. Bullock, *Hitler and Stalin* (1993), is a fascinating comparison by a master biographer, while I. Kershaw, *The "Hitler Myth": Image and Reality in the Third Reich* (1987), is a provocative reassessment of Hitler's power. P. Fritzsche, *Germans into Nazis* (1999), argues provocatively that Hitler embodied the hopes of both the lower and middle classes, and M. Mayer, *They Thought They Were Free* (1955), probes the minds of ten ordinary Nazis who supported Hitler. A. Speer, *Inside the Third Reich* (1970), contains the fascinating recollections of Hitler's wizard of the armaments industry. C. Koonz, *Mothers in the Fatherland: Women, the Family, and Nazi Politics* (1987), and D. Peukert, *Inside Nazi Germany: Conformity, Opposition, and Racism in Everyday Life* (1987), are pioneering forays into the social history of the Nazi era. Moving accounts of the Holocaust include Y. Bauer, *A History of the Holocaust* (1982); M. Gilbert, *The Holocaust: The History of the Jews During the Second World War* (1985); and R. Hilberg, *The Destruction of the European Jews, 1933–1945,* 3 vols., rev. ed. (1985), a monumental scholarly achievement. M. Marrus, *The Holocaust in History* (1987), is an excellent interpretive survey, and I. Clendinnen, *Reading the Holocaust* (1999), is an imaginative reconsideration of victims and perpetrators. Goldhagen's widely debated study, cited in the Notes, may be compared with C. Browning, *Ordinary Men: Reserve Police Battalion 101 and the Final Solution in Poland* (1992). E. Staub, *The Roots of Evil: The Origins of Genocide and Other Group Violence* (1989), is a profound study by a noted psychologist with a gift for history. Especially recommended are E. Weisel, *Night* (1961), a brief and compelling autobiographical account of a young Jew in a Nazi concentration camp; and A. Frank, *The Diary of Anne Frank,* is a remarkable personal account of a Jewish girl in hiding during the Nazi occupation of Holland. R. Gellately and N. Stolzfus, eds., *Social Outsiders in Nazi Germany* (2001), studies other groups that were oppressed in addition to the Jews, and A. Fraser, *The Gypsies* (1992), considers a misunderstood people decimated by Nazi terror.

J. Campbell, *The Experience of World War II* (1989), is attractively illustrated and captures the drama of global conflict, as does G. Keegan, *The Second World War* (1990). G. Wright, *The Ordeal of Total War, 1939–1945* (1990), and C. Emsley, *World War II and Its Consequences* (1990), are also recommended. G. Weinberg, *World at Arms: A Global History of World War II* (1994), is a masterful interconnected overview. Two dramatic studies of special aspects of the war are A. Dallin, *German Rule in Russia, 1941–1945* (1981), which analyzes the effects of Nazi occupation policies on the Soviet population, and L. Collins and D. La Pierre, *Is Paris Burning?* (1965), a best-selling account of the liberation of Paris and Hitler's plans to destroy the city.

Witness to the Holocaust

The Second World War brought mass murder to the innocent. The Nazis and their allies slaughtered 6 million Jews in addition to about 5 million Slavs, Gypsies, Jehovah's Witnesses, homosexuals, and mentally ill persons. On the Russian front, some Jews were simply mowed down with machine guns, but most Jews were arrested in their homelands and taken in freight cars to unknown destinations, which were in fact extermination camps. The most infamous camp—really two camps on different sides of a railroad track—was Auschwitz-Birkenau in eastern Poland. There 2 million people were murdered in gas chambers.

The testimony of camp survivors helps us comprehend the unspeakable crime known to history as the Holocaust. One eyewitness was Marco Nahon, a Greek Jew and physician who escaped extermination at Auschwitz-Birkenau along with several thousand other slave laborers in the camp. The following passage is taken from Birkenau: The Camp of Death, *which Nahon wrote in 1945 after his liberation. Conquered by Germany in 1941, Greece was divided into German, Italian, and Bulgarian zones of occupation. The Nahon family lived in Dimotika in the Bulgarian zone.*

Early in March 1943, disturbing news arrives from Salonika [in the German occupation zone]: the Germans are deporting the Jews [of Salonika]. They lock them up in railway cattlecars . . . and send them to an unknown destination—to Poland, it is said. . . . Relatives and friends deliberate. What can be done in the face of this imminent threat? . . . My friend Vitalis Djivré speaks with conviction: "We must flee, cross over into Turkey at once, go to Palestine, Egypt—anywhere at all—but leave immediately." . . . A few friends and I held a completely different opinion. . . . [I say that] I am not going to emigrate. They are going to take us away to Germany or Poland [to work]? If so, I'll work. . . . It is certain that the Allies will be the victors, and once the war is over, we'll go back home. . . .

Until the end we were deaf to all the warnings. . . . [None of the warnings] would be regarded as indicating the seriousness of the drama in preparation. But does not the human mind find inconceivable the total extermination of an innocent population? In this tragic error lay the main cause, the sole cause, of our perdition. . . .

On Monday May 10, 1943, the bugles awaken us at a very early hour. We [have already been arrested and] today we are leaving for Poland. . . . As soon as a freight car has been packed to capacity with people, it is quickly locked up, and immediately the remaining passengers are pushed into the next one. . . .

Every two days the train stops in some meadow in open country. The car doors are flung open, and the whole transport spreads out in the fields. Men and women attend to their natural needs, side by side, without any embarrassment. Necessity and common misfortune have made them part of one and the same family. . . .

We are now in a small station in Austria. Our car door half opens; a Schupo [German police officer] is asking for the doctor. . . . He leads me to the rear of the convoy and shuts me inside the car where the woman is in labor. She is very young; this is her first child. The car, like all the others, is overcrowded. The delivery takes place in deplorable conditions, in front of everybody—men, women, and children. Fortunately, everything turns out well, and a few hours later a baby boy comes into the world. The new mother's family is very happy and passes candy around. Surely no one realizes that two days later the mother and her baby and more than half of the company will pass through the chimney of a crematorium at Birkenau.

It is May 16, 1943. We have reached the end of our journey [and arrived at Auschwitz-Birkenau]. The train stops along a wooden platform. Through the openings of the cars we can see people wearing strange costumes of blue and white stripes [the prisoners who work in the camp]. We immediately notice that they are doing nothing voluntarily but are moving and acting on command. . . . The people in stripes . . . line us up five by five, the women on one side, the men on the other. I lose sight of my wife and little girl in the crowd. I will never see them again.

They make us march, swiftly as always, before a group of [German] officers. One of them, without uttering a word and with the tip of his forefinger, makes a rapid selection. He is, as we know later on, the Lagerarzt, the SS medical doctor of the camp [the notorious Dr. Mengele]. They call him here the "Angel of Death." [Mengele divides the men into two groups: those who are young and sturdy for work in the camp, and those who are old, sick, and children. The women are also divided and only healthy young women without children are assigned to work. All those not selected for work] are immediately loaded on trucks and driven off somewhere. Where? Nobody knows yet. . . .

[After being assigned to a crude windowless barrack,] we must file before the . . . scribes, who are responsible for receiving and registering the transport. Each prisoner must fill out a form in which he relinquishes his identity and becomes a mere number. . . . I am given the number 122274. My son, who is next, gets 122275. This tattoo alarms us terribly. . . . Each one of us now comes to realize in the deepest part of his conscious being, and with a bitter sense of affliction, that from this moment on he is no more than an animal. . . .

After our meal [of watery soup] Léon Yahiel, a veteran among the Lager inmates, . . . gives us this little speech: "My friends, here you must . . . forget your families, your wives, your children. You must live only for yourselves and try to last as long as possible." At these words our spirits plunge into grief and despair. Forget about our families? The hint is unmistakable. Our minds are confused. . . . Our families taken away from us forever? No, it is humanly not conceivable that we should pay such a penalty without having done anything to deserve it, without any provocation.

Jewish victims of Nazism, on the arrival platform at Auschwitz station. (*AKG London*)

What miserable wretches we prisoners are! We have no idea that while we entertain these thoughts, our wives, our children, our mothers and our fathers have already ceased to exist. They have arrived at Auschwitz this morning, healthy and full of life. They have now been reduced to smoke and ashes.

Questions for Analysis

1. How did the Jews of Dimotika react in early 1943 to the news of Jews being deported? Why?

2. Describe the journey to Auschwitz-Birkenau. Did those on the train know what was awaiting them there?

3. How did the Nazis divide the Jews at Auschwitz-Birkenau? Why?

4. What did you learn from Nahon's account? What parts of his testimony made the greatest impression on you?

Source: Slightly adapted from Marco Nahon, *Birkenau: The Camp of Death,* trans. J. Bowers (Tuscaloosa: University of Alabama Press, 1989), pp. 21, 23, 33–39. Copyright © 1989 by The University of Alabama Press. Used by permission of the publisher.

The youth revolution. London, ca 1980.
(Wellcome Photo Library/Anthea Seiveking)

chapter

30

Cold War Conflicts and Social Transformations, 1945–1985

chapter outline

- The Division of Europe

- The Western Renaissance, 1945–1968

- Soviet Eastern Europe, 1945–1968

- Postwar Social Transformations, 1945–1968

- Conflict and Challenge in the Late Cold War, 1968–1985

*T*he total defeat of the Nazis and their allies in 1945 laid the basis for one of Western civilization's most remarkable recoveries. A battered western Europe dug itself out from under the rubble and fashioned a great renaissance, building strong democracies, vibrant economies, and new societies. The United States also made solid progress, and the Soviet Union became more humane and less dictatorial. Yet there was also a tragic setback. The Grand Alliance against Hitler gave way to an apparently endless cold war in which tension between East and West threatened world peace.

In the late 1960s and early 1970s, the postwar Western renaissance came to an end. First, as cold war competition again turned very hot in Vietnam, postwar certainties such as domestic political stability and social harmony evaporated, and several countries experienced major crises. Second, the astonishing postwar economic advance came to a halt, and this had serious social consequences. Third, new roles for women after World War II led to a powerful "second wave" of feminist thought and action in the 1970s, resulting in major changes for women and gender relations. Thus the long cold war created an underlying unity for the years 1945–1985, but the first half of the cold war era was quite different from the second.

- What were the causes of the cold war?
- How and why, in spite of the cold war, did western Europe recover so successfully from the ravages of war and Nazism?
- To what extent did communist eastern Europe and the United States also experience such a recovery?
- How did political crisis strike many countries from the late 1960s on?
- Why, after a generation, did the economy shift into reverse gear, and what were some of the social consequences of the reversal?
- How did women's lives change and promote a revitalized women's movement?

These are the questions this chapter will seek to answer.

The Division of Europe

In 1945 triumphant American and Russian soldiers came together and embraced on the banks of the Elbe River in the heart of vanquished Germany. At home, in the United States and in the Soviet Union, the soldiers' loved ones erupted in joyous celebration. Yet victory was flawed. The Allies could not cooperate politically in peacemaking. Motivated by different goals and hounded by misunderstandings, the United States and the Soviet Union soon found themselves at loggerheads. By the end of 1947, Europe was rigidly divided. It was West versus East in a cold war that was waged around the world for forty years.

The Origins of the Cold War

The most powerful allies in the wartime coalition—the Soviet Union and the United States—began to quarrel almost as soon as the unifying threat of Nazi Germany disappeared. A tragic disappointment for millions of people, the hostility between the Eastern and Western superpowers was the sad but logical outgrowth of military developments, wartime agreements, and long-standing political and ideological differences.

In the early phases of the Second World War, the Americans and the British made military victory their highest priority. They consistently avoided discussion of Stalin's war aims and the shape of the eventual peace settlement. Stalin received only a military alliance and no postwar commitments. Yet the United States and Britain did not try to take advantage of the Soviet Union's precarious position in 1942, because they feared that hard bargaining would encourage Stalin to consider making a separate peace with Hitler. They focused instead on the policy of unconditional surrender to solidify the alliance.

By late 1943, discussion about the shape of the postwar world could no longer be postponed. The conference that Stalin, Roosevelt, and Churchill held in the Iranian capital of Teheran in November 1943 thus proved of crucial importance in determining subsequent events. There, the **Big Three** jovially reaffirmed their determination to crush Germany and searched for the appropriate military strategy. Churchill, fearful of the military dangers of a direct attack, argued that American

The Big Three In 1945 a triumphant Winston Churchill, an ailing Franklin Roosevelt, and a determined Joseph Stalin met at Yalta in southern Russia to plan for peace. Cooperation soon gave way to bitter hostility. (*F.D.R. Library*)

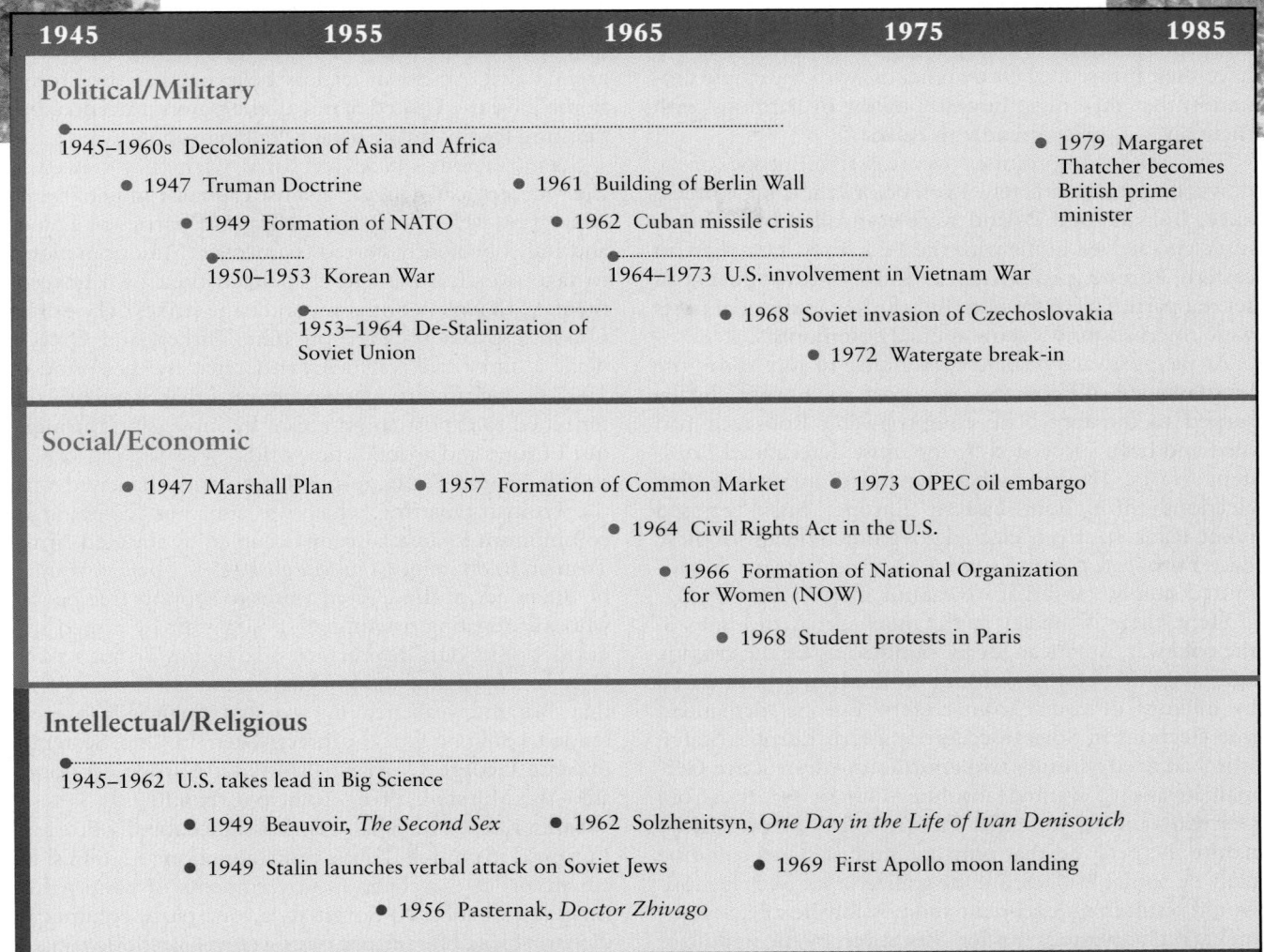

1945	1955	1965	1975	1985

Political/Military

- 1945–1960s Decolonization of Asia and Africa
- 1947 Truman Doctrine
- 1949 Formation of NATO
- 1950–1953 Korean War
- 1953–1964 De-Stalinization of Soviet Union
- 1961 Building of Berlin Wall
- 1962 Cuban missile crisis
- 1964–1973 U.S. involvement in Vietnam War
- 1968 Soviet invasion of Czechoslovakia
- 1972 Watergate break-in
- 1979 Margaret Thatcher becomes British prime minister

Social/Economic

- 1947 Marshall Plan
- 1957 Formation of Common Market
- 1973 OPEC oil embargo
- 1964 Civil Rights Act in the U.S.
- 1966 Formation of National Organization for Women (NOW)
- 1968 Student protests in Paris

Intellectual/Religious

- 1945–1962 U.S. takes lead in Big Science
- 1949 Beauvoir, *The Second Sex*
- 1949 Stalin launches verbal attack on Soviet Jews
- 1956 Pasternak, *Doctor Zhivago*
- 1962 Solzhenitsyn, *One Day in the Life of Ivan Denisovich*
- 1969 First Apollo moon landing

and British forces should follow up their Italian campaign with an indirect attack on Germany through the Balkans. Roosevelt, however, agreed with Stalin that an American-British frontal assault through France would be better. This agreement was part of Roosevelt's general effort to meet Stalin's wartime demands whenever possible, and it had momentous political implications. It meant that the Soviet and the American-British armies would come together in defeated Germany along a north-south line and that only Soviet troops would liberate eastern Europe. Thus the basic shape of postwar Europe was emerging even as the fighting continued.

When the Big Three met again in February 1945 at Yalta on the Black Sea in southern Russia, advancing Soviet armies were within a hundred miles of Berlin. The Red Army had occupied not only Poland but also Bul-

garia, Romania, Hungary, part of Yugoslavia, and much of Czechoslovakia. The temporarily stalled American-British forces had yet to cross the Rhine into Germany. Moreover, the United States was far from defeating Japan. In short, the Soviet Union's position was strong and America's weak.

There was little the increasingly sick and apprehensive Roosevelt could do but double his bet on Stalin's peaceful intentions. It was agreed at Yalta that Germany would be divided into zones of occupation and would pay heavy reparations to the Soviet Union. At American insistence, Stalin agreed to declare war on Japan after Germany was defeated. As for Poland and eastern Europe—"that Pandora's Box of infinite troubles," according to American secretary of state Cordell Hull—the Big Three struggled to reach an ambiguous compromise at Yalta: eastern

European governments were to be freely elected but pro-Russian. As Churchill put it at the time, "The Poles will have their future in their own hands, with the single limitation that they must honestly follow in harmony with their allies, a policy friendly to Russia."[1]

The Yalta compromise over eastern Europe broke down almost immediately. Even before the Yalta Conference, Bulgaria and Poland were controlled by communists who arrived home with the Red Army. Elsewhere in eastern Europe, pro-Soviet "coalition" governments of several parties were formed, but the key ministerial posts were reserved for Moscow-trained communists.

At the postwar Potsdam Conference of July 1945, the long-avoided differences over eastern Europe finally surged to the fore. The compromising Roosevelt had died and been succeeded by the more determined President Harry Truman, who demanded immediate free elections throughout eastern Europe. Stalin refused point-blank. "A freely elected government in any of these East European countries would be anti-Soviet," he admitted simply, "and that we cannot allow."[2]

Here, then, is the key to the much-debated origins of the cold war. American ideals, pumped up by the crusade against Hitler, and American politics, heavily influenced by millions of voters from eastern Europe, demanded free elections in Soviet-occupied eastern Europe. Stalin, who had lived through two enormously destructive German invasions, wanted absolute military security from Germany and its potential Eastern allies. Suspicious by nature, he believed that only communist states could be truly dependable allies, and he realized that free elections would result in independent and possibly hostile governments on his western border. Moreover, by the middle of 1945, there was no way short of war that the United States could determine political developments in eastern Europe, and war was out of the question. Stalin was bound to have his way.

West Versus East

The American response to Stalin's exaggerated conception of security was to "get tough." In May 1945, Truman abruptly cut off all aid to the U.S.S.R. In October he declared that the United States would never recognize any government established by force against the free will of its people. In March 1946, former British prime minister Churchill ominously informed an American audience that an "iron curtain" had fallen across the continent, dividing Germany and all of Europe into two antagonistic camps. Emotional, moralistic denunciations of Stalin and communist Russia emerged as part of American political life. Yet the United States also responded to

the popular desire to "bring the boys home" and demobilized its troops with great speed. Some historians have argued that American leaders believed that the atomic bomb gave the United States all the power it needed, but "getting tough" really meant "talking tough."

Stalin's agents quickly reheated what they viewed as the "ideological struggle against capitalist imperialism." The large, well-organized Communist parties of France and Italy obediently started to uncover "American plots" to take over Europe and challenged their own governments with violent criticisms and large strikes. The Soviet Union also put pressure on Iran, Turkey, and Greece, while a bitter civil war raged in China. By the spring of 1947, it appeared to many Americans that Stalin was determined to export communism by subversion throughout Europe and around the world.

The United States responded to this challenge with the Truman Doctrine, which was aimed at "containing" communism to areas already occupied by the Red Army. Truman told Congress in March 1947, "I believe it must be the policy of the United States to support free people who are resisting attempted subjugation by armed minorities or by outside pressure." To begin, Truman asked Congress for military aid to Greece and Turkey, countries that Britain, weakened by war and financially overextended, could no longer protect. Then, in June, Secretary of State George C. Marshall offered Europe economic aid—the **Marshall Plan**—to help it rebuild.

Stalin refused Marshall Plan assistance for all of eastern Europe. He purged the last remaining noncommunist elements from the coalition governments of eastern Europe and established Soviet-style, one-party communist dictatorships. The seizure of power in Czechoslovakia in February 1948 was particularly antidemocratic, and it greatly strengthened Western fears of limitless communist expansion. Thus, when Stalin blocked all traffic through the Soviet zone of Germany to Berlin, the former capital, which the occupying powers had also divided into sectors at the end of the war, the Western allies acted firmly but not provocatively. Hundreds of planes began flying over the Soviet roadblocks around the clock, supplying provisions to the people of West Berlin and thwarting Soviet efforts to swallow up the West Berliners. After 324 days, the Soviets backed down: containment seemed to work. In 1949, therefore, the United States formed an anti-Soviet military alliance of Western governments: the North Atlantic Treaty Organization (**NATO**). Stalin countered by tightening his hold on his satellites, later united in the Warsaw Pact. Europe was divided into two hostile blocs.

In late 1949, the communists triumphed in China, frightening and angering many Americans, who saw new

The Berlin Airlift   Standing in the rubble of their bombed-out city, a German crowd in the American sector awaits the arrival of a U.S. transport plane flying in over the Soviet blockade in 1948. The crisis over Berlin was a dramatic indication of growing tensions among the Allies, which resulted in the division of Europe into two hostile camps. *(Walter Sanders,* LIFE MAGAZINE © *Time Inc.)*

evidence of a powerful worldwide communist conspiracy. When the Russian-backed communist army of North Korea invaded South Korea in 1950, President Truman acted swiftly. American-led United Nations forces under General Douglas MacArthur intervened. Initially, the North Koreans almost conquered the entire peninsula, but the South Koreans and the Americans rallied and advanced until China suddenly entered the war. The bitter, bloody contest then seesawed back and forth near where it had begun, as President Truman rejected General MacArthur's call to attack China and fired him instead. In 1953 a fragile truce was negotiated, and the fighting stopped. Thus the United States extended its policy of containment to Asia but drew back from an attack on communist China and possible nuclear war.

The rapid descent from victorious Grand Alliance to bitter **cold war** was directly connected to the tragic fate of eastern Europe. After 1933, when the eastern European power vacuum invited Nazi racist imperialism, the appeasing Western democracies mistakenly did nothing. They did, however, have one telling insight: how, they asked themselves, could they unite with Stalin to stop Hitler without giving Stalin great gains on his western borders? After Hitler's invasion of the Soviet Union, the

Western powers preferred to ignore this question and hope for the best. But when Stalin later began to claim the spoils of victory, the United States began to protest and professed outrage. This belated opposition quite possibly encouraged even more aggressive measures by the always-suspicious Stalin, and it helped explode the quarrel over eastern Europe into a global confrontation. Thus the Soviet-American confrontation became institutionalized and formed the bedrock of the long cold war era, which lasted until the mid-1980s despite intermittent periods of relaxation.

The Western Renaissance, 1945–1968

As the cold war divided Europe into two blocs, the future appeared bleak on both sides of the iron curtain. European economic conditions were the worst in generations, and Europe was weak and divided, a battleground for cold war ambitions. Moreover, western European empires were crumbling in the face of nationalism in Asia and Africa. Yet Europe recovered, and the nations of

994

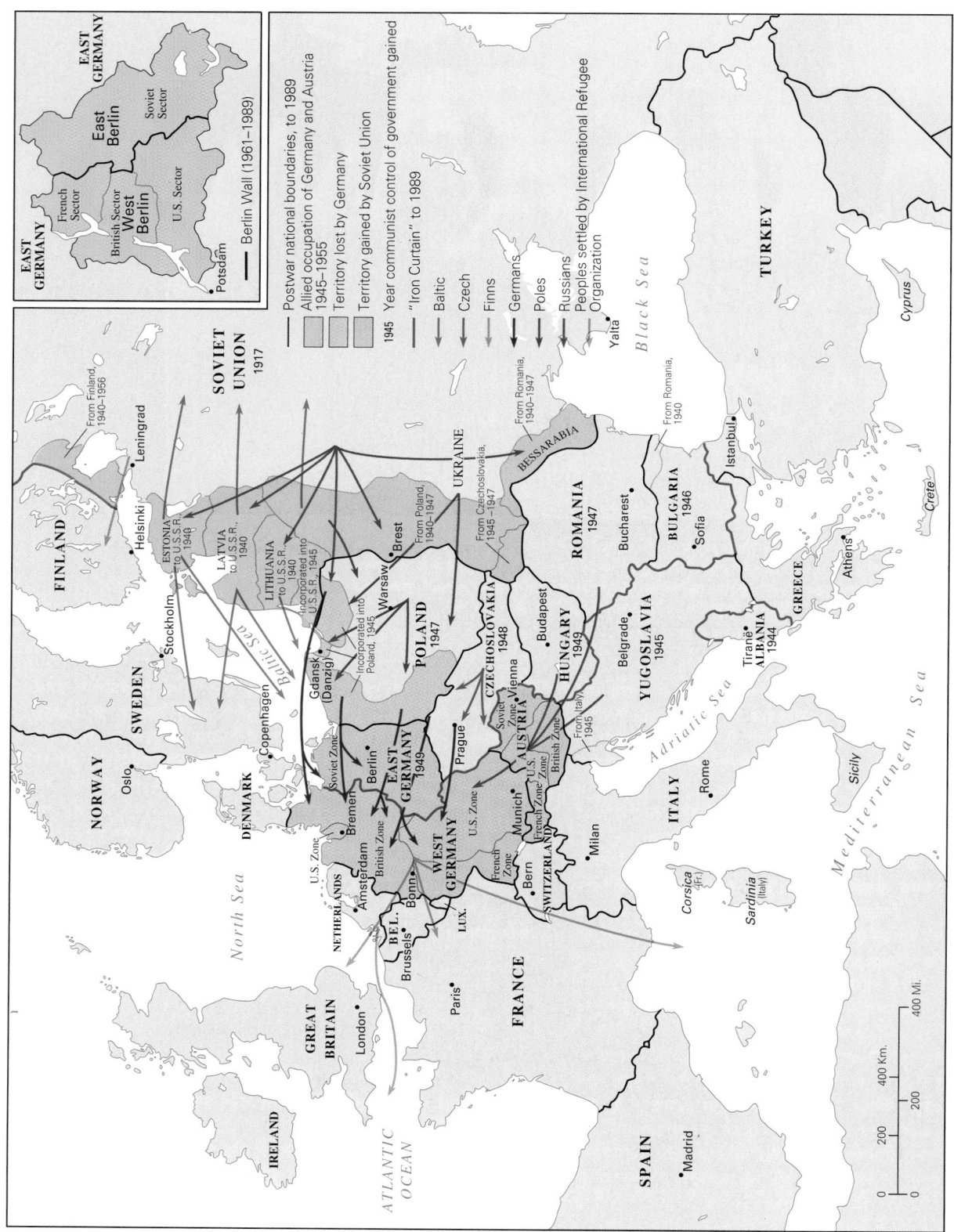

MAP 30.1 The Results of World War II in Europe Millions of refugees fled land from Germany, which the Allies of war and territorial changes. The Soviet Union and Poland took land from Germany, which the Allies partitioned into occupation zones. Those zones subsequently formed the basis of the East and West German states, as the iron curtain fell to divide both Germany and Europe. Austria was detached from Germany, but the Soviets subsequently permitted Austria to reunify as a neutral state.

western Europe led the way. In less than a generation, western Europe achieved unprecedented economic prosperity and peaceful social transformation, while the United States boomed and eventually experienced a wholesome social revolution. It was an amazing rebirth—a true renaissance.

The Postwar Challenge

After the war, economic conditions in western Europe were terrible. Runaway inflation and black markets testified to severe shortages and hardships. Many people believed that Europe was quite simply finished.

Suffering was most intense in defeated Germany. The major territorial change of the war had moved the Soviet Union's border far to the west. Poland was in turn compensated for this loss to the Soviets with land taken from Germany (see Map 30.1). To solidify these changes in boundaries, 13 million Germans were driven from their homes and forced to resettle in a greatly reduced Germany. The Russians were also seizing factories and equipment as reparations in their zone, even tearing up railroad tracks and sending the rails to the Soviet Union.

In 1945 and 1946, conditions were not much better in the Western zones, for the Western allies also treated the German population with severity at first. Countless Germans sold prized possessions to American soldiers to buy food. By the spring of 1947, refugee-clogged, hungry, prostrate Germany was on the verge of total collapse and threatening to drag down the rest of Europe. Yet western Europe was not finished. The Nazi occupation and the war had discredited old ideas and old leaders. All over Europe, many people were willing to change and experiment, and new groups and new leaders were coming to the fore to guide these aspirations. Progressive Catholics and revitalized Catholic political parties—the **Christian Democrats**—were particularly influential.

In Italy the Christian Democrats emerged as the leading party in the first postwar elections in 1946, and in early 1948 they won an absolute majority in the parliament in a landslide victory. Their very able leader was Alcide De Gasperi, a courageous antifascist firmly committed to political democracy, economic reconstruction, and moderate social reform. In France, too, the Catholic party also provided some of the best postwar leaders after January 1946, when General Charles de Gaulle, the inspiring wartime leader of the Free French, resigned after having re-established the free and democratic Fourth Republic. As Germany was partitioned by the cold war, a radically purified Federal Republic of Germany (as West Germany was officially known) found new and able leadership among its Catholics. In 1949 Konrad Adenauer, the former mayor of Cologne and a long-time anti-Nazi, began his long, highly successful democratic rule; the Christian Democrats became West Germany's majority party for a generation. In providing effective leadership for their respective countries, the Christian Democrats were inspired and united by a common Christian and European heritage. They steadfastly rejected authoritarianism and narrow nationalism and placed their faith in democracy and cooperation.

The socialists and the communists, active in the resistance against Hitler, also emerged from the war with increased power and prestige, especially in France and Italy. They, too, provided fresh leadership and pushed for social change and economic reform. In the immediate postwar years, welfare measures such as family allowances, health insurance, and increased public housing were enacted throughout continental Europe. Britain followed the same trend, as the newly elected socialist Labour party established a "welfare state." Many British industries were nationalized, and the government provided free medical service. Thus all across Europe, social reform complemented political transformation, creating solid foundations for a great European renaissance.

The United States also supplied strong and creative leadership, providing western Europe with both massive economic aid and ongoing military protection. Economic aid was channeled through the Marshall Plan, and military security was provided through NATO, which featured American troops stationed permanently in Europe and the American nuclear umbrella. Thus the United States assumed the international responsibilities it had shunned after 1919.

As Marshall Plan aid poured in, the battered economies of western Europe began to turn the corner in 1948. The outbreak of the Korean War in 1950 further stimulated economic activity, and Europe entered a period of rapid economic progress that lasted into the late 1960s. Never before had the European economy grown so fast. There were many reasons for western Europe's brilliant economic performance. American aid helped the process get off to a fast start. Moreover, economic growth became a basic objective of all western European governments, for leaders and voters were determined to avoid a return to the dangerous and demoralizing stagnation of the 1930s. Thus governments generally accepted Keynesian economics (see pages 938 and 944) and sought to stimulate their economies. They also adopted a variety of imaginative and successful strategies.

In postwar West Germany, Minister of Economy Ludwig Erhard, a roly-poly, cigar-smoking former professor,

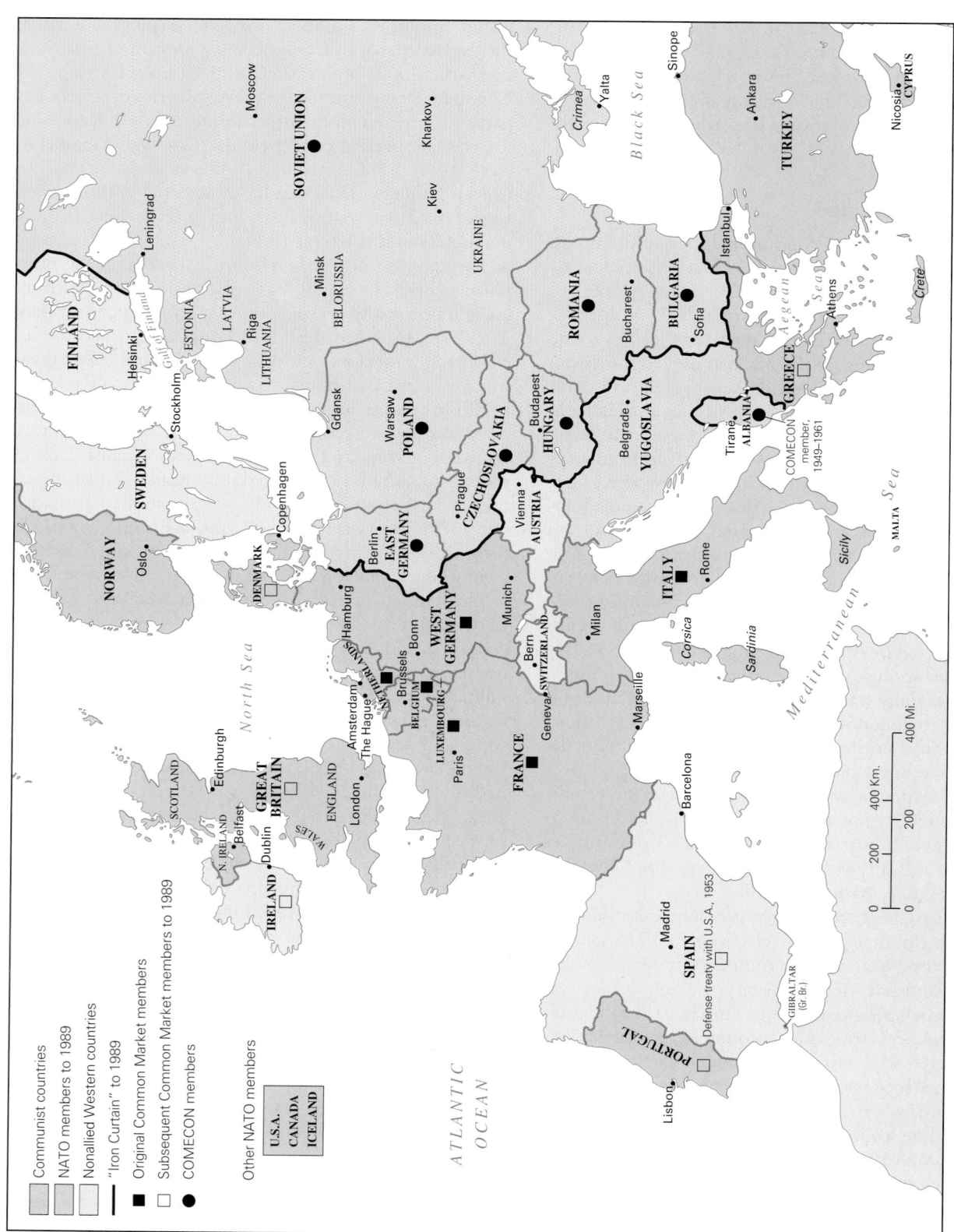

MAP 30.2 European Alliance Systems, 1949–1989 After the cold war divided Europe into two hostile military alliances, six western European countries formed the Common Market in 1957. The Common Market grew later to include most of western Europe. The communist states organized their own economic association—COMECON.

broke decisively with the straitjacketed Nazi economy. Erhard bet on the free-market economy while maintaining the extensive social welfare network inherited from the Hitler era. He and his teachers believed not only that capitalism was more efficient but also that political and social freedom could thrive only if there were real economic freedom. Erhard's first step was to reform the currency and abolish rationing and price controls in 1948. He boldly declared, "The only ration coupon is the Mark."[3] West Germany's success renewed respect for free-market capitalism.

The French innovation was a new kind of planning. Under the guidance of Jean Monnet, an economic pragmatist and apostle of European unity, a planning commission set ambitious but flexible goals for the French economy and used the nationalized banks to funnel money into key industries. Thus France combined flexible planning and a "mixed" state and private economy to achieve the most rapid economic development in its long history.

In most countries, there were many people ready to work hard for low wages and the hope of a better future. Moreover, although many consumer products had been invented or perfected since the late 1920s, few Europeans had been able to buy them. In 1945 the electric refrigerator, the washing machine, and the automobile were rare luxuries. There was a great potential demand, which the economic system moved to satisfy. Finally, western European nations abandoned protectionism and gradually created a large unified market known as the "Common Market." This historic action, which certainly stimulated the economy, was part of a larger search for European unity.

Toward European Unity

Western Europe's political recovery was spectacular in the generation after 1945. Republics were re-established in France, West Germany, and Italy. Constitutional monarchs were restored in Belgium, Holland, and Norway. Democratic governments, often within the framework of multiparty politics and shifting parliamentary coalitions, took root again and thrived. National self-determination was accompanied by civil liberties and individual freedom.

A similarly extraordinary achievement was the march toward a united Europe. The Christian Democrats, with their shared Catholic heritage, were particularly committed to "building Europe," and other groups shared their dedication. Many Europeans believed that only unity in a new "European nation" could reassert western Europe's influence in world affairs.

The close cooperation among European states required by the Americans for Marshall Plan aid led to the creation of both the Organization of European Economic Cooperation (OEEC) and the Council of Europe in 1948. European federalists hoped that the Council of Europe would quickly evolve into a true European parliament with sovereign rights, but this did not happen. Britain, with its empire and its "special relationship" with the United States, consistently opposed giving any real political power—any sovereignty—to the council. Many continental nationalists and communists felt similarly.

Frustrated in the direct political approach, European federalists turned toward economics as a way of working toward genuine unity. Two far-seeing French statesmen, the planner Jean Monnet and Foreign Minister Robert Schuman, took the lead in 1950 and called for a special international organization to control and integrate all European steel and coal production. West Germany, Italy, Belgium, the Netherlands, and Luxembourg accepted the French idea in 1952; the British would have none of it. The immediate economic goal—a single steel and coal market without national tariffs or quotas—was rapidly realized. The more far-reaching political goal was to bind the six member nations so closely together economically that war among them would eventually become unthinkable and virtually impossible.

In 1957 the six nations of the Coal and Steel Community signed the Treaty of Rome, which created the European Economic Community, generally known as the **Common Market** (see Map 30.2). The first goal of the treaty was a gradual reduction of all tariffs among the six in order to create a single market almost as large as that of the United States. Other goals included the free movement of capital and labor and common economic policies and institutions. The Common Market was a great success, encouraging companies and regions to specialize in what they did best.

The development of the Common Market fired imaginations and encouraged hopes of rapid progress toward political as well as economic union. In the 1960s, however, these hopes were frustrated by a resurgence of more traditional nationalism. France took the lead. Mired in a bitter colonial war in Algeria, the French turned in 1958 to General de Gaulle, who established the Fifth Republic and ruled as its president until 1969. De Gaulle was at heart a romantic nationalist, and he viewed the United States as the main threat to genuine French (and European) independence. He withdrew all French military forces from the "American-controlled" NATO, developed France's own nuclear weapons, and vetoed the scheduled advent of majority rule within the Common Market. Thus throughout the 1960s, the Common Market thrived economically but remained a union of sovereign states.

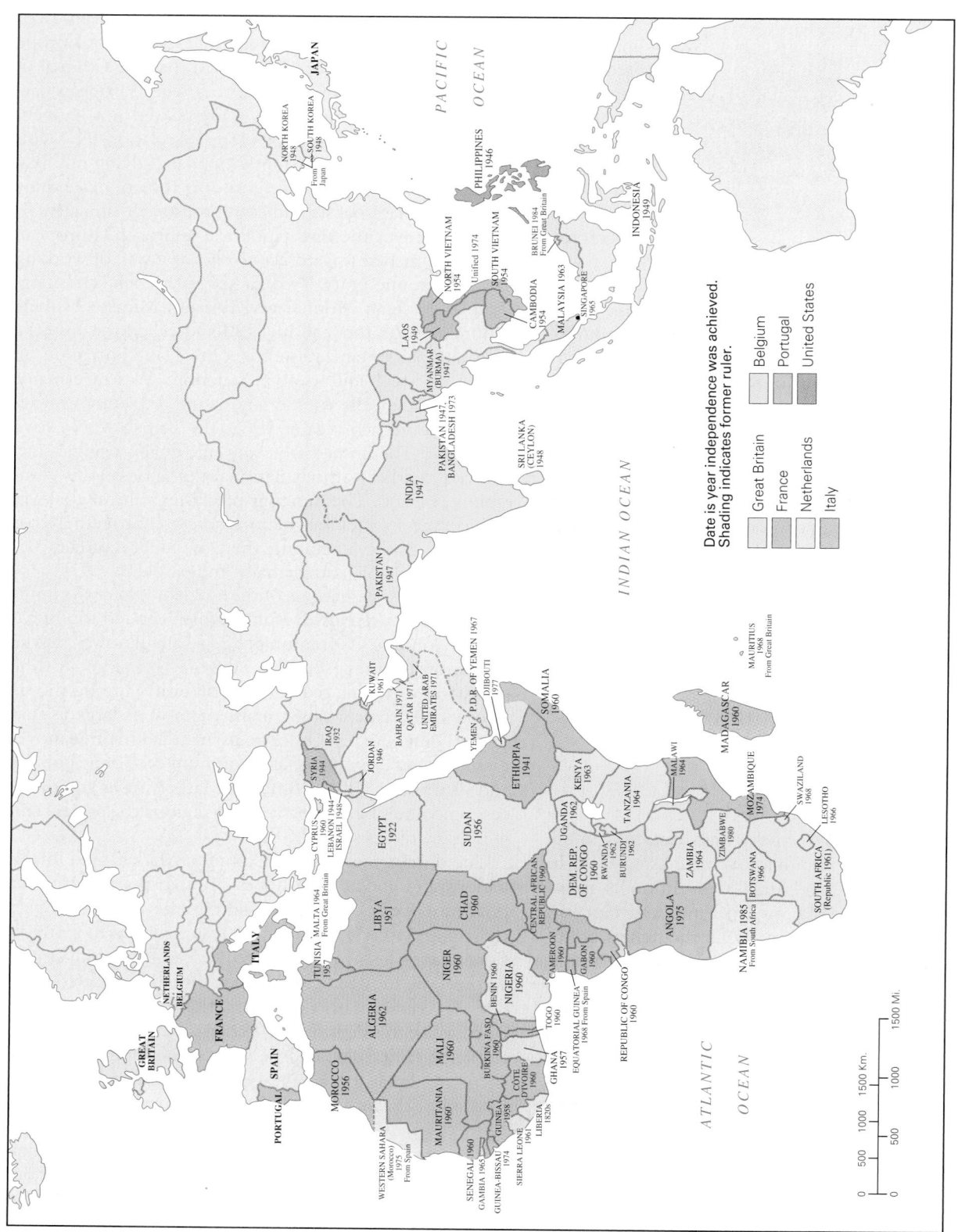

MAP 30.3 The New States in Africa and Asia   Divided primarily along religious lines into two states, British India led the way to political independence in 1947. Most African territories achieved statehood by the mid-1960s, as European empires passed away, unlamented.

Date is year independence was achieved.
Shading indicates former ruler.

Great Britain
France
Netherlands
Italy
Belgium
Portugal
United States

PACIFIC OCEAN

JAPAN

NORTH KOREA 1948
SOUTH KOREA 1948
From Japan

PHILIPPINES 1946

INDONESIA 1949

BRUNEI 1984 From Great Britain

NORTH VIETNAM 1954
Unified 1974
SOUTH VIETNAM 1954
CAMBODIA 1954
MALAYSIA 1963
SINGAPORE 1965
LAOS 1949
MYANMAR (BURMA) 1947

PAKISTAN 1947, BANGLADESH 1973

SRI LANKA (CEYLON) 1948

INDIA 1947

INDIAN OCEAN

PAKISTAN 1947

KUWAIT 1961
IRAQ 1932
JORDAN 1946
BAHRAIN 1971
QATAR 1971
UNITED ARAB EMIRATES 1971
YEMEN 1967 / P.D.R. OF YEMEN 1967
DJIBOUTI 1977

SYRIA 1944
CYPRUS 1960
LEBANON 1944
ISRAEL 1948

MAURITIUS 1968 From Great Britain

SOMALIA 1960

MADAGASCAR 1960

EGYPT 1922
SUDAN 1956
ETHIOPIA 1941
UGANDA 1962
KENYA 1963
RWANDA 1962
BURUNDI 1962
TANZANIA 1964
MALAWI 1964
MOZAMBIQUE 1974
SWAZILAND 1968
LESOTHO 1966

LIBYA 1951
CHAD 1960
CENTRAL AFRICAN REPUBLIC 1960
DEM. REP. OF CONGO 1960
ZAMBIA 1964
ZIMBABWE 1980
BOTSWANA 1966
SOUTH AFRICA (Republic) 1961

TUNISIA 1957
MALTA 1964 From Great Britain

NIGER 1960
NIGERIA 1960
CAMEROON 1960
GABON 1960
ANGOLA 1975
NAMIBIA 1985 From South Africa

ALGERIA 1962
MALI 1960
BENIN 1960
TOGO 1960
EQUATORIAL GUINEA 1968 From Spain
REPUBLIC OF CONGO 1960

MOROCCO 1956
MAURITANIA 1960
BURKINA FASO 1960
GHANA 1957
CÔTE D'IVOIRE 1960
LIBERIA 1820s

WESTERN SAHARA (Morocco) 1975 From Spain

SENEGAL 1960
GAMBIA 1965
GUINEA-BISSAU 1974
GUINEA 1958
SIERRA LEONE 1961

ATLANTIC OCEAN

GREAT BRITAIN
NETHERLANDS
BELGIUM
FRANCE
ITALY
SPAIN
PORTUGAL

0   500   1000   1500 Km.
0   500   1000   1500 Mi.

Decolonization

In the postwar era, Europe's long-standing overseas expansion was dramatically reversed. Future generations will almost certainly see this rolling back of Western expansion as one of world history's great turning points (see Map 30.3).

The most basic cause of imperial collapse—what Europeans called **decolonization**—was the rising demand of Asian and African peoples for national self-determination, racial equality, and personal dignity. This demand spread from intellectuals to the masses in virtually every colonial territory after the First World War. As a result, colonial empires had already been shaken by 1939, and the way was prepared for the eventual triumph of independence movements.

European empires had been based on an enormous power differential between the rulers and the ruled, a difference that had declined almost to the vanishing point by 1945. Not only was western Europe poor and battered immediately after the war, but most Europeans regarded their empires very differently after 1945 than before 1914, or even before 1939. Empire had rested on self-confidence and self-righteousness; Europeans had believed their superiority to be not only technical and military but also spiritual and moral. The horrors of the Second World War destroyed such complacent arrogance and gave opponents of imperialism much greater influence in Europe. With their political power and moral authority in tatters in 1945, many Europeans were willing to let go of their colonies more or less voluntarily and to concentrate on rebuilding at home.

Indian independence played a key role in decolonization. When the Labour party came to power in Great Britain in 1945, it was determined to leave India. British socialists had always opposed imperialism, and the heavy cost of governing India had become an intolerable burden. Empire in India ended in 1947, and most Asian colonies achieved independence shortly thereafter. Although the French obstinately tried to re-establish colonial rule in Indochina, they were defeated in 1954, and two independent Vietnamese states came into being.

In the Middle East, the movement toward political independence continued after World War II (see Map 30.3). In 1944 the French gave up their League of Nations mandates in Syria and Lebanon. In British-mandated Palestine, where after 1918 the British government established a Jewish homeland alongside the Arab population, violence and terrorism mounted on both sides. In 1947 the frustrated British decided to leave Palestine, and the United Nations then voted in a nonbinding resolution to divide Palestine into two states—one Arab and one Jewish, which became Israel. The Jews accepted the plan but the Arabs did not, and in 1948 they attacked the Jewish state as soon as it was proclaimed. The Israelis drove off the invaders and conquered more territory, as roughly 900,000 Arabs fled or were expelled. Holocaust survivors from Europe streamed into Israel, as Theodor Herzl's Zionist dream came true (see page 847). The next fifty years saw four more wars and innumerable clashes between Arabs and Israelis.

In North Africa, the French fought a long, dirty war to keep Algeria, but Algeria won its independence in 1962. In much of Africa south of the Sahara, decolonization proceeded much more smoothly. Beginning in 1957, Britain's colonies achieved independence with little or no bloodshed and then entered a very loose association with Britain as members of the British Commonwealth of Nations. In 1958 the clever de Gaulle offered the leaders of

African Independence   Britain's Queen Elizabeth II pays an official visit in 1961 to Ghana, the former Gold Coast colony. Accompanying the queen at the colorful welcoming ceremony is Ghana's popular Kwame Nkrumah, who was educated in black colleges in the United States and led Ghana's breakthrough to independence in 1957. (*Corbis*)

French black Africa the choice of a total break with France or immediate independence within a kind of French commonwealth. All but one of the new states chose association with France. As in the past, the French saw themselves as continuing their civilizing mission in black Africa. More important, they saw in Africa untapped markets for their industrial goods, raw materials for their factories, outlets for profitable investment, and good temporary jobs for their engineers and teachers. The British acted somewhat similarly.

As a result, western European countries actually managed to increase their economic and cultural ties with their former African colonies in the 1960s and 1970s. Above all, they used the lure of special trading privileges and heavy investment in French- and English-language education to enhance a powerful Western presence in the new African states. This situation led a variety of leaders and scholars to charge that western Europe (and the United States) had imposed a system of neocolonialism on the former colonies. According to this view, **neocolonialism** was a system designed to perpetuate Western economic domination and undermine the promise of political independence, thereby extending to Africa (and much of Asia) the economic subordination that the United States had established in Latin America in the nineteenth century. At the very least, enduring influence in black Africa testified to western Europe's resurgent economic and political power in international relations.

America's Civil Rights Revolution

The Second World War cured the depression in the United States and brought about an economic boom. Despite fears that peace would bring renewed depression, conversion to a peacetime economy went smoothly. As in western Europe, the U.S. economy proceeded to advance fairly steadily for a long generation.

The March on Washington, August 1963   The march marked a dramatic climax in the civil rights struggle. More than 200,000 people gathered at the Lincoln Memorial to hear the young Martin Luther King, Jr., deliver his greatest address, the "I have a dream" speech. *(Francis Miller/Timepix)*

Prosperity helps explain why postwar domestic politics consisted largely of modest adjustments to the status quo until the 1960s. Truman's upset electoral victory in 1948 demonstrated that Americans had no interest in undoing Roosevelt's social and economic reforms, and Truman's presidency consolidated the accomplishments of the New Deal. In 1952 the Republican party and the voters turned to General Dwight D. Eisenhower (1890–1969), a national hero and self-described moderate.

The federal government's only major new undertaking during the Eisenhower years (1953–1961) was the interstate highway system. Some Americans feared that the United States was becoming a "blocked society," obsessed with stability and incapable of wholesome change. This feeling contributed in 1960 to the election of the young John F. Kennedy (1917–1963), who promised to "get the country moving again." President Kennedy captured the popular imagination and revitalized the old Roosevelt coalition before he was struck down by an assassin's bullet in 1963.

Belatedly and reluctantly, complacent postwar America did experience a genuine social revolution. After a long struggle, African Americans (and their white supporters) threw off a deeply entrenched system of segregation, discrimination, and repression. Eloquent lawyers challenged school segregation and in 1954 won a landmark decision in the Supreme Court, which ruled in *Brown v. Board of Education* that "separate educational facilities are inherently unequal." Blacks effectively challenged institutionalized inequality with bus boycotts, sit-ins, and demonstrations. As civil rights leader Martin Luther King, Jr. (1929–1968), told the white power structure, "We will not hate you, but we will not obey your evil laws."[4]

In key northern states, African Americans used their growing political power to gain the support of the liberal wing of the Democratic party. A liberal landslide elected Lyndon Johnson (1908–1973) president in 1964. The Civil Rights Act of 1964 prohibited discrimination in public services and on the job; the Voting Rights Act of 1965 guaranteed all blacks the right to vote. By the 1970s, substantial numbers of blacks had been elected to public and private office throughout the southern states, proof positive that dramatic changes had occurred in American race relations.

President Johnson also declared "unconditional war on poverty." In the mid-1960s, Congress and the administration created a host of antipoverty projects, such as a domestic peace corps and free preschools for poor children. These programs were directed to all poor Americans—the majority of whom were white—but they were also intended to increase economic equality for

blacks. Thus the United States promoted in the mid-1960s the kind of fundamental social reform that western Europe had embraced immediately after the Second World War. The United States became more of a welfare state, as government spending for social benefits rose dramatically and approached European levels.

Soviet Eastern Europe, 1945–1968

While western Europe surged ahead economically after the Second World War and increased its political power as American influence gradually waned, eastern Europe followed a different path. The Soviet Union first tightened its grip on the "liberated" nations of eastern Europe under Stalin and then refused to let go. Thus postwar economic recovery in eastern Europe proceeded along Soviet lines, and political and social developments were strongly influenced by changes in the Soviet Union.

Stalin's Last Years, 1945–1953

Americans were not the only ones who felt betrayed by Stalin's postwar actions. The "Great Patriotic War of the Fatherland" had fostered Russian nationalism and a relaxation of dictatorial terror. It also had produced a rare but real unity between Soviet rulers and most Russian people. Having made a heroic war effort, the vast majority of the Soviet people hoped in 1945 that a grateful party and government would grant greater freedom and democracy. Such hopes were soon crushed.

Even before the war ended, Stalin was moving his country back toward rigid dictatorship. As early as 1944, the leading members of the Communist party were being given a new motivating slogan: "The war on Fascism ends, the war on capitalism begins."[5] By early 1946, Stalin was publicly singing the old tune that war was inevitable as long as capitalism existed. Stalin's new foreign foe in the West provided an excuse for re-establishing a harsh dictatorship. Many returning soldiers and ordinary citizens were purged in 1945 and 1946, as Stalin revived the terrible forced-labor camps of the 1930s.

Culture and art were also purged in violent campaigns that reimposed rigid anti-Western ideological conformity. Many artists were denounced, including the composers Sergei Prokofiev and Dimitri Shostakovich and the film director Sergei Eisenstein. In 1949 Stalin launched a savage verbal attack on Soviet Jews, accusing them of being pro-Western and antisocialist.

Sergei Eisenstein: Ivan the Terrible
Eisenstein's final masterpiece—one of the greatest films ever—was filmed during the Second World War and released in two parts in 1946. In this chilling scene, the crafty paranoid tyrant, who has saved Russia from foreign invaders, invites the unsuspecting Prince Vladimir to a midnight revel that will lead to his murder. The increasingly demonic Ivan seemed to resemble Stalin, and Eisenstein was censored and purged. *(David King Collection)*

In the political realm, Stalin reasserted the Communist party's complete control of the government and his absolute mastery of the party. Five-year plans were reintroduced to cope with the enormous task of economic reconstruction. Once again, heavy industry and the military were given top priority, and consumer goods, housing, and collectivized agriculture were neglected. Everyday life was very hard. In short, it was the 1930s all over again in the Soviet Union, although police terror was less intense.

Stalin's prime postwar innovation was to export the Stalinist system to the countries of eastern Europe. The Communist parties of eastern Europe had established one-party states by 1948, thanks to the help of the Red Army and the Russian secret police. Rigid ideological indoctrination, attacks on religion, and a lack of civil liberties were soon facts of life. Industry was nationalized, and the middle class was stripped of its possessions. Economic life was then faithfully recast in the Stalinist mold. Forced industrialization lurched forward without regard for human costs. The collectivization of agriculture began.

Only Josip Broz Tito (1892–1980), the resistance leader and Communist chief of Yugoslavia, was able to resist Soviet domination successfully. Tito stood up to Stalin in 1948, and since there was no Russian army in Yugoslavia, he got away with it. Yugoslavia prospered as a multiethnic state until it began to break apart in the 1980s (see page 1047). Tito's proclamation of independence infuriated Stalin. Popular Communist leaders who, like Tito, had led the resistance against Germany

were purged as Stalin sought to create absolutely obedient instruments of domination in eastern Europe. (See the feature "Individuals in Society: Tito and the Rise of Independent Communism.")

Reform and De-Stalinization, 1953–1964

In 1953 the aging Stalin finally died, and the dictatorship that he had built began to change. Even as Stalin's heirs struggled for power, they realized that reforms were necessary because of the widespread fear and hatred of Stalin's political terrorism. The power of the secret police was curbed, and many of the forced-labor camps were gradually closed. Change was also necessary for economic reasons. Moreover, Stalin's belligerent foreign policy had led directly to a strong Western alliance, which isolated the Soviet Union.

On the question of just how much change should be permitted in order to preserve the system, the Communist leadership was badly split. Conservatives wanted to make as few changes as possible. Reformers, who were led by Nikita Khrushchev, argued for major innovations. Khrushchev (1894–1971), who had joined the party as an uneducated coal miner in 1918 and rose to a high-level position in the 1930s, emerged as the new ruler in 1955.

To strengthen his position and that of his fellow reformers within the party, Khrushchev launched an all-out attack on Stalin and his crimes at a closed session of the Twentieth Party Congress in 1956. In gory detail, he

Individuals in Society

Tito and the Rise of Independent Communism

Josip Tito (1892–1980) was always a dedicated communist. But after fighting the Nazis and bringing revolution to Yugoslavia, he experienced Stalin's wrath. He then built an independent communist state and achieved remarkable influence as a world leader.

Tito was born into a peasant family of mixed ethnic background in northwest Croatia, in what was then Austria-Hungary. Leaving home as a teenager for work in towns, he became a communist labor organizer in the 1920s. Imprisoned for five years in the 1930s, Tito went to Moscow and in 1937 was charged by the Soviets to reorganize the Communist party of Yugoslavia and then to lead the resistance to Nazi and Italian occupation.

Communist revolution was always Tito's main goal. His guerrilla forces fought as much against the competing noncommunist resistance movement, centered in the Serbian region of Yugoslavia and loyal to the deposed monarchy, as against the Nazis and Italians and their collaborators in Croatia, Bosnia, and Serbia. Yet Tito played down his revolutionary objectives and appealed with some success to all ethnic groups in Yugoslavia. He promised "brotherhood and unity" when the carnage ended. Liberating Yugoslavia in 1945 in coordination with Stalin's Red Army, which moved on in pursuit of the retreating Germans, Tito and his followers quickly established the first Stalinist regime in eastern Europe. Yugoslavia's peasants were exploited to pay for heavy industry. Tito's picture was everywhere, and the Communists held all power.

Yet Stalin grew dissatisfied with his ally. Tito bubbled with revolutionary enthusiasm. He supported the Greek communists in their civil war, called for a communist federation in the Balkans, and enraged U.S. public opinion by shooting down an American "spy plane" over Yugoslavia. Stalin preferred cautious moderation in relations with the West, which would, he hoped, facilitate Soviet consolidation in eastern Europe and encourage a division of the world into spheres of influence. Above all, he demanded absolutely obedient Communist leaders. In 1948 he suddenly denounced Tito as a heretic and called on Yugoslavia's Communist party to oust him. Tito later described the rupture as his most traumatic experience, but he stayed calm, rallied party stalwarts, and survived.

At first, Tito's independent communism remained strictly Stalinist, imprisoning opponents and proclaiming its Marxist-Leninist orthodoxy. But Tito

Marshal Tito in 1940, planning operations for the liberation of Yugoslavia.
(Corbis)

soon steered a middle course between East and West. He approved the introduction of "workers' self-management" in Yugoslavia, which loosened the state's hold on the economy and was trumpeted internationally as a radical step toward genuine communism. In the 1950s and 1960s, Tito's one-party dictatorship allowed greater personal freedom and presented would-be communist reformers in eastern Europe with an intriguing model.

Yugoslavia's independent, "nonaligned" communism became an influential model in world politics. Tito adroitly negotiated indispensable military commitments from the United States to keep Stalin's armies at bay, and he received massive U.S. aid. But he also re-established generally good relations with the Soviet Union after Stalin's death. Finally, Tito joined with India's Jawaharlal Nehru and Egypt's Gamal Abdel Nasser to lead and inspire the movement of nonaligned, newly independent countries. Pressing his case on many fronts, Tito strengthened the idea that Third World nations should avoid crippling cold war alliances and concentrate instead on building independent socialist states like his.

Questions for Analysis

1. Does the rupture between Tito and Stalin throw light on the origins of the cold war? In what ways?
2. What were the characteristics of Tito's independent communism? How did it enhance his status as a leader?

described to the startled Communist delegates how Stalin had tortured and murdered thousands of loyal Communists, how he had trusted Hitler completely and bungled the country's defense, and how he had "supported the glorification of his own person with all conceivable methods." Khrushchev's "secret speech" was read at Communist party meetings held throughout the country, and it strengthened the reform movement.

The liberalization—or **de-Stalinization,** as it was called in the West—of the Soviet Union was genuine. The Communist party jealously maintained its monopoly on political power, but Khrushchev shook up the party and brought in new members. Some resources were shifted from heavy industry and the military toward consumer goods and agriculture, and Stalinist controls over workers were relaxed. The Soviet Union's very low standard of living finally began to improve and continued to rise substantially throughout the booming 1960s.

De-Stalinization created great ferment among writers and intellectuals who hungered for cultural freedom. The poet Boris Pasternak (1890–1960) finished his great novel *Doctor Zhivago* in 1956. Published in the West but not in Russia, *Doctor Zhivago* is both a literary masterpiece and a powerful challenge to communism. It tells the story of a prerevolutionary intellectual who rejects the violence and brutality of the revolution of 1917 and the Stalinist years. Even as he is destroyed, he triumphs because of his humanity and Christian spirit. Pasternak was denounced—but he was not shot. Other talented writers followed Pasternak's lead, and courageous editors let the sparks fly.

The writer Aleksandr Solzhenitsyn (b. 1918) created a sensation when his *One Day in the Life of Ivan Denisovich* was published in the Soviet Union in 1962. Solzhenitsyn's novel portrays in grim detail life in a Stalinist concentration camp—a life to which Solzhenitsyn himself had been unjustly condemned—and is a damning indictment of the Stalinist past.

Khrushchev also de-Stalinized Soviet foreign policy. "Peaceful coexistence" with capitalism was possible, he argued, and great wars were not inevitable. Khrushchev even made concessions, agreeing in 1955 to real independence for a neutral Austria after ten long years of Allied occupation. Thus there was considerable relaxation of cold war tensions between 1955 and 1957. At the same time, Khrushchev began wooing the new nations of Asia and Africa—even if they were not communist—with promises and aid.

De-Stalinization stimulated rebelliousness in the eastern European satellites. Having suffered in silence under Stalin, communist reformers and the masses were quickly emboldened to seek much greater liberty and national independence. Poland took the lead in 1956, when extensive rioting brought a new government that managed to win greater autonomy.

Hungary experienced a real and tragic revolution. Led by students and workers—the classic urban revolutionaries—the people of Budapest installed a liberal communist reformer as their new chief in October 1956. Soviet troops were forced to leave the country. But after the new government promised free elections and renounced Hungary's military alliance with Moscow, the Russian leaders ordered an invasion and crushed the national and democratic revolution. Fighting was bitter until the end, for the Hungarians hoped that the United States would come to their aid. When this did not occur, most people in eastern Europe concluded that their only hope was to strive for small domestic gains while following Russia obediently in foreign affairs.

The End of Reform

By late 1962, opposition in party circles to Khrushchev's policies was strong, and in 1964 Khrushchev fell in a bloodless palace revolution. Under Leonid Brezhnev (1906–1982), the Soviet Union began a period of stagnation and limited "re-Stalinization." The basic reason for this development was that Khrushchev's Communist colleagues saw de-Stalinization as a dangerous, two-sided threat. How could Khrushchev denounce the dead dictator without eventually denouncing and perhaps even arresting his still-powerful henchmen? Moreover, the widening campaign of de-Stalinization posed a clear threat to the dictatorial authority of the party. The party had to tighten up considerably while there was still time. Khrushchev had to go.

Another reason for conservative opposition was that Khrushchev's policy toward the West was erratic and ultimately unsuccessful. In 1958 he ordered the Western allies to evacuate West Berlin within six months. In response, the allies reaffirmed their unity in West Berlin, and Khrushchev backed down. Then in 1961, as relations with communist China deteriorated dramatically, Khrushchev ordered the East Germans to build a wall between East and West Berlin, thereby sealing off West Berlin in clear violation of existing access agreements between the Great Powers. The recently elected U.S. president, John F. Kennedy, acquiesced to the construction of the Berlin Wall. Emboldened and seeing a chance to change the balance of military power decisively, Khrushchev ordered missiles with nuclear warheads installed in Fidel Castro's communist Cuba in 1962. President Kennedy countered with a naval blockade of Cuba. After a tense diplomatic crisis, Khrushchev agreed to remove the Soviet missiles in return for American pledges not to disturb Castro's regime. Khrushchev looked like a bumbling buffoon; his influence, already slipping, declined rapidly after the Cuban fiasco.

After Brezhnev and his supporters took over in 1964, they started talking quietly of Stalin's "good points" and ignoring his crimes. This change informed Soviet citizens that further liberalization could not be expected at home. Soviet leaders, determined never to suffer Khrushchev's humiliation in the face of American nuclear superiority, also launched a massive arms buildup. Yet Brezhnev and company proceeded cautiously in the mid-1960s and avoided direct confrontation with the United States.

In the wake of Khrushchev's reforms, the 1960s brought modest liberalization and more consumer goods to eastern Europe, as well as somewhat greater national autonomy, especially in Poland and Romania. In January 1968, the reform elements in the Czechoslovak Communist party gained a majority and voted out the long-time Stalinist leader in favor of Alexander Dubček (1921–1992), whose new government launched dramatic reforms.

Educated in Moscow, Dubček was a dedicated Communist. But he and his allies believed that they could reconcile genuine socialism with personal freedom and internal party democracy. Thus local decision making by trade unions, managers, and consumers replaced rigid bureaucratic planning, and censorship was relaxed. The reform program proved enormously popular.

Although Dubček remembered the lesson of the Hungarian revolution and constantly proclaimed his loyalty to the Warsaw Pact, the determination of the Czechoslovak reformers to build what they called "socialism with a human face" frightened hard-line Communists. These fears were particularly strong in Poland and East Germany, where leaders knew full well that they lacked popular support. Moreover, the Soviet Union feared that a liberalized Czechoslovakia would eventually be drawn to neutrality or even to the democratic West. Thus the Eastern bloc countries launched a concerted campaign of intimidation against the Czechoslovak leaders, and in August 1968, 500,000 Russian and allied eastern European troops suddenly occupied Czechoslovakia. The Czechoslovaks made no attempt to resist militarily, and

The Invasion of Czechoslovakia   A Russian soldier holds his assault rifle on a young Czech student, who is greeting the invader with only a sign. In 1968 the Czechs and Slovaks knew that armed resistance would be suicidal. *(Joseph Koudelka/Magnum Photos)*

the arrested leaders surrendered to Soviet demands. The reform program was abandoned, and the Czechoslovak experiment in humanizing communism came to an end. Shortly after the invasion of Czechoslovakia, Brezhnev declared the so-called **Brezhnev Doctrine,** according to which the Soviet Union and its allies had the right to intervene in any socialist country whenever they saw the need.

The 1968 invasion of Czechoslovakia was the crucial event of the Brezhnev era, which really lasted beyond the aging leader's death in 1982 until the emergence in 1985 of Mikhail Gorbachev. The invasion demonstrated the determination of the ruling elite to maintain the status quo in the Soviet bloc. In the U.S.S.R. that determination resulted in further repression, but the Soviet Union appeared quite stable in the 1970s and early 1980s.

Postwar Social Transformations, 1945–1968

While Europe staged its astonishing political and economic recovery from the Nazi nightmare, the patterns of everyday life and the structure of Western society were changing no less rapidly and remarkably. Epoch-making inventions and new technologies profoundly affected human existence. Important groups in society formulated new attitudes and demands, which were closely related to the changing class structure and social reforms. An international youth culture took shape and rose to challenge established lifestyles and even governments.

Science and Technology

Ever since the scientific revolution of the seventeenth century and the Industrial Revolution at the end of the eighteenth century, scientific and technical developments had powerfully influenced attitudes, society, and everyday life. Never was this influence stronger than after about 1940. Science and technology proved so productive and influential because, for the first time in history, "pure theoretical" science and "practical" technology (or "applied" science) were effectively joined together on a massive scale.

With the advent of the Second World War, pure science lost its impractical innocence. Most leading university scientists went to work on top-secret projects to help their governments fight the war. The development by British scientists of radar to detect enemy aircraft was a particularly important outcome of this new kind of sharply focused research. A radically improved radar system played a key role in Britain's victory in the battle for air supremacy in 1940. The air war also greatly stimulated the development of jet aircraft and spurred further research on electronic computers, which calculated the complex mathematical relationships between fast-moving planes and anti-aircraft shells to increase the likelihood of a hit.

The most spectacular result of directed scientific research during the war was the atomic bomb. In August 1939, physicist Albert Einstein wrote to President Franklin Roosevelt that recent work in physics suggested that "it may become possible to set up a nuclear chain reaction in a large mass of uranium" and to construct "extremely powerful bombs of a new type."[6] This letter and ongoing experiments by nuclear physicists led to the top-secret Manhattan Project, which ballooned into a mammoth crash. After three years of intensive effort, the first atomic bomb was successfully tested in July 1945. In August 1945, two bombs were dropped on Hiroshima and Nagasaki, thereby ending the war with Japan.

The atomic bomb showed the world both the awesome power and the heavy moral responsibilities of modern science and its high priests. As one Los Alamos scientist exclaimed as he watched the first mushroom cloud rise over the American desert, "We are all sons-of-bitches now!"[7]

The spectacular results of directed research during World War II inspired a new model for science—**Big Science.** By combining theoretical work with sophisticated engineering in a large organization, Big Science could attack extremely difficult problems, from better products for consumers to new and improved weapons for the military. Big Science was extremely expensive, requiring large-scale financing from governments and large corporations.

Populous, victorious, and wealthy, the United States took the lead in Big Science after World War II. Between 1945 and 1965, spending on scientific research and development in the United States grew five times as fast as the national income, and by 1965 such spending took 3 percent of all U.S. income. It was generally accepted that government should finance science heavily in both the "capitalist" United States and the "socialist" Soviet Union.

One reason for the parallel between the two countries was that science was not demobilized in either country after the war. Scientists remained a critical part of every major military establishment, and a large portion of all postwar scientific research went for "defense." New weapons such as rockets, nuclear submarines, and spy satellites demanded breakthroughs no less remarkable than those of radar and the first atomic bomb. After

1945 roughly one-quarter of all men and women trained in science and engineering in the West—and perhaps more in the Soviet Union—were employed full-time in the production of weapons to kill other humans.

Sophisticated science, lavish government spending, and military needs all came together in the space race of the 1960s. In 1957 the Soviets used long-range rockets developed in their nuclear weapons program to put a satellite in orbit. In 1961 they sent the world's first cosmonaut circling the globe. Embarrassed by Soviet triumphs, President Kennedy made an all-out U.S. commitment to catch up with the Soviets and land a crewed spacecraft on the moon "before the decade was out." Harnessing pure science, applied technology, and up to $5 billion a year, the Apollo Program achieved its ambitious objective in 1969. Four more moon landings followed by 1972.

The rapid expansion of government-financed research in the United States attracted many of Europe's best scientists during the 1950s and 1960s. Thoughtful Europeans lamented this "brain drain" and feared that Europe was falling hopelessly behind the United States in science and technology. In fact, a revitalized Europe was already responding to the American challenge, with countries pooling their efforts on such Big Science projects as the *Concorde* supersonic passenger airliner and the peaceful uses of atomic energy.

The rise of Big Science and of close ties between science and technology greatly altered the lives of scientists. The scientific community grew much larger than ever before. There were about four times as many scientists in Europe and North America in 1975 as in 1945. Scientists, technologists, engineers, and medical specialists counted after 1945, in part because there were so many of them.

One consequence of the growth of science was its high degree of specialization, for no one could possibly master a broad field such as physics or medicine. Intense specialization in new disciplines and subdisciplines increased the rates at which both basic knowledge was acquired and practical applications were made.

Highly specialized modern scientists and technologists normally had to work as members of a team, which completely changed the work and lifestyle of modern scientists. A great deal of work therefore went on in large bureaucratic organizations, where the individual was very often a small cog in a great machine. The growth of large scientific bureaucracies in government and private enterprise suggested how scientists and technologists permeated the entire society and many aspects of life.

Modern science became highly, even brutally, competitive. This competitiveness is well depicted in Nobel Prize

winner James Watson's fascinating book *The Double Helix,* which tells how in 1953 Watson and an Englishman, Francis Crick, discovered the structure of DNA, the molecule of heredity. A brash young American Ph.D. in his twenties, Watson seemed almost obsessed by the idea that some other research team would find the solution first and thereby deprive him of the fame and fortune he desperately wanted. With so many thousands of like-minded researchers in the wealthy countries of the world, scientific and technical knowledge rushed forward in the postwar era.

The Changing Class Structure

Rapid economic growth went a long way toward creating a new society in Europe after the Second World War. European society became more mobile and more democratic. Old class barriers relaxed, and class distinctions became fuzzier.

Changes in the structure of the middle class were particularly influential in the general drift toward a less rigid class structure. In the nineteenth and early twentieth centuries, the model for the middle class had been the independent, self-employed individual who owned a business or practiced a liberal profession such as law or medicine. Ownership of property—very often inherited property—and strong family ties had often been the keys to wealth and standing within the middle class. After 1945 this pattern declined drastically in western Europe. A new breed of managers and experts replaced traditional property owners as the leaders of the middle class. Ability to serve the needs of a big organization largely replaced inherited property and family connections in determining an individual's social position in the middle and upper middle classes. At the same time, the middle class grew massively and became harder to define.

There were several reasons for these developments. Rapid industrial and technological expansion created in large corporations and government agencies a powerful demand for technologists and managers. Moreover, the old propertied middle class lost control of many family-owned businesses, and many small businesses (including family farms) simply passed out of existence as their former owners joined the ranks of salaried employees.

Top managers and ranking civil servants therefore represented the model for a new middle class of salaried specialists. Well paid and highly trained, often with backgrounds in engineering or accounting, these experts increasingly came from all social classes, even the working class. Pragmatic and realistic, they were primarily concerned with efficiency and practical solutions to concrete

Oldenburg: Fried Egg (1961)
The American Claes Oldenburg, a leader in the international pop art movement in the 1960s, said he wanted an art "that does something other than sit on its ass in a museum." In painting and music, fashion and dance, pop artists scoffed at elitist traditions and produced works intended for ordinary people. *(Private Collection/The Bridgeman Art Library International Ltd)*

problems. Managers and technocrats, of whom a small but growing number were women (see pages 1009–1010), could pass on the opportunity for all-important advanced education to their children, but only in rare instances could they pass on the positions they had attained. Thus the new middle class, which was based largely on specialized skills and high levels of education, was more open, democratic, and insecure than the old propertied middle class.

The structure of the lower classes also became more flexible and open. There was a mass exodus from farms and the countryside, as one of the most traditional and least mobile groups in European society drastically declined. Meanwhile, the industrial working class ceased to expand, and job opportunities for white-collar and service employees grew rapidly. Such employees bore a greater resemblance to the new middle class of salaried specialists than to industrial workers, who were also better educated and more specialized.

European governments were reducing class tensions with a series of social security reforms. Many of these reforms—such as increased unemployment benefits and more extensive old-age pensions—simply strengthened social security measures first pioneered in Bismarck's Germany before the First World War (see pages 839–840). Other programs were new, like comprehensive national health systems directed by the state. Most countries also

introduced family allowances—direct government grants to parents to help them raise their children. These allowances helped many poor families make ends meet. Most European governments also gave maternity grants and built inexpensive public housing for low-income families and individuals. These and other social reforms provided a humane floor of well-being. Reforms also promoted greater equality because they were expensive and were paid for in part by higher taxes on the rich.

The rising standard of living and the spread of standardized consumer goods also worked to level Western society, as the percentage of income spent on food and drink declined substantially. For example, the European automobile industry expanded phenomenally after lagging far behind the United States since the 1920s. In 1948 there were only 5 million cars in western Europe, but in 1965 there were 44 million. Car ownership was democratized and came within the range of better-paid workers.

Europeans took great pleasure in the products of the "gadget revolution" as well. Like Americans, Europeans filled their houses and apartments with washing machines, vacuum cleaners, refrigerators, dishwashers, radios, TVs, and stereos. The purchase of consumer goods was greatly facilitated by installment purchasing, which allowed people to buy on credit. With the expansion of social security safeguards, reducing the need to accumulate savings

POSTWAR SOCIAL TRANSFORMATIONS, 1945–1968

for hard times, ordinary people were increasingly willing to take on debt. This change had far-reaching consequences.

Leisure and recreation occupied an important place in consumer societies. The most astonishing leisure-time development was the blossoming of mass travel and tourism. With month-long paid vacations required by law in most European countries and widespread automobile ownership, beaches and ski resorts came within the reach of the middle class and much of the working class. By the late 1960s, packaged tours with cheap group flights and bargain hotel accommodations had made even distant lands easily accessible. A French company grew rich building imitation Tahitian paradises around the world. At Swedish nudist colonies on secluded West African beaches, office-workers from Stockholm fleetingly worshiped the sun in the middle of the long northern winter. Truly, consumerism had come of age.

New Roles for Women

A growing emancipation of women in Europe and North America was unquestionably one of the most significant transformations of the cold war era. This historic development grew out of long-term changes in the basic patterns of motherhood and paid work outside the home. These changing patterns altered women's experiences and expectations, preparing the way for the success of a new generation of feminist thinkers and a militant women's movement in the 1970s and 1980s (see pages 1017–1018).

Before the Industrial Revolution, most Europeans married late. Once a woman was married, however, she usually had children as long as she was fertile, and she bore several children, of whom one-third to one-half would not survive to adulthood. With the growth of industry, people began to marry earlier, death rates fell, and population grew rapidly. By the late nineteenth century, improved diet, higher incomes, and the use of contraception within marriage was producing the demographic transition from high birthrates and death rates to low birthrates and death rates.

These trends continued in the twentieth century. In the 1950s and 1960s, the typical woman in the West married early and bore her children quickly. The postwar baby boom did make for larger families and a fairly rapid population growth of 1 to 1.5 percent per year in many European countries. However, in the 1960s the long-term decline in birthrates resumed, and from the mid-1970s on in many European countries, the total population practically stopped growing from natural increase, with limited subsequent growth coming mainly from immigration.

The postwar culmination of the trends toward early marriage, early childbearing, and small family size in wealthy urban societies had revolutionary implications for women. Above all, pregnancy and child care occupied a much smaller portion of a woman's life than in earlier times. By the early 1970s, about half of Western women were having their last baby by the age of twenty-six or twenty-seven. When the youngest child trooped off to kindergarten, the average mother had more than forty years of life in front of her.

This was a momentous change. Throughout history male-dominated society insisted on defining most women as mothers or potential mothers, and motherhood was very demanding. Pregnancy followed pregnancy, and there were many children to nurse, guide, and bury. In the postwar years, however, the period devoted to having babies and caring for young children became a relatively short phase in most women's total life span. Motherhood no longer absorbed the energies of a lifetime, and more and more married women looked for new roles in the world of work outside the family.

For centuries before the Industrial Revolution, ordinary women worked hard and long on farms and in home industries while caring for their large families. With the growth of modern industry and much more rigid gender roles, few middle-class women worked outside the home for wages, although charity work was socially acceptable. Young unmarried women continued to work as wage earners, but poor married women typically earned their money at home in low-paid crafts as they looked after their children.

In the twentieth century and especially after World War II, the ever-greater complexity of the modern economy meant that almost all women had to go outside the home to find cash income. Three major forces helped women searching for jobs. First, the economy boomed from about 1950 to 1973 and created a strong demand for labor. Second, the economy continued its gradual shift away from the old, male-dominated heavy industries, such as coal, steel, and shipbuilding, to the more dynamic, "white-collar" service industries, such as government, education, trade, and health care. Women had always worked in these service fields. Third, young Western women shared fully in the postwar education revolution and could take advantage of the growing need for officeworkers and well-trained professionals. Thus more and more married women became full-time and part-time wage earners.

The trend went the furthest in communist eastern Europe, where women accounted for almost half of all employed·persons. In noncommunist western Europe and

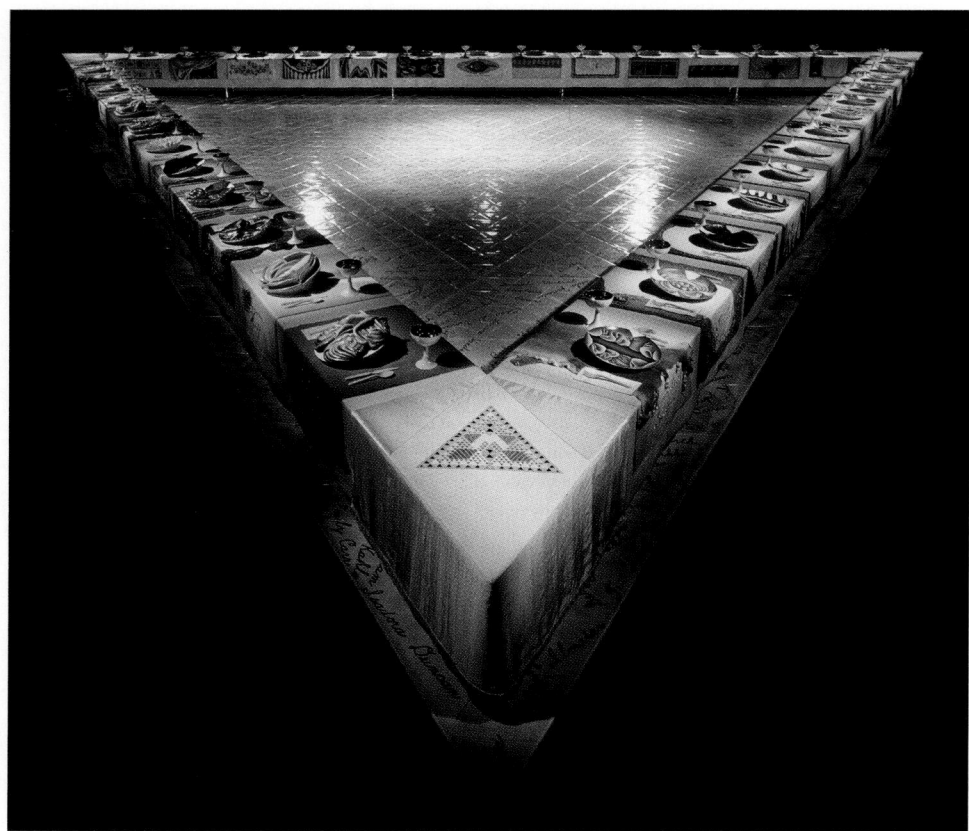

Celebrating Women's History
Judy Chicago's multimedia creation *The Dinner Party* features thirty-nine handcrafted placemats and ceramic plates, each embellished with a painted motif associated with the woman being honored. Begun in 1974 and completed in 1978 with the participation of more than one hundred women, Chicago wanted to represent the "historic struggle of women to participate in all the aspects of society." It attracted enormous crowds. (*© Judy Chicago, 1979; mixed media, 48' × 42' × 3'. Photo: © Donald Woodman*)

North America, there was a good deal of variation, with the percentage of married women in the workforce rising from a range of roughly 20 to 25 percent in 1950 to a range of 40 to 70 percent in the early 1980s.

Rising employment for married women went hand in hand with the decline of the birthrate (see Figure 30.1). Women who worked outside the home had significantly fewer children than women of the same age who did not. Raising a family while holding down a full-time job was a tremendous challenge and often resulted in a woman's being grossly overworked. The multiple demands of job, motherhood, and marriage became more manageable with fewer children.

Married women entering (or re-entering) the labor force faced widespread, long-established discrimination in pay, advancement, and occupational choice in comparison to men. Moreover, many women could find only part-time work. As the divorce rate rose in the 1960s, part-time work, with its low pay and scanty benefits, meant poverty for many women with teenage children. Finally, in the best of circumstances, married working women still carried most of the child-raising and house-keeping responsibilities. A reason for many to accept part-time employment, this gendered imbalance meant an exhausting "double day"—on the job and at home—for the full-time worker.

The injustices that married women encountered as wage earners contributed greatly to the subsequent movement for women's equality and emancipation. A young unmarried woman of seventy or a hundred years ago was more likely to accept such problems as temporary nuisances because she looked forward to marriage and motherhood for fulfillment. In the postwar era, a married wage earner in her thirties gradually developed a very different perspective. She saw employment as a permanent condition within which she, like her male counterpart, sought not only income but also psychological satisfaction. Sexism and discrimination in the workplace—and in the home—grew loathsome and evoked the sense of injustice that drives revolutions and reforms. When powerful voices arose to challenge the system, they found support among working women.

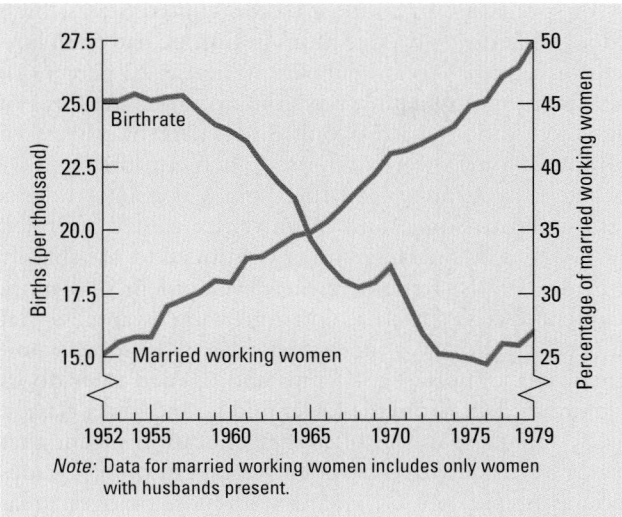

FIGURE 30.1 The Decline of the Birthrate and the Increase of Married Working Women in the United States, 1952–1979 The challenge of working away from home encouraged American wives to prefer fewer children and helped to lower the birthrate.

Youth and the Counterculture

Economic prosperity and a more democratic class structure had a powerful impact on youth throughout the Western world. The bulging cohort of youth born after World War II developed a distinctive and very international youth culture. Self-consciously different in the late 1950s, this youth culture became increasingly oppositional in the 1960s, interacting with a revival of leftist thought to create a "counterculture" that rebelled against parents, authority figures, and the status quo.

Young people in the United States took the lead. American college students in the 1950s were docile and often dismissed as the "Silent Generation," but some young people did revolt against the conformity of middle-class suburbs. These "young rebels" wore tightly pegged pants and idolized singer Elvis Presley and actor James Dean. The "beat" movement of the late 1950s expanded on the theme of revolt, and Jack Kerouac vividly captured the restless motion of the beatniks in his autobiographical novel *On the Road*. People like Kerouac clustered together in certain urban areas, such as the Haight Ashbury district of San Francisco or the Near North Side of Chicago. There the young (and the not-so-young) fashioned a highly publicized subculture that blended radical politics, unbridled personal experimentation (with drugs

and communal living, for example), and new artistic styles. This subculture quickly spread to major American and western European cities.

Rock music helped tie this international subculture together. Rock grew out of the black music culture of rhythm and blues, which was flavored with country and western to make it more accessible to white teenagers. The mid-1950s signaled a breakthrough as Bill Haley called on record buyers to "Rock Around the Clock" and Elvis Presley warned them to keep off of his "Blue Suede Shoes." In the 1960s, the Beatles thrilled millions of young people, often to their parents' dismay. Like Elvis, the Beatles suggested personal and sexual freedom that many older people found disturbing.

It was Bob Dylan, a young folksinger turned rock poet with an acoustic guitar, who best expressed the radical political as well as cultural aspirations of the "younger generation." In a song that became a rallying cry, Dylan sang that "the times they are a'changing."[8] Increasing discontent with middle-class conformity and the injustices of racism and imperialism fueled the young leaders of social protest and reflected a growing spirit of rebellion.

Certainly the sexual behavior of young people, or at least some young people, appeared to change dramatically in the 1960s and into the 1970s. More young people engaged in sexual intercourse, and they did so at an earlier age. For example, a 1973 study reported that only 4.5 percent of West German youths born in 1945 and 1946 had experienced sexual relations before their seventeenth birthday but that 32 percent of those born in 1953 and 1954 had done so.[9] Perhaps even more significant was the growing tendency of young unmarried people to live together in a separate household on a semi-permanent basis, with little thought of getting married or having children. Thus many youths, especially middle-class youths, defied social custom, claiming in effect that the long-standing monopoly of married couples on legitimate sexual unions was dead.

Several factors contributed to the emergence of the international youth culture in the 1960s. First, mass communications and youth travel linked countries and continents together. Second, the postwar baby boom meant that young people became an unusually large part of the population and could therefore exercise exceptional influence on society as a whole. Third, postwar prosperity and greater equality gave young people more purchasing power than ever before. This enabled them to set their own trends and patterns of consumption, which fostered generational loyalty. Finally, prosperity meant that good jobs were readily available. Students and young

The Beatles The older generation often saw sexual license and immorality in the group's frank lyrics and suggestive style. But in comparison with all that came after them in the world of pop music, the Beatles were sentimental and wholesome. *(John Zimmerman/Camera Press/Retna Ltd.)*

job seekers had little need to fear punishment from strait-laced employers for unconventional behavior.

The youth culture practically fused with the counter-culture in opposition to the established order in the late 1960s. Student protesters embraced romanticism and revolutionary idealism, dreaming of complete freedom and simpler, purer societies. The materialistic West was hopelessly rotten, but better societies were being built in the newly independent countries of Asia and Africa, or so many young radicals believed. Thus the Vietnam War took on special significance. Many politically active students believed that the older generation was fighting an immoral and imperialistic war against a small and heroic people. As the war in Vietnam intensified, so did world-wide student opposition to it.

Student protests in western Europe also highlighted more general problems of youth, education, and a soci-

ety of specialists. In contrast to the United States, high school and university educations in Europe had been limited for centuries to a small elite. Whereas 22 percent of the American population was going on to some form of higher education in 1950, only 3 to 4 percent of western European youths were doing so. Then enrollments sky-rocketed. By 1960 at least three times as many students were going to some kind of university as had attended before the war, and the number continued to rise sharply until the 1970s. Reflecting the development of a more democratic class structure and a growing awareness that higher education was the key to success, European universities gave more scholarships and opened their doors to more students from the lower middle and lower classes.

The rapid expansion of higher education meant that classes were badly overcrowded. Competition for grades became intense. Moreover, although more practical areas of study were gradually added, many students felt that they were not getting the kind of education they needed for jobs in the modern world. At the same time, some reflective students warned of the dangers of narrowly trained experts. They feared that universities would soon do nothing but turn out docile technocrats both to stock and to serve "the establishment."

The many tensions within the exploding university population came to a head in the late 1960s and early 1970s. As in the United States, European university students rose to challenge their university administrations and even their governments. The most far-reaching of these revolts occurred in France in 1968. Students occupied buildings and took over the University of Paris, which led to violent clashes with police. Most students demanded both changes in the curriculum and a real voice in running the university. Some student radicals went further, attacking capitalism and appealing to France's industrial workers for help. Rank-and-file workers ignored the advice of their cautious union officials, and a more or less spontaneous general strike spread across France in May 1968. It seemed certain that President de Gaulle's Fifth Republic would collapse.

In fact, de Gaulle stiffened, like an irate father. Declaring that he was in favor of university reforms and higher minimum wages but would oppose the "bed-wetting" of undisciplined students and workers, he moved troops toward Paris and called for new elections. Thoroughly frightened by the student-sparked upheaval and fearing an eventual communist takeover, the masses of France voted overwhelmingly for de Gaulle's party and a return to law and order. Workers went back to work, and the mini-revolution collapsed. Yet the proud de Gaulle and the post-war European renaissance that he represented had been

Student Rebellion in Paris   These rock-throwing students in the Latin Quarter of Paris are trying to force education reforms and even to topple de Gaulle's government. Throughout May 1968 students clashed repeatedly with France's tough riot police in bloody street fighting. De Gaulle remained in power, but a major reform of French education did follow. *(Bruno Barbey/Magnum Photos)*

shaken, and within a year he resigned. Growing out of the counterculture and youthful idealism, the student rebellion of 1968 signaled the end of an era and the return of unrest and uncertainty in the 1970s and early 1980s.

Conflict and Challenge in the Late Cold War, 1968–1985

Similar to but more important than the student upheaval in France and the crushing of socialist reform in Czechoslovakia, the Vietnam War marked the beginning of a new era of challenges and uncertainties in the late 1960s. The Vietnam War and its aftermath divided the people of the United States, shook the ideology of containment, and

weakened the Western alliance. A second major challenge appeared when the great postwar economic boom came to a close in 1973, opening a long period of economic stagnation, widespread unemployment, and social dislocation.

The United States and Vietnam

President Johnson wanted to go down in history as a master reformer and a healer of old wounds. Instead, he opened new ones with the Vietnam War.

Although many student radicals believed that imperialism was the main cause, American involvement in Vietnam was more clearly a product of the cold war and the policy of containment (see page 992). From the late 1940s on, most Americans and their leaders viewed the world in terms of a constant struggle to stop the spread of communism. As western Europe began to revive and China established a communist government in 1949, efforts to contain communism shifted to Asia. The bloody Korean War (1950–1953) ended in stalemate, but the United States did succeed in preventing a communist victory in South Korea. After the defeat of the French in Vietnam in 1954, the Eisenhower administration refused to sign the Geneva Accords that temporarily divided the country into two zones pending national unification by means of free elections. President Eisenhower then acquiesced in the refusal of the anticommunist South Vietnamese government to accept the verdict of elections and provided it with military aid. President Kennedy greatly

An Antiwar Rally   The signs and slogans of these anti–Vietnam War protesters highlight the widespread opposition to the draft on college campuses. The red sign quotes the Cuban revolutionary and anti-imperialist Che Guevara, a popular hero for young people on the left. *(Corbis)*

increased the number of American "military advisers" to sixteen thousand.

After winning the 1964 election on a peace platform, President Johnson greatly expanded the American role in the Vietnam conflict. American strategy was to "escalate" the war sufficiently to break the will of the North Vietnamese and their southern allies without resorting to "overkill," which might risk war with the entire Communist bloc. Thus South Vietnam received massive military aid, American forces in the South gradually grew to half a million men, and the United States bombed North Vietnam with ever-greater intensity. But there was no invasion of the North or naval blockade. In the end, the American strategy of limited warfare backfired. It was the American people who grew weary and the American leadership that cracked.

The undeclared war in Vietnam, fought nightly on American television, eventually divided the nation. Initial support was strong. The politicians, the media, and the population as a whole saw the war as part of a legitimate defense against communist totalitarianism in all poor countries. But an antiwar movement quickly emerged on college campuses, where the prospect of being drafted to fight savage battles in Asian jungles made male stomachs churn. In October 1965, student protesters joined forces with old-line socialists, New Left intellectuals, and pacifists in antiwar demonstrations in fifty American cities. By 1967 a growing number of critics denounced the war as a criminal intrusion into a complex and distant civil war.

Criticism reached a crescendo after the Vietcong Tet Offensive in January 1968. This, the communists' first comprehensive attack with conventional weapons on major cities in South Vietnam, failed militarily: the Vietcong suffered heavy losses, and the attack did not spark a mass uprising. But Washington had been claiming that victory in South Vietnam was in sight, and U.S. critics of the Vietnam War quickly interpreted the bloody combat as a decisive American defeat. America's leaders lost heart. In 1968, after a narrow victory in the New Hampshire primary, President Johnson called for negotiations with North Vietnam and announced that he would not stand for re-election.

Elected by a razor-slim margin in 1968, President Richard Nixon (1913–1994) sought to gradually disengage America from Vietnam and the accompanying national crisis. Intensifying the continuous bombardment of the enemy while simultaneously pursuing peace talks with the North Vietnamese, Nixon suspended the draft, so hated on college campuses, and cut American forces in Vietnam from 550,000 to 24,000 in four years. The cost of the war dropped dramatically. Moreover, President Nixon launched a flank attack in diplomacy. He journeyed to China in 1972 and reached a spectacular if limited reconciliation with the People's Republic of China. In doing so, Nixon took advantage of China's growing fears of the Soviet Union and undermined North Vietnam's position.

Fortified by the overwhelming endorsement of the voters in his 1972 electoral triumph, President Nixon and Secretary of State Henry Kissinger finally reached a peace agreement with North Vietnam. The agreement allowed remaining American forces to complete their withdrawal, and the United States reserved the right to resume bombing if the accords were broken. Fighting declined markedly in South Vietnam, where the South Vietnamese army appeared to hold its own against the Vietcong. The storm of crisis in the United States seemed to have passed.

On the contrary, the country reaped the **Watergate** whirlwind. Like some other recent American presidents, Nixon authorized spying activities that went beyond the law. Going further than his predecessors, he allowed special units to use various illegal means to stop the leaking of government documents to the press. One such group broke into the Democratic party headquarters in Washington's Watergate complex in June 1972 and was promptly arrested. Nixon and many of his assistants then tried to hush up the bungled job, but the media and the machinery of congressional investigation eventually exposed the administration's web of lies and lawbreaking. In 1974 a beleaguered Nixon was forced to resign in disgrace.

The consequences of renewed political crisis flowing from the Watergate affair were profound. First, Watergate resulted in a major shift of power away from the presidency and toward Congress, especially in foreign affairs. Therefore, as American aid to South Vietnam diminished in 1973 and as an emboldened North Vietnam launched a general invasion against South Vietnamese armies in early 1974, Congress refused to permit any American military response. A second consequence of the U.S. crisis was that after more than thirty-five years of battle, the Vietnamese communists unified their country in 1975 as a harsh dictatorial state. Third, the belated fall of South Vietnam in the wake of Watergate shook America's postwar confidence and left the country divided and uncertain about its proper role in world affairs.

Détente or Cold War?

One alternative to the badly damaged policy of containing communism was the policy of **détente,** or the progressive piecemeal relaxation of cold war tensions. Thus while the cold war continued to rage outside Europe and generally defined superpower relations between the Soviet Union and the United States, West Germany took a major step toward genuine peace in Europe.

West German chancellor Willy Brandt (1913–1992) took the lead when in December 1970 he flew to Poland for the signing of a historic treaty of reconciliation. In a dramatic moment rich in symbolism, Brandt laid a wreath at the tomb of the Polish unknown soldier and another at the monument commemorating the armed uprising of Warsaw's Jewish ghetto against occupying Nazi armies. Standing before the ghetto memorial, a somber Brandt fell to his knees and knelt as if in prayer. "I wanted," Brandt said later, "to ask pardon in the name of our people for a million-fold crime which was committed in the misused name of the Germans."[10]

Brandt's gesture at the Warsaw Ghetto memorial and the treaty with Poland were part of his policy of reconciliation with eastern Europe. Indeed, Brandt aimed at nothing less than a comprehensive peace settlement for central Europe and the two German states established after 1945. The Federal Republic of Germany (West Germany) had long claimed that the communist German Democratic Republic (East Germany) lacked free elections and hence any legal or moral basis. West Germany also refused to accept the loss of German territory taken by Poland and the Soviet Union after 1945. However, Brandt, the popular socialist mayor of West Berlin when the Berlin Wall was built in 1961, believed that the wall showed the painful limitations of West Germany's official hard line toward communist eastern Europe. A new foreign policy was needed.

Winning the chancellorship in 1969, Brandt negotiated treaties with the Soviet Union, Poland, and Czechoslovakia that formally accepted existing state boundaries in return for a mutual renunciation of force or the threat of force. Using the imaginative formula of "two German states within one German nation," Brandt's government also broke decisively with the past and entered into direct relations with East Germany. He aimed for modest practical improvements rather than reunification, which at that point was completely impractical.

The policy of détente reached its high point when all European nations (except isolationist Albania), the United States, and Canada signed the Final Act of the Helsinki Conference in 1975. The thirty-five nations participating agreed that Europe's existing political frontiers could not be changed by force. They also solemnly accepted numerous provisions guaranteeing the human rights and political freedoms of their citizens.

Optimistic hopes for détente in international relations gradually faded in the later 1970s. Brezhnev's Soviet

Willy Brandt in Poland, 1970   Chancellor Brandt's gesture at the Warsaw memorial to the Jewish victims of Nazi terrorism was criticized by some West Germans but praised by many more. This picture reached an enormous audience, appearing in hundreds of newspapers in both the East and the West. *(Bilderdienst Süddeutscher Verlag)*

Union ignored the human rights provisions of the Helsinki agreement, and East-West political competition remained very much alive outside Europe. Many Americans became convinced that the Soviet Union was taking advantage of détente, steadily building up its military might and pushing for political gains and revolutions in Africa, Asia, and Latin America. The Soviet invasion of Afghanistan in December 1979, which was designed to save an increasingly unpopular Marxist regime, was especially alarming. Many Americans feared that the oil-rich states of the Persian Gulf would be next, and once again they looked to the Atlantic alliance and military might to thwart communist expansion.

President Jimmy Carter (b. 1924), elected in 1976, tried to lead the Atlantic alliance beyond verbal condem-

nation and urged economic sanctions against the Soviet Union. Yet only Great Britain among the European allies supported the American initiative. The alliance showed the same lack of concerted action when the Solidarity movement rose in Poland. Some observers concluded that the alliance had lost the will to think and act decisively in dealing with the Soviet bloc.

The Atlantic alliance endured, however. The U.S. military buildup launched by Carter in his last years in office was greatly accelerated by President Ronald Reagan (b. 1911), who was swept into office in 1980 by a wave of patriotism and economic discontent. The new American leadership acted as if the military balance had tipped in favor of the Soviet Union, which Reagan anathematized as the "evil empire." Increasing defense spending enormously, the Reagan administration concentrated on nuclear arms and an expanded navy as keys to American power in the post-Vietnam age.

A broad swing in the historical pendulum toward greater conservatism in the 1980s gave Reagan invaluable allies in western Europe. In Great Britain a strong-willed Margaret Thatcher worked well with Reagan and was a forceful advocate for a revitalized Atlantic alliance. After a strongly pro-American Helmut Kohl (b. 1930) came to power with the conservative Christian Democrats in 1982, West Germany and the United States once again effectively coordinated military and political policy toward the Soviet bloc.

Passing in the 1970s and early 1980s from détente to confusion to regeneration, the Atlantic alliance bent, but it did not break. In maintaining the alliance, the Western nations gave indirect support to ongoing efforts to liberalize authoritarian communist eastern Europe and probably helped convince the Soviet Union's Mikhail Gorbachev that endless cold war conflict was foolish and dangerous.

The Women's Movement

The 1970s marked the birth of a broad-based feminist movement devoted to securing genuine gender equality and promoting the general interests of women. Three basic reasons accounted for this major development. First, ongoing changes in underlying patterns of motherhood and paid work created novel conditions and new demands (see pages 1009–1010). Second, a vanguard of feminist intellectuals articulated a powerful critique of gender relations, which stimulated many women to rethink their assumptions and challenge the status quo. Third, taking a lesson from the civil rights movement in the United States and worldwide student protest against the Vietnam War, dissatisfied individuals recognized that they had to band together if they were to influence politics and secure fundamental reforms.

One of the most influential works produced by this new feminist wave was *The Second Sex* (1949) by the French writer and philosopher Simone de Beauvoir (1908–1986). Characterizing herself as a "dutiful daughter" of the bourgeoisie in childhood, the adolescent Beauvoir came to see her pious and submissive mother as foolishly renouncing any self-expression outside of home and marriage and showing Beauvoir the dangers of a life she did not want. A brilliant university student, Beauvoir began at the Sorbonne a complex relationship with Jean-Paul Sartre, the future philosopher who became her lifelong intellectual companion and sometime lover.

Beauvoir analyzed the position of women within the framework of existential thought (see pages 924–925). She argued that women—like all human beings—were in essence free but that they had almost always been trapped by particularly inflexible and limiting conditions. (See the feature "Listening to the Past: A Feminist Critique of Marriage" on pages 1024–1025.) Only by means of courageous action and self-assertive creativity could a woman become a completely free person and escape the role of the inferior "other" that men had constructed for her gender. Drawing on history, philosophy, psychology, biology, and literature, Beauvoir's massive investigation inspired a generation of women intellectuals.

One such woman was Betty Friedan (b. 1924), who played a key role in reopening a serious discussion of women's issues in the United States. Unlike Beauvoir, who believed that each woman had to chart her own course, Friedan reflected the American faith in group action and political solutions. As a working wife and the mother of three small children in the 1950s, Friedan became acutely aware of the conflicting pressures of career and family. Conducting an in-depth survey of her classmates at Smith College fifteen years after their graduation, she concluded that many well-educated women shared her growing dissatisfaction. In her pathbreaking study *The Feminine Mystique* (1963), Friedan identified this dissatisfaction as the "problem that has no name." According to Friedan, the cause of this nameless problem was a crisis of identity. Women were not permitted to become mature adults and genuine human beings. Instead, they were expected to conform to a false, infantile pattern of femininity and live (like Beauvoir's mother) for their husbands and children. In short, women faced what feminists would soon call *sexism,* a pervasive social problem that required drastic reforms.

When long-standing proposals to treat sex discrimination as seriously as race discrimination fell again on deaf ears, Friedan took the lead in 1966 in founding the National Organization for Women (NOW) to press for women's rights. NOW flourished, growing from seven hundred members in 1967 to forty thousand in 1974. Many other women's organizations of varying persuasions rose to follow NOW in Europe and the United States. Throughout the 1970s, a proliferation of publications, conferences, and institutions devoted to women's issues reinforced the emerging international movement.

Although national peculiarities abounded, this movement generally shared the common strategy of entering the political arena and changing laws regarding women. First, advocates of women's rights pushed for new statutes in the workplace: laws against discrimination,

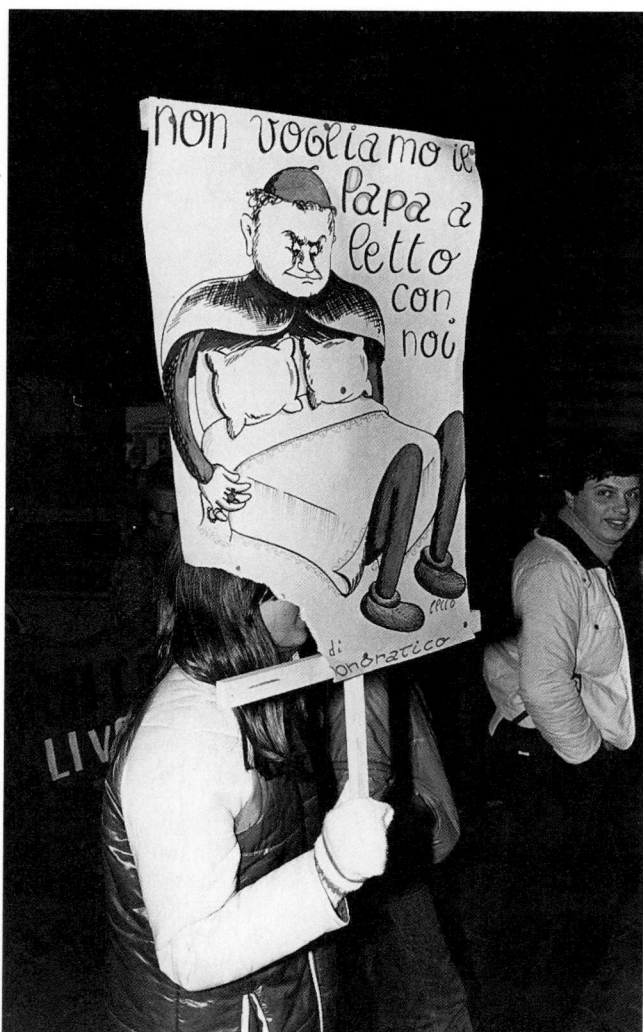

Italian Feminists These women demonstrate in Rome in 1981 for the passage of legislation legalizing abortion, which the pope and the Catholic church have steadfastly opposed. This woman's provocative sign says that she does not want the pope in her bed. *(Giansanti/Corbis SYGMA)*

women's movement (and in creating an opposition to it, as in the United States).

In countries that had long placed women in a subordinate position, the legal changes were little less than revolutionary. In Italy, for example, new laws abolished restrictions on divorce and abortion, which had been strengthened by Mussolini and defended energetically by the Catholic church in the postwar era. By 1988 divorce and abortion were common in Italy, which had the lowest birthrate in Europe. More generally, the sharply focused women's movement of the 1970s won new rights for women. Subsequently, the movement became more diffuse, a victim of both its successes and the resurgence of an antifeminist opposition.

The accomplishments of the women's movement encouraged mobilization by many other groups. Gay men and lesbian women pressed their own demands, organizing politically and calling for an end to legal discrimination and social harassment. People with physical disabilities joined together to promote their interests. Thus many subordinate groups challenged the dominant majorities, and the expansion and redefinition of human liberty—one of the great themes of modern Western and world history—continued.

The Troubled Economy

For twenty years after 1945, most Europeans were preoccupied with the possibilities of economic progress and consumerism. The more democratic class structure also helped to reduce social tension, and ideological conflict went out of style. In the late 1960s, sharp criticism and social conflict re-emerged, however, marking the passing of postwar stability.

Yet it was the reappearance of economic crisis in the early 1970s that brought the most serious challenges for the average person. The postwar international monetary system was based on the American dollar, valued in gold at $35 an ounce. Giving foreign aid and fighting foreign wars, the United States sent billions abroad. By early 1971, it had only $11 billion in gold left, and Europe had accumulated U.S. $50 billion. Foreigners then panicked and raced to exchange their dollars for gold. President Richard Nixon responded by stopping the sale of American gold. The value of the dollar fell sharply, and inflation accelerated worldwide. Fixed rates of exchange were abandoned, and great uncertainty replaced postwar predictability in international trade and finance.

Even more damaging was the dramatic reversal in the price and availability of energy. The great postwar boom was fueled by cheap oil from the Middle East, which

"equal pay for equal work," and measures such as maternal leave and affordable day care designed to help women combine careers and family responsibilities. Second, the movement concentrated on gender and family questions, including the right to divorce (in some Catholic countries), legalized abortion, the needs of single mothers, and protection from rape and physical violence. In almost every country, the effort to decriminalize abortion served as a catalyst in mobilizing an effective, self-conscious

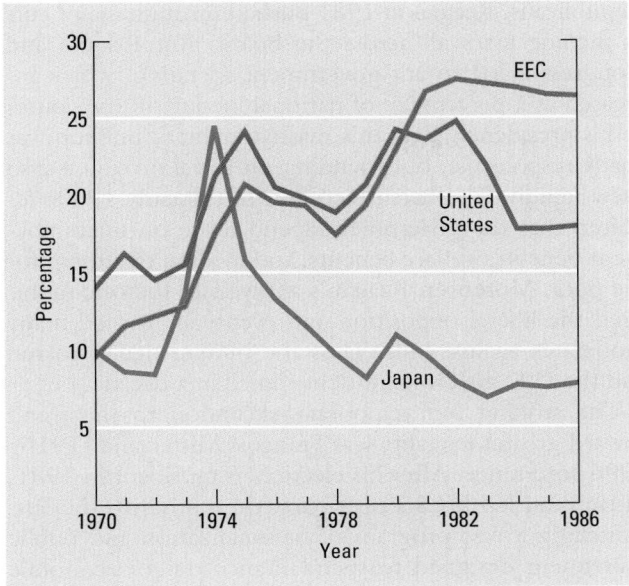

FIGURE 30.2 The Misery Index, 1970–1986
Combining rates of unemployment and inflation provided a simple but effective measure of economic hardship. This particular index represents the sum of two times the unemployment rate plus the inflation rate, reflecting the widespread belief that joblessness causes more suffering than higher prices. EEC = European Economic Community, or Common Market countries. *(Source: OECD data, as given in* The Economist, *June 15, 1985, p. 69.)*

permitted energy-intensive industries—automobiles, chemicals, and electric power—to expand rapidly and lead other sectors of the economy forward. By 1971 the Arab-led Organization of Petroleum Exporting Countries (**OPEC**) had watched the price of crude oil decline consistently compared with the rising price of manufactured goods and had decided to reverse that trend by presenting a united front against the oil companies. The stage was set for a revolution in energy prices during the fourth Arab-Israeli war in October 1973, when Egypt and Syria launched a surprise attack on Israel. OPEC then declared an embargo on oil shipments to the United States, Israel's ally, and within a year crude oil prices quadrupled. Western nations realized that the rapid price rise was economically destructive, but they did nothing. Thus governments, industry, and individuals had no other choice than to deal piecemeal with the so-called oil shock—a "shock" that turned out to be an earthquake.

Coming on the heels of upheaval in the international monetary system, the revolution in energy prices plunged the world into its worst economic decline since the 1930s. The energy-intensive industries that had driven the economy up in the 1950s and 1960s now dragged it down. Unemployment rose; productivity and living standards declined. By 1976 a modest recovery was in progress. But when a fundamentalist Islamic revolution struck Iran and oil production collapsed in that country, the price of crude oil doubled in 1979 and the world economy suc-

cumbed to its second oil shock. Unemployment and inflation rose dramatically before another uneven recovery began in 1982. In 1985 the unemployment rate in western Europe rose to its highest level since the Great Depression. Nineteen million people were unemployed.

One telling measure of the troubled economy was the **misery index,** which combined rates of inflation and unemployment in a single, powerfully emotional number. Figure 30.2 shows a comparison of misery indexes for the United States, Japan, and the Common Market countries between 1970 and 1986. "Misery" increased on both sides of the Atlantic, but the increase was substantially greater in western Europe, where these hard times were often referred to simply as "the crisis." Japan did better than both Europe and the United States in this period.

Throughout the 1970s and 1980s, anxious observers, recalling the disastrous consequences of the Great Depression, worried that the Common Market would disintegrate in the face of severe economic dislocation and that economic nationalism would halt steps toward European unity. Yet the Common Market—now officially known as the European Economic Community—continued to attract new members. In 1973 Denmark and Iceland, in addition to Britain, finally joined. Greece joined in 1981, and Portugal and Spain entered in 1986. The nations of the European Economic Community also cooperated more closely in international undertakings, and the movement toward unity for western Europe stayed alive.

Society in a Time of Economic Uncertainty

The most pervasive consequences of economic stagnation in the 1970s and early 1980s were probably psychological and attitudinal. Optimism gave way to pessimism; romantic utopianism yielded to sober realism. This drastic change in mood—a complete surprise only to those who had never studied history—affected states, institutions, and individuals in countless ways.

To be sure, there were heartbreaking human tragedies—lost jobs, bankruptcies, homelessness, and mental breakdowns. But on the whole, the welfare system fashioned in the postwar era prevented mass suffering and degradation through extended benefits for the unemployed, pensions for the aged, free medical care and special allowances for the needy, and a host of lesser supports. The responsive, socially concerned national state undoubtedly contributed to the preservation of political stability and democracy in the face of economic difficulties that might have brought revolution and dictatorship in earlier times.

The energetic response of governments to social needs helps explain the sharp increase in total government spending in most countries during the 1970s and early 1980s. In 1982 western European governments spent an average of more than 50 percent of all national income, as compared to only 37 percent fifteen years earlier. In all countries, people were much more willing to see their governments increase spending than raise taxes. This imbalance contributed to the rapid growth of budget deficits, national debts, and inflation. By the late 1970s, a powerful reaction against government's ever-increasing role had set in, however, and Western governments were gradually forced to introduce austerity measures to slow the growth of public spending and the welfare state.

Part of a broad cultural shift toward greater conservatism, growing voter dissatisfaction with government and government spending helped bring Margaret Thatcher (b. 1925) to power in Britain in 1979. Thatcher had some success in slowing government spending and in "privatizing" industry—that is, in selling off state-owned companies to private investors. Thatcher's Conservative government also encouraged low- and moderate-income renters in state-owned housing projects to buy their apartments at rock-bottom prices. This privatization initiative created a whole new class of property owners, thereby eroding the electoral base of Britain's socialist Labour party.

President Ronald Reagan's success in the United States was more limited. With widespread popular support and the agreement of most congressional Democrats as well as Republicans, Reagan in 1981 pushed through major cuts in income taxes all across the board. But Reagan and Congress failed to cut government spending, which increased as a percentage of national income in the course of his presidency. Reagan's massive military buildup was partly responsible, but spending on social programs also grew rapidly. The harsh recession of the early 1980s required that the government spend more on unemployment benefits, welfare benefits, and medical treatment for the poor. Moreover, Reagan's antiwelfare rhetoric mobilized the liberal opposition and eventually turned many moderates against him. Thus the budget deficit soared and the U.S. government debt tripled in a decade.

The striking but temporary exception to the trend toward greater frugality was François Mitterrand (1916–1996) of France. After his election as president in 1981, Mitterrand led his Socialist party on a lurch to the left, launching a vast program of nationalization and public investment designed to spend France out of economic stagnation. By 1983 this attempt had clearly failed. Mitterrand's Socialist government was then compelled to impose a wide variety of austerity measures and to maintain those policies for the rest of the decade.

When governments were forced to restrain spending, large scientific projects were often singled out for cuts. These reductions reinforced the ongoing computer revolution. This new scientific revolution thrived on the diffusion of ever-cheaper computational and informational capacity to small research groups and private businesses, which were both cause and effect of the revolution itself. Big organizations lost some of their advantages over small firms.

Individuals felt the impact of austerity at an early date, for unlike governments, they could not pay their bills by printing money and going ever further into debt. The energy crisis of the 1970s forced them to re-examine not only their fuel bills but also the whole pattern of self-indulgent materialism in the postwar years. The result in both Europe and North America was a leaner, tougher lifestyle in the 1970s and early 1980s, featuring more attention to nutrition and a passion for exercise. Correspondingly, there was less blind reliance on medical science for good health and a growing awareness that individuals had to accept a large portion of the responsibility for illness and disease. More people began to realize that they could substantially increase their life spans simply by eating regular meals, sleeping seven or eight hours each night, exercising two or three times a week, maintaining moderate weight, forgoing smoking, and using alcohol only in moderation. In the late 1970s, a forty-five-year-old American male who practiced three or fewer of these habits could expect to live to be sixty-seven; one who adhered to five or six could expect to live eleven years more, to age seventy-eight.

Economic troubles also strengthened the new trends within the family. Men and women were encouraged to postpone marriage until they had put their careers on a firm foundation, so the age of marriage rose sharply for both sexes in many Western countries. Indeed, the very real threat of unemployment—or "underemployment" in a dead-end job—seemed to shape the outlook of a whole generation. The students of the 1980s were serious, practical, and often conservative. As one young woman at a French university told a reporter in 1985, "Jobs are the big worry now, so everyone wants to learn something practical."[11] In France as elsewhere, the shift away from the romantic visions and the political activism of the late 1960s was astonishing.

Harder times also help explain why ever more women entered or remained in the workforce after they did marry. Although attitudes related to personal fulfillment were one reason for the continuing increase—especially for well-educated, upper-middle-class women—many wives in poor and middle-class families simply had to work outside the home because of economic necessity. As in preindustrial Europe, the wife's earnings provided the margin of survival for millions of hard-pressed families.

Postwar developments in eastern Europe displayed both similarities to and differences from developments in western Europe and North America. Perhaps the biggest difference was that Stalin imposed harsh one-party rule in the lands occupied by his armies, which led to the bitter cold war. Nevertheless, the Soviet Union became less dictatorial under Khrushchev, and the standard of living in the Soviet Union improved markedly in the 1950s and 1960s.

In the late 1960s and early 1970s, Europe and North America entered a time of crisis. Many nations, from France to Czechoslovakia to the United States, experienced major political difficulties, as cold war conflicts and ideological battles divided peoples and shook governments. Beginning with the oil shocks of the 1970s, severe economic problems added to the turmoil and brought real hardship to millions of people. Yet in western Europe and North America, the welfare system held firm, and both democracy and the movement toward European unity successfully passed through the storm. The women's movement also mobilized effectively and won expanded rights in the best tradition of Western civilization. Finally, efforts to achieve détente in central Europe while still maintaining a strong Atlantic alliance met some success. This modest progress helped lay the foundations for the sudden end of the cold war and the opening of a new era.

Summary

The recovery of western Europe after World War II was one of the most striking chapters in the long, uneven course of Western civilization. Although the dangerous tensions of the cold war frustrated hopes for a truly peaceful international order, the transition from imperialism to decolonization proceeded rapidly, surprisingly smoothly, and without serious damage to western Europe. Genuine political democracy gained unprecedented strength in western Europe, and rapid economic progress marked a generation.

Fundamental social changes accompanied the political recovery and economic expansion after World War II. Pure science combined with applied technology to achieve remarkable success. The triumphs of applied science contributed not only to economic expansion but also to a more fluid, less antagonistic class structure, in which specialized education was the high road to advancement for men and women. Married women entered the labor force in growing numbers.

Key Terms

Big Three
Marshall Plan
NATO
cold war
Christian Democrats
Common Market
decolonization
neocolonialism

de-Stalinization
Brezhnev Doctrine
Big Science
Watergate
détente
OPEC
misery index

Notes

1. Quoted in N. Graebner, *Cold War Diplomacy, 1945–1960* (Princeton, N.J.: Van Nostrand, 1962), p. 17.
2. Quoted ibid.
3. Quoted in J. Hennessy, *Economic "Miracles"* (London: Andre Deutsch, 1964), p. 5.
4. Quoted in S. E. Morison et al., *A Concise History of the American Republic* (New York: Oxford University Press, 1977), p. 697.
5. Quoted in D. Treadgold, *Twentieth Century Russia*, 5th ed. (Boston: Houghton Mifflin, 1981), p. 442.

6. Quoted in J. Ziman, *The Force of Knowledge: The Scientific Dimension of Society* (Cambridge: Cambridge University Press, 1976), p. 128.

7. Quoted in S. Toulmin, *The Twentieth Century: A Promethean Age,* ed. A. Bullock (London: Thames & Hudson, 1971), p. 294.

8. Quoted in N. Cantor, *Twentieth-Century Culture: Modernism to Deconstruction* (New York: Peter Lang, 1988), p. 252.

9. M. Mitterauer, *The History of Youth* (Oxford: Basil Blackwell, 1992), p. 40.

10. Quoted in Kessing's Research Report, *Germany and East Europe Since 1945: From the Potsdam Agreement to Chancellor Brandt's "Ostpolitik"* (New York: Charles Scribner's Sons, 1973), pp. 284–285.

11. *Wall Street Journal,* June 28, 1985, p. 1.

Suggested Reading

M. Eksteins, *Walking Since Daybreak: A Story of Eastern Europe, World War II, and the Heart of Our Century* (1999), is a powerful, partly autobiographical account that is highly recommended. Three valuable general studies with extensive bibliographies are W. Laqueur, *Europe in Our Time: A History, 1945–1992* (1992); C. Black, *Rebirth: A History of Europe Since World War II* (1992); and P. Johnson, *Modern Times: The World from the Twenties to the Eighties* (1983). Winston Churchill and Charles de Gaulle both wrote histories of the war in the form of memoirs. Other interesting memoirs are those of Dwight Eisenhower, *Crusade in Europe* (1948), and Dean Acheson, *Present at the Creation* (1969), a defense of American foreign policy in the early cold war. K. Sainsbury, *Churchill and Roosevelt at War: The War They Fought and the Peace They Hoped to Make* (1994), is an excellent, very readable introduction. Valuable works on the cold war include A. Winkler, *The Cold War: A Collection of Documents* (2000); P. de Senarclens, *From Yalta to the Iron Curtain: The Great Powers and the Origins of the Cold War* (1995); and M. Walker, *The Cold War: A History* (1993).

D. Urwin, *The Community of Europe: A History of European Integration,* 2d ed. (1995), and R. Mayne, *The Recovery of Europe, 1945–1973* (1973), focus on steps toward western European unity. W. Leuchtenberg, *In the Shadow of FDR: From Harry Truman to Ronald Reagan* (1989), ably discusses developments in the United States. Postwar economic and social developments are analyzed in G. Ambrosius and W. Hibbard, *A Social and Economic History of Twentieth-Century Europe* (1989), and F. Tipton and R. Aldrich, *An Economic and Social History of Europe from 1939 to the Present* (1986).

Two outstanding works on France are J. Ardagh, *The New French Revolution* (1969), which puts the momentous social changes since 1945 in human terms; and S. Bernstein, *The Republic of de Gaulle, 1958–1969* (1993). On postwar West Germany, H. Turner, *The Two Germanies Since 1945: East*

and West (1987), and W. Patterson and G. Smith, eds., *The West German Model: Perspectives on a Stable State* (1981), are good introductions. R. Dahrendorf, *Society and Democracy in Germany* (1971), is a classic interpretation. The spiritual dimension of West German recovery is probed by Günter Grass in his world-famous novel *The Tin Drum* (1963), as well as in the novels of Heinrich Böll. A. Marwick, *British Society Since 1945* (1982), and A. H. Halsey, *Change in British Society* (1981), are good on postwar developments. M. Chamberlain, *Decolonialization: The Fall of European Empires,* 2d ed. (1999), is a clear, up-to-date account. T. von Laue, *The World Revolution of Westernization: The Twentieth Century in Global Perspective* (1987), is a stimulating interpretation.

Z. Brzezinski, *The Grand Failure: The Birth and Death of Communism in the Twentieth Century* (1989), is a readable overview by a leading American scholar. L. Johnson, *Central Europe: Enemies, Neighbors, Friends* (1996), is an up-to-date synthesis discussing major developments. J. Ridley, *Tito* (1994), is lively and learned. P. Zinner, *National Communism and Popular Revolt in Eastern Europe* (1956) and *Revolution in Hungary* (1962), are excellent on the tragic events of 1956. A. Amalrik, *Will the Soviet Union Survive Until 1984?* (1970), is a fascinating and prophetic interpretation of Soviet society and politics in the 1960s.

Ziman's volume, cited in the Notes, which has an excellent bibliography, is a penetrating look at science by a leading physicist. A. Bramwell, *Ecology in the Twentieth Century: A History* (1989), examines negative aspects of technical and industrial development. Two more stimulating works on postwar technology are J. J. Servan-Schreiber, *The World Challenge* (1981), and H. Jacoby, *The Bureaucratization of the World* (1973).

In addition to previously mentioned country studies, A. Simpson, *The New Europeans* (1968), provides a good guide to Western society in the 1960s. Mitterauer and Cantor, both cited in the Notes, are excellent on the youth culture and the trends that made it possible. L. Wylie, *Village in the Vauclause* (1964), and P. J. Hélias, *The Horse of Pride* (1980), provide fascinating pictures of life in the French village before prosperity arrived. A. Kriegel, *The French Communists* (1972) and *Eurocommunism* (1978), are also recommended. D. Caute, *The Year of the Barricades: A Journey Through 1968* (1988), is a high-energy account that brings the upheavals of 1968 to life, while C. Fink et al., *1968: The World Transformed* (1998), is a stimulating reconsideration. Two outstanding works on the Vietnam War are N. Sheehan, *A Bright and Shining Lie: John Paul Vann and America in Vietnam* (1988), and A. Short, *The Origins of the Vietnam War* (1989). Among the many books to come out of the Czechoslovak experience in 1968, I. Svitak, *The Czechoslovak Experiment, 1968–1969* (1971), and Z. Zeman, *Prague Spring* (1969), are particularly recommended.

M. Boxer and J. Quartaert, *Connecting Spheres: European Women in a Globalizing World, 1500 to the Present,* 2d ed. (2000), is an excellent survey with up-to-date bibliographies. E. Sullerot, *Women, Society and Change* (1971), is a pioneering analysis of women's evolving roles after 1945. Two extremely influential books on women and their new awareness are S. de Beauvoir, *The Second Sex* (1962), and B. Friedan, *The Feminine Mystique* (1963). They may be compared with C. Lasch, *Haven in a Heartless World* (1977), an influential study of the family.

On feminism and the women's movement, see N. Cott, *The Grounding of Modern Feminism* (1987). J. Lovenduski, *Women and European Politics: Contemporary Feminism and Public Policy* (1986), provides an extremely useful compara-tive study of similar developments in different countries. C. Duchen, *Feminism in France: From May '68 to Mitterrand* (1986), is also recommended. L. Appignanesi, *Simone de Beauvoir* (1988), is a readable study of the life and thought of the famous thinker. Good studies on British women include E. Wilson, *Only Halfway to Paradise: Women in Postwar Britain, 1945–1968* (1980), and M. Barrett, *Women's Opposition Today* (1980). U. Frevert, *Women in German History: From Bourgeois Emancipation to Sexual Liberation* (1989), is both learned and engaging. Two good studies on Soviet women before the collapse of communism are F. DuPlessix Gray, *Soviet Women* (1989), and T. Mamonova, ed., *Women and Russia* (1986).

Listening to the Past

A Feminist Critique of Marriage

Having grown up in Paris in a middle-class family and become a teacher, novelist, and intellectual, Simone de Beauvoir (1908–1986) turned increasingly to feminist concerns after World War II. Her most influential work was The Second Sex *(1949), a massive declaration of independence for contemporary women.*

As an existentialist, Beauvoir believed that all individuals must accept responsibility for their lives and strive to overcome the tragic dilemmas they face. Studying the experience of women since antiquity, Beauvoir argued that men had generally used education and social conditioning to create a dependent "other," a negative nonman who was not permitted to grow and strive for freedom.

Marriage—on men's terms—was part of this unjust and undesirable process. Beauvoir's conclusion that some couples could establish free and equal unions was based in part on her experience with philosopher Jean-Paul Sartre, Beauvoir's encouraging companion and sometime lover.

Every human existence involves transcendence and immanence at the same time; to go forward, each existence must be maintained, for it to expand toward the future it must integrate the past, and while intercommunicating with others it should find self-confirmation. These two elements—maintenance and progression—are implied in any living activity, and for *man* marriage permits precisely a happy synthesis of the two. In his occupation and his political life he encounters change and progress, he senses his extension through time and the universe; and when he is tired of such roaming, he gets himself a home, a fixed location, and an anchorage in the world. At evening he restores his soul in the home, where his wife takes care of his furnishings and children and guards the things of the past that she keeps in store. But she has no other job than to maintain and provide for life in pure and unvarying generality; she perpetuates the species without change, she ensures the even rhythm of the days and the continuity of the home, seeing to it that the doors are locked. But she is allowed no direct influence upon the future nor upon the world; she reaches out beyond herself toward the social group only through her husband as intermediary.

Marriage today still retains, for the most part, this traditional form. . . . The male is called upon for action, his vocation is to produce, fight, create, progress, to transcend himself toward the totality of the universe and the infinity of the future; but traditional marriage does not invite woman to transcend herself with him; it confines her in immanence, shuts her up within the circle of herself. She can thus propose to do nothing more than construct a life of stable equilibrium in which the present as a continuance of the past avoids the menaces of tomorrow—that is, construct precisely a life of happiness. . . .

In domestic work, with or without the aid of servants, woman makes her home her own, finds social justification, and provides herself with an occupation, an activity, that deals usefully and satisfyingly with material objects—shining stoves, fresh, clean clothes, bright copper, polished furniture—but provides no escape from immanence and little affirmation of individuality. . . . Few tasks are more like the torture of Sisyphus than housework, with its endless repetition: the clean becomes soiled, the soiled is made clean, over and over, day after day. The housewife wears herself out marking time: she makes nothing, simply perpetuates the present. She never senses conquest of a positive

Good, but rather indefinite struggle against negative Evil. . . . Washing, ironing, sweeping, ferreting out rolls of lint from under wardrobes—all this halting of decay is also the denial of life; for time simultaneously creates and destroys, and only its negative aspect concerns the housekeeper. . . .

Thus woman's work within the home gives her no autonomy; it is not directly useful to society, it does not open out on the future, it produces nothing. It takes on meaning and dignity only as it is linked with existent beings who reach out beyond themselves, transcend themselves, toward society in production and action. That is, far from freeing the matron, her occupation makes her dependent upon husband and children; she is justified through them; but in their lives she is only an inessential intermediary. . . .

The tragedy of marriage is not that it fails to assure woman the promised happiness—there is no such thing as assurance in regard to happiness—but that it mutilates her; it dooms her to repetition and routine. The first twenty years of woman's life are extraordinarily rich, as we have seen; she discovers the world and her destiny. At twenty or thereabouts mistress of a home, bound permanently to a man, a child in her arms, she stands with her life virtually finished forever. Real activities, real work, are the prerogative of her man: she has mere things to occupy her which are sometimes tiring but never fully satisfying. . . .

Marriage should be a combining of two whole, independent existences, not a retreat, an annexation, a flight, a remedy. . . . The couple should not be regarded as a unit, a close cell; rather each individual should be integrated as such in society at large, where each (whether male or female) could flourish without aid; then attachments could be formed in pure generosity with another individual equally adapted to the group, attachments that would be founded upon the acknowledgment that both are free.

This balanced couple is not a utopian fancy: such couples do exist, sometimes even within the frame of marriage, most often outside it. Some mates are united by a strong sexual love that leaves them free in their friendships and in their work; others are held together by a friendship that does not preclude sexual liberty; more rare are

Simone de Beauvoir at home in Paris, June 1985. *(Gerard Gastand/Sipa Press)*

those who are at once lovers and friends but do not seek in each other their sole reasons for living. Many nuances are possible in the relations between a man and a woman: in comradeship, pleasure, trust, fondness, co-operation, and love, they can be for each other the most abundant source of joy, richness, and power available to human beings.

Questions for Analysis

1. How did Beauvoir analyze marriage and marriage partners in terms of existential philosophy?

2. To what extent does a married woman benefit from a "traditional" marriage, according to Beauvoir? Why?

3. What was Beauvoir's solution to the situation she described? Was her solution desirable? Realistic?

4. What have you learned about the history of women that supports or challenges Beauvoir's analysis? Include developments since World War II and your own reflections.

Source: Simone de Beauvoir, *The Second Sex,* trans. H. M. Parshley. Copyright © 1952 and renewed 1980 by Alfred A. Knopf, Inc. Reprinted by permission of the publisher.

Salt Lake City, 2002. International Olympic Committee president Jacques Rogge presents the Olympic flag to the mayor of Turin, Italy, site of the 2006 Winter Olympics. *(Elsa/Getty Images)*

Revolution, Rebuilding, and New Challenges: 1985 to the Present

chapter outline

- The Decline of Communism in Eastern Europe

- The Revolutions of 1989

- Building a New Europe in the 1990s

- New Challenges in the Twenty-first Century

- The Future in Perspective

In the late twentieth century, massive changes swept through eastern Europe and opened a new era in human history. Efforts in the late 1980s to reform and revitalize the communist system in the Soviet Union snowballed out of control, and in 1989 revolutions swept away communist rule throughout the entire Soviet bloc. The cold war came to a spectacular end, West Germany absorbed East Germany, and the Soviet Union broke into fifteen independent countries. Thus after forty years of cold war division, Europe regained an underlying unity, as faith in democratic government and some kind of market economy became the common European creed. In 1991 hopes for peaceful democratic progress throughout Europe were almost universal.

The post–cold war years saw the realization of some of these hopes, but the new era brought its own problems and tragedies. The cold war division of Europe had kept a lid on ethnic conflicts and nationalism, which suddenly burst into the open and led to a disastrous civil war in the former Yugoslavia. Moreover, most western European economies were plagued by high unemployment and struggling to adapt to the wide-open global economy, which undermined cherished social benefits and complicated the task of working together with the former communist states. Thus in eastern Europe, the process of rebuilding shattered societies was much more difficult than optimists had envisioned in 1991, and in western Europe, the road toward greater integration and eventual eastward expansion proved bumpy.

The new century brought a growing awareness of a new set of fundamental challenges, which were related to the prospect of population decline, the reality of large-scale immigration, and Europe's identity and place in the world. These challenges promised to preoccupy Europeans for years to come.

- Why did efforts to reform the communist system fail and result in successful anticommunist revolutions throughout eastern Europe?
- What were the consequences of these revolutions and the end of the cold war?
- How, in the 1990s, did the different parts of a unifying Europe meet the challenges of postcommunist reconstruction, resurgent nationalism, and economic union?

- What are the new challenges facing Europe as it proceeds through the twenty-first century?

These are the fundamental questions that this chapter will address.

The Decline of Communism in Eastern Europe

The Soviet bloc perplexed Western observers in the 1970s and early 1980s, and with good reason. On the one hand, attempts to liberalize the system continued, and the brutality of the Stalinist era was never re-established after Nikita Khrushchev fell from power in 1964. These changes encouraged Western hopes of gradual liberalization and of a more democratic, less threatening Soviet eastern Europe.

On the other hand, hard facts frequently intervened to undermine these hopes. In addition to periodic threats and military action, the Soviet Union repeatedly demonstrated that it remained a harsh and aggressive dictatorship that paid only lip service to egalitarian ideology and was determined to uphold its rule throughout eastern Europe. Periodic efforts to achieve fundamental political change were doomed to failure sooner or later—or so it seemed to most Western experts into the mid-1980s.

And then Mikhail Gorbachev burst on the scene. The new Soviet leader opened an era of reform that was as sweeping as it was unexpected. Although many believed that Gorbachev would soon fall from power, his reforms rapidly transformed Soviet culture and politics, and they drastically reduced cold war tensions. But communism, which Gorbachev wanted so desperately to revitalize in order to save it, continued to decline as a functioning system throughout the Soviet bloc.

The Soviet Union to 1985

The 1968 invasion of Czechoslovakia (see pages 1005–1006) was the crucial event of the Brezhnev era, a period that actually lasted beyond the aging leader's death in 1982 until the emergence in 1985 of Gorbachev. The invasion demonstrated the intense conservatism of the Soviet Union's ruling elite and its determination to maintain the status quo in the Soviet bloc. There was a certain **re-Stalinization** of the U.S.S.R., but now dictatorship was collective rather than personal and coercion replaced terror. This compromise seemed to suit the leaders and a majority of the people.

A slowly rising standard of living for ordinary people contributed to the apparent stability in the Soviet Union, although long lines and innumerable shortages persisted. Ambitious individuals had tremendous incentive to do as the state wished in order to gain access to special, well-stocked stores, to attend special schools, and to travel abroad.

Another source of stability was the enduring nationalism of ordinary **Great Russians.** Party leaders successfully identified themselves with Russian patriotism, stressing their role in saving the country during the Second World War and protecting it now from foreign foes, including eastern European "counter-revolutionaries." Moreover, the politically dominant Great Russians, who were concentrated in the central Russian heartland and held through the Communist party the commanding leadership positions in the non-Russian republics, constituted less than half of the total Soviet population. The Great Russians generally feared that greater freedom might result in demands for autonomy and even independence not only by eastern European nationalities but also by the non-Russian nationalities within the Soviet Union itself. Thus liberalism and democracy generally appeared to Great Russians as alien political philosophies designed to undermine the U.S.S.R.'s power and greatness.

The strength of the government was expressed in the re-Stalinization of culture and art. Free expression disappeared and Brezhnev and company made certain that Soviet intellectuals did not engage in public protest. Acts of open nonconformity and protest were severely punished, but with sophisticated, cunning methods.

Most frequently, dissidents were blacklisted and thus rendered unable to find decent jobs since the government was the only employer. This fate was enough to keep most in line. More determined protesters were quietly imprisoned, while celebrated nonconformists such as Aleksandr Solzhenitsyn were permanently expelled from the country. Eliminating the worst aspects of Stalin's dictatorship strengthened the regime, and almost all Western experts concluded that rule by a self-perpetuating Communist party elite in the Soviet Union appeared to be quite solid in the 1970s and early 1980s.

Yet beneath the dreary immobility of political life in the Brezhnev era, the Soviet Union was actually experiencing profound changes. As a perceptive British journalist put it in 1986, "The country went through a social revolution while Brezhnev slept."[1] Three aspects of this revolution, which was seldom appreciated by Western observers at the time, were particularly significant.

First, the growth of the urban population, which had raced forward at breakneck speed in the Stalin years, con-

1985	1991	1997	2003

Political/Military

- August 1989 Solidarity gains power in Poland
- November 1989 Collapse of the Berlin Wall
- December 1989 Velvet Revolution ends communism in Czechoslovakia
- 1990–1991 Gulf War
- October 1990 Reunification of Germany
- November 1990 Paris Accord
- 1991–2001 Civil war in Yugoslavia
- 1991 Chechnya declares independence from Russian Federation; Russian army begins war
- July 1991 Failed coup against Gorbachev in Russia
- December 1991 Dissolution of the Soviet Union
- 1993 Creation of the European Union
- September 2001 Terrorist attack on the United States by the al-Qaida terrorist network

Social/Economic

- 1985– Decline in birthrate in industrialized nations continues
- 1986 Single European Act lays groundwork for single currency
- 1991 Maastricht treaty sets financial criteria for European monetary union
- 1992–1997 "Shock therapy" in Russia causes decline of the economy
- 1993–1999 Growth of illegal immigration in Europe
- January 2002 New Euro (unified) currency goes into effect in the European Union

Intellectual/Religious

- 1985 Glasnost leads to greater freedom of speech and expression in the Soviet Union
- 1991–2000 Resurgence of nationalism and ethnic conflict in eastern Europe
- 1992 Fukuyama, *The End of History and the Last Man*
- 1996 Cronin, *The War the Cold War Made*
- 1998– Growing support for global human rights in Europe

tinued rapidly in the 1960s and 1970s. In 1985 two-thirds of all Soviet citizens lived in cities, and one-quarter lived in big cities. Of great significance, this expanding urban population lost its old peasant ways, exchanging them for more education, better job skills, and greater sophistication.

Second, the number of highly trained scientists, managers, and specialists expanded prodigiously, increasing fourfold between 1960 and 1985. Thus the class of well-educated, pragmatic, and self-confident experts, which played such an important role in restructuring industrial societies after World War II (see pages 1007–1009), developed rapidly in the Soviet Union. Moreover, leading Soviet scientists and technologists sought membership in the international "invisible college" of their disciplines.

"What's This? You Have Your Own Opinion?" This cartoon, published in the Soviet Union's enormously popular satirical magazine *The Crocodile,* shows a Soviet manager getting into trouble for drawing a nonstandard doodle at a meeting. Jokes poking fun at communist bosses and human foibles permeated Soviet culture, especially the oral culture, in the Brezhnev era. *(© Vneshtorgizdat, Moscow)*

They sought the intellectual freedom necessary to do significant work, and they often obtained it because their research had practical (and military) value.

Third, education and freedom for experts in their special areas helped foster the growth of Soviet public opinion. Educated people read, discussed, and formed definite ideas about social questions. And if caution dictated conventional ideas (at least in public), many important issues could be approached and debated in "nonpolitical" terms. Developing definite ideas on such issues as environmental pollution and urban transportation, educated urban people increasingly saw themselves as worthy of having a voice in society's decisions, even its political decisions.

Solidarity in Poland

Gorbachev's reforms interacted with a resurgence of popular protest in the Soviet Union's satellite empire. Developments in Poland were most striking and significant.

Poland had been an unruly satellite from the beginning. Stalin said that introducing communism to Poland was like putting a saddle on a cow. Efforts to saddle the cow—really a spirited stallion—led to widespread riots in 1956 (see page 1004). As a result, Polish Communists dropped their efforts to impose Soviet-style collectivization on the peasants and to break the Roman Catholic church. Most agricultural land remained in private hands, and the Catholic church thrived. Thus the Communists failed to monopolize society.

They also failed to manage the economy effectively. Even the booming 1960s saw little economic improvement. In 1970 Poland's working class rose again in angry protest. A new Communist leader came to power, and he wagered that massive inflows of Western capital and technology, especially from rich and now-friendly West Germany (see pages 1015–1017), could produce a Polish "economic miracle." Instead, bureaucratic incompetence and the first oil shock in 1973 put the economy into a nosedive. Workers, intellectuals, and the church became increasingly restive. Then the real Polish miracle occurred: Cardinal Karol Wojtyla, archbishop of Cracow, was elected pope in 1978. In June 1979, he returned from Rome, preaching love of Christ and country and the "inalienable rights of man." Pope John Paul II drew enormous crowds and electrified the Polish nation. The economic crisis became a moral and spiritual crisis as well.

In August 1980, the sixteen thousand workers at the gigantic Lenin Shipyards in Gdansk (formerly known as Danzig) laid down their tools and occupied the plant. As other workers joined "in solidarity," the strikers ad-

Lech Walesa and Solidarity An inspiration for fellow workers at the Lenin Shipyards in the dramatic and successful strike against the Communist bosses in August 1980, Walesa played a key role in Solidarity before and after it was outlawed. Speaking here to old comrades at the Lenin Shipyards after Solidarity was again legalized in 1988, Walesa personified an enduring opposition to Communist rule in eastern Europe. *(G. Merrillon/Gamma)*

vanced revolutionary demands, including the right to form free trade unions, freedom of speech, release of political prisoners, and economic reforms. After eighteen days of shipyard occupation, the government gave in and accepted the workers' demands in the **Gdansk Agreement.** In a state where the Communist party claimed to rule on behalf of the proletariat, a working-class revolt had won an unprecedented victory.

Led by feisty Lenin Shipyards electrician and devout Catholic Lech Walesa (b. 1943), the workers proceeded to organize their free and democratic trade union. They called it **Solidarity.** Joined by intellectuals and supported by the Catholic church, Solidarity became the union of a nation. By March 1981, a full-time staff of 40,000 linked 9.5 million union members together as Solidarity published its own newspapers and cultural and intellectual freedom blossomed in Poland. Solidarity's leaders had tremendous support, and the ever-present threat of call-

ing a nationwide strike gave them real power in ongoing negotiations with the Communist bosses.

But if Solidarity had power, it did not try to take the reins of government in 1981. History, the Brezhnev Doctrine, and virulent attacks from communist neighbors all seemed to guarantee the intervention of the Red Army and a terrible bloodbath if Polish Communists "lost control." Thus the Solidarity revolution remained a "self-limiting revolution" aimed at defending the cultural and trade-union freedoms won in the Gdansk Agreement, and it refused to use force to challenge directly the Communist monopoly of political power. (See the feature "Listening to the Past: A Solidarity Leader Speaks from Prison" on pages 1062–1063.)

Solidarity's combination of strength and moderation postponed a showdown, as the Soviet Union played a waiting game of threats and pressure. After a confrontation in March 1981, Walesa settled for minor government concessions, and Solidarity dropped plans for a massive general strike. Criticism of Walesa's moderate leadership grew, and Solidarity lost its cohesiveness. The worsening economic crisis also encouraged grassroots radicalism, as the Polish Communist leadership shrewdly denounced Solidarity for promoting economic collapse and provoking Soviet invasion. In December 1981, Communist leader General Wojciech Jaruzelski suddenly struck, proclaiming martial law, arresting Solidarity's leaders, and "saving" the nation.

Outlawed and driven underground, Solidarity fought successfully to maintain its organization and to voice the aspirations of the Polish masses after 1981. Part of the reason for the union's survival was the government's unwillingness (and probably its inability) to impose full-scale terror. Moreover, in schools and shops, in factories and offices, millions decided to continue acting as if they were free, even though they were not. Therefore, cultural and intellectual life remained extremely vigorous in spite of renewed repression. At the same time, the faltering Polish economy continued to deteriorate. Thus popular support for outlawed Solidarity remained strong and deep under martial law in the 1980s, preparing the way for the union's political rebirth toward the end of the decade.

The rise and survival of Solidarity showed the desire of millions of eastern Europeans for greater political liberty and the enduring appeal of cultural freedom, trade-union rights, patriotic nationalism, and religious feeling. Not least, Solidarity's challenge encouraged fresh thinking in the Soviet Union, ever the key to lasting change in the Eastern bloc.

Gorbachev's Reforms in the Soviet Union

Fundamental change in Russian history has often come in short, intensive spurts, which contrast vividly with long periods of immobility. The era of reform launched by Mikhail Gorbachev in 1985 was one such decisive transformation. Gorbachev's initiatives brought political and cultural liberalization to the Soviet Union, and they then permitted democracy and national self-determination to triumph spectacularly in the old satellite empire and eventually in the Soviet Union itself, although this was certainly not Gorbachev's original intention.

As we have seen, the Soviet Union's Communist party elite seemed secure in the early 1980s as far as any challenge from below was concerned. The long-established system of administrative controls continued to stretch downward from the central ministries and state committees to provincial cities, and from there to factories, neighborhoods, and villages. At each level of this massive state bureaucracy, the overlapping hierarchy of the Communist party, with its 17.5 million members, continued to watch over all decisions and manipulate every aspect of national life. Organized opposition was impossible, and average people simply left politics to the bosses.

Yet the massive state and party bureaucracy was a mixed blessing. It safeguarded the elite, but it promoted apathy in the masses. Therefore, when the ailing Brezhnev finally died in 1982, his successor, the long-time chief of the secret police, Yuri Andropov (1914–1984), tried to invigorate the system. Relatively little came of these efforts, but they combined with a sharply worsening economic situation to set the stage for the emergence in 1985 of Mikhail Gorbachev (b. 1931), the most vigorous Soviet leader in a generation.

Trained as a lawyer and working his way up as a Communist party official in the northern Caucasus, Gorbachev was smart, charming, and tough. Gorbachev believed in communism, but he realized it was failing to keep up with Western capitalism and technology. This was eroding the Soviet Union's status as a superpower. Thus Gorbachev (and his intelligent, influential wife, Raisa, a dedicated professor of Marxist-Leninist thought) wanted to save the Soviet system by revitalizing it with fundamental reforms. Gorbachev was also an idealist. He wanted to improve conditions for ordinary citizens. Understanding that the endless waste and expense of the cold war arms race had had a disastrous impact on living conditions in the Soviet Union, he realized that improvement at home required better relations with the West.

In his first year in office, Gorbachev attacked corruption and incompetence in the bureaucracy, and he consolidated his power. He attacked alcoholism and drunkenness, which were deadly scourges of Soviet society, and elaborated his ambitious reform program.

The first set of reform policies was designed to transform and restructure the economy, in order to provide for the real needs of the Soviet population. To accomplish this economic "restructuring," or **perestroika,** Gorbachev and his supporters permitted an easing of government price controls on some goods, more independence for state enterprises, and the setting up of profit-seeking private cooperatives to provide personal services for consumers. These timid economic reforms initially produced a few improvements, but shortages then grew as the economy stalled at an intermediate point between central planning and free-market mechanisms. By late 1988, widespread consumer dissatisfaction posed a serious threat to Gorbachev's leadership and the entire reform program.

Gorbachev's bold and far-reaching campaign "to tell it like it is" was much more successful. Very popular in a country where censorship, dull uniformity, and outright lies had long characterized public discourse, the new-found "openness," or **glasnost,** of the government and the media marked an astonishing break with the past. Long-banned and vilified émigré writers sold millions of copies of their works in new editions, while denunciations of Stalin and his terror became standard fare in plays and movies. Thus initial openness in government pronouncements quickly went much further than Gorbachev intended and led to something approaching free speech and free expression, a veritable cultural revolution.

Democratization was the third element of reform. Beginning as an attack on corruption in the Communist party, it led to the first free elections in the Soviet Union since 1917. Gorbachev and the party remained in control, but a minority of critical independents was elected in April 1989 to a revitalized Congress of People's Deputies. Millions of Soviets then watched the new congress for hours on television as Gorbachev and his ministers saw their proposals debated and even rejected. Thus millions of Soviet citizens took practical lessons in open discussion, critical thinking, and representative government. The result was a new political culture at odds with the Communist party's monopoly of power and control.

Democratization ignited demands for greater autonomy and even for national independence by non-Russian minorities, especially in the Baltic region and in the Caucasus. In April 1989, troops with sharpened shovels charged into a rally of Georgian separatists in Tbilisi and left twenty dead. But whereas China's Communist leaders brutally massacred similar prodemocracy demonstrators in Beijing in June 1989 and reimposed rigid authoritarian rule, Gorbachev drew back from repression. Thus nationalist demands continued to grow in the non-Russian Soviet republics.

Finally, the Soviet leader brought "new political thinking" to the field of foreign affairs and acted on it. He withdrew Soviet troops from Afghanistan and sought to reduce East-West tensions. Of enormous importance, he sought to halt the arms race with the United States and convinced President Ronald Reagan of his sincerity. In December 1987, the two leaders agreed in a Washington summit to eliminate all land-based intermediate-range missiles in Europe, setting the stage for more arms reductions. Gorbachev also encouraged reform movements in Poland and Hungary and pledged to respect the polit-

Mikhail Gorbachev   In his acceptance speech before the Supreme Soviet (the U.S.S.R.'s parliament), newly elected president Mikhail Gorbachev vowed to assume "all responsibility" for the success or failure of perestroika. Previous parliaments were no more than tools of the Communist party, but this one actively debated and even opposed government programs. *(Vlastimir Shone/Gamma)*

ical choices of the peoples of eastern Europe, repudiating the Brezhnev Doctrine. By early 1989, it seemed that if Gorbachev held to his word, the tragic Soviet occupation of eastern Europe might well wither away, taking the long cold war with it once and for all.

MAP 31.1 Democratic Movements in Eastern Europe, 1989 With Gorbachev's repudiation of the Brezhnev Doctrine, the revolutionary drive for freedom and democracy spread throughout eastern Europe. Countries that had been satellites in the orbit of the Soviet Union began to set themselves free to establish their own place in the universe of free nations.

The Revolutions of 1989

Instead, history accelerated. In 1989 Gorbachev's plan to reform communism in order to save it snowballed out of control. A series of largely peaceful revolutions swept across eastern Europe (see Map 31.1), overturning existing communist regimes and ending the communists' monopoly of power. Watched on television in the Soviet Union and around the world, these stirring events marked the triumph and the transformation of long-standing opposition to communist rule and foreign domination in eastern Europe.

The revolutions of 1989 had momentous consequences. First, the peoples of eastern Europe joyfully reentered the mainstream of contemporary European life and culture, after having been conquered and brutalized by Nazis and communists for almost sixty years. Second, Gorbachev's reforms boomeranged, and a complicated anticommunist revolution swept through the Soviet Union, as the multinational empire broke into a large Russia and fourteen other independent states. Third, West Germany quickly absorbed its East German rival and emerged as the most influential country in Europe. Finally, the long cold war came to an abrupt end, and the United States suddenly stood as the world's only superpower.

The Collapse of Communism in Eastern Europe

Solidarity and the Polish people led the way to revolution in eastern Europe. In 1988 widespread labor unrest, raging inflation, and the outlawed Solidarity's refusal to cooperate with the military government had brought Poland to the brink of economic collapse. Thus Solidarity skillfully pressured Poland's frustrated Communist leaders into another round of negotiations that might work out a sharing of power to resolve the political stalemate and the economic crisis. The subsequent agreement in early 1989 legalized Solidarity and declared that a large minority of representatives to the Polish parliament would be chosen by free elections in June 1989. Still guaranteed a parliamentary majority and expecting to win many of the contested seats, the Communists believed that their rule was guaranteed for four years and that Solidarity would keep the workers in line.

Lacking access to the state-run media, Solidarity succeeded nonetheless in mobilizing the country and winning most of the contested seats in an overwhelming victory. Moreover, many angry voters crossed off the names of unopposed party candidates, so that the Communist party failed to win the majority they had anticipated. Solidarity members jubilantly entered the Polish parliament, and a dangerous stalemate quickly developed. But Solidarity leader Lech Walesa, a gifted politician who always repudiated violence, adroitly obtained a majority by securing the allegiance of two minor procommunist parties that had been part of the coalition government after World War II. In August 1989, the editor of Solidarity's weekly newspaper was sworn in as Poland's new noncommunist leader.

In its first year and a half, the new Solidarity government cautiously introduced revolutionary political changes. It eliminated the hated secret police, the Communist ministers in the government, and finally Jaruzelski himself, but it did so step by step in order to avoid confrontation with the army or the Soviet Union. However, in economic affairs, the Solidarity-led government was radical from the beginning. It applied **shock therapy** designed to make a clean break with state planning and move quickly to market mechanisms and private property. Thus the Solidarity government abolished controls on many prices on January 1, 1990, and reformed the monetary system with a "big bang."

Hungary followed Poland. Hungary's Communist party boss, János Kádár, had permitted liberalization of the rigid planned economy after the 1956 uprising in exchange for political obedience and continued Communist control. In May 1988, in an effort to retain power by granting modest political concessions, the party replaced Kádár with a reform communist. But opposition groups rejected piecemeal progress, and in the summer of 1989 the Hungarian Communist party agreed to hold free elections in early 1990. Welcoming Western investment and moving rapidly toward multiparty democracy, Hungary's Communists now enjoyed considerable popular support, and they believed, quite mistakenly it turned out, that they could defeat the opposition in the upcoming elections. In an effort to strengthen their support at home and also put pressure on East Germany's hard-line Communist regime, the Hungarians opened their border to East Germans and tore down the barbed-wire "iron curtain" with Austria. Thus tens of thousands of dissatisfied East German "vacationers" began pouring into Hungary, crossed into Austria as refugees, and continued on to immediate resettlement in thriving West Germany.

The flight of East Germans led to the rapid growth of a homegrown protest movement in East Germany. Intellectuals, environmentalists, and Protestant ministers took the lead, organizing huge candlelight demonstrations and arguing that a democratic but still socialist East Germany was both possible and desirable. These "stayers" failed to convince the "leavers," however, who continued to flee the country en masse. In a desperate attempt to stabilize the situation, the East German government opened the Berlin Wall in November 1989, and people danced for joy atop that grim symbol of the prison state. East Germany's aging Communist leaders were swept aside, and a reform government took power and scheduled free elections.

In Czechoslovakia, communism died in December 1989 in an almost good-humored ousting of Communist bosses in only ten days. This so-called **Velvet Revolution** grew out of popular demonstrations led by students, intellectuals, and a dissident playwright turned moral revolutionary named Václav Havel. (See the feature "Individuals in Society: Václav Havel.") The protesters practically took control of the streets and forced the Communists into a power-sharing arrangement, which quickly resulted in the resignation of the Communist

The Fall of the Berlin Wall   The sudden opening of the Berlin Wall in November 1989 dramatized the spectacular collapse of Communism throughout eastern Europe. Built by the Soviet leader Nikita Khrushchev in 1961, the hated barrier had stopped the flow of refugees from East Germany to West Germany. (*Patrick Piel/Gamma*)

government. As 1989 ended, the Czechoslovakian assembly elected Havel president.

Only in Romania was revolution violent and bloody. There ironfisted Communist dictator Nicolae Ceauşescu (1918–1989) had long combined Stalinist brutality with stubborn independence from Moscow. Faced with mass protests in December, Ceauşescu, alone among eastern

European bosses, ordered his ruthless security forces to slaughter thousands, thereby sparking a classic armed uprising. After Ceauşescu's forces were defeated, the tyrant and his wife were captured and executed by a military court. A coalition government emerged from the fighting, although the legacy of Ceauşescu's oppression left a very troubled country.

Individuals in Society

Václav Havel

O n the night of November 24, 1989, the revolution in Czechoslovakia reached its climax. Three hundred thousand people had poured into Prague's historic Wenceslas Square to continue the massive protests that had erupted a week earlier after the police savagely beat student demonstrators. Now all eyes were focused on a high balcony. There an elderly man with a gentle smile and a middle-aged intellectual in jeans and sport jacket stood arm in arm and acknowledged the cheers of the crowd. "Dubček-Havel," the people roared. "Dubček-Havel!" Alexander Dubček, who represented the failed promise of reform communism in the 1960s (see page 1005), was symbolically passing the torch to Václav Havel, who embodied the uncompromising opposition to communism that was sweeping the country. That very evening, the hard-line Communist government resigned, and soon Havel was the unanimous choice to head a new democratic Czechoslovakia. Who was this man to whom the nation turned in 1989?

Born in 1936 into a prosperous, cultured, upper-middle-class family, the young Havel was denied admission to the university because of his class origins. Loving literature and philosophy, he gravitated to the theater, became a stagehand, and emerged in the 1960s as a leading playwright. His plays were set in vague settings, developed existential themes, and poked fun at the absurdities of life and the pretensions of communism. In his private life, Havel thrived on good talk, Prague's lively bar scene, and officially forbidden rock-and-roll.

In 1968 the Soviets rolled into Czechoslovakia, and Havel watched in horror as a tank commander opened fire on a crowd of peaceful protesters in a small town. "That week," he recorded, "was an experience I shall never forget."[*] The free-spirited artist threw himself into the intellectual opposition to communism and became its leading figure for the next twenty years. The costs of defiance were enormous. Purged and blacklisted, Havel lifted barrels in a brewery and wrote bitter satires that could not be staged. In 1977 he and a few other dissidents publicly protested Czechoslovakian violations of the Helsinki Accord on human rights, and in 1989 this Charter '77 group became the inspiration for Civic Forum, the democratic coalition that toppled communism. Havel spent five years in prison and was constantly harassed by the police.

Václav Havel, playwright, dissident leader, and the first postcommunist president of the Czech Republic. (Chris Niedenthal/Black Star)

Havel's thoughts and actions focused on truth, decency, and moral regeneration. In 1975, in a famous open letter to Czechoslovakia's Communist boss, Havel wrote that the people were indeed quiet, but only because they were "driven by fear. . . . Everyone has something to lose and so everyone has reason to be afraid." Thus Havel saw lies, hypocrisy, and apathy undermining and poisoning all human relations in his country. "Order has been established—at the price of a paralysis of the spirit, a deadening of the heart, and a spiritual and moral crisis in society."[†]

Yet Havel saw a way out of the Communist quagmire. He argued that a profound but peaceful revolution in human values was possible. Such a revolution could lead to the moral reconstruction of Czech and Slovak society, where, in his words, "values like trust, openness, responsibility, solidarity and love" might again flourish and nurture the human spirit. Havel was a voice of hope and humanity, a voice who inspired his compatriots with a lofty vision of a moral postcommunist society. As president of his country, Havel continued to speak eloquently on the great questions of our time.

Questions for Analysis

1. Why did Havel oppose Communist rule? How did his goals differ from those of Dubček and other advocates of reform communism?
2. Havel has been called a "moralist in politics." Is this a good description of him? Why? Can you think of a better one?

[*]Quoted in M. Simmons, *The Reluctant President: A Political Life of Václav Havel* (London: Methuen, 1991), p. 91.
[†]Quoted ibid., p. 110.

The Disintegration of the Soviet Union

As 1990 began, revolutionary changes had triumphed in all but two eastern European states—tiny Albania and the vast Soviet Union. The great question now became whether the Soviet Union would follow its former satellites and whether reform communism would give way to a popular anticommunist revolution.

In February 1990, as competing Russian politicians noisily presented their programs, and nationalists in the non-Russian republics demanded autonomy or independence from the Soviet Union, the Communist party suffered a stunning defeat in local elections throughout the country. As in the eastern European satellites, democrats and anticommunists won clear majorities in the leading cities of the Russian Federation. Moreover, in Lithuania the people elected an uncompromising nationalist as president, and the newly chosen parliament declared Lithuania an independent state. Gorbachev responded by placing an economic embargo on Lithuania, but he refused to use the army to crush the separatist government. The result was a tense political stalemate, which undermined popular support for Gorbachev. Separating himself further from Communist hard-liners, Gorbachev asked Soviet citizens to ratify a new constitution, which formally abolished the Communist party's monopoly of political power and expanded the power of the Congress of People's Deputies. Retaining his post as party secretary, Gorbachev convinced a majority of deputies to elect him president of the Soviet Union.

Gorbachev's eroding power and his unwillingness to risk a universal suffrage election for the presidency strengthened his great rival, Boris Yeltsin (b. 1931). A radical reform communist who had been purged by party conservatives in 1987, Yeltsin embraced the democratic movement, and in May 1990 he was elected leader of the Russian Federation's parliament. He boldly announced that Russia would put its interests first and declare its in-

Celebrating Victory, August 1991   A Russian soldier flashes the victory sign in front of the Russian parliament, as the last-gasp coup attempt of Communist hard-liners is defeated by Boris Yeltsin and an enthusiastic public. The soldier has cut the hammer and sickle out of the Soviet flag, consigning those famous symbols of proletarian revolution to what Trotsky once called the "garbage can of history." *(Filip Horvat/Saba)*

dependence from the Soviet Union, thereby broadening the base of the anticommunist movement as he joined the patriotism of ordinary Russians with the democratic aspirations of big-city intellectuals. Gorbachev tried to save the Soviet Union with a new treaty that would link the member republics in a looser, freely accepted confederation, but six of the fifteen Soviet republics rejected Gorbachev's pleas.

Opposed by democrats and nationalists, Gorbachev was also challenged again by the Communist old guard. Defeated at the Communist party congress in July 1990, a gang of hard-liners kidnapped a vacationing Gorbachev and his family in the Caucasus and tried to seize the Soviet government in August 1991. But the attempted coup collapsed in the face of massive popular resistance, which rallied around Yeltsin, recently elected president of the Russian Federation by universal suffrage. As the world watched spellbound on television, Yeltsin defiantly denounced the rebels from atop a stalled tank in central Moscow and declared the "rebirth of Russia." The army supported Yeltsin, and Gorbachev was rescued and returned to power as head of the Soviet Union.

The leaders of the coup wanted to preserve Communist power, state ownership, and the multinational Soviet Union, but they succeeded only in destroying all three. An anticommunist revolution swept the Russian Federation as Yeltsin and his supporters outlawed the Communist party and confiscated its property. Locked in a personal and political duel with Gorbachev, Yeltsin and his democratic allies declared Russia independent and withdrew from the Soviet Union. All the other Soviet republics also left. The Soviet Union—and Gorbachev's job—ceased to exist on December 25, 1991 (see Map 31.2). The independent republics of the old Soviet

MAP 31.2 Russia and the Successor States   After the attempt in August 1991 to depose Gorbachev failed, an anticommunist revolution swept the Soviet Union. Led by Russia and Boris Yeltsin, the republics that formed the Soviet Union declared their sovereignty and independence. Eleven of the fifteen republics then formed a loose confederation called the Commonwealth of Independent States, but the integrated economy of the Soviet Union dissolved into separate national economies, each with its own goals and policies.

Union then established a loose confederation, the Commonwealth of Independent States, which played only a minor role in the 1990s.

German Unification and the End of the Cold War

The revolutions of 1989 and the collapse of communism transformed eastern Europe, as people tore down the walls and the liberation of eastern Europe enhanced the prospect of ending the cold war. Yet the sudden death of communism in East Germany in 1989 also reopened the "German question," and renewed cold war conflict over Germany was still possible.

Taking power in October 1989, East German reform communists, enthusiastically supported by leading East German intellectuals and former dissidents, wanted to preserve socialism by making it genuinely democratic and responsive to the needs of the people. They argued for a **third way,** which would go beyond the failed Stalinism they had experienced and the ruthless capitalism they saw in the West. These reformers supported closer ties with West Germany, but they feared unification and wanted to preserve a distinct East German identity.

These efforts failed, and within a few months East Germany was absorbed into an enlarged West Germany, much like a faltering company is merged into a stronger rival and ceases to exist. Three factors were particularly important in this sudden absorption. First, in the first week after the Berlin Wall was opened, almost 9 million East Germans—roughly one-half of the total population—poured across the border into West Germany. Almost all returned to their homes in the East, but the joy of warm welcomes from long-lost friends and loved ones and the exhilarating experience of shopping in the well-stocked stores of the much wealthier West aroused long-dormant hopes of unity among ordinary citizens.

Second, West German chancellor Helmut Kohl and his closest advisers skillfully exploited the historic opportunity on their doorstep. Sure of support from the United States, whose leadership he had steadfastly followed, in November 1989 Kohl presented a ten-point plan for a step-by-step unification in cooperation with both East Germany and the international community. Kohl then promised the struggling citizens of East Germany an immediate economic bonanza—a one-for-one exchange of all East German marks in savings accounts and pensions into much more valuable West German marks. This generous offer helped a well-financed conservative-liberal **Alliance for Germany,** which was set up in East Germany and was closely tied to Kohl's West German Christian Democrats, to overwhelm those who argued for the preservation of some kind of independent socialist society in East Germany. In March 1990, the Alliance outdistanced the Socialist party and won almost 50 percent of the votes in an East German parliamentary election. (The Communists ignominiously fell to fringe-party status.) The Alliance for Germany quickly negotiated an economic union on favorable terms with Chancellor Kohl.

Finally, in the summer of 1990, the crucial international aspect of German unification was successfully resolved. Unification would once again make Germany the strongest state in central Europe and would directly affect the security of the Soviet Union. But Gorbachev swallowed hard—Western cartoonists showed Stalin turning over in his grave—and negotiated the best deal he could. In a historic agreement signed by Gorbachev and Kohl in July 1990, a uniting Germany solemnly affirmed its peaceful intentions and pledged never to develop nuclear, biological, or chemical weapons. Germany also sweetened the deal by promising to make enormous loans to the hard-pressed Soviet Union. In October 1990, East Germany merged into West Germany, forming henceforth a single nation under the West German laws and constitution.

The peaceful reunification of Germany accelerated the pace of agreements to liquidate the cold war. In November 1990, delegates from twenty-two European countries joined those from the United States and the Soviet Union in Paris and agreed to a scaling down of all their armed forces. The delegates also solemnly affirmed that all existing borders in Europe—from unified Germany to the newly independent Baltic republics—were legal and valid. The **Paris Accord** was for all practical purposes a general peace treaty, bringing an end to World War II and the cold war that followed.

Peace in Europe encouraged the United States and the Soviet Union to scrap a significant portion of their nuclear weapons in a series of agreements. In September 1991, a confident President George H. W. Bush also canceled the around-the-clock alert status for American bombers outfitted with atomic bombs, and a floundering Gorbachev quickly followed suit. For the first time in four decades, Soviet and American nuclear weapons were no longer standing ready to destroy capitalism, communism, and life itself.

As anticommunist revolutions swept eastern Europe and East-West tensions rapidly disappeared, the Soviet Union lost both the will and the means to be a global superpower. Yet the United States retained the strength and the desire to influence political and economic developments on a global scale. Thus the United States, still flanked by many allies, emerged rather suddenly as the world's only surviving superpower.

In 1991 the United States used its military superiority on a grand scale in a quick war with Iraq in western Asia. Emerging in 1988 from an eight-year war with neighboring Iran with a big, tough army equipped by the Soviet bloc, western Europe, and the United States, Iraq's strongman Saddam Hussein (b. 1937) set out to make himself the leader of the entire Arab world. Eyeing the great oil wealth of his tiny southern neighbor, Saddam Hussein's forces suddenly invaded Kuwait in August 1990 and proclaimed the annexation of Kuwait.

"Saddam, Surrender!"   So reads the caption under the image of an advancing U.S. soldier on the cover of a leading Italian newsmagazine, which repeatedly featured the crisis over Kuwait and the war with Iraq. This heavy Italian coverage was symptomatic of enormous coverage worldwide. Although U.S. forces provided most of the muscle, twenty-eight countries, including Italy, participated in Operation Desert Storm. (*U.S. News & World Report/PANORAMA/Mondadori. Courtesy, Madeline Grimoldi*)

Reacting vigorously to free Kuwait, the United States mobilized the U.N. Security Council, which in August 1990 imposed a strict naval blockade on Iraq. Receiving the support of some Arab states, as well as of Great Britain and France, the United States also landed 500,000 American soldiers in Saudi Arabia near the border of Kuwait. When a defiant Saddam Hussein refused to withdraw from Kuwait, the Security Council authorized the U.S.-led military coalition to attack Iraq. The American army and air force then smashed Iraqi forces in a lightning-quick desert campaign, although the United States stopped short of toppling Saddam because it feared a sudden disintegration of Iraq more than Saddam's hanging on to power.

The defeat of Iraqi armies in the Gulf War demonstrated the awesome power of the U.S. military, rebuilt and revitalized by the spending and patriotism of the 1980s. Little wonder that in the flush of yet another victory, President Bush spoke of a **"new world order,"** an order that would apparently feature the United States and a cooperative United Nations working together to impose stability throughout the world.

Building a New Europe in the 1990s

The fall of communism, the end of the cold war, and the collapse of the Soviet Union opened a new era in European and world history. Yet the dimensions and significance of this new era, opening suddenly and unexpectedly, are far from clear. We are so close to what is going on that we lack vital perspective. Thus it is particularly difficult to interpret intelligently recent events.

Yet the historian must take a stand and try to find patterns of development and explanation. Thus in this section we shall concentrate on two main themes of European development since the end of the cold war. First, since Europe has taken giant strides toward a loose unification of fundamental institutions and beliefs, we shall examine broad economic, social, and political trends that operated all across the continent in the 1990s. These trends include national economies increasingly caught up in global capitalism, the defense of social achievements under attack, and a resurgence of nationalism and ethnic conflict. Second, with these common themes providing an organizational framework, we shall examine the course of development in the three overlapping but still distinct regions of contemporary Europe. These are Russia and the western states of the old Soviet Union, previously communist eastern Europe, and western Europe.

Common Patterns and Problems

The end of the cold war and the disintegration of the Soviet Union ended the division of Europe into two opposing camps with two different political and economic systems. Thus, although Europe in the 1990s was a collage of diverse peoples with their own politics, cultures, and histories, the entire continent shared an underlying network of common developments and challenges.

Of great importance, in economic affairs European leaders embraced, or at least accepted, a large part of the neoliberal, free-market vision of capitalist development. This was most strikingly the case in eastern Europe, where states such as Poland and Hungary implemented market reforms and sought to create vibrant capitalist economies. Thus postcommunist governments in eastern Europe freed prices, turned state enterprises over to private owners, and sought to move toward strong currencies and balanced budgets. Milder doses of this same free-market medicine were administered by politicians and big business to the lackluster economies of western Europe. These initiatives and proposals for further changes marked a considerable modification in western Europe's still-dominant welfare capitalism, which featured government intervention, high taxes, and high levels of social benefits.

Two factors were particularly important in accounting for this ongoing shift from welfare state activism to tough-minded capitalism. First, Europeans were only following practices and ideologies revived and enshrined in the 1980s in the United States and Great Britain (see page 1020). Western Europeans especially took American prescriptions more seriously because U.S. prestige and power were so high after the United States "won the cold war" and because the U.S. economy continued to outperform its western European counterparts in the Clinton years. Second, the deregulation of markets and the privatization of state-controlled enterprises were an integral part of the powerful trend toward a wide-open, wheeler-dealer global economy. The rules of the global economy, which were laid down by Western governments, multinational corporations, and international financial organizations such as the International Monetary Fund (IMF), called for the free movement of capital and goods and services, as well as low inflation and limited government deficits. Accepting these rules and attempting to follow them was the price of full participation in the global economy.

The ongoing computer and electronics revolution strengthened the move toward a global economy. That revolution thrived on the diffusion of ever-cheaper computational and informational capacity to small research groups and private businesses, which were both cause and effect of the revolution itself. By the 1990s, an inexpensive personal computer had the power of a 1950s mainframe that filled a room and cost hundreds of thousands of dollars. The computer revolution reduced the costs of distance, speeding up communications and helping businesses tap cheaper labor overseas. Reducing the friction of distance made threats of moving factories abroad ring true and helped hold down wages at home.

The freer global economy, which probably did speed up world economic growth as enthusiasts invariably claimed, had powerful social consequences. Millions of ordinary citizens in western Europe saw global capitalism and freer markets as challenging hard-won social achievements. As in the United States and Great Britain in the 1980s, the public in other countries generally opposed the unemployment that accompanied corporate downsizing, the efforts to reduce the power of labor unions, and, above all, government plans to reduce social benefits. The reaction was particularly intense in France and Germany, where unions remained strong and socialists championed a minimum of change in social policies.

Indeed, the broad movement toward neoliberal global development produced a powerful backlash as the 1990s ended. Financial crises, which devastated many of Asia's smaller economies and threatened to spread, sparked the reaction. The damage was contained, but critics and protesters charged that multinational corporations and international financial organizations sacrificed the world's poor for corporate interests and harsh balanced budgets. These attacks shook global neoliberalism, but it remained dominant.

Political developments across Europe also were loosely unified by common patterns and problems. The demise of European communism brought the apparent triumph of liberal democracy everywhere. All countries embraced genuine electoral competition, with elected presidents and legislatures and the outward manifestations of representative liberal governments. With some notable exceptions, such as discrimination against Gypsies, countries also guaranteed basic civil liberties. Thus, for the first time since before the French Revolution, almost all of Europe followed the same general political model, although the variations were endless.

The triumph of the liberal democratic program led the American scholar Francis Fukuyama to discern the "end of history" in an influential book by that title. According to Fukuyama, first fascism and Nazism and then commu-

Guggenheim Museum, Bilbao, Spain   Praised by admirers as the "first great building of the twenty-first century," Bilbao's exotic undulating museum of contemporary art is intended to revitalize the Basque region of northwestern Spain through international prestige, cultural renaissance, and tourism. Selected in a global competition, Frank Gehry's design relies heavily on three-dimensional computer modeling to hold dramatic opposites in delicate balance, as well as to translate complex forms into construction blueprints. *(Jeff Goldberg/Esto. All rights reserved.)*

nism had been definitively bested by liberal democratic politics and market economics. Conversely, as James Cronin perceptively noted, the fall of communism also marked the return of nationalism and national history.[2] The cold war and the superpowers generally kept their allies and clients in line, either by force or by granting them conditional aid. As soon as the cold war was over, nationalism and ethnic conflict re-emerged, and history, as the story of different peoples, began again.

The resurgence of nationalism in the 1990s led to terrible tragedy and bloodshed in parts of eastern Europe, as it did in several hot spots in Africa and Asia. During the civil wars in Yugoslavia, many observers feared that national and ethnic hatreds would spread throughout eastern Europe and infect western Europe in the form of racial hostility toward minorities and immigrants. Yet if nationalist and racist incidents were a recurring European theme, they remained limited in the extent of their damage. Of critical importance in this regard was the fact that all European states wished to become or remain full-fledged members of the European society of nations and to join eventually an ever-expanding European Community, renamed the **European Union** in 1993. States that embraced national hatred and ethnic warfare, most notably Serbia, were branded as outlaws and boycotted and isolated by the European Union and the international community. The process of limiting resurgent nationalism in Europe was almost as significant as the resurgence itself.

Recasting Russia

Politics and economics were closely intertwined in Russia after the attempted Communist coup in 1991 and the dissolution of the Soviet Union. President Boris Yeltsin, his democratic supporters, and his economic ministers wanted to create conditions that would prevent forever a return to communism and would also right the faltering economy. Following the example of some postcommunist governments in eastern Europe and agreeing with those Western advisers who argued that private economies were always best, the Russian reformers opted in January 1992 for breakneck liberalization. Their "shock therapy" freed prices on 90 percent of all Russian goods, with the exception of bread, vodka, oil, and public transportation. The government also launched a rapid privatization of industry and turned thousands of factories and mines over to new private companies. Each citizen received a voucher worth 10,000 rubles (about $22) to buy stock in private companies, but control of the privatized companies usually remained in the hands of the old bosses, the managers and government officials from the communist era.

President Yeltsin and his economic reformers believed that shock therapy would revive production and bring prosperity after a brief period of hardship. The results of the reforms were in fact quite different. Prices increased 250 percent on the very first day, and they kept on soaring, increasing twenty-six times in the course of 1992. At the same time, Russian production fell a staggering 20 percent. Nor did the situation stabilize quickly. Throughout 1995 rapid but gradually slowing inflation raged, and output continued to fall. According to most estimates, in 1996 the Russian economy produced at least one-third and possibly as much as one-half less than in 1991. Only in 1997 did the economy stop declining, before crashing yet again in 1998 in the wake of Asia's financial crisis.

Rapid economic liberalization worked poorly in Russia for several reasons. Perhaps most important, Soviet industry had been highly monopolized and strongly tilted toward military goods. Production of many items had been concentrated in one or two gigantic factories or interconnected combines that supplied the entire economy. With privatization these powerful state monopolies simply became powerful private monopolies, which then cut production and raised prices in order to maximize their financial returns.

This was not what Yeltsin and the free-market ideologues around him had expected. According to standard economic theory, monopoly prices and profits should have encouraged new firms to enter production, thereby increasing Russian output and pushing down prices through competition. But this desirable process developed very slowly. Powerful managers and bureaucrats forced Yeltsin's government to hand out enormous subsidies and credits to reinforce the positions of big firms and to avoid bankruptcies and the discipline of a free market. The managerial elite also combined with criminal elements to intimidate would-be rivals and prevent the formation of new businesses. Not that most ordinary Soviet citizens were eager to start businesses. For decades they had been told that all capitalists were "speculators" and "exploiters," and as Russian business became associated in popular culture with crime, corruption, and national decline, most people had little reason to change their minds. In short, enterprise directors and politicians combined to subvert Yeltsin's unrealistic "radical" liberalization. This group then succeeded in eliminating worker ownership and converted large portions of previously state-owned industry into their own private property.

Runaway inflation and poorly executed privatization brought a profound social revolution to Russia. A new capitalist elite acquired great wealth and power, while large numbers of people fell into abject poverty, and the majority struggled in the midst of decline to make ends meet.

Managers, former officials, and financiers who came out of the privatization process with large shares of the old state monopolies stood at the top of the reorganized elite. The richest plums were found in Russia's enormous oil and natural resources industries, where unscrupulous enterprise directors pocketed enormous dishonest gains. From all indications, crime and corruption permeated Russian business big and small. Russian (and foreign) business leaders always moved with their bodyguards, but murders of executives were nonetheless common. The new elite was more highly concentrated than ever before. By 1996 Moscow, with 5 percent of Russia's population, accounted for 35 percent of the country's national income and controlled 80 percent of its capital resources.

At the other extreme, the vast majority saw their savings become practically worthless. Pensions lost much of

Russia's New Rich   Members of Moscow's exclusive Chimney Club dine in privacy and extravagance in 1994. Club members paid an annual membership fee of U.S.$1000—an astronomical sum for the vast majority of Russians, who had no opportunity to loot the economy. *(Anthony Suau/Getty Images)*

their value, and whole markets were devoted to people selling off their personal goods to survive. Perhaps the most telling statistic, summing up millions of hardships and tragedies, was the truly catastrophic decline in the life expectancy of the average Russian male from sixty-nine years in 1991 to only fifty-eight years in 1996. Only in 2000 did living conditions for ordinary people finally begin to improve a bit as manufacturing showed signs of life and oil exports boomed.

Yeltsin and his supporters proved more successful in politics. Rapid economic decline in 1992 and 1993 increased popular dissatisfaction. This encouraged the Russian parliament, dominated by former Communists elected in 1990, to oppose Yeltsin's plan for constitutional reform. Yeltsin and his coalition of democratic reformers and big business interests pressed for a strong presidential system, while an opposition of communists, nationalists, and populists defended the authority of the parliament. Winning in April 1993 the support of 58 percent of the population in a referendum on his pro-

posed constitution, Yeltsin then brought in tanks to crush a parliamentary mutiny in October 1993 and literally blew away the last vestiges of Soviet power. Although Yeltsin's allies in the reform parties lost ground to the communists and the nationalists in two subsequent elections, in 1996 Yeltsin won re-election as president in an impressive come-from-behind victory.

Yeltsin's victory in 1996 suggested to some observers that free elections had become a regular and accepted core of Russian political life. To be sure, the constitution concentrated power in the hands of the president, and Russia still lacked a rule of law and a reorganized court system to deal with crime and corruption. Yet all politicians looked to the ballot box for legitimacy, as the election of President Vladimir Putin, Yeltsin's hand-picked successor, clearly indicated in 2000. Putin's stress on public order and economic reform was popular.

Russia's moderation in relations with foreign countries also provided reasons for guarded optimism after the fall of communism. First, military spending continued to

Battling to Survive   These impoverished Russian women are selling their clothing and personal possessions in order to buy food for themselves and their families. Today's Russia is a relatively free society with a competitive electoral system, but begging, homelessness, and high crime rates have also taken root. *(Sovfoto)*

decline under Yeltsin. Second, Russia reluctantly accepted the enlargement of NATO in 1997 to include Poland, Hungary, and the Czech Republic and negotiated a treaty with NATO to provide a framework for cooperation in the future. Third, Russia generally respected the independence of the Soviet successor states and usually played a moderating role in the bitter ethnic conflicts that abounded in Central Asia and the Caucasus. Seldom did Russia use its position as dominant regional power to make matters worse.

The notable exception to this pattern was in Chechnya. In 1991 this tiny republic of 1 million Muslims on Russia's southern border declared its independence from the Russian Federation (see Map 31.2). After a three-year stalemate, Yeltsin ordered the Russian army to crush the separatists. But Chechnya resisted with ferocious valor, and in 1996 a wily Yeltsin accepted a face-saving truce and withdrew Russian soldiers to help win re-election. Unfortunately, the brutal war was subsequently resumed, and it continued unabated under Vladimir Putin.

Progress and Tragedy in Eastern Europe

Developments in eastern Europe shared important similarities with those in Russia, as many of the problems were the same. Thus the postcommunist states of the former satellite empire worked to replace state planning and socialism with market mechanisms and private property.

Western-style electoral politics also took hold, and as in Russia, these politics were marked by intense battles between presidents and parliaments and by weak political parties. The social consequences of these revolutionary changes were similar to those in Russia. Ordinary citizens and the elderly were once again the big losers, while the young and the ex-Communists were the big winners. Inequalities between richer and poorer regions also increased. Capital cities such as Warsaw, Prague, and Budapest concentrated wealth, power, and opportunity as never before, while provincial centers stagnated and old industrial areas declined. Crime and gangsterism increased in the streets and in the executive suites.

Yet the 1990s saw more than a difficult transition, with high social costs, to market economies and freely elected governments in eastern Europe. Many citizens had never fully accepted communism, which they equated with Russian imperialism and the loss of national independence. The joyous crowds that toppled communist regimes in 1989 believed that they were liberating the nation as well as the individual. Thus communism died and nationalism was reborn.

The surge of nationalism in eastern Europe recalled a similar surge of state creation after World War I. Then, too, authoritarian multinational empires had come crashing down in defeat and revolution. Then, too, nationalities with long histories and rich cultures had drawn upon ideologies of popular sovereignty and national self-determination to throw off foreign rule and found new democratic states.

The response to this opportunity in the former communist countries was quite varied in the 1990s, but most observers agreed that Poland, the Czech Republic, and Hungary were the most successful (see Map 31.3). Each of these three countries met the critical challenge of economic reconstruction more successfully than Russia, and each could claim to be the economic leader in eastern Europe, depending on the criteria selected. The reasons for these successes included considerable experience with limited market reforms before 1989, flexibility and lack of dogmatism in government policy, and an enthusiastic embrace of capitalism by a new entrepreneurial class. In the first five years of reform, Poland created twice as many new businesses as Russia, with a total population only one-fourth as large.

The three northern countries in the former Soviet bloc also did far better than Russia in creating new civic institutions, legal systems, and independent broadcasting networks that reinforced political freedom and national revival. Lech Walesa in Poland and Václav Havel in Czechoslovakia were elected presidents of their countries and proved as remarkable in power as in opposition. After Czechoslovakia's "Velvet Revolution" in 1989, Havel and the Czech parliament accepted a "velvet divorce" in 1993 when Slovakian nationalists wanted to break off and form their own state. All three northern countries managed to control national and ethnic tensions that might have destroyed their postcommunist reconstruction.

The popular goal of "rejoining the West" reinforced political moderation and compromise. Seeing themselves as heirs to medieval Christendom and liberal democratic values in the 1920s, Poles, Hungarians, and Czechs hoped to find security in NATO membership and economic prosperity in western Europe's ever-tighter union. Membership required many proofs of character and stability, however. Providing these proofs and endorsed by the Clinton administration, Poland, Hungary, and the Czech Republic were accepted into the NATO alliance in 1997. Gaining admission to the European Union (EU) proved more difficult, because candidates also had to accept EU rules and regulations.

Slovakia, Romania, and Bulgaria were the eastern European laggards in the postcommunist transition. Western traditions were much weaker there, and all three countries were much poorer than their neighbors to the north. In 1993 Bulgaria and Romania had per capita national incomes of $1,140, in contrast to Hungary ($3,830) and the Czech Republic ($2,710). There was no going back, however, and progress was eventually made. In 2001 full membership for Slovakia, Romania, and Bulgaria in either NATO or the EU still lay far in the future.

The great postcommunist tragedy was Yugoslavia, which under Josip Tito had been a federation of republics and regions under strict communist rule (see pages 1002 and 1003). After Tito's death in 1980, power passed increasingly to the sister republics, which encouraged a revival of regional and ethnic conflicts that were exacerbated by charges of ethnically inspired massacres during World War II and a dramatic economic decline in the mid-1980s.

The revolutions of 1989 accelerated the breakup of Yugoslavia. Serbian president Slobodan Milosevic intended to grab land from other republics and unite all Serbs, regardless of where they lived, in a "greater Serbia." In 1989 Milosevic arbitrarily abolished self-rule in the Serbian province of Kosovo, where Albanian-speaking people constituted the overwhelming majority. Milosevic's moves strengthened the cause of separatism, and in June 1991 Slovenia and Croatia declared their independence. Slovenia repulsed a Serbian attack, but Milosevic's armies managed to take about 30 percent of Croatia. In 1992 the civil war spread to Bosnia-Herzegovina, which had declared its independence. Serbs—about 30 percent

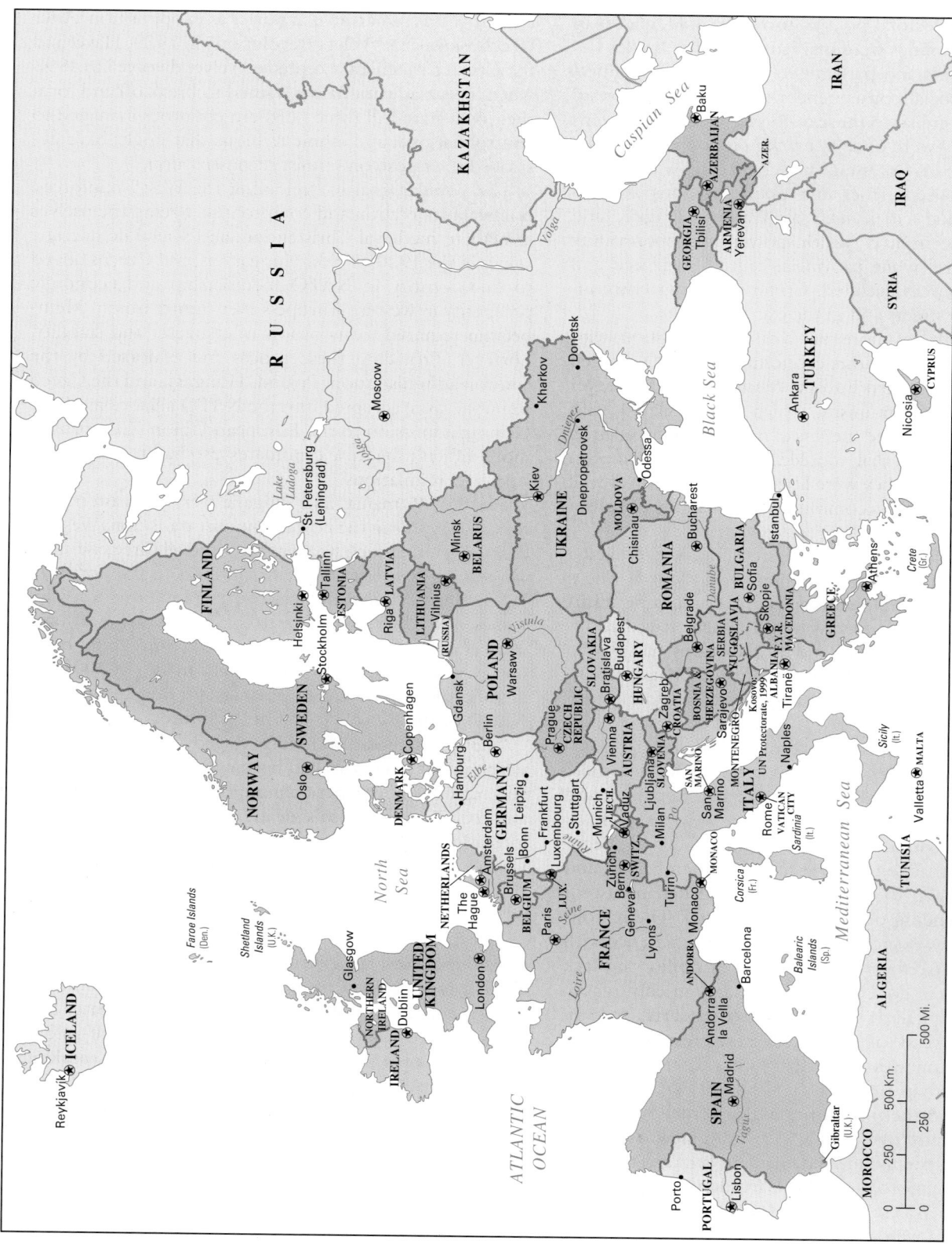

MAP 31.3 Contemporary Europe No longer divided by ideological competition and the cold war, today's Europe features a large number of independent states. Several of these states were previously part of the Soviet Union and Yugoslavia, both of which broke into many different countries. Czechoslovakia also divided on ethnic lines, while a reunited Germany emerged, once again, as the dominant nation in central Europe.

MAP 31.4 The Ethnic Composition of Yugoslavia, 1991   Yugoslavia had the most ethnically diverse population in eastern Europe. The Republic of Croatia had substantial Serbian and Muslim minorities. Bosnia-Herzegovina had large Muslim, Serbian, and Croatian populations, none of which had a majority. In June 1991, Serbia's brutal effort to seize territory and unite all Serbs in a single state brought a tragic civil war.

of that region's population—refused to live under the more numerous Bosnian Muslims (see Map 31.4). Yugoslavia had once been a tolerant and largely successful multiethnic state, with different groups living side by side and often intermarrying. The Bosnian civil war unleashed ruthless brutality, with murder, rape, destruction, and the herding of refugees into concentration camps.

While scenes of horror shocked the world, the Western nations had difficulty formulating an effective response. The turning point came in July 1995, when Bosnian Serbs overran Srebrenica—a Muslim city previously declared a United Nations "safe area"—and killed several thousand civilians. World outrage prompted NATO to bomb Bosnian Serb military targets intensively, and the Croatian army drove all the Serbs from Croatia. In No-

vember 1995, President Bill Clinton helped the warring sides hammer out a complicated accord that gave the Bosnian Serbs about 49 percent of Bosnia and the Muslim-Croatian peoples the rest. Troops from NATO countries patrolled Bosnia to try to keep the peace.

The Albanian Muslims of Kosovo had been hoping for a restoration of self-rule, but they gained nothing from the Bosnian agreement. In early 1998, frustrated Kosovar militants formed the **Kosovo Liberation Army (KLA)** and began to fight for independence. Serbian repression of the Kosovars increased, and in 1998 Serbian forces attacked both KLA guerrillas and unarmed villagers, displacing 250,000 people within Kosovo. By January 1999, the Western powers, led by the United States, were threatening Milosevic with heavy air raids if he did

Escape from Srebrenica   A Bosnian Muslim refugee arrives at the United Nations base in Tuzla and with her anguished screams tells the world of the Serbian atrocities. Several thousand civilians were murdered at Srebrenica, and Western public opinion finally demanded decisive action. Efforts continue to arrest those Serbs believed responsible and to try them for crimes against humanity. *(J. Jones/Corbis SYGMA)*

not withdraw Serbian armies from Kosovo and accept self-government (but not independence) for Kosovo. Milosevic refused, and in March 1999 NATO began bombing Yugoslavia. Serbian paramilitary forces responded by driving about 780,000 Kosovars into exile. NATO redoubled its highly destructive bombing campaign, which eventually forced Milosevic to withdraw and allowed the joyous Kosovars to regain their homeland. The impoverished Serbs eventually voted the still-defiant Milosevic out of office, and in July 2001 a new pro-Western Serbian government turned him over to the war crimes tribunal in the Netherlands, to stand trial for crimes against humanity. The civil wars in the former Yugoslavia were a monument to human cruelty and evil in the worst tradition of the twentieth century. But ongoing efforts to preserve peace, repatriate refugees, and try war criminals also testified to the regenerative power of liberal values and human rights as the new century opened.

Unity and Identity in Western Europe

The movement toward western European unity, which since the late 1940s had inspired practical politicians seeking economic recovery and idealistic visionaries imagining a European identity that transcended destructive national rivalries, received a powerful second wind in the mid-1980s. The Single European Act of 1986 laid down a detailed legal framework for establishing a single market, which would add the free movement of labor, capital, and services to the existing free trade in goods.

With work proceeding vigorously toward the single market, which went into effect in 1993 as the European Community proudly rechristened itself the European Union (EU), French president François Mitterrand and German chancellor Helmut Kohl took the lead in pushing for a monetary union of EU members. After long negotiations and compromises, designed especially to overcome Britain's long-standing reluctance to cede aspects of sovereignty, in December 1991 the member states reached an agreement in the Dutch town of Maastricht. The **Maastricht treaty** set strict financial criteria for joining the proposed monetary union, with its single currency, and set 1999 as the target date for its establishment. The treaty also anticipated the development of common policies on defense and foreign affairs after achieving monetary union.

Western European elites and opinion makers generally supported the decisive step toward economic integration embodied in the Maastricht treaty. They saw monetary union as a means of coping with Europe's ongoing economic problems, imposing financial discipline, cutting costs, and reducing high unemployment. European elites also viewed monetary union as a historic, irreversible step toward a basic political unity. This unity would allow western Europe as a whole to regain its rightful place in world politics and to deal with the United States as an equal.

The Maastricht plan for monetary union encountered widespread skepticism and considerable opposition from ordinary people, leftist political parties, and patriotic nationalists. Ratification votes were close, especially when the public rather than the politicians could vote yes or no on the question.

There were several interrelated reasons for this widespread popular opposition. Many people resented the unending flow of rules handed down by the EU's ever-growing bureaucracy in Brussels, which sought to impose common standards on everything from cheese to day care and undermined national practices and local traditions. Moreover, increased unity meant yielding still more power to distant "Eureaucrats" and political insiders, thereby undermining popular sovereignty and democratic control through national politics and electoral competition. Above all, many ordinary citizens feared that the new Europe was being made at their expense. Joining the monetary union required national governments to meet stringent fiscal standards and impose budget cuts. The resulting reductions in health care and social benefits hit ordinary citizens and did nothing to reduce western Europe's high unemployment rate.

Events in France dramatically illustrated these developments. Mitterrand's Socialist government had been forced to adopt conservative financial policies in the 1980s (see pages 1020–1021), and more cuts followed the Maastricht treaty. In early 1993, frustrated French voters elected Jacques Chirac president and gave a coalition of conservatives and moderates an overwhelming victory over the Socialist party. Chirac had won by promising a vigorous attack on unemployment, but the Maastricht criteria demanded that he continue the unpopular retrenchment of the Socialists. After some hesitation, Chirac's government chose deficit-reducing cuts in health benefits and transportation services. France's powerful unions and railroad workers, seconded by the Socialist opposition, responded with massive protest marches and a crippling national strike that simply shut down rail traffic throughout France for almost a month. Paris freeways became creeping parking lots as exhausted workers struggled with nightmare commutes. Yet despite the enormous inconvenience and economic damage, the public supported the strike. Many people felt that the transport workers were also fighting for them. The government had to back down, although it continued its austerity program with less provocative measures until disgruntled French voters again gave the Socialists control of the National Assembly. The Socialists quickly passed a controversial new law to reduce the legal workweek to thirty-five hours, in an attempt to reduce France's stubborn 12 percent unemployment rate without budget-busting spending. More generally, much of the western European public increasingly saw laws to cut the workweek and share the work as a way to reconcile desires for social welfare and a humane market economy with financial discipline and global competition.

Battles over budgets and high unemployment throughout the European Union in the 1990s raised profound questions about the meaning of European unity and identity. Would the European Union remain an exclusive Western club, or would it expand as promised to include the postcommunist nations of eastern Europe? If some of them were admitted, how could Muslim Turkey's long-standing application be ignored? Conversely, how could a European Union of twenty-five to thirty countries have any real cohesion and common identity?

The merging of East Germany into the German Federal Republic suggested the enormous difficulties of full East-West integration under the best conditions. After 1991 Helmut Kohl's Germany pumped massive investments into its new eastern provinces, but Germans in the east still saw factories closed and social dislocation. Unemployment in Germany reached a postwar high of 12.8 percent in late 1997, and it soared to 20 percent in the eastern region. Germany's generous social benefits cushioned the economic difficulties, but many ordinary citizens felt hurt and humiliated.

Eastern German women suffered in particular. Before unification, the overwhelming majority had worked outside the home, effectively supported by cheap child care, flexible hours, and the prevailing socialist ideology. Now they faced expensive child care and a variety of pressures to stay at home and let men take the hard-to-find jobs. Many of these women, who had found autonomy and self-esteem in paid work, felt a keen sense of loss. They helped vote Kohl out of office in 1998.

Instructed by the serious difficulties of unification in Germany, western Europeans proceeded cautiously in considering new requests for EU membership. Sweden, Finland, and Austria were admitted because they had strong capitalist economies and because they no longer needed to maintain the legal neutrality that the Soviet Union had required during the cold war. But of the former communist states in the 1990s, only Poland, the Czech Republic, and Hungary had any foreseeable chance of becoming EU members. In December 2000, the EU's fifteen members agreed "in principle" to begin "final negotiations" to admit the three leading eastern candidates by 2006. When on January 1, 2002, brand-new Euros entered the billfolds of all Euro-zone citizens as their unified common currency, a host of complex issues still needed to be resolved before the European Union expanded into eastern Europe.

New Challenges in the Twenty-first Century

As the twenty-first century opened and the historic movement toward European unity crept forward, European society faced new uncertainties. Of great significance, Europe continued to experience a remarkable **baby bust,** as birthrates fell to levels that seemed to promise a shrinking and aging population in the future. At the same time, the peaceful, wealthy European Union attracted rapidly growing numbers of refugees and illegal immigrants. The unexpected arrival of so many newcomers raised many perplexing questions and prompted serious thinking about European identity and Europe's place in the world. For some western Europeans, the promotion of freedom and human rights emerged increasingly

as Europe's calling in the global era. The terrorist attack on the United States on September 11, 2001, reinforced European commitment to this cause.

The Prospect of Population Decline

Population is still growing rapidly in many poor countries, but this is not the case in the world's industrialized nations. In 2000 women in developed countries had only 1.6 children on average; only in the United States did women have, almost exactly, the 2.1 children necessary to maintain a stable population. In European countries, where women have been steadily having fewer babies since the 1950s, national fertility rates ranged from 1.2 to 1.8 children per woman. Italy, once renowned for big Catholic families, had achieved the world's lowest birthrate—a mere 1.2 babies per woman. Spain, Germany, and Russia were only slightly higher, while France, Poland, and Britain were clustered around 1.6 children per woman.

If the current baby bust continues, the long-term consequences could be dramatic, though hardly predictable. At the least, Europe's population would decline and age. Projections for Germany are illustrative. Total German population, barring immigration, would gradually decline from 82 million in 2001 to only 62 million around 2050. The number of people of working age would drop by a third, and almost half of the population would be over sixty. Social security taxes paid by the shrinking labor force would need to soar for the skyrocketing costs of pensions and health care for seniors to be met—a recipe for generational tension and conflict. As the premier of Bavaria, Germany's biggest state, warned in 2001, the prospect of demographic decline was a "ticking time bomb under our social welfare system and entire economy."[3]

Why, in time of peace, were Europeans failing to reproduce themselves? Certainly the uneven, uninspiring European economic conditions of the 1980s and much of the 1990s played some role. High unemployment fell heavily on young people and often frustrated their plans to settle down and have children. Some observers also argued that a partial rejection of motherhood and parenting was critical. They noted that many women chose to have no children or only one child. In 2000, 30 percent of German women born in 1965 were childless, whereas 90 percent would have had children in earlier generations. In the Catholic countries of southern Europe, where strong pressures to have children still exist, a quarter of the couples were fulfilling their "social duty" with a single child.

Terrorism in Spain Flames from a powerful car bomb engulf the booby-trapped vehicle of a Spanish army officer and take another life in Madrid in January 2000. The bombing was attributed to the Basque separatist organization ETA, which assassinates officials and ordinary citizens in a violent campaign to obtain political independence for the Basque region in northern Spain. Similar terrorist attacks plague many countries divided by political and ethnic conflicts. *(AFP/Corbis)*

In our view, the ongoing impact of careers for married women and the related drive for gender equality remained the decisive factors in the long-term decline of postwar birthrates. After World War II, Western women married early, had their children early, and then turned increasingly to full-time employment, where they suffered from the discrimination that drove the women's movement (see pages 1017–1018). By the 1990s, women had attained many (but not all) of their objectives. They did as well or better than men in school, and educated young women earned almost as much as their male counterparts.

Yet research showed that European women (and men) in their twenties, thirties, and early forties still wanted to have two or even three children—about the same number as their parents had wanted. But unlike their parents, young couples had not realized their ideal family size. This was because many women had postponed the birth of their first child into their thirties in order to finish their education and establish themselves in their careers. Finding that raising even one child was more difficult and time-consuming than anticipated, new mothers tended to postpone and eventually forgo a second child. This was especially true of professional women. The better educated and the more economically successful a woman was, the more likely she was to stop with a single child or to have no children at all.

In 2001 some population experts believed that European women were no longer postponing having children further into the future. Birthrates appeared to have stabilized and may even have begun to rise. More-over, the frightening implications of dramatic population decline emerged as a major public issue. Opinion leaders, politicians, and the media started to press the case for more babies and more support for families with children.

To summarize, indigenous Europeans will quite possibly fail to reproduce themselves in the early twenty-first century—a momentous development. But Europeans may respond with enough vigor to limit the extent of their population decline and avoid societal disaster.

The Growth of Immigration

As European demographic vitality waned in the 1990s, a surge of migrants from Africa, Asia, and eastern Europe headed for western Europe. Some migrants entered the European Union legally, but increasing numbers were smuggled in past beefed-up border patrols. Large-scale immigration emerged as a contentious and critical challenge.

Historically a source rather than a destination of immigrants, western Europe drew heavily on North Africa and Turkey for manual laborers until 1973, when unemployment started to rise and governments abruptly stopped the inflow. Many foreign workers stayed on, however, eventually bringing their families to western Europe and establishing permanent immigrant communities there.

A new and different surge of migration into western Europe began in the 1990s. The collapse of communism in the East and savage civil wars in Yugoslavia sent hundreds of thousands of refugees fleeing westward. Equally brutal conflicts in Afghanistan, Iraq, Somalia, and Rwanda—to name only four countries—brought thousands more from Asia and Africa. Illegal immigration into the European Union also exploded, rising from an estimated 50,000 people in 1993 to perhaps 500,000 in 1999 and thereafter. This movement exceeded the estimated 300,000 unauthorized foreigners entering the United States each year.

As the new century opened, many migrants still applied for political asylum and refugee status, but most were eventually rejected and classified as illegal job seekers. Certainly, greater economic opportunities exerted a powerful pull. Germans earned on average six times more than neighboring Poles, who in turn earned much more than those farther east and in North Africa. In 1995 a tearful Moroccan woman captured the poignant drama of migration and spoke for millions when she explained to her American friend why she had left her little

boy in Morocco to work as a maid in France. "There are no jobs at home," she said, "just no jobs."

Illegal immigration also soared because powerful criminal gangs turned to "people smuggling" for big, low-risk profits. Ruthless Russian-speaking gangs dominated much of the trade, passing their human cargo across Russia and through the war-torn Balkans to western Europe. A favorite final leg involved Albanian smugglers with speedy motorboats, who slipped across the narrow Adriatic Sea past Italian coastal patrols and landed their high-paying passengers on the beaches of southern Italy. From there new arrivals could head off unimpeded in almost any direction, because in 1998 the European Union abolished all border controls between member states. Substantial numbers tried similar entries across the Strait of Gibraltar into southern Spain.

A large portion of the illegal immigrants were young women from eastern Europe, especially Russia and Ukraine. Often lured by criminals promising jobs as maids or waitresses and sometimes simply kidnapped and sold like slaves from hand to hand for a few thousand dollars, these women were smuggled into the most prosperous parts of central Europe and into the European Community and forced into prostitution or worse. Each year the mutilated bodies of hundreds of trafficked women turned up across Europe, tragic testimony to the feminization of poverty in postcommunist eastern Europe.

Illegal immigration generated intense debate and discussion in western Europe. A majority opposed the new-comers, who were accused of taking jobs from the unemployed and somehow undermining national unity. The idea that cultural and ethnic diversity could be a force for vitality and creativity ran counter to deep-seated beliefs. As busy mosques came to outnumber dying churches in parts of some European cities, rightist politicians especially tried to exploit widespread doubts that immigrants from Muslim countries would never assimilate to the different national cultures.

An articulate minority challenged the anti-immigrant campaign and its racist overtones. They argued that Europe badly needed newcomers—preferably talented newcomers—to limit the impending population decline and provide valuable technical skills. European leaders also focused on improved policing of EU borders and tougher common procedures to combat people smuggling and punish international crime. Above all, growing illegal immigration pushed Europeans to examine the whys of this dramatic human movement and to consider how it related to Europe's proper role in world affairs.

Protesting Against Racism   This was one of many demonstrations organized by SOS-Racism, a leading French force in the fight against hostility and violence toward immigrants in Europe. "Don't touch my pal" warns the slogan on the uplifted hand. *(G. Merillon/Gamma)*

Europe's Role in the Global Era

The tide of refugees and illegal job seekers made thinking people in western Europe acutely aware of their current good fortune, the sweet fruit of more than fifty years of peace, security, and rising standards of living. The nearby agonies of barbarism and war in the former Yugoslavia vividly recalled the horrors of World War II, and they cast in bold relief the ever-present reality of collective violence in today's world. At the same time, western European countries were generally doing their best to limit or expel the foreigners arriving at their gates, as we have seen. This ongoing rejection gave some Europeans a guilty conscience and a feeling that they needed to do more when they had so much and so many others had so little. As a result, European intellectuals and opinion makers began to envision a new historic mission for Europe—the promotion of domestic peace and human rights in those lands plagued by instability, violence, and oppression.

European leaders and humanitarians believed that Europe's mission required more global agreements and new international institutions to set moral standards and to regulate countries, political leaders, armies, corporations, and individuals. In practice, this meant more curbs on the sovereign rights of the world's states, just as the states of the European Union had imposed increasingly strict standards of behavior on themselves in order to secure the rights and welfare of EU citizens. As Nicole Gnesotto, the director of the European Union's institute, concluded, the EU has a "historical responsibility" to make morality "a basis of policy," because "human rights are more important than states' rights."[4] In general, the United States reacted coolly to the idea of preferring human rights to states' rights. American leaders stressed the preservation of U.S. freedom of action in world affairs, particularly after George Walker Bush was elected president in 2000.

In practical terms, western Europe's evolving human rights mission meant, first of all, humanitarian interventions to stop civil wars and to prevent tyrannical gov-

Humanitarian Aid to Africa   A German worker from the privately funded French group Médecins Sans Frontières (Doctors Without Borders) helps a young victim of a bad flood in Mozambique in 2000. Doctors Without Borders provides free and effective emergency services to poor countries stricken by natural disasters and civil wars. *(Per-Anders Pettersson/Prestige/Getty Images)*

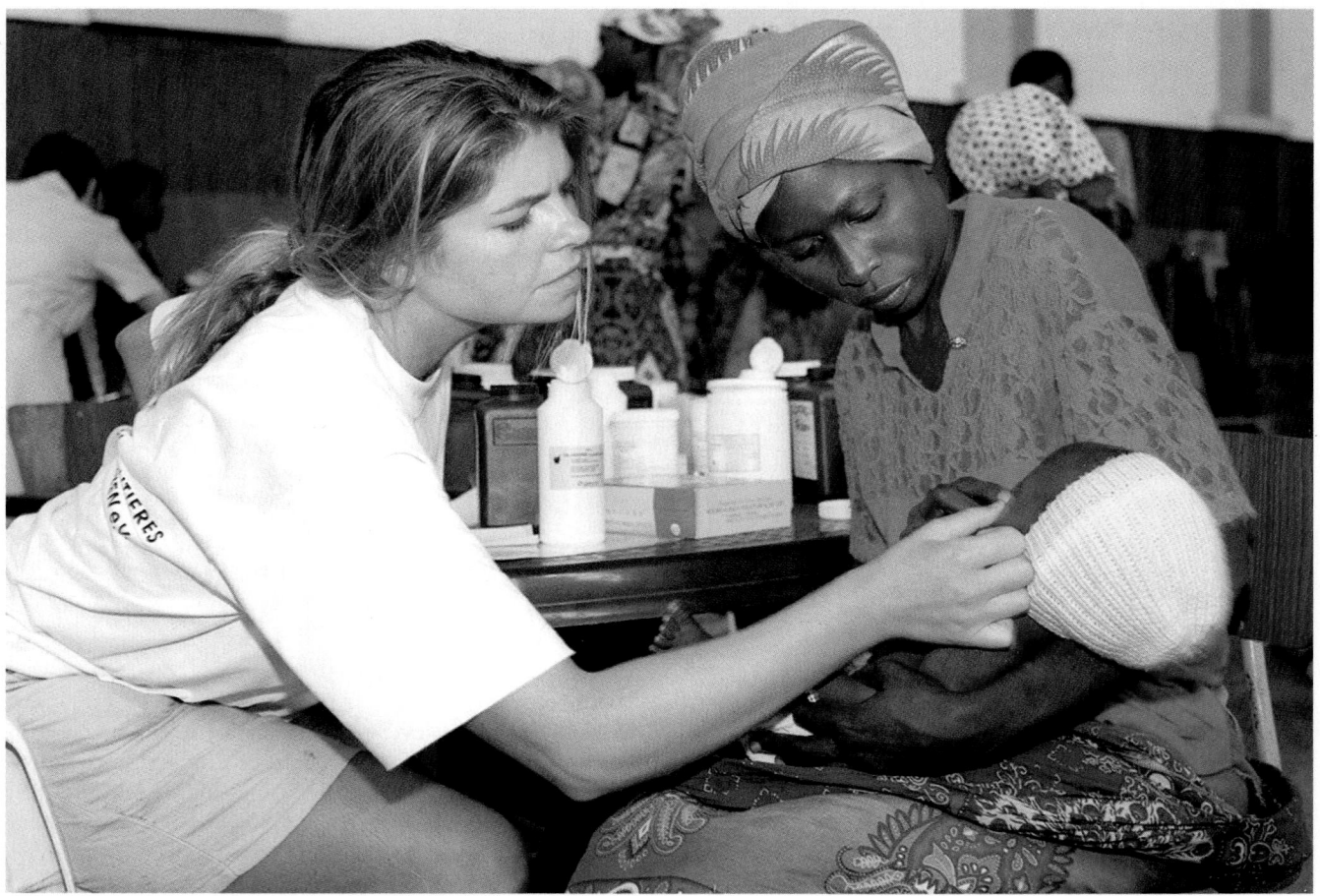

ernments from slaughtering their own people. Thus the European Union joined with the United States to intervene militarily to stop the killing in Bosnia, Kosovo, and Macedonia and to protect the rights of embattled minorities. The states of the EU also vigorously supported U.N.-sponsored conferences and treaties that sought to verify the compliance of anti–germ warfare conventions, outlawed the use of hideously destructive land mines, and established a new international court to prosecute war criminals. Moreover, individual states acted on their own. In June 2001, the jurors of a Belgian court, acting on the basis of a Belgian law asserting "universal jurisdiction" in cases involving crimes against humanity, sentenced four Rwandan Hutus to long prison terms for their roles in the genocidal massacres of about 500,000 Tutsis in Rwanda in 1994. Some observers thought that this judgment might have set a historic precedent for the concept that "justice has no border."

Europeans also pushed for broader definitions of individual rights. Abolishing the death penalty in the European Union, for example, they condemned its continued use in China, the United States, Saudi Arabia, and some other countries as inhumane and uncivilized. Rights for Europeans in their personal relations also continued to expand. In the pacesetting Netherlands, for example, a growing network of laws gave prostitutes (legally recognized since 1917) pensions and full workers' rights and legalized gay and lesbian marriages, the smoking of pot in licensed coffee shops, and assisted suicide (euthanasia) for the terminally ill.

As the new century opened, western Europeans also pushed as best they could to extend their broad-based concept of social and economic rights to the world's poor countries. These efforts were related to sharp criticism of globalization and unrestrained capitalism (see pages 1041–1042), criticism that in 2001 helped socialists regain power in twelve of the fifteen countries in the European Union. Quite typically, Europe's moderate social democrats combined with human rights campaigners in 2001 to help African governments secure drastic price cuts from the big international drug companies on the drug cocktails needed to combat Africa's AIDS crisis. Strong advocates of greater social equality and state-funded health care, European socialists embraced morality as a basis for action and the global expansion of human rights as a primary goal.

On the morning of September 11, 2001, two hijacked passenger planes from Boston crashed into and destroyed the World Trade Center towers in New York City. Shortly thereafter, a third plane crashed into the Pentagon, and a fourth, believed to be headed for the White House or the U.S. Capitol, crashed into a field in rural Pennsylvania. These terrorist attacks took the lives of more than three thousand people from many countries and put the personal safety of ordinary citizens at the top of the West's agenda.

The United States, led by President George W. Bush, launched a military campaign to destroy the perpetrators of the crime, Saudi-born millionaire Osama bin Laden's al-Qaida network of terrorists and Afghanistan's reactionary Muslim government, the Taliban. Building a broad international coalition that included western Europe, Russia, and Pakistan, the United States joined its tremendous airpower with the faltering Northern Alliance in Afghanistan, which had been fighting the Taliban for years. By mid-October American special forces on the ground were directing precision air strikes that devastated Taliban and al-Qaida troops, and a rejuvenated Northern Alliance took the offensive. In mid-November the Taliban retreated and then suddenly collapsed. Jubilant crowds in the capital of Kabul welcomed Northern Alliance soldiers as liberators. In December Afghan opposition leaders and United Nations mediators worked out plans for a new broad-based government, while American planes and tribal fighters decimated bin Laden's die-hard supporters in their mountain hideaways.

The swift punishment of al-Qaida and its Afghan supporters dramatically reaffirmed the West's commitment to the most basic of all human rights—the right to life itself. Sincere concerns about human rights also underlay American and European support during the war effort. The American military tried hard to avoid accidental bombings of Afghan civilians. Women's groups highlighted the Taliban's barbaric treatment of Afghan women, who were not permitted to work outside the home, go to school, or in many cases even appear in public. Moreover, an undeniable yearning for greater freedom in Afghanistan, so evident in liberation celebrations in Kabul reminiscent of Germans dancing joyously on the Berlin Wall in 1989, contributed greatly to the Taliban's defeat. Eruptions of joy testified yet again to a universal desire for freedom from oppression. As foreign governments, private aid organizations, and the United Nations turned to the awesome task of helping the Afghans get themselves back on their feet in early 2002, it seemed possible that the Western movement for a global expansion of human rights and human dignity had gained added strength.

Dancing in Kabul, January 2002 These joyful guests are celebrating a young couple's engagement, but they are also reveling in the sudden collapse of Taliban rule. The ultrapuritanical Taliban outlawed mixed gatherings of men and women, and it prohibited every type of music, theater, and dance. *(Paula Bronstein/Getty Images)*

The Future in Perspective

For centuries astrologers and scientists, experts and ordinary people, have sought to peek into the future. And although it may seem that the study of the past has little to say about the future, the study of history over a long period is actually very useful in this regard. It helps put the future in perspective.

Certainly, history is full of erroneous predictions, a few of which we have mentioned in this book. Yet lack of success has not diminished the age-old desire to look into the future. Self-proclaimed experts even pretend that they have created a new science of futurology. With great pomposity, they often act as if their hunches and guesses about future human development are inescapable realities. Yet the study of history teaches healthy skepticism regarding such predictions, however scientific and learned they may appear. Past results suggest that most such predictions will simply not come true, or at least not in the anticipated ways. Thus history provides some psychological protection from the visions of modern prognosticators.

This protection is particularly valuable when we realize that views of the future tend to swing between pessimistic and optimistic extremes from one generation, or even from one decade, to the next. These swings back and forth between optimism and pessimism, which one historian has aptly called "the great seesaw" in the development of the Western world, reflect above all the current situation of the observers.[5] Thus in the economic stagnation and revived cold war of the 1970s and 1980s, many projections into the future were quite pessimistic, just as they were very optimistic in the 1950s and 1960s. Many people in the Western world feared that conditions were going to get worse rather than better. For example, there were fears that pollution would destroy the environment and that the traditional family would disappear. Some gloomy experts predicted that twenty to thirty states might well have nuclear weapons by the end of the twentieth century. Many forecasters and politicians predicted that the energy crisis—in the form of skyrocketing oil prices—meant disaster in the form of lower standards of living at best and the collapse of civilization at worst. In fact, oil prices collapsed in the early 1980s and stayed low thereafter. It was heartening in that time of pessimism to know that most dire predictions do not prove true, just as the same knowledge of likely error is sobering in times of optimistic expectations.

Optimistic visions of the future were certainly in the air after the end of the cold war. The pendulum had definitely swung, most notably in the United States. Untroubled in the late 1990s by the high unemployment and the early stages of corporate downsizing that soured the mood in western Europe, the United States celebrated its dynamic economy and its booming stock market. U.S. military power, leadership in world affairs, and excellence in advanced technologies also encouraged optimism and rosy projections.

In 2000 the American mood shifted. The dot-com bubble burst, and in 2001 the U.S. economy slid into a recession. The attack of September 11, 2001, accentuated economic problems, brought national grief and fear, and led to many pessimistic forecasts of a long uphill struggle against global terrorism. Most frightening of all were grim warnings by some self-described experts who predicted that terrorist groups were likely to succeed in developing biological and nuclear weapons of mass destruction, which they would then turn on millions of innocent people with unspeakable cruelty. Such nightmare scenarios are not impossible, but we should remember that modern governments possess tremendous resources that they can mobilize to control individuals and small opposition groups, especially when the leading states decide to work together, as they did after September 11. Once again, just as it is sobering to know that the rosiest predictions in optimistic times usually do not prove true, so is it heartening to know that the direst projections in pessimistic times normally do not come to pass.

Whatever does or does not happen, the study of history puts the future in perspective in other ways. We have seen that every age has its problems and challenges. Others before us have trodden the paths of uncertainty and crisis. This knowledge helps save us from exaggerated self-pity in the face of our own predicaments.

Perhaps our Western heritage may rightly inspire us with pride and measured self-confidence. We stand, momentarily, at the head of the long procession of Western civilization. Sometimes the procession has wandered, or backtracked, or done terrible things. But it has also carried the efforts and sacrifices of generations of toiling, struggling ancestors. Through no effort of our own, we are the beneficiaries of those sacrifices and achievements. Now that it is our turn to carry the torch onward, we may remember these ties with our forebears.

To change the metaphor, we in the West are like a card player who has been dealt many good cards. Some of them are obvious, such as our technical and scientific heritage or our commitment to human rights and the individual. Others are not so obvious, sometimes half-forgotten or even hidden up the sleeve. Think, for example, of the Christian Democrats, the moderate Catholic party that emerged after World War II to play such an important role in the western European renaissance. And in the almost miraculous victory of peaceful revolution in eastern Europe in 1989—in what Czech playwright turned president Václav Havel called "the power of the powerless"—we see again the regenerative strength of the Western ideals of individual rights, representative government, and nationhood in the European homeland. We hold a good hand.

Our study of history, of mighty struggles and fearsome challenges, of shining achievements and tragic failures, gives a sense of the essence of life itself: the process of change over time. Again and again we have seen how peoples and societies evolve, influenced by ideas, human passions, and material conditions. As surely as anything is sure, this process of change over time will continue as the future becomes the present and then the past. And students of history are better prepared to make sense of this unfolding process because they have already observed it. They know how change is rooted in existing historical forces, and their projections will probably be better than many of the trendy speculations of futurologists. Students of history are also prepared for the new and unexpected in human development, for they have already seen great breakthroughs and revolutions. They have an understanding of how things really happen.

Key Terms

re-Stalinization
Great Russians
Gdansk Agreement
Solidarity
perestroika
glasnost
shock therapy
Velvet Revolution
third way

Alliance for Germany
Paris Accord
"new world order"
European Union
Kosovo Liberation Army
  (KLA)
Maastricht treaty
baby bust

Notes

1. M. Walker, *The Waking Giant: Gorbachev's Russia* (New York: Pantheon Books, 1987), p. 175.
2. F. Fukuyama, *The End of History and the Last Man* (New York: Free Press, 1992); and J. Cronin, *The War the Cold War Made: Order, Chaos, and Return of History* (New York: Routledge, 1996), pp. 267–281.
3. Quoted in *The Economist,* January 6, 2001, p. 6.
4. Quoted by Flora Lewis, *International Herald Tribune,* June 15, 2001, p. 6.
5. G. Blainey, *The Great Seesaw: A New View of the Western World* (London: Macmillan, 1988).

Suggested Reading

Many of the studies cited in the Suggested Reading for Chapters 29 and 30 are of value for the years since 1985 as well. Among other general works, F. Gilbert, *The End of the European Era: 1890 to the Present* (1991), is particularly helpful with its evenhanded account and extensive bibliography. Journalistic accounts in major newspapers and magazines are also invaluable tools for an understanding of recent developments. *Current History,* which devotes each monthly issue to either a geographical region or a contemporary topic, is especially recommended. The December 2001 issue, "America at War," provides a valuable overview of terrorism and its history.

M. Dobbs, *Down with Big Brother: The Fall of the Soviet Empire* (1997), is a superb firsthand account by an inspired journalist who covered events in Russia and eastern Europe between 1977 and 1993. On the Soviet Union, in addition to works cited in Chapter 30, the book by Walker cited in the Notes is a fascinating eyewitness account of Soviet life in the mid-1980s. R. Suny, *The Soviet Experiment: Russia, the USSR, and the Successor States* (1998), is outstanding on Russia in the 1990s and has up-to-date bibliographies. M. Lewin, *The Gorbachev Phenomenon: A Historical Interpreta-*

tion (1988), is excellent on the origins of the reforms. Two valuable studies by leading authorities on Russia after communism are M. Goldman, *Lost Opportunity: What Has Made Economic Reform in Russia So Difficult?* (1996), and R. Brady, *Kapitalizm: Russia's Struggle to Free Its Economy* (1999).

N. Naimark, *Fires of Hate: Ethnic Cleansing in Twentieth-Century Europe* (1999), argues that recent nationalism rather than "ancient hatreds" is decisive, while L. Johnson, *Central Europe: Enemies, Neighbors, Friends* (1996), ably interprets developments in eastern Europe before and after the revolutions of 1989. For developments in Poland, R. Leslie, *The History of Poland Since 1863* (1981), provides a long-term perspective. T. Ash, *The Magic Lantern: The Revolution of '89 Witnessed in Warsaw, Budapest, Berlin, and Prague* (1990), is exciting instant history, as is Ash's earlier book, *The Polish Revolution: Solidarity* (1983). G. Stokes, ed., *From Stalinism to Pluralism: A Documentary History of Eastern Europe Since 1945,* 2d ed. (1996), is another excellent collection. V. Havel, *The Art of the Impossible: Politics as Morality in Practice, Speeches and Writings, 1990–1996* (1997), reflects the hopes and worries of the Czech leader since 1989. Two excellent, judicious studies on the tragedy in Yugoslavia are J. Lampe, *Yugoslavia as History: Twice There Was a Country,* 2d ed. (2000), and T. Judah, *The Serbs: History, Myth and the Destruction of Yugoslavia* (1997). T. Rosenberg, *The Haunted Land: Facing Europe's Ghosts After Communism* (1995), is a moving look at people's lives in postcommunist eastern Europe.

The work by Cronin cited in the Notes provides a stimulating view of the late cold war and the massive changes following it. P. Zelikow and C. Rice, *Germany Unified and Europe Transformed: A Study in Statecraft* (1995), is an award-winning study of relations between the Great Powers and the peaceful resolution of the German question. G. Rose, *Jacques Delors and European Integration* (1995), analyzes the controversies surrounding the European Union in the 1990s. W. Laqueur, *The Germans* (1985), is a contemporary report by a famous historian. J. Ardagh, *Germany and the Germans: The United Germany in the Mid-1990s,* is another insightful study.

The contemporary resurgence of nationalism is analyzed by R. Brubaker, *Nationalism Reframed: Nationhood and the National Question* (1996), and R. Caplan and John Feffer, *Europe's New Nationalism: States and Minorities in Conflict* (1996). N. Cantor, *The American Century: Varieties of Culture in Modern Times* (1997), is a lively consideration of many cultural developments that includes the 1990s. Important books on globalization include P. O'Meara et al., eds., *Globalization and the Challenges of the New Century* (2000); M. Hardt and A. Negri, *Empire* (2000); and S. Strange, *The Retreat of the State: The Diffusion of Power in the World Economy* (1996). P. Kennedy, *Preparing for the Twenty-first Century* (1993), is a look into the future by a leading historian of international power politics. The work by Fukuyama cited in the Notes illustrates the widespread euphoria after the collapse of communism, arguing that democratic capitalism has defeated all its competitors. This optimistic projection may be compared with the somber future envisioned a generation ago in the influential and representative works by R. Heilbroner, *An Inquiry into the Human Prospect* (1974), and J. Revel, *The Totalitarian Temptation* (1977). The pathbreaking study of Blainey cited in the Notes examines the cycle of pessimism and optimism in Western history in fascinating detail.

A Solidarity Leader Speaks from Prison

*S*olidarity built a broad-based alliance of
intellectuals, workers, and the Catholic church,
which was one reason it became such a powerful
movement in Poland. Another reason was Solidarity's
commitment to social and political change through
nonviolent action. This enabled Solidarity to avoid a
bloodbath in 1981 and thus maintain its structure
after martial law was declared, although at the time
foreign observers often criticized Lech Walesa's
leadership for being too cautious and unrealistic.

One of Walesa's closest coworkers was Adam
Michnik. Walesa was a skilled electrician and a devout
Catholic, whereas Michnik was an intellectual and
disillusioned Communist. But their faith in nonviolence
and gradual change bound them together. Trained as a
historian but banned from teaching because of his
leadership in student strikes in 1968, Michnik earned
his living as a factory worker. In 1977 he joined with
others to found the Committee for the Defense of
Workers (KOR), which supported workers fired for
striking. In December 1981, Michnik was arrested with
the rest of Solidarity's leadership. While in prison until
July 1994, he wrote his influential Letters from
Prison, *from which the following is taken.*

Why did Solidarity renounce violence? This
question returned time and again in my
conversations with foreign observers. I would like
to answer it now. People who claim that the use of
force in the struggle for freedom is necessary must
first prove that in a given situation it will be
effective and that force, when it is used, will not
transform the idea of liberty into its opposite.

No one in Poland is able to prove today that
violence will help us to dislodge Soviet troops
from Poland and to remove the communists from
power. The U.S.S.R. has such enormous military
power that confrontation is simply unthinkable.
In other words, we have no guns. Napoleon,
upon hearing a similar reply, gave up asking

further questions. However, Napoleon was above
all interested in military victories and not building
democratic, pluralistic societies. We, by contrast,
cannot leave it at that.

In our reasoning, pragmatism is inseparably
intertwined with idealism. Taught by history, we
suspect that by using force to storm the existing
Bastilles we shall unwittingly build new ones. It is
true that social change is almost always
accompanied by force. But it is not true that social
change is merely a result of the violent collision of
various forces. Above all, social changes follow
from a confrontation of different moralities and
visions of social order. Before the violence of
rulers clashes with the violence of their subjects,
values and systems of ethics clash inside human
minds. Only when the old ideas of the rulers lose
this moral duel will the subjects reach for force—
sometimes. This is what happened in the French
Revolution and the Russian Revolution—two
examples cited in every debate as proof that
revolutionary violence is preceded by a moral
breakdown of the old regime. But both examples
lose their meaning when they are reduced to such
compact notions, in which the Encyclopedists are
paired with the destruction of the Bastille, and the
success of radical ideologies in Russia is paired
with the storming of the Winter Palace. An
authentic event is reduced to a sterile scheme.

In order to understand the significance of these
revolutions, one must remember Jacobin and
Bolshevik terror, the guillotines of the sans-culottes,
and the guns of the commissars. Without reflection
on the mechanisms in victorious revolutions that
gave birth to terror, it is impossible to even pose the
fundamental dilemma facing contemporary freedom
movements. Historical awareness of the possible
consequences of revolutionary violence must be
etched into any program of struggle for freedom.
The experience of being corrupted by terror must
be imprinted upon the consciousness of everyone
who belongs to a freedom movement. [Or], as

Simone Weil wrote, freedom will again become a refugee from the camp of the victors. . . .

Solidarity's program and ethos are inextricably tied to this strategy. Revolutionary terror has always been justified by a vision of an ideal society. In the name of this vision, Jacobin guillotines and Bolshevik execution squads carried out their unceasing, gruesome work. The road to God's Kingdom on Earth led through rivers of blood.

Solidarity has never had a vision of an ideal society. It wants to live and let live. Its ideals are closer to the American Revolution than to the French. . . . The ethics of Solidarity, with its consistent rejection of the use of force, has a lot in common with the idea of nonviolence as espoused by Gandhi and Martin Luther King, Jr. But it is not an ethic representative of pacifist movements.

Pacifism as a mass movement aims to avoid suffering; pacifists often say that no cause is worth suffering or dying for. The ethics of Solidarity are based on an opposite premise: that there are causes worth suffering and dying for. Gandhi and King died for the same cause as the miners in Wujek who rejected the belief that it is better to remain a willing slave than to become a victim of murder [and who were shot down by police for striking against the imposition of martial law in 1981]. . . .

But ethics cannot substitute for a political program. We must therefore think about the future of Polish-Russian relations. Our thinking about this key question must be open; it should consider many different possibilities. . . .

The Soviet state has a new leader; he is a symbol of transition from one generation to the next within the Soviet elite. This change may offer an opportunity, since Mikhail Gorbachev has not yet become a prisoner of his own decisions. No one can rule out the possibility that an impulse for reform will spring from the top of the hierarchy of power. This is exactly what happened in the time of Alexander II and, a hundred years later, under Khrushchev. Reform is always possible, even in the face of resistance by the old apparatus. . . .

So what can now happen [in Poland]?

The "fundamentalists" say, no compromises. Talking about compromise, dialogue, or understanding demobilizes public opinion, pulls the wool over the eyes of the public, spreads illusions. Walesa's declarations about readiness for dialogue were often severely criticized from this point of view. I do not share the fundamentalist point of view. . . . The logic of fundamentalism precludes any attempt to find compromise, even in the future. It harbors not only the belief that communists are ineducable but also a certainty that they are unable to behave rationally, even in

Solidarity activist Adam Michnik in 1984, appearing under police guard in the military court that sentenced him to prison. *(Wide World Photos)*

critical situations—that, in other words, they are condemned to suicidal obstinacy.

This is not so obvious to me. Historical experience shows that communists were sometimes forced by circumstances to behave rationally and to agree to compromises. Thus the strategy of understanding must not be cast aside. We should not assume that a bloody confrontation is inevitable and, consequently, rule out the possibility of evolutionary, bloodless change. This should be avoided all the more inasmuch as democracy is rarely born from bloody upheavals. We should be clear in our minds about this: The continuing conflict may transform itself into either a dialogue or an explosion. The TKK [the underground Temporary Coordinating Committee of outlawed Solidarity] and [Lech] Walesa are doing everything in their power to make dialogue possible. Their chances of success will be greater if the level of self-organization of independent Polish society increases. For street lynchings, angry crowds are enough; compromise demands an organized society.

Questions for Analysis

1. What arguments does Michnik present for opposing the government with nonviolent actions? Are his arguments convincing?

2. How did Michnik's study of history influence his thinking? What lessons did he learn?

3. Analyze Michnik's attitudes toward the Soviet Union and Poland's Communist leadership. What policies did he advocate? Why?

Source: Adam Michnik, *Letters from Prison and Other Essays,* trans. Maya Latynski (Berkeley and Los Angeles: University of California Press, 1985), pp. 86–89, 92, 95, by permission of the University of California Press. Copyright © 1985 by The Regents of the University of California.

Index

Abandoned children: as factory workers, 729, 744; decrease in, 810

Aborigines (Australia), 860

Abortion, 1018

Abstract art, 958(illus.)

Adams, John, 694

Adenauer, Konrad, 995

Adult education: Soviet, 962, 962(illus.)

Afghanistan, 1054; Soviets and, 1016; warfare and Taliban in, 1057

Africa: German colonies in, 841; imperialism in, 869–872, 877; partition of, 870(map); France in, 889; decolonization in, 998(map), 999–1000; Khrushchev and, 1004; humanitarian aid to, 1056(illus.); AIDS crisis in, 1057. *See also* North Africa

African Americans: Revolution and, 694; U.S. Civil War and, 833–835; civil rights of, 1001

Afrikaners, 869, 873

Age of anxiety, 921–948

Agoult, Marie d', 771

Agricultural Adjustment Act (1933), 946

Agriculture: Industrial Revolution and, 726; Russian, 835; five-year plans and, 959–961. *See also* Farms and farming

AIDS crisis: in Africa, 1057

Air force: in Second World War, 975

Albania, 1038

Albanian Muslims: in Kosovo, 1049–1050

Albert (England), 822(illus.)

Alcohol: among workers, 804; in Soviet Union, 1032

Alexander I (Russia), 715, 758(illus.), 759, 905; Napoleon and, 714, 718

Alexander II (Russia), 836, 836(illus.)

Alexander III (Russia), 836, 890

Alexandra (Russia), 905

Alexis (Russian heir to throne), 905

Algeciras Conference, 890

Algeria, 871, 983, 997, 999

Alliance for Germany, 1040

Alliance of the Three Emperors, 889

Alliances: Quadruple Alliance and, 718; Holy, 759; after 1871, 888(illus.); Russian-French, 888(illus.), 890; defensive military, 889, 914, 916, 994, 996; Three Emperors' League, 889; Triple Alliance, 889, 890; before First World War, 890–891; Triple Entente, 894–895; postwar, 996(map). *See also* specific alliances

Allies (First World War): in Russian civil war, 910; peace settlement and, 911; at Versailles, 912(illus.), 912–914; at peace conference, 912–914

Allies (Second World War), *see* Grand Alliance

All Quiet on the Western Front (Remarque), 896

Al-Qaida network: terrorism of, 1057

Alsace, 841

Alsace-Lorraine: after Franco-Prussian War, 888, 889; after First World War, 914. *See also* Lorraine

American Indians, 860

American Revolution, 693–697

Amiens, Treaty of, 714

Anarchy, 850

Anaximander, 814

Andropov, Yuri, 1032

Anglo-French Entente, 888(illus.), 890

Anglo-German naval agreement, 972

Anglo-Japanese Alliance, 890

Anglo-Russian Agreement, 888(illus.), 890

Angola, 869

Animals: energy from, 729

Anti-Corn Law League (England), 775

Antifederalists, 697

Anti-Semitism: after 1880, 839; Dreyfus affair and, 842, 842(illus.); modern, 845–846; of Hitler, 967, 970. *See also* Jews and Judaism

Antiseptic principle, 792

Antiwar movement, 1014, 1014(illus.)

Apartheid policy, 873

Apollo Program, 1007

Appeasement: of Hitler, 971–975, 974(illus.)

Arabi, Ahmed (Egypt), 862

Arab-Israeli wars, 999, 1019

Arabs and Arab world: nationalists in First World War, 899. *See also* Islam; Muslims

Arago, François, 779

Archangel, 910

Architecture, 797; Chicago school of, 930; modern, 930–931; Guggenheim Museum, Bilbao, Spain, 1043(illus.)

Argentina, 864, 866

Aristocracy: in post-revolutionary France, 777; of labor, 799, 802(illus.). *See also* Elites; Nobility

Arkwright, Richard, 728

Armed forces: Prussian, 830; Russian, 835; in Japan, 880(illus.); Russia and, 906; in Nazi Germany, 970; Paris Accord and, 1040. *See also* Military

Armistice: for First World War, 911

Arms race: before First World War, 895; Soviet Union and, 1032; Gorbachev-Reagan agreement and, 1033

Army Order No. 1 (Russia), 906

Arsenal of democracy: U.S. as, 979

Art(s): romanticism in, 767(illus.), 767–770; expressionist, 922(illus.), 932(illus.), 932–933; modern, 931–933; impressionist, 932; cubism, 933; dadaism, 933; surrealism, 933; French, 940; realism in, 945(illus.); abstract, 958(illus.); Soviet, 963, 1001, 1002(illus.); Nazi, 970; de-Stalinization and, 1004; pop art, 1008(illus.); women in, 1010(illus.); re-Stalinization in, 1028. *See also* Intellectual thought; Literature; Music; Painting

Artisans: labor movement and, 748; working classes and, 799

Ashley Mines Commission, 752

Asia: migration from, 867–868; imperialism in, 872, 877; in 1914, 874(map); Second World War in, 977, 982(map); U.S. containment policy in, 993; decolonization in, 998(map), 999; Khrushchev and, 1004; financial crises in, 1042. *See also* specific countries

Assassinations: of Francis Ferdinand, 892–893; in Germany, 938

Assemblies: in American colonies, 695

Atomic power, 926–927, 927(illus.), 1006; bombings of Hiroshima and Nagasaki, 983, 983(illus.). *See also* Nuclear power

Auden, W. H., 926

Auerstädt, battle at, 715

Auschwitz-Birkenau, 979, 986–987, 987(illus.)

Austerlitz, Battle of, 714

Australia, 899, 982; aborigines in, 860

Austria, 914, 954, 971; Declaration of Pillnitz and, 705–706; First Coalition and, 706; Napoleon and, 714, 717; Second Coalition and, 714; Third Coalition and, 714; Fourth Coalition and, 718; at Congress of Vienna, 758; Metternich and, 758, 759–761; Prussia and, 782; Italy and, 826, 828; Germany and, 829, 974; Zollverein and,

Austria (*cont.*)
829–830; Jews in, 845, 846; Triple Alliance and, 889; political tensions in, 903–904; republic of, 911; after Second World War, 994(map), 1004; Hungary and, 1035; in EU, 1052. *See also* Austro-Hungarian Empire (Austria-Hungary)
Austria-Hungary, *see* Austro-Hungarian Empire (Austria-Hungary)
Austrian Empire: 1848 revolutions and, 780. *See also* Austro-Hungarian Empire (Austria-Hungary); Habsburg dynasty
Austrian Netherlands, 706, 707, 708, 714
Austro-Hungarian Empire (Austria-Hungary), 844, 892(map); Alliance System and, 888–889; Balkan nationalism and, 891–894; revolution and national states in, 911; nationalism in, 967. *See also* First World War
Austro-Prussian War: Bismarck and, 830
Authoritarianism, 836(illus.), 880, 954–957
Authoritarian nationalism: French, 824–825
Autocracy: Holy Alliance and, 759
Auxiliary Service Law (1916), 901, 904
Axis powers, 974, 983

Baby boom, 1009, 1011
Bacteria: disease and, 792–794
Balance of power: in 1815, 756(map); at Congress of Vienna, 757–759, 758(illus.)
Baldwin, Stanley, 942; radio and, 937
Balfour Declaration (1917), 847
Balkans: migration from, 865; Alliance System and, 889; after Congress of Berlin, 891–892, 892(map); nationalism and war in, 891–892; in 1914, 892(map); in First World War, 899
Balzac, Honoré de, 815
Banks and banking: British, 726; continental industrialization and, 740; Great Depression and, 944
Barth, Karl, 926
Basques, 1053(illus.)
Bastille (Paris), 701–702, 702(illus.)
Battles, *see* Wars and warfare; specific battles and wars
Bauhaus, 931
Baumgarten, Hermann, 831
Beatles, 1011, 1012(illus.)
"Beat" movement, 1011
Beauvoir, Simone de, 1017, 1024–1025, 1025(illus.)
Bechuanaland (Botswana), 869
Beethoven, Ludwig van, 770, 771(illus.)
Beijing (Peking), 860, 1033
Belgium: France and, 715; industrialization in, 736, 738; railroads in, 738; banking in, 740; dynastic change in, 759; Congo and, 869; invasion of, 894, 894(illus.), 895; Ruhr and, 938; constitutional monarchy

in, 997; European unity and, 997. *See also* Austrian Netherlands; Netherlands
Belorussia, 910
Bentham, Jeremy, 791
Benthamites, 791, 843
Berg, Alban, 933
Berlin: Soviet blockade of, 992
Berlin airlift, 992, 993(illus.)
Berlin conference, 871
Berlin Wall, 1004, 1015; opening of, 1035, 1036(illus.), 1037
Bernstein, Edward, 849
Bethmann-Hollweg, Theobald von, 893, 901
Big Four, 912
Big Science, 1006–1007
Big Three: wartime conferences of, 990–992
Bill of Rights: in U.S., 696; English, 697
Bin Laden, Osama, 1057
Biology: Pasteur and, 812
Birkenau: The Camp of Death (Nahon), 986–987
Birth of a Nation (movie), 937
Birthrate: decline of, 1009, 1052–1054; and married working women, 1010, 1011(illus.)
Bismarck, Otto von, 797, 831(illus.), 890; Austro-Prussian War and, 830; Prussian leadership by, 831; German Empire and, 839; Africa and, 869–871; Alliance System of, 888–889
Black Hand, 893
Blacklisting: of Soviet dissidents, 1028
Blacks: American Revolution and, 694; U.S. Civil War and, 833–834. *See also* Africa; African Americans; Slaves and slavery
Black Sea: Russia and, 835
Black Shirts, 965
Blanc, Louis, 765, 778
Blitzkrieg (lightning war), 975
Blockade(s): in First World War, 899–900, 901(illus.), 904, 914; of Berlin, 992; of Cuba, 1004; of Iraq, 1041
Blocs: pre-First World War, 890–891; in cold war, 992. *See also* Alliances
Bloody Sunday massacre: in Russia, 838
Blum, Léon, 948
Boer War, 869, 873, 890; critics of, 876
Bolsheviks, 906–910. *See also* Communists and communism; Lenin, Vladimir Ilyich; Russian Revolution (1917)
Bombings: of Hiroshima and Nagasaki, 983, 983(illus.), 1006; in Second World War, 983; of Bosnian Serb targets, 1049. *See also* Terrorism
Borders: Locarno agreements and, 939, 941; Paris Accord and, 1040; of EU, illegal immigrants and, 1054
Borodino, Battle of, 718, 719
Bosnia, 891, 893; annexation of, 892; intervention in, 1057
Bosnia-Herzegovina, 1047–1049, 1049(map)

Bosnian Muslims, 1049, 1050(illus.)
Bosnian Serbs, 1049
Boston Tea Party, 694(illus.), 695
Botswana, 869
Boundaries, *see* Borders
Bourbon dynasty: restoration of, 718, 757, 759; Naples and Sicily ruled by, 827
Bourgeoisie, 692; French, 699; Marx on, 766
Bourne, J. C., 724(illus.)
Boxer Rebellion, 882
Brain drain, 1007
Brandt, Willy: Poland, détente and, 1015, 1016(illus.)
Brassey, Thomas, 733
Brazil: migration to, 864, 866
Brazza, Pierre de, 869
Bread: French, 708
Breast-feeding, *see* Nursing of children
Brest-Litovsk: Treaty of, 909, 911
Brezhnev, Leonid, 1004–1005, 1015–1016
Brezhnev Doctrine, 1006, 1033, 1034(illus.)
Briand, Aristide, 939, 941(illus.)
Britain: Battle of, 975. *See also* England (Britain)
British Broadcasting Corporation (BBC), 937
British Commonwealth of Nations, 999
British East India Company, 694
British Empire, 890; in India, 878–879, 879(illus.). *See also* England (Britain)
Brothers Karamazov, The (Dostoevski), 812
Brown, Ford Maddox, 741(illus.)
Brown v. Board of Education, 1001
Broz, Josip, *see* Tito (Josip Broz)
Brunel, Isambard Kingdom, 733, 733(illus.)
Brüning, Heinrich, 969, 970
Brussels: EU bureaucracy in, 1051
Budget deficit: in U.S. (1980s), 1020
Bulgaria, 892, 914, 954, 991; First World War and, 899; Second World War and, 975; postcommunist transition in, 1047
Bulgarians, 844
Bureaucracy: Soviet, 1032; of EU, 1051
Burke, Edmund, 705
Bush, George H. W., 1040, 1041
Bush, George W., 1056, 1057
Business: women and, 742, 743; Russian, 1044
Byron, George Gordon, 771(illus.)

Camus, Albert, 925
Canada: migration to, 864
Canals, 726; international trade and, 859
Cape Colony, 869, 873
Capital (financial): on Continent, 738, 740; industrialization and, 740–749; export of, 860
Capital (Marx), 846
Capitalism: global, 1041; shift from welfare state to, 1042; criticism of, 1057

Car bomb, 1053(illus.)
Carlsbad Decrees (1819), 759
Carter, Jimmy, 1016
Cartwright, Edmund, 729
Caste: in India, 878
Castle, The (Kafka), 930
Castlereagh, Robert, 758, 759
Castro, Fidel, 1004
Casualties: of First World War, 896, 899, 905; of Second World War, 983
Catherine the Great (Russia): League of Armed Neutrality and, 695
Catholic Center party (Germany), 839
Catholicism, *see* Roman Catholic church
Catholic party (Germany): Treaty of Versailles and, 914
Cavour, Camillo Benso di, 828
Ceauşescu, Nicolae, 1036
Censorship: in First World War, 902–903; Gorbachev and, 1033
Central Powers, 899, 903–904
Cézanne, Paul, 933
Chadwick, Edwin, 742, 791
Chamberlain, Neville, 974, 975
Chamber of Deputies (France), 777
Champagne: attack on, 896
Chaplin, Charlie, 936
Charles X (France), 777
Chartist movement, 749, 775
Chaumont, Treaty of, 718
Chechnya: Russia in, 1046
Checks and balances: in U.S. government, 696
Cheka (secret police), 910
Chemistry: organic, 813
Chicago: architecture in, 930, 931
Chicago, Judy, 1010(illus.)
Child labor, 744, 745; in factories, 729; in mines, 752–753, 753(illus.)
Children: in industrial Britain, 745; gender roles, family life, and, 807; rearing of, 810–812; First World War and, 901; as forced labor, 901; in postwar period, 1009
China, 914; industrialization and, 736; opening to West, 860–861; immigrants from, 867; imperialism in, 868, 872, 874(map), 877, 880; revolution in (1912), 880–881; Tzu Hsi in, 881, 881(illus.); civil war in, 992; communism in, 992–993; Nixon in, 1014–1015; massacre of prodemocracy demonstrators in, 1033
Chirac, Jacques, 1051
Cholera, 792
Chopin, Frédéric, 770
Christian Democrats: in western Europe, 995, 997; in West Germany, 1017, 1040
Christian existentialism, 926
Christianity: French, 704; working class and, 804; revival of, 925–926. *See also* Church; Religion
Christian socialists: anti-Semitism and, 846

Church: working-class attendance in, 804. *See also* Christianity
Churchill, Winston, 871; wartime leadership of, 975, 979; Yalta Conference and, 990(illus.), 991–992; at Teheran Conference, 990–991; "iron curtain" speech of, 992
Cities and towns: European, 788(map); industrialization and, 788–790; disease in, 789, 790(illus.), 791–792; apartment living in, 793(illus.); Madrid landscape and, 795(illus.). *See also* Urban society
Civil Code (1804, France), 712
Civilization(s): European spread of, 875, 876(illus.). *See also* Culture(s)
Civil liberties: in 1990s, 1042
Civil Rights Act (1964), 1001
Civil rights movement (U.S.), 1000(illus.), 1000–1001
Civil war(s): in U.S., 833–834, 834(map); in Russia, 910; Spanish, 974; in China, 992; in Yugoslavia, 1043, 1047–1050
Classes: industrialization and, 740; factory owners as, 741–742; Marx on, 765–766; in Parisian apartments, 793(illus.); lifestyles of, 796–804; urban social hierarchy of, 799(illus.); working, 799–805; women's fashion and, 800(illus.), 800–801, 801(illus.); in India, 878; in Italy, 964, 965; in Nazi Germany, 970; in postwar period, 1007–1009
Classical economists: Marx as, 766. *See also* Ricardo, David; Smith, Adam
Classical liberalism, 762; American government and, 697; compared to totalitarianism, 956
Clemenceau, Georges, 903; at Versailles peace conference, 912, 912(illus.), 914
Clergy: French, 698, 700
Clermont (steamship), 858
Clinical psychiatry, 929
Clinton, Bill: Bosnian agreement of, 1049
Clothing: underwear and, 729; of workers, 744; women's fashion and, 800(illus.), 800–801, 801(illus.); women workers and, 803
Coal and Steel Community, 997
Coal industry, 730–731, 747–748, 837
Cobden, Richard, 872
Cockerill family: John, 738; William, 738
Coercive Acts, 695
Coke, 732; in Germany, 739(illus.)
Cold war, 990–992; Truman Doctrine and, 992; Stalin and, 992–993; Khrushchev and, 1004–1005; 1968-1985, 1013–1017; end of, 1027, 1040–1041
Coleridge, Samuel Taylor, 768
Collective bargaining, 849
Collectivization: in Soviet Union, 960–961
Colleges, *see* Universities and colleges
Cologne, Germany, 792

Colonies and colonization: German, 841, 869, 871, 914; decolonization and, 998(map), 999–1000; neocolonialism and, 1000. *See also* Imperialism; New imperialism
Combination Acts, 748–749
COMECON, 996(map)
Commerce, *see* Trade
Committee for the Defense of Workers (KOR), 1062
Committee of Public Safety, 708
Commoners: French, 698–699
Common Market, 996(map), 997; misery index for, 1019(illus.). *See also* European Economic Community
Commons, *see* House of Commons (England)
Common Sense (Paine), 695
Commonwealth of Independent States, 1039(map), 1040
Communal living: Fourier and, 764
Communications: trade and, 859; totalitarian state and, 955
Communist Manifesto, The (Marx and Engels), 765–766, 846, 906
Communist party: German, 912, 940, 969; French, 992; in Italy, 992
Communists and communism: in Russia, 909–910; war, 910; in Soviet Union, 956–957, 1002, 1038(illus.), 1038–1040, 1039(map); Second World War and, 980; in eastern Europe, 992, 993, 1002, 1003, 1004–1006, 1028–1033, 1035–1036; in China, 992–993; in postwar western Europe, 995; in Poland, 1030–1032; Gorbachev and, 1032–1033. *See also* Soviet Union
Composers, 770, 933
Computers, 1006, 1020, 1042
Comte, Auguste, 813
Concentration camps, 978(illus.), 978–979, 986–987, 987(illus.)
Concord: fighting at, 695
Concordat of 1801, 714
Concorde supersonic airliner, 1007
Condition of the Working Class in England, The (Engels), 742
Confederate States of America, 833–834
Congo region, 869
Congress (U.S.), 697
Congress of Berlin (1878), 889, 891–892, 892(map)
Congress of People's Deputies (Soviet Union), 1033, 1038
Congress of Vienna, 757–761, 758(illus.); Italy and, 826
Congress system of diplomacy, 759
Conrad, Joseph, 877
Conservatism: Metternich and, 759–761; in Austrian Empire, 780; of Bismarck, 833; anti-Semitism and, 846; in 1980s, 1017, 1020; in 1970s, 1020

Conservative authoritarianism, 954

Conservative party: German, 839; British, 843, 942, 1020

Constable, John, 767, 770

Constituent Assembly: French, 778–779, 780; Prussian, 782; Russian, 910

Constitution(s): in U.S., 696–697; French, 703, 704, 825; 1848 revolutions and, 780; German, 782; Prussian, 782; in North German Confederation, 831; Russian, 904; Soviet, 1038

Constitutional Charter (France), 718, 762, 777

Constitutional Convention, 696–697

Constitutional monarchy: French, 704; Russian, 838; postwar, 997

Constitutional reform: in Russia, 1045

Consumers and consumerism: after Second World War, 1008–1009

Containment policy: of U.S., 992, 993, 1013–1014

Continental Congress, 695

Continental Europe: industrialization in, 734–740, 737(map). See also Europe

Continental system: of Napoleon, 717–718

Coral Sea: Battle of the, 982

Corinne (Staël), 769

Corn Laws (England), 773, 777, 858

Coronation: of Napoleon I, 715(illus.)

Corporate downsizing, 1042

Corporations: banks as, 740

Corruption: in Soviet bureaucracy, 1032

Cort, Henry, 732

Cottage industry: in 18th century, 726(map); workers in, 744

Cotton industry, 727; inventions in, 728; spinning of yarn for, 728, 728(illus.), 729; mills in, 744–746, 745(illus.); trade in British Empire and, 858. See also Textile industry

"Cottonopolis": Manchester as, 730(illus.)

Council(s): of Europe, 997

Counterculture, 1012–1013

Counter-cyclical policy (Keynes), 944

Counter-revolutionaries: of eastern Europe, 1028

Coup(s): French, 824; in Soviet Union, 1039, 1044

Crafts: urban workers and, 802

Craft unions: gender separation and, 747

Crane, Diana, 801

Crédit Mobilier, 740

Crick, Francis, 1007

Crimean War, 835, 836

Criminals: people smuggling by gangs, 1054

Crisis of the mind: Valéry on, 923

Croatia, Republic of: civil war in, 1047, 1049; ethnic composition of, 1049(map)

Croats, 780

Crompton, Samuel, 728

Cronin, James, 1043

Crown, see England (Britain); Monarchs and monarchies

Crystal Palace exhibition, 733, 735(illus.)

Cuba: Chinese migrants in, 867; missile crisis in, 1004–1005

Cubells y Ruiz, Enrique Martinez, 795(illus.)

Cubism, 933, 934

Culture(s): middle-class, 798; political changes and, 842; Soviet, 961–963, 1001; de-Stalinization and, 1004; youth culture, 1011–1012; counterculture, 1012–1013; re-Stalinization in, 1028. See also Intellectual thought

Curie, Marie, 926

Czechoslovakia, 914, 938, 954, 991; republic of, 911; Hitler and, 972(map); Nazi aggression toward, 975; communism in, 992; Soviet invasion of, 1005–1006, 1006(illus.), 1028; West German treaty with, 1015; Václav Havel in, 1035–1036, 1037; Velvet Revolution in, 1035–1036, 1047

Czech people: in Austria, 761, 844

Czech Republic, 1046, 1047, 1052

Dadaism, 933

"Daffodils" (Wordsworth), 768

Dance: after First World War, 933

Dance of Life, The (Munch), 928(illus.)

Danhauser, Josef, 771(illus.)

Danton, Georges Jacques, 707, 711

Dardanelles: in First World War, 899

Dar es Salaam, 876(illus.)

Darwin, Charles, 814–815; satire of, 814(illus.)

David, Jacques-Louis, 701(illus.), 715(illus.)

Dawes, Charles G., 939

Dawes Plan, 939

Dean, James, 1011

Death penalty: EU and, 1057

Death rate, see Mortality

Deaths: First World War and, 902

De Beers Mining Company, 873

Declaration of Independence (U.S.), 693, 695, 696(illus.)

Declaration of Pillnitz, 705–706

Declaration of the Rights of Man (France), 692, 703, 722

Declaration of the Rights of Woman (Gouges), 722–723

Declassé, Théophile, 890

Decline of the West, The (Spengler), 930

Decolonization: in Asia and Africa, 998(map), 999–1000

Defense mechanisms: Freud on, 812

Defense spending: Reagan and, 1016–1017

De Gaulle, Charles, 980, 997, 999–1000, 1012–1013, 1013(illus.)

Delacroix, Eugène, 770, 772(illus.)

Democracy: democratic republics and, 779(illus.); in Weimar Republic, 940; postwar, 997

Democracy in America (Tocqueville), 778

Democratic nationalism: of Mazzini, 784–785

Democratic republicanism, 764

Democratization: in Soviet Union, 1033

Denmark: Germany and, 782; Schleswig-Holstein and, 830; Second World War and, 975; in European Economic Community, 1019

Dentistry, 798

Depression, see Great Depression

Deregulation: of markets, 1042

De-Stalinization, 1004

Détente policy, 1015–1016

Determinism, 815

Developed regions, 856

Dialectic: Marx and Hegel on, 766

Dictatorship, 953; nationalism and, 823–824; German, 911; conservative authoritarianism and, 954–957; radical totalitarianism and, 954–957; in Soviet Union, 957–964, 1001–1002; in Italy, 964–966; of Tito, 1003. See also Nazi Germany

Diet (food): of workers, 744. See also Food

Dinner Party, The (Judy Chicago), 1010(illus.)

Diphtheria, 792

Diplomacy: congress system and, 759; of Bismarck, 888–889; outbreak of First World War and, 894; of France, 938; Nixon, Vietnam War, and, 1014–1015

Directory (France), 712

Disarmament conference: Hitler and, 971

"Disasters of the War, The" (Goya), 717(illus.)

Discrimination: gender, 807, 1010, 1017; against Asian immigrants, 868

Disease: in cities, 788; miasmatic and germ theories of, 791–792

Disraeli, Benjamin, 843, 872

Dissidents: re-Stalinization and, 1028; Václav Havel as, 1037

Divine right of kings: Louis XVI (France) and, 700

Division of labor: by gender, 746–748, 807

Divorce: in 1960s, 1010; in Italy, 1018

Dix, Otto, 897(illus.)

Doctors, see Medicine; Physicians

Doctors Without Borders, 1056(illus.)

Doctor Zhivago (Pasternak), 1004

Domestic servants, 802–803, 803(illus.)

Dostoevski, Feodor, 812

Double Helix, The (Watson), 1007

Dowry, 805

Draft (military): in U.S., 1014

Drama, see Theater

Dreiser, Theodore, 817

Dreyfus, Alfred, 842, 842(illus.)

Drinking, see Alcohol

Droz, Gustave, 808, 810

Dual government: in Nazi Germany, 969–970

Dual revolution, 755; Holy Alliance against, 759

Dubček, Alexander, 1005

Duma (Russia), 838, 905–906

Dumas, Alexander, 768, 771

Dunkirk: battle at, 975

Dupin, Amandine Aurore Lucie, *see* Sand, George (Amandine Aurore Lucie Dupin)

Dutch: in South Africa, 869; in East Indies, 872; empire of, 874(map). *See also* Holland; Netherlands

Duties of Man, The (Mazzini), 784–785

Dylan, Bob, 1011

East, *see* Asia; Middle East

East Berlin, 1004

Eastern Europe, 1027; anti-Semitism in, 846; French diplomacy and, 938; authoritarianism, 954; division of, 991–992; COMECON in, 996(map); Soviet, 1001–1006; de-Stalinization and, 1004; women in postwar period, 1009; decline of communism in, 1028–1033; democratic movements in, 1034(illus.); revolutions in, 1034–1037; Soviet Union and, 1038–1040; German unification and, 1040; markets and capitalism in, 1042; nationalism and warfare in, 1043–1044; liberalization in, 1046–1047; illegal immigrants from, 1054

Eastern front: in First World War, 897–900

East Germany, 1027; Brandt and, 1015; Hungary and, 1035; protest movement in, 1035; reunification of, 1040. *See also* Germany

East Indies, 872

Economic Consequences of the Peace (Keynes), 938

Economic liberalism, 762; in Russia, 1044–1045; in eastern Europe, 1046–1047

Economic nationalism: in Germany, 740

Economy and economics: inequality in, 692; French, 711, 997; industrialization and, 740; specialization in, 796; in German Empire, 839–841; Marx on, 846; global, 855–857; world market and, 857–860; new imperialism and, 872; in Japan, 880; First World War and, 900–902; German, 938, 970; Dawes Plan and, 939; Great Depression and, 942–948; Keynesian, 944, 995; five-year plans, 957, 959–961; Soviet, 957–959, 1032–1033; Hitler and, 968; after Second World War, 995–997; Common Market and, 996(map), 997; in West Germany, 997; decolonization, neocolonialism, and, 1000; service economy and, 1009; women workers and, 1009–1010; in 1970s and 1980s, 1018–1019; misery index and, 1019(illus.); in Poland, 1030,

1032, 1035; in former Soviet Union, 1042, 1044–1045; global economy in 1990s, 1042; baby bust and, 1052–1054

Education: of middle class, 797–798; of women, 807–808; French, 841; in India, 878; Soviet, 962, 962(illus.); for middle class, 1007–1008; higher education and, 1012; Soviets and, 1030. *See also* Intellectual thought

Ego: in Freudian psychology, 929

Egypt, 890; England and, 862–863, 863(illus.), 869, 872; West and, 862–863; Khartoum massacre and, 871; responses to imperialism in, 877; Second World War in, 983; 1973 attack on Israel, 1019

Egyptian Nationalist party, 862

Einstein, Albert, 926–927, 1006

Eisenhower, Dwight D., 983, 1001, 1014

Eisenstein, Sergei, 937, 1001, 1002(illus.)

El Alamein: Battle of, 983

Elba: Napoleon and, 718

Elbe River, 983

Elections: in Russia, 1045

Electoral system: of Napoleon III, 824, 825

Electric streetcars, 792–794

Electromagnetism, 813

Electronics revolution, 1042

Elimination of Poverty, The (Napoleon III), 824

Eliot, George (Mary Ann Evans), 816

Eliot, T. S., 926, 930

Elites: after 1871, 839; in Nazi Germany, 970; Soviet, 1028; in Russia, 1044, 1045(illus.); Maastricht treaty and, 1051

Elizabeth II (England), 999(illus.)

Emigrant Ship, The (Staniland), 854(illus.)

Emigration: from Europe, 864–866, 865(illus.); origin and destination of migrants, 866(illus.). *See also* Immigrants and immigration; Migration

Emile, or On Education (Rousseau), 704

Empires: of France, 715–718, 824; of Napoleon I, 715–718; of Hitler, 975; after Second World War, 993–995; decolonization and, 998(map), 999–1000. *See also* Colonies and colonization; Imperialism; New imperialism

Employment: First World War impact on, 902; part-time, for women, 1010

Employment Agency (Soyer), 945(illus.)

Enabling Act, 969

Enclosure movement, 726

"End of history": triumph of liberal democracies and, 1042–1043

Energy: for Industrial Revolution, 729–730; crisis in, 1018–1019. *See also* Coal industry; Oil and oil industry; Steam engine

Engels, Friedrich, 742, 765(illus.), 765–766

Engineering: of railroads, 733; on Continent, 738; middle class and, 797

England (Britain): freedom and equality in, 692; American Revolution and, 694–696; conservatism in, 705; Napoleon and, 714, 717–718; Industrial Revolution in, 725, 726–734, 734(map), 736, 737; cottage industry in, 726(map); transportation in, 726(map); factories in, 727–729; iron industry in, 732; railroads in, 732–733; industry and population growth in, 733–734; workers in, 744–746, 849; labor movement in, 748–749; at Congress of Vienna, 758; liberalism in, 762; reforms in, 773–776; cities in, 788(map), 788–790; overcrowding in, 795; literary realism in, 816; Ireland and, 843–844; Jewish homeland and, 847; Labour party and, 850; income in, 856; empire and trade of, 857–859; shipping and, 858(illus.); Egypt and, 862–863, 863(illus.), 869, 872; Suez Canal and, 862; migration from, 864; Rhodes and, 869, 873, 873(illus.); South Africa and, 869; Asian imperialism of, 872; in Sudan, 872; empire of, 874(map); India and, 878–879, 998(map), 999; alliances and, 890; Boer War and, 890; Germany and, 890–891, 938; First World War home front of, 902; France and, 938; German reparations and, 939; democratic government in, 940–942; Great Depression and, 943(map), 944, 947, 950–951; in Grand Alliance, 971; Hitler and, 972–974; Battle of Britain in, 975; Second World War and, 979–980; welfare state in, 995; European unity and, 997; Africa and, 999(illus.); Palestine and, 999; Thatcher and Atlantic alliance, 1017; in European Economic Community, 1019. *See also* First World War; Second World War

Enlightenment: classical liberalism and, 692

Entertainment: movies as, 936–937

Entrepreneurs: industrialization and, 738

Equality: in revolutionary era, 691–693; of women, 769, 963; during First World War, 902

Era of Tyrannies, The (Halévy), 954–955

Erhard, Ludwig, 995–997

Essay on Logical Philosophy (Wittgenstein), 925

Essay on the Principle of Population (Malthus), 734

Estates (classes): in France, 698(illus.), 698–699

Estates General (France), 699–700

Estonia, 954

ETA (Basque separatists), 1053(illus.)

Ethiopia: Italy and, 974

Ethnicity: in Austrian Empire, 761; nationalism and, 762; in Yugoslavia, 1049(map)

EU, *see* European Union (EU)

Eugénie (France), 822(illus.)

Eureaucrats, 1051

Europe: American Revolution and, 697; defense of conservatism in, 705; Napoleonic, 715–718, 716(map); Grand Empire and, 716(map), 716–718; industrialization in, 725–740, 737(map); in 1815, 756(map); cities in, 788(map), 788–790; foreign investment by, 859(map), 859–860; Great Migration from, 863–868, 865(illus.); origin and destination of emigrants from, 866(illus.); partition of Africa by, 870(map); First World War in, 898(map); after First World War, 915(map); Great Depression in, 943(map); Second World War in, 975–979, 976(map), 994(map); New Order in, 977–978; division of, 990–993; American aid to, 992, 995; alliance systems in, 996(map); brain drain of, 1007; in 1990s, 1041–1052; contemporary, 1048(map); baby bust in, 1052; population decline in, 1053–1054; immigration to, 1054; in global era, 1055–1057; future of, 1058–1059

European Community, 1044, 1051. See also European Union (EU)

European Economic Community, 1019. See also Common Market

European federalists: unity and, 997

European Union (EU), 1044, 1047; Maastricht treaty and, 1051; illegal immigration in, 1054; human rights mission of, 1056–1057

Europe first policy, 979

Euros, 1052

Evans, Mary Ann, see Eliot, George (Mary Ann Evans)

Evolution, 814–815, 926

Evolutionary Socialism (Bernstein), 849

Exercise: in 1970s and 1980s, 1020–1021

Existentialism, 925; Christian, 926; women, Beauvoir, and, 1017, 1024–1025

Expansion: of West, 864; of Nazi Germany, 971–975, 972(map); of Japan, 977. See also Imperialism; New imperialism

Expressionist art, 922(illus.)

Extermination camps, 978(illus.), 978–979, 986–987, 987(illus.)

Factories, 727–729; conditions in, 729, 740–749; sexual division of labor in, 747; working classes and, 799

Factory Act (1833), 746

Fagus shoe factory (Gropius), 931

Fairy tales: of Grimm brothers, 770

Family: under Napoleonic Code, 714; in Britain, 745; working-class women and, 747; industrialization and, 805–812; in 1970s and 1980s, 1021

Family allowances, 1008

Family monarchy: French, 714

Famine: in Ireland, 775, 776–777, 843; in Soviet Union, 961

Faraday, Michael, 813

Farms and farming: in England, 726. See also Agriculture

Fascism: in France, 947–948; totalitarianism and, 954; radical dictatorships and, 957; in Italy, 964–967

Fashoda, 872

Father: role of, 811–812

Faulkner, William, 929

Federalism: in U.S., 696–697

Federal Republic of Germany, see West Germany

Feminine Mystique, The (Friedan), 1017

Feminism, 807, 1024–1025; in 1970s, 1017–1018, 1018(illus.)

Feminization of poverty: in eastern Europe, 1054

Ferdinand I (Austrian Empire), 780

Ferry, Jules, 841, 869–871; imperialism and, 872, 884–885, 885(illus.)

Fifth Republic (France), 997, 1012–1013

Films, see Movies

Final Act: of Helsinki Conference, 1015

"Final solution": Hitler and, 978–979

Finance(s): French, 697; crash in (1873), 839, 845–846

Finland: in EU, 1052

Finland Station: Lenin at, 908

First Balkan War, 892

First Coalition, 707, 708

First Continental Congress, 695

First estate: in France, 698

First French Republic, 778

First International, 846–848

First World War, 887–888; youth and sexuality before, 820–821, 821(illus.); origins of, 888–891, 894–895; outbreak of, 891–894; western front in, 895–896, 898(map); stalemate and trench warfare, 895–897, 896(illus.), 897(illus.); casualties of, 896, 899, 905; eastern front in, 897–900, 898(map); widening of, 897–900; U.S. in, 899–900, 911; home front in, 900–904; Russian Revolution and, 904–910; peace settlement after, 911–916, 915(map); experiences of, 918–919; Hitler and, 967

Fisher, Irving, 942

Five-year plans: Soviet, 957, 959–961, 1002

Food: prices of, 744; rationing in First World War, 901. See also Diet (food); Famine

Forced-labor camps: Soviet, 1001

Forced-labor law: in First World War Germany, 901

Foreign affairs: from 1924-1929, 939; Watergate affair and, 1015; Russia and, 1045–1046

Foreign investment: by Europe (to 1914), 859(map), 859–860

Foreign policy: of Napoleon, 714–718; German, 888–889; of Britain, 890; containment (U.S.), 992, 993, 1013–1014;

Truman Doctrine and, 992; de-Stalinization and, 1004; Brezhnev Doctrine, 1006; détente, 1015–1016

Formosa: Japan and, 880

Fourier, Charles, 764–765

Fourth Coalition, 718

France, 1042; freedom and equality in, 692; American Revolution and, 695; breakdown of old order in, 697–698; estates in, 698(illus.), 698–699; revolt of poor in, 700–703; storming of Bastille in, 701–702, 702(illus.); limited monarchy in, 703–704; in European war (1792), 706; as republic, 707; planned economy in, 708; Reign of Terror in, 708–711, 710(illus.); Thermidorian Reaction and Directory in, 711–712; Napoleon I in, 712; industrialization in, 736, 737; at Congress of Vienna, 757–758; nationalism in, 764; utopian socialism in, 764–765; 1830 revolution in, 777; First Republic in, 778; 1848 revolution in, 778–780; literary realism in, 815–816; Napoleon III and, 823–825; Second Empire in, 824–825, 826(illus.); Third Republic in, 841–842; Dreyfus affair in, 842, 842(illus.); Jews in, 845; socialism in, 846; workers in, 849; revisionism in, 850; Congo and, 869; North Africa and, 871; Sudan and, 872; Alsace-Lorraine and, 888; Russia and, 888(illus.), 890; Alliance System and, 888–889; Britain and, 890; German invasion of, 894; home front in First World War, 900, 903; Versailles Treaty and, 914, 937–938; Germany and, 937, 938, 939; diplomacy of, 938; democratic government in, 940; Great Depression and, 947–948; Popular Front in, 947–948; Rhineland occupation and, 970; Second World War and, 975, 977; Vichy government in, 975; Christian Democrats in, 995; De Gaulle in, 997; recovery in, 997; decolonization and, 999; Africa and, 999–1000; student rebellion in, 1012–1013, 1013(illus.); Mitterrand in, 1020; conservatism in, 1021; economics and society in, 1051; national strike in, 1051. See also Ferry, Jules; First World War; Second World War

Francis II (Austria): Napoleon and, 714

Francis II (Habsburg): French war against, 706

Francis Ferdinand (Austro-Hungarian Empire), 892–893

Francis Joseph I (Austro-Hungarian Empire), 780, 844, 903

Franco, Francisco, 974

Franco-Prussian War, 832–833, 841, 888

Frankfurt: fighting in, 781(illus.)

Frankfurt Assembly, 763(illus.), 782; Jewish rights and, 845

Franklin, Benjamin, 695

Frederick VII (Denmark), 782
Frederick William III (Prussia), 715
Frederick William IV (Prussia), 781–782
Freedom(s): in revolutionary era, 691–693; under Napoleonic Code, 714; liberalism and, 762. *See also* Rights
"Free French" government, 980
Free love: Fourier on, 765
Free market: First World War and, 900; in postwar West Germany, 997; in former Soviet republics, 1042
French-Algerian war, 999
French Revolution, 692, 697–705, 755; Second, 706–708; legacies of, 720; women's rights and, 722–723, 723(illus.); industrialization and, 737
French Section of the Workers International, 846
Freud, Sigmund, 812, 928–929
Friedan, Betty, 1017
Fried Egg (Oldenburg), 1008(illus.)
Friedrich, Caspar David, 767(illus.)
Führer: Hitler as, 967
Fukuyama, Francis, 1042–1043
Fulton, Robert, 858
Functionalism: in architecture, 930
Fundamental Laws (Russia), 838

Gambetta, Léon, 841
Gapon (Father), 838
Garibaldi, Giuseppe, 828–829, 829(illus.)
Gas chambers, 979
Gassed (Sargent), 886(illus.)
Gauguin, Paul, 933
Gays, *see* Homosexuality and homosexuals
Gdansk Agreement, 1031
Gehry, Frank: Guggenheim Museum of, 1043(illus.)
Gender: division of labor by, 746–748, 807; women's fashion and, 800(illus.), 800–801, 801(illus.); family life and, 807–810. *See also* Men; Women
Generators, 813
Geneva Accords (1954), 1014
George III (England), 695
Georgia: separatists in, 1033
German Confederation, 714–715, 759, 782, 829; dissolution of, 830
German Democratic Republic, *see* East Germany
German Empire, 839–841, 888; Jews in, 845
German Revolution, 911–912
Germans: in Austria, 844
German Trade Union Congress, 849
German Workers' party: Hitler in, 967
Germany, 739(illus.), 1042; France and, 714, 841; Napoleon and, 714–715, 719; industrialization in, 736, 738, 739(illus.); *Zollverein* in, 739–740; Prussia and, 759; nationalism in, 764; unified state in, 782;

women in universities in, 807–808; unification of, 829–833, 832(map); socialism in, 839, 840–841, 846, 850; unions in, 849; migration from, 864, 865; Berlin Conference in, 871; Asia and, 872; German Empire and, 888; alliances and, 888–889; Triple Alliance and, 889; before First World War, 890–891, 894; aggression of, 894–895; rationing in, 900, 901(illus.); in First World War, 900–901, 904; Lenin and, 906; Russia and, 909; Treaty of Versailles and, 912–914, 937–938; reparations and, 914, 938; after First World War, 915, 915(map); existentialism in, 925; films in, 936; Western powers and, 937–939; inflation in, 938; Weimar Republic in, 938, 940; Dawes Plan and, 939; political divisions in, 940; Stresemann in, 941; Great Depression in, 943(map); Hitler and, 967–969; division of, 991; after Second World War, 994(map), 995; reunification of, 1040, 1051–1052; baby bust in, 1052; unemployment in, 1052. *See also* East Germany; First World War; German Empire; Nazi Germany; Prussia; Second World War; West Germany
Germinal (Zola), 816
Germ theory of disease, 791–792
Gestapo, 970
Ghana, 999(illus.)
Gibraltar, 714
Gioberti, Vincenzo, 828
Girls, *see* Women
Girondists (France), 706, 707, 708
Gladstone, William, 843
Glasnost (openness), 1033
Global capitalism, 1041
Global economy, 1042
Globalization: West and, 855–863; criticism of, 1057
Gnesotto, Nicole, 1056
GNP, *see* Gross National Product (GNP)
Goethe, Johann Wolfgang von, 768
Gold Coast, 999(illus.)
Goldhagen, Daniel, 979
Gold standard, 944, 946, 1018
Gorbachev, Mikhail, 1006, 1017, 1033(illus.); reforms of, 1028, 1032–1033; disintegration of Soviet Union and, 1038–1039; German unification and, 1040
Gorbachev, Raisa, 1032
Gotz von Berlichingen (Goethe), 768
Gouges, Olympe de, 705, 722–723
Gouze, Marie, *see* Gouges, Olympe de
Government: representative, 692; in U.S., 696–697; French, 704; liberals on, 762; Russian, 835; in Japan, 880; in First World War, 900; post-First World War democratic, 940–942; conservative authoritarian, 954; radical totalitarian, 954–957; in Nazi Germany, 969–970; after Second

World War, 997; spending by, 1020. *See also* specific countries
Goya, Francisco, 717(illus.)
Grains: mills and, 729
Grand Alliance: Second World War and, 971, 979–980
Grand Empire: of Napoleon, 715–718, 716(map)
Grand National Consolidated Trades Union, 749
Great Britain, *see* England (Britain)
Great Depression: in Britain, 943(map), 947–948; in France, 943(map), 947–948; in U.S., 943(map); economic crisis and, 943–944; unemployment in, 944–945; New Deal and, 945–946; Scandinavia and, 946–947; Hitler and, 967–968
Greater Germany, 972(map), 974
Greater Serbia: Milosevic and, 1047
Great Exposition (London, 1851), 733, 735(illus.)
Great Famine: in Ireland, 777
Great Fear (France), 702–703
Great Migration: from Europe, 863–868
"Great Patriotic War of the Fatherland," 980, 1001
Great Powers, 888, 888(illus.); Prussia and, 756(map), 833; at Congress of Vienna, 758; Greek independence and, 771–772
Great Rebellion (India), 878
Great Reforms: in Russia, 835
Great Russians: nationalism of, 1028
Great Trek (South Africa), 869
Great War, *see* First World War
Great Western Railway, 724(illus.)
Greece, 891, 892, 899, 954, 992; independence of, 771–772, 772(illus.); Second World War in, 975, 986; in European Economic Community, 1019
Greene, Graham, 926
Grimm, Jacob and Wilhelm, 770
Grimshaw, Atkinson, 800, 801(illus.)
Gropius, Walter, 930–931
Gross national product (GNP): in England, 734; developed nations and, 856
Guernica (Picasso), 934–935, 934–935(illus.)
Guggenheim Museum, Bilbao, Spain, 1043(illus.)
Guillotine: and French Revolution, 706
Gulf War, 1041, 1041(illus.)
Gypsies: Nazis and, 986; discrimination against, 1042

Habsburg dynasty: Austrian Empire of, 760(map), 761; Germans and, 760(map), 761; Hungary and, 760(map), 761; peoples under rule of, 760(map); 1848 revolutions and, 780. *See also* Austro-Hungarian Empire (Austria-Hungary)
Halévy, Elie, 954–955

Hancock, John, 695
Hardy, Thomas, 816
Hargreave, James, 728, 728(illus.)
Harkort, Fritz, 738, 741
Haussmann, Georges, 792
Havel, Václav, 1035–1036, 1037, 1037(illus.), 1047
Health: in cities, 789–790. *See also* Disease; Medicine; Public health movement
Heart of Darkness (Conrad), 877
Hébert, Jacques, 711
Hegel, Georg, 766
Heidegger, Martin, 925
Heine, Heinrich, 715
Heisenberg, Werner, 928
Helsinki Accord: on human rights, 1037
Helsinki Conference: Final Act of, 1015
Herzegovina, 891, 892
Herzl, Theodor, 846, 847, 847(illus.), 999
Hierarchy: urban social, 799(illus.)
Higher education: comparison in U.S. and Europe, 1012. *See also* Universities and colleges
Himmler, Heinrich, 970, 977
Hindenburg, Paul von, 899, 901, 969
Hindus: in India, 878–879, 879(illus.)
Hiroshima: atomic bombing of, 983, 983(illus.), 1006
Historians: on social conflict in pre-revolutionary France, 699; Eric Hobsbawm, 755; on nationalism, 763–764; Diana Crane, 801; Treitschke, 872–874; on origins of First World War, 894–895; on extermination of European Jews, 979
History: as dialectic process, 766
Hitler, Adolf, 846, 937, 966–967; rise to power, 940, 967–969; dictatorship of, 969–970; Nazi state and, 969–970; popularity of, 970–971; empire of (1939-1942), 975; New Order of, 977; suicide of, 983. *See also* Nazi Germany; Second World War
Hitler Youth, 968(illus.)
Hobsbawm, Eric, 755
Hobson, J. A., 876
Holland: France and, 714, 715; Second World War in, 975; constitutional monarchy in, 997. *See also* Netherlands
Holocaust, 978(illus.), 978–979, 986–987, 987(illus.); survivors in Israel, 999
Holstein, 782
Holy Alliance, 759
Holy Roman Empire. *See also* German Empire
Home front: in First World War, 900–902; in Russian civil war, 910
Home rule: for Ireland, 843, 844(illus.)
Homestead Act (1862), 834
Homosexuality and homosexuals: Nazis and, 986; activism of, 1018
Hong Kong, 860
Hoover, Herbert, 945

Household: women and, 808
House of Commons (England), 843
House of Commons, The, 1833 (Hayter), 775(illus.)
House of Lords (England), 843
Housing: of workers, 744; of middle class, 797; Soviet, 962; in postwar period, 1008
Hugo, Victor, 768, 771
Hull, Cordell, 991
Human Comedy, The (Balzac), 815
Humanitarian aid, 1056(illus.); EU and, 1056–1057
Human rights: Final Act of Helsinki Conference and, 1015, 1016; in EU policy, 1056–1057
Hunchback of Notre Dame (Hugo), 768
Hundred Days (France), 718, 777
Hungarians: as Magyars, 761
Hungary, 938, 991, 1052; revolutionaries in, 780; nationalism in, 844; republic of, 911; Treaty of Versailles and, 914; Second World War and, 975; revolution in, 1004; reform movement in, 1033; collapse of communism in, 1035; in NATO, 1046; economic reconstruction and civic institutions, 1047. *See also* Austro-Hungarian Empire (Austria-Hungary)
Hussein, Saddam, 1041
Huxley, Aldous, 926
Hygiene, *see* Sanitation

Iberian Peninsula, *see* Portugal; Spain
Ibo people, 875
Iceland: in European Economic Community, 1019
Id: in Freudian psychology, 929
Ideologies: revolts and, 755–782; conservatism as, 759–761; liberalism as, 761, 762; nationalism as, 762–764; romantic movement and, 766–770; 1848 revolutions and, 779
Illegal immigration: in western Europe, 1054
Illegitimacy: explosion in, 805; abandonment and, 810
Immigrants and immigration: from Ireland, 776; Jews and, 846; from Europe, 854(illus.), 863–868; origin and destination of, 866(illus.); from Asia, 867–868; growth into 21st century, 1054; illegal, 1054
Imperialism: Russian Revolution of 1905 and, 837; western, 868–882; Ferry's defense of, 884–885; Boer War and, 890; Treaty of Versailles and, 914. *See also* New imperialism
Imperialism (Hobson), 876
Impressionist art, 932
Income: lifestyle and, 796; growth of, 856(illus.); disparities in, 856–857. *See also* Wages
Independence: of U.S., 695–696; of Greece, 771–772, 772(illus.); of India, 878–879;

and decolonization in Asia and Africa, 998(map), 999–1000
India: industrialization and, 736; Britain and, 874(map); imperialism in, 878–879; soldiers from, 899, 899(illus.); independence in, 998(map), 999
Indian National Congress, 878
Indians (American), *see* American Indians
Individual rights: death penalty in EU and, 1057
Indochina: France in, 999
Indoctrination: through radio and movies, 937
Industrialization, 734–740, 737(map); capital and labor for, 740–749; urban society and, 787–795; middle classes and, 796, 797–798; working classes and, 799–805; family life and, 805–812; of Russia, 835–837; Soviet, 961; in eastern Europe, 1002. *See also* Factories; Industry; Labor; Workers
Industrial Revolution, 725–740; in England, 726–734, 734(map), 755; in continental Europe, 734–740; global inequity after, 856–857
Industry: growth of, 727; steam engine in, 731–732; population and, 733–734; working conditions in, 740–749; Russian, 835; accidents in, 840(illus.); in First World War, 900; British, 947. *See also* Factories; Industrial Revolution; Labor; Workers
Infant mortality, 810. *See also* Mortality
Infection, *see* Disease
Inflation: in Germany, 938, 941; in Russia, 1044
Inquiry into the Nature and Causes of the Wealth of Nations (Smith), 762
Intellectual thought: uncertainty in, 921–930; on dictatorships, 954–957; Soviet, 963, 1030; Nazi, 970; Beauvoir, existentialism, and, 1017, 1024–1025; on domestic peace and human rights, 1056(illus.), 1056–1057. *See also* Marxism
International Monetary Fund (IMF), 1042
International monetary system, 1018, 1019
International organizations: League of Nations as, 912; financial, 1042. *See also* United Nations
International relations, *see* Foreign policy
Internationals (communist): First, 846–848; Second, 850. *See also* Marxism
International style: of architecture, 930–931
International youth culture, 1011–1013
Interstate highway system: in U.S., 1001
Inventions, *see* Industrial Revolution; Technology
Investment: in industry, 740; European to 1914, 859(map), 859–860
Ipatescu, Ana, 754(illus.)

Iran, 992; fundamentalist Islamic revolution in, 1019; war with Iraq, 1041. *See also* Persia

Iraq, 914; Saddam Hussein and war with U.S., 1041, 1041(illus.); refugees from, 1054

Ireland: workers from, 746; Great Famine in, 775, 776–777, 843; England and, 843–844, 844(illus.); migration from, 865; Easter Rebellion in, 903; autonomy in southern, 942

Iron and iron industry: energy for, 730; coke in, 732; German, 739(illus.)

Iron curtain: speech by Churchill, 992; collapse of, 1035

Iron law of wages (Ricardo), 734

Isabey, J.-B., 769(illus.)

Islam: fundamentalist revolution in Iran, 1019

Ismail (Egypt), 862, 877

Isolationism: of U.S. after First World War, 916

Israel: Arab wars with, 999, 1019. *See also* Jews and Judaism; Palestine

Italy: France and, 714, 715, 825; Mazzini and, 784–785, 827–828; nationalism and unification in, 826–829; socialism in, 850; migration from, 864, 866; Triple Alliance and, 889; in First World War, 899; Treaty of Versailles and, 914; Mussolini and fascism in, 964–966; Ethiopia and, 974; Rome-Berlin Axis and, 974; Allied invasion of, 983; Christian Democrats in, 995; European unity and, 997; political recovery in, 997; feminists in, 1018, 1018(illus.). *See also* Rome (city)

Ivan the Terrible (movie), 1002(illus.)

Jacobins (France), 706

Jager, Hugo, 952(illus.)

Japan: industrialization in, 736; Russian war with, 837; trade with West, 861, 861(illus.); imperialism in, 868–869, 877, 879–880; in First World War, 899; Treaty of Versailles and, 914; Rome-Berlin Axis and, 974; Asian expansion of, 977; in Second World War, 977, 982(map), 982–983; atomic bombing of, 983; misery index for, 1019(illus.)

Jaruzelski, Wojciech, 1032

Jaspers, Karl, 925

Jaurès, Jean, 850

Java, 872

Jefferson, Thomas, 692, 695

Jehovah's Witnesses: Nazis and, 986

Jena: battle at, 715

Jewish State, The: .... (Herzl), 847

Jews and Judaism: in Russia, 835; modern anti-Semitism and, 839; Dreyfus affair and, 842, 842(illus.); emancipation of, 845; in eastern Europe, 846; Zionism and, 846, 847; migration from Europe, 865–866; immigrants in New York, 867(illus.); pogroms against, 913; national home in Palestine for, 914; in fascist Italy, 966; Nazis, Holocaust, and, 970, 978(illus.), 978–979, 986–987, 987(illus.); in Soviet Union, 1001. *See also* Anti-Semitism

Joad, Cyril, 926

Joffre, Joseph, 895

Johann of Austria, 763(illus.)

John Paul II (pope), 1030

Johnson, Lyndon B., 1001, 1014

Johnson, Samuel, 767

Joyce, James, 930

June Days (1848, France), 779

Junkers, 839

Justice. *See also* Law codes; Legislation

Kabul, 1057, 1058(illus.)

Kádár, János, 1035

Kafka, Franz, 930

Kandinsky, Wassily, 933

Kellogg, Frank B., 939

Kellogg-Briand Pact, 939

Kennedy, John F., 1001, 1007; Cuba and, 1004–1005; Vietnam and, 1014

Kerensky, Alexander, 905–906, 908

Kerouac, Jack, 1011

Keynes, John Maynard, 734, 938, 944

Khartoum: battle at, 871

Khedive, 862

Khrushchev, Nikita, 1002–1004, 1028; Cuba and, 1004–1005

Kiel: mutiny at, 911

Kierkegaard, Søren, 926

King, Martin Luther, Jr., 1001

Kingdom of the Two Sicilies, 759

Kings and kingdoms: divine right and, 700; in French Empire, 715–717, 716(map). *See also* Empires; Monarchs and monarchies; specific rulers and countries

Kinship: family life and, 807. *See also* Family

Kipling, Rudyard, 875, 877

Kirov, Sergei, 964

Kissinger, Henry, 1015

Kitchener, Horatio H., 871–872, 878

Klimt, Gustav, 787(illus.)

Koch, Robert, 792

Kohl, Helmut, 1017, 1040, 1051, 1052

Kollontai, Alexandra, 963

Korea: Japanese imperialism and, 880

Korean War, 993, 995, 1014

Kornilov, Lavr, 908

Kosovo: warfare in, 1047–1050; intervention in, 1057

Kosovo Liberation Army (KLA), 1049

Kristallnacht, 970

Kronstadt: sailors' rebellion in, 958

Kulaks: in Soviet Union, 960

Kulturkampf, 839

Kuwait: Iraqi invasion of, 1041

Labor: industrialization and, 740–749; sexual division of, 746–748; aristocracy of, 799, 802(illus.); of immigrants, 1054. *See also* Child labor; Labor movement; Labor unions

Labor movement: in England, 748–749

Labor strikes, *see* Strikes

Labor unions, 848–850; during First World War, 902; in Great Depression, 946; French, 948; Solidarity as, 1030–1032; in 1990s, 1042. *See also* Labor movement

Labouchère, Henry, 877

Labour party (Britain), 850, 942, 995, 999, 1020

Lafayette, marquis de (Marie-Joseph-Paul-Yves-Roch-Gilbert du Motier de), 695, 697, 702, 703

Laissez faire doctrine, 762

Lake Shore Apartments (Mies van der Rohe), 931

Lamarck, Jean Baptiste, 814

Lamartine, Alphonse-Marie-Louis de Prat, 768

Land: in cities, 789. *See also* Agriculture; Farms and farming

Languages: Magyar, 844

Lateran Agreement, 966

Latin America: Spain and, 759; military dictatorships in, 954

Latvia, 954

Law(s), *see* Law codes; Legislation

Law codes: Civil Code of France (1804), 712

Law of wages (Ricardo), 734

Lawrence, Thomas, 761(illus.)

Lawrence of Arabia, 899

Laws (scientific): law of conservation of energy, 812–813

League of Armed Neutrality, 695

League of Nations, 914, 915, 916; mandates, 914, 999; Germany and, 939, 971; Italy, Ethiopia, and, 974

Learning, *see* Intellectual thought

Lebanon, 914; decolonization and, 999

Le Chambon: during Second World War, 979, 981

Le Corbusier, 931

Legal orders: in France, 698–699, 703–704

Legislation: feminist movement and, 1017–1018

Legislative Assembly (France), 706; Louis XVI and, 706

Lehmus, Emilie, 809

Leisure: working-class, 804; in postwar period, 1009

Lélia (Sand), 770

Lenin, Vladimir Ilyich, 905, 937; Bolshevik Revolution and, 906–908; formation of government by, 909–910; dictatorship and, 955; Soviet economy and, 957–959

Leningrad: siege of, 977

Lenin Shipyards (Poland): strike in, 1030–1031

Leo XIII (Pope), 842

Leonardo da Vinci, 933

Leopold II (Belgium): Africa and, 869, 871(illus.)

Lesbians, *see* Homosexuality and homosexuals

Les Demoiselles d'Avignon (Picasso), 934–935, 934–935(illus.)

Leseur, Pierre Antoine, 690(illus.)

Lewis, C. S., 926

Lexington: fighting at, 695

Liberalism, 762; classical, 692, 697; Metternich on, 761; nationalism and, 764; reform in England and, 773–776; Prussian, 830, 831; compared with totalitarianism, 956

Liberalization: in former Soviet Union, 1044–1046; in eastern Europe, 1046–1047

Liberal party (Britain), 942

Liberty: in revolutionary era, 691–693

Liberty Leading the People (Delacroix), 770

Liberty party (England), 843

Liebknecht, Karl, 903, 912

Liège: industry in, 738

Life expectancy: decline in Russian, 1045. *See also* Mortality

"Life Is Everywhere" (Yaroshenko), 816(illus.)

Lifestyle: social class and, 796–804; of workers, 849; Soviet, 961–963, 1002; in 1970s and 1980s, 1020–1021. *See also* Standard of living

Lightning war, *see* Blitzkrieg (lightning war)

Lincoln, Abraham, 833, 834(map)

List, Friedrich, 739, 836, 865

Lister, Joseph, 792

Liszt, Franz, 770, 771(illus.)

Literature: realism in, 815–817; in Age of Anxiety, 929–930; stream-of-consciousness technique in, 929–930; anti-utopian, 930; de-Stalinization and, 1004; feminist, 1017. *See also* Historians; History

Lithuania: reform in, 1038

Little Entente, 938

Lloyd George, David, 843, 890, 902, 912, 912(illus.)

Locarno agreements, 939, 941, 971

Locke, John, 692

Locomotives, 732

Lodge, Henry Cabot, 915

Logical empiricism, 925

Lombardy, 758, 826; Sardinia and, 828

London: Great Exhibition in, 733, 735(illus.); blitz of, 977(illus.)

Lorraine, 841, 895

Louis XV (France), 697

Louis XVI (France), 704, 705, 705(illus.); Estates General and, 699–700; death of, 706

Louis XVIII (France, Bourbon dynasty), 718, 757, 759; Constitutional Charter of, 718, 762, 777

Louis Philippe (France), 777, 778–780

Low, David, 974(illus.)

Low Countries: at Congress of Vienna, 758. *See also* Netherlands

Lower classes: in postwar period, 1008

Lower middle class, 797

Loyalists: and American Revolution, 695

Luddites, 742

Ludendorff, Erich, 899, 901, 911

Lueger, Karl, 846, 967

Lunéville, Treaty of, 714

Lusitania (passenger ship), 900

Luxembourg: European unity and, 997

Luxemburg, Rosa, 895, 912, 913

Lyell, Charles, 814, 815

Lyrical Ballads (Wordsworth and Coleridge), 768

Maastricht treaty, 1051

MacArthur, Douglas, 993

MacDonald, Ramsay, 942, 947

Macedonia: intervention in, 1057

MacMahon, Marshall, 841

Madame Bovary (Flaubert), 816

Madrid, 795(illus.)

Magyars, 761, 844. *See also* Hungary

Malthus, Thomas, 734, 815

Management: as profession, 797

Manchester, England: industrialization in, 730(illus.)

Manchu Dynasty (China), 860

Mandates: of League of Nations, 914, 999

Manorial rights, 698

Manufacturing: factories and, 727–728. *See also* Textile industry

Marcel, Gabriel, 926

March on Washington (1963), 1000(illus.)

Marconi, Guglielmo, 937

Marie Antoinette (France), 703, 705, 705(illus.)

Maritain, Jacques, 926

Market(s): worldwide, 857–860

Marne: First Battle of, 895, 898(map); Second Battle of, 911

Marriage: Fourier on, 765; premarital sex and, 805; relationships in, 808–810; of teachers in France, 841–842; in postwar period, 1009; in 1970s and 1980s, 1021; feminist critique of, 1024–1025

Married women: in work force, 1009, 1010, 1011(illus.)

Marshall, Alfred, 813

Marshall, George C., 992

Marshall Plan, 992, 995, 997

Marx, Karl, 742, 765(illus.), 813; socialism and, 765–766, 824

Marxism, 846–850; class-consciousness and, 740; women and, 808; German, 840; Lenin and, 906; Luxemburg and, 913; Sorel and, 924–925

Marxism-Leninism, 963. *See also* Lenin, Vladimir Ilyich; Marxism; Soviet Union

Massacre at Chios (Delacroix), 772(illus.)

Mass communications: youth culture and, 1011

Mass transportation, 795(illus.); urban planning and, 792–795

Master race: of Hitler, 975

Masurian Lakes: Battle of, 899

Materialism: in postwar period, 1020

Mathematics, *see* Science

Matisse, Henri, 933

Matteotti, Giacomo, 965

May Day, 848, 848(illus.)

Mazzini, Giuseppe, 764, 827–828; democratic nationalism of, 784–785, 785(illus.)

McDonald, Daniel, 776(illus.)

Médecins Sans Frontières (Doctors Without Borders), 1056(illus.)

Medicine: antiseptic principle and, 792; women in, 809; advances in, 812. *See also* Disease

Meiji Restoration (Japan), 879–880

Mein Kampf (Hitler), 940, 967, 968

Melba, Nellie, 937

Men: division of labor and, 746–748

Mendeleev, Dmitri, 813

Mengele, Josef (Angel of Death), 987

Mensheviks, 906

Mental illness: Nazis and, 986

Methodism, 804

Metric system: French, 704

Metternich, Klemens von, 718, 758, 759–761, 761(illus.), 771; 1848 revolutions and, 780

Mexico: U.S. and, 833

Miasmatic theory of disease, 791

Michelet, Jules, 764

Michnik, Adam, 1062–1063, 1063(illus.)

Middle classes: French, 698; liberalism of, 762; in England, 775–776; industrialization and, 796, 797–798; feminists in, 807; children of, 811; youth and sexuality among, 821; German, 831; Russian, 838; Jews in, 845; in Nazi Germany, 970–971; in postwar period, 1007–1008

Middle East: Alliance System and, 889; decolonization and independence in, 998(map), 999

Middlemarch: A Study of Provincial Life (Eliot), 816

Midlands (England), 734(map)

Midway Island: Battle of, 982

Mies van der Rohe, Ludwig, 931

Migration: Irish, 776; European, 854(illus.), 863–868; vs. immigration, 865; migrant characteristics, 865–866, 866(illus.); Asian, 867–868; rural, 1008; in 1990s, 1054

Military: Russian, 835, 1045–1046; imperialism and, 875; in Second World War, 979. *See also* Armed forces; specific battles and wars

Mill, John Stuart, 843

Mills: cotton, 728, 744–746, 745(illus.); for grain, 729. *See also* Water mills

Milosevic, Slobodan, 1047–1050

Mines Act (1842), 748, 752, 753(illus.)

Mines and mining: coal and, 730–731; sexual division of labor and, 748; child labor in, 752–753

Minorities: in Austrian Empire, 780; in Russia, 837–838, 1033

Misery index, 1019, 1019(illus.)

Missions and missionaries: imperialism and, 875–876, 876(illus.). *See also* Christianity

Mitterrand, François, 1020; EU and, 1051

Mobilization: First World War and, 893, 894, 900–902

Modern art, 931–933

Moltke, Helmuth von, 894

Mona Lisa (Leonardo da Vinci): dadaist reproduction of, 933

Monarchs and monarchies: French, 703–704, 718; English, 726; Austrian, 780. *See also* specific rulers

Monet, Claude, 733, 932

Monetary union: Maastricht treaty and, 1051

Monnet, Jean, 997

Monopolies: in Russia, 1044

Montesquieu, baron de (Charles-Louis de Secondat), 692, 696

Moon: landings on, 1007

Morality: of middle class, 798; Nietzsche and, 924

Moratorium: on German reparations, 938

Morocco, 890, 983

Mortality: decline in, 791, 791(illus.). *See also* Infant mortality

Moscow: Napoleon and, 718, 719(illus.). *See also* Russia

Mothers: role of, 811–812; in postwar period, 1009

Mountain, the (France), 706, 707, 708

Movies: after First World War, 936–937

Mozambique, 869

Mr., Mrs., and Baby (Droz), 808

Muhammad Ali (general), 862

Multinational corporations, 1042

Munch, Edvard, 928(illus.)

Munich: Hitler's uprising in, 940, 967

Munich Conference, 975

Music: romantic, 770; modern, 933; rock, 1011

Music halls, 798(illus.), 804

Muslims: and British in Africa, 871–872; in India, 878–879, 879(illus.); in former Yugoslavian states, 1049(map), 1049–1050; as immigrants, 1054. *See also* Islam

Mussolini, Benito, 937, 954, 964–966, 966(illus.), 971, 974, 983

Mutual defense pact: French-Polish, 938

My Secret Life, 806

Nagasaki: atomic bombing of, 983, 1006

Nahon, Marco, 986–987

Nanking: Treaty of, 860

Naples, 778, 827

Napoleon I (Napoleon Bonaparte), 712–714, 715(illus.); empire of, 715–718; Jakob Walter and, 719; Egypt and, 862

Napoleon III (Louis Napoleon), 780, 822(illus.); Paris and, 792; nationalism and, 823–825; Sardinia and, 828; social issues and, 841

Napoleonic Code, 712, 714, 807

Napoleonic Era, 713

Napoleonic Ideas (Napoleon III), 824

Napoleonic wars, 714–718; peace settlement after, 757–761

Nasmyth, James: steam hammer of, 731(illus.)

Nasser, Gamal Abdel, 1003

Nast, Thomas, 814(illus.)

Natal, 869

Nation, *see* State (nation)

National Assembly (France), 702, 703–704, 706; Estates General as, 700; Napoleon III and, 824–825; after Franco-Prussian War, 841; Ferry's speech to, 884–885

National Assembly (Frankfurt), 782

National Convention (France), 706, 707, 708, 712; Thermidorian reaction and, 711

National health systems, 1008

Nationalism, 762–764, 763(illus.), 875; French, 708, 823–825; economic, 740; Irish, 777, 843–844; Czech, 780; democratic, 784–785; Italian, 784–785, 826–829; in U.S., 833–835; Russian, 836, 837–838; Bismarck and, 839; Magyar, 844; socialism and, 846; Zionism as, 847; Egyptian, 862; Indian, 878; Balkan, 891–893; First World War and, 895, 904; of Hitler, 967, 971; European unity and, 997; Great Russian, 1028; in 1990s, 1043–1044; eastern European, 1047

Nationalization: during Russian civil war, 910

National Labor Relations Act, 946

National Liberals (Germany), 839

National Organization for Women (NOW), 1017

National Recovery Administration (NRA), 946

National socialism: in Germany, 967

National Socialist German Workers' party, 940, 967. *See also* Nazi Germany

National states: 1871-1914, 838–846

National System of Political Economy (List), 739

Nation-states: nationalism and, 763–764

Native Americans, *see* American Indians

NATO, 992, 995; France and, 997; Poland, Hungary, and Czech Republic in, 1046, 1047; Russia and, 1046; Bosnia and, 1049; Yugoslavia and, 1050

Naturalism, *see* Realism

Natural selection, *see* Darwin, Charles

Nature: romanticism and, 767–768, 770

Nature and the Meaning of Life (Friedrich), 767(illus.)

Navarino: battle at, 772

Navy: British, 890; German, 890, 891(illus.); in Second World War, 982–983

Nazi Germany, 937, 952(illus.), 956(illus.), 957; Hitler and, 966–971; Jews in, 970; Second World War and, 971–983, 972(map); Rome-Berlin Axis and, 974; empire of, 975–979; New Order and, 977–978; Allied invasion of, 983. *See also* Second World War

Nazi Labor Front, 970

Nazism: defined, 967

Nazi-Soviet nonaggression pact, 975

Necker, Jacques, 769

Nehru, Jawaharlal, 1003

Nelson, Horatio: at Trafalgar, 714

Neocolonialism, 1000

NEP, *see* New Economic Policy (NEP)

Netherlands: First Coalition and, 706; European unity and, 997. *See also* Holland

Neutrality: of Belgium, 894

Neutron, 927

Newcomen, Thomas, 731

"New conservatism": of Bismarck, 833

New Deal, 945–946

New Economic Policy (NEP), 958, 959

New imperialism, 855, 869; of Leopold (Belgium), 869, 871(illus.); Rhodes and, 869, 873, 873(illus.); in Africa, 870(map); in Asia, 872, 874(map); causes of, 872–876; critics of, 876–877

New Lanark, 746

New Order: of Hitler, 977–978

Newspapers: of working class, 749

New world order: George H. W. Bush and, 1041

New York (city): Jewish immigrants in, 867(illus.); World Trade Center attack in, 1057

New Zealand, 899

Nice, France, 828

Nicholas I (Russia): 1848 revolutions and, 780

Nicholas II (Russia), 838, 894, 905–906

Nietzsche, Friedrich, 924, 924(illus.)

Nigeria, 875

Nile River region, 871

1984 (Orwell), 930

Nivelle, Robert, 896, 903

Nixon, Richard: Vietnam War and, 1014–1015

Nkrumah, Kwame, 999(illus.)

Nobility: French, 698, 699, 703–704

Normandy invasion, 980(illus.), 983

North Africa: France and, 871; Second World War in, 983; French-Algerian war in, 999; immigrants from, 1054

North America, *see* Canada; Mexico; United States

North Atlantic Treaty Organization (NATO), *see* NATO

Northern Alliance: in Afghanistan, 1057

North German Confederation, 830

North Korea: invasion of South Korea, 993

North Vietnam: Vietnam War and, 1014–1015

Norway: women in, 838; nationalism in, 844; socialism in, 946; Second World War in, 975; constitutional monarchy in, 997. *See also* Scandinavia

Novels, *see* Literature

NOW, *see* National Organization for Women (NOW)

Nuclear power: French nuclear weapons, 997; Soviet arms buildup, 1005; U.S./Soviet agreement on, 1040

Nurses, 798

Nursing of children, 810

Nutrition: in 1970s and 1980s, 1020–1021

Oath of the Tennis Court, 700, 701(illus.)

Occupation zones: after Second World War, 991, 994(map), 995

October Manifesto (Russia), 838

Oedipal conflict, 812

OEEC, *see* Organization of European Economic Cooperation (OEEC)

Oil and oil industry: energy crisis and, 1018–1019; Islamic revolution in Iran and, 1019; oil shocks in, 1019, 1021, 1030

Oldenburg, Claes, 1008(illus.)

Omdurman: battle of, 871

One Day in the Life of Ivan Denisovich (Solzhenitsyn), 1004

On Germany (Staël), 768, 769

On Liberty (Mill), 843

On the Origin of Species by the Means of Natural Selection (Darwin), 815

On the Road (Kerouac), 1011

OPEC: energy crisis and, 1019

Operation Desert Storm, 1041, 1041(illus.)

Opium trade, 860

Orders, *see* Legal orders

Organic chemistry, 813

Organization of European Economic Cooperation (OEEC), 997

Organization of Petroleum Exporting Countries (OPEC), *see* OPEC

Organization of Work (Blanc), 765

Orphans, 729. *See also* Abandoned children

Orwell, George, 930, 950

Ottoman Empire, 892(map); nationalism in, 844, 891–892; as sick man of Europe, 889; end of, 899. *See also* Ottoman Turks

Ottoman Turks: Greece and, 771; Egypt and, 862

Owen, Robert, 746, 749, 849

Pacific region: World War II in, 977, 982(map), 982–983

Paganini, Nicolo, 771

Paine, Thomas, 695

Painting: of railroads, 733; romantic, 767(illus.), 767–768, 770; modern, 932

Palermo, 828

Palestine: Jewish homeland in, 846, 847, 914, 999. *See also* Arab-Israeli wars

Panama Canal, 859

Pankhurst, Emmeline, 838

Papacy: Italy and, 827. *See also* Christianity; Roman Catholic Church

Papal infallibility doctrine, 839

Papal States: Italian unification and, 828

Paris: in 1848, 778–779; modernization of, 792, 794(map), 824; apartment living in, 793(illus.); prostitution in, 806, 806(illus.); in Second Empire, 826(illus.); intellectuals and artists in, 940; rebellion in, 1012–1013, 1013(illus.). *See also* Paris, Treaty of

Paris, Treaty of: 1783, 696

Paris Accord, 1040

Paris Commune (1871), 841

Parliament: Prussian, 830; in North German Confederation, 831

Parliament (England): American Revolution and, 694; reforms and, 843. *See also* England (Britain)

Passchendaele: battle at, 896

Pasternak, Boris, 1004

Pasteur, Louis, 791–792, 812

Patriotism: German, 938; Soviet, 1028. *See also* Nationalism

Paupers: as workers, 744

Peace: First World War and, 911–916; search for, 937–942; Kellogg-Briand Pact and, 939; Paris Accord and, 1040

Peaceful coexistence policy, 1004

Pearl Harbor: Japanese attack on, 977, 979

Peasants: French, 703, 707–708; in Ireland, 776; Soviet, 958, 959–961, 960(illus.). *See also* Serfs and serfdom

Peel, Robert, 775

Pennsylvania: September 11, 2001, terrorist attack in, 1057

Pensions: German, 839–840

Pentagon: terrorist attack on, 1057

People, The (Michelet), 764

People's Budget, 843, 890

People's Charter of 1838 (England), 775

People's Republic of China, *see* China

Père Goriot, Le (Balzac), 815–816

Pereire, Isaac and Emile, 740

Perestroika (restructuring), 1032–1033

Périer, Casimir, 777

Perry, Matthew, 861

Persia, 890

Persian Gulf region, 1016

Personal computer, 1042

Peru, 867

Pétain, Henri-Philippe, 903, 975

Peterloo: Battle of, 773

Petrograd: demonstrations in, 908(illus.)

Petrograd Soviet, 906, 908

Philippines, 872

Philosophes, 813

Philosophy: in Age of Anxiety, 924–925; existentialism and, 925; logical empiricism in, 925. *See also* Intellectual thought

Physically disabled: activism of, 1018

Physicians: women as, 809. *See also* Medicine

Physics: thermodynamics and, 812–813; after First World War, 926–928, 927(illus.)

Picasso, Pablo, 933, 934–935, 934–935(illus.)

Pickford, Mary, 936

Piedmont, 826

Pietism, 804

Pissarro, Camille, 932

Pius VII (Pope), 715(illus.); Napoleon I and, 714

Pius IX (Pope), 828, 839

Planck, Max, 926

Planned economy: in France, 708. *See also* Five-year plans

Planting of a Liberty Tree, The (Leseur), 690

Plants: energy from, 729

Plays and playwrights, *see* Theater

Poets and poetry: romantic, 768, 770

Pogroms, 846, 913

Poincaré, Raymond, 938

Poland, 914, 1005, 1033, 1052; and Congress of Vienna, 758, 758(illus.), 759; revolution in (1846), 778; Treaty of Versailles and, 914; Nazis and, 972(map), 975; Second World War in, 978; Yalta Conference and, 991–992; after Second World War, 994(map), 995; de-Stalinization and, 1004; West Germany, détente, and, 1015, 1016(illus.); Solidarity movement in, 1030–1032, 1031(illus.), 1035, 1062–1063; martial law in, 1032; in NATO, 1046; economy and institutions in, 1047

Polish people: in Austria, 844

Political parties: in England, 775(illus.); in German Empire, 839. *See also* specific parties

Political stability: after First World War, 937–942

Politics: liberty and equality in, 691–693; women in (France), 704; economy and, 755; search for peace and stability in, 940–942; Hitler and, 969; feminists and, 1017–1018; Soviet, 1028; Gorbachev and, 1033; in 1990s, 1042–1043; Russian, 1045

Poorhouses, 744

Poor Laws (England), 773, 791

Pop art, 1008(illus.)

Pope(s), *see* Papacy; specific popes

Popp, Adelheid, 852–853

Popular Front (France), 948

Popular sovereignty: after collapse of Soviet Union, 1047

Population: industry and, 733–734; in Ireland, 776–777; European migration and, 863–864; growth of, 864(illus.), 1009, 1028–1029; baby boom and, 1009, 1011; decline of, 1009, 1052–1054. *See also* Cities and towns; Urban society

Portugal: Africa and, 869; in European Economic Community, 1019

Positivist method, 813–814

Postimpressionist art, 932–933

Potato: Irish famine and, 775, 776–777; blight in, 776(illus.), 777

Potsdam Conference, 992

Poverty: revolt of poor in France, 700–703; Industrial Revolution and, 729–730; of working-class women, 747; wealth and, 796–804, 860; illegitimacy and, 805; in Third World, 856; First World War and, 902; in Great Depression, 944; war on, 1001; in global economy, 1042; feminization of, 1054

Power loom, 729

Power plants: steam power and, 732

Prague, 780

Pregnancy: marriage and, 805

Premarital sex, 805

Presley, Elvis, 1011

Priests and priesthood, *see* Clergy; Papacy

Principle of uncertainty, 928

Privatization: of state-controlled enterprises, 1042; in former Soviet Union, 1044

Production: industrial, 727–728; Great Depression and, 944

Professions: management as, 797; of middle class, 797–798

Prokofiev, Sergei, 1001

Proletariat: Marx on, 766

Propaganda: in First World War, 902–903; Mussolini and, 966(illus.)

Property ownership: in postwar period, 1007

Property rights: for women, 807

Prosperity: international youth culture and, 1011–1012

Prostitution, 806, 806(illus.); of female illegal immigrants, 1054; in Netherlands, 1057

Protective tariff: *Zollverein* and, 739–740; in Germany, 839

Protestantism: in Ireland, 776, 843; in Germany, 839; Christian existentialism in, 926

Protests: student, 1012; against Vietnam War, 1012, 1014, 1014(illus.); re-Stalinization and, 1028

Proudhon, Pierre Joseph, 765

Proust, Marcel, 929

Provisional government: in Russia, 905–906, 909

Prussia, 718; Declaration of Pillnitz and, 705–706; war against France, 706–707; Napoleon and, 715; industrialization in, 738, 739(illus.); as Great Power, 756(map), 758; at Congress of Vienna, 758, 759; Holy Alliance and, 759; Frankfurt assembly and, 763(illus.), 782; France and, 825; Germany and, 829; Bismarck and, 830; parliament in, 830; Franco-Prussian War and, 832–833. *See also* Germany

Psychiatry and psychology: family dynamics and, 812; Freudian, 928–929; clinical, 929

Public health movement, 791–792

Public opinion: Napoleon III and, 825; before First World War, 891; Soviet education and, 1030, 1030(illus.)

Public transportation, *see* Mass transportation

Public works programs: of Hitler, 970. *See also* New Deal

Puddling furnace, 732

Punch (magazine): on urban conditions, 790(illus.)

Purges: in Soviet Union, 963–964, 1001

Pushkin, Aleksander, 770

Putin, Vladimir, 1045, 1046

Putting-out system, 738

Qing (Manchu) Dynasty (China), 860, 882

Quadruple Alliance, 718, 757–759

Queens, *see* Monarchs and monarchies; specific queens

Race and racism: in India, 878; Hitler and, 967, 977–979; immigration and, 1054, 1055(illus.)

Racial imperialism: in New Order, 977–978

Racial segregation: apartheid as, 873

Radar, 1006

Radical ideas: liberalism and, 762; nationalism and, 762–764; socialism and, 764–766, 840–841, 849

Radio: after First World War, 937

Radium, 926

Railroads, 859; in England, 732–733; bridges for, 733(illus.); in Belgium, 738; Prussian, 739; in Russia, 836–837; trade and, 858

Rasputin, Grigori, 905, 905(illus.)

Rathenau, Walter, 900–901

Rationing: in First World War, 900–901, 904

Raw materials: world market for, 859; rationing of, 901

Reagan, Ronald, 1016–1017, 1020, 1033

Realism, 945(illus.); in literature, 815–817

Rebellions: in India, 878; in China, 881; Easter Rebellion (Ireland), 903. *See also* Revolts; Revolution(s)

Reception Room in the Brothel on the Rue des Moulins (Toulouse-Lautrec), 806(illus.)

Recovery programs: postwar, 995–997

Recreation, *see* Leisure

Recycling: in First World War, 901

Red Army, 959, 991, 992, 1002

Reds: in Russian civil war, 910

Red Shirts: of Garibaldi, 828

Reflections on the Revolution in France (Burke), 705

Reform(s): by Napoleon, 714; in England, 773–776; Meiji (Japan), 879–880; in China, 882; in France, 948; after Second World War, 995; in U.S., 1000–1001; in Soviet Union, 1002–1004; in postwar period, 1008; Solidarity movement and, 1030–1032, 1035; Gorbachev and, 1033; 1989 revolutions and, 1034–1037

Reform Bill of 1832 (England), 773–774

Refrigerated ships, 859

Refugees: after Second World War, 994(map), 995; in Serbian civil war, 1049; migration to western Europe, 1054

Reichstag (Germany), 839–841; Social Democrats in, 841; socialists in, 846; in First World War, 904; Hitler and, 969

Reign of Terror, in France, 708–711, 710(illus.)

Relief programs: in New Deal, 946

Religion: in France, 704; in French Revolution, 711–712; Napoleon I and, 713–714; in Ireland, 776; working-class, 804–805; positivism and, 813–814; imperialism and, 875–876, 876(illus.); revival of, 925–926

Remarque, Erich, 896, 897

Remembrance of Things Past (Proust), 929

Renoir, Pierre Auguste, 932

Reparations, 914; Germany and, 938, 941; moratorium on, 938; Dawes Plan for, 939

Representative government, 692, 762; American Revolution and, 694–695

Republic: democratic, 779(illus.); in China, 882; postwar, 997. *See also* France

Republicanism: in France, 778, 841–842

Research: and development (R&D), 813; during and after Second World War, 1006–1007

Re-Stalinization, 1004, 1028

Restoration: of Bourbon dynasty, 718, 757, 759

Return of the Native, The (Hardy), 816

Reunification, *see* Unification

Revisionism, 849–850

Revolts: Boston Tea Party and, 694(illus.); of poor in France, 700–703; ideology and, 755–782; in Italy, 828; Paris Commune as, 841

Revolution(s): in U.S., 693–697; French, 697–705, 777; Russian, 754(illus.), 837(illus.), 837–838, 890, 904–910, 909;

Revolution(s) (*cont.*)
in Greece, 771–772; of 1848, 774, 778–782; in Austria, 780; in Hungary, 780, 1004; socialist, 846–848; in China (1912), 882; German, 911–912, 938; administrative, 916; of Solidarity, 1031; of 1989, 1034(map), 1034–1037; Velvet Revolution, 1035–1036, 1047; in computers and electronics, 1042. *See also* Industrial Revolution
Revolutionaries: German, 841
Revolutionary terror, 910
Rhineland, 707, 708; French occupation of, 938; Hitler in, 972
Rhodes, Cecil, 869, 873, 873(illus.)
Rhodesia, 869
Ricardo, David, 734, 766
Riefenstahl, Leni, 937
Rights: of women, 807, 963; social, 922
Riots: in Russia, 905
Rite of Spring, The (Stravinsky), 933
Rivers: transportation and, 726
Road to Wigan Pier, The (Orwell), 950–951
Roberts, Robert, 902
Robespierre, Maximilien, 704, 706, 711(illus.); Reign of Terror and, 708; Thermidorian reaction and, 711
Rocket (locomotive), 732
Rock music, 1011
Rolling mills, 732
Roman Catholic church: in France, 704, 712, 841; Napoleon I and, 713–714; in Ireland, 776, 843; in Germany, 839; Dreyfus affair and, 842; Christian existentialism in, 926. *See also* Christianity; Church; Papacy; Religion
Romania, 772, 891–892, 914, 938, 954, 1005; Second World War and, 975; anti-Communist revolution in, 1036; postcommunist transition in, 1047
Romanians, 780, 844
Romantic movement, 766–770; painting of, 767(illus.), 767–768, 770; literature of, 768–770; heroes of, 771(illus.); realism and, 815
Rome (city): Italian unification and, 828–829; Treaty of, 997
Rome-Berlin Axis, 974
Roosevelt, Franklin D., 937, 979, 1006; New Deal of, 945–946; Yalta and, 990(illus.), 991–992; Teheran and, 990–991
Rossini, Gioacchino, 771
Rousseau, Jean-Jacques, 766; on education of children, 704
Roux, Jacques, 708
Royalty, *see* Kings and kingdoms; Monarchs and monarchies; specific rulers
Ruhr crisis, 938, 939(illus.), 941
Rule by decree: in Germany, 969
Rural areas, *see* Farms and farming

Russia, 714; Napoleon and, 714, 715, 718; at Congress of Vienna, 758; Holy Alliance and, 759; poetry in, 770; Greece and, 772; literary realism in, 816; modernization of, 835–838; terrorism in, 836(illus.); 1905 revolution in, 837(illus.), 837–838; pogroms in, 846; Jews and, 865–866; imperialism of, 872; alliances and, 888–889, 890; Balkans and, 892; before First World War, 894; fall of Romanovs in, 904–905; peace settlement with Germany, 909; Constituent Assembly in, 910; after August, 1991, 1039(map); in 1990s, 1044–1046, 1045(illus.), 1046(illus.). *See also* First World War; Second World War; Soviet Union
Russian Federation, 1038–1039
Russian-French Alliance, 888(illus.), 890
Russian-German Reinsurance Treaty (1887), 889, 890
Russian Revolution (1905), 890
Russian Revolution (1917), 906–909, 913, 965; provisional government and, 905–906; chronology of, 907(illus.); Trotsky and, 908–909. *See also* Lenin, Vladimir Ilyich
Russo-Japanese War (1904-1905), 837
Rutherford, Ernest, 927
Rwanda: refugees from, 1054

SA, *see* Storm troopers (SA)
St. Helena: Napoleon on, 718
Saint-Simon, Henri de (socialist), 764, 765, 813
Salons: during romantic movement, 769
Saltash Bridge, 732(illus.)
Samurai, 879
Sand, George (Amandine Aurore Lucie Dupin), 768–770, 771
Sanitation: in cities, 789–790; public health movement and, 791–792
Sans-culottes, 707(illus.), 707–708
Sardinia, 826; Cavour in, 828
Sardinia-Piedmont, 828
Sargent, John Singer, 886(illus.)
Sartre, Jean-Paul, 925, 1017, 1024
Sasson, Siegfried, 896
Savery, Thomas, 731
Savoy: France and, 828
Saxony, 759
Scandinavia: Great Depression and, 946–947
Schacht, Hjalmar, 970
Schleswig-Holstein, 830
Schlieffen, Alfred von, 894
Schlieffen plan, 894, 895
Scholarship, *see* Intellectual thought
Schönberg, Arnold, 933
Schools: French, 841. *See also* Education; Universities and colleges
Schuman, Robert, 997

Science: germ theory of disease, 791–792; before World War I, 812–815; social science and, 813–815; evolution and, 814–815; new physics, 926–928, 927(illus.); in postwar period, 1006–1007; computer revolution in, 1020. *See also* Philosophy
Scientists: Soviet, 1029–1030
Scott, Walter, 768
Second Balkan War, 892
Second Coalition, 714
Second Continental Congress, 695
Second Empire (France), 824–825, 826(illus.), 832–833
Second estate (France), 698
Second International, 850, 913
Second Revolution (France), 706–708
Second Sex, The (Beauvoir), 1017, 1024–1025
Second World War: German expansion and appeasement, 971–975, 972(map); in Europe, 975–979, 976(map); in Pacific region, 977, 982(map), 982–983; Le Chambon and, 979, 981; Grand Alliance in, 979–980; Normandy invasion, 980(illus.), 983; in Soviet Union, 980–982; atomic bombings in, 983, 983(illus.); end of, 983; in North Africa, 983; Big Three conferences during, 990(illus.), 990–992; results in Europe, 994(map); research during, 1006
Secularism: of working classes, 804; Darwin and, 815
Security Council, 1041
Sedan: battle at, 833, 841
Self-determination, 1047; Russia and, 835; Treaty of Versailles and, 914; after Second World War, 997
Sennett, Mack, 936
Separate spheres concept, 747, 807, 808
Separatism: in former Yugoslavia, 1047
September 11, 2001: terrorist attacks on U.S., 1052, 1057
Serbia, 891–892, 899; war declared on, 893; as Yugoslavia, 911; Milosevic and warfare in, 1047–1050; ethnic composition of, 1049(map); NATO bombing of, 1050
Serbian people, 780, 844; in former Yugoslavian states, 1047–1048, 1048(map); Bosnian, 1049
Serfs and serfdom: in Austria, 780; in Russia, 835. *See also* Peasants
Servants: of middle class, 798; domestic, 802–803, 803(illus.). *See also* Peasants
Service economy: women and, 1009
Seven Years' War: American Revolution and, 694; France and, 695
Sewer system: in Paris, 792. *See also* Sanitation
Sex and sexuality: premarital sex and, 805; of women, 808–810; child rearing and, 811–812; Freud on, 812, 929; of middle class,

820–821; counterculture and, 1011. *See also* Homosexuality and homosexuals

Sexism: women and, 1010; feminist movement and, 1017

Sexual division of labor, 746–748

Ships and shipping: British, 858(illus.); refrigerated ships and, 859; German battleships, 890, 891(illus.); in First World War, 900

Shock therapy: in Poland, 1035; in former Soviet Union, 1044–1046

Shogun (Japan), 861(illus.), 879

Shostakovich, Dimitri, 1001

Show trials: in Soviet Union, 964

Sicily, 827; Kingdom of the Two Sicilies, 759; Second World War in, 983

Sick man of Europe: Ottoman Empire as, 889

Sickness, *see* Health; Medicine; Physicians

Sieyès, Emmanuel Joseph, 700, 712

Silent Generation, 1011

Single European Act (1986), 1050

Sino-Japanese War, 881

Sister Carrie (Dreiser), 817

Six Acts (England), 773

Skilled workers, 802

Slave labor: of Nazis, 978

Slaves and slavery: in U.S., 833–834, 834(map)

Slavic people: in Austria, 761, 844; in Second World War, 977; Nazis and, 986

Slovakia: postcommunist transition in, 1047

Slovenia: civil war in, 1047

Smith, Adam, 762

Smolensk, 718, 719

Social and economic rights: EU and, 1057

Social classes, *see* Classes

Social Darwinism, 815; imperialism and, 875

Social Democrats (Germany), 840–841, 846, 913; German Revolution and, 911–912; Treaty of Versailles and, 914

Social Democrats (Scandinavia): Great Depression and, 946–947

Socialism and socialists: utopian, 764–765; Marxism and, 765–766, 846–850; Hegel and, 766; 1848 revolutions and, 778, 779; women and, 808; Russian, 837(illus.); German, 839, 840–841; nationalism and, 839; unions and, 848–850; revisionism and, 849–850; in First World War, 900–901; in Scandinavia, 946–947, 947(illus.); after Second World War, 995; in EU countries, 1057

Socialist party: in Poland, 913; in Italy, 964, 965; French, 1020, 1051

Socialist Revolutionaries (Russia), 910

Social reform, *see* Reform(s)

Social rights, 922

Social science, 813–815

Social security, 840(illus.); in Germany, 839–840; in U.S., 946; postwar, 1008

Social welfare: in Germany, 839–840, 840(illus.); French, 841–842; in England, 843

Society: classes in, 692; equality concept and, 693; French legal orders and, 698–699; Industrial Revolution and, 727–728; industrialization and, 740, 742–744; literary realism and, 815–817; First World War impact on, 902; Soviet, 961–963; in Nazi Germany, 969–970; postwar, 1006–1012; in 1970s and 1980s, 1020–1021. *See also* Urban society

Soldiers: in First World War, 896(illus.), 896–897, 903, 918. *See also* Armed forces; Military; Wars and warfare

Solidarity movement, 1030–1032, 1031(illus.), 1035, 1062–1063, 1063(illus.)

Solzhenitsyn, Aleksandr, 1004, 1028

Somalia: refugees from, 1054

Somme: Battle of the, 896, 899(illus.), 901

Sophia (Austrian Empire), 780

Sophie (Austria-Hungary), 893

Sorel, Georges, 924–925

SOS-Racism, 1055(illus.)

Sound and the Fury, The (Faulkner), 929

South Africa, 869; apartheid in, 873

South Korea: North Korean invasion of, 993

South Vietnam: Vietnam War and, 1014–1015

Sovereignty: revolutionaries and, 692

Soviet bloc: revolutions in, 1027; liberalization in, 1028; disintegration of Soviet Union and, 1038(illus.), 1038–1040, 1039(map)

Soviets: in Petrograd, 906

Soviet Union, 1027; five-year plans in, 957, 959–961; totalitarianism in, 957–964; collectivization in, 960–961; forced labor in, 961(illus.); terror and purges in, 963–964; in Grand Alliance, 971; Nazi-Soviet nonaggression pact, 975; German attack on, 975–977, 976(map); in Second World War, 980; eastern Europe and, 991–992, 993, 1028; after Second World War, 994(map), 995, 1001–1002; de-Stalinization in, 1002–1004; end of reform in, 1004–1006; Brezhnev and, 1006; West Germany and, 1015; Afghanistan and, 1016; human rights and, 1016; Great Russians in, 1028; re-Stalinization in, 1028; to 1985, 1028–1030; Gorbachev and, 1032–1033; perestroika in, 1032–1033; glasnost in, 1033; collapse of communism and, 1035–1036; disintegration of, 1038(illus.), 1038–1040, 1039(map); end of cold war and, 1040. *See also* Cold war; Russia; Russian Federation; Russian Revolution (1917); Second World War

Soyer, Isaac, 945

Space program, 1007

Spain: debt repudiated by, 698; war with France in, 717, 717(illus.); Latin America and, 759; nationalism in, 764; Franco-Prussian War and, 832; socialism in, 850; fascism in, 974; in European Economic Community, 1019; Basque terrorism in, 1053(illus.)

Spanish civil war, 974

Special-interest groups: imperialism and, 875

Specialization: economic, 796; in science and technology, 1007

Spencer, Herbert, 815

Spengler, Oswald, 930

Spinning jenny, 728, 728(illus.)

Sports: working class and, 804

Srebrenica: massacre at, 1050(illus.)

SS corps (Germany), 970, 977–978

Staël, Germaine de, 768, 769, 769(illus.)

Stalin, Joseph: five-year plans of, 957, 959–961; rise to power, 959; terror and purges of, 963–964; at Yalta Conference, 990(illus.), 991–992; Teheran Conference and, 990–991; cold war and, 992, 993; Soviet Union under, 1001–1002

Stalingrad: Battle of, 976(map)

Stamp Act, 694

Standard of living: of workers, 744, 849; after Industrial Revolution, 856; Soviet, 962, 1004, 1021, 1028; postwar, 1008. *See also* Lifestyle

Staniland, Charles J., 854(illus.)

Stanley, Henry M., 869

Starry Night (Van Gogh), 932(illus.)

Starvation: in First World War, 901, 914. *See also* Famine

State (nation): national states and, 838–846

State monopolies: as private monopolies in Russia, 1044

State socialism: during First World War, 900–901

States' rights: vs. human rights, 1056

Steam engine, 730(illus.), 730–732, 858

Steam hammer, 731(illus.)

Steamships, 858

Steel industry: Russian, 837

Stein, Gertrude, 940

Stern, Karl, 926

Stock market crash: of 1873, 845–846; of 1929, 942–944

Storm troopers (SA), 970

Strasser, Gregor, 969

Stravinsky, Igor, 933

Stream-of-consciousness technique: in novels, 929–930

Streetcars, 792–794

Stresemann, Gustav, 938, 939, 941, 941(illus.), 971

Strikes: labor movement and, 748; British, 849; in Germany, 849, 911; during student rebellion in France, 1012–1013; national strike in France, 1051. *See also* Labor

Strutt family: Elizabeth, 742, 743; Jedediah, 743, 745

Student protests, 1012

Sturm und Drang, 766

Submarine warfare: in First World War, 900, 904; in Second World War, 980

Subsidies: in Russia, 1044

Sudan, 877; British in, 872

Sudetenland: German takeover of, 975

Suez Canal, 859, 862, 872

Suffrage: in England, 775; in France, 824; woman, 838. *See also* Voting and voting rights

Sullivan, Louis H., 930

Summer (Atkinson), 800, 801(illus.)

Sun Yat-sen (China), 882

Superego: in Freudian psychology, 929

Superpowers: U.S. as, 1040–1041. *See also* Cold war; Soviet Union; United States

Surgeons: antiseptic principle and, 792

Surrealism, 933

Swallows: Italian migrants as, 866

Sweated industries: women in, 803

Sweden, 714; Norwegian nationalism and, 844; socialism in, 946–947; in EU, 1052. *See also* Scandinavia

Syllabus of Errors (Pius IX), 828

Synthetics: development of, 901

Syria, 914; decolonization and, 999; 1973 attack on Israel, 1019

System of Positive Philosophy (Comte), 813

Tai Ping rebellion (China), 881

Taliban, 1057

Talleyrand, Charles, 758

Tannenburg: Battle of, 899

Tariffs: protection and industrialization, 738; *Zollverein* and, 739–740; in Germany, 839; imperialism and, 872; Common Market and, 997

Taxation: American Revolution and, 694; by Napoleon, 717; in First World War, 901

Tbilisi, Georgia: separatists in, 1033

Technology: steam engine and, 731–732; British protection of, 738; middle class and, 797; R&D and, 813; imperialism and, 875; in Japan, 880; totalitarian state and, 955; in postwar period, 1006–1007. *See also* Industrial Revolution; Science; Weapons

Teheran Conference, 990–991

Teke people, 869

Telegraph, 859

Ten Hours Act (1847), 775

Terror, The (France), *see* Reign of Terror

Terrorism: in Russia, 836(illus.); in Soviet Union, 963–964, 1002; of September 11, 2001, 1052, 1057; in Spain, 1053(illus.)

Tess of the D'Urbervilles (Hardy), 816

Tet Offensive, 1014

Tewfiq (Egypt), 862

Textile industry: factories in, 729; British trade and, 858. *See also* Cotton industry

Thatcher, Margaret, 1017, 1020

Theater: German, 798(illus.); working class and, 804

Theis, Edouard, 981

Theology, *see* Religion

Thermidorian Reaction, 711–712

Thermodynamics, 812–813

Thiers, Adolphe, 841

Third Balkan War, 894

Third Coalition, 714

Third estate (France), 698(illus.), 698–699, 700

Third Reform Bill (England), 843

Third Republic (France), 841–842

Third World, 856; Tito and, 1003

Three Emperors' League, 889

Three Musicians (Picasso), 934–935, 934–935(illus.)

Tiburtius, Franziska, 809, 809(illus.)

Tito (Josip Broz), 1002, 1003, 1003(illus.)

Tocqueville, Alexis de, 778–779

Tokyo: Perry in, 861

Tolstoy, Leo, 816–817

Tory party (England), 773, 775–776

Totalitarianism, 954–957; in First World War Germany, 901. *See also* Communists and communism; Nazi Germany; Soviet Union

Total war: First World War as, 899, 900–902, 903(illus.); Second War World as, 983

Toulouse-Lautrec, Henri de, 806(illus.)

Towns, *see* Cities and towns

Toynbee, Arnold, 926

Tractatus Logico-Philosophicus (Wittgenstein), 925

Trade: world market and, 857–860; with China, 860–861; imperialism and, 872

Trade unions, 748, 749; in Poland, 1031

Trafalgar: Battle of, 714

Transportation: in England, 726(map); in cities, 789–790, 792–795; in Russia, 835, 836–837; trade and, 858–859; interstate highway system and, 1001. *See also* Railroads

Trans-Siberian railway, 837

Transylvania, 754(illus.)

Travel, 1009

Treaties: Paris (1783), 696; Amiens, 714; Lunéville, 714; Chaumont, 718; Nanking, 860; with China, 860–861; Russian-German Reinsurance, 889, 890; Brest-Litovsk, 909, 911; Versailles, 937–938, 971; Rome-Berlin Axis, 974; Nazi-Soviet nonaggression pact, 975; Rome, 997; Paris Accord as, 1040; Maastricht, 1051

Treitschke, Heinrich von, 872–874

Trench warfare, 895–897, 896(illus.), 897(illus.)

Trial, The (Kafka), 930

Trials: in Soviet Union, 964

Triple Alliance, 888(illus.), 889, 890, 899

Triple Entente, 894–895, 899

Triumph of the Will, The (movie), 937

Trocmé, André and Magda, 981

Trotsky, Leon, 908–909, 910, 959

Truman, Harry, 992, 993, 1001

Trumbull, John, 696(illus.)

Tse-hsü, Lin, 860

Turkey, 899, 914, 992; Greece and, 771–772; immigrants from, 1054. *See also* Ottoman Empire; Ottoman Turks

Turks, *see* Ottoman Turks; Turkey

Turner, Joseph M. W., 733, 770

Tuscany, 826–827

Twentieth Party Congress, 1002–1004

Two Sicilies: kingdom of, 759

Typhoid, 792

Typhus, 792

Tzu Hsi (China), 881, 881(illus.)

Ukraine, 837, 910; collectivization in, 961

Ulster, 776

Ulysses (Joyce), 929–930

Uncertainty principle, 921–930

Underemployment, 1021

Unconditional surrender policy: of Allies, 979, 990

Unemployment: British, 942, 950–951; in Great Depression, 944–945, 945(illus.), 946; Soviet, 962; energy crisis and, 1019; in 1970s and 1980s, 1021; downsizing and, 1042; EU and, 1051; German, 1052

Unification: Prussia and, 782; of Italy, 826–829, 829(illus.); of Germany, 829–833, 832(map), 1040, 1051–1052; of Europe, 1041

Uniformitarianism, 814

Union of South Africa, 869

Unions, *see* Labor unions

United Nations: Palestine division by, 999; Iraqi war and, 1041

United States: revolutionary era in, 693–697; industrialization in, 734, 736; religion in, 804–805; literary realism in, 817; nationalism in, 833–835; women's voting rights in, 838; immigration to, 846, 864, 866; Asian imperialism of, 872; Britain and, 890; in First World War, 899–900, 911; Treaty of Versailles and, 914–916; film industry in, 936; Dawes Plan and, 939; Depression and, 943(map), 944; New Deal in, 945–946; in Grand Alliance, 971; Pearl Harbor and, 977, 979; atomic bombing of Japan by, 983; eastern Europe and, 991–992; Marshall Plan of, 992, 995; March on Washington (1963), 1000(illus.); civil rights movement in, 1000–1001; Vietnam War and, 1013–1015; Watergate and, 1015; misery index for, 1019(illus.); as superpower, 1040–1041; war with Iraq and, 1041; September 11, 2001, attack on, 1052, 1057; human vs. states' rights and,

1056; former Yugoslavia and, 1057. *See also* Cold war; First World War; Second World War

Unity movement: in western Europe, 996(map), 997, 1050–1053

Universal suffrage: in England, 775; in France, 824

Universe: uncertainty and, 928

Universities and colleges: women in, 807–808; rebellions at, 1012–1013, 1013(illus.)

University of Paris, 1012–1013, 1013(illus.)

Upper classes, *see* Elites

Upper middle class, 797

Urban areas: working classes in, 799–804; Soviet population in, 1028–1029. *See also* Cities and towns

Urbanization, *see* Cities and towns; Urban society

Urban planning, 792–795

Urban society: from 1848 to 1914, 787–817

Ure, Andrew, 742

USSR, *see* Soviet Union

Utopian socialism, 808

Valentino, Rudolf, 936

Valéry, Paul, 923–924

Valmy, Battle of, 706

Van Gogh, Vincent, 932(illus.), 932–933

Vatican, 966. *See also* Papacy; Roman Catholic church

Vaudeville, 804

Velvet Revolution, 1035–1036, 1047

Venetia, 758, 826

Venice, 829

Verdun: Battle of, 896, 901

Versailles: Oath of the Tennis Court and, 700, 701(illus.); Louis XVI and, 703; peace conference at, 912–914; Treaty of, 914–916, 937–938, 971

Vichy government, 975

Victor Emmanuel II (Italy), 828, 829, 829(illus.)

Victor Emmanuel III (Italy), 965

Victoria (England), 822(illus.), 905

Vienna, 792; Congress of, 757–761

Vietcong, 1014, 1015

Vietnam, 999

Vietnam War, 1012, 1013–1015, 1014(illus.)

Vigny, Alfred-Victor de (Comte), 769

Vindication of the Rights of Man, A (Wollstonecraft), 705

Vindication of the Rights of Women, A (Wollstonecraft), 705

Vladivostok, 910

Voting and voting rights: in Massachusetts, 694; liberals on, 762; in France, 777, 778; for women, 838, 902. *See also* Suffrage

Voting Rights Act (1965), 1001

Wages: of weavers, 729; Ricardo on, 734; industrialization and, 744. *See also* Income

Walesa, Lech, 1047, 1062; Solidarity movement and, 1031(illus.), 1031–1032, 1035

Walking cities, 788

Walter, Jakob, 719

War (Dix), 897(illus.)

War, As I Saw It, The, 922(illus.)

War and Peace (Tolstoy), 816–817

War communism: in Russia, 910

War crimes tribunal (Netherlands): Milosevic at, 1050

War Raw Materials Board, 901

Warrior castes: of India, 899(illus.)

Wars and warfare: Napoleonic, 714–718; trench warfare, 895–897, 896(illus.), 897(illus.); total war and, 899, 900–902, 903(illus.), 983; submarine warfare, 900. *See also* Armed forces; Military; Revolution(s)

Warsaw ghetto, 978(illus.); Brandt at, 1015, 1016(illus.)

Warsaw Pact, 992, 1005

Washington, D.C.: September 11, 2001, attack on, 1057

Washington, George, 695

Waste Land, The (Eliot), 930

Water frame, 728

Watergate affair, 1015

Waterloo, Battle of, 718

Water mills, 729, 732

Watson, James, 1007

Watt, James: steam engine and, 731

Waugh, Evelyn, 926

Wealth: poverty and, 796–804, 860; in developed regions, 856; First War World and, 895; in Russia, 1044, 1045(illus.). *See also* Classes; Trade

Wealth of Nations, The (Smith), *see Inquiry into the Nature and Causes of the Wealth of Nations* (Smith)

Weapons: imperialism and, 875; research and, 1006–1007

Weavers, 729. *See also* Textile industry

Weimar Republic, 938, 940, 941; Hitler and, 967–969

Welfare state: in Britain, 995; shift to capitalism, 1042

Welfare system: in 1970s and 1980s, 1020, 1021

West Africa: Portugal and, 869; imperialism in, 871

West Berlin, 1004. *See also* Berlin; Germany

Western Europe, 1027; postwar, 993–997; Common Market in, 996(map); unity in, 996(map), 997, 1050–1053; decolonization by, 998(map), 999–1000; energy and, 1019; capitalism in, 1042

Western front: in First World War, 895–896

Western world: industrialization in, 736; Russia and, 837; global society and, 855–863; imperialism by, 868–882

West Germany, 1027; economy in, 995–997; political recovery in, 997; détente and, 1015; U.S., Soviet bloc, and, 1017; refugees to, 1035; reunification of, 1040. *See also* Germany

What Is Property? (Proudhon), 765

What Is the Third Estate? (Sieyès), 700

Whig party (England), 773, 775

Whites: U.S. Civil War and, 833–834

Whites (faction): in Russian civil war, 910

William I (Germany), 831, 833, 839

William II (Germany), 840, 876(illus.), 889, 893, 911

Wilson, Woodrow, 900, 912, 912(illus.); Versailles Treaty and, 914, 915–916

Witte, Serge, 836–837

Wittgenstein, Ludwig, 925

Wojtyla, Karol, *see* John Paul II (pope)

Wollstonecraft, Mary, 705, 807

Woman's suffrage movement, 838

Women: French, 703, 704; rights of, 705; in Napoleonic France, 714; in business world, 742, 743; sexual division of labor and, 746–748; Fourier and, 764–765; equal rights for, 769; middle-class, 798; fashion of, 800(illus.), 800–801, 801(illus.); as domestic servants, 802–803, 803(illus.); in workforce, 807, 808; careers of, 809; suffrage movement and, 838; as French teachers, 841–842; as forced labor, 901; during First World War, 902, 918–919; Soviet, 963; in fascist Italy, 966; in Nazi Germany, 970, 971; in postwar period, 1009–1010; intellectuals, 1017; in Russia, 1046(illus.); birthrate and, 1052, 1053–1054; East German after unification, 1052; as illegal immigrants, 1054; in Afghanistan, 1057

Women's movement: in 1970s, 1017–1018, 1018(illus.)

Women's rights, 807–808; French Revolution and, 722–723, 723(illus.)

Wood: as energy source, 730

Woolf, Virginia, 929, 929(illus.)

Wordsworth, William, 742, 768

Workers: French, 704, 707–708; industrial, 741(illus.), 742–749, 745(illus.); Engels on, 742; labor movement and, 748; social security for, 839–840, 840(illus.); socialism and, 846; May Day and, 848, 848(illus.); in Berlin, 853(illus.). *See also* Labor; Socialism and socialists

Workers International, *see* Internationals (communist)

Workforce: women in, 807, 808, 902, 1009–1010, 1021; Soviet, 962, 963(illus.); Nazi, 970

Working classes: industrialization and, 742–744, 799–805; sexual division of labor and, 746–748; labor movement and, 748;

Working classes (*cont.*)
  newspapers of, 749(illus.); home of,
  810(illus.); family life of, 812
Workplace: women in, 1017–1018
Works Progress Administration (WPA),
  946
World markets, 857–860, 890
World of Yesterday, The (Zweig), 820–821
World War I, *see* First World War
World War II, *see* Second World War
Wozzeck (Berg), 933
Wright, Frank Lloyd, 930, 931(illus.)
Writers, 940, 954–957. *See also* Literature

Xhosa people, 869

Yalta Conference, 990(illus.), 991–992
Yamagata, Yasuko, 983(illus.)
Yaroshenko, N. A., 816(illus.)
Yellow fever, 792
Yeltsin, Boris, 1038–1040, 1044–1046
Yokohama, 879
Young Italy, 784
Young people: before World War I, 820–821,
  821(illus.); counterculture of, 1011–
  1013
Youth movement: of Italian fascists, 965; of
  Nazis, 968(illus.), 969
Yugoslavia, 911, 914, 938, 954, 991; Second
  World War in, 975; Tito in, 1002, 1003,
  1003(illus.); civil wars in, 1043, 1047–

1050, 1050(illus.), 1054; revolutions of
  1989 and, 1047; ethnicity, 1049(map)

Zambia, 869
Zanzibar, 871
Zemstvo, 835
Zimbabwe, 869
Zionism: Herzl and, 846, 847; Israel and,
  999
Zola, Emile, 815, 816, 842
Zollverein, 739–740, 829–830
Zones of occupation, *see* Occupation zones
Zoning: urban, 792
Zulu people, 869
Zweig, Stephan, 820–821

	Government	Society and Economy
3200 B.C.	Dominance of Sumerian cities in Mesopotamia, ca 3200–2340 Unification of Egypt; Archaic Period, ca 3100–2660 Old Kingdom of Egypt, ca 2660–2180 Dominance of Akkadian empire in Mesopotamia, ca 2331–2200 Middle Kingdom in Egypt, ca 2080–1640	Neolithic peoples rely on settled agriculture, while others pursue nomadic life, ca 7000–ca 3000 Development of wheeled transport in Mesopotamia, by ca 3200 Expansion of Mesopotamian trade and culture into modern Turkey, the Middle East, and Iran, ca 2600
2000 B.C.	Babylonian empire, ca 2000–1595 Hyksos invade Egypt, ca 1640–1570 Hittite Empire, ca 1600–1200 New Kingdom in Egypt, ca 1570–1075	First wave of Indo-European migrants, by 2000 Extended commerce in Egypt, by ca 2000 Horses introduced into western Asia, by ca 2000
1500 B.C.	Third Intermediate Period in Egypt, ca 1100–700 Unified Hebrew Kingdom under Saul, David, and Solomon, ca 1025–925	Use of iron increases in western Asia, by ca 1300–1100 Second wave of Indo-European migrants, by ca 1200
1000 B.C.	Hebrew Kingdom divided into Israel and Judah, 925 Assyrian Empire, ca 900–612 Phoenicians found Carthage, 813 Kingdom of Kush conquers and reunifies Egypt, 8th c. Medes conquers Persia, 710 Babylon wins independence from Assyria, 626 Dracon issues law code at Athens, 621 Cyrus the Great conquers Medes, founds Persian Empire, 550 Solon's reforms at Athens, ca 549 Persians complete conquest of ancient Near East, 521–464 Reforms of Cleisthenes in Athens, 508	Concentration of landed wealth in Greece, ca 750–600 Greek overseas expansion, ca 750–550 Beginning of coinage in western Asia, ca 640
500 B.C.	Battle of Marathon, 490 Xerxes' invasion of Greece, 480–479 Delian Confederacy, 478/7 Twelve Tables in Rome, 451/0 Valerio-Horatian laws in Rome, 449 Peloponnesian War, 431–404 Rome captures Veii, 396 Gauls sack Rome, 390 Roman expansion in Italy, 390–290 Conquests of Alexander the Great, 334–323 Punic Wars, 264–146 Reforms of the Gracchi, 133–121	Building of the Via Appia begins, 312 Growth of Hellenistic trade and cities, ca 300–100 Beginning of Roman silver coinage, 269 Growth of slavery, decline of small farmers in Rome, ca 250–100 Agrarian reforms of the Gracchi, 133–121

Religion and Philosophy	Science and Technology	Arts and Letters
Growth of anthropomorphic religion in Mesopotamia, ca 3000–2000	Development of wheeled transport in Mesopotamia, by ca 3200	Sumerian cuneiform writing, ca 3200
Emergence of Egyptian polytheism and belief in personal immortality, ca 2660	Use of widespread irrigation in Mesopotamia and Egypt, ca 3000	Egyptian hieroglyphic writing, ca 3100
Spread of Mesopotamian and Egyptian religious ideas as far north as modern Anatolia and as far south as central Africa, ca 2600	Construction of the first pyramid in Egypt, ca 2600	
Emergence of Hebrew monotheism, ca 1700	Construction of the first ziggurats in Mesopotamia, ca 2000	*Epic of Gilgamesh,* ca 1900
Mixture of Hittite and Near Eastern religious beliefs, ca 1595	Widespread use of bronze in the ancient Near East, ca 1900	Code of Hammurabi, ca 1790
	Babylonian mathematical advances, ca 1800	
Exodus of the Hebrews from Egypt into Palestine, 13th c.	Hittites introduce iron technology, ca 1400	Phoenicians develop alphabet, ca 1400
Religious beliefs of Akhenaten, ca 1367		Naturalistic art in Egypt under Akhenaten, ca 1367
		Egyptian Book of the Dead, ca 1300
Era of the prophets in Israel, ca 1100–500	Babylonian astronomical advances, ca 750–400	Beginning of the Hebrew Bible, ca 9th c.
Intermixture of Etruscan and Roman religious cults, ca 753–509		First Olympic Games, 776
Growing popularity of local Greek religious cults, ca 700 B.C.–A.D. 337		Babylonian astronomical advances, ca 750–400
Babylonian Captivity of the Hebrews, 586–539		Homer, traditional author of the *Iliad* and *Odyssey,* ca 700
		Hesiod, author of the *Theogony* and *Works and Days,* ca 700
		Archilochos, lyric poet, 648
		Aeschylus, first significant Athenian tragedian, 525/4–456
Pre-Socratic philosophers, 5th c.	Hippocrates, formal founder of medicine ca 430	Sophocles, tragedian who used his plays to explore moral and political problems, ca 496–406
Socrates, 469–399	Theophrastus, founder of botany, ca 372–288	Euripides, the most personal of the Athenian tragedians, ca 480–406
Plato, 429–347	Aristarchos of Samos, advances in astronomy, ca 310–230	
Diogenes, leading proponent of cynicism, ca 412–323	Euclid codifies geometry, ca 300	Thucydides, historian of the Peloponnesian War, ca 460–400
Aristotle, 384–322	Herophilus, discoveries in medicine, ca 300–250	Aristophanes, the greatest writer of Old Comedy, ca 457–ca 385
Epicurus, 340–270	Archimedes, works on physics and hydrologics, ca 287–212	Herodotus, the father of history, ca 450
Zeno, founder of Stoic philosophy, 335–262		
Emergence of Mithraism, ca 300		
Spread of Hellenistic mystery religions, 2nd c.		
Greek cults brought to Rome, ca 200		

	Government	Society and Economy
100 B.C.	Dictatorship of Sulla, 88–79 Civil war in Rome, 78–27 Dictatorship of Caesar, 45–44 Principate of Augustus, 31 B.C.–A.D. 14	Reform of the Roman calendar, 46
A.D. 300	Constantine removes capital of Roman Empire to Constantinople, ca 315 Visigoths defeat Roman army at Adrianople (378), signaling massive German invasions into the empire Bishop Ambrose asserts church's independence from the state, 380 Death of emperor Romulus Augustus marks end of Roman Empire in the West, 476 Clovis issues Salic law of the Franks, ca 490	Growth of serfdom in Roman Empire, ca 200–500 Economic contraction in Roman Empire, 3rd c.
500	Law Code of Justinian, 529 Dooms of Ethelbert, king of Kent, ca 604 Spread of Islam across Arabia, the Mediterranean region, Spain, North Africa, and Asia as far as India, ca 630–733	Gallo-Roman aristocracy intermarries with Germanic chieftains Decline of towns and trade, ca 500–700 Agrarian economy predominates in the West, ca 500–1500
700	Charles Martel defeats Muslims at Tours, 732 Pippin III anointed king of the Franks, 754 Charlemagne secures Frankish crown, r. 768–814	Height of Muslim commercial activity, ca 700–1300
800	Imperial coronation of Charlemagne, Christmas 800 Treaty of Verdun, 843 Viking, Magyar, and Muslim invasions, ca 845–900	Byzantine commerce and industry, ca 800–1000 Invasions and unstable conditions lead to increase of serfdom
1000	Seljuk Turks conquer Muslim Baghdad, 1055 Norman conquest of England, 1066 Penance of Henry IV at Canossa, 1077	Agrarian economy predominates in the West, 1000–1500 Decline of Byzantine free peasantry, ca 1025–1100 Growth of towns and trade in the West, ca 1050–1300 Domesday Book, 1086
1100	Henry I of England, r. 1100–1135 Louis VI of France, r. 1108–1137 Frederick I of Germany, r. 1152–1190 Henry II of England, r. 1154–1189 Thomas Becket murdered, 1170 Philip Augustus of France, r. 1180–1223	Henry I of England establishes the Exchequer, 1130 Beginnings of the Hanseatic League, 1159

Religion and Philosophy	Science and Technology	Arts and Letters
Mithraism spreads to Rome, 27 B.C.–A.D. 270 Dedication of the Ara Pacis Augustae, 9 Traditional birth of Jesus, ca 3	Pliny the Elder, student of natural history, 23 B.C.–A.D. 79 Frontinus, engineering advances in Rome, 30 B.C.–A.D. 104	Virgil, 70–19 B.C. Livy, ca 59 B.C.–A.D. 17 Ovid, 43 B.C.–A.D. 17
Constantine legalizes Christianity, 312 Theodosius declares Christianity the official state religion, 380 Donatist heretical movement at its height, ca 400 St. Augustine, *The City of God,* ca 425 Clovis adopts Roman Christianity, 496		St. Jerome publishes the Latin *Vulgate,* late 4th c. St. Augustine, *Confessions,* ca 390 Byzantines preserve Greco-Roman culture, ca 400–1000
Rule of St. Benedict, 529 Monasteries established in Anglo-Saxon England, 7th c. Muhammad preaches reform, ca 610 Publication of the Qu'ran, 651 Synod of Whitby, 664	Using watermills, Benedictine monks exploit energy of fast-flowing rivers and streams Heavy plow and improved harness facilitate use of multiple-ox teams; harrow widely used in northern Europe	Boethius, *The Consolation of Philosophy,* ca 520 Justinian constructs church of Santa Sophia, 532–537 Pope Gregory the Great publishes *Dialogues, Pastoral Care, Moralia,* 590–604
Missionary work of St. Boniface in Germany, ca 710–750 Iconoclastic controversy in Byzantine Empire, 726–843 Pippin III donates Papal States to the papacy, 756	Byzantines successfully use "Greek fire" in naval combat against Arab fleets attacking Constantinople, 673, 717	Lindisfarne Gospel Book, ca 700 Bede, *Ecclesiastical History of the English Nation,* ca 700 *Beowulf,* ca 700 Carolingian Renaissance, ca 780–850
Foundation of abbey of Cluny, 909 Byzantine conversion of Russia, late 10th c.	Stirrup and nailed horseshoes become widespread in shock combat Paper, invented in China ca 2d c., enters Europe through Muslim Spain in 10th c.	Byzantines develop the Cyrillic script, late 10th c.
Beginning of reformed papacy, 1046 Schism between Roman and Greek Orthodox churches, 1054 Pope Gregory VII, 1073–1085 Peter Abelard, 1079–1142 St. Bernard of Clairvaux, 1090–1153 First Crusade, 1095–1099	Arab conquests bring new irrigation methods, cotton cultivation, and manufacture to Spain, Sicily, southern Italy Avicenna, Arab scientist, d. 1037	Romanesque style in architecture and art, ca 1000–1200 *Song of Roland,* ca 1095 Muslim musicians introduce lute, rebec—stringed instruments and ancestors of violin
Universities begin, ca 1100–1300 Concordat of Worms ends investiture controversy, 1122 Height of Cistercian monasticism, 1125–1175 Aristotle's works translated into Latin, ca 1140–1260 Third Crusade, 1189–1192 Pope Innocent III, 1198–1216	In castle construction Europeans, copying Muslim and Byzantine models, erect rounded towers and crenelated walls Windmill invented, ca 1180 Some monasteries, such as Clairvaux and Canterbury Cathedral Priory, supplied by underground pipes with running water and indoor latrines, elsewhere very rare until 19th c.	*Rubaiyat of Umar Khayyam,* ca 1120 Dedication of abbey church of Saint-Denis launches Gothic style, 1144 Hildegard of Bingen, 1098–1179 Court of troubador poetry, especially that of Chrétien de Troyes, circulates widely

	Government	Society and Economy
1200	Spanish victory over Muslims at Las Navas de Tolosa, 1212 Frederick II of Germany and Sicily, r. 1212–1250 Magna Carta, 1215 Louis IX of France, r. 1226–1270 Mongols end Abbasid caliphate, 1258 Edward I of England, r. 1272–1307 Philip IV (the Fair) of France, r. 1285–1314 England and France at war, 1296	Economic revival, growth of towns, clearing of wasteland contribute to great growth of personal freedom, 13th c. Crusaders capture Constantinople (Fourth Crusade) and spur Venetian economy, 1204 Agricultural expansion leads to population growth, ca 1225–1300
1300	Philip IV orders arrest of Pope Boniface at Anagni, 1303 Hundred Years' War, 1337–1453 Political chaos in Germany, ca 1350–1450 Merchant oligarchies or despots rule Italian city-states	European economic depression, ca 1300–1450 Black Death appears ca 1347; returns intermittently until 18th c. Height of the Hanseatic League, 1350–1450 Peasant and working-class revolts: France, 1358; Florence, 1378; England, 1381
1400	Joan of Arc rallies French monarchy, 1429–1431 Medici domination of Florence begins, 1434 Princes in Germany consolidate power, ca 1450–1500 Ottoman Turks under Mahomet II capture Constantinople, May 1453 Wars of the Roses in England, 1453–1471 Ferdinand and Isabella complete reconquista in Spain, 1492 French invasion of Italy, 1494	Population decline, peasants' revolts, high labor costs contribute to decline of serfdom in western Europe Christopher Columbus reaches the Americas, October 1492 Portuguese gain control of East Indian spice trade, 1498–1511 Flow of Balkan slaves into eastern Mediterranean; of African slaves into Iberia and Italy, ca 1400–1500
1500	Charles V, Holy Roman emperor, 1519–1556 Imperial sack of Rome, 1527 Philip II of Spain, r. 1556–1598 Revolt of the Netherlands, 1566–1609 St. Bartholomew's Day massacre, August 24, 1572 Defeat of the Spanish Armada, 1588 Henry IV of France issues Edict of Nantes, 1598	Balboa discovers the Pacific, 1513 Magellan's crew circumnavigates the earth, 1519–1522 Spain and Portugal gain control of regions of Central and South America, ca 1520–1550 Peasants' Revolt in Germany, 1524–1525 "Time of Troubles" in Russia, 1598–1613
1600	Thirty Years' War, 1618–1648 Richelieu dominates French government, 1624–1643 Frederick William, Elector of Brandenburg, r. 1640–1688 English Civil War, 1642–1649	Chartering of British East India Company, 1600 Famine and taxation lead to widespread revolts, decline of serfdom in western Europe, ca 1600–1650 English Poor Law, 1601

Religion and Philosophy	Science and Technology	Arts and Letters
Maimonides, d. 1204 Founding of Franciscan order, 1210 Fourth Lateran Council, 1215 Founding of Dominican order, 1216 Thomas Aquinas (1225–1274) marks height of Scholasticism Pope Boniface VIII, 1294–1303	*Notebooks* of Villard de Honnecourt, a master mason (architect), a major source for Gothic engineering, ca 1250 Development of double-entry bookkeeping in Florence and Genoa, ca 1250–1340 Venetians purchase secrets of glass manufacture from Syria, 1277 Mechanical clock invented, ca 1290	*Parzifal, Roman de la Rose, King Arthur and the Round Table* celebrate virtues of knighthood Height of Gothic style, ca 1225–1300
Babylonian Captivity of the papacy, 1307–1377 John Wyclif, ca 1330–1384 Great Schism in the papacy, 1377–1418	Edward III of England uses cannon in siege of Calais, 1346	Petrarch, 1304–1374 Paintings of Giotto, ca 1305–1337 Dante, *Divine Comedy*, ca 1310 Boccaccio, *The Decameron*, ca 1350 Jan van Eyck, 1366–1441 Brunelleschi, 1377–1446 Chaucer, *Canterbury Tales*, ca 1385–1400
Council of Constance, 1414–1418 Pragmatic Sanction of Bourges, 1438 Expulsion of Jews from Spain, 1492	Water-powered blast furnaces operative in Sweden, Austria, the Rhine Valley, Liège, ca 1400 Leonardo Fibonacci's *Liber Abaci* (1202) popularizes use of Hindu-Arabic numerals, "a major factor in the rise of science in the Western world" Paris and largest Italian cities pave streets, making street cleaning possible Printing and movable type, ca 1450	Masaccio, 1401–1428 Botticelli, 1444–1510 Leonardo da Vinci, 1452–1519 Albrecht Dürer, 1471–1528 Michelangelo, 1475–1564 Raphael, 1483–1520 Rabelais, ca 1490–1553
Lateran Council attempts reforms of church abuses, 1512–1517 Machiavelli, *The Prince*, 1513 Concordat of Bologna, 1516 More, *Utopia*, 1516 Luther, *Ninety-five Theses*, 1517 Henry VIII of England breaks with Rome, 1532–1534 Loyola establishes Society of Jesus, 1540 Calvin establishes theocracy in Geneva, 1541 Merici establishes Ursuline order for education of women, 1544 Council of Trent, 1545–1563 Peace of Augsburg, 1555 Hobbes, 1588–1679 Descartes, 1596–1650	Copernicus, *On the Revolutions of the Heavenly Bodies*, 1543 Galileo, 1564–1642 Kepler, 1571–1630 Harvey, 1578–1657	Erasmus, *The Praise of Folly*, 1509 Castiglione, *The Courtier*, 1528 Cervantes, 1547–1616 Baroque movement in the arts, ca 1550–1725 Shakespeare, 1564–1616 Rubens, 1577–1640 Montaigne, *Essays*, 1598 Velazquez, 1599–1660
Huguenot revolt in France, 1625	Bacon, *The Advancement of Learning*, 1605 Boyle, 1627–1691 Leeuwenhoek, 1632–1723	Rembrandt van Rijn, 1606–1669 Golden Age of Dutch culture, 1625–1675 Vermeer, 1632–1675 Racine, 1639–1699

	Government	Society and Economy
1600 (cont.)	Louis XIV, r. 1643–1715 Peace of Westphalia, 1648 The Fronde in France, 1648–1660	Chartering of Dutch East India Company, 1602 Height of Dutch commercial activity, ca 1630–1665
1650	Protectorate in England, 1653–1658 Leopold I, Habsburg emperor, r. 1658–1705 Treaty of the Pyrenees, 1659 English monarchy restored, 1660 Siege of Vienna, 1683 Glorious Revolution in England, 1688–1689 Peter the Great of Russia, r. 1689–1725	Height of mercantilism in Europe, ca 1650–1750 Principle of peasants' "hereditary subjugation" to their lords affirmed in Prussia, 1653 Colbert's economic reforms in France, ca 1663–1683 Cossack revolt in Russia, 1670–1671
1700	War of the Spanish Succession, 1701–1713 Peace of Utrecht, 1713 Frederick William I of Prussia, r. 1713–1740 Louis XV of France, r. 1715–1774 Maria Theresa of Austria, r. 1740–1780 Frederick the Great of Prussia, r. 1740–1786	Foundation of St. Petersburg, 1701 Last appearance of bubonic plague in western Europe, ca 1720 Enclosure movement in England, ca 1730–1830 Jeremy Bentham, 1748–1823
1750	Seven Years' War, 1756–1763 Catherine the Great of Russia, r. 1762–1796 Partition of Poland, 1772–1795 Louis XVI of France, r. 1774–1792 American Revolution, 1776–1783 Beginning of the French Revolution, 1789	Start of general European population increase, ca 1750 Growth of illegitimate births, ca 1750–1850 Adam Smith, *The Wealth of Nations*, 1776 Thomas Malthus, *Essay of the Principle of Population*, 1798
1800	Napoleonic era, 1799–1815 Congress of Vienna, 1814–1815 "Battle of Peterloo," Great Britain, 1819	European economic imperialism, ca 1816–1880
1825	Greece wins independence, 1830 Revolution in France, 1830 Great Britain: Reform Bill of 1832; Poor Law reform, 1834; Chartists, repeal of Corn Laws, 1838–1848 British complete occupation of India, 1848 Revolutions in Europe, 1848	Height of French utopian socialism, 1830s–1840s German Zollverein founded, 1834 European capitalists begin large-scale foreign investment, 1840s Great Famine in Ireland, 1845–1851 Marx, *Communist Manifesto*, 1848
1850	Second Empire in France, 1852–1870 Crimean War, 1853–1856 Unification of Italy, 1859–1870 Civil War, United States, 1861–1865 Bismarck leads Germany, 1862–1890 Unification of Germany, 1864–1871 Britain's Second Reform Bill, 1867 Third Republic in France, 1870–1940	Crédit Mobilier founded in France, 1852 Japan opened to European influence, 1853 Mill, *On Liberty*, 1859 Russian serfs emancipated, 1861 First Socialist International, 1864–1871 Marx, *Das Capital*, 1867

Religion and Philosophy	Science and Technology	Arts and Letters
Patriarch Nikon's reforms split Russian Orthodox church, 1652 Test Act in England excludes Roman Catholics from public office, 1673 Revocation of Edict of Nantes, 1685 James II tries to restore Catholicism as state religion, 1685–1688 Montesquieu, 1689–1755 Locke, *Second Treatise on Civil Government,* 1690 Pierre Bayle, *Historical and Critical Dictionary,* 1697	Tull (1674–1741) encourages innovation in English agriculture Newton, *Principia Mathematica,* 1687 Newcomen develops steam engine, 1705	Construction of baroque palaces and remodeling of capital cities throughout central and eastern Europe, ca 1650–1725 J. S. Bach, 1685–1750 Fontenelle, *Conversations on the Plurality of Worlds,* 1686 The Enlightenment, ca 1690–1790 Voltaire, 1694–1778
Wesley, 1703–1791 Hume, 1711–1776 Diderot, 1713–1784 Condorcet, 1743–1794	Charles Townsend introduces four-year crop rotation, 1730	Montesquieu, *The Spirit of Laws,* 1748
Ricardo, 1772–1823 Fourier, 1772–1837 Papacy dissolves the Jesuits, 1773 Church reforms of Joseph II in Austria, 1780s Reorganization of the church in France, 1790s	Hargreaves's spinning jenny, ca 1765 Arkwright's water frame, ca 1765 Watt's steam engine promotes industrial breakthroughs, 1780s War widens the gap in technology between Britain and the continent, 1792–1815 Jenner's smallpox vaccine, 1796	*Encyclopedia,* edited by Diderot and d'Alembert, published, 1751–1765 Mozart, 1756–1791 Rousseau, *The Social Contract,* 1762 Beethoven, 1770–1827 Wordsworth, 1770–1850 Romanticism, ca 1790–1850 Wollstonecraft, *A Vindication of the Rights of Women,* 1792
Napoleon signs Concordat with Pope Pius VII regulating Catholic church in France, 1801 Spencer, 1820–1903		Staël, *On Germany,* 1810 Liszt, 1811–1886
Comte, *System of Positive Philosophy,* 1830–1842 List, *National System of Political Economy,* 1841 Nietzsche, 1844–1900 Sorel, 1847–1922	First railroad, Great Britain, 1825 Faraday studies electromagnetism, 1830–1840s	Balzac, *The Human Comedy,* 1829–1841 Delacroix, *Liberty Leading the People,* 1830 Hugo, *Hunchback of Notre Dame,* 1831
Decline in church attendance among working classes, ca 1850–1914 Pope Pius IX, *Syllabus of Errors,* denounces modern thoughts, 1864 Doctrine of papal infallibility, 1870	Modernization of Paris, ca 1850–1870 Great Exhibition, London, 1851 Darwin, *Origin of Species,* 1859 Pasteur develops germ theory of disease, 1860s Suez Canal opened, 1869 Mendeleev develops the periodic table, 1869	Realism, ca 1850–1870 Freud, 1856–1939 Flaubert, *Madame Bovary,* 1857 Tolstoy, *War and Peace,* 1869 Impressionism in art, ca 1870–1900 Eliot (Mary Ann Evans), *Middlemarch,* 1872

	Government	Society and Economy
1875	Congress of Berlin, 1878 European "scramble for Africa," 1880–1900 Britain's Third Reform Bill, 1884 Berlin conference on Africa, 1884 Dreyfus affair in France, 1894–1899 Spanish-American War, 1898 Boer War, 1899–1902	Full property rights for women, Great Britain, 1882 Social welfare legislation, Germany, 1883–1889 Second Socialist International, 1889–1914 Witte directs modernization of Russian economy, 1892–1899
1900	Russo-Japanese War, 1904–1905 Revolution in Russia, 1905 Balkan wars, 1912–1913	Women's suffrage movement, England, ca 1900–1914 Social welfare legislation, France, 1904, 1910; England, 1906–1914 Agrarian reforms in Russia, 1907–1912
1914	World War I, 1914–1918 Easter Rebellion, 1916 U.S. declares war on Germany, 1917 Bolshevik Revolution, 1917–1918 Treaty of Versailles, 1919	Planned economics in Europe, 1914 Auxiliary Service Law in Germany, 1916 Bread riots in Russia, March 1917
1920	Mussolini seizes power, 1922 Stalin uses forced collectivization, police terror, ca 1929–1939 Hitler gains power, 1933 Rome-Berlin Axis, 1936 Nazi-Soviet Non-Aggression Pact, 1939 World War II, 1939–1945	New Economic Policy in the Soviet Union, 1921 Dawes Plan for reparations and recovery, 1924 The Great Depression, 1929–1939 Rapid industrialization in Soviet Union, 1930s Roosevelt's "New Deal," 1933
1940	United Nations, 1945 Cold war begins, 1947 Fall of colonial empires, 1947–1962 Communist government in China, 1949 Korean War, 1950–1953 "De-Stalinization," 1955–1962	The Holocaust, 1941–1945 Marshall Plan, 1947 European economic progress, ca 1950–1969 European Coal and Steel Community, 1952 European Economic Community, 1957
1960	The Berlin Wall goes up, 1961 United States in Vietnam, ca 1961–1973 Student rebellion in France, 1968 Soviet tanks end Prague Spring, 1968 Détente, 1970s Soviets in Afghanistan, 1979	Civil rights movement in United States, 1960s Collapse of postwar monetary system, 1971 OPEC oil price increases, 1973 and 1979 Stagflation, 1970s Women's movement, 1970s
1980	U.S. military buildup, 1980s Solidarity in Poland, 1980 Gorbachev takes power, 1985 Unification of Germany, 1989 Revolutions in eastern Europe, 1989–1990 End of Soviet Union, 1991 War in former Yugoslavia, 1991–1995	Growth of debt, 1980s Economic crisis in Poland, 1988 Maastricht Treaty proposes monetary union, 1990 Conservative economic policies in western Europe, 1990s European Community becomes European Union, 1993 Migration to western Europe grows, 1990s
2000	Terrorist attack on United States, Sept. 11, 2001 War in Afghanistan, 2001	Euro note enters circulation, 2002

Religion and Philosophy	Science and Technology	Arts and Letters
Growth of public education in France, ca 1880–1900 Growth of mission schools in Africa, 1890–1914	Emergence of modern immunology, ca 1875–1900 Trans-Siberian Railroad, 1890s Marie Curie, discovery of radium, 1898 Electrical industry: lighting and streetcars, 1880–1900	Zola, *Germinal,* 1885 Kipling, "The White Man's Burden," 1899
Separation of church and state, France, 1901–1905 Jean-Paul Sartre, 1905–1980	Planck develops quantum theory, ca 1900 First airplane flight, 1903 Einstein develops relativity theory, 1905–1910	"Modernism," ca 1900–1929 Conrad, *Heart of Darkness,* 1902 Cubism in art, ca 1905–1930 Proust, *Remembrance of Things Past,* 1913–1927
Schweitzer, *Quest of the Historical Jesus,* 1906	Submarine warfare, 1915 Ernest Rutherford splits the atom, 1919	Spengler, *The Decline of the West,* 1918
Emergence of modern existentialism, 1920s Wittgenstein, *Essay on Logical Philosophy,* 1922 Revival of Christianity, 1920s and 1930s	"Heroic age of physics," 1920s First major public radio broadcasts in Great Britain and the United States, 1920 Heisenberg, "principle of uncertainty," 1927 Talking movies, 1930 Radar system in England, 1939	Gropius, the Bauhaus, 1920s Dadaism and surrealism, 1920s Woolf, *Jacob's Room,* 1922 Joyce, *Ulysses,* 1922 Eliot, *The Waste Land,* 1922 Remarque, *All Quiet on the Western Front,* 1929 Picasso, *Guernica,* 1937
De Beauvoir, *The Second Sex,* 1949 Communists fail to break Catholic church in Poland, 1950s	Oppenheimer, 1904–1967 "Big Science" in United States, ca 1940–1970 U.S. drops atomic bombs on Japan, 1945 Watson and Crick discover structure of DNA molecule, 1953 Russian satellite in orbit, 1957	Cultural purge in Soviet Union, 1946–1952 Van der Rohe, Lake Shore Apartments, 1948–1951 Orwell, *1984,* 1949 Pasternak, *Doctor Zhivago,* 1956 The "beat" movement in the U.S., late 1950s
Catholic church opposes the legalization of divorce and abortion, 1970 to present Pope John Paul II electrifies Poland, 1979	European Council for Nuclear Research (CERN), 1960 Space race, 1960s Russian cosmonaut first to orbit globe, 1961 American astronaut first person on the moon, 1969	The Beatles, 1960s Solzhenitsyn, *One Day in the Life of Ivan Denisovitch,* 1962 Friedan, *The Feminine Mystique,* 1963 Servan-Schreiber, *The American Challenge,* 1967
Revival of religion in Soviet Union, 1985 to present Fukuyama proclaims "end of history," 1991 Growth of Islam in Europe, 1990s	Reduced spending on Big Science, 1980s Computer revolution continues, 1980s and 1990s "Dolly," first genetically cloned sheep, 1996 U.S. Genome Project begins, 1990	Solzhenitsyn returns to Russia, 1994 Author Salman Rushdie is exiled from Iran, 1989